CIVIL PARTNERSHIP –
THE NEW LAW

Mark Harper
Withers LLP, London

Martin Downs
1 Crown Office Row, London

Gerald Wilson
Tanfield Chambers, London

Katharine Landells
Withers LLP, London

Family Law

2005

Published by Family Law
a publishing imprint of
Jordan Publishing Limited
21 St Thomas Street
Bristol BS1 6JS

British Library Cataloguing-in-Publication Data
A catalogue record for this book is available from the British Library.

ISBN 0 85308 933 7

Typeset by MFK-Mendip, Frome, Somerset
Printed and bound in Great Britain by Antony Rowe Ltd, Chippenham, Wilts

CIVIL PARTNERSHIP – THE NEW LAW

*This book is dedicated to those that paved the way
and, in particular:*

*Rob Wintemute
Angela Mason
Anthony Lester QC (Lord Lester of Herne Hill)*

Preface

In this book we aim to explain the new law on civil partnership, drawing where appropriate, on statute and case law and, in particular, the relevant European Convention of Human Rights jurisprudence. The purpose of the book is to place the Civil Partnership Act 2004 into perspective and to provide such guidance as is possible into its likely meaning, consequences and difficulties. In addition the book examines the position of cohabitees left outside the civil partnership regime – by choice or otherwise. It is aimed at solicitors and barristers who practise in family, housing and chancery (as it relates to the intestacy provisions). It should also be of real interest to all concerned with the registration of marriages and deaths and those concerned with drawing up employment and other policies which are concerned with family relationships – for example, those in the NHS and Prison Service.

The Civil Partnership Act 2004 is a major piece of legislation. This book concentrates on the law as it concerns England and Wales and the text of those sections can be found as an appendix to this book. The text draws on the explanatory notes, discussion papers and submissions that were sent to the government in preparation for the Bill as well as the parliamentary debates.

The Government announced in a press release on 21 February 2005 that the Act will be brought into force on 5 December 2005. As was emphasised in the course of parliamentary debate, it will be necessary for secondary legislation to be prepared prior to this. The Finance Bill in the Spring of 2005 will encompass the necessary changes to the system of taxation. Although neither the secondary legislation nor the Finance Bill was available at the time of going to press it is believed that the material currently available gives a very clear picture of how the legislation is likely to operate when it comes into force.

We are extremely grateful to Martin West, Greg Woodgate and Diane Acon at Jordans for their help and guidance. We are also very grateful to Jennifer Cowan for dealing with our text and getting it into proper order and being patient when cases sometimes intruded. We are also indebted to those at the Women and Equality Unit and the Department of Trade and Industry and Department for Constitutional Affairs for their assistance in answering our queries. However, should this book contain any error it is entirely of our own making and for which we accept full responsibility.

The law is stated as it stood on 31 January 2005.

Mark Harper	Martin Downs	Katharine Landells	Gerald Wilson
Withers LLP	*1 Crown Office Row*	*Withers LLP*	*Tanfield Chambers*
London	*London*	*London*	*London*

Contents

List of Abbreviations

ACAS	Advisory, Conciliation and Arbitration Service
CPA 2004	Civil Partnership Act 2004
CSA 1991	Child Support Act 1991
DPP	Director of Public Prosecutions
DTI	Department for Trade and Industry
EAT	Employment Appeals Tribunal
ECHR	European Court of Human Rights
ECJ	European Court of Justice
EOC	Equal Opportunities Commission
ETD	Equal Treatment Directive 76/207/EEC
FLA 1996	Family Law Act 1996
GLA	Greater London Authority
IBJSA	Income-based Jobseekers Allowance
ICTA 1988	Income and Corporation Taxes Act 1988
IPFDA 1975	Inheritance (Provision for Family and Dependants) Act 1975
IS	Income Support
MHA 1983	Mental Health Act 1983
PACS	Civil Solidarity Pacts (France)
s 28	Local Government Act 1988, s 28
SFLA	Solicitors' Family Law Association
SSAA 1992	Social Security Administration Act 1992
SSCBA 1992	Social Security Contributions and Benefits Act 1992
TCGA 1992	Taxation and Chargeable Gains Act 1992
WEU	Women and Equality Unit at the DTI

TABLE OF CASES

References are to paragraph number.

INTERNATIONAL

Canada

New Zealand

United States

TABLE OF STATUTES

References are to paragraph numbers.

TABLE OF STATUTORY INSTRUMENTS

References are to paragraph numbers.

Chapter 1

INTRODUCTION

1.1 The Civil Partnership Act 2004 is both a piece of legislation concerning family law and a civil rights or equality[1] measure. Parliament was concerned about the potentially serious problems that can arise with the unreformed law under which same sex relationships were largely ignored. The example given by Baroness Scotland of Asthal in her speech at the beginning of the Second Reading debate in the House of Lords is typical:

> 'where an accident causes the death of a person in a same-sex relationship, the other person in that relationship may find that he or she faces specific difficulties in obtaining access to the body, information about circumstances leading to or surrounding the death, or, indeed, compensation. Following a partner's death, they may find themselves unable to stay in the home they have shared with that partner for many years. Sometimes there have even been difficulties about attending events as intimate as funerals.'[2]

1.2 However, the fact that Parliament chose to enact legislation which makes provision for the surviving civil partners of those who hold a knacker's yard license[3] speaks volumes for the determination of the government and Parliament to equalise the position of same sex couples with those of married couples. In some respects the history of the legislation is relatively brief as it could be dated back to the commitment made by the government to conduct a review of the feasibility of such reform in response to the private member's Bill introduced by Lord Lester of Herne Hill. In other respects it is one of the last in a long line of reforms undertaken by government in recognition of a civil rights struggle which has been acted out in the streets, fought out in the courts in the UK and in Europe, and adopted by political parties. It might also be seen as representing a landmark in the acceptance not only of lesbians and gay men as individuals but also of their relationships and families. To this end it is instructive to examine the reform brought about by this Act as well as the changing legal status of lesbians and gay men more generally. This book seeks to examine the legal changes introduced by the Civil Partnership Act 2004 and the rights and responsibilities that it offers to those who register under the scheme, as well as to examine the law as it relates to cohabitants so that the legislation can be seen in context. The legislation makes provision for Scotland and Northern Ireland but this work will confine its analysis to the implications for the law of England and Wales.

---

1   In the discussion document, *Civil Partnership: A Framework for the Legal Recognition of Same-Sex Couples* (Women and Equality Unit, June 2003), civil partnership registration was described as an important equality measure for same sex couples who are unable to marry each other.
2   *Hansard*, HL Deb, col 387 (22 April 2004).
3   Civil Partnership Act 2004, Sch 27, para 48.

1.3   The seminal event of the modern history of lesbians and gay men in the UK was the passing of s 28 of the Local Government Act 1988 ('s 28'). This stated that:

'(1) A Local Authority shall not—

(a)   intentionally promote homosexuality or publish material with the intention of promoting homosexuality;

(b)   promote the teaching in any maintained school of the acceptability of homosexuality as a pretended family relationship.'

It was introduced to regulate the resort to an identity politics within local government and in particular the way that identity was represented.[1] The principal *cause célèbre* which justified its introduction in the eyes of its proponents was the publication in English of the Danish picture book for children, *Jenny lives with Eric and Martin* (originally *Mette bor hos Morten og Erik*),[2] and subsequent discussion around sex education. Section 28 was only repealed by the Local Government Act 2003 which was given Royal Assent on 18 September 2003.

1.4   It is striking to compare the text of s 28 and its reference to pretended family relationships with the minority judgment of Ward LJ in *Fitzpatrick v Sterling Housing Association Ltd*[3] less than 10 years later which began by considering the manner by which the Applicant and his deceased lover lived together and concluded that:[4]

'No distinction can sensibly be drawn between the two couples in terms of love, nurturing, fidelity, durability, emotional and economic interdependence – to name but some and no means all of the hallmarks of a relationship between a husband and his wife.'

He next went on to consider the familial nexus in terms of its structures or components and said:[5]

'A family unit is a social organisation which functions through linking its members closely together. The functions may be procreative, sexual, sociable, economic, and emotional. The list is not exhaustive. Not all families function in the same way. Save for the ability to procreate, these functions were present in the relationship between the deceased and the appellant.'

On that basis Ward LJ appears to be hinting at a functional rather than a moral analysis for the purposes of jurisprudential analysis.

1.5   The judgment of Ward LJ also gives some clue to the change in social attitudes. This phenomenon has not been unique to the UK. On the international stage the revised stance of Amnesty International in 1993 and 1994[6] was a major landmark. The example of the Republic of Ireland is also instructive. Upon independence it inherited British legislation on the criminality of homosexual behaviour and the new state took on a

---

1   L Moran *The Homosexuality of Law* (London and New York: Routledge, 1996).

2   The book was written by Susanne Bosche in 1981 in Danish and was translated into English in 1983. The connection between the book and the introduction of s 28 was confirmed by the now Baroness Knight (then Dame Jill Knight) in a House of Lords debate on its repeal on 6 December 1999: *Hansard*, HL Deb, col 1103.

3   [1997] 4 All ER 991, CA.

4   At 1022.

5   At 1023.

6   Amnesty International *First Steps: Amnesty International's Work On Behalf of Lesbians and Gay Men* (London, 1993); Amnesty International *Breaking the Silence: Human Rights Violations based on Sexual Orientation* (New York, 1994).

determinedly conservative outlook.[1] Decriminalisation only came about after the successful challenge to Irish law in *Norris v Ireland*.[2] However, the last 15 years have seen a significant legal and cultural revolution which included the election of Senator Norris's leading counsel, Mary Robinson SC, to the position of President of Ireland and no less than eight separate pieces of legislation from 1989 to 1998 which have replaced illegality with legal protection in the form of anti-discrimination legislation.[3]

1.6 In the UK, the judiciary has openly acknowledged the change in climate. It is noticeable that in the judgments of both Lord Bingham MR (as he was then) and Henry LJ in *R v Ministry of Defence, ex parte Smith*[4] there were explicit references to the discernible trend towards tolerance in the UK since the Sexual Offences Act 1967. Similar statements can also be found in the judgment of Singer J in *Re W (a minor) (adoption: homosexual adopter)*.[5]

1.7 Against such a background of international change, the Dutch academic Kees Waaldijk[6] has developed his analysis of the progressive development of lesbian and gay rights in Europe. From his comparative survey of the legal status of lesbians and gay men and the history of reform in each country in Europe he concludes that almost all European states, at different times, go through a standard sequence of steps in recognising homosexuality: After decriminalisation there is legislation for an equal age of consent, followed by anti-discrimination measures and then formal recognition and ultimately the creation of formal same sex partnerships including the legal status of parenthood. He concludes that four distinct features are characteristic of this process of legal recognition: There should be steady progress,[7] in standard sequences (he notes that with the exception of Ireland and Finland all countries have decriminalised homosexuality before introducing anti-discrimination laws), the process of change tends to be gradual and it usually involves some element of symbolic preparation.

1.8 In the UK, the election of an unsympathetic Conservative government in 1979 blocked legislative change for 18 years. The effect was to channel energies into a litigation strategy based on the European Convention for the Protection of Human Rights and EC law and ultimately on trying to achieve constitutional and legislative change in EC level. With the election of a Labour government on 1 May 1997, reform by way of legislation was again possible. The reality was that the Blair government was very cautious about change in public and preferred to be seen to legislate as a result of the case law of the

---

1 Kevin O'Higgins proudly boasted: 'We were probably the most conservative minded revolutionaries that ever put through a successful revolution.' K Rose *Diverse Communities* (Cork: Cork University Press, 1994) at p 35.
2 (1988) 13 EHHR 186.
3 L Flynn 'From Individual Protection to Recognition of Relationships? Same-Sex Couples and the Irish Experience of Sexual Orientation Law Reform' in R Wintemute and M Andenas (eds) *Legal Recognition of Same-Sex Partnerships – A Study of National, European and International Law* (Hart Publishing, 2001).
4 [1996] QB 517, CA.
5 [1997] 2 FLR 406.
6 K Waaldijk 'Towards the Recognition of Same-Sex Partners in European Union Law: Expectations Based on Trends in National Law' in T Wintemute and M Andenas (eds) *Legal Recognition of Same-Sex Partnerships* (Hart Publishing, 2001).
7 Waaldijk admits there are a few exceptions to this 'rule' but he is not really prepared to acknowledge s 28 as one such example as it was ineffective.

European Court of Human Rights. This was partly a product of the problems the party had in getting reform legislation passed unscathed in the House of Lords. Reformers had the enthusiastic support of many backbenchers in the Labour Party, and MPs from most of the smaller parties in Britain were particularly sympathetic. It is arguable that the real breakthrough occurred with the passage of the Adoption and Children Act 2002 through Parliament. This was amended by backbenchers in the House of Commons to permit unmarried couples, whether homosexual or heterosexual, to adopt. Although this was reversed in the House of Lords, the resulting splits in the Conservative Party appeared to invigorate the Labour Party frontbench. The result was that same sex partners will be able to adopt when the relevant sections of the Act come into force.

1.9   By this stage the government was already under pressure to legislate to protect the position of cohabitants, whether heterosexual or homosexual, as a result of the introduction of a Civil Partnership Bill by Lord Lester in the House of Lords and the spread of such schemes throughout much of Europe. In addition, particular injustices were coming to light as a result of cases supported by Stonewall, Liberty and others in domestic courts and in the European Court of Human Rights and the European Court of Justice. One of the other beneficial side-effects of the Adoption and Children Act 2002 for campaigners and the government was that it removed from the debate one of the most contentious arguments of all, that if lesbians and gay men were allowed to enter civil partnerships should they not also be allowed to adopt children?[1] It still left open the argument that the introduction of civil partnerships for all regardless of sexual orientation would undermine marriage.

1.10   The solution adopted by the government was to propose a Bill to create civil partnerships for same sex couples only. This had the advantage of not creating a possible rival for marriage, as the only people who would benefit were those who were not entitled to get married in the first place. Over the course of debate of the Civil Partnership Bill, a scheme which had been designed to give many of the advantages of marriage to lesbian and gay men developed into one in which every right and responsibility arising from marriage, in the power of the state, was made available to civil partners, with the exception of a church ceremony. The title would be different. This would not be without its significance, as marriage carries with it particular popular conceptions as well as a unique status in international law. This is not an issue which should arise in the Netherlands, which opened up marriage to same sex couples on 1 April 2001,[2] and Belgium which followed in 2002.[3] On 1 October 2004 the Spanish government published a Bill to legalise same sex marriage. The opening up of marriage to same sex couples has, since May 2004, had the support of the French Socialists. In the UK, the government has not sought to alter the position as concerns marriage but wished to

---

1   In the table of partnership registration schemes in EU member states that the Women and Equality Unit presented in its consultation paper, *Civil Partnership: A Framework for the Legal Recognition of Same-Sex Couples* (June 2003), it is very noticeable that of the nine countries of the then 15 member EU states that had at that stage had some form of civil union, only 10 of the schemes incorporated adoption.

2   Act of 21 December 2000 amending Book 1 of the Civil Code, concerning the opening up of marriage for persons of the same sex (Act on the Opening up of Marriage).

3   In 2002.

provide recognition of same sex couples in the light of the legal difficulties they faced. In the words of Baroness Scotland:[1]

> 'What same-sex couples seek now is an acknowledgement of their relationship ... At second reading we heard of many difficulties that same-sex couples can face. They face them because their long-term mutually supportive relationships are, at the moment, invisible in law. They have chosen to share their lives together, emotionally and financially, separately from other financial ties, but as same-sex couples are unable to marry. That is the acknowledgement that we have to make.'

1.11 The Civil Partnership Act 2004 is a radical piece of social legislation and represents an important reform in the field of family law in the UK. This book will concern itself with the effects on the law of England and Wales. It includes an analysis of some of the parliamentary debates many of which could be relevant in future arguments about the meaning of the statute in accordance with the rule in *Pepper (Inspector of Taxes) v Hart*.[2] In addition there is consideration of some wider material for the purpose of evaluating compatibility of the legislation with Convention rights, including the value judgments inherent in the test of proportionality as suggested in *Wilson v First County Trust Ltd*.[3]

1.12 The main area left untouched by the reforms is the legal position of cohabitants of whatever sexual orientation. It remains to be seen whether the government will legislate in the future to protect their position. The Employment Equality (Sexual Orientation) Regulations 2003[4] almost certainly make any different treatment of same sex and lesbian and gay partners either direct or indirect discrimination, but this only applies to employment. Otherwise protection is only available through existing statute law interpreted so as to conform to the UK's obligations under the European Convention on Human Rights. This task might be considered to have been made considerably easier after the decision of the European Court of Human Rights in *Karner v Austria*[5] and the judgment of the House of Lords in *Ghaidan v Godin-Mendoza*.[6] This book will seek to explore the implication of these and other decisions with a view to exploring the legal rights and responsibilities of lesbian and gay couples whether in registered partnerships or not.

---

1 *Hansard*, HL Deb, col GC5 (10 May 2004).
2 [1993] AC 593.
3 [2003] UKHL 40, [2004] 1 AC 816.
4 SI 2003/1660.
5 [2003] 2 FLR 623, ECHR.
6 [2004] UKHL 30, [2004] 2 AC 557.

Chapter 2

THE CONTEXT: LESBIAN AND GAY LAW REFORM

INTRODUCTION

2.1 It is arguable that the origins of the Civil Partnership Act 2004 lay in events 50 years previously,[1] with the conviction and imprisonment of Lord Montagu of Beaulieu, Michael Pitt-Rivers and Peter Wildblood in March 1954.[2] The furore generated by that trial led directly to the Wolfenden Report of 1957[3] which represented the first substantial achievement of the reformers who began to organise to achieve law reform. As with race, sex and disability discrimination, parliamentarians and campaigners alike were much influenced by the civil rights movement in the United States.[4] However, the Wolfenden Report[5] presaged 10 years of bitter argument before the resulting Sexual Offences Act 1967 was enacted. This was an extremely limited measure in that it decriminalised homosexual acts (in England and Wales only) where the activity took place in private between men who were both over the age of 21. As the Court of Appeal confirmed in *R v Knuller*,[6] 'There is a material difference between merely exempting certain conduct from criminal penalties and making it lawful in the full sense'.

2.2 A good indication of the status conferred on homosexuals can be found in the speech of Lord Arran, one of the Bill's main sponsors, during the Third Reading debate in the House of Lords: [7]

> 'Any form of ostentatious [gay] behaviour now, or in the future, any form of public flaunting, would be utterly distasteful and would, I believe, make the sponsors of the Bill regret that they have done what they have done. Homosexuals must remember that while there is nothing bad in being homosexual, there is certainly nothing good.'

2.3 It is perhaps not surprising, therefore, that, after such struggle, it was not until 1980 that there was any variation in this legal regime when the provisions were extended to

---

1   A coincidence that was remarked upon in the speech by Baroness Gould of Potternewton in the Second Reading debate in *Hansard*, HL Deb, col 401 (22 April 2004).
2   See A Barlow and others *Advising Lesbian and Gay Clients* (Butterworths, 1999).
3   Cmnd 247.
4   S Jeffrey-Poulter *Peers, Queers and Commons: The Struggle for Gay Law Reform from 1950 to the Present* (London: Routledge, 1991).
5   Cmnd 247.
6   [1973] AC 435 at 457.
7   Cited in A Grey *Quest for Justice: Towards Homosexual Emancipation* (London: Sinclair-Stevenson, 1992) pp 125–126.

Scotland.[1] This was, in part, a response[2] to the decision in *Saunders v Scottish National Camps Association*,[3] where the Scottish Employment Appeals Tribunal (EAT) upheld an Industrial Tribunal decision that a considerable proportion of employers would have taken the view that the applicant, as a homosexual, should not have been employed in close proximity to children.

2.4   Northern Ireland had to wait until October 1982 and even this move was as a result of a challenge mounted under the European Convention on Human Rights in the case of *Dudgeon v United Kingdom*.[4] Even after the decision the government struggled to amend the law. At the time, Enoch Powell MP commented, 'I would sooner receive injustice in the Queen's courts than justice in a foreign court and I hold that a man or woman to be a scoundrel who goes abroad to a foreign court to have the judgments of the Queen's courts overturned'.[5]

2.5   What marks the UK out as being unique in the EU was that the next legislative development was restrictive, in the form of s 28 of the Local Government Act 1988 ('s 28'). As Kees Waaldijk[6] has argued, most jurisdictions move from decriminalisation to an equal age of consent to anti-discrimination legislation. Very few have sought to tighten legislation in the way that was attempted in the UK. The fall of Margaret Thatcher in November 1990 coincided with renewed lesbian and gay activism brought about by the campaign against the then Clause 28. The pressure group Stonewall was founded in May 1989 and Outrage! (a direct action organisation) a year later.[7] In 1991 the Prime Minister announced that homosexual orientation would not preclude appointment to sensitive posts in the Home Civil Service and the Lord Chancellor made a similar announcement as concerns judicial office.[8] In 1994 homosexuality was decriminalised in the armed forces, but this did not prevent discharge of the service personnel involved on the ground of their homosexuality.[9]

2.6   In May 1997 a Labour government was elected with a large majority including six openly gay or lesbian MPs. The party's manifesto contained no specific commitment on sexual orientation discrimination but hope was generated early on with the introduction of a 'concession'[10] on the operation of immigration control which recognised same sex partners, based on a 4-year relationship (reduced to 2 years in 1999). However, the new government still instructed lawyers to argue against the concept of equal pay for same sex partners in the case of *Grant v South West Trains*[11] in February 1998 and *Smith and Grady*[12] in September 1999. It appeared that the new Labour government was following a

1   Criminal Justice (Scotland) Act 1980.
2   S Jeffrey-Poulter *Peers, Queers and Commons: The Struggle for Gay Law Reform from 1950 to the Present* (London: Routledge, 1991).
3   [1980] IRLR 174.
4   [1981] 4 EHRR 149.
5   *Belfast Telegraph* 15 March 1982.
6   K Waaldijk 'Small Change: How the Road to Same-Sex Marriage Got Paved in the Netherlands' in R Wintemute and M Andenas (eds) *Legal Recognition of Same-Sex Partnerships* (Hart Publishing, 2001).
7   I Cassell Lucas *Outrage!* (London and New York, 1998).
8   See the judgment of Sir Thomas Bingham MR in *R v Ministry of Defence, ex parte Smith* [1996] IRLR 100 at para 10.
9   Criminal Justice and Public Order Act 1994.
10   Immigration Directorate's Instructions Ch 8, annexe Z.
11   [1998] IRLR 206, ECJ.
12   [1999] IRLR 734, ECHR.

well-worn path, as Jeff Dudgeon, the applicant who brought the UK before the European Court of Human Rights[1] over the criminalisation of homosexual behaviour in Northern Ireland 8 years before, commented:[2]

'The knowledge that the European Court will eventually force change has given the government unprecedented extra powers of delay and disinterest. It no longer needs to participate in standard democratic argument and discussion, rather it has exported its power.'

2.7 In January 1998, the Equal Opportunities Commission, having failed to persuade a court to decide that sexual orientation discrimination was also sex discrimination in the case of *Grant*,[3] proposed amending the Sex Discrimination Act 1975 and Equal Pay Act 1970 in its consultative document entitled 'Equality in the 21st Century: a new approach'.[4] However the government indicated that it was not minded to make major changes to the present discrimination laws, confining itself instead to the recommendations of the Better Regulation Task Force.[5]

2.8 What progress there was seemed largely as a result of litigation or devolution. A generic sexual conduct code for the Armed Forces[6] was introduced as a result of *Smith and Grady v United Kingdom*.[7] In *ADT v United Kingdom*[8] the European Court of Human Rights found that the privacy provisions in the offence of gross indecency violated Article 8 of the Convention. A Sex Offences Review Team at the Home Office produced a report, 'Setting the Boundaries',[9] in July 2000 which recommended the repeal of specific gay male offences. The pace of change in Scotland was somewhat quicker. The Adults with Incapacity (Scotland) Act 2000, s 87(2) provides 'next of kin' rights to same sex partners, which is the first time such statutory recognition has been given in the UK. The Ethical Standards in Public Life (Scotland) Act 2000, s 25 repealed the Scottish equivalent of s 28 after a divisive debate.

2.9 If law reform by the use of legislation proved difficult in Scotland, it proved doubly so in England and Wales, where the government failed to get the support of the House of Lords for reform. When gay male sex was partially decriminalised in 1967, an age of consent was set at 21 years of age. This was challenged in *Wilde v United Kingdom*,[10] an action which was commenced in 1993. The next year the age of consent was reduced to 18 years[11] after a fierce campaign which, at one point, involved civil disobedience taking place at the House of Commons.[12] The limited legal reform still meant that the legal action had to be re-started.

---

1   *Dudgeon v United Kingdom* [1981] IRLR 174.
2   Jeff Dudgeon, quoted in S Jeffrey-Poulter *Peers, Queers and Commons: The Struggle for Gay Law Reform from 1950 to the Present* (London: Routledge, 1991) at 154.
3   The EOC funded the case with assistance from UNISON.
4   (Manchester: EOC, 1998).
5   www.cabinet-office.gov.uk/regulation/1999/task-force/anti-discrimination.pdf
6   Armed Forces Code of Conduct 2000.
7   [1999] IRLR 734, ECHR.
8   [2000] 2 FLR 697, ECHR.
9   www.homeoffice.gov.uk/new.htm – pp vii–viii.
10   (1995) 80 AD & R 132.
11   Criminal Justice and Public Order Act 1994.
12   I Cassell Lucas *Outrage!* (London and New York, 1998).

2.10 In July 1997 the European Human Rights Commission reported in *Sutherland and Morris v United Kingdom*[1] that the unequal age of consent was discriminatory. In October 1997 the Labour government reached an agreement to make time available for a further free vote on the subject but the attempt by Ann Keen MP to secure an equal consent was defeated in the House of Lords despite passing the House of Commons with a majority of 207. A Sexual Offences (Amendment) Bill was introduced in 1999 only to be lost in the House of Lords. The reform only passed into law on 8 January 2001[2] after the Speaker of the House of Commons in November 2000 certified that the Parliament Acts could be invoked, the measure having been passed in two successive Parliaments.[3] Discrimination was only removed from the criminal law by the Sexual Offences Act 2003.[4]

2.11 It is hardly surprising that, against this background, Baroness Turner of Camden encountered difficulties when she introduced a Sexual Orientation Discrimination Bill in three parliamentary sessions.[5] This measure would have amended both s 3 of the Sex Discrimination Act 1975 and s 1(3) of the Equal Pay Act 1970 to cover sexual orientation. However, the Bill fell on each occasion because of lack of debating time. Speaking on behalf of the Labour government and opposing the Bill in 1998, Baroness Blackstone emphasised:[6]

> '. . . the importance that this government place on the family . . . For generations, marriage has provided for millions of people a strong and stable base for the bringing up of children in a rapidly changing world. This Bill goes to the heart of that issue. It invites us to treat same sex couples as the equivalent of a family unit. What we must do is tread a careful path between taking account of social reality and at the same time ensuring that we do not undermine the family.'

2.12 On 18 September 2003 the Local Government Act 2003 received Royal Assent. This Act finally repealed s 28[7] after 15 years of campaigning. It is not difficult to see why, against that background, so much emphasis was given to a litigation strategy based on the use of the European Convention on Human Rights and EC law.

EUROPEAN CASE LAW

2.13 One of the most striking developments came in the field of employment law. In the UK, traditionally, lesbians and gay men were given very little protection against unfair dismissal by Industrial Tribunals who tended to give great weight to submissions by employers that they felt obliged to act on the feelings and prejudices (actual or assumed) of their customers or employees, however objectively unreasonable such prejudices might be. This approach was confirmed in *Saunders v Scottish National Camps*

---

1   [1998] EHRLR 117.
2   Sexual Offences (Amendment) Act 2000.
3   Parliament Act 1911 and Parliament Act 1949.
4   The Sexual Offences Act 2003 eventually made the criminal law non-discriminatory, with the exception of s 71 which makes sexual activity in a public toilet an offence. It is arguable that this is indirectly discriminatory.
5   1995, 1996 and 1998.
6   HL Official Report (6th Series) col 655 (5 June 1998).
7   Local Government Act 1986, s 2(a).

Association Ltd[1] and *Boychuk v HJ Symons Holdings Ltd*[2] and given a particular twist with the emergence of HIV in the 1980s and the accompanying 'AIDS phobia' by the EAT in *Buck v The Letchworth Palace*.[3] In that instance, the employer dismissed an employee on the basis that other employees refused to work with him since they felt he posed a health risk to them. Industrial Tribunals appeared to compound this prejudice. In *Boychuk*, the IT Chairman, in the course of proceedings, asked the applicant whether she was trying to bring other women into the 'cult … of lesbianism'.[4]

2.14   The Ministry of Defence used the argument about the potential reaction of other service personnel to justify its policy of automatic discharge on grounds of homosexuality. In the early 1990s, the lobbying group Stonewall, who from their inception had placed emphasis on the 'European dimension',[5] having failed to persuade the government to reform this policy at the time of the renewal of the Armed Services Act 1991, determined that it would support challenges to the legality of such discrimination as and when cases arose. In June 1995 they backed four ex-service personnel who sought judicial review of their discharges in the High Court[6] on the grounds that they breached both Article 8 of the European Convention on Human Rights and the Equal Treatment Directive (ETD).[7] The Application failed but Simon Brown LJ gave a very sympathetic judgment, particularly as regards the possible infringement of Article 8.[8] His judgment began with the words, 'Lawrence of Arabia would not be welcome in today's armed forces'.[9]

2.15   The service personnel appealed and the matter was heard in November 1995.[10] The leading judgment was given by Sir Thomas Bingham MR who, whilst impressed with the merits of the human rights argument, said that he felt obliged to reject it because at that stage the Convention was not incorporated into UK domestic law. He also rejected the argument based on the Equal Treatment Directive, on the basis that the drafters of the Directive would not have had sexual orientation in mind at the time it was drafted, and said he was similarly not persuaded of the merits of the argument based on *Toonen v Australia*,[11] which was decided on Article 26 of the International Covenant on Civil and Political Rights 1966, where the Human Rights Committee decided that the word 'sex' includes sexual orientation.

2.16   At this stage campaigners for reform were given a boost by the decision of the European Court of Justice in *P v S and Cornwall County Council*[12] where the court ruled

---

1   [1981] IRLR 277 CS.

2   [1977] IRLR 395 EAT.

3   Unreported.

4   P Crane *Gays and the Law* (London: Pluto Press, 1982).

5   S Jeffrey-Poulter *Peers, Queers and Commons: The Struggle for Gay Law Reform from 1950 to the Present* (London: Routledge, 1991) at 154.

6   *R v Ministry of Defence, ex parte Smith and others* [1996] QB 517.

7   76/207/EEC.

8   76/207/EEC at para 70.

9   76/207/EEC at 567 para 1.

10   *R v Ministry of Defence, ex parte Smith and Grady; R v Admiralty Board of the Defence Council, ex parte Lustig-Prean and Beckett* [1996] IRLR 100.

11   (1994) 1–3 IHRR 97.

12   Case No C-13/94 [1996] IRLR 347 ECJ.

that Article 5(1) of the ETD precludes dismissal of a transsexual for a reason related to his gender re-assignment. They argued that:

> 'he or she is treated unfavourably by comparison with persons of the sex to which he or she was deemed to belong before undergoing gender reassignment. To tolerate such discrimination would be tantamount, as regards such a person, to a failure to respect the dignity and freedom to which he, or she, is entitled and which the Court has a duty to respect.'

The court's emphasis on the primacy of equality was supported by its contention that this formed a fundamental principle of Community law and that it was 'one of the fundamental human rights whose observance the court has a duty to ensure'. As a consequence of the ruling, the Sex Discrimination Act 1975 was amended by the Employment Rights Act 1999 to provide a new s 2A covering gender re-assignment.

2.17   Despite the optimism generated by *P v S*,[1] in February 1998 the European Court of Justice in *Grant v South West Trains*[2] held that a female employee of a railway company had not been discriminated against because her lesbian partner had been denied travel concessions under a company policy, a condition of which restricted such concessions to workers living in a stable relationship with a person of the opposite sex. The court dismissed her claim, holding that since the condition applied in the same way to male and female workers; it could not be regarded as constituting discrimination based directly on sex, since a male homosexual would also have been refused a travel concession for his male partner. This was the reasoning which had been described by Cherie Booth QC as the 'equality of misery argument' in oral argument before the court.[3] The court noted that the position might change with the signing of the Treaty of Amsterdam on 2 October 1997.

2.18   The decision proved a serious setback for campaigners in the UK. The reference in *R v Secretary of State for Defence, ex parte Perkins*,[4] which concerned the armed forces, was withdrawn reluctantly by Lightman J,[5] on the basis that the European Court of Justice had already settled the issue. In some respects *Perkins* was a far stronger case than *Grant*, as it involved the loss of a job, not just the loss of certain fringe benefits for a partner, and, with hindsight, it was perhaps unfortunate that it was *Grant* which was heard first.[6] Lightman J held out the prospect of a favourable ruling once the Human Rights Bill became law. *Grant* was followed by the Court of Appeal in July 1998 in *Smith v Gardner Merchant Ltd*.[7]

2.19   With the domestic and EU litigation having proved unfruitful, the only avenue remaining was under the European Convention on Human Rights. This had not always proved a happy path. In 1955, in a case brought against Germany, the European Commission of Human Rights held that Article 8(2) of the Convention 'allows a high

---

1   See the judgment of Lightman J in *R v Secretary of State for Defence, ex parte Perkins* [1997] IRLR 297 per Lightman J; and IT Smith and G Thomas *Industrial Law* (London: Butterworths, 8th edn, 2003).

2   Case No C-249/96 [1998] IRLR 206, ECJ.

3   Barlow et al *Advising Lesbian and Gay Clients* (London: Butterworths, 1999) p 10.

4   [1997] IRLR 297 (referring the matter to the ECJ), (No 2) [1998] IRLR 508, QBD (withdrawing the reference).

5   See *R v Secretary of State for Defence, ex parte Perkins* [1997] IRLR 297 per Lightman J.

6   Barlow et al *Advising Lesbian and Gay Clients* (London: Butterworths, 1999) p 38.

7   [1998] IRLR 510, CA.

contracting party to punish homosexuality ... for the protection of health and morals'.[1] However it had brought decriminalisation in Ireland in *Dudgeon v United Kingdom*[2] and *Norris v Ireland*.[3]

2.20 In *Smith and Grady v UK*[4] the majority of the European Court of Human Rights, in September 1999, found that the government had breached Article 8 as a result of over-intrusive investigations.[5] The UK government had argued that the interference was justified under Article 8(2) but the court rejected the argument, observing that when the restrictions concern 'a most intimate aspect of an individual's private life', there must be 'a particularly serious reason before such interference can be justified'. The court rejected the arguments of the Ministry of Defence[6]

> 'founded solely upon the negative attitudes of heterosexual personnel towards those of homosexual orientation'

and declared that

> 'these attitudes even if sincerely felt by those who expressed them, ranged from stereotypical expressions of hostility to those of homosexual orientation, to vague expressions of unease about the presence of homosexual colleagues. To the extent that they represent a predisposed bias on the part of a heterosexual majority against a homosexual minority, those negative attitudes cannot, of themselves, be considered by the Court to amount to sufficient justification for the interference with the applicant's rights ... any more than similar negative attitudes towards those of a different race, origin or colour.'

2.21 This was followed in December 1999 by the finding by the European Court of Human Rights, in a family case, that a difference of treatment on grounds of sexual orientation was discriminatory. In *Salgueiro da Silva Mouta v Portugal*[7] the court concluded that Portugal had breached Articles 8 and 14 in a private law children's case. The facts were that the parents of M had agreed that their daughter should live with her mother. When it transpired that M was actually being cared for by the maternal grandparents, the father applied for and was granted custody and care of the child despite the mother's contentions that the father was homosexual and living with another man. After various allegations and counter-allegations the case reached the Lisbon Court of Appeal.

2.22 The Portuguese Court of Appeal was quoted as stating:

> 'It is well known that society is becoming more and more tolerant of such situations. However, it cannot be agreed that an environment of this kind is the healthiest and best suited to the child's psychological, social and mental development, especially given the dominant model in our society ... The child should live in ... a traditional Portuguese family.'

The court added that:

---

1 *X v Germany* (No 104/55) (1955), 1 Yearbook of the European Conv HR 228.
2 (1981) 4 EHRR 149, ECHR.
3 (1988) 13 EHRR 186, ECHR.
4 [1999] IRLR 734.
5 It found that the complaints under Article 14 did not give rise to a separate issue.
6 [1999] IRLR 734at 748 para 97.
7 [2001] 1 FCR 653, ECHR.

'it is not our task here to determine whether homosexuality is or is not an illness or whether it is a sexual orientation towards persons of the same sex. In both cases it is an abnormality and children should not grow up in the shadow of abnormal situations.'

It did not prove very difficult for the European Court of Human Rights to conclude that the decision of the Lisbon Court constituted an interference with the father's right to respect for his family life. It further concluded that the decision of the Court of Appeal had turned on the father's sexual orientation and on that basis had made a distinction on the grounds of sexual orientation, which was not acceptable under the Convention, relying on the decision in *Hoffman v Austria*.[1] It concluded that it couldn't find a reasonable relationship of proportionality between the means employed and the aim pursued. The facts of the case were relatively extreme, like the earlier decision of the court in *Smith and Grady*, but the sentiments in the Portuguese judgment might have been expressed in not too dissimilar terms in English County Courts not very many years before.

2.23 A more traditional decision of the court in this sensitive area of family law was arrived at by the European Court of Human Rights by a majority of four to three[2] in *Frette v France*[3] in February 2002. The Conseil D'Etat rejected the application of a single gay man to adopt, on the basis that his lifestyle did not provide the requisite safeguards for adopting a child. The European Court of Human Rights found that Article 8, in conjunction with Article 14, was engaged. Following *Salgueiro da Silva Mouta v Portugal*[4] the court reiterated that Article 14 covered a difference in treatment based on the applicant's sexual orientation[5] but the court took into account the fact that it felt the law in this area in the member states of the Council of Europe was in a state of transition and therefore a wide margin of appreciation must be left to the authorities of each state. It concluded that the justification given by France appeared objective and reasonable and the difference in treatment was not discriminatory.

DOMESTIC CASE LAW

2.24 It is not surprising that the decision in *Salgueiro da Silva Mouta v Portugal*[6] was being cited almost as soon as it became known. In particular it was used in argument in the Scottish case of *MacDonald v Ministry of Defence*[7] which was another armed forces case heard in September 2000 just before the Convention was enshrined in domestic law by the Human Rights Act 1998. Using Scottish precedents dealing with the status of the Convention, Lord Johnston found that the word 'sex' was ambiguous in that:

---

1   (1994) 17 EHRR 293.
2   The minority felt that if a country were to go beyond its Article 8 obligations and entitle single persons to apply for adoption, France was under a duty to implement the system in such a way that there was no unwarranted discrimination on Article 14 grounds.
3   [2003] 2 FLR 9, ECHR. The Canadian academic, Robert Wintemute, was one of the two who addressed the court.
4   [2001] 1 FCR 653, ECHR.
5   [2003] 2 FLR 9 paras 32 and 33.
6   [2001] 1 FCR 653, ECHR.
7   [2000] IRLR 748 EAT.

'The Oxford University Dictionary (sic) (1989) inter alia includes a definition under the word 'sex' of a 'third sex' which undoubtedly refers to homosexuality in both men and women.'

2.25 On the basis that 'sex' under Convention law now included sexual orientation, the EAT found that the Sex Discrimination Act 1975 should be interpreted accordingly. However, the judgment was hopelessly compromised by the fact the Scottish EAT would not appear to have had a proper report of the *Salgueiro* judgment.[1] In *Hallam v Basford Plant Ltd and Anthony Kirk*,[2] an English Employment Tribunal case heard in January 2001, the Employment Tribunal analysed a French transcript of the judgment which made it clear that the ECHR had intended that discrimination on grounds of sexual orientation was to be treated as discrimination on the grounds of 'other status' under Article 14.

2.26 The matter was revisited by the Scottish Court of Session in June 2001 in the appeal of *Macdonald v Secretary of State for Defence*.[3] All the judges had little difficulty in rejecting the reasoning of the EAT that there was ambiguity in the meaning of the word 'sex'. The issue was then considered by the English Court of Appeal on 31 July 2001 in the case of *Pearce v Governing Body of Mayfield Secondary School*.[4] Although the matter was heard after the implementation of the Human Rights Act 1998, the House of Lords in *R v Lambert*[5] had, by that time, determined that 'There is nothing to show that it was intended by s 3 that the meaning given to a statutory provision by a court prior to 2 October 2000 should be changed in the event of an appeal against that decision being heard on or after that date'. As a result, the Court of Appeal had little difficulty in following *Smith v Gardner Merchant*[6] and *Grant v South West Trains*.[7]

2.27 In a lengthy (and largely obiter) judgment, Hale LJ (as she was then) went on to consider whether, if the Human Rights Act 1998 had been effective, it would have made a difference. She concluded that the experience suffered by the Appellant was incompatible with Articles 8 and 14 and that the Convention not only afforded her protection against arbitrary action by public authorities but also created positive obligations. She placed reliance on the judgment of Sachs J in the case of *National Coalition for Gay and Lesbian Equality and another v Ministry of Justice and others*[8] where he contended that a right to privacy was a complex notion which included protection for that which gives a person an autonomous identity. That can include family life and sexual preference, for the Constitution of South Africa does not 'presuppose that a holder of rights is an isolated, lonely and abstract figure possessing a disembodied and socially disconnected self'. Hale LJ concluded that a remedy might exist for cases whose factual matrix arises after 1 October 2000 under ss 6 and 7 of the Human Rights Act 1998, or it may be possible to give effect to the Sex Discrimination Act 1975 compatible with the Convention by regarding sexual orientation as an irrelevant circumstance for the purpose of s 5(3) of the Sex Discrimination Act.

1   *MacDonald* [2000] IRLR 750 at para 12.
2   Unreported ET.
3   [2001] IRLR 431 CS.
4   [2001] IRLR 669, CA.
5   [2001] UKHL 37, HL.
6   [1998] IRLR 510, CA.
7   Case C-249/96 [1998] IRLR 206, ECJ.
8   [2000] 4 LRC 292.

SUCCESSION RIGHTS

2.28 It was to transpire that the question of lesbian and gay cohabitation rights was to prove a remarkable testing ground for Human Rights Convention jurisprudence and of the efficacy of the Human Rights Act 1998. In October 1999 the case of *Fitzpatrick v Sterling Housing Association*[1] reached the House of Lords. The case concerned the succession rights of a surviving partner to a same sex relationship under the Rent Act 1977.[2] The Rent Act 1977 (as amended by the Housing Act 1988), provided that a surviving spouse would inherit the statutory tenancy provided that they were residing in the dwelling-house immediately before the death of the previous tenant. The same rights were provided for a person if they were living with the original tenant 'as his or her wife or husband'. The Act went on to provide that a person could acquire an assured tenancy if they were a member of the original tenant's family residing with him at the time of and for the period of 2 years immediately before the original tenant's death.

2.29 The Law Lords were unanimous in their view that the Act could not be read so that a same sex partner could be treated as living with the original tenant 'as his or her wife or husband'. In his speech Lord Slynn said:

> 'Whether that result is discriminatory against same-sex couples in the light of the fact that non-married different sex couples living together are to be treated as spouses so as to allow one to succeed to the tenancy of the other may have to be considered when the Human Rights Act 1988 is in force. Whether the result is socially desirable in 1999 is a matter for Parliament.'

However, by a majority of three to two the House of Lords decided that 'family' was a word that had not been given a statutory meaning but had been left to the courts to decide.

2.30 Lord Clyde in his speech considered what was required to evidence the common bond in a partnership of two adult persons that may entitle them to be considered a member of the other's family. He concluded:

> 'the bond must be one of love and affection, not of a casual or transitory nature, but in a relationship which is permanent or at least intended to be so. As a result of that personal attachment to each other, other characteristics will follow, such as a readiness to support each other emotionally and financially, to care, to care for and look after the other in times of need, and to provide a companionship in which mutual interests and activities can be shared and enjoyed together. It would be difficult to establish such a bond unless the couple were living together in the same house. It would also be difficult to establish it without an active sexual relationship between them or at least the potentiality of such a relationship.'

2.31 A strikingly similar case was then heard by the European Court of Human Rights in July 2003, *Karner v Austria*.[3] It concerned the succession of a tenancy by a same sex partner and whether he could be considered to be a 'life-companion' in Austrian law. The court permitted the European Region of the International Lesbian and Gay Association, Liberty and Stonewall to intervene as third parties and they were represented before the court by Rob Wintemute. The court was prepared to hear the case despite the fact that the original applicant had died.[4] The court found that Article 8 was engaged and that there

---

1   [2000] 1 FLR 271, HL.
2   Sch 1, para 2.
3   [2003] 2 FLR 623, ECHR.
4   It was this issue which led to Judge Grabenwarter to produce a dissenting opinion.

had been a difference of treatment on the ground of sexual orientation. Of particular importance is the fact that:

(1) the court found that differences based on sexual orientation require particularly serious reasons by way of justification; and

(2) it accepted that the protection of the family in the traditional sense is, in principle, a weighty and legitimate reason which might justify a difference in treatment but it has to be seen in each case whether the principle of proportionality is respected. This is particularly because the aim is rather narrow and this is an area in which the margin of appreciation available to member states is narrow.

2.32 The court concluded that it must be shown that it was necessary to exclude persons living in a homosexual relationship from the scope of application of the particular section in the Austrian Rent Act. It is not particularly surprising, therefore, that when the House of Lords had an opportunity to reconsider the question of the interpretation of Sch 1 to the Rent Act 1977 after the implementation of the Human Rights Act 1998 it found that it was able to go further than it had in *Fitzpatrick v Sterling Housing Association*.[1] That occasion arose in June 2004 when the House of Lords decided the case of *Ghaidan v Mendoza*.[2] By a majority of four to one, the Law Lords found that they were required by s 3 of the Human Rights Act 1998 to read the relevant section of the Rent Act 1977 as though the survivor of a homosexual relationship was the surviving souse of the original tenant. The government did not seek to put any argument before the court that the Rent Act restriction of succession rights to heterosexual cohabitees pursued a legitimate aim and it was left to counsel for the leaseholder to argue that its aim was the protection of the traditional family. This was an argument which did not find favour, as the Law Lords were unable to find any connection between the restriction in the legislation and any aim because the Schedule as it stood put heterosexual cohabitants in a privileged position regardless of parenthood or the presence of children in the home or procreative potential.

THE TREATY OF AMSTERDAM

2.33 The judgment of the European Court of Justice in *Grant*[3] represented a very serious defeat for lesbian and gay campaigners but the court did recognise that a potential remedy lay with Article 13 of the Treaty as amended at Amsterdam:[4]

'Without prejudice to the other provisions of this treaty and within the limits of the powers conferred by it upon the Community, the Council, acting unanimously on a proposal from the Commission and after consulting the European Parliament, may take appropriate action to combat discrimination based on sex, racial or ethnic origin, religion or belief, disability, age or sexual orientation.'

---

1   [2000] 1 FLR 271, HL.

2   [2004] 2 FLR 600, HL.

3   Case C-249/96[1998] IRLR 206 ECJ.

4   The provision was initially numbered 6a following the numbering of the EC Treaty as used in the body of the Amsterdam Treaty. It is now commonly referred to as Article 13, in accordance with the renumbering of the Treaty, which followed the Amsterdam revision.

2.34 On 27 November 2000 the EU adopted a Framework Directive[1] under the mechanism of Article 13. The Framework Directive covers discrimination on the grounds of religion or belief, disability, age or sexual orientation. It only covers employment and occupation.[2] The way the Directive was transposed into domestic law was and is controversial. In particular, it was unclear to what extent it offered protection to those in same sex relationships.

2.35 The Directive would appear to make discrimination against couples unlawful in certain circumstances. In the government's consultation paper,[3] it noted that the scope of the Directive includes 'employment and working conditions ... and pay' and conceded that the Directive may therefore make it unlawful to discriminate against same sex couples where benefits are paid out to a surviving partner on death. This would have an impact on schemes where benefits are paid to a partner on death.[4] However, it argued[5] that, where the rules of the scheme restrict benefits to surviving spouses, this would probably survive scrutiny as the Directive is expressed to be 'without prejudice to national laws on marital status and the benefits dependent thereon'.[6]

2.36 Mark Bell[7] argues that these vague restrictions were placed in the Directive as they were politically necessary to achieve unanimity but that they flatly contradict Article 2(2) in that the 'apparently neutral' criterion of marital status, 'puts ... at a disadvantage' gay and lesbian couples because they are barred from marriage by means of s 11(c) of the Matrimonial Causes Act 1973. He notes, in support of his contention that this is likely to be a troublesome area of law, the fact that, since 1994, two-thirds of all complaints brought under the Dutch General Equal Treatment Act have been related to the non-availability for same sex couples of the privileges available for married couples.

2.37 The most notorious problem arose as a result of the EU's own internal staff regulations which contain a non-discrimination clause which was, at that time, said to be without prejudice to the relevant provision requiring a specific marital status.[8] In the case of *D and Sweden v EU Council*[9] D, an employee of the Council, supported by the governments of Sweden, Denmark and the Netherlands, complained that his partner had been denied employee benefits even though their relationship was registered in Sweden. The European Court of Justice published its judgment at the end of May 2001 and gave five main reasons for dismissing the appeal:

---

1   Council Directive 2000/78/EC of 27 November 2000 establishing a general framework for equal treatment in employment and occupation.

2   Including vocational training.

3   Office of the Deputy Prime Minister *Towards Equality and Diversity: Implementing the Employment and Race Directives* (London, 2001).

4   Recital 22.

5   Recital 22.

6   Preamble at (22).

7   Bell 'Sexual Orientation Discrimination in Employment: An Evolving Role for the European Union' in R Wintemute and M Andenas (eds) *Legal Recognition of Same-Sex Partnerships* (Hart Publishing, 2001) at 668.

8   Article 1a Council Regulation (EC, ECSC, Euratom) No 781/98 of 7 April 1998, amending the Staff Regulations of Officials and Conditions of Employment of Other Servants of the European Communities in respect of Equal treatment, OJ [1998] L 113/4 15 April 1998.

9   Joined Cases C-122/99 P, C-125/99 P *D and Sweden v Council of the European Union* 2001 ECR 1–4319.

(1) 'married official' could not be interpreted to cover registered partnerships according to the definition generally accepted by member states, which is that it is a union between two persons of the opposite sex;

(2) registered partnerships are legally distinct from marriages where they apply and are limited to a few jurisdictions only;

(3) it does not involve sex discrimination with regard to Article 141, because a woman with a female partner would have been treated the same way (in other words, adopting the reasoning in *Grant*);

(4) it does not involve sexual orientation discrimination because, 'it is not the sex of the partner which determines whether the household allowance is granted, but the legal nature of the ties between the official and the partner';[1] and

(5) it does not violate the general principle of equal treatment as it was not comparing like with like.

2.38 This may not be the last such case, as the European Court of Justice ruled inadmissible an argument based on nationality discrimination and the obstacle that such discrimination might pose to the free movement of workers, on the ground that it was not argued before the Court of First Instance and raised only on appeal. Further, neither Article 13 EC nor Article 21 of the Charter of Fundamental Rights and Freedoms was relied upon. A further consolidation of the position of member states on this issue may influence the European Court of Justice.[2] It is interesting to note that a month before the judgment in *D*, the Netherlands opened up marriage to same sex couples.[3] It is likely that there will be a challenge in an EU member state as to the consequences of such a marriage for freedom of movements and rights flowing from being an EU citizen or the spouse of such a citizen.

SEXUAL ORIENTATION REGULATIONS

2.39 The UK government chose to implement the Directive by means of the European Communities Act 1972, s 2(2) which placed restrictions on what was possible by means of expanding upon the rights provided for in the Directive. In fact, the way the Directive was transposed was the subject of considerable controversy and led to a judicial review by Amicus and others in April 2004.[4]

2.40 The Employment Equality (Sexual Orientation) Regulations 2003[5] make discrimination unlawful on grounds of sexual orientation. A good illustration of the operation of the Regulations as they concern the rights of lesbians and gay men is

---

1   Para 47.

2   Bell 'Sexual Orientation Discrimination in Employment: An Evolving Role for the European Union' in R Wintemute and M Andenas (eds) *Legal Recognition of Same Sex Partnerships* (Hart Publishing, 2001) at 670.

3   Act of 21 December 2000 amending Book 1 of the Civil Code, concerning the opening up of marriage for persons of the same sex (Act on the Opening up of Marriage).

4   *R (on the application of Amicus – MSF section and others) v Secretary of State for Trade and Industry and Christian Action Research Education (Interveners)* [2004] IRLR 430 HC.

5   SI 2003/1661.

provided in the ACAS Guidelines *Sexual Orientation and the Workplace*[1] which give the following example of direct discrimination contrary to the Regulations: [2]

> 'Whilst being interviewed, a job applicant says that she has a same sex partner, although she has all the skills and competences required of the job holder, the organisation decides not to offer her the job because she is a lesbian.'

2.41 The ACAS Guidelines also offer the following advice about benefits for same sex partners:

> 'If organisations give benefits such as insurance or private health care to opposite sex unmarried partners then refusing to give the same benefits to same sex partners would be discrimination. If benefits specify "married" partners or "spouse" then they do not have to cover unmarried partners.'

2.42 However, reg 25 of the Employment Equality (Sexual Orientation) Regulations 2003 provides that nothing in Part II or III of the Regulations 'shall render unlawful anything which prevents or restricts access to a benefit by reference to marital status'. Its effect was that employment benefits defined by reference to marital status, such as a surviving spouse's pension, are not prohibited by the Regulations. In the *R (on the application of Amicus – MSF Section) v Secretary of State for Trade and Industry*[3] case, Richards J decided that the UK Regulations were correctly implementing the Directive in this regard, largely on the evidence of recital (22) which states that the Directive 'is without prejudice to national laws on marital status and the benefits dependent thereon'. It is not clear that that clarified the law any further than it had been in the course of parliamentary debate. It is interesting that the EU Charter of Fundamental Rights as agreed at Nice, while cited in *R (on the application of Amicus – MSF Section) v Secretary of State for Trade and Industry*,[4] was thought to add nothing material in a case which was almost entirely concerned with EU law concepts.

THE FUTURE

2.43 Article 21 of the Charter expressly prohibits discrimination on grounds of sexual orientation, despite the best efforts of the UK government to have it deleted from the draft.[5] Article 9 of the EU Charter of Fundamental Rights guarantees the 'Right to marry and the right to found a family ... in accordance with the national laws governing the exercise of these rights'. However, it is thought unlikely that it will generate much case law in this area because of the influence of an explanatory memorandum of the drafting Convention which states that there is no obligation to recognise same sex couples as a

---

1   Published in April 2004 by the Advisory, Conciliation and Arbitration Service (ACAS).
2   *Sexual Orientation and the Workplace* para 1.1.
3   *R (on the application of Amicus – MSF section and others) v Secretary of State for Trade and Industry and Christian Action Research Education (Interveners)* [2004] IRLR 430.
4   [2004] IRLR 430 at 436 HC p 27.
5   Contribution of Lord Goldsmith on behalf of the government, Charter 4344/00 at http://db.consilium.eu.int/df/default.asp?lang=eng (search: Show All Documents, 31 May 2000), proposed Article 22(2).

result of the Charter.[1] Further developments are largely reliant on the Treaty of Rome 2004 being ratified by the member states.

2.44 It is envisaged that in the UK much of the impetus behind a litigation strategy to establish legal recognition of lesbian and gay partnership rights will be lost because of the success of the campaign to establish a statutory same sex scheme for civil union.[2] In the Republic of Ireland, however, the struggle continues. On 9 November 2004 Mr Justice McKechnie in the Irish High Court gave leave to Katherine Zappone (a Human Rights Commissioner in the Republic of Ireland) and her partner, Ann Louise Gilligan, judicially to review a decision by the Revenue Commissioner to refuse them tax relief available to married couples. Ms Zappone and Ms Gilligan had been married in British Columbia, Canada in September 2003.

---

1   Carracciolo di Torella and Reid 'The Changing face of 'the European Family' and Fundamental Rights' (2002) European Law Review 80.
2   Campaigning energy is likely to focus on the requirement for equal anti-discrimination legislation to cover all the Article 13 protected categories and for law reform to protect heterosexual as well as homosexual cohabitants.

Chapter 3

THE GENESIS AND SCOPE OF THE CIVIL PARTNERSHIP ACT 2004

INTRODUCTION

3.1   In common law the assumption has always been that marriage is a heterosexual institution. A commonly cited authority for this is *Hyde v Hyde and Woodmansee*[1] where Lord Penzance spoke of marriage as 'the voluntary union for life of one man to one woman to the exclusion of all others' – although it needs to be remembered that this was in the context of a consideration of the problems of entertaining a divorce petition concerning a potentially polygamous marriage. *Rayden on Divorce*[2] puts it succinctly: 'Marriage requires the participation of two persons, one a man, the other a woman.' The Matrimonial Causes Act 1973, s 11(c) specifies that a marriage shall be void if 'the parties are not respectively male and female'. As Stephen Cretney[3] has pointed out, though, in contrast with the United States, there is no reported case in which anyone in the UK has sought to persuade a court that a relationship between persons of the same sex was capable of constituting a 'marriage'.

3.2   That comment needs some qualification since the recent case law concerning the rights of transsexuals both in the UK[4] and before the European Court of Human Rights.[5] That led to the Gender Recognition Act 2004 which received Royal Assent on 1 July 2004. This is after an earlier history of cases in which the European Court remained unconvinced of the arguments.[6]

3.3   In the absence of marriage or a system of registered partnership, same sex couples faced the same difficulties as heterosexual cohabitants. That is to say, they had to take deliberate steps to protect their legal rights, such as making wills, entering cohabitation agreements[7] and, if they had any children, obtaining a shared residence order. All of this is more complex and expensive than registering a marriage or a civil partnership. In the absence of orders or explicit agreements between the parties there was the real possibility of injustice. Parliament, however, was reluctant to legislate to give more protection for

---

1   (1866) LR 1 P&D 130, 133.
2   (17th edn) p 102.
3   S Cretney *Family Law in the Twentieth Century: A History* (OUP, 2003).
4   *Bellinger v Bellinger* [2003] 1 FLR 1043, HL.
5   *Goodwin v UK* (Application Number 28957/95) [2002] 2 FLR 487, ECHR.
6   *Rees v UK* [1987] 2 FLR 111; *Cossey v UK* [1991] 2 FLR 492.
7   The general enforceability of which was confirmed in *Sutton v Mishcon de Reya* [2004] 3 All ER 411, HL.

cohabitants, for fear that it would undermine marriage. The history of parliamentary reform of family law in the 1990s is illuminating in this regard.

FAMILY LAW REFORM

3.4   In 1992 the Law Commission had proposed reform of the complex competing jurisdictions of the courts as concerned the protection of adults and children from 'domestic violence'. It recommended synthesising the available legal remedies into a clear, simple and comprehensible civil code.[1] Its report generated considerable criticism from certain MPs and a press campaign led by the *Daily Mail*.[2] The Major government sought to give effect to the Law Commission's proposals in its Family Homes and Domestic Violence Bill in 1995. After the Bill faced a hostile reception in the House of Commons, on the ground that it undermined marriage, it was withdrawn.

3.5   The clauses of the Family Homes and Domestic Violence Bill then found themselves inserted as Part IV of the Family Law Bill introduced in the following parliamentary session. The whole process of putting this Bill through Parliament proved to be a traumatic experience for the then Conservative government. The Bill required 137 amendments during its passage through the Commons alone and many of these amendments were specifically concerned with protecting the institution of marriage by making divorce more difficult. The consequence of this was that the Act was of such complexity that large portions of it were never put into force when a Labour government was elected on 1 May 1997. What did survive, though, were clauses stressing the importance of whether a couple had given each other 'the commitment involved in marriage'.[3]

3.6   Under the Adoption Act 1976 a joint application for an adoption order could only be made by a married couple. This is a position that had been clear in statute from the Adoption of Children Act 1926. This didn't prevent one member of a couple applying for an adoption order on their own or an application being made by one member of a couple together with a joint residence order in favour of both of them. This was a position that was confirmed by Singer J in *Re W (a minor) (adoption: homosexual adopter)*.[4]

3.7   The 1992 Report, *Review of Adoption Law*,[5] had recommended that formal statutory restrictions be maintained, and that was the basis upon which the Adoption and Children Bill was originally drafted. On the second day of the Report stage of the Bill, David Hinchcliffe MP successfully introduced an amendment to extend the right to adopt to unmarried and same sex couples. This was widely seen as the subject of serious disagreement within the government which was only successfully resolved by a decision

1   *Domestic Violence and Occupation of the Family Home* (Law Com No 207).
2   In 'Unmarried Couples in Family Law' [2004] Fam Law, Baroness Hale recalled the *Daily Mail* headline for 1 November 1995: 'Legal commissars subverting family values'.
3   Family Law Act 1996, ss 36 and 41.
4   [1997] 2 FLR 406.
5   Department of Health and Welsh Office, *Review of Adoption Law, Report to Ministers of an Interdepartmental Working Group: A Consultation Document* (HMSO, 1992).

to allow a free vote on the question.[1] It was highly significant as it was the first occasion in which formal recognition in law was given to 'partners'.

3.8 In turn, the House of Lords adopted by 34 votes an amendment proposed by Earl Howe to restrict the right to adopt jointly to married couples. When the Bill returned to the House of Commons and the matter was debated on 4 November, the Conservative Party imposed a three-line whip on the vote on the amendment. This was ignored by, amongst others, Michael Portillo MP, amidst rumours of a leadership bid and splits based on cultural values. The Bill became a litmus test of whether the Conservative Party needed to adapt to certain social and cultural norms, and the debate generated intense media interest. It is arguable that it proved a major turning point in that the Labour government realised that, despite all their fraught discussion about the terms of the proposals, they actually caused more political difficulties for their Conservative opponents than for their own party. In the end the Commons version of the Bill prevailed but in an echo of the subsequent arguments over the Civil Partnership Bill it was only approved by the House of Lords on 5 November and given Royal Assent on 7 November. The complexity of the Act and the desire of the government to produce Regulations (which need to be consulted on) led to a substantial delay in the implementation of most of the Act.

3.9 One of the issues that emerged in the last debates on the Bill was the role of the European Convention on Human Rights. The Report of the Joint Committee on Human Rights on the Bill[2] concluded that the Bill (as amended in the House of Lords) would violate Article 14 of the Convention. In fact, when the European Court of Human Rights had to confront the problem in *Frette v France*[3] its reaction was equivocal. It found that Article 14 in conjunction with Article 8 was applicable, as the appellant's right to apply for adoption had been infringed on grounds of his sexual orientation. By four votes to three, though, the court decided that the case was within the margin of appreciation because it raised a delicate issue upon which there was little common ground amongst the member states of the Council of Europe and the refusal to authorise adoption did not infringe the principle of proportionality. It is likely that this is a question to which the court will return.

INTERNATIONAL CONTEXT

3.10 It is not possible in a book like this to provide a comprehensive survey of international developments in the recognition of civil unions or marriages between lesbians and gay men. It is interesting to note, though, the cultural difference between developments in Europe, which have largely been borne of legislative change, compared with the situation in many common law countries, where change has frequently been the product of case law.

---

1   C Bridge and H Swindells *Adoption – The Modern Law* (Family Law, 2003) p 26.

2   *Twenty-fourth Report of the Joint Committee on Human Rights on the Adoption and Children Bill as amended by the House of Lords on Report*, published as 177/HL/HC Paper 979, 30 October 2002.

3   [2003] 2 FLR 9, ECHR.

Denmark

3.11 Despite its pioneering role in opening up marriage to lesbians and gay men, the leader in the field of civil partnerships for same sex couples was not the Netherlands but Denmark. On 7 June 1989 Denmark adopted a Civil Partnership Act which gave to registered partners the same legal privileges and responsibilities as married couples, save for the right to a wedding in a state church, the right to adopt children jointly and for joint custody of children.[1] In 1999 the Act was amended so that a registered partner was permitted to adopt a partner's child and arrangements were made for the recognition of equivalent relationships in other countries.

3.12 Beyond its originality, the Danish scheme has been particularly influential in the UK. Because of the length of time that such a scheme has been in existence it has proved possible to make some statistical analysis of the numbers of persons who have registered their partnerships and make some predictions for the UK. In addition, Ingrid Lund-Anderson argued that the passing of the legislation changed public opinion on homosexuals in Denmark.[2] This was cited in support of the UK government's contention that the introduction of civil partnerships would bring about cultural change, in its consultation paper, *Civil Partnership: A Framework for the Legal Recognition of Same Sex Couples*, published in June 2003.[3]

Common law countries

3.13 The case law of South Africa[4] and Canada[5] was quoted repeatedly in parliamentary debate and cited in *R (on the application of Amicus – MSE Section) v Secretary of State for Trade and Industry*.[6] On 9 December 2004 the Canadian Supreme Court ruled that it would be *intra vires* for the Canadian Parliament to legislate to the effect that marriage, for civil purposes, is the lawful union of two persons to the exclusion of all others.[7] This is in a country where a substantial number of provinces already recognise same sex marriage rights.[8] However, the decision makes it much more likely that Canada will join Belgium and the Netherlands in opening up marriage to same sex couples. A same sex marriage Bill was introduced in the Canadian Parliament on 1 February 2005.[9]

3.14 On the same day as the decision of the Supreme Court of Canada, the Parliament of New Zealand passed a Civil Union Act. This is very similar to the UK legislation save that it is open to same sex and de facto couples. In fact a challenge to the New Zealand

---

1   L Neilsen 'Family Rights and the Registered Partnership in Denmark' (1990) 4 International Journal of Law and the Family 297.
2   'The Danish Registered Partnership Act, 1989: Has the Act Meant a Change in Attitudes?' in R Wintemute and M Andenas (eds) *Legal Recognition of Same-Sex Partnerships* (Hart Publishing, 2001).
3   WEU p 13.
4   In particular the judgment of the Constitutional Court of South Africa in *Satchwell v President of the Republic of South Africa* 2002 (9) BCLR 986.
5   In particular, the judgment of the Court of Appeal of Ontario in *Halpern v Attorney General of Canada* 60 DR (3d) 321.
6   [2004] IRLR 430.
7   2004 SCC 79.
8   Newfoundland and Labrador became the seventh province to legalise same-sex marriage on 21 December 2004.
9   An Act respecting certain aspects of legal capacity for marriage for civil purposes.

Marriage Act 1955 had already failed[1] but the New Zealand Human Rights Amendment Act 2001 required government activities to be subject to anti-discrimination standards. The particular point of reference in this context is s 21 of the Human Rights Act 1993 which prohibits discrimination on grounds of sexual orientation. A serious attempt to deal with the problems surrounding the status of de facto couples in other contexts, and remove discriminatory provisions was introduced as well as the Relationships (Statutory References) Bill. This has had a more troubled history and will not be considered until 2005.

United States

3.15   In the United States many individual states have faced legal challenges in an effort to open up marriage. Many of these have proved to be highly controversial and it is argued may have played a role in the 2004 re-election of George W Bush, who in February 2004 endorsed a proposed constitutional amendment that would ban same sex marriages. The first major victory by campaigners was in the Supreme Court of Hawaii in *Baehr v Lewin*[2] where it was established that the exclusion of same sex partners from marriage was prima facie sex discrimination unless it could be justified by a 'compelling state interest'. One of the most successful outcomes of a litigation strategy for same sex marriage campaigners in the US was that embarked upon in Vermont which led to the decision of the State Supreme Court on 20 December 1999, in *Baker v State*,[3] that same sex couples can no longer be denied full and equal protections, benefits and responsibilities under the law. The court gave the legislature the option of deciding how to provide equality, while retaining jurisdiction over the case to assess what the legislature did in the session beginning January 2000. The court left open the question whether a 'separate but equal' approach would satisfy the constitution's standard of equality, or whether only ending discrimination in marriage itself would suffice.

3.16   After extensive hearings, the House and Senate enacted a new marital status, called 'civil union', which provides virtually all the state-sponsored protections, responsibilities and benefits afforded through civil marriage. Gov Howard Dean signed the Act into law on 26 April 2000, and it took effect on 1 July 2000.

3.17   An even more dramatic development occurred on 17 May 2004[4] when the State of Massachusetts began issuing marriage certificates to same sex couples as a result of the ruling by the Massachusetts supreme judicial court in *Goodridge v Department of Public Health*[5] that the state constitution guarantees gay and lesbian couples the right to marry. The advantage for British campaigners of these developments was that the UK government's scheme was starting to look moderate by comparison. Indeed, when serious doubt began to be cast on the possibility of a Bill being passed by the House of Lords, Stephen Cretney commented, 'let there be no doubt: if civil registration is lost, there will

1   *Quilter v Attorney General* [1998] 1 NZLR 523.
2   853 P 2d 44.
3   744 A 2d 864.
4   *The Times* estimated that 110 couples applied for registration from Provincetown alone, including British émigrés Trevor Pinker and Stephen Mascillo.
5   SJC-08860.

be pressure for much more radical – and potentially more divisive – change of the Dutch and American kind which will be more difficult to resist'.[1]

United Kingdom

3.18   The UK was influenced by both Northern European models and by the Danish Civil Registration scheme in particular, as well as by the common law experience. Of particular significance was the publicity that surrounded the publication of *Virtually Normal* by the conservative columnist Andrew Sullivan[2] and the public debate organised in London by his publishers and visits to the UK by Evan Wolfson, who at the time was Director of the Marriage Project at the Lambda Legal Defense and Education Fund and who had been co-counsel in *Baehr v Lewin*.[3] At the time of the publication of the consultation paper[4] nine other EU member states had either same sex marriage or civil partnerships schemes or similar. In the case of Denmark the civil partnership legislation had been in place since 1993.

3.19   Between 1 and 13 July 1999, Robert Wintemute and Mads Andenas organised a major international conference on the legal recognition of same sex partnerships, at the School of Law at King's College, London. This brought together many of the most distinguished academics and jurists in the field and stimulated intense debate and activity. The papers given at the conference formed the foundation of a serious book, *Legal Recognition of Same Sex Partnerships*.[5] It was not purely symbolic that the book launch was organised at the House of Commons, for it became the research background of the legislative activity that was to follow.

OPTING IN OR OPTING OUT

3.20   The significance of these developments was that they strongly boosted the cause of registered partnerships as a means of dealing with the acknowledged deficiencies of the legal regime for protecting the rights of couples who were not married. However, it was not completely obvious that any scheme would not be restricted to same sex partners nor that greater statutory protection for cohabitants would not also be provided. The problem is fairly striking. Between 1979 and 1995 the percentage of married women in the British population decreased from 74% to 56%.[6] Yet the potential for injustice on relationship breakdown is very substantial[7] and the improving legal situation of wives as concerns ancillary relief on divorce only accentuates the difference.[8] The concern is that to improve the rights of cohabitants would make marriage less attractive, yet there is evidence that despite the relatively superior differential between Scotland and England

---

1   [2004] Fam Law 777.
2   (Picador, 1995).
3   853 P 2d 44.
4   *Civil Partnership: A Framework for the Legal Recognition of Same Sex Couples* WEU, June 2003.
5   (Hart, 2001).
6   *Social Trends* 33 (London: The Stationery Office, 2003).
7   *Burns v Burns* [1984] Ch 317, CA.
8   *White v White* [2001] 1 AC 596 HL; *Lambert v Lambert* [2003] 1 FLR 139, CA.

and Wales as concerns the rights of cohabitants, the proportion of cohabitants in both jurisdictions is very similar.[1]

3.21 April 1999 saw the publication of the Report of the Solicitors' Family Law Association (SFLA) Cohabitation Committee, and September of the same year *Cohabitation: Proposals for Reform of the Law* by the Family Law Committee of the Law Society. In July 2002 the Law Society published *Cohabitation: The Case for Clear Law*[2] in which they called for the following:

— a standard definition of 'cohabitation';[3]
— that the rights should come about after a set period of time;
— that same sex and opposite sex couples should be treated equally;
— that the rights should not be the same as those acquired through marriage;
— that cohabitants should have a limited right to apply for maintenance on separation; and
— that cohabitants should have the right to apply for capital provision on separation, having regard to the principle that 'fair account should be taken of any economic advantage derived by either party from contributions by the other, and of any economic disadvantages suffered by either party in the interests of the other party or of the family'.

3.22 Baroness Hale has contended that intimate domestic relationships face particularly acute problems if there are children involved. There is an argument that this is really an equality issue, as the parties frequently compromise their respective economic positions, and this can be compounded by domestic violence.[4] Baroness Hale turns the old argument that, in adoption, the absence of a responsibility to maintain one another was a good reason for not allowing unmarried couples to adopt,[5] and raises the question whether adults should be prepared to take on responsibility for one another, as well as for the child, in the interests of them all.[6]

3.23 In 2003 the SFLA tackled some of the more commonly raised practical problems in *Fairness for Families* in which they proposed that the definition of 'cohabitation' should be:

> 'A couple living together in the same household who have a personal relationship of an intimate nature (other than a legal marriage) in which one or both of them provides financial commitment, and/or support of a domestic nature, for the benefit of the other.'

The SFLA recommended that the qualifying period should be that the couple should have been cohabiting for a period of at least 2 years and that limited benefits and/or relief should be available to them, short of the rights that were provided by marriage.

3.24 Both the SFLA and the Law Society supported the principle of civil partnership legislation for same sex couples but did not believe that that detracted from the need for some form of law reform of the recognition of the rights of unmarried (and unregistered)

---

1   A Barlow and G James 'Regulating Marriage in 21st Century Britain' (2004) 67 (2) MLR at 146.
2   (Representation and Law Reform Directorate, The Law Society 2002).
3   A good summary of the differing definitions currently to be found in law can be found in A Barlow and G James 'Regulating Marriage in 21st Century Britain' (2004) 67 (2) MLR at 146.
4   B Hale 'Unmarried Couples in Family Law' [2004] Fam Law 419.
5   Adoption Law Review 1992.
6   B Hale 'Homosexual Rights' (2004) 16 (2) Child and Family Law Quarterly 134.

cohabitants. The proposals that appeared to generate most political support, though, were the registered partnership (opt-in) models. The difficulties faced by the government of New Zealand with their Relationships (Statutory References) Bill may make the UK government relieved they did not follow that country's twin-track approach to the problem.

3.25 On 24 October 2001 Jane Griffith MP submitted a Relationships (Civil Registration) Bill in the House of Commons, under the 10-minute rule. This would have granted rights to same sex couples and different sex couples. It granted them all the rights of spouses. This was followed by the introduction by Lord Lester of his formidable Civil Partnerships Bill on 9 January 2002 (which again was not confined to same sex couples). The Bill was supported by the Law Society, the SFLA and the Liberal Democrats and was accompanied by an opinion that had been commissioned by David Pannick QC as to its compatibility with the Human Rights Act 1998. Lord Lester's Bill provided that persons were eligible to register their partnership on condition that they lived in the same household for a period of at least 6 months otherwise than merely by reason of one of them being the other's employee, tenant, lodger or boarder. The scheme was not open to close relatives. This meant that the Bill was not confined to same sex couples but was open to all cohabitants.

3.26 Debate on the Second Reading of the Bill took place on 25 January 2002. Lord Lester argued for the rights of same sex couples, noting particularly the judgment of Justice Ackermann in the Constitutional Court of South Africa in *National Coalition for Gay and Lesbian Equality v Ministry of Home Affairs* where he observed that the message of the denial of equal rights to same sex as to opposite sex partners:

> 'is that gays and lesbians lack the inherent humanity to have their families … respected or protected. It serves in addition to perpetuate and reinforce existing prejudices and stereotypes.'

Lord Lester withdrew the Bill on 6 February 2002 after Second Reading, having been given assurances that the government was conducting an inter-departmental review of civil partnerships.

3.27 Lord Lester's Bill came under sustained attack from various quarters. None was better organised that the Christian Institute, who published a pamphlet opposing his proposals on 17 January 2002.[1] They were particularly concerned as the provisions of Lord Lester's Bill extended to heterosexual cohabitees (who they pointed out had freely chosen not to marry) all the rights and privileges that apply to married couples. They believed that this devalued marriage, with all the consequences that would have for children. The difference in treatment in the law of married couples as it stood was justified because they make a commitment to be together to the exclusion of all others for life and because marriage is a union for raising children. They believed that Stonewall was really fighting for civil partnerships as part of its struggle to reclaim the idea of the family as including lesbians and gay men. Even at that stage they were raising the possibility in Lord Lester's Bill of two contrasting scenarios:

---

1   *Counterfeit Marriage. How 'Civil Partnerships' devalue the currency of marriage* (The Christian Institute, 17 January 2002).

(i)   The drug-taking heir of a wealthy industrialist is picked up at a gay nightclub by a man 20 years his senior, who takes him back to his flat. After 6 months the older man threatens to kick him out unless they register. They do so. The young man dies of AIDS. His partner inherits the whole estate.

(ii) A daughter gives up her well-paid job to care for her elderly and infirm mother for 15 years. She moves into her mother's London home where the family has lived for generations. Her mother dies and the daughter inherits. She is then faced with a large bill for inheritance tax, which forces her to sell the family home and move out of London.

3.28   In March 2003 the Congregation for the Doctrine of the Faith issued, with the approval of Pope John Paul II, *Considerations regarding proposals to give legal recognition to unions between homosexual persons*. In this document the Congregation argued:

> 'Society owes its continued survival to the family, founded on marriage. The inevitable consequence of legal recognition of homosexual unions would be the redefinition of marriage, which would become, in its legal status, an institution devoid of essential reference to factors linked to heterosexuality; for example, procreation and raising children. If, from the legal standpoint, marriage between a man and a woman were to be considered just one possible form of marriage, the concept of marriage would undergo a radical transformation, with grave detriment to the common good. By putting homosexual unions on a legal plane analogous to that of marriage and the family, the State acts arbitrarily and in contradiction with its duties.'

3.29   Countervailing pressures were also at work, though. In June 2001 the Liberal Democrats included in their manifesto for the general election (on 7 June) a commitment to establish a scheme for the civil registration of partnerships, giving legal rights at present only available to married couples to unrelated adults. In August 2001 the Greater London Authority (GLA) began accepting applications for a London Partnerships Register. This was essentially symbolic as it was not accompanied by any rights or responsibilities but was a service offered by the GLA in common with many of the largest cities in England. In the meantime, the Law Commission conceded it had failed to come up with any ready answers to the complex problems faced by cohabitants.[1]

CIVIL PARTNERSHIP CONSULTATION

3.30   In November 2001 the then Minister for Women and Equality, Barbara Roche MP announced that the government would look at the issue of civil partnership registration with its associated rights and responsibilities. The work was given to a dedicated team of officials at the Women and Equality Unit (WEU) at the DTI. In June 2003 the WEU published *Civil Partnership: A Framework for the Legal Recognition of Same Sex Couples*. This envisaged a scheme which very largely mimicked marriage and excluded heterosexual cohabitants. Specifically the WEU envisaged an opt-in same sex only entity. The government took the view that the problems of opposite-sex couples who cohabit and those others who chose to live together in a close supportive family background were significantly different from same sex couples who desire to formalise

---

1   Law Commission *Sharing Homes: A Discussion Paper* (London: Law Commission for England and Wales, July 2002).

their relationships but are prevented by law from doing so. In addition, the government argued that they favoured an opt-in system rather than a mechanism of recognition of cohabitation because of the greater legal certainty that would be created for those who chose to register their relationships. The government recognised that a problem existed because of misperceptions about the supposed existence of legal recognition of 'common-law' husbands and wives[1] but believed that another form of opt-in commitment was not the answer. It went on to say that 'the rights of other home-sharers (siblings, flatmates etc) are a separate issue, and there are currently no plans for changes to the law in that area'.[2]

3.31   The document stressed that the Government 'has no plans to introduce same-sex marriage'.[3] This was consistent with an earlier statement in October 2000 made by Jack Straw MP, then Home Secretary, who gave an assurance that:[4]

> '[marriage is] . . . about a union for the procreation of children, which by definition can only happen between a heterosexual couple. So I see no circumstances in which we would ever bring forward proposals for so-called gay marriages.'

In the discussion document there were also other elements of social conservatism, such as the assertion that the scheme would encourage more stable family life.[5] However, the civil rights aspects of the proposals were emphasised by the stress on the possibility that the plan might bring about a cultural change in social attitudes.[6] This was not an entirely theoretical concept as it was hoped that the mere existence of the legislation might lessen the difficulties faced by same sex couples when dealing with situations such as problems over defining the 'next of kin' in the NHS when there is no legal definition.

3.32   After a period of consultation the government published, in November 2003, *Responses to Civil Partnership*[7] in which it summarised the representations the government received to its original consultation paper. This showed a broadly sympathetic reaction by organisations that participated in the process. The government re-iterated its proposal to introduce an opt-in scheme for same sex couples only but it did also state that the Department of Constitutional Affairs is leading a cross-government working group to explore how best to raise public awareness about the rights and responsibilities of opposite sex cohabitants and to dispel the myths around 'common law marriage'.[8] Perhaps the most striking conclusion that the government reached as a result

---

1   This had been starkly illustrated in the British Social Attitudes Survey, *Public policy, Social Trends* 18th Report: 2001–02 edn.
2   *Civil Partnership: A Framework for the Legal Recognition of Same Sex Couples* (WEU, June 2003) p 18.
3   *Civil Partnership* para 1.3. This was re-iterated in the publication *Responses to Civil Partnership* (WEU, November 2003, DT) p 14.
4   *The Times* 2 October 2000.
5   The discussion paper contained the rather utilitarian argument that a Cabinet Office Life Satisfaction Survey in December 2002 had found that marriage increases people's life satisfaction and happiness by an amount equivalent to an additional annual income of £72,000. In addition the 1998 Consultation document *Supporting Families* was quoted as saying, 'strong and stable families provide the best basis for raising children and for building strong and stable communities': *Civil Partnership: A Framework for the Legal Recognition of Same Sex Couples* p 69.
6   The discussion paper relied on I Lund-Anderson 'The Danish Registered Partnership Act 1989: Has the Act meant a change in Attitudes?' in R Wintemute and M Andenas (eds) *Legal Recognition of Same-Sex Partnerships* (Hart Publishing, 2001).
7   (WEU, November 2003, DT).
8   *Responses to Civil Partnership* (WEU, November 2003, DT) p 16.

of their research was that cohabiting, but unregistered, same sex couples should be treated the same as unmarried different sex cohabitants for the purpose of income-related benefits and child support to ensure fairness and so there was no financial disincentive to registration.[1]

3.33 As with Lord Lester's Bill, there was serious criticism of this Bill. The criticism was largely confined to socially conservative groups and religious organisations such as the Evangelical Alliance. As before, the most organised resistance was provided by the Christian Institute who published a pamphlet in May 2004 entitled, *'Gay marriage' in all but name*.[2] Their arguments centred on their concern at the possible consequences of such legislation for the status of marriage and some scepticism as to the purpose of such reforms when the government had by that stage downgraded its estimates of the numbers who would be affected by such reforms.

3.34 The government signalled its intention to introduce the Bill in the Queen's Speech on 26 November 2003. On 9 February 2004, Michael Howard MP, in a major departure from the stance of previous Conservative Party leaders, announced in his 'British Dream' speech that he would give his MPs a free vote on the incoming Bill. He went further than that, as stated:[3]

> 'Civil partnership differs from marriage. Marriage is a separate and special relationship which we should continue to celebrate and sustain. To recognise civil partnership is not, in any way, to denigrate or downgrade marriage. It is to recognise and respect the fact that many people want to live their lives in different ways.'

THE PASSAGE OF THE BILL

3.35 The Bill originated in the House of Lords and began its progress there on 30 March 2004, with the Bill being published the following day. The Bill was greeted by a largely supportive Chamber with cross-party support.[4] On the same day the Inland Revenue issued a press release stating that the question of the tax implications of the Bill would be dealt with in the first available Finance Bill. In her closing speech at the end of the Second Reading debate, Baroness Scotland of Asthal stated:[5]

> 'I should also make clear that the intention in relation to social security and tax credits legislation is that in general same sex couples in civil partnerships will be treated in a similar way as married couples.'

3.36 The Bill was debated in committee in the House of Lords on 10, 12, 13, 17 and 25 May 2004. The Bill ran into difficulties in the House of Lords at the Report stage on 24 June 2004 where a new clause 2 was added which provided that two people are eligible to register as civil partners of each other where they are within specified degrees of family relationship, are both over 30 years of age and have lived together in a continuous period

---

1   *Responses to Civil Partnership* (WEU, November 2003, DT) p 27.
2   (The Christian Institute, Newcastle upon Tyne, May 2004).
3   *The Guardian* 10 February 2004.
4   Speaking for the Conservative frontbench, Baroness Wilcox quoted Michael Howard MP in support of the Bill on a number of occasions but was concerned about the circumstances of people living together platonically: *Hansard*, HL Deb, col 393 (22 April 2004).
5   *Hansard*, HL Deb, col 431 (22 April 2004).

of 12 years immediately prior to the date of registration. This had some interesting unintended consequences. For example, a daughter who formed a civil partnership with her mother but subsequently wished to marry would need to prove irretrievable breakdown of the relationship with her mother in order to dissolve their civil partnership. She could do that only by separation from the mother for whom she wished to care, or by proving her mother's unreasonable behaviour.

3.37   The other points of contention centred on the fact that the regime was restricted to same sex couples only and not open to heterosexuals as Lord Lester's Bill had been. This was one of the points considered in the report of the Joint Committee on Human Rights.[1] This recorded that the government maintained there was an objective justification for any difference of treatment because unmarried heterosexuals were free to marry but this was not an option available to same sex couples. The Joint Committee contended that this was called into question by the decision of the Supreme Court of Canada in *Miron v Trudel*.[2] This concerned the rights of an unmarried male partner to make a claim for loss of income against his female partner's insurance policy. However, it is not apparent that the answer to the problems of cohabitants was to establish another opt-in scheme.[3] It might be supposed that this is more of an argument for granting cohabitants more rights. It should be noted that the Committee's report noted the government's commitment to refer this matter to the Law Commission.[4] In the Stonewall Lecture on 8 December 2004 Barbara Roche MP said that the government was faced with a choice between enacting a scheme similar to that proposed by Lord Lester for everybody, which provided less rights and responsibilities than marriage, or a scheme for same sex partners only which, as far as possible, mirrored marriage in every particular.

3.38   A further problem concerned survivors' pension rights, where the Bill contained a clause which provided that the government could change or make subordinate legislation to require occupations pension schemes to provide such benefits but the government only envisaged requiring such schemes to calculate the value of such benefits on the basis of contributions made from the commencement of the Civil Partnership Act. The Joint Committee expressed the view that without proper evidence they considered there was a risk that this was incompatible with Article 14 of the Convention in conjunction with Article 1, Protocol 1. On 12 October, Anne McGuire MP, in the Second Reading debate in the House of Commons, announced that the government proposed to adopt the same approach for survivor pensions in public service schemes as with tax and to treat civil partners in the same way as married couples.[5]

---

1   Fifteenth Report.
2   (1995) SCR 124 DLR (4th) 693 The implications of the decision was discussed in the speech of Lord Lester in debate at Grand Committee in the House of Lords on 10 May 2004: *Hansard*, HL Deb, col GC3.
3   In any event it is clear that the government were concerned that opening up the civil partnership scheme to heterosexuals might be seen to undermine marriage. This point was underlined by Baroness Scotland of Asthal in the second reading debate in the House of Lords: *Hansard*, HL Deb, col 388 (22 April 2004).
4   Jacqui Smith MP, in debate in the Standing Committee on 21 October 2004, stated that the Law Commission were considering including opposite sex and same sex cohabitation in its next programme of law reform: *Hansard*, HC Deb, col 053.
5   *Hansard*, HC Deb, col 248 (12 October). The government said they would introduce regulations after Royal Assent that would allow registered same sex partners to accrue survivor pensions in public service schemes from 1988.

3.39   Another recurring theme of the debates was the status of marriage and civil partnership and whether the latter was, in fact, simply a contract, as Lord Tebbit contended. For her part, on behalf of the government in the House of Lords, Baroness Scotland saw civil partnership as a new legal entity[1] and as being more properly distinguished as a status rather than a contract.[2] On 24 June 2004 she went on to say:[3]

'Civil Partnership is not governed by the law of contract and there is no room for individual variation of the statutory rules governing eligibility, or governing formation or dissolution of a civil partnership, nor of those setting out its consequences. The change of status from single person to civil partner affects a couple's relationship with each other. After the formation of their civil partnership they would have an entirely new legal relationship with each other. Forming a civil partnership also affects their status; in other words, their position as an individual in relation to everyone else. Each would now be a civil partner. This change of status is permanent in that on the ending of a civil partnership, civil partners do not revert to being single people. They will be marked by having been in a civil partnership in that they will be former civil partners or a surviving civil partner.'

3.40   The amended Bill was unopposed at Third Reading in the House of Lords on 1 July 2004 and the Bill was introduced in the House of Commons on 5 July 2004. It had its Second Reading in the House on Commons on 12 October 2004. It was considered by a Standing Committee between 19 and 26 October 2004. The Bill was restored to one concerning itself with same sex couples only on the first day in Committee. The Bill returned to the House of Lords on 17 November 2004 where the Commons amendments to the Bill were accepted. An attempt to delay the Act from coming into force until some of the rights afforded to civil partners were extended to some family members under a separate scheme was defeated by 251 votes to 136. By the end of the passage of the Bill through Parliament it had been greatly expanded so that on the last day of debate in Committee Jacqui Smith MP was able to say, when asked about the difference between civil partnership and marriage:[4]

'we have used civil marriage as the template for creating a completely new legal relationship ... our view was that, unless there was an objective justification for a difference in the approaches taken to civil marriage and civil partnership, no difference should exist ... It is not marriage, but it is, in many ways ... akin to marriage.'

The Civil Partnership Act 2004 received Royal Assent on 18 November 2004.

OUTLINE OF THE CIVIL PARTNERSHIP ACT 2004

3.41   The Act is a behemoth, containing 264 sections and 30 schedules. It grew steadily over the time in which it was debated. The principal reason for the Bill's huge size is the incorporation of Scotland and Northern Ireland into the scheme, but another significant factor has been the desire to bring about as much equality as possible with marriage.[5] The

---

1   *Hansard*, HL Deb, col GC 4 (10 May 2004).

2   *Hansard*, HL Deb, col GC 9 (10 May 2004).

3   *Hansard*, HL Deb, col 1361 (24 June 2004).

4   *Hansard*, HC Deb, col 776 (9 November 2004). When pressed in the House of Lords, the only difference that Baroness Scotland could come up with was the lack of need for a civil partnership to be consummated: *Hansard*, HL Deb, col 1479 (17 November 2004).

5   In Committee, Angela Eagle MP referred to this as adding the last pieces to the equality jigsaw.

Danish Registered Partnership Act, which was enacted on 1 June 1989, contained only seven sections.[1] The difference can be partially explained as being one of approach. The Nordic countries have adopted a 'subtraction' model which provides that registered partners shall have all the rights and obligations of married persons save for the following, whereas the Dutch and German models have adopted an 'enumeration' method which provides for very long statutes setting out the precise rights and obligations provided by the civil partnership. The Vermont approach is one of 'belt and braces' in that it contains a general statement of equality but is also enumerated for greater certainty.[2]

3.42 There are very few differences between civil partnership and marriage. In general a civil partnership is formed when two people have signed the civil partnership document in the presence of each other, and the place at which the two people register must not be in religious premises.[3] The precise form of the ceremony is likely to be subject to guidance. The whole process is currently under review.[4]

3.43 Most of the other differences are ones of nomenclature. Divorce is deemed to be dissolution. The grounds for dissolution are the same as for marriage, with the exception that no provision is made for adultery.[5] On the last day of the Committee stage the government also introduced a series of amendments ensuring that references to couples who are living together as husband and wife are clearly understood to apply to cohabiting same sex couples; this was in response to the judgment on 21 June 2004 in *Ghaidan v Mendoza*.[6] The intention was to ensure that the drafting changes make it clear to courts and legal advisers how Parliament intends phrases such as 'living together as husband and wife' to be interpreted after the Bill takes effect. Without the amendments, the risk is that the Bill could be seen as removing the equal treatment that already exists following that judgment.

3.44 Overseas relationships are also afforded recognition under the Act. To qualify, they must either be registered in accordance with one of the defined schemes set out in Sch 20 to the Act or meet the general conditions set down by the Act. Schedule 20 recognises specific relationships which include marriage in Belgium and the Netherlands, registered partnership in Norway and Sweden, civil union in Vermont and civil solidarity pacts in France. In both cases the overseas relationship must have been registered outside the UK by two people, both of whom are of the same sex and neither of whom is already a civil partner or already married.

3.45 So long as two people have registered a valid overseas relationship, they will be treated as having formed a civil partnership[7] subject to the overriding exception that there will be no recognition of an overseas relationship if to do so would be manifestly

---

1   The Act to amend the Danish Marriage (Formation and Dissolution) Act, the Inheritance Act, the Penal Code and the Inheritance Tax Act enacted on 7 June the same year was little longer.
2   R Wintemute 'Conclusion' in R Wintemute and M Andenas (eds) *Legal Recognition of Same-Sex Partnerships* (Hart Publishing, 2001) p 766.
3   Civil Partnership Act 2004, s 6.
4   The matter was the subject of a White Paper, 'Civil Registration: Vital Change', in January 2002.
5   In divorce law, sexual intercourse with a person of the same sex does not amount to adultery: *Clarkson v Clarkson* (1930) TLR 623.
6   [2004] 2 FLR 600, HL.
7   Civil Partnership Act 2004, Part 5, Chapter 2.

contrary to public policy. Problems are likely to arise as a consequence of the fact that some of the European registered partnership regimes are more meaningful than others.[1]

PROJECTED TAKE-UP

3.46   The problem faced by the government was that there is little reliable data available as to the size of the lesbian, gay and bisexual population. The Consultation Paper *Civil Partnership: A Framework for the Legal Recognition of Same Sex Couples* which was published in June 2003 proceeded on the basis that 5% of the population is lesbian, gay or bisexual. In the higher of two estimates they made, calculations were made on the assumption that eventually the same proportion of the lesbian, gay and bisexual population will enter into civil partnerships as the wider population enters into marriage, ie 33%. In the lower assumption this was assumed to be only 10% of the lesbian, gay and bisexual population.

3.47   The Christian Institute, in their pamphlet published in May 2004 entitled, *'Gay Marriage' in all but Name*,[2] cast doubt on the projected numbers of civil partnerships. They noted that the 2001 census showed that there are fewer than 40,000 same sex households in England and Wales. They, like the government, cited statistics from Denmark that between 1 January 1990 and 1 January 1998 there had been a cumulative total of only 2,168 partnerships registered in Denmark.[3] Additionally, they cited survey evidence from March 2004 that since September 2001, 15 local authorities including Manchester have established their own same sex partnership ceremonies but since their inception there had been only 849 ceremonies.[4]

3.48   Only provisional figures are available for Massachusetts where same sex couples have been above to marry since 17 May 2004 but an Associated Press review of all 8,158 wedding certificates publicly recorded with the state since 17 May shows that at least 2,980 were filed by same sex couples in 290 of the state's 351 cities and towns. According to unofficial data compiled by the Registry of Vital Records, 4,266 same sex marriage certificates have been sent to the agency, but not all have been reviewed or officially recorded[5]

3.49   At the time that the Civil Partnership Act was presented to Parliament, the government produced revised estimates of projected take-up of civil partnerships by reference to the popularity of marriage.[6] By 2050, under the low estimate, they calculate that the numbers in civil partnerships might amount to 5% of the heterosexual population who are married and in the high figure that proportion rises to 10%. The number of civil partnerships registered is likely to be relatively high in the first year as

---

1   *International Aspects of Civil Partnerships* June [2004] IFL 111.

2   (Newcastle upon Tyne: The Christian Institute, May 2004).

3   I Lund Anderson 'The Danish Registered Partnership Act, 1989: Has the Act Meant a Change in Attitudes?' in R Wintemute and M Andenas (eds) *Legal Recognition of Same-Sex Partnerships* (Hart Publishing, 2001).

4   *The Independent on Sunday* 21 March 2004.

5   *The Advocate* 18 November 2004.

6   *Final Regulatory Impact Assessment: Civil Partnership* (WEU, 2004).

established couples take advantage of the reform. This would reflect the experience of countries such as Sweden, Norway and Denmark.

COMMENCEMENT

3.50   The Civil Partnership Act 2004 received Royal Assent on 18 November 2004. It is likely that it will not come into force for a further year. This is because of the requirement for there to be amendments to the tax and benefits regime, consultation on and drafting of regulations (including transitional arrangements) and the provision of training for registrars amongst others.[1] In addition, it will be necessary for the next Finance Bill to deal with all the financial implications of the legislation.

---

1   This was confirmed by Jacqui Smith MP on 26 October in debate in Committee: *Hansard*, HC Deb, col 208.

Chapter 4

REGISTRATION AND DISSOLUTION

INTRODUCTION

4.1   In January 2003 the government published a White Paper *Civil Registration: Vital Change*. This White Paper was followed by a consultation paper, *Civil Registration: Delivering Vital Change*. The main proposals of the consultation paper are designed to effect a modernisation of the system of registration of births, deaths and marriages and, to a large extent, the system of registration of civil partnership reflects the system that will be implemented in respect of civil marriage in accordance with the *Civil Registration: Delivering Vital Change* proposals. The way in which the change in relation to civil marriage is to be implemented is by way of Regulatory Reform Order (pursuant to the Regulatory Reform Act 2001) and where there are differences between the framework of civil partnership and the new framework of civil marriage, the Civil Partnership Act 2004 provides for any changes made to civil marriage to be assimilated into the procedures for civil partnership.[1]

4.2   Chapters 1 and 2 of Part 2 of the Act deal with the registration of a civil partnership and proceedings relating to the dissolution and annulment of civil partnerships. The purpose of this chapter is to examine and explain these provisions.

4.3   Section 1 of the Act sets out the real starting point by defining a 'civil partnership'. A 'civil partnership' is defined as a relationship between two people of the same sex, having been formed by registration in England and Wales, or a relationship which has been formed overseas but is afforded recognition in England and Wales by virtue of the Act. A civil partnership can be ended only by death, dissolution or annulment, and provisions for termination are included in the Act (and dealt with in detail in Chapter 5).[2] The consequences of the formation of a civil partnership and the rights and responsibilities flowing from it are dealt with in the other chapters of this book. Similar schemes for civil registration exist in both Scotland and Northern Ireland, but they are outside the scope of this book.

---

1   Civil Partnership Act 2004 (CPA 2004), s 35. See **4.14**.
2   CPA 2004, s 1.

REGISTRATION

Formation

4.4   In order to understand the nature of a civil partnership it is necessary to look at the government's reasons behind the legislation. In the words of Jacqui Smith MP, Deputy Minister for Women and Equality, in the Second Reading of the Bill in the House of Commons on 12 October 2004, the Act is designed to send a clear and unequivocal message that same sex couples deserve recognition and respect. She acknowledged the legal and financial insecurities that absence of recognition can bring. The Act is an equality measure, not to introduce same sex marriage, because of the religious connotations of holy matrimony, but to introduce a twenty-first century approach, a new legal institution, equivalent and parallel to civil marriage. The Act is intended to end the 'legal invisibility' of same sex couples, and give to civil partners the same rights and responsibilities as those who enter civil marriage.[1] On Third Reading in the House of Commons, Jacqui Smith MP went so far as to say civil partnership was 'akin to marriage'.[2] In contrast, one of the main opponents of the Bill, a Conservative backbench peer, Baroness O'Cathain, on 10 May 2004 in the House of Lords described the Bill as 'a parody of marriage for homosexuals'.[3] The truth of the matter from a legal perspective is that civil partnership to all intents and purposes is civil marriage in all but name. It is nonetheless a different institution from civil marriage. The effective legal differences between civil partnership and civil marriage are few. Civil partnership is a legal status which ends only on death, dissolution or annulment. The legal rights and responsibilities flow from statute rather than any religious tradition or status as a contract.

The status of civil partnership was a subject hotly debated in the House of Lords when the Civil Partnership Bill was introduced. One amendment moved by Lord Higgins in the Grand Committee of the House of Lords was that the word 'relationship' appearing in s 1(1) of the Act (which reads: 'a civil partnership is a relationship between two people of the same sex') be replaced with the word 'contract'.[4] The amendment was moved by Lord Higgins on the basis that it was more appropriate, given the complicated legal ramifications of civil partnership, than the word 'relationship'. The amendment was supported by Lord Tebbit.[5] However, it was resisted by Lord Lester on the ground that defining a civil partnership as a contract would have the effect of downgrading the loving and committed relationships which civil partnership had been designed to recognise and afford validity to.[6] Baroness Scotland for the government stated in response that she accepted 'straightaway that marriage is a contract' but went on to say that marriage is 'also an expression of a relationship' and the purpose of the legislation was to afford same sex couples acknowledgement of their relationship, not just a recognition of a contract. She made the further point that a fundamental part of a contract was that it could be flexible to the circumstances of the contracting parties, whereas civil partnership had prescribed rights and responsibilities flowing from it which were identified by the state, and that was

---

1   *Hansard*, HL Deb, col 180 (12 October 2004).
2   *Hansard*, HL Deb, col 776 (9 November 2004).
3   *Hansard*, HL Deb, col GC54 (10 May 2004).
4   *Hansard*, HL Deb, col GC1 (10 May 2004).
5   *Hansard*, HL Deb, col GC5 (10 May 2004).
6   *Hansard*, HL Deb, col GC4 (10 May 2004).

the clear difference.[1] The leading case in relation to the status of marriage is *Niboyet v Niboyet*.[2] The case contains the best known definition of 'marriage', which is recited in *Halsbury's Laws*:[3]

> '[marriage] is the fulfilment of a contract [to marry] satisfied by the solemnisation of the marriage, but marriage, directly it exists, creates by law a relation between the parties and what is called a status of each. .... That relation between the parties, and that status of each of them with regard to the community, which are constituted on marriage are not imposed or defined by contract or agreement but by law.'

Arguably, the same definition is applicable to civil partnership. Indeed, Baroness Scotland said:[4]

> 'Civil partnership is not governed by the law of contract and there is no room for individual variation of the statutory rules governing eligibility, or governing formation or dissolution of a civil partnership, nor of those setting out its consequences. The change of status from single person to civil partner affects a couple's relationship with each other. After the formation of their civil partnership they would have an entirely new legal relationship with each other. Forming a civil partnership also affects their status; in other words, their position as an individual in relation to everyone else. Each would now be a civil partner. This change of status is permanent in that on the ending of a civil partnership, civil partners do not revert to being single people. They will be marked by having been in a civil partnership in that they will be former civil partners or a surviving civil partner.'

However, whilst emphasising that civil partnership affected the individuals' status, the government was also keen to play down the similarity between civil partnership and marriage, stating on several occasions that civil partnership was not same sex marriage. During the final debate in the House of Lords on the Bill, the issue was raised by Lord Tebbit. He referred to a written question that he had asked the government:[5]

> 'In what respects, other than its availability to persons of the same sex, a civil partnership as envisaged in the Civil Partnership Bill differs from a civil marriage?'

The reply that Baroness Scotland gave in her answer was that there were a number of differences, one of them being that a civil partnership is formed when the second civil partner signs the civil partnership document, whereas a civil marriage is formed when the couple exchange spoken words.[6] During the course of the debate Baroness Scotland emphasised that marriage was not affected in any way by the civil partnership regime.[7] However, marriage being unaffected by civil partnership is not quite the same as civil partnership not effectively being same sex marriage, which arguably it is. Two other differences highlighted by Baroness Scotland in the Lords on 17 November 2004 were that non-consummation was not a ground for the annulment of a civil partnership and there was no ability to dissolve a civil partnership based on adultery.[8] The reason for this, Baroness Scotland stated, was that, 'the nature of the sexual relationship that enters into

---

1   *Hansard*, HL Deb, col GC7 (10 May 2004).
2   (1878) 4 PD 1, CA.
3   *Halsbury's Laws of England* Vol 29(3) (4th edn) para 33.
4   *Hansard*, HL Deb, col 1361 (24 June 2004).
5   *Hansard*, HL Deb, col 1470 (17 November 2004).
6   *Official Report* col WA 161 (16 July 2004).
7   *Hansard*, HL Deb, col 1477 (17 November 2004).
8   See **4.48**.

the civil partnership ... is totally different in nature'.[1] However, the presumption that a sexual relationship would exist between civil partners means that the doctrine of consanguinity necessarily still applies. Civil partners will presumably also not be bound by the common law duty of cohabitation for spouses. The reason for this was not discussed in Parliament but, in the modern world, it is becoming increasingly clear that the traditional 'conjugal rights' associated with marriage are less and less appropriate. In spite of these differences, what is clear is that a civil partnership is exclusive, and may not be entered into by anyone already married or a civil partner.[2] This is a very important aspect of civil partnership and its exclusivity, among other things, brings it far closer to civil marriage than the differences mentioned above distinguish it.

4.5 A civil partnership is formed when two people have signed a civil partnership document in the presence of each other, the registrar and two witnesses. The witnesses and the registrar must then also sign the civil partnership document.[3] The civil partnership document will be either a Registrar General's licence, in the case of the special procedure,[4] or a civil partnership schedule in any other case.[5] It is intended that there will be guidance issued to registration authorities dealing with the reading out of words on the civil partnership document. These words will not have any legal effect in the sense that it will be the signing of the civil partnership document which will form the civil partnership itself.

Eligibility

4.6 In order to be eligible to register a civil partnership the parties must not be:

— of the opposite sex;
— already a civil partner or already married;
— under 16; or
— within prohibited degrees of relationship.[6]

4.7 People within a prohibited degree of relationship are not permitted to register as civil partners. This reflects the doctrine of consanguinity in marriage. Two people are within prohibited degrees of relationship if one falls within the list below in relation to the other:

— adoptive child;
— adoptive parent;
— child;
— former adoptive child;
— former adoptive parent;
— grandparent;
— grandchild;
— parent;
— parent's sibling;

---

1   *Hansard*, HL Deb, col 1479 (17 November 2004).
2   See **4.6**.
3   CPA 2004, s 2.
4   See **4.24**.
5   CPA 2004, s 7(1). See **4.25**.
6   CPA 2004, s 3.

— sibling; or
— sibling's child.[1]
'Sibling' means brother or sister or half-brother or half-sister.

4.8 Backbench Conservative peers and MPs wanted the category of those who could register their civil partnership extended to family members. Baroness O'Cathain successfully tabled an amendment in the Lords, before the Bill went to the Commons, which would have enabled close relatives, of the same or opposite sex, who had lived together for at least 12 years, and were both over the age of 30, to register their partnerships. That amendment was removed in the Commons. It would have meant that a son caring for his elderly mother, who registered his partnership with her, in order to marry someone would have had to prove unreasonable behaviour of his mother to dissolve the partnership, or rely on 2 years' separation and consent, obviously an absurdity. The amendment inflicted in the Lords was described by Resolution, formerly the Solicitors Family Law Association, as 'unworkable in both family law and family life'.[2] Lord Tebbit admitted to John Bercow MP earlier in 2004, regarding the amendment, that 'the effect of the cleverly conceived amendments would be to cause the Government no end of trouble and that Gordon's [Gordon Brown MP, the Chancellor of the Exchequer] sums would be thrown into disarray, providing the opportunity for a great deal of fun'.[3] It is obvious that the amendment was designed to be a wrecking amendment.

That amendment was re-tabled by Edward Leigh MP, a backbench Conservative, in modified form in the Commons on Third Reading, restricting the additional category only to siblings of the same or opposite sex, who had lived together for at least 12 years, and were both over the age of 30, and providing for dissolution of those partnerships by notice alone. That amendment was defeated in the Commons by 381 votes to 74. At the final stage of the Bill in the Lords on 17 November 2004 Baroness O'Cathain re-tabled a further modified version of that amendment, which would have prevented the Act from being brought into force unless the government had devised and brought into force a similar scheme of registration for carers and family members, designed mainly to save inheritance tax. That amendment was defeated by 251 votes to 136.

4.9 Also included within the definition of a 'prohibited relationship' are two people who fall within the list below in relation to each other, unless both of them have reached the age of 21 when they register and the younger of the two has not at any time before the age of 18 been a child of the family in relation to the other:

— child of former civil partner;
— child of former spouse;
— former civil partner of grandparent;
— former civil partner of parent;
— former spouse of grandparent;
— former spouse of parent;
— grandchild of former civil partner; or

---

1   CPA 2004, Sch 1, para 1.
2   Resolution (formerly known as the Solicitors' Family Law Association) Briefing Note *The Civil Partnership Bill: House of Commons Second Reading* (September 2004).
3   *Hansard*, HC Deb SC D 017 (19 October 2004).

— grandchild of former spouse.[1]

A 'child of the family' in relation to the prohibitions means someone who has lived in the same household as the other person concerned and has been treated by that person as a child of his or her family.[2] Where there is a relationship between the two civil partners that would be prohibited on the grounds of their affinity, save for the fact that both of them are over the age of 21 and the younger of them has not at any time been a child of the family in relation to the other before the age of 18, notice of the proposed civil partnership may not be recorded in the register unless the registration authority has received evidence that both parties are over 21 and a declaration in the required form.[3] Such declaration must contain details of the relationship, and a declaration that the exception applies.[4] Further information that should be included may be prescribed by regulations. Once received, the declaration must be recorded in the register. Such a declaration may be challenged by a third party.[5] If an objection is recorded, the registration authority must note it on the register and must not issue a civil partnership schedule unless either one of the proposed civil partners has obtained a confirmatory High Court declaration of no impediment, or the objection has been withdrawn.[6] Either one of the proposed civil partners may apply to the High Court at any time, whether or not an objection has been made.[7] Unlike objections made under s 13,[8] any person making a frivolous objection under paras 5 to 7 of Sch 1 will not be liable to any costs or damages in relation to that objection.

4.10 Two people will also be within prohibited degrees of relationship if one of the people is the former civil partner or spouse of the other person's child and the child and the child's other parent are still living. There is also a prohibited degree of relationship where one person is the parent of the other's former civil partner or former spouse and the former spouse or civil partner and their other parent is still living. This prohibition will cease upon the death of either the former civil partner, former spouse, child or other parent and the persons concerned having reached the age of 21.[9]

4.11 These provisions, which reflect marriage in preventing relationships which challenge the doctrine of consanguinity, have been questioned in the context of a same sex relationships. It was argued that the biological rationale for refusing such relationships the endorsement of civil partnership cannot be the same as for marriage and, therefore, consanguinity was not applicable in the case of civil partnership. This argument is flawed. Given that two civil partners are likely to be sexually active, and human relationships are more sophisticated than simple matters of biology, the public policy argument against the registration of relationships which offend principles of consanguinity must still stand.[10]

---

1   CPA 2004, Sch 1, para 2(1).
2   CPA 2004, Sch 1, para 2(2).
3   CPA 2004, Sch 1, para 5(1).
4   CPA 2004, s 5(1)(a).
5   CPA 2004, Sch 1, para 6(1)(a).
6   CPA 2004, s 7(1).
7   CPA 2004, s 7(2).
8   See **4.18**.
9   CPA 2004, Sch 1, para 3.
10   See **4.4** for a discussion of the debate in the House of Lords on this matter.

Procedure

Generally

4.12   In order to register a civil partnership, there are four distinct procedures which may be followed: (i) the standard procedure; (ii) the procedure for housebound persons; (iii) the procedure for detained persons; or (iv) the special procedure (where one person is terminally ill).[1] These procedures are modified in the case of non-residents and where a former spouse has undergone a sex change.[2] They are also subject to the supplementary provisions discussed at **4.9** in relation to declarations where there is an exception to the prohibition of civil partnership between persons who have an affinal relationship.[3] The registration of civil partnerships overseas in British consulates is dealt with at **4.35**.

4.13   The registration of a civil partnership must take place in England and Wales and may not be in religious premises.[4] 'Religious premises' are any places that are used solely or mainly for religious purposes or places whose main use has been for religious purposes and which have not been used since for any other main purpose. The place to be used must be open to anyone wishing to attend the registration and must be agreed by the registration authority (this will be either the County Council or a London Borough Council, the Common Council of the City of London or the Council of the Isles of Scilly).[5] If it is not, then the notice is void.[6] There is no requirement that a registration authority provide a place in its area for the registration of civil partnerships, although it may provide such a place and may approve a place specified in the notice.[7] It is not clear how any failure to provide a place by a registration authority would be challenged and it is likely that registration authorities will simply make the facilities currently available for civil marriages available to those wishing to register a civil partnership. The fact that a civil partnership may not be registered in religious premises could be considered to have been a concession by the government to protect the establishment of religious marriage. This puts civil partnerships on a par with civil marriage. However, given the debate within the Church of England in particular, any other provision may well have caused insurmountable obstacles to the passage of the Act through Parliament. The place to be used must be specified in the notice of civil partnership.[8]

4.14   The scheme of the Civil Partnership Act 2004 broadly reflects the framework envisaged by the government consultation paper, *Civil Registration: Delivering Vital Change.*[9] However, as the proposals put forward in the consultation paper have not yet been formulated and the Regulatory Reform Order planned has not yet been introduced, s 35 gives the Chancellor of the Exchequer power to make such amendments to the Act by order as appear appropriate to assimilate any provision connected with the formation or recording of civil partnerships to any provision made in relation to civil marriage in England and Wales. This section is particularly important. It underlines the similarity

---

1   CPA 2004, s 5(1).
2   CPA 2004, s 20 and Sch 3.
3   CPA 2004, s 5(3).
4   CPA 2004, s 6.
5   CPA 2004, s 28.
6   CPA 2004, s 6(5). See **4.15**.
7   CPA 2004, s 6(5). See **4.26**.
8   See **4.15**.
9   See **4.1**.

between civil marriage and civil partnership and the government's intention that they work and are treated in the same way.

The standard procedure

4.15   Each of the would-be civil partners must give notice of the proposed partnership to a registration authority.[1] It is important to note that partners can choose in which registration authority they wish to register their partnership. This mirrors proposed changes to civil marriage as set out in *Delivering Vital Change*. The information that should be contained in the notice may be prescribed by regulations[2] but the registration authority may require a proposed civil partner to provide evidence of:

— name and surname;
— age;
— any former civil partnerships or marriage and proof of their termination;
— nationality; and
— residence in England and Wales for the 7 days preceding the giving of a notice of proposed civil partnership by that person.[3]

Both proposed civil partners must have resided in England and Wales for at least 7 days prior to giving the notice.[4] This is not to say that after a week of living in England and Wales, two people may register as civil partners. After giving notice, the parties are obliged to wait a further 15 days. The waiting period is dealt with at **4.17**. These two provisions are likely to mean that 'registration tourism' in England and Wales is unlikely to happen, but it remains to be seen how rigorously registration officers enforce the definition of 'usual place of residence'. There is no requirement that proposed civil partners who wish to register, for example, in Brighton, have their usual place of residence somewhere within the geographical area covered by the Brighton and Hove registration authority. In contrast, as with civil marriage, in Scotland the 'Gretna Green'[5] ability will exist; s 88 mirrors the ability under Scottish marriage law for a marriage to take place without residence anywhere in Scotland. This is likely to mean that there will be registration tourism in Scotland.

4.16   The Civil Partnership Act 2004, s 249 incorporates Sch 23, which contains provisions relation to the formation of civil partnerships by persons subject to immigration control.[6] Someone subject to immigration control is someone who is not an EEA national and who requires leave to enter or remain in the UK (regardless of whether or not leave has been given).[7] Schedule 23 is not applicable to the special procedure.[8] In order for someone subject to immigration control to be able to register a civil partnership in England and Wales, he or she must give notice to a specified registration authority, which will be designated for the purpose of regulating civil partnerships involving persons subject to immigration control, and the notice must be

---

1   CPA 2004, s 8.
2   CPA 2004, s 8(2).
3   CPA 2004, s 9(3).
4   CPA 2004, s 8(1).
5   A town just over the English border in Scotland.
6   See **4.24**. See Chapter 8.
7   CPA 2004, Sch 23, para 1(2).
8   See **4.24**. CPA 2004, Sch 23, para 3.

delivered in person by both of the proposed civil partners.[1] The notice of civil partnership must contain a declaration that the person subject to immigration control:

— has an entry clearance granted expressly for the purpose of enabling him to form a civil partnership in the UK; or
— has the written permission of the Secretary of State to form a civil partnership in the UK; or
— falls within a class specified for the purpose of this paragraph by regulations made by the Secretary of State.[2]

It is likely that the registration officer will require evidence from the proposed civil partners, of identity and may also require evidence of nationality and place of residence. This requirement is currently in place in respect of civil marriage and will continue after the introduction of the proposals in *Civil Registration: Delivering Vital Change*.[3] Failure to comply with these requirements will render the civil partnership void.[4] If the registration authority is satisfied by the notice, it must be recorded in the register and the process then continues in line with the standard procedure. Regulations are likely to provide that registration authorities report to the Home Office any civil partnerships they suspect of being contracted in order to evade immigration control.[5] This mirrors changes introduced under the Asylum and Immigration (Treatment of Claimants, etc) Act 2004 for civil marriage as part of the government's attempts to reduce the numbers of alleged bogus marriages for immigration purposes.

4.17 The notice must be signed by the proposed civil partner in the presence of a registration officer or someone similar authorised to attest notices. The notice declaration will declare that the proposed civil partner believes that there is no impediment of kindred or affinity (ie that the provisions relating to prohibited degrees of relationship do not apply[6]) or any other lawful hindrance to the formation of the civil partnership and will also state that each of the proposed civil partners has had a usual place of residence in England and Wales for at least 7 days before giving notice.[7]

4.18 Once the notice has been given to a registration authority, it must be publicised during the waiting period, both in the registration authority's area in which the registration is to take place, and in the registration authority area in which both partners live. The details to be published will include the name of the person giving notice and that person's proposed civil partner, along with any other information prescribed by regulations.[8] After notice has been given, the proposed civil partners must wait until the expiry of the waiting period before being able to register their partnership. The waiting period is the period of 15 days beginning with the day that the notice was recorded, although the Registrar General may shorten the period in special cases where he is satisfied that there are compelling reasons and exceptional circumstances in which the

---

1   CPA 2004, Sch 23, para 4(1).
2   CPA 2004, Sch 23, para 2.
3   *Civil Registration: Delivering Vital Change*, 3.3.17.
4   CPA 2004, s 49(b)(i).
5   *Civil Registration: Delivering Vital Change*, 3.3.28.
6   See **4.6** and **4.7**.
7   CPA 2004, s 8(4).
8   CPA 2004, s 10.

period should be shortened.[1] An example would be where one of the proposed civil partners was in Her Majesty's Forces and was due to be posted abroad to somewhere FN where he or she is at risk of losing his or her life. Regulations will prescribe means by which certain classes of case may be afforded these shortenings of the waiting period and particularise the situations in which applications for the shortening of time should be made and granted.[2]

4.19 During the waiting period, any person may object to a proposed civil partnership by giving notice of an objection.[3] This exists currently in respect of civil marriage and will continue to do so after the changes proposed by *Civil Registration: Delivering Vital Change* are introduced. The notice of objection must state where the objector lives and be signed by him or her.[4] Where notice is given of an objection, it must be recorded in the register as soon as possible.[5] The objection will then be investigated and either dismissed or upheld, in which case the Registrar may refuse to issue a civil partnership schedule.[6] A decision to uphold an objection may be appealed.[7] If the objector is found to have made a frivolous objection, that person may be liable for the costs of the Registrar General and possibly damages, recoverable by the civil partner to whom the objection relates.[8] The determination of whether or not an objection is frivolous is made by the Registrar General.[9] Therefore, spurious or politically motivated objections to the formation of a civil partnership should be discouraged, although it may require a test case on top of the legislation to give this provision its full weight.

4.20 As soon as the waiting period is over, the Registrar is under a duty, at the request of one or both of the proposed civil partners, to issue a civil partnership schedule.[10] However, this duty does not apply if an objection has been recorded, or where the registration authority believes that there may be a lawful impediment to the formation of a civil partnership. An example of such an impediment may be a notice of an objection on the grounds of affinity under Sch 1, para 6(1) of the Act.[11] The proposed civil partners have 12 months from the day the first civil partner's notice of proposed civil partnership was recorded to sign the civil partnership schedule. Once the proposed civil partners have signed it, a civil partnership will have been formed.[12] There is no prescribed ceremony as such or standard wording to be spoken set out in the Act. The registration will simply be two partners signing the civil partnership document. Regulations are likely to be introduced under ss 14(2) and 25(5), after consultation, to provide for an appropriate form of words which in practice may be read out at the signing of the civil partnership document. Concern was expressed in the House of Lords that no provision was made in the Act for words of commitment to be exchanged by civil partners.

---

1   CPA 2004, s 11 and s 12.
2   CPA 2004, s 12(2) and (3).
3   CPA 2004, s 13.
4   CPA 2004, s 13(2).
5   CPA 2004, s 13(3).
6   CPA 2004, s 14(4).
7   CPA 2004, s 15(1)(a).
8   CPA 2004, s 16.
9   CPA 2004, s 16(1)(b).
10   CPA 2004, s 14(1).
11   See **4.7**.
12   CPA 2004, s 17.

Other registration procedures

4.21   There are several other procedures that may be used to register a civil partnership: the procedure for house-bound persons; the procedure for detained persons; and the special procedure. Separate provisions also govern the situation where one of the proposed civil partners is serving with Her Majesty's Forces outside the UK, or where one of them is living in Scotland or Northern Ireland. There are is also a separate procedure for the registration of civil partnerships between persons who are overseas and the recognition of partnerships formed in jurisdictions other than England and Wales, both of which are dealt with in detail at **4.35** et seq.

House-bound persons

4.22   A person is house-bound if, in relation to that person, a doctor has made a statement that that person is someone who, by reason of their illness or disability, should not be moved from the place that he or she is for at least the following 3 months.[1] The content of the doctor's statement may be prescribed by regulations.[2] In this situation, the two proposed civil partners may register at the place where the person is house-bound. The procedure is the same as the standard procedure, except that both notices of proposed civil partnership must be accompanied by the doctor's statement ('a medical statement'), which should have been made less than 14 days before the notice is recorded by the registration authority.[3] The only other difference in the case of a housebound person is that the period in which the proposed civil partners must register after the civil partnership schedule has been issued is 3 months, instead of 12, from the date the first notice was recorded.[4]

Detained persons

4.23   The procedure differs again in relation to detained persons. A detained person is someone who is detained in a hospital under the Mental Health Act 1983 (although short-term detentions under this Act are excluded) or who is in prison or another place to which the Prison Act 1952 applies.[5] Where two people wish to register a civil partnership in the case where one of them is detained, each person's notice of proposed civil partnership must be accompanied by a supporting statement made by the authority responsible for the detained person, no more than 21 days before the day on which the notice was recorded by the registration authority, giving details of the place where the person is detained, and stating that there is no objection to that place being the place at which the person is to register as a civil partner.[6] Regulations may also prescribe the contents of the supporting statement.[7] The 'authority responsible' within the meaning of the section means either the hospital manager or the prison governor.[8] The only other difference is that the period during which the proposed civil partners may register their

---

1   CPA 2004, s 18(2).
2   CPA 2004, s 4.
3   CPA 2004, s 18(3)(a).
4   CPA 2004, s 18(3)(c).
5   CPA 2004, s 19(2).
6   CPA 2004, s 19(3).
7   CPA 2004, s 19(5).
8   CPA 2004, s 19(6).

partnership by signing the civil partnership schedule is 3 months from the day the first notice was recorded, as opposed to 12.[1] Where someone is detained, they are to be treated for the purposes of the provisions in relation to the formation of a civil partnership under the Act as being resident at the place where they are detained, if they would not otherwise be so treated.[2]

SPECIAL PROCEDURE

4.24   An important additional procedure under the Act is the special procedure. The special procedure is to be used where one of the proposed civil partners is seriously ill. In this situation, the procedure may be changed in order to speed up the registration process. Only one of the proposed civil partners need give notice of the proposed civil partnership to the registration authority. The notice must be accompanied by such evidence as the Registrar General may require to be satisfied that:

— one of the proposed civil partners is seriously ill and not expected to recover (a registered medical practitioner's certificate will be sufficient evidence for those purposes);
— the civil partner understands the effect of signing a Registrar General's licence;
— there is no lawful impediment to the formation of the civil partnership; and
— there is sufficient reason for a licence to be granted.[3]

Any notice under the special procedure must be reported to the Registrar General, who may give directions in relation to the verification of the evidence given.[4] Instead of a civil partnership schedule being issued, the Registrar General grants a licence. Once a Registrar General's licence has been issued, the signing of it by both parties will register the civil partnership. The time limit for the signing of the licence is one month from the day that notice was given.[5] Objections to the granting of a licence may be made, and the penalties for frivolous objections are the same as with the standard procedure.[6] There is no provision allowing for procedures to be combined so, for example, if someone is house-bound and terminally ill, it would not be possible to combine the procedure for house-bound persons with the special procedure. However, it is possible for the waiting period time to be abridged under s 12, and so in the case mentioned, the procedure for housebound persons could be used and combined with an application to the Registrar General for a shortening of the waiting period.

4.25   The registration process is altered slightly in relation to the general procedure and the procedure in respect of house-bound persons and detained persons where one or other of the proposed civil partners is living in either Scotland or Northern Ireland, or is a member of Her Majesty's forces serving outside the United Kingdom. In these circumstances, the proposed civil partner living outside England and Wales or serving in Her Majesty's forces is not required to give notice of the proposed civil partnership.

---

1   CPA 2004, s 19(3)(c).
2   CPA 2004, s 19(8).
3   CPA 2004, s 22.
4   CPA 2004, s 23.
5   CPA 2004, s 27.
6   CPA 2004, s 26.

Instead only the proposed civil partner living in England and Wales has to give notice.[1] The date of that notice, is the date by reference to which the waiting period and the period during which the civil partners may sign the civil partnership schedule will be calculated.[2] Before the civil partnership schedule is issued, either of the proposed civil partners must produce a certificate of no impediment. A certificate of no impediment will be either a certificate issued by the authority empowered to issue such a certificate to the proposed civil partner living in Scotland or Northern Ireland on his or her application, or a certificate issued by the proposed civil partner's commanding officer. In either case, the issuing body must be satisfied that there is nothing which makes the parties ineligible to register as civil partners before issuing a certificate of no impediment.[3]

Hierarchy of registration organisation

4.26 Every council in England and Wales will also be a registration authority for the purposes of the Act.[4] Each registration authority must designate a civil partnership registrar and ensure that there are sufficient civil partnership registrars available to perform the functions required.[5] The Registrar General is the Registrar General for England and Wales and is responsible for providing a system by which any records required by the Act are made and kept. The Act provides in particular that the system of record keeping should enable those records to be kept with other records kept by the Registrar General.[6] This is in line with the proposals envisaged by the consultation document *Civil Registration: Delivering Vital Change* and the uniformity of approach visualised in it.

Offences

4.27 If someone issues a partnership schedule before the waiting period is over, or after the end of the period during which the civil partnership schedule may be signed by the proposed civil partners or where the issue of the partnership schedule has been forbidden under Sch 2 (on grounds of a prohibited degree of relationship) he or she will have committed an offence.[7] If someone, in his or her actual or purported capacity as civil partnership registrar, officiates at the signing of a civil partnership schedule by proposed civil partners, knowing that the place is a different one than was specified in the notices of civil partnership, or in the absence of a civil partnership registrar, or before the waiting period has expired, he or she will be guilty of an offence, not withstanding the fact that the civil partnership is void under s 49(b) or (c).[8] If someone is convicted on indictment of any of these offences, he or she will be liable to imprisonment for a maximum of 5 years or to a fine or both.[9]

---

1   CPA 2004, s 20(5)(a).
2   CPA 2004, s 20(5)(c) and (e).
3   CPA 2004, s 20(5)(d) and s 20(6).
4   CPA 2004, s 28. See **4.13**.
5   CPA 2004, s 29.
6   CPA 2004, s 30.
7   CPA 2004, s 31(1).
8   CPA 2004, s 31(2).
9   CPA 2004, s 31(3).

4.28   The offences are similar in relation to a Registrar General's licence. A person commits an offence if he or she gives evidence in support of a notice of a proposed civil partnership in accordance with s 22(1) or provides a certificate of no lawful impediment under s 22(3), knowing that the information or the certificate is false.[1] A person also commits an offence if he or she, in his or her actual or purported capacity as civil partnership registrar, officiates at the signing of a Registrar General's licence, knowing that the place is a different one than was specified in the notices of civil partnership, or in the absence of a civil partnership registrar, or before the waiting period has expired. He or she will be guilty of an offence, notwithstanding the fact that the civil partnership is void under s 49(b) or (c).[2] A person guilty of an offence in relation to a Registrar General's licence is liable on conviction on indictment to imprisonment not exceeding 3 years or to a fine or both or, on summary conviction, to a fine not exceeding the statutory maximum.[3]

4.29   An offence will be committed under the Act if a civil partnership registrar fails to comply with any of the provisions relating to the registration of civil partnerships or any of the supplementary regulations.[4] The sanction for the committal of such an offence is, on conviction on indictment, a maximum of 2 years' imprisonment or a fine or both[5] and, on summary conviction, a fine not exceeding the statutory maximum.[6]

4.30   A person also commits an offence if he or she is responsible under s 2(4) to ensure that the fact that two people have registered as civil partners of each other (and any other information prescribed by regulations) is recorded in the register, and omits to do so.[7] Someone who is guilty of such an offence will be liable on summary conviction to a fine not exceeding level 3 on the standard scale.[8]

4.31   An offence will also be committed if someone records in the register information relating to the formation of a civil partnership by the signing of a civil partnership schedule if he or she knows that the civil partnership is void under s 49(b) or (c).[9] Someone who is guilty of such an offence will be liable on conviction on indictment, to imprisonment for a term not exceeding 5 years or a to a fine, or both.[10]

4.32   An offence is also committed if someone records in the register information relating to the formation of a civil partnership by the signing of a civil partnership licence if she or she knows that the civil partnership is void under section 49(b) or (c).[11] Someone who is guilty of such an offence is liable on conviction on indictment to imprisonment for a term not exceeding 3 years or to a fine or both[12] and on summary conviction to a fine not exceeding the statutory maximum.[13]

---

1   CPA 2004, s 32(1). See **4.24**.
2   CPA 2004, s 32(2).
3   CPA 2004, s 32(3).
4   CPA 2004, s 33(1).
5   CPA 2004, s 33(2)(a).
6   CPA 2004, s 33(2)(b).
7   CPA 2004, s 32(5).
8   CPA 2004, s 33(3).
9   CPA 2004, s 33(5). See **4.51**.
10   CPA 2004, s 33(6).
11   CPA 2004, s 33(7). See **4.51**.
12   CPA 2004, s 33(8)(a).
13   CPA 2004, s 33(8)(b).

4.33   A prosecution under ss 31, 32 or 33 may not be commenced more than 3 years after the commission of the offence.[1]

4.34   If anyone makes a statement for the purpose of procuring the formation of a civil partnership that he or she knows to be false, or represents him or herself to be a person whose consent is required for a civil partnership to take place between another person and a child that person will be guilty of an offence and will be liable on conviction on indictment to imprisonment for a term not exceeding 7 years or to a fine or both, and on summary conviction to a fine not exceeding the statutory maximum.[2]

Registration and recognition of partnerships formed overseas

4.35   There are two situations in which a partnership formed overseas will be afforded recognition under the Act. The first is where two people register a civil partnership other than in England, Wales, Scotland or Northern Ireland, at the British Consulate in that country or, in the case of armed forces personnel, at their barracks. The second is where the parties have registered a relationship 'overseas' (under that country's jurisdiction) and, by reason either of being a specified relationship, or because that relationship satisfies the general conditions, that relationship is afforded recognition as a civil partnership in England and Wales.

4.36   Unusually, the Act provides that it is possible to register a relationship as a civil partnership overseas under the law of England and Wales. Section 210 of the Act provides that the Queen, by an Order in Council, may make provision for two people to register as civil partners of each other in certain prescribed countries or territories, in the presence of a prescribed officer of Her Majesty's Diplomatic Service. In this context, 'prescribed' means prescribed in the Order in Council, so it may effectively be anywhere where there is an active diplomatic mission.[3] The conditions that must be met before such a registration may take place are that:

— at least one of the proposed civil partners is a UK national;
— the proposed civil partners would have been eligible to register as civil partners of each other in the UK;
— the authorities in the country or territory in which is it proposed that the people are registered would not object to the registration; and
— insufficient facilities exist for them to enter into a similar relationship under the law of that country or territory.[4]

There is no requirement that an officer allow two people to register as civil partners of each other if to do so would be inconsistent with international law or the comity of nations.[5] If a civil partnership is registered in this way, for the purposes of its termination, it will be treated as having been registered in whichever part of the United Kingdom the civil partners would otherwise have been eligible to register, that is England and Wales, Scotland or Northern Ireland.[6]

---

1   CPA 2004, s 31(4), s 32(4), s 33(9).
2   CPA 2004, s 80.
3   CPA 2004, s 210(1).
4   CPA 2004, s 211(1).
5   CPA 2004, s 210(3).
6   CPA 2004, s 210(5).

4.37   Armed forces personnel or their children living with them may also register as civil partners of another person where they are serving outside the UK where the Queen makes provision by Order in Council.[1] The place of registration is again to be prescribed by the Order in Council. The registration should take place before an officer appointed by virtue of the Registration of Births, Deaths and Marriages (Special Provisions) Act 1957.[2] The conditions that must be satisfied in order for an Order in Council to be made are that:

—   at least one of the proposed civil partners is a member or a part of Her Majesty's forces serving in the territory; or
—   is employed in the country in another capacity as may be prescribed by the Order; or
—   is the child of someone who falls into the two categories above and has his or her home with that person in that country; and
—   the proposed civil partners would have been eligible to register as civil partners in the UK; and
—   any other requirements prescribed by the Order have been complied with.[3]

A 'child' for these purposes is someone who is or was treated as a child of the serving member's family.[4] If a civil partnership is registered in this way, for the purposes of its termination, it will be treated as having been registered in whichever part of the UK the civil partners would otherwise have been eligible to register in.[5] This provision in particular represents a sea change in government policy. Having been forced by the ruling in *Smith and Grady v United Kingdom*[6] to suspend the policy of discharging gay men and women from the armed forces, the government seems, finally, to be embracing the concept by enabling the registration of civil partnerships at barracks.

4.38   Overseas relationships are also given recognition under the Act. As Jacqui Smith MP, Deputy Minister for Women and Equality, said at the Third Reading of the Bill in the House of Commons, the Act is 'ground-breaking, in that it is the first Bill of its kind to include comprehensive international recognition provisions that could be used as a template by other countries in the years to come'.[7] 'Overseas relationships' are defined as either one of the relationships listed in Sch 20 or a relationship which meets the general conditions set down by the Act.[8] Schedule 20 affords recognition to specific relationships, which include marriage in Belgium and the Netherlands, registered partnerships in Norway and Sweden and Civil Solidarity Pacts (known as PACS) in France. In both cases the overseas relationship must have been registered outside the UK by two people, both of whom are of the same sex and neither of whom is already a civil partner or already married.[9] The exception to this rule is where a gender recognition certificate has been issued under the Gender Recognition Act 2004. In this situation, there will be no bar to an overseas relationship being treated as a civil partnership where at the relevant time the two people were not of the same sex under UK law, provided that

---

1   CPA 2004, s 211(1).
2   CPA 2004, s 211(2).
3   CPA 2004, s 210(2).
4   CPA 2004, s 210(3).
5   CPA 2004, s 211(4).
6   [2000] 29 EHRR 493, ECHR.
7   *Hansard*, HC Deb, col 798 (9 November 2004).
8   CPA 2004, s 212.
9   CPA 2004, s 213.

they were regarded as being of the same sex under the relevant law.[1] The subsequent issue of the gender recognition certificate, which recognises the change of gender of one of the parties under UK law, will enable the parties to the overseas relationship to be treated as civil partners.

4.39   If the overseas relationship is not a specified relationship under Sch 20, the general conditions that an overseas relationship must meet in order to be recognised are that:

— the relationship may not be entered into by parties already party to a relationship of that kind or married;
— the relationship is of indeterminate duration; and
— the effect of entering into the relationship on the parties is that the parties are treated as a couple or treated as married; and
— the relationship has been registered.[2] The requirement that the relationship be registered will be satisfied where the two people concerned had capacity to enter into the relationship under the relevant law, defined as 'the law of the country or territory where the relationship is registered (including its rule of private international law)',[3] usually the law of the overseas country, and have met all of the requirements necessary to ensure the formal validity of the relationship.[4]

However, where one of the parties was domiciled in England and Wales when the overseas relationship was registered, it will not be recognised as a civil partnership if either of the parties was under 16 or they would have been within prohibited degrees of relationship if they had been registering in England and Wales.[5] It is interesting to note that there is no distinction made in the Act between overseas relationships treated as marriage in the jurisdiction in which they were formed, and registered partnerships. All relationships between same sex partners are converted into civil partnerships, regardless of any higher status they may have in the home country. The fact that same sex marriage in Belgium and the Netherlands will be treated as a civil partnership is unfair, but causes no real practical disadvantages given how alike civil partnership is to civil marriage.

4.40   The recognition of any overseas relationship is subject to the overriding exception that there will be no recognition of an overseas relationship if to do so would be manifestly contrary to public policy to recognise the capacity, under the relevant law, of one or both of the partners to enter into the relationship.[6]

4.41   These provisions may cause complications, and possible unfairness, in practice as some forms of foreign civil partnership give far fewer rights and responsibilities than a civil partnership in England and Wales. For example, a PACS in France gives few rights on relationship breakdown; rather it gives mainly tax and inheritance benefits 3 years after registration. A number of the registration systems in parts of Spain, such as Catalonia, give housing and other limited rights. Whilst not afforded recognition under Sch 20, by virtue of ss 212 and 215 such a registered relationship, if it fulfils the general conditions, may be recognised. If couples who have registered their relationship under regimes such as those mentioned come to live in England or Wales then they will have

1   CPA 2004, s 216.
2   CPA 2004, s 212(1)(b) and s 214.
3   CPA 2004, s 212(2).
4   CPA 2004, s 215.
5   CPA 2004, s 217. See **4.6** and **4.7**.
6   CPA 2004, s 218.

imposed on them a whole series of obligations, and procedures to dissolve their partnership which would not have applied in their home country. On the other hand, marriage between same sex couples in Belgium and the Netherlands is only afforded civil partnership status under the Act. This raises interesting conflict of law points. Rule 67 of Dicey and Morris states that marriage is formally valid if the marriage is celebrated in accordance with the form required or recognised as sufficient in the country in which the marriage was celebrated.[1] The reason for this is that the law of England and Wales gives effect to the principle that contracts will be governed by the law of the country in which the contract was made and, for these purposes at least, marriage can be seen as a form of contract. Rule 68 states that the parties' capacity to marry will be determined in accordance with the law of each of the parties' ante-nuptial domicile. The exception to this rule is that the courts of England and Wales will not recognise a marriage where to do so would be 'offensive to the conscience of the English court'.[2] In practice, although open to challenge, it is unlikely that any challenge will be made to the Act's refusal to recognise same sex marriage when the rights afforded to civil partners are so extensive, unless the challenge is on ground of principle.

4.42   There is no concept of mutual recognition of civil partnership in the Act. Whilst overseas relationships fulfilling the criteria set out by the Act will be recognised in England and Wales, there is no guarantee that such recognition will be reciprocated and civil partnerships formed in England and Wales will be recognised in any other country. However, whilst the courts of England and Wales clearly cannot compel recognition of a civil partnership formed in this jurisdiction in any other jurisdiction, the Act does make provision for the courts to be given jurisdiction to dissolve a civil partnership formed in England and Wales if the partners live outside the United Kingdom and if dissolution cannot be obtained abroad and to hear proceedings for the termination of a civil partnership in England and Wales where it was formed abroad.[3]

TERMINATION OF A CIVIL PARTNERSHIP

Generally

4.43   A civil partnership may be terminated on the ground of nullity, or it may be terminated by either party bringing an action for dissolution or legal separation or applying for a presumption of death order.[4] The fact that a civil partnership can only be terminated in these ways is a sign of how serious a commitment civil partnership is intended to be. Orders for dissolution, annulment or presumption of death will be conditional in the first instance, and may not be made final before the end of the period of 6 weeks from the date the order was made conditional. If that day is a day when the

---

1   Dicey and Morris *The Conflict of Laws* (13th edn) p 688.
2   *Cheni (otherwise Rodriquez) v Cheni* [1965] P 85.
3   See **4.61**.
4   CPA 2004, s 37(1).

register office is closed, it will be the first working day after that date.[1] The court has power to shorten the period by order where it is dealing with the case.[2]

4.44 Where an application has been made for the dissolution or annulment of a civil partnership, or for a presumption of death order, the Queen's Proctor may intervene if the court thinks it would be fit for him to do so or if any person during the proceedings gives him information before a final order that may affect the outcome of the case.[3] If so requested by the court, the Queen's Proctor must, having taken directions from the Attorney General, instruct counsel to argue before the court any question that the court feels it is necessary to have argued. Where another person gives him information relating to the case, he may take such steps as the Attorney General thinks necessary or expedient. The costs of the Queen's Proctor's intervention may be borne either by the parties involved or by himself. He may also be ordered to bear the costs of either of the parties incurred as a result of his intervention.[4]

4.45 If either the Queen's Proctor or a third party has succeeded in showing that the order should not be made final on the ground that material facts have not been brought before the court, or 3 months have passed since the earliest date on which the conditional order could have been made final and the other civil partner makes an application, the court may make the order final, rescind the order, require further enquiry, or otherwise deal with the case as it thinks fit.[5]

4.46 Where an application is made for a dissolution or separation order, rules of court are to make provision requiring the solicitor acting for the applicant to certify whether or not he or she has discussed the possibility of reconciliation with the applicant and whether or not he or she has given the applicant names and addresses of people qualified to help effect such a reconciliation.[6] Proceedings for a dissolution or separation order may be suspended at any point if it appears to the court that there is a reasonable possibility of a reconciliation being effected between the parties.[7]

Dissolution

4.47 As with divorce, no application may be made for a dissolution order before a year has elapsed from the date of the formation of a civil partnership. However, the time bar does not prevent an application being made on the basis of events that occurred during that first year.[8]

4.48 Subject to the one-year time bar, an application for a dissolution order may be made to court by either party to a civil partnership, on the ground that the partnership has irretrievably broken down.[9] This ground may be proved only by the existence of one of four facts, and the court may make enquiries into any facts alleged by the applicant and

---

1   CPA 2004, s 37(2) and s 38(1).
2   CPA 2004, s 38(4).
3   CPA 2004, s 39(2) and (3).
4   CPA 2004, s 39(4).
5   CPA 2004, s 40.
6   CPA 2004, s 42(2).
7   CPA 2004, s 42(3).
8   CPA 2004, s 41.
9   CPA 2004, s 44(1).

the respondent.[1] If the court is satisfied that any of the facts alleged is true, it must make a dissolution order unless it is satisfied that the civil partnership has not broken down irretrievably.[2] The four facts are:

(1) behaviour such that the applicant cannot reasonably be expected to live with the respondent;
(2) the parties have lived apart for a period of 2 years and the respondent consents to the dissolution;
(3) the parties have lived apart for 5 years; or
(4) desertion.[3]

Missing from the list is adultery. This would seem to restrict the facts upon which a party may rely to prove the irretrievable breakdown of a civil partnership. One party's unfaithfulness is just as likely to be the cause of an irretrievable breakdown of a relationship between same sex couples as opposite sex couples. However, the definition of 'adultery' in the *Oxford English Dictionary* is 'voluntary sexual intercourse between a married person and someone other than his or her spouse'. In Rayden and Jackson[4] the definition given is:

> 'Consensual sexual intercourse between a married person and a person of the opposite sex, not the other spouse, during the subsistence of the marriage. There must be at least partial penetration of the female by the male for the act of adultery to be proven. The attempt to commit adultery must not be confused with the act itself, and if there is no such penetration, some lesser act of sexual gratification does not amount to adultery.'

The Biblical definition can be found in Leviticus Chapter 18, verse 20, which states 'You shall not have sexual relations with your kinsman's wife, and defile yourself with her'. The physical and biological problems with these definitions in same sex cases rightly meant that the fact of adultery was not included in the legislation. In any event, it is likely that in the case of civil partnership, infidelity will be regarded as unreasonable behaviour.

4.49 A dissolution order will not be precluded by a previous separation order, occupation order or financial order under Sch 6 and it may be made on the same facts as those orders.[5] However, although an order may have been granted, and the court can treat the order as proof of any fact by reference to which it was made, the applicant must still adduce evidence in support of his or her application.[6] As with divorce, a dissolution in 5-year separation cases will not be ordered if it would cause grave financial or other hardship to the respondent and it would be wrong in all the circumstances to dissolve the civil partnership.[7] The circumstances considered will include the conduct and interests of the civil partners together with the interests of any children or any other persons concerned.[8] Hardship includes the loss of the chance of acquiring any benefit which the respondent might acquire if the civil partnership were not dissolved.[9] If the court is

---

1   CPA 2004, s 44(2).
2   CPA 2004, s 44(4).
3   CPA 2004, s 44(5).
4   Rayden and Jackson *Divorce and Family Matters* (17th edn) Chapter 8, Section 1, para 5.2.
5   CPA 2004, s 46(1) and (2).
6   CPA 2004, s 46(3).
7   CPA 2004, s 47(1).
8   CPA 2004, s 47(3).
9   CPA 2004, s 47(4).

satisfied that hardship would be caused, the court must dismiss the application for the dissolution order.[1]

4.50 Conditional orders for dissolution on the basis of 2 years' separation and consent will not be made final where the court finds on an application made by the respondent that the applicant misled the respondent about any matter which led to the respondent giving his or her consent to a dissolution.[2] An order for dissolution where the applicant has relied on 2 years' separation and consent or 5 years' separation will also only be made final where the court, on the respondent's application, having considered all the circumstances of the case (including the age, earning capacity, health of the parties and their respective financial positions), is satisfied that the applicant should not be required to make any financial provision for the respondent or the financial provision made is reasonable and fair or the best that can be made in the circumstances.[3] If the court has a satisfactory undertaking from the applicant to make appropriate financial provision, it may nevertheless make a conditional order final.[4]

Nullity

4.51 A civil partnership will be void if the parties to the civil partnership were not eligible to register as civil partners, or if there was a procedural irregularity of which both parties were aware at the time of registration. There will be a procedural irregularity where:

— notice of the proposed civil partnership has not been given; or
— the civil partnership document has not been duly issued; or
— the place of registration was a place other than the place specified in the notice of proposed civil partnership; or
— the registrar was not present.[5]

A civil partnership will also be void if it takes place between a child and another person.[6] A civil partnership that is void *ab initio* in these circumstances can only be validated at a later date by an order of the Lord Chancellor and can only be validated in circumstances where the reason for the invalidity is a procedural irregularity (ie not where it is void because one of the parties is a child).[7] An order of the Lord Chancellor may include provisions for the relief of a person from criminal liability under s 33.[8]

4.52 There are five reasons which will make a civil partnership voidable as opposed to void *ab initio*:

(1) either of the parties did not validly consent to its formation (which could be as a result of duress, mistake, unsoundness of mind or some other reason);

---

1   CPA 2004, s 47(3)(b).
2   CPA 2004, s 48(1).
3   CPA 2004, s 48(2), (3), (4).
4   CPA 2004, s 48(5).
5   CPA 2004, s 49.
6   CPA 2004, s 49.
7   CPA 2004, s 53.
8   See **4.27**.

(2)   at the time of the formation of the civil partnership either of the parties was suffering from a mental disorder of such a kind or to such an extent as to be unfit for civil partnership (even if that party was capable of giving valid consent);[1]

(3)   at the time of the formation of the civil partnership one of the parties was pregnant by another person other than the other party to the partnership;

(4)   after the time of formation, an interim gender recognition certificate has been issued under the Gender Recognition Act 2004; or

(5)   if one of the parties is a person whose gender at the time of the formation of the civil partnership had become the acquired gender under the Gender Recognition Act 2004.[2]

It is important to note that there is no requirement in the Act for the civil partnership to be consummated, and no requirement for the relationship to be sexual, unlike for marriage (unless the parties to a marriage consent to non-consummation). Baroness Scotland emphasised this point as a significant difference from marriage, in the Lords on 17 November 2004.[3] Whether this will mean that a dissolution cannot be obtained based on a civil partner refusing to engage in any form of sexual relations remains to be seen, but is probably unlikely in most cases. It is interesting to note that a mental disorder, whilst it may not invalidate the consent given by a person, may make that person unfit for civil partnership. Another slightly odd provision is that which states that the fact that at the time of the formation one of the parties was pregnant by some person other than the applicant will make the civil partnership voidable. As civil partnerships are between two people of the same sex, it is inevitable (and in the case of civil partnerships between men, impossible) that if one of the parties was pregnant, it would be by some other person than the applicant. Furthermore, there is no provision stating that if, in the case of two men, a third party was pregnant by one of them, the civil partnership should be voidable. The applicant will be estopped from bringing an action for a nullity order if the court is not satisfied that the applicant was, at the time of the formation of the partnership, ignorant of the respondent's pregnancy by someone other than the applicant. One ground of nullity not brought into civil partnership that exists for marriage is if one of the parties is suffering from venereal disease. The Matrimonial Causes Act 1973 provides that if at the time of the marriage 'the respondent was suffering from venereal disease in a communicable form' the marriage will be voidable.[4] The ability of the applicant to rely on this ground depends on him or her not having known of the disease at the time of the marriage.[5] There has not been any clarification of why this provision was omitted, no doubt because of its somewhat archaic nature.

---

1   This provision does not seem to be quite in keeping with the ratio of *Sheffield County Council v E and Others* (The Times 20 January 2005, and [2004] EWHC 2808 (Fam)). In his judgment, Munby J drew a distinction between an individual's capacity to marry and the question of whether or not that marriage was objectively wise. It was held that the court had no jurisdiction to consider whether it was in a particular person's best interests to marry. Whether or not 'best interests' would have the same meaning as fitness in the context of this provision is not clear. However, at a glance, it seems that whilst this provision of the CPA 2004 is saying that the validity of a civil partnership may be dependent on a person's fitness for civil partnership, regardless of whether or not valid consent has been given, the validity of a marriage is dependent only on the person's ability to give valid consent.

2   CPA 2004, s 50.

3   *Hansard*, HL Deb, col 1479 (17 November 2004).

4   Matrimonial Causes Act 1973, s 12(e).

5   Matrimonial Causes Act 1973, s 13(3).

4.53 A civil partnership that has been registered somewhere other than England and Wales may also be void or voidable under the Act. If a civil partnership is formed either in Scotland or Northern Ireland or by an Order in Council, it will be void if it would be void under the law relating to Scotland and Northern Ireland, and in relation to a civil partnership formed by Order in Council, it will be void if the pre-conditions or the requirements prescribed by the Order have not been met.[1] In relation to an alleged overseas relationship, it will be void if it is not in actual fact an overseas relationship, or if the parties are not treated as having formed a civil partnership under the provisions of Chapter 2 of Part 5 of the Act (discussed at **4.35**). An overseas relationship will be voidable if it is voidable under the law of the country in which it was registered or if an interim gender recognition certificate has been issued to either civil partner under the Gender Recognition Act 2004.[2] It will also be voidable if either of the parties was domiciled in England and Wales or Northern Ireland (but not Scotland) at the time the overseas relationship was registered and it would be voidable if it had been registered in England and Wales.[3]

4.54 Even where a civil partnership is voidable, the court must not make a nullity order if the respondent satisfies the court that the applicant, while knowing that the civil partnership was voidable, conducted himself in relation to the respondent in such a way as to lead the respondent reasonably to believe that the nullity order would not be sought. The court must further be satisfied that it would be unjust to the respondent to make such an order.[4]

4.55 Proceedings in respect of a nullity order must be commenced within 3 years of the date of formation of the civil partnership, unless the leave of the court is given.[5] Leave will only be given if the applicant has at some point during the 3-year period suffered from a mental disorder and the granting of leave would be just in all the circumstances.[6] Furthermore, the court must not make a nullity order on the ground that an interim gender recognition certificate has been issued since the formation of the civil partnership, or on the ground of the respondent's pregnancy by someone other than the applicant, without being satisfied that the applicant was at the time of the formation of the civil partnership ignorant of the facts alleged.[7] It is hard to see how this particular provision can be applicable to the issuing of a gender recognition certificate after the formation of the civil partnership, as the applicant will always be ignorant of the issuing of the certificate at the time of the formation of the civil partnership in this situation.

4.56 It will not be necessary for the court to be presented with any evidence that proves that any person whose consent to the civil partnership was required gave that consent or that the civil partnership registrar had the necessary authority. However, a civil partnership between a child and another person will always be void, regardless of that child's parent or guardian having given consent.[8]

---

1   CPA 2004, s 54(1)–(5).
2   CPA 2004, s 54(8)(a), (b).
3   CPA 2004, s 54(8)(c).
4   CPA 2004, s 51(1).
5   CPA 2004, s 51(2).
6   CPA 2004, s 51(3).
7   CPA 2004, s 51(6).
8   CPA 2004, s 52.

Presumption of death orders and separation orders

4.57 The Act provides for presumption of death orders to be made where the court is satisfied that there are reasonable grounds for supposing that the other civil partner is dead.[1] The fact that the other civil partner has been absent for a period of 7 years or more and the applicant has no reason to believe that the other civil partner has been living within that time will be sufficient evidence that the other civil partner is dead.[2] However, that is not to say that there may not be other grounds on which a court could make a presumption of death order. Such a presumption, having been established, will stand until the contrary is proved.

4.58 Separation orders may be made on the basis of the same facts as dissolution.[3] On an application for a separation order the court must enquire into the circumstances of the facts alleged by the application. However, whether the civil partnership has broken down irretrievably or not is irrelevant.[4] If the court is satisfied that one of the four facts alleged is true, it may make a separation order. The same restrictions in relation to consent and subsequent cohabitation that apply to the making of an order for dissolution apply in relation to the making of a separation order.[5] While the separation order continues in force and the separation is continuing, for the purposes of intestacy, the other civil partner will be treated as being dead.

4.59 Any civil partner may apply to the High Court or County Court for a declaration that the civil partnership was at its inception valid (but not that at its inception it was void[6]), that it subsisted, that it did not subsist, that a dissolution is valid or that a dissolution or legal separation is not recognisable.[7] The court must make such a declaration if it is satisfied of the truth of the proposition to be declared, unless to do so would be contrary to public policy.[8] The court may not, on the dismissal of an application made under s 58, make any other declaration.[9] Any declaration made under s 58 should be made in such a form as may be prescribed by rules of court.[10] No proceedings under s 58 should affect any final judgment or order already pronounced or made by any court of competent jurisdiction (presumably including overseas courts).[11] Any application under s 58 should be heard in private.[12]

Jurisdiction for termination including termination of civil partnerships registered overseas

4.60 As discussed at **4.35**, civil partnerships formed abroad will be afforded recognition by the Act by virtue of the sections contained in Chapter 2 of the Act.

---

1   CPA 2004, s 55.
2   CPA 2004, s 55(2).
3   CPA 2004, s 56(1).
4   CPA 2004, s 56(2).
5   CPA 2004, s 56(4).
6   CPA 2004, s 59(5).
7   CPA 2004, s 58.
8   CPA 2004, s 59(1).
9   CPA 2004, s 59(3).
10   CPA 2004, s 61(2).
11   CPA 2004, s 61(3).
12   CPA 2004, s 61(5).

Chapter 3 of the Act deals with their termination and also with the recognition of the termination of civil partnerships abroad.

4.61 Section 219 of the Act gives the Lord Chancellor the power to make provision by regulations for the jurisdiction of the courts of England and Wales for proceedings for dissolution, separation or annulment of a civil partnership, or the recognition of the termination of a civil partnership by another EU member state in the following circumstances:

— where a civil partner is or has been habitually resident in an EU member state; or
— is a national of a member state; or
— is domiciled in a part of the UK or Republic of Ireland.[1]

The regulations may also make provision for the recognition in England and Wales of the termination of a civil partnership by another EU member state.[2] Section 219(3) states that the regulations may in particular make provision corresponding to that made in Council Regulation (EC) No 2201/2003 of 27 November 2003 (known as the new Brussels II). Arguably, this is a novel provision. There is currently no Europe-wide scheme of mutual recognition of civil partnerships, or jurisdiction for their termination, despite a number of EU countries having adopted legislation creating a status akin to civil partnership, although not the same. Due to the political influences in each country in which the concept of civil partnership has been introduced, each regime is different, and in each country differing rights and responsibilities will arise from the creation and termination of a civil partnership. However, it appears that the government has decided that the jurisdiction for termination of a civil partnership is to be as if on divorce, namely the new Brussels II criteria and, where a non-EU member state (including Denmark) is the competing jurisdiction, the ground that either party is domiciled in England and Wales. No doubt this is in the hope that in due course there may be EU-wide recognition of jurisdiction for termination of a civil partnership, and possibly even EU-wide recognition of civil partnerships.

4.62 The courts of England and Wales will have jurisdiction to hear proceedings for a dissolution, nullity or separation order only if:

— it is so provided for by the regulations enacted pursuant to s 219; or
— no court has jurisdiction under the s 219 regulations and either civil partner is domiciled in England and Wales on the date proceedings are begun; or
— the parties registered as partners in England and Wales and no court has or is recognised as having jurisdiction under s 219 regulations, and it appears in the interests of justice for the court to assume jurisdiction.[3]

The third category of jurisdiction is a novel one. This was included so as to prevent a situation where a couple having registered in England and Wales are not able to obtain a termination of their civil partnership in the country where they are living, meaning that to do so one or both of them would have to return to live in England and Wales.

---

1   CPA 2004, s 219(1)(a).
2   CPA 2004, s 219(1)(b).
3   CPA 2004, s 221.

4.63 The court will have jurisdiction to hear proceedings for a presumption of death order only if the applicant had been habitually resident for the period of one year before proceedings were begun and is domiciled in England and Wales on the date proceedings were begun; the two people registered as civil partners in England and Wales; and it appears to be in the interests of justice for the court to assume jurisdiction.

Delaying of a Final Order

4.64 If in any proceedings for a dissolution, nullity or separation order it appears to the court that there are children of the family in respect of which the court has been or is likely to be asked to exercise any of its powers under the Children Act 1989, the court must take into account the circumstances of the case and consider, with respect to any such child, whether it is in a position to exercise its power without giving further consideration to the case and if there are any exceptional circumstances which make it desirable in the interests of the child that the court should give a direction. Such direction may be that the order is not to be made final or, in the case of a separation order, is not to be made, until the court orders otherwise.[1]

Parties to proceedings

4.65 Rules of the court may be made to enable parties to be joined if there are allegations of improper conduct made in the dissolution proceedings. The court may also allow a third party whose interests are affected by the proceedings to intervene upon such terms as the court thinks fit.[2]

---

1   CPA 2004, s 63.
2   CPA 2004, s 64.

Chapter 5

FINANCIAL CONSEQUENCES OF TERMINATION

INTRODUCTION

5.1 Whilst the civil partnership subsists, and upon the commencement of proceedings for the termination of a civil partnership, relief will be mutually available to applicants or respondents regardless of who has made the application for the termination of the civil partnership.[1] Chapters 3 and 4 and Schs 5, 6 and 7 to the Civil Partnership Act 2004 deal with financial proceedings between parties to a civil partnership and these provisions are discussed below in detail.

PROPERTY AND FINANCIAL ARRANGEMENTS

5.2 Outside any proceedings for termination of the civil partnership, the court may make an order in relation to property where a civil partner has contributed to the improvement of real or personal property and where either or both of the civil partners has an interest in the property or the proceeds of its sale.[2] The contribution has to have been of a substantial nature,[3] and the contributing partner will be treated as having acquired by virtue of the contribution a share (or a larger share as the case may be) in the property in such shares may seem in all the circumstances just.[4] This may be overridden by any agreement, either express or implied, between the civil partners to the contrary.[5]

5.3 Where there is a dispute between civil partners about the title or possession of property, either party may apply to court for determination of their application and the court may make such an order as it deems fit in respect of the property. This could include an order for sale.[6] The court may make an order even where the applicant does not have the property in his or her possession or under his or her control or where the applicant does not know where the property is.[7] This provision would be particularly useful in circumstances where the respondent civil partner has sold a property, but where the

---

1 Civil Partnership Act 2004 (CPA 2004), s 62.
2 CPA 2004, s 65.
3 CPA 2004, s 65(1)(b).
4 CPA 2004, s 65(2).
5 CPA 2004, s 65(3).
6 CPA 2004, s 66.
7 CPA 2004, s 67.

applicant does not know the whereabouts of the sale proceeds. Provided that the applicant civil partner has a beneficial interest in the sale proceeds, or a share of them, it does not matter how that beneficial interest was acquired.[1] Where the respondent has disposed of property (by way of sale or otherwise) and has money or other property in which the applicant has a beneficial interest and has not made an appropriate payment or disposition to the applicant, the court may make an order to redress this balance.[2] However, this remedy is available only where the respondent holds money or other property in which the applicant has a beneficial interest. If the respondent civil partner has gifted the property to another person, there is no provision in accordance with which he or she may be ordered to pay to the applicant such sum as represents the value of the applicant's share. Applications under s 66 may be made by former civil partners, provided that the action is begun within 3 years of the date of dissolution or annulment.[3]

ACTIONS IN TORT BETWEEN PARTNERS

5.4   The court may stay proceedings in tort where it appears that no substantial benefit would accrue to either civil partner from the continuation of an action or if such proceedings could be more conveniently disposed of under s 66.[4]

CIVIL PARTNERSHIP AGREEMENTS

5.5   Chapter 4 deals with civil partnership agreements. These should not be confused with pre-nuptial or pre-partnership agreements.[5] A civil partnership agreement is an agreement between two people to register as civil partners or to enter into an overseas relationship. This is unenforceable under the Act and no action may be brought in respect of its breach.[6] However, where a civil partnership agreement has been made and is subsequently terminated, a civil partner may have recourse to the provisions of the Act in relation to property in s 66 or s 67 where either or both of the parties had a beneficial interest in the property while the agreement was in force and provided that any action is brought within 3 years of the termination of the agreement.[7] A party who gifts another property on the condition that it be returned if the agreement is terminated is not precluded from having the property returned to him or her, merely because it was he or she who terminated the agreement.[8]

5.6   What is interesting here is that relief is available for a civil partner only on termination of the agreement, rather than in circumstances where the agreement is not fulfilled (ie the civil partnership is not registered). It would be contrary to public policy to compel anyone to enter into a civil partnership on the basis of an agreement to do so, and,

---

1   CPA 2004, s 67(2).
2   CPA 2004, s 67(4).
3   CPA 2004, s 68.
4   CPA 2004, s 69. See **5.7**.
5   See **5.7**.
6   CPA 2004, s 73.
7   CPA 2004, s 74(3), (4).
8   CPA 2004, s 74(5).

therefore, it also stands that it would be contrary to public policy to give one party a remedy for the other's breach of the agreement and, therefore, the relief available is not so broad as to be able to put the parties back into their pre-agreement position if some reliance has been placed on the agreement by one party to his or her detriment.

5.7   Where there is a pre-partnership agreement, akin to a pre-nuptial agreement, it is likely that ancillary relief case law on pre-nuptial agreements will be followed. Although a significant number of same sex couples have children, many do not. Where there are no children of the partnership then there may be strong arguments for the terms of a pre-partnership agreement, properly entered into, to be given significant weight in resolving financial claims. Such an agreement would need to have been signed at least 21 days before the registration, with full financial disclosure and independent legal advice for both partners.

FINANCIAL CONSEQUENCES OF DISSOLUTION, NULLITY OR SEPARATION

5.8   The Civil Partnership Act 2004, s 72 makes provision for financial relief for civil partners generally. Subsection (1) states that Sch 5, which contains the 'ancillary relief' provisions, 'corresponds to provision made for financial relief in connection with marriages by Part 2 of the Matrimonial Causes Act 1973' (which deals with financial relief for parties to a marriage and children of the family). This is an important declaration. Having such a declaration on the face of the Act gives the clearest indication possible that the purpose of the civil partnership regime is to extend all of those rights and responsibilities invoked by a marriage between opposite sex couples at least as regards ancillary relief to same sex couples who choose to register a civil partnership. Section 72 also incorporates any rule of law under which a married person would be entitled to relief under Part 2 of the Matrimonial Causes Act on the ground of presumed death and applies it to civil partners, as well as incorporating provision for financial relief in magistrates courts and provision for financial relief in England and Wales after a civil partnership has been terminated abroad.

5.9   Schedule 5 to the Act sets out the framework of financial relief in relation to the breakdown of civil partnerships. Orders available resemble the orders available under the Matrimonial Courses Act 1973 and come in the form of orders for:

—   the payment of periodical payments to a civil partner or to any person for the benefit of a child of the family or to a child of the family (any of these periodical payments may be secured);
—   the payment of a lump sum or sums to a civil partner or to any person for the benefit of a child of the family or to a child of the family (any lump sum or sums may be secured);
—   property adjustment;
—   variation of settlement;
—   sale of property; and
—   pension sharing.

Part 1 of Sch 5 deals with periodical payments and lump sums, Part 2 deals with property adjustment, Part 3 deals with the sale of property and Part 4 deals with pension sharing.

5.10   The court may make orders for periodical payments or lump sums on making a dissolution, nullity or separation order, or at any time afterwards.[1] Where an order is made for the benefit of a child of the family, it may be made before the making of a dissolution, nullity or separation order final, or if proceedings for any of those orders are dismissed.[2] Where a court makes an order under Sch 5 in favour of a child, it may from time to time make a further order for the payment of periodical payments or a lump sum in favour of that child.[3]

5.11   Lump sum orders may be made in respect of liabilities incurred before a civil partner made an application for financial relief, where those liabilities were incurred in the maintenance of the civil partner or a child of the family.[4] Any lump sum payment that is ordered may be paid in instalments, and such instalments may be secured. The court may also direct that interest be payable on any amount deferred.[5]

5.12   No order for the payment of lump sums or periodical payments for the benefit of a civil partner made on or after the making of a dissolution or nullity order can take effect until the order has been made final.[6]

5.13   A court may make a property adjustment order on the making of a dissolution nullity or separation order or at any time afterwards.[7] A property adjustment order is an order for the transfer or settlement of property by one of the civil partners to the other or to a child of the family, or to someone else for the benefit of a child of the family. 'Property adjustment' also encompasses the variation of a settlement for the benefit of either or any of the civil partners or the children of the family, or to extinguish or reduce the interest of either or the civil partners under a settlement.[8] As with variation of settlement orders in the context of divorce and nullity proceedings following the breakdown of a marriage, the Act requires any settlement to be varied to have a 'nuptial' element. Settlements that are capable of variation are settlements made during the subsistence of a civil partnership, in anticipation of its formation, on the civil partners, including one made by will or codicil, but not including one in the form of a pension arrangement. This definition unintentionally may be more restrictive than on divorce.[9]

5.14   As with orders for the payment of periodical payments and lump sums, an order for property adjustment for the benefit of a civil partner may only take effect on the making of a dissolution or nullity order final.[10]

5.15   On making an order for the payment of secured periodical payments or an order for the payment of a lump sum or a property adjustment order, the court may also order the sale of property and such consequential or supplementary provisions as are appropriate in the circumstances.[11] A sale of property order may be made in respect of

---

1   CPA 2004, Sch 5, para 1(1).
2   CPA 2004, Sch 5, para 1(2).
3   CPA 2004, Sch 5, para 1(4).
4   CPA 2004, Sch 5, para 3(1), (2).
5   CPA 2004, Sch 5, para 3(3) to (7).
6   CPA 2004, Sch 5, para 4(1).
7   CPA 2004, Sch 5, para 6.
8   CPA 2004, Sch 5, para 7.
9   CPA 2004, Sch 5, para 3.
10   CPA 2004, Sch 5, para 8(1).
11   CPA 2004, Sch 5, para 10.

such property in which either or both of the civil partners have a beneficial interest.[1] In particular, the court may make provisions requiring the payment out of the proceeds of the sale of the property a sum of money to a specified person or class of persons. Such an order may take effect only once the dissolution or nullity order has been made final and the court may, in addition, specify that it should take effect only after the occurrence of a specified event, or at the end of a specified period.[2] A sale of property order which secures periodical payments will cease on the death or remarriage of the civil partner to whom the payments are made.[3]

5.16 Where a third party has an interest in a property, that third party must be given an opportunity to make representations to the court before the court makes any order for the sale of the property. The court must take these representations into account when deciding whether or not to make such an order.[4]

5.17 Pension sharing orders may also be made by the court on the making or a dissolution or nullity order or at any time afterwards.[5] A pension sharing order is an order which provides that one civil partner's sharable rights under a specified pension arrangement or under sharable state scheme rights be shared for the benefit of the other civil partner. The percentage value of the amount to be shared should be specified in the order.[6] Sharable rights under a pension arrangement or state scheme rights are rights in relation to which pension sharing is available under Chapter 1 of Part 4 of the Welfare Reform and Pensions Act 1999. A pension arrangement is:

— an occupational pension scheme; or
— a personal pension scheme; or
— a retirement annuity contract; or
— an annuity or insurance policy bought or transferred for the purpose of giving effect to pension rights; or
— an annuity purchased for the purpose of discharging a liability in respect of a pension credit.

Charges in relation to the pension sharing order may be apportioned as appropriate.[7] Pension sharing orders will not be made in relation to a pension which is already subject to a pension sharing order between the civil partners or where the court has required a lump sum to be paid to one of the civil partners out of the pension scheme under Sch 5, para 26. A pension sharing order will not take effect unless the dissolution or nullity order in relation to which it is made has been made final.[8]

---

1   CPA 2004, Sch 5, para 11(1).
2   CPA 2004, Sch 5, para 12.
3   CPA 2004, Sch 5, para 13.
4   CPA 2004, Sch 5, para 14.
5   CPA 2004, Sch 5, para 15.
6   CPA 2004, Sch 5, para 16(1)(b).
7   CPA 2004, Sch 5, para 17.
8   CPA 2004, Sch 5, para 19.

MATTERS TO BE TAKEN INTO CONSIDERATION WHEN MAKING A FINANCIAL ORDER

5.18 As with the Matrimonial Causes Act 1973, there are a number of factors that must be considered by the court when it exercises its powers in relation to financial orders made on the termination of a civil partnership. When considering making an order for periodical payments, the payment of lump sums, property adjustment, the sale of property and pension sharing orders, the court must take into account all of the circumstances of the case, giving first consideration to the welfare of any child of the family who is under 18.[1] More specifically, the court must take into account the factors contained in Sch 5, para 21(2), which mirror the factors set out in s 25 of the Matrimonial Causes Act 1973 almost identically. In deciding whether or not to exercise any of its powers under Parts 1, 2, 3 or 4, the factors to which the court must have particular regard are:

— the income, earning capacity, property and other financial resources which each partner has or is likely to have in the foreseeable future (this includes any increase in earning capacity which it would be reasonable to expect a civil partner to take steps to acquire);[2]
— the financial needs, obligations, responsibilities which each civil partner has or is likely to have in the foreseeable future;[3]
— the standard of living enjoyed by the family before the breakdown of the civil partnership;[4]
— the age of each civil partnership and the duration of civil partnership;[5]
— any physical or mental disability of either of the civil partners;[6]
— the contributions which each of the civil partners has made or is likely to make in the foreseeable future to the welfare of the family;[7]
— the conduct of each civil partner (if that conduct is such that it would be inequitable to disregard it);[8] and
— the value to each civil partner of any benefit which, because of the dissolution or annulment of the civil partnership, that civil partner will lose the chance of acquiring[9] (including pension benefits).[10]

5.19 It is likely that the interpretation of these factors will be based on the current interpretation of the factors in the Matrimonial Causes Act and that the case law in respect of those factors (in particular *White*[11] and *Lambert*[12]) will be applicable equally to civil partners as to spouses. How that case law is interpreted will be interesting

---

1   CPA 2004, Sch 5, para 20.
2   CPA 2004, Sch 5, para 21(2)(a).
3   CPA 2004, Sch 5, para 21(2)(b).
4   CPA 2004, Sch 5, para 21(2)(c).
5   CPA 2004, Sch 5, para 21(2)(d).
6   CPA 2004, Sch 5, para 21(2)(e).
7   CPA 2004, Sch 5, para 21(2)(f).
8   CPA 2004, Sch 5, para 21(2)(g).
9   CPA 2004, Sch 5, para 21(2)(h).
10 CPA 2004, Sch 5, para 24(2).
11 *White v White* [2000] 2 FLR 981, HL.
12 *Lambert v Lambert* [2003] 1 FLR 139, CA.

to see. However, it is likely that, in the absence of any preconceptions regarding the 'traditional' roles of home making or child caring which have affected the way in which husbands' and wives' contributions have been dealt with on divorce, the 'yardstick of equality'[1] will be even easier to apply.

The duration of the civil partnership is likely to include a period of seamless cohabitation. It is likely that case law on ancillary relief will be followed on this point, such as *GW v RW*[2] and *CO v CO*.[3]

5.20 Where the court is asked to exercise its powers in relation to a child of the family, it must have particular regard to the following factors:

— the financial needs of the child;[4]
— the income, earning capacity (if any), property and other financial resources of the child;[5]
— any physical or mental disability of the child;[6] and
— the way in which the child was being and the civil partners expect the child to continue to be educated or trained;[7] and
— the financial circumstance of the civil partners and any mental or physical disability on their part.[8]

Unless an adoption order has been made in favour of the non-biological parent, it is likely that the child will not be the child of both civil partners and, therefore, the additional factors in Sch 5, para 22(3) will come into play where one of the civil partners is ordered to make payments in relation to a child of the family who is not that civil partner's child. These factors are as follows:

— whether the civil partner has assumed responsibility for the child's maintenance;
— the extent and the basis upon which that responsibility has been assumed and the length of time for which it has been assumed;
— whether, in assuming and discharging such responsibility, the civil partner did so knowing that the child was not his or her child; and
— the liability of any other persons to maintain the child.

5.21 When making an order for the payment of periodical payments or a lump sum (secured or otherwise) under Part 1 of Sch 5, the court must also have regard to any pension benefits or pension protection fund entitlement that a civil partner has or is likely to have and any consideration of these benefits should be made under Sch 5, para 21(2)(a) as if the paragraph did not require future financial benefits to be 'foreseeable'.[9] Where the court makes an order under Part 1 for the payment of periodical payments or lump sums, having had regard to the civil partners' pension benefits, it may require the payment out of the pension of payments to one of the civil partners in order to discharge the other civil

---

1 *White v White*, per Lord Nicholls.
2 [2003] 2 FLR 108.
3 [2004] 1 FLR 1095.
4 CPA 2004, Sch 5, para 22(2)(a).
5 CPA 2004, Sch 5, para 22(2)(b).
6 CPA 2004, Sch 5, para 22(2)(c).
7 CPA 2004, Sch 5, para 22(2)(d).
8 CPA 2004, Sch 5, para 22(2)(d).
9 CPA 2004, Sch 5, paras 23(1) and 30(1).

partner's liability under the Part 1 order.[1] The court may also order any lump sum payable to a civil partner from his or her pension on that civil partner's death to be paid to the other civil partner, or it may require the civil partner to nominate the other civil partner as the person to whom the sum should be paid (Sch 5, para 26). Where the order is made in relation to an occupational pension scheme, there are provisions made in Part 7 of Sch 5 that govern the situation where the Pension Protection Fund Board has assumed responsibility for the scheme. Paragraph 28 of Sch 5 gives the Lord Chancellor power to enact regulations governing the valuation of pensions, and the logistical arrangements for payment.

5.22 Paragraph 23 of Sch 5 relates to the termination of financial obligations. The overriding objective of the court is to ensure that the party's financial inter-dependence is terminated as soon as possible, without giving rise to any undue hardship to either party. This principle originates from that of the 'clean break' in marriage and has been transferred into the civil partnership sphere. To this end, the court must consider the most appropriate timescale for the termination of the financial obligations of the civil partners towards each other when making any order. The court may also bar any future applications for the making or variation of orders for periodical payments.[2] The variation of orders made on dissolution or annulment is dealt with at **5.29**.

MAINTENANCE PENDING THE OUTCOME OF PROCEEDINGS

5.23 This is dealt with in Sch 5, para 38 to the Act. It provides that on an application for a dissolution, nullity or separation order, the court may make an order requiring either civil partner to make periodical payments to the other for the other's maintenance for any term that the court thinks reasonable, provided that it is no earlier than the date of the application or later than the date of the determination of the proceedings. Therefore, the financially weaker civil partner who, before the breakdown of the relationship relied on the other for his or her maintenance, may make an application for interim maintenance pending the making of any final order.

APPLICATIONS FOR FAILURE TO MAINTAIN

5.24 Even outside the context of an application for dissolution, nullity or legal separation, either civil partner to a civil partnership may apply to court for an order for periodical payments, secured periodical payments, or lump sum for the benefit of the applicant or any child in respect of whom the application is made, on the ground that the other civil partner has failed to provide reasonable maintenance for the applicant or make a proper contribution towards the maintenance of any child of the family.[3] An interim order may also be made.[4] In making the order, the court must have regard to all of the circumstances of the case, including the para 21(2) factors. If an application is made in

---

1   CPA 2004, Sch 5, para 25.
2   CPA 2004, Sch 5, paras 23(4) and 47(5).
3   CPA 2004, Sch 5, para 39.
4   CPA 2004, Sch 5, para 40.

respect of a child, the court must give first consideration to the welfare of that child. Where application is made on behalf of the child, the court must also take into account the para 22(2) factors. In order to make an application for maintenance under this paragraph, both civil partners must be domiciled in England and Wales on the date of the application. The applicant must have been habitually resident in England and Wales for the period of one year before the making of the application or the respondent must be habitually resident on the date of the application.[1]

5.25 Orders that may be made on an application for failure to maintain are:

— an order for periodical payments;
— an order for the payment of a lump sum;
— an order for the payment of periodical payments or secured periodical payments for the benefit of a child; or
— an order for the payment of a lump sum or secured lump sum for the benefit of a child.[2]

COMMENCEMENT AND DURATION OF PROCEEDINGS AND ORDERS

5.26 Orders for the payment of periodical payments or lump sums or for a property adjustment order or for maintenance pending the outcome of proceedings may be begun anytime after the presentation of the application for a dissolution, nullity or separation order.[3] Rules of court may be made to provide that an application for any relief should be made in the application for the dissolution, nullity or separation order or the response to that application and, if it is not made then, time limits within which it should be made.[4]

5.27 An order for the payment of periodical payments or secured periodical payments in favour of a civil partner must not begin before the date of the application for the order or extend beyond the death of either civil partner (or, in the case of secured periodical payments, the death of the civil partner in whose favour the order was made) or the subsequent formation of a civil partnership or marriage by the partner in whose favour the order was made.[5] The subsequent marriage or formation of a civil partnership by one of the civil partners will bar that person from making an application for the payment of periodical payments or a lump sum against the other civil partner in respect of the civil partnership previously dissolved or annulled.[6]

5.28 There are specific time limits in relation to orders made in favour of children. Generally, no order is to be made in favour of a child who is over the age of 18[7] and no order made in favour of a child should extend beyond the date of the child's seventeenth birthday unless the welfare of the child requires it to be extended to the date of the child's

1   CPA 2004, Sch 5, para 39(2).
2   CPA 2004, Sch 5, para 41(1).
3   CPA 2004, Sch 5, para 46.
4   CPA 2004, Sch 5, para 46(3).
5   CPA 2004, Sch 5, para 47.
6   CPA 2004, Sch 5, para 48.
7   CPA 2004, Sch 5, para 49(1).

eighteenth birthday.[1] The exception to that rule is that where a child is, or would be if the order was made, in education or undergoing training or there are special circumstances which justify the making of an order, the time limit may be extended.[2] In any event, periodical payments in favour of a child will cease to have effect on the death of the person liable to make the payments.[3] If a child is the subject of a 'maintenance calculation' under the Child Support Act 1991 and an application is made under Sch 5 for periodical payments or secured periodical payments in respect of that child in accordance with s 8 of the Child Support Act 1991 and before the end of the 6-month period beginning with the date of the current calculation, the term to be specified on any order made on that application may begin on the later of 6 months before the date of the application or the date on which the current calculation took effect.[4] Where a maintenance calculation has ceased to have effect, the term may begin on the date that that maintenance calculation ceased to have effect, or any later date.[5]

APPLICATIONS TO VARY OR DISCHARGE ORDERS

5.29   Provisions relating to the variation or discharge of orders made under Sch 5 are contained in Part 11. Paragraph 50 states that this part applies to financial orders made in the context of proceedings for financial provision on dissolution, nullity or legal separation and also failure to maintain. In any case where a court has made such an order, it may vary or discharge it, suspend any of its provisions or revive the operation of any provision previously suspended.[6] The court may also remit the payment of any arrears due under the order.[7] Where the court varies or discharges an order for periodical payments or secured periodical payments, it may make supplemental provisions providing for a different financial order to take its place (a lump sum, property adjustment, pension sharing or periodical payments order).[8] When making any replacement order, the court may require a lump sum ordered to be secured, or to be paid in instalments. It may also provide for interest to be paid on any deferred instalments. If the court makes a property adjustment order, and there was already such an order in the original order in the proceedings, the further property adjustment order must fall within a different category to the first one.[9]

5.30   Where an application is made for the variation of an order made under Part 9 (failure to maintain), if the original order was made in favour of the child, the child may apply him or herself for variation of that order if he or she is over 16.[10] If the child in relation to whom the order was originally made has reached 16, then the court will have

---

1   CPA 2004, Sch 5, para 49(3), (5).
2   CPA 2004, Sch 5, para 49(5).
3   CPA 2004, Sch 5, para 49(6).
4   CPA 2004, Sch 5, para 49(7), (8).
5   CPA 2004, Sch 5, para 49(9).
6   CPA 2004, Sch 5, para 51.
7   CPA 2004, Sch 5, para 52.
8   CPA 2004, Sch 5, para 53.
9   CPA 2004, Sch 5, para 54.
10   CPA 2004, Sch 5, para 55(1).

to take into account the all of the circumstances of the case, including whether or not that child is till in full time education, before making a revised order.[1]

5.31 Property adjustment and pension sharing orders have special rules applicable to them. The court may not vary a property adjustment order or vary a settlement except on an application made in proceedings for the rescission of a separation order or for a dissolution order following a separation order in which a property adjustment or variation of settlement order was made.[2] The restriction is similar for pension sharing orders. The court may make an order varying a pension sharing order only if it has not yet taken effect. No variation may take effect before the order for dissolution or annulment is made final.[3]

5.32 No order for the payment of a lump sum or periodical payments may be made on an application for the variation of a property adjustment order or a pension sharing order. Orders for the payment of lump sums or periodical payments may be made only where an application has been made to vary an order that provided for their payment in the first place.[4]

5.33 In considering an application for the variation or discharge of any financial order, the court must take into account all of the circumstances of the case, and, in particular, must give first consideration to the welfare of any child of the family who has not reached 18.[5] The circumstance of the case include any matters to which the court was required to have regard when making the original order to which the application relates.[6] If the court decides to vary an order, it must consider what period would be sufficient to enable the civil partner in whose favour the order was made to adjust to the termination of the payments required to be made under the order, without undue hardship.[7]

5.34 Where the person liable to make secured periodical payments has died, an application may be made relating to the order by the person to whom the payments were made or the personal representatives of the deceased person.[8] The court may also direct when such variation or discharge is to take effect, if it is to take effect at some future date.[9] Any order that provides for the payment of periodical payments or secured periodical payments in favour of a child must take into account any maintenance calculation made under the Child Support Act 1991.

ARREARS AND REPAYMENTS

5.35 Where any arrears are due under a final or interim financial order made on dissolution or annulment or legal separation or under an order made pursuant to an application for failure to maintain and the arrears became due more than 12 months

---

1   CPA 2004, Sch 5, para 55(3).
2   CPA 2004, Sch 5, para 56.
3   CPA 2004, Sch 5, para 57.
4   CPA 2004, Sch 5, para 58.
5   CPA 2004, Sch 5, para 59(1).
6   CPA 2004, Sch 5, para 59(2).
7   CPA 2004, Sch 5, para 59(4).
8   CPA 2004, Sch 5, para 60.
9   CPA 2004, Sch 5, para 61.

before enforcement proceedings began, leave must be obtained before commencing proceedings for enforcement.[1]

5.36 Where an order has been made for the payment of periodical payments, secured periodical payments or interim maintenance, an application for the repayment of sums paid in accordance with such an order may be made where a change in circumstances means that the initial term of the order exceeds the term that is appropriate. If, as a result, the amount that the former civil partner or the former civil partner's representatives are paid an excess, the former civil partner, or his or her personal representatives, may be ordered to repay such an amount is just, such amount not exceeding the amount of the excess.[2]

5.37 Where, by reason of the formation of a subsequent civil partnership or marriage by a former civil partner in whose favour an order for periodical payments was made, the order ceases to subsist, any payments made by the other former civil partner in the belief that the order still subsisted may be ordered to be repaid.[3]

CONSENT ORDERS AND MAINTENANCE AGREEMENTS

5.38 The Civil Partnership Act 2004, s 43 provides that rules of court may be made so as to enable civil partners to refer an agreement relating to an order for dissolution or separation to the court for the court's opinion as to the reasonableness of the agreement and to give such directions as it thinks fit. This mirrors s 7 of the Matrimonial Causes Act 1973, although no such rules of court have ever been made.[4]

5.39 The court may make an order in terms agreed regarding financial relief, provided it does not think that there are circumstances which should be investigated, after provision of prescribed financial information.[5]

5.40 Schedule 5 to the Act also makes provisions in relation to the validity of maintenance agreements and financial arrangements. A 'maintenance agreement' is defined by para 67 of Sch 5 as any agreement in writing between the civil partners which is made during the civil partnership or after the dissolution or annulment of it and contains financial arrangements or is a separation agreement which contains no financial arrangements but is made in the case where no other agreement in writing between the civil partners contains financial arrangements. 'Financial arrangements' are subsequently defined as provisions governing the rights and liabilities of the civil partners towards one another when they are living separately in respect of the making or securing of payments or the disposition or use of any property. This includes the rights and liabilities in respect of the maintenance or education of a child, whether or not that child is a child of the family. These agreements are valid so long as they do not purport to include any provision restricting either party to apply to court for an order containing financial arrangements, in which case, that provision is struck out.[6] Either party to a maintenance agreement may

---

1 CPA 2004, Sch 5, para 63.
2 CPA 2004, Sch 5, para 64.
3 CPA 2004, Sch 5, para 65.
4 CPA 2004, s 43.
5 CPA 2004, Sch 5, para 66.
6 CPA 2004, Sch 5, para 68.

apply to court for its discharge and the court will take into account any change of circumstances in light of which any financial arrangements were made or not made and alter the agreement accordingly.[1] Where the court does alter the agreement, it has a wide scope of alterations that it may make, including the provision of periodical payments and secured periodical payments for such a term as it thinks fit. It may also alter the agreement so as to make provision for the maintenance of a child of the family.[2] Maintenance agreements may be altered by the court on the death of one party, and, if so altered, the maintenance agreement is treated as having been altered by agreement by both parties immediately prior to the death for valuable consideration.[3]

5.41 The court's power to vary a maintenance agreement does not preclude it from making any other order in the context of any proceedings brought for financial relief under any other part of the Act.[4]

TRANSACTIONS INTENDED TO FRUSTRATE A CLAIM FOR FINANCIAL RELIEF

5.42 Any transaction made by one civil partner which has the purpose of defeating any claim that the other may make for financial relief under the provisions of Sch 5 may be reviewed and set aside. If the court is satisfied that a civil partner, with the intention of defeating the other's claim for financial relief, is about to make any disposition or transfer any property out of the jurisdiction or otherwise deal with any property, it may make such an order as it thinks fit, restraining that civil partner from doing so, or any other order that may be necessary to protect the claim.[5] That intention of defeating claims is presumed if the application is made within 3 years of the transaction. If the disposition has been made and, if the disposition were set aside, different financial relief would be granted to the civil partner whose claim the disposition was intended to frustrate, the disposition may be set aside by the court.[6] If the disposition has been made after the granting of an order for financial relief, it may also be set aside.[7]

5.43 'Disposition' does not include any provision contained in a will or codicil.[8] Any disposition made is a reviewable disposition unless it was made for valuable consideration to a person who acted in good faith.[9]

OTHER PROVISIONS

5.44 Where the court has made an order for financial relief, it may direct that the matter be referred to one of the conveyancing counsel of the court for him or her to draw

---

1   CPA 2004, Sch 5, para 69.
2   CPA 2004, Sch 5, para 71.
3   CPA 2004, Sch 5, para 73.
4   CPA 2004, Sch 5, para 72.
5   CPA 2004, Sch 5, para 74(2).
6   CPA 2004, Sch 5, para 74(3).
7   CPA 2004, Sch 5, para 74(4).
8   CPA 2004, Sch 5, para 74(2).
9   CPA 2004, Sch 5, para 75(3).

up the instrument to be executed by all necessary parties. The making of any dissolution, nullity or separation order may be deferred until the instrument has been duly executed.[1]

5.45 Any settlement made in compliance with a property adjustment order may be avoided on the bankruptcy of the settlor.[2]

FINANCIAL RELIEF IN MAGISTRATES' COURTS

5.46 Whilst a civil partnership is still subsisting, civil partners may make an application to a magistrates' court for maintenance where the court is satisfied that the other partner has failed to provide reasonable maintenance for the applicant or any child of the family or the other civil partner has behaved in such a way that the applicant cannot reasonably be expected to live with the respondent, or that the respondent has deserted the applicant.[3]

5.47 The financial orders that can be made include orders for periodical payments for the applicant or child of the family, or a lump sum to the applicant or for the benefit of a child of the family.[4] The amount of lump sum must not exceed £1,000 (or such larger amount as the Lord Chancellor may from time to time fix).[5] The factors to be taken into account are the same as the factors to be taken into account in making orders under Sch 5, save that the relevant point in time before which the standard of living of the parties is to be considered is the date of the occurrence of the conduct which is alleged which leads to the application.[6] When exercising powers in relation to children, the court must take into account the same factors as in Sch 5.[7] As under Sch 5, proceedings may be held up if there is any prospect of reconciliation between the partners.[8]

5.48 Such orders may also be made by consent where both parties agree the financial provision either for the applicant or for a child of the family. However, in considering whether or not to make the order, the court may also consider whether or not an alternative order is appropriate.[9]

5.49 Orders under Sch 6 may be made where the civil partners are living apart by agreement if they have been living apart for a continuous period of more than 3 months and one of the civil partners has been making periodical payments for the benefit of the other civil partner or a child of the family. If these circumstances exist, then the court may order those periodical payments to be made. However, the payments ordered cannot exceed the amount of the payments made by the respondent to the applicant during the 3 months preceding the date of the application. The matters to be taken into consideration are those that should be taken into consideration for applications to a court in respect of

---

1 CPA 2004, Sch 5, para 76.
2 CPA 2004, Sch 5, para 77.
3 CPA 2004, Sch 6, para 1(1).
4 CPA 2004, Sch 6, para 2(1).
5 CPA 2004, Sch 6, para 2(2).
6 CPA 2004, Sch 6, paras 4, 5.
7 CPA 2004, Sch 6, para 6.
8 CPA 2004, Sch 6, para 7.
9 CPA 2004, Sch 6, paras 9, 13.

failure to maintain where the parties are living together.[1] The court may refuse to make an order where the parties are living apart if it feels that it would be more appropriate to make an order under the provisions of Part 1 of Sch 6 in respect of a failure to maintain.[2]

5.50 Part 4 of Sch 6 provides that interim orders may be made at any time before the making of a final order, or a dismissal or refusal of the application. Such interim order may provide for payments to be made from such date as the court may specify, providing that it is not before the date of the application. An interim order will cease to have effect on the date specified in the order or 3 months after the making of the order or such a date that the order is made final or the application is dismissed.

5.51 The court may specify the term for which periodical payments should be made in its order, except that such a term does not begin on any date before the making of the application, and must not extend beyond the death of either one of the civil partners. If an order continues beyond the dissolution or annulment of a civil partnership, it will continue until such time as the civil partner in whose favour the order was made marries or enters into a subsequent civil partnership.[3]

5.52 Unless a child is in education or is undergoing training, any order made in favour of a child may not extend beyond his or her eighteenth birthday.[4]

5.53 Orders made pursuant to Sch 6 will be enforceable even where the civil partners are living together at the date of the making of the order or where, if they were not living together at the date of the making of the order, they resume living together. However, the order will cease to have effect if the parties continue to live together for a period exceeding 6 months. This will not be the case if the order is made in favour of a child of the family. In this situation the order will continue to have effect and be enforceable even if the civil partners are living together at the date of the making of the order or they subsequently resume living together.[5]

5.54 The court will have power to vary, revoke, suspend or revive any order on the application of one of the partners. Any variation of an order for periodical payments may include the order for the payment of a lump sum instead. On variation, the court is to have regard to all of the circumstances of the case, including any change in circumstances which includes any change in any of the matters to which the court was required to have regard on making the order originally or, in the case of an application for the variation or revocation of an order, to which the court would have been required to have regard if that order had been made under the provisions of Part 1 of Sch 6 (failure to maintain).[6]

5.55 The magistrates' court may order the enforcement of the order under its powers under s 59(3)(a)–(d) of the Magistrates' Courts Act 1980.[7]

---

1   CPA 2004, Sch 6, paras 15 to 17.
2   CPA 2004, Sch 6, para 18.
3   CPA 2004, Sch 6, para 26.
4   CPA 2004, Sch 6, para 27.
5   CPA 2004, Sch 6, para 29.
6   CPA 2004, Sch 6, paras 30 to 42.
7   CPA 2004, Sch 6, para 43.

5.56 As with orders made under Sch 5, the magistrates' court may order the repayment of sums paid in accordance with orders if it considers that there has been an excess payment in the circumstances.[1]

FINANCIAL RELIEF IN ENGLAND AND WALES AFTER THE TERMINATION OF A CIVIL PARTNERSHIP OVERSEAS

5.57 This is dealt with in Sch 7 to the Civil Partnerships Act 2004. Where a civil partnership has been dissolved or annulled or there has been a legal separation by means of judicial proceedings or other proceedings in a country or territory outside the British Isles, the dissolution, annulment or legal separation is entitled to be recognised as valid in England and Wales.[2] Flowing from this recognition is the right of either of the civil partners to make an application to the courts of England and Wales for an order for financial provision, property adjustment and pension sharing orders, just as if the partnership had been dissolved in England and Wales.[3] However, any such application will be barred if either of the civil partners has formed a subsequent civil partnership or marriage.[4] One prerequisite is that the court must have granted leave and the court will not grant leave unless it considers that there is substantial ground for the making of an application for such an order. Leave may be granted notwithstanding that there is a financial order outside of England and Wales and may be granted subject to such conditions as the court thinks fit.[5]

5.58 Where leave has been granted, the court may also make an interim order for maintenance requiring one civil partner to pay the other such periodical payments as the court thinks fit to the applicant or for the benefit of a child.[6]

5.59 At least one of the following jurisdictional requirements must be satisfied:[7]

— either of the civil partners must have been domiciled in England and Wales on the date when leave was applied for or must have been domiciled in England and Wales on the date when the dissolution, annulment or legal separation took effect in the overseas country in which it was obtained;[8] or

— either of the civil partners was habitually resident in England and Wales throughout the period of one year ending with the date when leave was applied for or was habitually resident in England and Wales throughout the period of one year ending with the date on which the dissolution, annulment or legal separation took effect in the overseas country in which it was obtained;[9] or

---

1   CPA 2004, Sch 6, para 44.
2   CPA 2004, Sch 7, para 1(1).
3   CPA 2004, Sch 7, para 2.
4   CPA 2004, Sch 7, para 3.
5   CPA 2004, Sch 7, para 4.
6   CPA 2004, Sch 7, para 5.
7   CPA 2004, Sch 7, para 7(1).
8   CPA 2004, Sch 7, para 7(2).
9   CPA 2004, Sch 7, para 7(3).

— either or both of the civil partners had, at the date when the leave was applied for, the beneficial interest in possession of a house situated in England and Wales which was at some point the home of the civil partners during the civil partnership.[1]

5.60 The court has a duty, before deciding the application, to consider whether in all the circumstances of the case it is appropriate for an order of the kind applied for to be made by a court in England and Wales.[2] If the court is not satisfied that it would be appropriate for it to hear the application, it must dismiss the application.[3] When considering the appropriateness or otherwise of the court to hear the application, it must consider the following matters:[4]

— the connection that the civil partners have with England and Wales;
— the connection which the civil partners have with the country in which the civil partnership was dissolved or annulled or in which they were legally separated;
— the connection which the civil partners have with any other country outside England and Wales;
— any financial benefit which, as a consequence of the dissolution, the applicant or a child of the family has received or is likely to receive by virtue of any agreement or the operation of the law of any country outside England and Wales;
— the extent to which any financial order in another country has been complied with or is likely to be complied with;
— any right which the applicant has or has had to apply for financial relief under the law of any other country apart from England and Wales;
— the availability of property in England and Wales in respect of which an order could be made;
— the enforceability of such an order; and
— the length of time which has elapsed since the date of the dissolution.

5.61 Where the court decides that it is appropriate for it to hear the application, it may make any of the orders under Parts 1, 2 or 4 of Sch 5 (financial provision, property adjustment and pension sharing) as if a dissolution order or a nullity order had been made in England and Wales.[5]

5.62 In making such an order the court must have regard to all the circumstances of the case, including the welfare of any child of the family under 18, and should consider the factors listed in para 21(2) of Sch 5 for orders in favour of a civil partner, and the factors listed in para 22(2) and (3) of Sch 5 for orders made in favour of a child of the family. The court is under a duty to consider the termination of financial obligations as under para 23(2) and (3) of Sch 5.[6]

5.63 Where the court has jurisdiction to make an order only because a dwelling house which was a former home of the civil partner is situated in England and Wales, but there is no other ground for jurisdiction, the court may not make any order for periodical

---

1   CPA 2004, Sch 7, para 7(4).
2   CPA 2004, Sch 7, para 8(1).
3   CPA 2004, Sch 7, para 8(2).
4   CPA 2004, Sch 7, para 8(3).
5   CPA 2004, Sch 7, para 9.
6   CPA 2004, Sch 7, para 10.

payments or pension sharing, but may only make orders in relation to that property or order the payment of a lump sum.[1]

5.64   The court may also make consent orders pursuant to para 12 of Sch 7. The provisions of that paragraph mirror the provisions set out in Sch 5 and the procedure for the making of consent orders is dealt with above at **5.39**. All of the other relevant provisions of Sch 5 apply in relation to an order made under Sch 7, including where transactions are designed to defeat claims.[2]

FINANCIAL PROVISION FOR CHILDREN

5.65   Section 78 of the Civil Partnership Act 2004 amends the Children Act 1989 ('the Children Act') to expand it to include references to civil partners where there are currently references to 'husband or wife' and to include periodical payments made in accordance with Sch 5 to the Act.[3] Paragraph 16(2) of Sch 1 to the Children Act 1989 is also revised to extend the definition of 'parent' for the purposes of all parts of the schedule, save for paras 2(4) (provision that no order shall be made for periodical payments in respect of a person over 18 where his or her parents still live with each other) and 15 (local authority not obliged to make contributions toward the maintenance of a child where that child lives with a parent or husband or wife of a parent). The extended definition of 'parent' includes any civil partner in a civil partnership (whether or not subsisting) in relation to whom the child concerned is a child of the family.

5.66   Although an application under Sch 1 to the Children Act will be rare where there has been a financial order following the dissolution or annulment of a civil partnership, the equalisation of provision under the Children Act means that a civil partner or a former civil partner may make an application under Sch 1 for child maintenance in the same way that a spouse of former spouse may.

---

1   CPA 2004, Sch 7, para 11.
2   CPA 2004, Sch 7, paras 15, 17.
3   See **5.20**.

Chapter 6

CHILDREN

INTRODUCTION

6.1   Since the implementation of the Family Law Reform Act 1987 and the Children Act 1989 the relevance of the marital status of parents has been greatly diminished, but same sex relationships still throw up complex problems in this regard and parties have been dependent on discretionary remedies from courts. The attitudes of the judiciary and the parties have historically reflected the moral and social attitudes of their day. In principle, at least, the appellate courts in England and Wales from the early 1980s were prepared to declare that problems that arise in the courts which concern lesbian or gay parents should be treated on their own merits in a non-discriminatory way. As early as 1980 in *E v E*[1] Ormrod LJ said:

> 'The mere fact of this homosexual way of life on the part of the mother is not, in itself, a reason for refusing to give her control of the children. There is no rule or principle that a lesbian mother or homosexual father cannot be granted custody of a child.'

6.2   It was, though, considered to be a relevant consideration.[2] This was generally the attitude of the Court of Appeal in the later case of *C v C*[3] but tempered by a concern that it was a factor that had to be brought into the equation and did represent a departure from the ideal. Cases around this time were very concerned with whether or not the lesbian or gay parent 'flaunted' their sexuality or could be considered to be 'militant'.[4]

6.3   At the conclusion of the consultation process, in advance of the publication of the Bill, the government announced in November 2003 that they proposed that civil partners would acquire parental responsibility in respect of their partners' children.[5] By the conclusion of the passage of the Civil Partnership Act 2004 through both Houses of Parliament, the law in England and Wales now provides all the rights and responsibilities concerning children of a civil partnership as are provided by marriage. This was relatively uncontroversial as adoption had already been dealt with in the Adoption and Children Act 2002. Complications are still likely to arise in international law – especially in

---

1   (Unreported CA) 27 November 1980 cited in Barlow et al *Advising Lesbian and Gay Clients* (Butterworths, 1999) p 42.

2   'The possible effect on a young child living in proximity to that practice is of crucial importance to that child and to the public interest': *Re P (A Minor) (Custody)* [1983] 4 FLR 401 per Watkins LJ at 405 G. See also *Re P (A Minor) (Custody)* [1993] 4 FLR 401 CA.

3   [1991] FCR 254, CA. The case was remitted for a further rehearing and the mother was granted custody – partly because of the level of hostility the father demonstrated towards the mother's lesbianism.

4   See *B v B* [1991] 1 FLR 402.

5   *Responses to Civil Partnership* (WEU, November 2003 DT) p 29.

jurisdictions which do not recognise civil partnerships between same sex couples and where same sex couples cohabit but do not enter into a civil partnership.

PARENTAL RESPONSIBILITY

6.4 'Parental responsibility' is the phrase used in the Children Act 1989 to refer to all the legal rights, duties, powers, responsibilities and authority which a parent has over a child and his property.[1] The Act[2] makes provision for the acquisition of parental responsibility for the children of civil partners akin to the mechanism used for the acquisition of parental responsibility by step-parents after marriage.[3] In a situation in which a civil partner (A) has parental responsibility for a child and is in a civil partnership with somebody (B) who does not have parental responsibility for that child, that other person is a step-parent. Civil partner (B) may acquire parental responsibility in one of two ways: either by agreement with (A), if he or she is the sole person having parental responsibility for the child, or with the agreement of both parents. In the alternative, the step-parent could acquire parental responsibility by order of the court on the application of the step-parent.

6.5   A parental responsibility agreement is made on a prescribed form which must be taken to a local Family Proceedings Court or county court or to the Principal Registry where the parties' agreement should be witnessed by a justice of the peace, a justice's clerk or an authorised court officer. The completed form with two copies should then be sent to the Principal Registry. Sealed copies will then be sent to the parties.

6.6   A parental responsibility agreement, once made, can be brought to an end only by court order. This would require the application of a person with parental responsibility or the child himself with the leave of the court (if it is satisfied that the child has sufficient understanding to make such an application).[4]

SHARED RESIDENCE ORDERS

6.7   In the absence of a civil partnership more creative methods are required to protect the interests of children and same sex couples concerned with their care. One of the principal difficulties that arose, assuming that one member of a same sex couple was the parent of a child or children, or had assumed the care of a child, was how to obtain parental responsibility for a same sex partner. It was obviously desirable that, as far as possible, the adults who were actually caring for a child should actually be in possession of parental responsibility. With the introduction of the Children Act 1989 the solution

---

1   Children Act 1989, s 3(1).
2   Civil Partnership Act 2004 (CPA 2004), s 75(2).
3   This was a mechanism that was inserted into the Children Act 1989 by s 112 of the Adoption and Children Act 1989 but has yet to come into force.
4   Children Act 1989, s 4A(3) and (4).

appeared to be to make a joint or shared residence order.[1] On 24 June 1994 Douglas Brown J made such an order in favour of two women in circumstances in which they were in a relationship and reached an agreement with a man who wanted no involvement in the child's life. The partner of the birth mother applied for a residence order after the child's birth so that she could acquire parental responsibility giving her equal legal status to the child's mother. The Official Solicitor was appointed to act for the child, who was by then 22 months old, and supported the application.[2] This is a solution that has now been used many times and is relatively common in the areas of main lesbian and gay population density such as Brighton.

6.8 Absent a civil partnership, a non-biological parent would not need to seek permission to make an application or any Children Act 1989, s 8 order, provided that the applicant has:

— lived with the child for a period of at least 3 years;
— if there is a residence order in force, the consent of each person in whose favour such an order has been made;
— in the case of a child who is in local authority care, the consent of the local authority;
— the consent of those with parental responsibility.[3]

Other persons, not so covered by the criteria above, would need to seek the permission of the court to make such an application.[4] The Civil Partnership Act 2004 provides that any civil partner is entitled to apply for a residence or contact order in relation to a civil partnership to whom the child is a child of the family, without having to seek leave.[5]

6.9 Over time, obtaining such permission, even when not consensual, has proved easier. It has been greatly assisted by the judgment of Bracewell J in *G v F (Shared Residence: Parental Responsibility)*[6] where she said:

'the fact that the relationship between the applicant and the respondent was a lesbian relationship, in my judgment, is to be seen as background circumstances of the case and there is no need for discriminating against the applicant in her wish to pursue these proceedings on the basis that she and the respondent lived together in a lesbian relationship. It would be entirely wrong ... and unsustainable to seek, in any way, to reflect against the applicant by reason of the nature of her relationship with the respondent.'

EXPERT EVIDENCE

6.10 Shared residence orders were a mechanism which got round the inadequacies of the then law, but they had disadvantages. The process was cumbersome and stressful (the fear being that an unsympathetic judge might put obstacles in the way of the

---

1   This had its limitations as, unlike a parental responsibility agreement or order, it did not allow the party with such an order to consent to adoption or appoint a guardian, as the Lesbian and Gay Lawyers Association pointed out in their submissions to the WEU during the consultation exercise leading to the publication of the Civil Partnership Bill.

2   [1994] Fam Law 468.

3   Children Act 1989, s 10(5).

4   The criteria that will apply is to be found in the Children Act 1989, s 10(9).

5   CPA 2004, s 77.

6   [1998] 2 FLR 799.

arrangement). Up until very recently, the obtaining of the right sort of expert evidence and filing of research papers was a considerable concern.[1] In *C v C*[2] the Court of Appeal noted the particular difficulty it had in deciding the case in the absence of expert evidence in assessing the consequence for the child's sexual development. This is also a problem that can arise in cases where co-parents without parental responsibility seek contact after relationship breakdown and in adoption cases where parents have withheld their consent on the ground of the sexual orientation of the applicant. It is quite possible that the existence of rights under the Civil Partnership Act 2004 and the recent case law of the European Court of Human Rights, including *Salgueiro da Silva Mouta v Portugal*,[3] might make this less likely.

6.11   The body of research in this area is now growing and was recently summarised by Dr Clare Murray.[4] Much of it has been conducted by Susan Golombok and Fiona Tasker. Dr Murray makes two principal conclusions:

— children growing up in lesbian families show no evidence of problems in either overall psychological adjustment or gender development;
— a positive family environment matters more for healthy psychological development than a particular family structure.[5]

It is to be hoped that continuing social change will mean it is less likely in future that any stigma will attach at school for the children of same sex couples. It is possible that the passing of the Civil Partnership Act 2004 might help bring about further social change.

ADOPTION

6.12   The attitudes of the courts in cases of adoption and in cases of residence and contact have been chequerered. The judgment of Stephenson LJ,[6] in an appeal concerning a father who was in a homosexual relationship, on the question of whether he was unreasonably withholding his consent to the adoption of his son by his wife and her then husband, is frequently cited, when he said:

'I cannot avoid using the terms "normal" and "abnormal" in relation to the fact of this case, because men's homosexual practices, though no longer illegal are still commonly regarded as abnormal, if not unnatural or immoral.'

Liberal criticism of the decision needs to be tempered by an appreciation of the fact that Stephenson LJ, with Orr LJ and Sir Gordon Willmer, upheld the appeal. It was only when the case went to the House of Lords that the original judgment was upheld, with

---

1   Lesbian and Gay Lawyers Association Conference 1998. Seminar given by Gill Butler and Elizabeth Woodcraft.
2   [1991] FCR 254, CA.
3   [2001] 1 FCR 653, ECHR.
4   'Same-Sex Families: Outcomes For Children and Parents' [2004] Fam Law 136.
5   Above 139.
6   In *Re D (An Infant) (Parent's Consent)* [1977] AC 602 at 614, HL.

the consequence that the adoption was approved. In the House of Lords Lord Wilberforce said:[1]

'Whatever new attitudes Parliament, or public tolerance, may have chosen to take as regards the behaviour of consenting adults over 21 inter se, these should not entitle the courts to relax, in any degree, the vigilance and severity with which they should regard the risk of children, at critical ages, being exposed or introduced to ways of life which, as this case illustrates, may lead to severance from normal society, to psychological stresses and unhappiness and possibly even to physical experiences which may scar them for life.'

Nevertheless, the Lords were anxious to stress that the homosexuality of a parent is not in itself a reason for depriving a parent access to his or her child.[2]

6.13 The mid-1990s saw a shift in the attitudes of the Court of Appeal on questions of same sex adoption. In *Re E (Adoption: Freeing Order)*[3] the Court of Appeal declined to interfere with a freeing order made by a county court judge who had dispensed with the mother's agreement The freeing order was made with a view to adoption by the child's existing foster carer, a lesbian who proposed to care for the child as a single parent.

6.14 By 1997 in *Re W (Adoption: Homosexual Adopter)*,[4] Singer J, relying on the Scottish authority of *T Petitioner*,[5] was prepared to take a significantly more liberal position in a case concerning a application for a freeing order where the mother objected to the child being adopted by the prospective single adopter who was a lesbian and in a same sex relationship. Singer J concluded that:

'The Adoption Act 1976 permits an adoption application to be made by a single applicant, whether her or she at that time lives alone, or cohabits in a heterosexual, homosexual or even an asexual relationship with another person who it is proposed should fulfil a quasi-parental role towards the child. Any other conclusion would be both illogical, arbitrary and inappropriately discriminatory in a context where the court's duty is to give first consideration to the need to safeguard and promote the welfare of the child throughout his childhood.'

The Adoption and Children Act 2002

6.15 Formerly a joint application for an adoption order could be made only by a married couple. This restriction had been put in place by the Adoption of Children Act 1926. The 1992 Review of Adoption Law had recommended that this prohibition should be maintained. However, the Adoption and Children Act 2002,[6] s 49(1)(a) allowed an adoption application to be made by 'a couple'. This is defined by s 144(4) as 'two people

---

1 In *Re D (An Infant) (Parent's Consent)* [1977] AC 602 at 629, HL. In fact the father was having a relationship with an 18-year-old man at the relevant time which was likely to have included unlawful acts under the law as it stood at the time.

2 See, for example, Lord Simon of Glaisdale in *In Re D (An Infant) (Parent's Consent)* [1977] AC 602 at 640, HL.

3 [1995] 1 FLR 382, CA.

4 [1997] 2 FLR 406.

5 1997 SLT 724, involving a single male adopter.

6 Large portions of the Act were still to come into force at the time this book was published. On 23 February 2004, in an answer to a written question, provided in *Hansard*, from Dr Jenny Tonge MP, Margaret Hodge, Children's Minister, expected the preponderance of the legislation to come into force in September 2005.

(whether of different sexes or the same sex) living together as partners in an enduring family relationship'. The stability and permanence of the relationship are still the subject of assessment, as they are for any applicant.[1] The Civil Partnership Act 2004 amends s 144(4) of the Adoption and Children Act 2002 so that it is made quite explicit that this includes two people who are civil partners of one another.[2]

6.16   The Civil Partnership Act 2004 makes a number of amendments to the Adoption and Children Act 2002. Given the major reforms in the 2002 Act which permitted same sex couples to adopt, such amendments that are made are confined to putting civil partnerships on an equal footing with marriage as concerns status in the adoption process. This includes sections which carefully re-define the term 'relative' to include, in each instance, relationships created by way of civil partnerships.

6.17   The Adoption and Children Act 2002 is amended so that it is not possible for a person in a civil partnership to adopt as a single person,[3] save if that person has attained the age of 21 and one of the following applies:

— that person is the partner of a parent of the person to be adopted;[4]
— the civil partners have separated and are living apart and this separation is likely to be permanent;

— the person's civil partner is incapable of making an application for an adoption order for reasons of physical or mental ill-health.[5]

6.18   In addition, the Adoption and Children Act 2002, s 21 is amended so that a placement order will also be terminated by a child entering into a civil partnership.[6] The Act as amended also makes clear that it is not permissible to adopt a person who is or has been in a civil partnership (this prevents anybody from trying to adopt their civil partners).[7]

6.19   The status conferred by adoption on a person and its consequences are not altered by the Civil Partnership Act 2004, save that, like marriage, it has consequences as concern kindred or affinity.[8] The definition of 'relative' is amended in the 2004 Act so that it explicitly includes relationships created by means of civil partnership as well as marriage.[9] Information for these purposes must be made available to an adopted person by the Registrar General for the purposes of those under 18 who wish to marry.[10] In addition, the definition of 'relative' is expanded for the purposes of the Adoption Contact Register which is maintained by the Registrar General in accordance with s 80 of the Adoption and Children Act 2002, so that includes those related by means of civil partnership.[11] Regulations   are   still   awaited   on   the   provision   of   information   to   adopted

---

1   *Civil Partnership: A Framework for the Legal Recognition of Same-sex Couples* (Women and Equality Unit, June 2003) p 37.
2   CPA 2004, s 79(12).
3   CPA 2004, s 79(4); Adoption and Children Act 2002, s 51.
4   Adoption and Children Act 2002, s 51(2).
5   CPA 2004, s 79(5).
6   CPA 2004, s 79(2).
7   CPA 2004, s 79(4).
8   CPA 2004, s 79(7).
9   CPA 2004, s 79(11).
10   CPA 2004, s 79(8).
11   CPA 2004, s 79(9).

persons who have attained the age of 18, to facilitate contact with their relatives. This latter category is expanded by the Civil Partnership Act 2004 to include relatives by way of civil partnerships.[1]

RELATIVES AND FAMILY

6.20   The Adoption and Children Act 2002 gives relatives more significance than they have had hitherto in modern children's law. The most obvious way in which this is signalled is the inclusion in the checklist of matters to which the court or adoption agencies should have regard under s 1(4) 'the relationship which the child has with relatives'. In addition, an application for contact under the Act can be made by relatives.[2] The Civil Partnership Act 2004 also makes similar amendments to the Children Act 1989.[3]

6.21   The Act expands the concept of 'child of the family' under the Children Act 1989[4] so that it also encompasses a child or children who is treated by the civil partners as a child of their family with the exception of children being placed with them as foster parents by either a local authority or a voluntary organisation.[5]

6.22   The definition of 'relative' in relation to a child in the Children Act 1989[6] is also amended by the Act[7] so that it means a grandparent, brother, sister, uncle or aunt (whether of the full blood or half blood or by marriage or civil partnership). The practical effect of this is that the brother or sister of a civil partner will become the uncle or aunt of a child irrespective of whether there is any blood relationship between them. This could have some significance if a local authority were to become involved with a child and were looking for family members with whom to place the child either permanently, temporarily or on a respite basis.

6.23   The Civil Partnership Act 2004 also amends 53 Acts of Parliament and makes provision for further amendments by way of an Order[8] so that civil partnerships will create step relationships[9] and in-laws.[10] By way of example, A's stepchild includes a person who is the child of A's civil partner (but is not A's child).

---

1   CPA 2004, s 79(19).
2   Adoption and Children Act 2002, s 26(3)(b).
3   CPA 2004, s 75(3)–(4).
4   Children Act 1989, s 105(1).
5   CPA 2004, s 75(3).
6   The definition of 'relative' in the Children Act 1989, s 105(1) means, for a child, a grandmother, brother, sister, uncle or aunt (whether of the full blood or half blood or by marriage or civil partnership) or step-parent.
7   CPA 2004, s 75(4).
8   CPA 2004, s 247(2).
9   CPA 2004, ss 246(1), 247 and Sch 21.
10   CPA 2004, ss 246(2), 247 and Sch 21.

THE CHILDREN ACT 1989

6.24 In addition to the matters specified above, the Civil Partnership Act 2004[1] provides that any civil partner in a civil partnership is entitled to apply for a residence or contact order[2] (ie they do not need to seek the leave of the court to make such an application). This will be of significance if a civil partnership were to founder and it was not possible to reach agreement as to arrangements for any children of the family. The present situation is that a non-birth parent has to apply for leave. That can sometimes involve a substantial hearing with the hearing of evidence if there is no consensus.

6.25 As with civil marriage, when the court is dealing with dissolution, nullity or separation proceedings the court must consider, where there are children of the family,[3] whether, in the light of the proposed arrangements, it should exercise any of its powers under the Children Act 1989.[4] It may conclude that it is not in a position to make a final order.[5]

6.26 The Civil Partnership Act 2004 reforms the law concerning the revoking of guardianships under the Children Act 1989. In this context it is referring to the arrangement by which somebody is formally appointed to take the place of a deceased parent. Under s 5(3) of the Children Act 1989 a parent who has parental responsibility for a child may appoint another individual to be the child's guardian in the event of their parent's death and under s 5(4) a duly appointed guardian may appoint another individual to take his or her place in the event of the guardian's death. Under the Civil Partnership Act 2004 such an appointment is revoked if the person appointed is a civil partner and the civil partnership is dissolved or revoked. It does not matter for these purposes whether the dissolution or revocation comes about by way of an order of a court in England and Wales or the legitimate recognition of a foreign dissolution or revocation.[6]

CHILD ABDUCTION

6.27 The power[7] possessed by the courts to order persons to disclose information about the whereabouts of children is specifically amended by the Civil Partnership Act 2004[8] so as to specify that a civil partner shall not be excused from complying with an order to disclose any information notwithstanding that it might tend to incriminate their civil partner. The Family Law Act 1986, s 33(2) specifies that any such statement shall not be admissible in evidence against either of them as to proceedings concerning any offence save for perjury.

---

1   CPA 2004, s 77.
2   Children Act 1989, ss 8–10.
3   As defined in CPA 2004, s 63(3).
4   CPA 2004, s 63(1)(b).
5   CPA 2004, s 63(2).
6   CPA 2004, s 76.
7   Family Law Act 1986, s 33(1).
8   CPA 2004, Sch 27.

6.28 The Civil Partnership Act 2004[1] makes a similar amendment to the Child Abduction and Custody Act 1985[2] which applies where there is an application concerning recognition, registration or enforcement of a Part I order which concerns international abduction. Private international law operates so that parental responsibility is a key concept. It is to be hoped that this proves to be more significant than the fact that it is granted by civil partnership or arises in a same sex relationship. Many of the Hague Convention countries have civil partnership schemes in any event.

HUMAN FERTILISATION AND EMBRYOLOGY

6.29 It is believed that increasing numbers of lesbians are having recourse to donor insemination, whether informally or through a clinic. Licensed clinics are subject to regulations and, in particular, s 13(5) of the Human Fertilisation and Embryology Act 1990 which provides that:

> 'a woman shall not be provided with treatment services unless account has been taken of the welfare of any child who may be born as a result of treatment (including the need of that child for a father) and of any other child who may be affected by the birth.'

6.30 Where a child is conceived by donor insemination at a licensed clinic the unmarried mother of such a child becomes the child's only legal parent by virtue of s 28 of the Act. The consequence of this is that no claims can be made against the donor or his estate and the donor is not under any legal obligations or responsibilities. Where the insemination is unlicensed and done outside marriage then the legal consequences are the same as if it involved any other heterosexual father.[3] Parties might be wise to consider entering into a written agreement. Although this would not oust the jurisdiction of the court it might prove influential in any dispute and would certainly assist the court in establishing what the relevant expectations were at the time any agreement was reached.

6.31 The Chair of the Human Fertilisation and Embryology Authority told the Annual Meeting of the Authority in January 2004 that she felt this should be reviewed. This was mainly because of her concern about the possibility of people increasingly circumventing the whole formal legal process. It is not clear whether, in the current climate of concern that fathers are being excluded, any review by the Authority of this aspect of the law would be acted upon. It is not clear whether the Civil Partnership Act 2004 might influence any review. It is likely that the research at **6.11** would be highly persuasive.

---

1 CPA 2004, Sch 27.
2 Child Abduction and Custody Act 1985, s 24A.
3 *Re M (Sperm Donor Father)* [2003] Fam Law 94.

Chapter 7

INCAPACITY AND DEATH

7.1 The lack of legal recognition of same sex partnerships had its most profound effect when one partner became incapable or died. At the very time that the survivor was suffering the loss of a partner and the emotional and financial support of the relationship, he could, and often did, find himself treated as a stranger by the family, the hospital, the authorities, the law. Having visited the hospital daily, at the end, when his partner had lost consciousness, the family could insist on taking charge and exclude him from medical decisions, from the death and finally from the funeral. A surviving partner might lose her home, whether because of the absence of succession rights to the tenancy, because her partner had made no will or because a sale was needed to pay inheritance tax. If her partner had been killed, her dependency would not be recognised under the Fatal Accidents Act 1976 or by the Criminal Injuries Compensation Board. Although she had forgone a career in order to look after the couple's children, she was not entitled to a widow's pension.

7.2 It was these striking injustices that, more than anything else, made the case for the legal recognition of same sex partnerships. Nevertheless, many of them could be and had been mitigated to some degree before the passing of the Civil Partnership Act 2004. Unregistered partners can ensure that property passes to their surviving partner by means of a will, a joint tenancy of the home or a deed of trust or cohabitation agreement,[1] or a nomination under a private pension scheme. They can grant their partner an enduring power of attorney to control their finances in the event of incapacity and give them a say in their treatment by means of a 'living will' or naming them as 'next of kin' upon admission to hospital. In practice, however, most people do not exercise such foresight.

7.3 Increased social recognition of same sex couples has resulted in their increased recognition by hospitals and the extension of survivors' pensions to them in most private sector schemes. The Employment Equality (Sexual Orientation) Regulations 2003[2] banned discrimination in the provision of benefits as against unmarried opposite-sex partners, but not as against married couples.

7.4 The decision in *Ghaidan v Mendoza*[3] has substantially improved the position of same sex partners, giving them the same rights as opposite-sex partners to succeed to tenancies, to compensation under the Fatal Accidents Act 1976, to act as the 'nearest relative' under the Mental Health Act 1983 and probably also to claim under the

---

1   The enforceability of the financial provisions of same sex cohabitation agreements was confirmed in *Sutton v Mishcon de Reya* [2004] 1 FLR 837.

2   SI 2003/1661.

3   [2004] 3 All ER 411, HL; [2004] 2 FLR 600, HL.

Inheritance (Provision for Family and Dependants) Act 1975 without having to prove a dependency.

7.5 Now, the Civil Partnership Act 2004 seeks to give broadly the same rights and recognition to registered civil partners as to married couples. 'Next of kin' rights are poorly defined at present, even in respect of spouses, and this remains the case for civil partners. However, civil partners will have the same rights on intestacy and for provision out of the estate as surviving spouses and should benefit from the same exemption from inheritance tax.[1] They will have an unlimited insurable interest in each other's life and need not prove cohabitation to qualify under the Fatal Accidents Act 1976. Civil partnership will have the same effect on wills as marriage does. In respect of pensions, differences with marriage remain. In respect of state, public sector and contracted-out pensions, civil partners will have the same rights as widowers, rather than widows. In respect of private sector occupational pensions, it is unclear whether they should have the same rights as married or unmarried couples.

MENTAL INCAPACITY

7.6 Under the Enduring Powers of Attorney Act 1985, a person may nominate someone to manage his financial affairs in the event that he loses mental capacity, by means of an enduring power of attorney which must be set out in writing. This can be either a general power or one limited by the terms of the document. Under the Mental Health Act 1983, an application can also be made to the Court of Protection, who can make decisions for the person directly or appoint a 'receiver' to do so. Spouses and cohabitants do not have any statutory precedence before the Court of Protection, although in practice the court will usually recognise their special connection. Similar recognition is likely to be accorded to civil partners (and should already be accorded to same sex partners in any event).

7.7 The Enduring Powers of Attorney Act 1985 has been amended to treat civil partnership in the same way as marriage. The attorney may make gifts at the formation of a civil partnership or on an anniversary thereof. Civil partners, like spouses, must be given notice before an enduring power of attorney is registered. These changes apply equally to enduring powers of attorney created before the Civil Partnership Act 2004.[2]

7.8 A person may also compile a 'living will' expressing in advance what medical treatment he would want in the event that he loses mental capacity, or nominating a person to take such decisions on his behalf. This is not binding on doctors, but can be persuasive.

7.9 The Mental Capacity Bill currently before Parliament would extend the nature of an enduring power of attorney (renamed a 'lasting power of attorney'). A person could use this to grant powers over his personal as well as his financial affairs. This could include decisions as to medical treatment. The Court of Protection would also be similarly empowered, either directly or by appointing a 'deputy'. Unlike a living will, decisions

---

1   See **8.50–8.52**.
2   Civil Partnership Act 2004 (CPA 2004), Sch 27, paras 106–108 amending Enduring Powers of Attorney Act 1985, s 3 and Sch 1, para 2(1).

made under a lasting power of attorney or by a deputy would be binding on the patient's doctors, subject to challenge in court. However, by clause 27 of the Bill, such powers could not extend to matters of personal relationship, such as formation of a marriage or civil partnership or consent to sexual relations.

7.10   Medical treatment for mental illness is governed by the Mental Health Act 1983. By s 26(6) of the Act, a same sex partner is a 'relative', provided that the partners cohabit and have done so for a period of 6 months.[1] He will be the 'nearest relative', provided that his partner is unmarried, separated or deserted. The Civil Partnership Act 2004 makes no changes as regards a civil partner, who is in the same position as any other cohabitant and so remains a relative only so long as the partners cohabit. By contrast, where a marriage is subject to a desertion or a permanent separation (whether under an agreement or a court order), the spouses will remain relatives but cease to be nearest relatives. The nearest relative has important powers under the Mental Health Act 1983 to apply for admission to hospital for assessment or for treatment, for the appointment of a guardian, to discharge from hospital and to apply to the Mental Health Review Tribunal.[2] The status of relative is much less important, so in practice the positions of a spouse and of a civil partner are very little different.

7.11   Like a spouse, a civil partner may not provide a medical recommendation for compulsory admission to hospital for assessment or treatment. Nor may he provide a written recommendation for aftercare under supervision.[3]

HOSPITAL VISITING AND CONSENT TO TREATMENT

7.12   In the first instance, decisions over who may visit a patient and what treatment he should receive will be taken by the patient himself. If the patient is incapable, another person may in future be able to take such decisions on his behalf if granted that power under a lasting power of attorney or by the Court of Protection in accordance with the current Mental Capacity Bill, subject to the restrictions set out in that Bill.

7.13   Otherwise, such decisions will be taken by the hospital caring for the patient. The hospital will usually try to consult those nearest to the patient if possible. It will also give weight to the expressed wishes of the patient, eg in a living will. However, a person's relationship to another adult does not give that person the power to decide treatment on his behalf. 'Next of kin' is not a status recognised in this area of law. It is a term used by hospitals on admission forms to identify the person to contact in an emergency. A patient may specify a same sex partner as 'next of kin'.

7.14   Hospitals are likely to give particular recognition to civil partners, as they do to spouses. The government in its White Paper has expressed the belief that the existence of civil partnership will also increase the recognition of unregistered same sex relationships. It has also stated it will ensure the guidance given to medical staff ensures same sex

---

1   Following *Ghaidan v Mendoza* [2004] 3 All ER 411, HL; [2004] 2 FLR 600, HL.
2   Mental Health Act 1983 (MHA 1983), ss 11, 23–25 and 69.
3   CPA 2004, Sch 27, para 86 amending MHA 1983, ss 12 and 25C.

partners are adequately recognised.[1] It remains unclear whether and how this will apply to private hospitals and care homes.

REGISTRATION OF DEATH

7.15 Where a person dies, their civil partner or other relative by civil partnership may give information about the death to a Registrar of births and deaths under the Births and Deaths Registration Act 1953, ss 16 and 17.[2] An unregistered same sex partner can do so only if present at the death or responsible for the funeral arrangements.[3]

INQUESTS AND BURIAL

7.16 Where a person has made a will, upon his death custody and possession of his body pass to his executors,[4] who will have charge of the funeral arrangements. Where the deceased has left directions regarding his funeral, these will usually be respected, especially where they are set out in the will, but they are not binding on the executors.[5]

7.17 Where the deceased dies intestate, it is customary for his nearest relations and friends to arrange the funeral. This has caused problems where the rest of the family refuse to recognise a same sex partner. No specific provision has been made in the Civil Partnership Act 2004 to resolve such conflict. Indeed, it would be difficult to impose hard and fast rules of precedence in such situations. However, the status of civil partner is likely to confer similar social precedence to that of a spouse. It is hoped this will also increase the recognition of unregistered same sex partners.

7.18 In its White Paper, the government has proposed extending to civil partners:

— the rights of spouses to be notified of inquests and to question witnesses;
— the right to access to relevant records and documents from the coroner;
— the rights of relatives with respect to burial, exhumation and cremation.

It is expected that this will be effected by delegated legislation and guidance.[6]

7.19 Where the place of burial of the deceased has become disused, his surviving civil partner may object to the land being re-used under the Disused Burial Grounds (Amendment) Act 1981.[7] The deceased's personal representative and certain other relatives have the same right, but cohabitants do not.

7.20 The retention and use of human tissue are governed by the Human Tissue Act 2004. Consent is required before a human body can be stored or used or tissue taken from

---

1   *Civil Partnership: A Framework for the Legal Recognition of Same-Sex Couples* (June 2003) paras 7.17–7.18.
2   CPA 2004, Sch 27, para 19 amending Births and Deaths Registration Act 1953, s 41.
3   *R v Liverpool City Council* (unreported) 22 October 2002.
4   *Dobson v North Tyneside Health Authority and Newcastle Health Authority* [1996] 4 All ER 474, CA.
5   *Williams v Williams* (1882) 20 Ch D 659.
6   *Civil Partnership: A Framework for the Legal Recognition of Same-Sex Couples* (June 2003) paras 9.4–9.6.
7   CPA 2004, Sch 27, para 66 amending Disused Burial Grounds (Amendment) Act 1981, s 9.

it, stored or used. This does not affect the powers of coroners to order post-mortems. Section 3 of the Act provides that a person may give such consent before his death, which need only be in writing if it is consent to public display or to anatomical examination of the body or of tissue taken from it after death. Where the deceased has neither consented nor refused consent, this may be supplied by a person appointed by him as his 'nominated representative' (see s 4) or, in the case of a child, by a person with parental responsibility for him (see s 2(7)). In the absence of such a person, a person in a 'qualifying relationship' may give consent. This is defined in the Human Tissue Act 2004, s 54(9) as a 'spouse, partner, parent, child, brother, sister, grandparent, grandchild, child of a brother or sister, stepfather, stepmother, half-brother, half-sister and friend of long standing'. The order of the list may be taken to indicate precedence, but this is not expressly provided in the Act. Civil partners are not included in this list and no amendment has been made by the Civil Partnership Act 2004, but the Secretary of State may in future amend the list by order under s 54(10). However, a civil partner is clearly included within the definition of 'partner' under s 54(8): 'a person is another's partner if the two of them (whether of different sexes or the same sex) live as partners in an enduring family relationship'.

WILLS

7.21 The Civil Partnership Act 2004, Sch 4, paras 1–5 amend the Wills Act 1837 by the insertion of ss 18B and 18C to treat the formation and termination of civil partnership in the same way as marriage.

7.22 By s 18B(1), a will is revoked by the formation of a civil partnership in the same circumstances as by marriage. As the recognition of a foreign civil partnership does not constitute the 'formation' of a civil partnership, the coming into force of the Civil Partnership Act 2004 should not result in the revocation of wills between existing civil partners who have registered abroad. By s 18B(2), a disposition in a will in the exercise of a power of appointment takes effect regardless, unless the property so appointed would in default of appointment pass to the testator's personal representatives. By s 18B(3), a will is not revoked if it names the testator's intended civil partner and shows that the testator intended to form a civil partnership with him and intended the will not to be revoked by the formation of the civil partnership. If the will evinces an intention that a particular disposition not be revoked, all other dispositions will stand unless a contrary intention appears from the will.[1]

7.23 Section 18C provides that, unless the contrary intention appears in the will, any former civil partner will be treated as having died upon the dissolution or annulment of the civil partnership. He will be bypassed as beneficiary, executor and trustee and in respect of any power of appointment. However, he will still be entitled to apply for financial provision under the Inheritance (Provision for Family and Dependants) Act 1975.

7.24 Similar amendments are made in respect of witnesses of wills. A gift to an attesting witness to a will or his civil partner will be null and void, unless the attested signature is

---

1   Wills Act 1837, s 18B(4)–(6).

not required to validate the will.[1] This should not apply to a gift to person who subsequently becomes the civil partner of a witness.[2] However, the civil partner of a creditor of the deceased may witness the will.[3]

7.25 The Civil Partnership Act 2004, Sch 4, para 5 provides that where the deceased leaves some property absolutely to his civil partner and also an interest in the same property to his issue, the civil partner takes free of the purported gift to the issue, unless the contrary intention appears.

7.26 Occasionally a will provides for a gift to the spouse of some named person without naming that spouse. It is unlikely that this will be apt to cover a civil partner, although this will depend on the particular wording by which the intended beneficiary is identified. The Civil Partnership Act 2004 creates no express presumption that such a gift may also pass to the civil partner of the named person; it never refers to a civil partner as 'spouse', 'married', 'husband' or 'wife'; it creates no general bar on discrimination as between married persons and civil partners.

ADMINISTRATION OF ESTATES AND INTESTACY

7.27 A surviving civil partner may be granted probate or letters of administration in priority over the Public Trustee under the Public Trustee Act 1906.[4] Presumably, consequential amendment will be made to the Non-Contentious Probate Rules 1987 to provide for civil partners to take out letters of administration upon intestacy and to give them first priority under Rule 22(1).

7.28 The Civil Partnership Act 2004, Sch 4, paras 7–14 amend the Administration of Estates Act 1925, the Intestates' Estates Act 1952 and the Family Provision Act 1966 to treat civil partnership in the same way as marriage:

— A surviving civil partner will have the same rights on intestacy as a surviving spouse. If the deceased leaves no issue, the civil partner will be entitled to the personal chattels, £200,000 and half the residue absolutely, the other half of the residue going to other relatives. If the deceased leaves issue, the civil partner's share is reduced to the personal chattels, £125,000 and a life interest in half the residue, the remainder going to the children absolutely. (Paras 7, 14.)

— If a minor forms a civil partnership, his entitlement will survive his death and accrue to his own estate, both in respect of a statutory trust of the residuary estate and his beneficial entitlement to land under a settlement. (Paras 8, 11.)

— A surviving civil partner may redeem his life interest in the deceased's residuary estate to the same extent as a surviving spouse. He may elect within 12 months of representation being taken out (unless the court extends this period) to capitalise the life interest, provided the property is in possession and not subject to a partial intestacy. The value is calculated in accordance with the Intestate Succession

---

1   CPA 2004, Sch 4, para 3 applying Wills Act 1837, s 15 and Wills Act 1968, s 1 to civil partners as to spouses.
2   *Thorpe v Bestwick* (1881) 6 QBD 311.
3   CPA 2004, Sch 4, para 4 amending Wills Act 1837, s 16.
4   CPA 2004, Sch 4, para 6.

(Interest and Capitalisation) Order 1977, [1] art 3. The sums required may be raised by charging the estate. (Paras 9, 10.)

— Civil partnership, like marriage, amounts to valuable consideration for the purposes of the Administration of Estates Act 1925. (Para 12.)

— A surviving civil partner has the same rights as a spouse to acquire the family home when his partner dies intestate. He may set off his entitlement under the intestacy against the value of the deceased's interest in the property and pay any balance due to the estate. (Para 13.)

INHERITANCE ACT CLAIMS

7.29   The Inheritance (Provision for Family and Dependants) Act 1975 allows certain persons to apply for reasonable provision out of a deceased person's estate. It is now amended by the Civil Partnership Act 2004, Sch 4, paras 15–27 to treat a civil partnership in the same way as a marriage.

7.30   The court has the same or equivalent powers upon an application by a surviving civil partner as by a surviving spouse.[2] Provision for civil partners, like spouses, is not restricted to what is required for their maintenance. However, it is not necessarily the same as for spouses. In the case of a civil partner, it means 'such financial provision as it would be reasonable in all the circumstances of the case for a *civil partner* to receive';[3] in the case of a spouse, 'such financial provision as it would be reasonable in all the circumstances of the case for a *husband or wife* to receive'.[4] It seems unlikely, however, that any distinction in provision is intended to be drawn. In both cases, the court is to have regard to what the survivor would have received in ancillary relief.[5]

7.31   As with marriage, the duration of the civil partnership is likely to be a very important factor in determining the appropriate provision. In the immediate future, any civil partner who applies for provision will only be able to rely on a registered civil partnership of short duration, whereas the couple's cohabitation may well have predated the civil partnership by many years. Following *Co v Co (Ancillary Relief: Pre-marriage Cohabitation)*,[6] it seems likely that the courts will take the whole relationship into account. The arguments for taking the period of cohabitation into account are all the stronger for same sex couples who were unable to register before the Civil Partnership Act 2004: their failure to register can be no reflection on the quality of the relationship or the interdependence or expectations of the parties to it.

7.32   A former civil partner may also apply, provided he has not subsequently married or registered a civil partnership.[7] The right of a former spouse to apply now ends if he

---

1   SI 1977/1491.

2   Inheritance (Provision for Family and Dependants) Act 1975 (IPFDA 1975), s 1(1)(a) as replaced by CPA 2004, Sch 4, para 15(2).

3   IPFDA 1975, s 1(2)(aa) inserted by CPA 2004, Sch 4, para 15(6).

4   IPFDA 1975, s 1(2)(a).

5   CPA 2004, Sch 4, para 17(5) amending IPFDA 1975, s 3(2)(b).

6   [2004] 1 FLR 1095; see also *GW v RW* [2003] 2 FLR 108 and *M v M (Ancillary Relief: division of assets accrued post-separation)* [2004] 2 FLR 236.

7   IFPDA 1975, s 1(1)(b) as replaced by CPA 2004, Sch 4, para 15(2).

forms a civil partnership as well as if he re-marries. Where the deceased has died within 12 months of the termination of a civil partnership (or a separation order, where the separation is continuing) and no final order for ancillary relief has been made, the court may treat the survivor as if the civil partnership had not been terminated. Otherwise a former civil partner will be restricted to provision for his maintenance only. Upon ancillary relief (whether under the Civil Partnership Act 2004, Sch 5 or Sch 7), the court may terminate a former spouse's right to apply under the Inheritance (Provision for Family and Dependants) Act 1975.[1]

7.33   A person may apply against the estate of his parent's civil partner if he was a child of the family.[2]

7.34   The right of cohabitants to apply is expressly extended to same sex cohabitants.[3] The survivor must show they lived together as if they were civil partners for the 2 years up to the deceased's death. Provision is limited to what is required for his maintenance. Previously, a same sex partner could apply only if he could show that he was dependent on the deceased[4] and provision was usually restricted in practice to the value of his lost dependency, quantified in rather narrow terms.

LIFE INSURANCE

7.35   Where a person takes out a policy of insurance on his own life for the benefit of his civil partner, the proceeds will not form part of his estate; similarly where a civil partner does so for the benefit of his children.[5] Accordingly, any debts in the estate will not be deductible from the proceeds of the policy; nor may the proceeds be transferred to a claimant under the Inheritance (Provision for Family and Dependants) Act 1975 (although the court may take them into account when determining the financial resources of any beneficiary of the estate under s 3(1)(c) of that Act).

7.36   Civil partners are presumed to have an unlimited insurable interest in the life of each other.[6] This does not apply to a contract of assurance entered into before the coming into force of the Civil Partnership Act 2004. Unregistered partners need to show a legitimate insurable interest in each other's life (eg where they are jointly liable under a mortgage).

7.37   Funds held by trade unions for the purposes of providing for the funeral expenses of a member's civil partner are protected from enforcement of awards against the trade union.[7]

---

1   IFPDA 1975, ss 15ZA and 15B as inserted by CPA 2004, Sch 4, paras 21 and 22.
2   IFPDA 1975, s 1(1)(d) as amended by CPA 2004, Sch 4, para 15(4).
3   IFPDA 1975, s 1(1B) as inserted by CPA 2004, Sch 4, para 15(5). This result has probably already been achieved by the decision in *Ghaidan v Mendoza* [2004] 3 All ER 411, HL; [2004] 2 FLR 600, HL. (See also the decision of the ECHR in *Karner v Austria* (2003) 2 FLR 623.)
4   IFPDA 1975, s 1(1)(e).
5   CPA 2004, s 70, applying Married Women's Property Act 1882, s 11 to civil partners.
6   CPA 2004, s 253, applying Life Assurance Act 1774, s 1 to civil partners.
7   CPA 2004, Sch 27, para 144 amending Trade Union and Labour Relations Act 1992, s 23(3)(b).

FATAL ACCIDENTS

7.38   The Civil Partnership Act 2004, s 83 extends the category of dependants who may claim for the loss of their dependency under the Fatal Accidents Act 1976 to include the deceased's civil partner, his former civil partner, his same sex cohabitant, a child of the family created by the deceased's civil partnership and an immediate relative of the deceased's civil partner. An unregistered cohabitant has to show at least 2 years' cohabitation with the deceased in order to qualify.[1]

7.39   Section 3(3) of the 1976 Act, which provides that a widow's re-marriage or prospects of re-marriage shall not be taken into account in quantifying her dependency, has not been extended to cover either a surviving civil partner or a widow subsequently forming a civil partnership. It is unlikely that this is intended to create any difference in treatment. Prior to the Civil Partnership Act 2004 and the institution of civil partnership, there could be no question of taking into account a person's prospects of forming a civil partnership. Accordingly, there is no rule that a court should do so. It should not be possible for the courts to infer such a rule after the institution of civil partnership as that would create discrimination contrary to the European Convention on Human Rights, Article 14.

7.40   Civil partners, like spouses, may now also claim damages for bereavement.[2]

7.41   The Criminal Injuries Compensation Scheme provides (as from 3 April 2001) for compensation to be paid to a surviving same sex partner who has lived with the deceased for at least 2 years. The government has not yet indicated whether it will require civil partners, unlike spouses, to show 2 years' cohabitation.

SURVIVORS' PENSIONS

7.42   Pensions come in a number of forms, which are each treated differently under the Civil Partnership Act 2004:

— the state pension;
— public sector employment pensions;
— contracted-out benefits within a private scheme;
— private sector employment pensions;
— private pensions.

With the exception of private pensions and some private sector schemes, survivor benefits are generally only paid to spouses (and in some cases to children). The Civil Partnership Act 2004 seeks to extend these survivor benefits to civil partners, but it has not been wholly successful in respect of private sector schemes.

---

1   This confirms the position of same sex cohabitants following *Ghaidan v Mendoza* [2004] 3 All ER 411, HL; [2004] 2 FLR 600, HL.
2   CPA 2004, s 83(7).

State provision

7.43 In respect of state pensions, a civil partner becomes entitled to a pension equal to his deceased partner's if both partners were over pension age at the time of the death. If only the surviving partner was over pension age at the time of the death, he will only be entitled as from 2010. Thus civil partners are treated the same as widowers. A civil partner who is under pension age at the time of the death has the same entitlement as a widow or widower.[1] The same provisions for uprating apply.[2]

7.44 A civil partner also becomes entitled to bereavement payment, bereavement allowance and widowed parent's allowance in the same circumstances as a surviving spouse. The formation of a new civil partnership or same sex cohabitation has the same effect as remarriage.[3] Late claims will be treated in the same way as for marriage.[4]

Public sector schemes and contracted-out rights

7.45 In public sector schemes and in respect of contracted-out rights in private sector schemes, the deceased's service from 1988 onwards will be taken into account when calculating the survivor's pension due to his civil partner. By the Civil Partnership Act 2004, s 255, the government has taken wide powers to amend pension legislation by statutory instrument to make provision for pensions, allowances and gratuities for surviving civil partners and other dependants under a civil partnership in both the public and private sectors. By s 255(4)(a), such provision may be different for civil partners and spouses. However, the government has stated that it will treat civil partners in public sector schemes in the same way as widowers.[5] This is reinforced by s 255(4)(b) – the result of a late government amendment to the Bill – which allows such provision to take account of rights and service before the coming into force of the Civil Partnership Act 2004. The government particularly intends to use this power in respect of contracted-out pensions.[6] This is a change from its previous policy that only contributions made to pension schemes after the date of coming into force of the Civil Partnership Act 2004 should be taken into account in determining any survivor's pension.[7]

7.46 Where public sector schemes require amendment of statutes in order to provide for civil partners, this has been effected in the Civil Partnership Act 2004, Sch 25. Amendment of legislation in respect of the armed forces is effected in Sch 26. The war widow's pension, when it becomes payable to civil partners, will attract the Christmas bonus[8] and may be disregarded in calculating council tax benefit.[9]

1　CPA 2004, Sch 24, paras 23, 26–28, 30–33 and 51 amending Social Security Contributions and Benefits Act 1992 (SSCBA 1992), ss 46, 48B, 48BB, 51, 52, 60, 61A and 62 and Sch 4A respectively.
2　CPA 2004, Sch 24, para 66 amending Social Security Administration Act 1992 (SSAA 1992), s 156.
3　CPA 2004, Sch 24, paras 16–22 amending SSCBA 1992, ss 36–39C.
4　CPA 2004, Sch 24, para 55 amending SSAA 1992, s 2AA(7).
5　Anne McGuire – *Hansard*, HC Second Reading, col 250 (12 October 2004).
6　Jacqui Smith – *Hansard*, HC Standing Committee D, col 184 (26 October 2004).
7　Explanatory notes to the Bill, para 339.
8　CPA 2004, Sch 24, para 49 amending SSCBA 1992, s 150.
9　CPA 2004, Sch 24, para 65 amending SSAA 1992, s 139.

Private sector occupational pensions

7.47 In respect of private sector schemes, the government at present intends to issue regulations in respect of only contracted-out rights. It remains unclear to what extent civil partners will receive the same benefits as spouses in respect of the additional rights under such schemes.

7.48 Employment discrimination regulations require an employer not to discriminate on the grounds of sexual orientation.[1] These provisions extend to the trustees and managers of occupational pension schemes with regard to rights accruing and benefits payable in respect of periods of service from 1 December 2003. Any provision for opposite-sex partners must equally be made for same sex partners and any discretion to provide benefits must be exercised without discrimination. The rules of these schemes are to be treated as amended accordingly. It is to be hoped that schemes which currently do not discriminate on the ground of sexual orientation do not begin to do so in respect of rights accruing in respect of periods of service before 1 December 2003.

7.49 By contrast, reg 25[2] of the Regulations expressly allows employers to discriminate in favour of married persons in the provision of benefits:

> 'Nothing in Part II or III shall render unlawful anything which prevents or restricts access to a benefit by reference to marital status.'

Although married persons may receive better treatment than unregistered same sex couples and unmarried opposite sex couples, it is unclear whether they may receive better treatment than civil partners following the Civil Partnership Act 2004, s 251, which amends the Sex Discrimination Act 1975, s 3 to bar discrimination against a civil partner compared with a person who is not civil partner and discrimination against a married person compared with a unmarried person. In debate in the House of Lords, Baroness Hollis of Heigham on behalf of the government stated: [3]

> 'In this Bill, the reference scheme test that provides a floor of benefits at least as good as what is provided by the state second pension is covered. Spouses and similar partners will be treated equally. If trustees offer no more than that, they do not have to do any more, but if they offer benefits above that—as most of them do within that headspace—they will come under the framework of the European regulations. What they do for spouses they must do for civil partners, and what they do for unmarried opposite-sex couples they must do for unmarried same-sex couples. If regulations from the DTI are needed to make that clear, we shall bring those forward.'

This suggests that the government intended s 251 to prevent discrimination in employment between civil partners and married persons and vice versa. However, even if

---

1   Employment Equality (Sexual Orientation) Regulations 2003 (SI 2003/1661) and Employment Equality (Sexual Orientation) Regulations 2003 (Amendment) Regulations 2003 implementing the European Equal Treatment Directive, Council Directive 2000/78/EC of 27 November 2000. (See also **8.61**.)

2   Implementing Recital 22 of the Directive: 'This Directive is without prejudice to national laws on marital status and the benefits dependent thereon.' In *R (on the application of Amicus – MSF Section) v Secretary of State for Trade & Industry* [2004] EWHC 860 (Admin), the court accepted that the Regulation constituted a proper implementation of the Directive.

3   *Hansard*, HL Grand Committee, cols GC507–8 (25 May 2004). See also the comments of Baroness Crawley – *Hansard*, HL Grand Committee, cols GC457–8 (25 May 2004) – as to the effect of s 251 on the employment of couples, noted at **8.63**.

this is not so, it would appear that the government will rectify this by regulation. Any continuing discrimination between spouses and civil partners under the Directive sits very uneasily with Civil Partnership Act 2004, s 260, which allows the government to apply to civil partners European legislation relating to spouses.

7.50 Where a scheme makes particular provision for a spouse, it will need to amend its rules if it is to extend these benefits to civil partners. However, where this will affect the accrued rights of other beneficiaries (eg children who may be entitled if there is no spouse) the trustees are likely to have to comply with the requirements of the Pensions Act 1995, s 67, which may make the amendment difficult to put into effect in practice.

7.51 The procedure for a registered civil partner to claim survivor benefits will be much simpler than for an unregistered partner as he can establish his status by producing his registration certificate.

Private pensions

7.52 In respect of private pensions, these usually allow the member to elect whether to have survivor benefits and who to nominate as the beneficiary. No change is envisaged in consequence of the Civil Partnership Act 2004.

TENANCY SUCCESSION

7.53 The Civil Partnership Act 2004, Sch 8 amends housing law to treat civil partners as if they were married. Surviving civil partners will have the same rights as widows and widowers to succeed to the following :

— a statutory tenancy under the Rent Act 1977 (para 13);
— a secure tenancy or periodic secured tenancy under the Housing Act 1985 (paras 20–22);
— an assured periodic tenancy under the Housing Act 1988 (para 41);
— an introductory or demoted tenancy under the Housing Act 1996 (paras 53, 55);
— as a protected occupier or statutory tenant of agricultural land under the Rent (Agriculture) Act 1976 (paras 8–9);
— a tenancy of an agricultural holding under the Agricultural Holdings Act 1986 (this also applies to succession upon retirement of the tenant, save where the civil partnership is subject to a separation order or a conditional order of dissolution, nullity or presumption of death) (paras 36–39);
— an assured agricultural occupancy under Chapter III of the Housing Act 1988 (para 44).

The civil partner will need to show that he was occupying the property at the time of the deceased's death, in most cases (depending on the type of tenancy) as his only or principal home.

7.54 A cohabitant (namely, 'a person who was living with the original occupier as if they were civil partners')[1] may also succeed to the same interests, except a tenancy of an

---

1   CPA 2004, Sch 8, paras 10(4), 13(3), 27(2), 41(3) and 44(4); see also para 61(5).

agricultural holding under the Agricultural Holdings Act 1986. The Civil Partnership Act 2004 thus confirms the decision of the House of Lords in *Ghaidan v Godin-Mendoza*[1] that cohabitants in such cases include those of the same sex. In the case of a secure tenancy, the cohabitation must have lasted at least 12 months prior to the death.[2]

7.55 Relatives by civil partnership are entitled to succeed to a secure tenancy under the Housing Act 1985 or an introductory or demoted tenancy under the Housing Act 1996.[3]

7.56 A surviving civil partner may also succeed to an agreement affording security of tenure under the Mobile Homes Act 1983 on the same basis as surviving spouses.[4]

7.57 A surviving civil partner will also be entitled to the same protection from eviction and harassment as a widow or widower in respect of:

— a caravan occupied under a residential contract;[5]
— agricultural land occupied under a contract of employment not amounting to a statutory tenancy.[6]

REGULATED OCCUPATIONS

7.58 A surviving civil partner, like a surviving spouse, may continue to carry on his partner's business as a dentist or optician for 3 years after the death.[7] (This does not allow him to practise in person as a dentist or optician, unless so qualified.) He may also operate under a knacker's yard licence issued under the Slaughterhouses Act 1974 for 2 months after the death[8] and a licence issued under the Food Safety Act 1990 for 3 months after the death (or for such longer period as the enforcement authority may allow).[9]

7.59 A surviving civil partner is eligible for provision under the Royal Pharmaceutical Society's benevolent fund.[10]

7.60 A surviving civil partner will not be regarded as a business partner of the deceased under the Partnership Act 1890, s 2 merely because he receives payments from the business after the deceased's death.

---

1   Above.
2   Housing Act 1985, s 87.
3   Housing Act 1985, s 87(b), together with s 113 as amended by CPA 2004, Sch 8, para 27; Housing Act 1996, s 131(b) and 143H(3), together with s 140 and s 143P as amended by CPA 2004, Sch 8, paras 51 and 59.
4   CPA 2004, Sch 27, paras 87 and 88.
5   CPA 2004, Sch 8, para 8 amending Caravan Sites Act 1968, s 3.
6   CPA 2004, Sch 8, para 15 amending Protection from Eviction Act 1977, s 4(2)(b).
7   CPA 2004, Sch 27, paras 89 and 135 amending Dentists Act 1984, s 41 and Opticians Act 1989, s 29.
8   CPA 2004, Sch 27, para 48.
9   CPA 2004, Sch 27, para 136.
10   CPA 2004, Sch 27, para 20 amending Pharmacy Act 1954, s 17(c).

7.61   An officer or servant of an industrial and provident society or friendly society may benefit from a deceased member's nomination of his property in the society only if he was a member of the deceased member's family, which class includes a civil partner.[1]

LEGAL PROCEEDINGS

7.62   A surviving civil partner may bring or continue an appeal against his deceased's partner's criminal conviction or sentence without having to show a substantial financial or other interest in the appeal.[2] He will still require the approval of the Court of Appeal under the Criminal Appeal Act 1968, s 44A.

7.63   He may also bring or continue proceedings before an employment tribunal on behalf of his deceased civil partner.[3]

7.64   He may bring or continue an appeal under the Courts-Martial (Appeals) Act 1968, s 48A on behalf of his deceased civil partner.[4] This will be particularly important if any survivor's pension is at risk in the proceedings.

---

1   CPA 2004, Sch 27, paras 24 and 52 amending Industrial and Provident Societies Act 1965, ss 23 and 25 and Friendly Societies Act 1974, s 66.
2   CPA 2004, Sch 27, para 26.
3   CPA 2004, Sch 27, para 146 amending Trade Union and Labour Relations Act 1992, s 146.
4   CPA 2004, Sch 26, para 33.

Chapter 8

RIGHTS AND RESPONSIBILITIES

8.1   The status of marriage affects almost every aspect of life and of law. It brings with it rights and responsibilities, not just with respect to each other but also with respect to the state (in taxation, pensions, social security, immigration, prisons, the courts) and to third parties, such as employers, clients, creditors, landlords, tenants and trustees.

8.2   The government has repeatedly stressed its policy that any difference between marriage and civil partnership must be justified objectively. Its determination to ensure that civil partnership should mirror marriage wherever possible is demonstrated by the thoroughness with which almost every statutory reference to marriage or to married persons or to widows or widowers has been amended to include civil partners. This thoroughness has led many parliamentarians in debate to ask what difference there is between civil partnership and marriage. Indeed, it is apparent that the essential difference is simply that civil partners must be of the same sex and married persons of different sex.

8.3   Nonetheless, Parliament has insisted on this difference. If it had not, the Civil Partnerships Act 2004 might have been a very short document indeed. Same sex partners would have been allowed to marry, with certain incidences of marriage (such as church weddings and the concepts of adultery and consummation) excepted. There would have been no need to amend the myriad statutes that refer to marriage and this chapter would be unnecessary.

8.4   Instead, the Civil Partnerships Act 2004 has created a compendium of existing matrimonial law. This chapter sets out the wider statutory implications of marriage in respect of housing, property, insolvency, social security, taxation, employment, business, immigration, elections, government information, prisons, witnesses and crime. It identifies some omissions in the provision which has been made for civil partnerships, but there must be many more oversights that will only be identified over time. Most, despite the government's stated policy, will have no objective justification and will cause real and unnecessary injustice. This is an inevitable consequence of the form the legislation has taken. However, there is express power in the Civil Partnerships Act 2004, s 259 to correct these omissions by statutory instrument.

8.5   One further result of this insistence that marriage and civil partnership are different and that civil partners are not spouses is that legal documents created by private individuals – contracts, trusts, rules – which refer to marriage and spouses will probably not be reinterpreted to include civil partners. It is less clear whether they will include parties to a same sex marriage contracted abroad, although the recognition of such marriages as civil partnerships under the Civil Partnerships Act 2004 may make this less likely.

8.6   There are areas that the Civil Partnerships Act 2004 deliberately does not deal with. Taxation (with the exception of tax credits) must await the 'next available' Finance Bill, on the ground that the Bill started in the House of Lords, which may not concern itself with taxation. In addition, where the relevant existing law is contained in delegated legislation, which applies particularly in relation to immigration and social security, the necessary changes will be effected by delegated legislation. The government has made a broad commitment to treat civil partners in the same way as married persons in these fields. This chapter tries to anticipate the likely changes in these areas. They are likely to come into effect at the same time as the Civil Partnerships Act 2004.

8.7   In general, the Civil Partnerships Act 2004 avoids dealing with unregistered same sex couples, save to repeat the effect of the decision in *Ghaidan v Mendoza*,[1] which the Act is at pains to support. However, the non-recognition of same sex couples gave them one important advantage: with respect to social security and tax credits their finances were treated independently. The Civil Partnerships Act 2004 has ended this and the financial impact on many couples will be severe. This change is, perhaps, a natural consequence of the recognition of same sex couples through civil partnership and, in the absence of this change, unmarried opposite sex couples might have been able to challenge the existing rules on the ground of discrimination under Article 14 of the European Convention on Human Rights.

THE FAMILY HOME

Home rights

8.8   Pursuant to the Family Law Act 1996, s 30, a spouse is entitled to occupy any dwelling which the other spouse is entitled to occupy (save under a non-contractual licence). These matrimonial home rights have been relabelled 'home rights' and are extended to civil partners under the Civil Partnerships Act 2004, Sch 9, para 1. Thus a civil partner will be entitled to occupy the family home and to meet any mortgage payments. His occupation will satisfy the occupation condition for protected, secure and assured tenancies, whether he or his civil partner is the tenant.

8.9   Home rights are a charge on the property and, if the chargee is in actual occupation, may be protected at the Land Registry by an agreed notice[2] (although only in respect of one property at any one time), affording protection against both a subsequent transfer of the other civil partner's interest in the property and a subsequent charge upon it. Home rights afford only limited rights of occupation to one civil partner upon the other's bankruptcy under the Insolvency Act 1986, s 336.[3] They also afford a right to compensation upon compulsory purchase under the Land Compensation Act 1973.

8.10   An unregistered same sex cohabitant will also have home rights for the duration of an occupation order in his favour under the Family Law Act 1996, s 36 (see below), but these do not take effect as a charge on the property.

---

1   [2004] 3 All ER 411, HL; [2004] 2 FLR 600, HL.
2   Under the Land Registration Act 2002. Despite its name, such a notice does not need to be agreed.
3   See also **8.30** below.

Injunctions

8.11 By reason of their home rights, civil partners are entitled to apply as against each other for an occupation order under the Family Law Act 1996, s 33 (or s 37 if neither has a right to occupy the home[1]). An application under s 33 may be made in respect of a home which they both either occupy or have intended to occupy. An occupation order can enforce the applicant's right to occupy the property, require the respondent to leave and not return to the home or a defined vicinity, define how the home is to be shared, or restrict or terminate home rights. By s 40, ancillary orders may be made with regard to the upkeep and outgoings of the property and the use and care of its contents.

8.12 Any other person with a right to occupy the property may also apply for an occupation order (save in respect of home rights) against an 'associated person' under s 33. An 'associated person' now includes a former civil partner, a same sex cohabitant or former cohabitant, a relative of a civil partner or cohabitant and a party to a civil partnership agreement.[2] Evidence of the agreement to form a civil partnership may be in writing, by the gift of some token or by some ceremony before others in accordance with s 44(3) and (4). The agreement may be relied upon for 3 years after its termination.[3]

8.13 A former civil partner without any right to occupy the property may apply for an occupation order under s 35; a same sex cohabitant or former cohabitant under s 36. Previously, a same sex partner did not count as a cohabitant and was unable to apply if he had no right to occupy the property, though he might persuade a court to make a non-molestation order in similar terms to an occupation order. However, the definition in s 62 has now been changed both by the Civil Partnership Act 2004, Sch 9, para 13 and by the Domestic Violence, Crime and Victims Act 2004, s 3. The Domestic Violence, Crime and Victims Act 2004 is likely to come into force before the Civil Partnership Act 2004.

8.14 A civil partner or other associated person may apply for a non-molestation injunction under s 42.

8.15 Where a person is likely to be subject to violence at home, the local authority normally has a duty to re-house them under homelessness legislation pursuant to the Housing Act 1996, s 177. This now covers conflict between civil partners or former civil partners, even if they have never lived together.[4] It also covers unregistered partners or former partners, provided they have lived together in the same household.

Tenancies

8.16 Assignments of public sector tenancies and disposals of land previously owned by local authorities (eg under the right to buy or in protected areas) or by Housing Action Trusts are subject to statutory restrictions. The exemptions for spouses are extended to civil partners as follows:

---

1   Family Law Act 1996 (FLA 1996), s 37(1A) inserted by the Civil Partnership Act 2004 (CPA 2004), Sch 4, para 8.
2   FLA 1996, ss 62 and 63, as amended by CPA 2004, Sch 4, paras 13 and 14. Previously, same sex partners had to 'live or have lived in the same household' to be associated.
3   FLA 1996, s 33(2A) and s 42(4ZA) inserted by CPA 2004, Sch 4, paras 4(3) and 9 respectively.
4   CPA 2004, Sch 8, para 61.

— An assignment of a tenancy to a civil partner or unregistered same sex cohabitant where the assignee would be qualified to succeed the tenant if the tenant died (see **7.53** and **7.54** above). This does not apply to a demoted tenancy.

— A disposal between civil partners or former civil partners of land which has been purchased from the local authority[1] or was subject to a grant under the Housing Grants, Construction and Regeneration Act 1996.[2]

— A property adjustment order or order for sale upon the ending of a civil partnership.[3] After a property adjustment order in respect of a secure tenancy, the new tenant will be entitled to the benefit of improvements made by his former civil partner;[4] in respect of a secure, introductory or demoted tenancy, the new tenant will not count as a successor unless his civil partner was a successor.[5]

A civil partner[6] or cohabitant (which includes a same sex cohabitant)[7] may apply for a transfer of the family home from their partner under the Family Law Act 1996, Sch 7 if it is held under a statutory, protected, secure or assured tenancy or assured agricultural occupancy. For civil partners, such an order may be made only upon ancillary relief; for cohabitants, upon the breakdown of their cohabitation.

8.17   Grounds for possession of tenancies are extended under the Civil Partnership Act 2004, Sch 8. Where it is a ground for possession that a landlord requires the demised premises as a residence for himself or a member of his family, this includes his civil partner.[8] The ground for possession of a secure or assured tenancy on the basis of domestic violence is extended to same sex couples, whether registered as civil partners or not.[9]

8.18   The duty on a landlord not to discriminate on the grounds of sex, race or disability does not apply in respect of small dwellings shared by the landlord or his near relatives, which class is extended to include a civil partner.[10]

8.19   Civil partners and former civil partners of secure and assured tenants may delay or suspend enforcement of a possession order if they have home rights and are in

---

1   CPA 2004, Sch 8, paras 18 and 30 amending Housing Act 1985, ss 39(2)(b), 160(2)(b) and 160(3).

2   Such a disposal may be to any member of the transferor's family as defined by Housing Act 1985, s 113 as amended by CPA 2004, Sch 8, para 27 to include a civil partner or same sex cohabitant.

3   CPA 2004, Sch 8, paras 16, 19, 23–24, 50, 53–54, 56, 58, 60 and 63 amending Housing Act 1980, s 54(2), Housing Act 1985, s 39(3), Housing Act 1985, s 90(3)(a) and Housing Act 1988, s 91(3)(b), Sch 11, para 4, s 15, s 133(3), s 134(2)(a), s 143I(3) and s 143K(2) and Housing Act 1996, s 160 and Housing Grants, Construction and Regeneration Act 1996, s 54(3) respectively.

4   CPA 2004, Sch 8, paras 25–26 and Sch 10, paras 19–20 amending Housing Act 1985, s 99B(2) and s 101(3).

5   CPA 2004, Sch 8, paras 21, 52 and 57 amending Housing Act 1985, s 88 and Housing Act 1996, s 132 and s 143J(5) respectively.

6   CPA 2004, Sch 9, para 16 amending FLA 1996, Sch 7, para 1.

7   See **8.13**.

8   CPA 2004, Sch 8, paras 2, 12, 14, 43 and 46 amending Landlord and Tenant Act 1954, Sch 3, para 1(e), Rent (Agriculture) Act 1976, Sch 4, Part 1, Case 9, para 1, Rent Act 1977, Sch 15, Part 1, Case 9 and Local Government and Housing Act 1989, Sch 2, Part 1, Ground 1, and Sch 10, para 5(1)(c) respectively.

9   CPA 2004, Sch 8, paras 33, 43 amending Housing Act 1985, Sch 2, Part 1, Ground 2A and Housing Act 1988, Sch 2, Part 2, Ground 14A respectively.

10   CPA 2004, Sch 27, paras 54, 55 and 150 amending Sex Discrimination Act 1975, s 82(5), Race Relations Act 1976, s 78(5) and Disability Discrimination Act 1995, s 23.

occupation.[1] Cohabitants and former cohabitants with an occupation order under the Family Law Act 1996, s 36 in respect of an assured tenancy are similarly protected. The Civil Partnership Act 2004 has not extended this protection to protected and statutory tenancies under the Rent Act 1977. This is probably an oversight and may be corrigible by reinterpretation of the Rent Act 1977, s 100(4A) and (4B) under the Human Rights Act 1998, s 3, as it appears to be contrary to Articles 8 (right to one's home) and 14 (prohibition of discrimination) of the European Convention on Human Rights.[2]

8.20   Under the right to buy, a civil partner of the tenant is to be treated in the same way as a spouse.[3] In addition, same sex cohabitants and relatives by civil partnership are treated as members of a secure tenant's family under Parts 4 and 5 of the Housing Act 1985 and Part 1 and Part 5, Chapter 1 of the Housing Act 1996.[4]

8.21   The requirement under Housing Act 1985, s 554(2A) on a registered social landlord to grant a secure tenancy to a spouse or former or surviving spouse upon acquiring his home is extended to civil partners, former and surviving civil partners.[5]

8.22   In relation to Housing Action Trusts, legal assistance may be extended to the civil partner of a tenant whose home sold and who is in dispute with the new landlord.[6]

8.23   Where a tenant is in arrears of rent, his landlord may levy distress on his civil partner's possessions at the property.[7]

PROPERTY AND FINANCE

8.24   The Law of Property Act 1925, s 205(1)(xxi) defines 'valuable consideration' as including marriage. The Civil Partnership Act 2004, Sch 27, para 7 extends this to include civil partnership. Schedule 27, para 153 extend the definition of 'family charges' under the Trusts of Land and Appointment of Trustees Act 1996 to include charges granted in consideration of the formation of a civil partnership.

8.25   The Law of Property Act 1925, s 149(6) is amended by the Civil Partnership Act 2004, Sch 8, para 1 to make provision for leases determinable upon formation of civil partnership in the same way as for those determinable upon marriage. (But leases determinable on marriage will not thereby be determinable upon the formation of a civil partnership or vice versa.) Consequential amendments are made to provide for commonholds in respect of such leases[8] and their extension or enfranchisement.[9] A landlord may defeat a tenant's right to extension or enfranchisement and exclude the right to manage on the ground that he or a member of his family (including a civil

---

1   CPA 2004, Sch 9, paras 18 and 23 amending Housing Act 1985, s 85 and Housing Act 1988, s 9.
2   See *Ghaidan v Mendoza* [2004] 3 All ER 411, HL; [2004] 2 FLR 600, HL.
3   CPA 2004, Sch 8, paras 28–31 and 34–35.
4   CPA 2004, Sch 8, paras 27 and 51.
5   CPA 2004, Sch 8, para 32.
6   CPA 2004, Sch 8, para 42.
7   CPA 2004, Sch 27, para 3 amending Law of Distress Amendment Act 1908, s 4(1).
8   CPA 2004, Sch 8, paras 64–65 amending Commonhold and Leasehold Reform Act 2002.
9   CPA 2004, Sch 8, paras 3–6 and 47 amending Leasehold Reform Act 1967 and Leasehold Reform, Housing and Urban Development Act 1993.

partner) needs to occupy the premises.[1] Notice to determine an agricultural lease determinable upon formation of civil partnership need not comply with the Agricultural Tenancies Act 1995, s 7.[2]

8.26   The disposal of the landlord's interest under a property adjustment order or order for sale upon the ending of a civil partnership or by gift to his civil partner, his same sex cohabitant or a relative by civil partnership will not trigger his tenants' right of first refusal under the Landlord and Tenant Act 1987.

8.27   The statutory power under the Trustee Act 1925 to advance trust property to a minor upon his marriage is extended to cover the formation of a civil partnership as well. The claims of spouses under a protective trust are extended to civil partners.[3]

8.28   Friendly societies may provide insurance policies which pay out in the event of the beneficiary forming a civil partnership.[4]

8.29   A credit union may provide that, where a person is a member of a credit union, his civil partner, former civil partner and relations by civil partnership shall be automatically entitled to membership.[5]

INSOLVENCY

8.30   Where a trustee in bankruptcy applies under the Trusts of Land and Appointment of Trustees Act 1996, s 14 for the sale of property in which the bankrupt's civil partner or former civil partner lives, the court may take into account the latter's needs and resources and his conduct in so far as it has contributed to the bankruptcy in deciding whether to order a sale.[6] However, after one year from the vesting of the property in the trustee, the creditors' interest will prevail save in circumstances which are exceptional.

8.31   Where the home of the bankrupt's civil partner or former civil partner has vested in the trustee in bankruptcy for 3 years, it will automatically revert to the bankrupt pursuant to the Insolvency Act 1986, s 283A unless the trustee takes specified steps to prevent this.[7]

8.32   Under the Insolvency Act 1986, transactions and preferences made by a bankrupt or by a company subject to winding-up may be set aside or adjusted if they were not genuine and for value. The formation of civil partnership is not sufficient valuable consideration for these purposes.[8] A civil partner or another 'associate' of the bankrupt or of an officer of the company who benefits from the transaction or preference has the burden of showing that it should not be set aside.[9] Where the trustee in bankruptcy

---

1   CPA 2004, Sch 8, paras 7, 48 and 66.
2   CPA 2004, Sch 8, para 49.
3   CPA 2004, Sch 27, paras 5 and 6 amending Trustee Act 1925, ss 31(2)(i) and 33(1)(ii).
4   CPA 2004, Sch 27, para 143 amending Friendly Societies Act 1992, Sch 2, Head A, class II.
5   CPA 2004, Sch 27, para 61 amending Credit Unions Act 1979, s 31(1).
6   CPA 2004, Sch 27, para 118 amending Insolvency Act 1986, s 335A.
7   CPA 2004, Sch 27, para 113.
8   CPA 2004, Sch 27, paras 112, 119 and 121 amending Insolvency Act 1986, ss 215, 339 and 423 respectively.
9   CPA 2004, Sch 27, para 122 amending Insolvency Act 1986, s 435.

transfers property to the bankrupt's civil partner, he must give notice to any creditors' committee.[1]

8.33 Credit advanced by a person to his civil partner who becomes bankrupt is postponed to all other unsecured debts under the bankruptcy.[2] At a creditors' meeting under a voluntary arrangement, the votes of a civil partner of the bankrupt may be discounted.[3]

SOCIAL SECURITY AND TAX CREDITS

8.34 The Civil Partnership Act 2004, s 254 and Sch 24 place civil partners in the same position as spouses and same sex cohabitants in the same position as opposite-sex cohabitants with regard to social security, tax credits and child support (under the old regime). The relevant regulations will be amended accordingly.

8.35 This represents a very significant change for same sex couples, whether registered as civil partners or not. Previously they have been treated much more favourably than heterosexual couples in respect of social security payments and tax credits because they were not treated as a single economic unit. The government will publicise this change to claimants. However, it has also stated that it will:[4]

'seek to avoid asking for repayments from someone who has inadvertently made a mistake and failed to appreciate that, although they have not entered into a civil partnership, nonetheless they are affected because they now form a same-sex couple.'

8.36 The definition of 'same sex cohabitation' for these purposes is likely to prove one of the more controversial aspects of the Civil Partnership Act 2004 in practice:[5]

'two people of the same sex are to be regarded as living together as if they were civil partners if, but only if, they would be regarded as living together as husband and wife were they instead two people of the opposite sex.'

Given how closely civil partnership mirrors marriage, the proviso in this definition appears tautologous. However, its purpose is to ensure that existing case law on cohabitation will apply equally to two persons living in the same household, whether they are of the same or different sex.

8.37 Case law has identified the following 'signposts' to establish cohabitation:

— a shared home;
— shared tasks and duties of daily life;
— stability and a degree of permanence in the relationship;

---

1   CPA 2004.
2   CPA 2004, Sch 27, para 16 amending Insolvency Act 1986, s 329.
3   CPA 2004, Sch 27, para 122 amending Insolvency Act 1986, s 435.
4   Baroness Hollis of Heigham – *Hansard*, HL Grand Committee, col GC490 (25 May 2004).
5   CPA 2004, Sch 24, paras 5, 41(3), 124(5), 127, 138, 143 and 147 inserting Child Support Act 1991, Sch 1, para 6(5A), Social Security Contributions and Benefits Act 1992, s 122(1A), Jobseekers Act 1995, s 35(1A), Child Support Act 1995, s 10(7A) in respect of child maintenance bonus, Social Security Act 1998, s 72(3) in respect of child benefit for lone parents, State Pension Credits Act 2002, s 17(1A) and Tax Credits Act 2002, s 48(2) respectively.

— financial support or a mixing of funds;
— a sexual relationship;
— a bond with the other's children;
— a financial motive for the parties' denial of cohabitation;
— public acknowledgement and the perception of friends.[1]

The most important of these is clearly a sexual relationship (although a past sexual relationship may be sufficient). However, the Department for Work and Pensions has tended not to enquire about this for reasons of privacy. In practice, it tends to assume a sexual relationship between two home-sharers of different sex, to some extent leaving it up to the claimants to protest and, if necessary, appeal on the basis that they are just friends.

8.38 Home-sharing between friends of the same sex is likely to be much more common than between friends of the opposite sex; the assumption that they have a sexual relationship is much less likely to be justified. Claimants may object very strongly to being labelled a same sex couple. Because of the sensitivity of the matter, the government intends to re-draft the test which they will apply for cohabitation (whether between persons of the same or opposite sex).[2] In the meantime, they are giving special training to their staff at the Department for Work and Pensions and the Inland Revenue.

8.39 Thus, civil partners and same sex couples will be treated in the same way as spouses and heterosexual cohabitants for the purposes of income-related benefits, in particular income support, housing benefit, council tax benefit, income-based jobseeker's allowance, pension credits and tax credits. Relations by civil partnership will also be treated in the same way as relations by marriage (eg step-children).

8.40 More specific statutory changes have been required to ensure that civil partners who live together and cohabitants may make only a single claim for Income Support (IS) or Income-based Jobseekers Allowance (IBJSA), mortgage interest payments,[3] housing benefit and council tax. The needs and resources of both will taken into account in assessing benefit.[4] This will be reduced where one or both is engaged in a trade dispute.[5] Adjustments to benefits may be made where a couple's benefits overlap.[6] If a person applies for IBJSA, his partner's IS may terminate[7] and the claim be treated as a joint claim, where both partners have to comply with directions to improve their job prospects.[8]

8.41 Adult dependency increases apply to civil partners, but these will not be payable whilst the civil partner is absent from Great Britain or in custody.[9]

1   *Crake v Supplementary Benefits Commission* [1982] 1 All ER 498; *Kimber v Kimber* [2000] 1 FLR 383.
2   Baroness Hollis of Heigham – *Hansard,* HL Grand Committee, col GC466 (25 May 2004).
3   CPA 2004, Sch 24, para 57 amending Social Security Administration Act 1992, s 15A.
4   CPA 2004, Sch 24, paras 42,45 and 46 amending Social Security Contributions and Benefits Act 1992 (SSCBA 1992), ss 124, 132 and 137 respectively.
5   CPA 2004, Sch 24, paras 43, 44, 120 and 121 amending SSCBA 1992, ss 126 and 127 and Jobseekers Act 1995, ss 15 and 15A respectively.
6   CPA 2004, Sch 24, para 59 amending SSCBA 1992, s 73.
7   CPA 2004, Sch 24, para 23 amending Jobseekers Act 1995, s 31.
8   CPA 2004, Sch 24, paras 118 and 119 amending Jobseekers Act 1995, ss 1 and 3 respectively.
9   CPA 2004, Sch 24, paras 38 and 39 amending SSCBA 1992, ss 113 and 114 respectively.

Child support, civil partner's maintenance and child benefit

8.42 The Secretary of State may retain any maintenance he collects in respect of a child, spouse or civil partner for whom benefit is payable, save to the extent it exceeds such benefit.[1] He may recover IS or IBJSA from the claimant's civil partner if the latter is liable to maintain him.[2] A failure to maintain a civil partner resulting in a claim for IS or IBJSA can amount to an offence contrary to the Social Security Administration Act 1992, s 105.[3]

8.43 To the extent that a spouse or cohabitant's means are taken into account in a Child Support Act assessment under the old rules, so too will a civil partner's or same sex cohabitant's.[4] Where a child marries or forms a civil partnership, he will cease to be the subject of a Child Support Act claim.[5]

8.44 In calculating guardian's allowance, account will be taken of payments to the guardian by the civil partner of the parent as if they had been made by the parent.[6]

8.45 In determining whether a parent should receive child benefit, the fact that the parent's civil partner is meeting some of the costs of the child will be taken into account.[7] Where child benefit continues to be payable following a child's death and the parent also dies, the entitlement will devolve upon his civil partner.[8] Child benefit ceases to be payable in respect of a child who forms a civil partnership.[9]

Incapacity

8.46 Entitlement to incapacity benefit may take account of the contributions of a deceased civil partner and may disregard certain increases in a civil partner's state pension.[10] Entitlement to disablement pension and industrial diseases benefit may take into account the needs of a civil partner or same sex cohabitant.[11]

8.47 A relative by civil partnership is included within the class of relatives who may be entitled to carer's allowance.[12]

8.48 Means-testing for renovation grants and disabled facilities grants may take into account the means and needs of a civil partner.[13]

---

1   CPA 2004, Sch 24, para 60 amending Social Security Administration Act 1992 (SSAA 1992), s 74A.
2   CPA 2004, Sch 24, paras 63 and 122 amending SSAA 1992, s 107 and Jobseekers Act 1995, s 23.
3   As amended by CPA 2004, Sch 24, para 62.
4   CPA 2004, Sch 24, para 4 amending Child Support Act 1991 (CSA 1991), Sch 1, para 6(5)(b).
5   CPA 2004, Sch 24, para 3 amending CSA 1991, s 55.
6   CPA 2004, Sch 24, para 34 amending SSCBA 1992, s 77.
7   CPA 2004, Sch 24, para 47 amending SSCBA 1992, s 143.
8   CPA 2004, Sch 24, para 48 amending SSCBA 1992, s 145A.
9   CPA 2004, Sch 24, para 54 amending SSCBA 1992, Sch 9, para 3.
10   CPA 2004, Sch 24, paras 14 and 15 amending SSCBA 1992, ss 30A and 30B.
11   CPA 2004, Sch 24, paras 52 and 53 amending SSCBA 1992, Schs 7A and 8.
12   CPA 2004, Sch 24, para 41(2) amending SSCBA 1992, s 122.
13   CPA 2004, Sch 8, para 62, amending Housing Grants, Construction and Regeneration Act 1996, s 30(6)(a).

State pension

8.49   When both civil partners have reached pension age, each will be entitled to rely on the other's National Insurance contributions if the other was born after 6 April 1950. Because of the different retirement ages for men and women, female civil partners will qualify from 2010 onwards, males from 2015 onwards.[1] As with divorce, where a civil partnership has been dissolved or annulled, a person will be entitled to rely on his former civil partner's contributions to the date of dissolution or annulment.[2] Adult dependency increases will apply to civil partners from 2010.[3]

TAXATION

8.50   The Civil Partnership Act 2004 makes almost no changes to taxation, except for tax credits[4] and council tax (both of which changes are disadvantageous to civil partners). However, the government has stated that it will treat civil partnerships in the same way as marriage for the purpose of tax and will make the relevant changes in the next Finance Bill. These changes are likely to take effect at the same time as the Civil Partnership Act 2004 is brought into effect. They are likely to include the extension of the exemptions from inheritance tax, capital gains tax and stamp duty land tax and perhaps also the married couples' age allowances. This will have important consequences for tax planning.

8.51   Lifetime gifts and gifts upon death between spouses are exempt from inheritance tax (unless the donor is domiciled in the UK and the donee is domiciled outside the UK, when only the first £55,000 is exempt).[5]

8.52   Lifetime gifts and transfers at an undervalue within 7 years of the death of the donor are generally liable to inheritance tax. However, there are exemptions for gifts in consideration of marriage (currently £5,000 by a parent, £2,500 by a grandparent and £1,000 by any other person) and for maintenance of a spouse and children.

8.53   For the purposes of capital gains tax, where a person transfers a capital asset to another (eg his partner) he will normally be treated as if he had received full value for the asset in return and be taxed on the notional profit accordingly. Spouses who live together are exempt from this rule.[6] Upon a transfer, the donee steps into the shoes of the donor with respect to the asset: the acquisition cost and period of ownership of the donor are treated as those of the donee. This exemption ends at the end of the tax year in which the spouses separate, save in respect of the family home.[7] The exemption is very useful in tax planning as one spouse may have an unused annual capital gains allowance or pay capital gains tax at a lower rate or be able to set off capital gains tax losses. Intending civil partners may therefore benefit from waiting until they have registered their civil partnership before they realise assets or transfer assets between themselves.

---

1   CPA 2004, Sch 24, paras 25 and 29 amending SSCBA 1992, ss 48A and 51A respectively.
2   CPA 2004, Sch 24, paras 24 and 40 amending SSCBA 1992, ss 48 and 121 respectively.
3   CPA 2004, Sch 24, paras 36 and 37 amending SSCBA 1992, ss 83A and 85 respectively.
4   Above.
5   Inheritance Tax Act 1984, s 18.
6   Taxation and Chargeable Gains Act 1992, s 58.
7   Inland Revenue concession D6.

8.54 There is a further exemption from capital gains tax in respect of a person's 'only or main residence'. However, spouses may claim this exemption in respect of only one property between them,[1] whereas unmarried partners may each elect a property to exempt. Intending civil partners who each own a home may therefore benefit from the disposal of one of the properties before registering their civil partnership (especially if a sizable capital gain has already accrued).

8.55 Where a person creates a settlement, unless both he and his spouse are excluded they will be liable for income tax on any income and capital gains tax on any capital gain.[2] This does not apply to a future spouse.[3] It is therefore important to create any settlement intended to benefit an intended civil partner before registering the civil partnership.

8.56 Transfers between 'connected persons' attract particular attention from the Inland Revenue lest they should be at an undervalue. Capital gains tax may therefore be charged upon the market price assessed by the Revenue. 'Connected persons' include a spouse's brother, sister, ancestor or lineal descendant.[4] If a person proposes to enter a transaction with a relative of his intended civil partner, he should consider doing so before registering the civil partnership.

8.57 Stamp duty land tax is not payable where property is transferred between spouses under a divorce settlement or by gift. However, where the parties to a transfer are 'connected persons', stamp duty land tax will be payable on the market value of the asset rather than the price paid.

8.58 With respect to income tax, the married couple's allowance has been abolished save where one spouse was aged 65 or over at 5 April 2000. As the allowance is being phased out, it is doubtful whether the government will extend it to civil partners.

8.59 The Civil Partnership Act 2004, Sch 27, para 140 provides that civil partners are jointly and severally liable for council tax in the same way as married couples.

EMPLOYMENT

8.60 Employers commonly extend a number of benefits to their staff in relation to their spouses and partners. The most important is the payment of death in service benefits or a survivor's pension (which is dealt with at **7.48** and **7.49**). In addition, they may provide bereavement, parental, adoption or carer's leave, relocation allowances, travel benefits, private healthcare and discounts on company services and products. Some of these benefits are required by the Employment Rights Act 1996. In particular, an employee has the right to take time off work to deal with certain emergencies involving his civil partner, as for a spouse or other dependants.[5]

---

1   Taxation and Chargeable Gains Act 1992 (TCGA 1992), s 222(6)(a).
2   Income and Corporation Taxes Act 1988 (ICTA 1988), s 660A and TCGA 1992, s 77 respectively.
3   ICTA 1988, s 660(3)(a) and TCGA 1992, s 77(3)(a).
4   TCGA 1992, s 286(2).
5   CPA 2004, Sch 27, para 151 amending Employment Rights Act 1996, s 57A(3).

8.61 The Employment Equality (Sexual Orientation) Regulations 2003 require employers not to discriminate on the grounds of sexual orientation.[1] Thus, the benefits available to unmarried opposite-sex couples must also be applied to same sex couples. Indirect discrimination, where a benefit is more likely to benefit couples of one sexuality, is also forbidden unless the employer can justify it as a proportionate means of achieving a legitimate aim.

8.62 However, Regulation 25 expressly allows employers to discriminate in favour of married persons in the provision of benefits. It is not clear how this affects civil partnership following the Civil Partnership Act 2004, s 251,[2] which extends the protection of married persons from discrimination in employment under the Sex Discrimination Act 1975, s 3 to civil partners. This provision probably allows employers to favour civil partners over unmarried and unregistered couples. It may also bar discrimination between civil partners and married couples. If it does not, it seems likely that the government will amend the Regulations to rectify this. In any event, married couples will remain privileged over unregistered and unmarried couples.

8.63 Section 251 also allows an employer to offer jobs to a couple who are married or registered as civil partners without that amounting to discrimination on the ground of sex. The government has expressed the view that this provision also prevents an employer from discriminating between a married couple and civil partners in offers of dual employment.[3]

8.64 The civil partner of an employee of a public airport company may take part in an employees' share scheme, under the Airports Act 1986, s 20.[4]

8.65 An employer is not required to insure an employee who is his civil partner.[5] The health and safety requirements of the Offices, Shops and Railway Premises Act 1963 are excluded where the only employees are family members of the employer, which class is extended to include civil partners.

8.66 It is an offence contrary to the Trade Union and Labour Relations Act 1992, s 241 to intimidate or annoy a person's civil partner in connection with industrial action.[6]

8.67 A person is disqualified from being a member of the Valuation Tribunal Service if his civil partner is an employee thereof.[7]

---

1   SI 2003/1661 implementing the European Equal Treatment Directive, Council Directive 2000/78/EC of 27 November 2000. See also Employment Equality (Sexual Orientation) (Amendment) Regulations 2003.
2   See **2.6** and **7.49**.
3   Baroness Crawley – *Hansard*, HL Grand Committee, cols GC457–8 (25 May 2004).
4   CPA 2004, Sch 27, para 111.
5   CPA 2004, Sch 27, para 33 amending Employer's Liability (Compulsory Insurance) Act 1969, s 2(2)(a).
6   CPA 2004, Sch 27, para 145.
7   CPA 2004, Sch 27, para 171 amending Local Government Act 2003, Sch 4, para 2(1)(a).

BUSINESS REGULATION AND LICENSING

8.68 An estate agent must fully disclose to their clients any direct or indirect personal interest. This includes an interest of their civil partner or relatives by civil partnership.[1] The rules regarding disclosure of spouses' interests by members of Transport for London, company directors, members of local authorities, building society directors and actuaries appointed by friendly societies and restricting dealings by their spouses are extended by the Civil Partnership Act 2004 to include civil partners.[2] The controls in relations to persons connected to a charity are extended to cover civil partners and any corporate body or institution in which they have an interest.[3]

8.69 In determining whether a person is a 'controller' of an undertaking under the Financial Services and Markets Act 2000, the holdings of his civil partner and other 'associates' will be taken into account.[4] Similarly, in determining whether two enterprises are under common control or what business a persons carries on under the Enterprise Act 2002, the holdings of a civil partner, a former civil partner, a relative of a civil partner or former civil partner and a business partner's civil partner or former civil partner will be taken into account.[5] In determining whether a person controls a body corporate under the Enterprise Act 2002, s 222, the holdings of a cohabitant or former cohabitant will also be taken into account.[6]

8.70 Where a trustee in bankruptcy or a member of a creditors' committee deals with his own civil partner in respect of the bankrupt's estate, the transaction is liable to be set aside or compensation may be payable.[7]

8.71 The Office of Fair Trading licenses individuals under the Consumer Credit Act 1974. They may take into account the conduct not only of the individual but also of their associates, which class is extended to include civil partners and relatives by civil partnership.[8] Where a spouse is barred from holding a broadcasting licence under the Broadcasting Act 1990, so too is a civil partner.[9] In respect of certificates of consent under the Gaming Act 1968, the Gaming Board may take into account the holdings of a civil partner in assessing who controls a corporate body.

8.72 Under the Licensing Act 2003, s 101, temporary events at the same venue held by the same person or by an associate of his (including his civil partner) must be at least 24 hours apart.[10]

---

1   CPA 2004, Sch 27, para 62.
2   CPA 2004, Sch 27, paras 38, 39, 99–105, 123, 128, 133, 134, 141 and 142 amending Local Government Act 1972, ss 95 and 96, Companies Act 1985, ss 203, 327, 328, 346, 430E, 742A and Sch 7, para 2B(3), Building Society Act 1986, s 70, Companies Act 1989, s 52, Local Government and Housing Act 1989, ss 19 and 69 and Friendly Societies Act 1992, ss 77 and 119A .
3   CPA 2004, Sch 27, para 147 amending Charities Act 1993, Sch 5, para 1(e).
4   CPA 2004, Sch 27, para 165 amending Financial Services and Markets Act 2000, s 422(4)(a).
5   CPA 2004, Sch 27, para 168 amending Enterprise Act 2003, s 127.
6   CPA 2004, Sch 27, para 169.
7   CPA 2004, Sch 27, para 122 amending Insolvency Act 1986, s 435.
8   CPA 2004, Sch 27, para 51.
9   CPA 2004, Sch 27, para 139.
10   CPA 2004, Sch 27, para 170.

IMMIGRATION

8.73 Most immigration law is contained in the Immigration Rules. As a result, few changes are effected by the Civil Partnership Act 2004. However, it is envisaged that the government will amend the Rules to treat civil partnership in the same way as marriage.

8.74 Where one same sex partner is a British citizen or has indefinite leave to remain, the other partner currently needs to show 2 years' prior cohabitation before the Home Office will grant leave to enter and remain. Thereafter, he must wait a further 2 years before he can apply for indefinite leave to remain. In its White Paper, the government has stated that it will remove the initial 2-year requirement for civil partners, placing them in the same position as married persons.[1] The other requirements remain, namely that the couple intend to live together permanently in the UK and will be self-supporting and have a home of their own. A person with leave to remain is also free to take up employment in the UK.

8.75 A spouse must apply from abroad for leave to enter and remain. An overstayer or illegal entrant or a person with leave of 6 months or less will almost always have to leave the UK first. It is likely that this will apply to civil partners too. It is not possible to switch from one basis for leave to another in order to remain in the UK.

8.76 A fiancé(e), however, may be granted leave to enter for 6 months in order to marry and then apply for leave to remain as a spouse whilst remaining in the UK.[2] The government has indicated that it will extend this concession to the intended civil partner of a UK national.[3] There seems to be no reason why this should not also apply to the intended civil partner of someone with indefinite leave to remain. This concession is likely to be particularly valuable for same sex couples, as it is much easier to marry abroad than to register a civil partnership. The Civil Partnership Act 2004, s 210 does provide for the registration of civil partnerships in British consulates abroad where that country does not provide sufficient facilities for registration. However, this is subject to the proviso that the local authorities do not object. This may prove problematic even in some states of the USA, let alone Iran or Saudi Arabia.

8.77 The Civil Partnership Act 2004, Sch 23 restricts registration of civil partnership where one partner is subject to immigration control in the same way as the Asylum and Immigration (Treatment of Claimants, etc) Act 2004 does for civil registration of marriage. Registration will be allowed only if the person:

— has entry clearance granted expressly for the purpose of enabling him to form a civil partnership in the UK; or
— has the written permission of the Secretary of State to form a civil partnership in the UK; or
— falls within a class specified for the purpose in regulations.

---

1   *Civil Partnership: A Framework for the Legal Recognition of Same-sex Couples* (June 2003) para 7.2.
2   Immigration Rules, paras 290–295.
3   *Responses to Civil Partnership* (WEU, November 2003 DT) p 38.

The government has indicated that those with less than 6 months' leave to remain will not normally be granted permission to register, but will have to leave the UK and apply for permission to enter in order to register a civil partnership.[1]

8.78 The provisions of the Asylum and Immigration (Treatment of Claimants etc) Act 2004 may be contrary to Articles 12 and 14 of the European Convention on Human Rights in that they restrict the right to marry on the basis of religion. Church weddings are not affected by the Act. The purpose of the Act is to prevent sham marriages in order to evade immigration controls.[2] It is doubtful whether this is a sufficient justification for the discrimination: why should someone prepared to marry in the Church of England be more likely to be genuine than someone who will only marry by civil ceremony? If the Act is found to be incompatible, this will not necessarily affect the Civil Partnership Act 2004, Sch 23, which does not discriminate on the ground of religion. However, discriminating between intended spouses and civil partners in this area appears to be contrary to government policy, if not necessarily contrary to the European Convention on Human Rights, so repeal is possible.

8.79 Where the officers involved in registering a civil partnership suspect that it is a sham, they must report their suspicions to the Home Office.[3]

8.80 Under the current Rules, unmarried partners (including same sex partners) of British citizens and of people settled in the UK may apply for leave to enter and remain if their relationship is of at least 2 years' standing. This is subject to requirements that the couple will be self-supporting and that any other marriage or similar relationship of the parties has broken down. The government has not indicated any intention to alter these provisions, although it is envisaged that the reference to marriage will be extended to include civil partnership.

8.81 The Immigration Rules also make particular provision for spouses in a number of other contexts, in particular in relation to bereavement, domestic violence and foreign nationals with work permits or student visas who wish to bring their spouses. The government has not yet indicated whether it will extend such provision to civil partners.

8.82 Civil partners have the same rights as spouses to acquire or resume British nationality by registration or naturalisation and to renounce British nationality.[4]

8.83 The Immigration Act 1971, s 3 provides for the deportation of members of the family of a person subject to a deportation order. This is extended to civil partners.[5]

ELECTIONS AND STATISTICS

8.84 The Representation of the People Acts 1983 and 2000 apply certain rights and responsibilities to spouses, in particular in relation to the electoral register, voting by

---

1   Lord Rooker – *Hansard*, HL Deb, col 75 (15 June 2004).
2   Lord Rooker – *Hansard*, HL Deb, col 685 (15 June 2004).
3   CPA 2004, Sch 27, para 162 inserting Immigration and Asylum Act 1999, s 24A.
4   CPA 2004, Sch 27, paras 71–78 amending British Nationality Act 1981.
5   CPA 2004, Sch 27, para 37.

proxy, assisting disabled spouses to cast their vote, and attending election events with a candidate. These are extended to civil partners.[1]

8.85 The government has indicated that on most government forms it will no longer ask about 'marital status' but about 'civil status' and no distinction will be made between marriage and civil partnership. Thus, civil partners will not be required to disclose their sexual orientation every time they fill out a form.[2]

8.86 However, during a census information may be collected in connection with civil partnerships as it is with marriage under the Census Act 1920, Sch, para 5.[3] Upon registration of death, information may be collected on the civil partnership status of the deceased and the age of the surviving civil partner under the Population (Statistics) Act 1938, Sch, para 2.[4] When persons enter and leave the UK by air, information may be collected about their civil partnership status under the Statistics of Trade Act 1947, s 10.[5]

PRISON VISITING

8.87 The present rules treat unmarried partners (whether heterosexual or same sex) as close relatives entitled to visit prisoners and to means-tested assistance with the cost of visiting. The government has indicated in its White Paper that it intends to amend the rules to include civil partners within the definition of close relatives regardless of whether the relationship subsisted immediately prior to imprisonment.[6]

COMPELLABILITY

8.88 The Civil Partnership Act 2004, s 84 provides that a civil partner will not be compellable as a witness in circumstances where a spouse is not. Schedule 24 specifically extends the following statutory privileges against incriminating a spouse to cover civil partners:

— the Child Support Act 1991, s 15, in respect of an inspector's investigation (para 2);
— the Social Security Administration Act 1992, s 109B (para 64).

8.89 Schedule 27 does likewise as follows:

— the Civil Evidence Act 1968 in respect of civil proceedings (para 30);
— the Medicines Act 1968, s 114(4) in respect of an investigation regarding the regulation of medicines (para 32);
— the Criminal Damage Act 1971, s 9 (para 36);

---

1   CPA 2004, Sch 27, paras 80–85 and 164 amending Representation of the People Act 1983, ss 14, 16, 59, 61, 141 and Sch 1, rules 11(4), 35(2) and 39(3)(b) and RPA 2000, Sch 4, paras 3(3)(c) and 6(6).
2   *Responses to Civil Partnership* (WEU, November 2003 DT) p 41.
3   CPA 2004, Sch 27, para 4.
4   CPA 2004, Sch 27, para 9.
5   CPA 2004, Sch 27, para 12.
6   *Civil Partnership: A Framework for the Legal Recognition of Same-sex Couples* (June 2003) paras 7.10–7.11.

— the Fair Trading Act 1973, s 30(6) in respect of contraventions of orders under s 22 thereof (para 47);
— the Consumer Credit Act 1974, s 165(3) (para 50);
— the Estate Agents Act 1979, s 27(4) (para 62);
— the Consumer Protection Act 1987, s 47 (para 126);
— the Civil Procedure Act 1997, s 7 in respect of orders for preserving evidence, etc (para 154);
— the National Minimum Wage Act 1998, s 14 in respect of official requests for information (para 155).

8.90 Conversely, Sch 27 provides that a person will be compellable in the following circumstances, even though he may incriminate his civil partner:

— an inquiry under the Explosive Substances Act 1883, s 6(2) (para 1);
— under the Supreme Court Act 1981, s 72 in respect of civil proceedings in the High Court relating to infringement of intellectual property or passing off (para 68);
— under the Police and Criminal Evidence Act 1984, s 80 in respect of an offence of violence against the witness where the witness was under 16 or a sexual offence against any person under 16 (although s 80A provides that the prosecution may not comment on a failure of a person to give evidence against their civil partner) (paras 96–97);
— under the Food and Environment Protection Act 1985, Sch 2, para 2A(1), in respect of an officer's investigation (para 109);
— an order under the Family Law Act, s 33 to disclose the whereabouts of a child (para 124);
— the duties under the Children Act 1989, ss 48(2) and 50(11) to assist in the recovery of a child who may be in need of emergency protection and to comply with a request in connection with an order for the recovery of an abducted child (paras 130–131).

8.91 A civil partner is also compellable in the following circumstances, but the evidence elicited is not admissible in criminal proceedings:

— proceedings relating to property or trusts, pursuant to the Theft Act 1968, s 31 (but the evidence elicited may be admissible in criminal proceedings outwith the Theft Act) (para 28);
— a statement taken by an inspector under the Health and Safety at Work Act 1974, s 20(2) (para 49);
— under an order under the Child Abduction and Custody Act 1985 to disclose information relating to the whereabouts of a child subject to an application for his return under the Hague Convention (but such evidence is admissible in proceedings for perjury) (para 110);
— in care proceedings and other public law proceedings under the Children Act 1989, Parts IV and V (but similarly admissible in proceedings for perjury) (para 132);
— where a person or his civil partner may have committed an offence under the Land Registration Act 2002 (para 167).

8.92 A person may be required to answer questions about spent convictions in proceedings relating to the formation of a civil partnership by a minor.[1]

---

1 CPA 2004, Sch 27, para 53 amending Rehabilitation of Offenders Act 1974, s 7(2)(c).

OFFENCES

8.93 The Civil Partnerships Act 2004 creates several offences with respect to registration, which are dealt with in Chapter 4. Offences relating to other particular areas are dealt with in the appropriate part of this work. However, the Act also makes changes to existing criminal law to treat civil partnership in the same way as marriage.

8.94 It is a defence to a charge under the Sexual Offences Act 2003, ss 16–19, 25 or 26 (sexual offences in relation to children under 18) that the child in question was aged 16 or over and was married to or the civil partner of the defendant.[1]

8.95 For offences relating to the possession of indecent photographs of a child under the Protection of Children Act 1978, s 1A and under the Criminal Justice Act 1988, s 160, where the child was aged 16 or over, a defendant who was married to the child or living with the child as his partner in an enduring family relationship will not be guilty of an offence unless the child did not consent and the defendant did not reasonably believe that the child consented. The Civil Partnership Act 2004, Sch 27, paras 60 and 127 clarify that this also applies to civil partners. Presumably it will also apply to unregistered same sex partners 'in an enduring family relationship'.[2]

8.96 It is a defence to an offence under the Sexual Offences Act 2003, ss 38–41 (sexual activity by a care worker involving a person with a mental disorder) for the care worker to show that he was married to the person with a mental disorder and that the latter was over 16.[3]

8.97 The consent of the Director of Public Prosecutions (DPP) is required for criminal proceedings for theft of property from a civil partner in the same circumstances as regards the property of a spouse.[4]

8.98 Parties to a civil partnership will not be guilty of conspiracy with each other in the same circumstances as married persons, namely unless the conspiracy includes some one else.[5]

FUTURE RIGHTS AND RESPONSIBILITIES

8.99 The Civil Partnership Act 2004 applies most of the legal incidences of marriage to civil partnership. The policy of the Act is that civil partners should be treated equally to spouses wherever possible and that any differences from marriage must be objectively justifiable. It will also be arguable in many instances that this is also required by the Human Rights Act 1998 and Article 14 of the European Convention on Human Rights. The Civil Partnership Act 2004 provides two powers of delegated legislation to ensure continuing consistency between marriage and civil partnership.

---

1   CPA 2004, Sch 27, paras 173 and 174 amending Sexual Offences Act 2003, ss 23 and 28.
2   See *Ghaidan v Mendoza* above.
3   CPA 2004, Sch 27, para 175 amending Sexual Offences Act 2003, s 43.
4   CPA 2004, Sch 27, para 27 amending Theft Act 1968, s 30.
5   CPA 2004, Sch 27, para 56 amending Criminal Law Act 1977, s 2.

8.100 The Civil Partnership Act 2004, s 259 gives the government a wide general power to make further provision in respect of civil partnership by statutory instrument in order to further the general and particular purposes of the Act, in consequence of any provision of the Act or of any delegated legislation made under it or to give full effect to the Act and its provisions. This is particularly intended to allow any legal incidence of marriage which has been overlooked in the Act to be applied to civil partnership where that is appropriate.[1]

8.101 The Civil Partnership Act 2004, s 260 enables the government, when implementing European legislation which affects spouses, to make similar provision for civil partners. The European Union has no standard for the legal recognition of same sex unions, so future European legislation may well fail to deal with the position of civil partners, creating a danger that in consequence English law relating to marriage and civil partnership would diverge without justification.

---

1   Jacqui Smith – *Hansard*, HC Standing Committee D, col 188 (26 October 2004).

Appendix

CIVIL PARTNERSHIP ACT 2004

2004 c 33

CONTENTS

CHAPTER 2
DISSOLUTION, NULLITY AND OTHER PROCEEDINGS

Nullity

Presumption of death orders

Separation orders

Declarations

General provisions

CHAPTER 3
PROPERTY AND FINANCIAL ARRANGEMENTS

CHAPTER 4
CIVIL PARTNERSHIP AGREEMENTS

CHAPTER 5
CHILDREN

CHAPTER 4
INTERDICTS

CHAPTER 5
DISSOLUTION, SEPARATION AND NULLITY

Dissolution and separation

Nullity

Financial provision after overseas proceedings

CHAPTER 6
MISCELLANEOUS AND INTERPRETATION

Miscellaneous

PART 4
CIVIL PARTNERSHIP: NORTHERN IRELAND

CHAPTER 1
REGISTRATION

Formation and eligibility

Preliminaries to registration

Young persons

Supplementary

CHAPTER 2
DISSOLUTION, NULLITY AND OTHER PROCEEDINGS

Introduction

Dissolution of civil partnership

Nullity

Presumption of death orders

Separation orders

Declarations

General provisions

The court

CHAPTER 3
PROPERTY AND FINANCIAL ARRANGEMENTS

CHAPTER 4
CIVIL PARTNERSHIP AGREEMENTS

CHAPTER 5
CHILDREN

CHAPTER 6
MISCELLANEOUS

PART 5
CIVIL PARTNERSHIP FORMED OR DISSOLVED ABROAD ETC

CHAPTER 1
REGISTRATION OUTSIDE UK UNDER ORDER IN COUNCIL

CHAPTER 2
OVERSEAS RELATIONSHIPS TREATED AS CIVIL PARTNERSHIPS

CHAPTER 3
DISSOLUTION ETC: JURISDICTION AND RECOGNITION

Introduction

Jurisdiction of courts in England and Wales

Jurisdiction of Scottish courts

Jurisdiction of courts in Northern Ireland

Recognition of dissolution, annulment and separation

CHAPTER 4
MISCELLANEOUS AND SUPPLEMENTARY

PART 6
RELATIONSHIPS ARISING THROUGH CIVIL PARTNERSHIP

PART 7
MISCELLANEOUS

PART 8
SUPPLEMENTARY

PART 1
INTRODUCTION

1 Civil partnership

(1) A civil partnership is a relationship between two people of the same sex ('civil partners')—

  (a) which is formed when they register as civil partners of each other—
    (i)   in England or Wales (under Part 2),
    (ii) in Scotland (under Part 3),
    (iii) in Northern Ireland (under Part 4), or
    (iv) outside the United Kingdom under an Order in Council made under Chapter 1 of Part 5 (registration at British consulates etc or by armed forces personnel), or
  (b) which they are treated under Chapter 2 of Part 5 as having formed (at the time determined under that Chapter) by virtue of having registered an overseas relationship.

(2) Subsection (1) is subject to the provisions of this Act under or by virtue of which a civil partnership is void.

(3) A civil partnership ends only on death, dissolution or annulment.

(4) The references in subsection (3) to dissolution and annulment are to dissolution and annulment having effect under or recognised in accordance with this Act.

(5) References in this Act to an overseas relationship are to be read in accordance with Chapter 2 of Part 5.

PART 2
CIVIL PARTNERSHIP: ENGLAND AND WALES
CHAPTER 1
REGISTRATION

Formation, eligibility and parental etc consent

2 Formation of civil partnership by registration

(1) For the purposes of section 1, two people are to be regarded as having registered as civil partners of each other once each of them has signed the civil partnership document—

    (a) at the invitation of, and in the presence of, a civil partnership registrar, and

    (b) in the presence of each other and two witnesses.

(2) Subsection (1) applies regardless of whether subsections (3) and (4) are complied with.

(3) After the civil partnership document has been signed under subsection (1), it must also be signed, in the presence of the civil partners and each other, by—

    (a) each of the two witnesses, and

    (b) the civil partnership registrar.

(4) After the witnesses and the civil partnership registrar have signed the civil partnership document, the relevant registration authority must ensure that—

    (a) the fact that the two people have registered as civil partners of each other, and

    (b) any other information prescribed by regulations,

is recorded in the register as soon as is practicable.

(5) No religious service is to be used while the civil partnership registrar is officiating at the signing of a civil partnership document.

(6) 'The civil partnership document' has the meaning given by section 7(1).

(7) 'The relevant registration authority' means the registration authority in whose area the registration takes place.

3 Eligibility

(1) Two people are not eligible to register as civil partners of each other if—

    (a) they are not of the same sex,

    (b) either of them is already a civil partner or lawfully married,

    (c) either of them is under 16, or

    (d) they are within prohibited degrees of relationship.

(2) Part 1 of Schedule 1 contains provisions for determining when two people are within prohibited degrees of relationship.

4 Parental etc consent where proposed civil partner under 18

(1) The consent of the appropriate persons is required before a child and another person may register as civil partners of each other.

(2) Part 1 of Schedule 2 contains provisions for determining who are the appropriate persons for the purposes of this section.

(3) The requirement of consent under subsection (1) does not apply if the child is a surviving civil partner.

(4) Nothing in this section affects any need to obtain the consent of the High Court before a ward of court and another person may register as civil partners of each other.

(5) In this Part 'child', except where used to express a relationship, means a person who is under 18.

Registration procedure: general

5 Types of pre-registration procedure

(1) Two people may register as civil partners of each other under—

    (a) the standard procedure;
    (b) the procedure for house-bound persons;
    (c) the procedure for detained persons;
    (d) the special procedure (which is for cases where a person is seriously ill and not expected to recover).

(2) The procedures referred to in subsection (1)(a) to (c) are subject to—

    (a) section 20 (modified procedures for certain non-residents);
    (b) Schedule 3 (former spouses one of whom has changed sex).

(3) The procedures referred to in subsection (1) (including the procedures as modified by section 20 and Schedule 3) are subject to—

    (a) Part 2 of Schedule 1 (provisions applicable in connection with prohibited degrees of relationship), and
    (b) Parts 2 and 3 of Schedule 2 (provisions applicable where proposed civil partner is under 18).

(4) This section is also subject to section 249 and Schedule 23 (immigration control and formation of civil partnerships).

6 Place of registration

(1) The place at which two people may register as civil partners of each other—

    (a) must be in England or Wales,
    (b) must not be in religious premises, and
    (c) must be specified in the notices, or notice, of proposed civil partnership required by this Chapter.

(2) 'Religious premises' means premises which—

    (a) are used solely or mainly for religious purposes, or
    (b) have been so used and have not subsequently been used solely or mainly for other purposes.

(3) In the case of registration under the standard procedure (including that procedure modified as mentioned in section 5), the place—

    (a) must be one which is open to any person wishing to attend the registration, and
    (b) before being specified in a notice of proposed civil partnership, must be agreed with the registration authority in whose area that place is located.

(4) If the place specified in a notice is not so agreed, the notice is void.

(5) A registration authority may provide a place in its area for the registration of civil partnerships.

7 The civil partnership document

(1) In this Part 'the civil partnership document' means—

(a) in relation to the special procedure, a Registrar General's licence, and
(b) in relation to any other procedure, a civil partnership schedule.

(2) Before two people are entitled to register as civil partners of each other—

(a) the civil partnership document must be delivered to the civil partnership registrar, and
(b) the civil partnership registrar may then ask them for any information required (under section 2(4)) to be recorded in the register.

The standard procedure

8 Notice of proposed civil partnership and declaration

(1) For two people to register as civil partners of each other under the standard procedure, each of them must—

(a) give a notice of proposed civil partnership to a registration authority, and
(b) have resided in England or Wales for at least 7 days immediately before giving the notice.

(2) A notice of proposed civil partnership must contain such information as may be prescribed by regulations.

(3) A notice of proposed civil partnership must also include the necessary declaration, made and signed by the person giving the notice—

(a) at the time when the notice is given, and
(b) in the presence of an authorised person;

and the authorised person must attest the declaration by adding his name, description and place of residence.

(4) The necessary declaration is a solemn declaration in writing—

(a) that the proposed civil partner believes that there is no impediment of kindred or affinity or other lawful hindrance to the formation of the civil partnership;
(b) that each of the proposed civil partners has had a usual place of residence in England or Wales for at least 7 days immediately before giving the notice.

(5) Where a notice of proposed civil partnership is given to a registration authority in accordance with this section, the registration authority must ensure that the following information is recorded in the register as soon as possible—

(a) the fact that the notice has been given and the information in it;
(b) the fact that the authorised person has attested the declaration.

(6) 'Authorised person' means an employee or officer or other person provided by a registration authority who is authorised by that authority to attest notices of proposed civil partnership.

(7) For the purposes of this Chapter, a notice of proposed civil partnership is recorded when subsection (5) is complied with.

9 Power to require evidence of name etc

(1) The registration authority to which a notice of proposed civil partnership is given may require the person giving the notice to provide it with specified evidence—

(a) relating to that person, or

(b) if the registration authority considers that the circumstances are exceptional, relating not only to that person but also to that person's proposed civil partner.

(2) Such a requirement may be imposed at any time before the registration authority issues the civil partnership schedule under section 14.

(3) 'Specified evidence', in relation to a person, means such evidence as may be specified in guidance issued by the Registrar General—

(a) of the person's name and surname,

(b) of the person's age,

(c) as to whether the person has previously formed a civil partnership or a marriage and, if so, as to the ending of the civil partnership or marriage,

(d) of the person's nationality, and

(e) as to the person's residence in England or Wales during the period of 7 days preceding the giving of a notice of proposed civil partnership by that person.

10 Proposed civil partnership to be publicised

(1) Where a notice of proposed civil partnership has been given to a registration authority, the relevant information must be publicised during the waiting period—

(a) by that registration authority,

(b) by any registration authority in whose area the person giving the notice has resided during the period of 7 days preceding the giving of the notice,

(c) by any registration authority in whose area the proposed civil partner of the person giving the notice has resided during the period of 7 days preceding the giving of that notice,

(d) by the registration authority in whose area the place specified in the notice as the place of proposed registration is located, and

(e) by the Registrar General.

(2) 'The relevant information' means—

(a) the name of the person giving the notice,

(b) the name of that person's proposed civil partner, and

(c) such other information as may be prescribed by regulations.

11 Meaning of 'the waiting period'

In this Chapter 'the waiting period', in relation to a notice of proposed civil partnership, means the period—

(a) beginning the day after the notice is recorded, and

(b) subject to section 12, ending at the end of the period of 15 days beginning with that day.

12 Power to shorten the waiting period

(1) If the Registrar General, on an application being made to him, is satisfied that there are compelling reasons because of the exceptional circumstances of the case for shortening the period of 15 days mentioned in section 11(b), he may shorten it to such period as he considers appropriate.

(2) Regulations may make provision with respect to the making, and granting, of applications under subsection (1).

(3) Regulations under subsection (2) may provide for—

(a) the power conferred by subsection (1) to be exercised by a registration authority on behalf of the Registrar General in such classes of case as are prescribed by the regulations;

(b) the making of an appeal to the Registrar General against a decision taken by a registration authority in accordance with regulations made by virtue of paragraph (a).

13 Objection to proposed civil partnership

(1) Any person may object to the issue of a civil partnership schedule under section 14 by giving any registration authority notice of his objection.

(2) A notice of objection must—

(a) state the objector's place of residence and the ground of objection, and

(b) be signed by or on behalf of the objector.

(3) If a notice of objection is given to a registration authority, it must ensure that the fact that it has been given and the information in it are recorded in the register as soon as possible.

14 Issue of civil partnership schedule

(1) As soon as the waiting period in relation to each notice of proposed civil partnership has expired, the registration authority in whose area it is proposed that the registration take place is under a duty, at the request of one or both of the proposed civil partners, to issue a document to be known as a 'civil partnership schedule'.

(2) Regulations may make provision as to the contents of a civil partnership schedule.

(3) The duty in subsection (1) does not apply if the registration authority is not satisfied that there is no lawful impediment to the formation of the civil partnership.

(4) If an objection to the issue of the civil partnership schedule has been recorded in the register, no civil partnership schedule is to be issued until—

(a) the relevant registration authority has investigated the objection and is satisfied that the objection ought not to obstruct the issue of the civil partnership schedule, or

(b) the objection has been withdrawn by the person who made it.

(5) 'The relevant registration authority' means the authority which first records that a notice of proposed civil partnership has been given by one of the proposed civil partners.

15 Appeal against refusal to issue civil partnership schedule

(1) If the registration authority refuses to issue a civil partnership schedule—

(a) because an objection to its issue has been made under section 13, or

(b) in reliance on section 14(3),

either of the proposed civil partners may appeal to the Registrar General.

(2) On an appeal under this section the Registrar General must either confirm the refusal or direct that a civil partnership schedule be issued.

16 Frivolous objections and representations: liability for costs etc

(1) Subsection (3) applies if—

(a) a person objects to the issue of a civil partnership schedule, but

(b) the Registrar General declares that the grounds on which the objection is made are frivolous and ought not to obstruct the issue of the civil partnership schedule.

(2) Subsection (3) also applies if—

    (a) in reliance on section 14(3), the registration authority refuses to issue a civil partnership schedule as a result of a representation made to it, and

    (b) on an appeal under section 15 against the refusal, the Registrar General declares that the representation is frivolous and ought not to obstruct the issue of the civil partnership schedule.

(3) The person who made the objection or representation is liable for—

    (a) the costs of the proceedings before the Registrar General, and

    (b) damages recoverable by the proposed civil partner to whom the objection or representation relates.

(4) For the purpose of enabling any person to recover any such costs and damages, a copy of a declaration of the Registrar General purporting to be sealed with the seal of the General Register Office is evidence that the Registrar General has made the declaration.

17 Period during which registration may take place

(1) The proposed civil partners may not register as civil partners of each other on the production of the civil partnership schedule until the waiting period in relation to each notice of proposed civil partnership has expired.

(2) Subject to subsection (1), under the standard procedure, they may register as civil partners by signing the civil partnership schedule at any time during the applicable period.

(3) If they do not register as civil partners by signing the civil partnership schedule before the end of the applicable period—

    (a) the notices of proposed civil partnership and the civil partnership schedule are void, and

    (b) no civil partnership registrar may officiate at the signing of the civil partnership schedule by them.

(4) The applicable period, in relation to two people registering as civil partners of each other, is the period of 12 months beginning with—

    (a) the day on which the notices of proposed civil partnership are recorded, or

    (b) if the notices are not recorded on the same day, the earlier of those days.

The procedures for house-bound and detained persons

18 House-bound persons

(1) This section applies if two people wish to register as civil partners of each other at the place where one of them is house-bound.

(2) A person is house-bound at any place if, in relation to that person, a statement is made by a registered medical practitioner that, in his opinion—

    (a) because of illness or disability, that person ought not to move or be moved from the place where he is at the time when the statement is made, and

    (b) it is likely to be the case for at least the following 3 months that because of the illness or disability that person ought not to move or be moved from that place.

(3) The procedure under which the two people concerned may register as civil partners of each other is the same as the standard procedure, except that—

(a) each notice of proposed civil partnership must be accompanied by a statement under subsection (2) ('a medical statement'), which must have been made not more than 14 days before the day on which the notice is recorded,

(b) the fact that the registration authority to whom the notice is given has received the medical statement must be recorded in the register, and

(c) the applicable period (for the purposes of section 17) is the period of 3 months beginning with—

    (i) the day on which the notices of proposed civil partnership are recorded, or

    (ii) if the notices are not recorded on the same day, the earlier of those days.

(4) A medical statement must contain such information and must be made in such manner as may be prescribed by regulations.

(5) A medical statement may not be made in relation to a person who is detained as described in section 19(2).

(6) For the purposes of this Chapter, a person in relation to whom a medical statement is made is to be treated, if he would not otherwise be so treated, as resident and usually resident at the place where he is for the time being.

19 Detained persons

(1) This section applies if two people wish to register as civil partners of each other at the place where one of them is detained.

(2) 'Detained' means detained—

(a) as a patient in a hospital (but otherwise than by virtue of section 2, 4, 5, 35, 36 or 136 of the Mental Health Act 1983 (c 20) (short term detentions)), or

(b) in a prison or other place to which the Prison Act 1952 (c 52) applies.

(3) The procedure under which the two people concerned may register as civil partners of each other is the same as the standard procedure, except that—

(a) each notice of proposed civil partnership must be accompanied by a supporting statement, which must have been made not more than 21 days before the day on which the notice is recorded,

(b) the fact that the registration authority to whom the notice is given has received the supporting statement must be recorded in the register, and

(c) the applicable period (for the purposes of section 17) is the period of 3 months beginning with—

    (i) the day on which the notices of proposed civil partnership are recorded, or

    (ii) if the notices are not recorded on the same day, the earlier of those days.

(4) A supporting statement, in relation to a detained person, is a statement made by the responsible authority which—

(a) identifies the establishment where the person is detained, and

(b) states that the responsible authority has no objection to that establishment being specified in a notice of proposed civil partnership as the place at which the person is to register as a civil partner.

(5) A supporting statement must contain such information and must be made in such manner as may be prescribed by regulations.

(6) 'The responsible authority' means—

(a) if the person is detained in a hospital, the hospital's managers;

(b) if the person is detained in a prison or other place to which the 1952 Act applies, the governor or other officer for the time being in charge of that prison or other place.

(7) 'Patient' and 'hospital' have the same meaning as in Part 2 of the 1983 Act and 'managers', in relation to a hospital, has the same meaning as in section 145(1) of the 1983 Act.

(8) For the purposes of this Chapter, a detained person is to be treated, if he would not otherwise be so treated, as resident and usually resident at the place where he is for the time being.

Modified procedures for certain non-residents

20 Modified procedures for certain non-residents

(1) Subsection (5) applies in the following three cases.

(2) The first is where—

(a) two people wish to register as civil partners of each other in England and Wales, and

(b) one of them ('A') resides in Scotland and the other ('B') resides in England or Wales.

(3) The second is where—

(a) two people wish to register as civil partners of each other in England and Wales, and

(b) one of them ('A') resides in Northern Ireland and the other ('B') resides in England or Wales.

(4) The third is where—

(a) two people wish to register as civil partners of each other in England and Wales, and

(b) one of them ('A') is a member of Her Majesty's forces who is serving outside the United Kingdom and the other ('B') resides in England or Wales.

(5) For the purposes of the standard procedure, the procedure for house-bound persons and the procedure for detained persons—

(a) A is not required to give a notice of proposed civil partnership under this Chapter;

(b) B may give a notice of proposed civil partnership and make the necessary declaration without regard to the requirement that would otherwise apply that A must reside in England or Wales;

(c) the waiting period is calculated by reference to the day on which B's notice is recorded;

(d) the civil partnership schedule is not to be issued by a registration authority unless A or B produces to that registration authority a certificate of no impediment issued to A under the relevant provision;

(e) the applicable period is calculated by reference to the day on which B's notice is recorded and, where the standard procedure is used in the first and second cases, is the period of 3 months beginning with that day;

(f) section 31 applies as if in subsections (1)(a) and (2)(c) for 'each notice' there were substituted 'B's notice'.

(6) 'The relevant provision' means—

(a) if A resides in Scotland, section 97;

(b) if A resides in Northern Ireland, section 150;

(c) if A is a member of Her Majesty's forces who is serving outside the United Kingdom, section 239.

(7) 'Her Majesty's forces' has the same meaning as in the Army Act 1955 (3 & 4 Eliz. 2 c 18).

The special procedure

21 Notice of proposed civil partnership

(1) For two people to register as civil partners of each other under the special procedure, one of them must—

    (a) give a notice of proposed civil partnership to the registration authority for the area in which it is proposed that the registration take place, and

    (b) comply with any requirement made under section 22.

(2) The notice must contain such information as may be prescribed by regulations.

(3) Subsections (3) to (6) of section 8 (necessary declaration etc), apart from paragraph (b) of subsection (4), apply for the purposes of this section as they apply for the purposes of that section.

22 Evidence to be produced

(1) The person giving a notice of proposed civil partnership to a registration authority under the special procedure must produce to the authority such evidence as the Registrar General may require to satisfy him—

    (a) that there is no lawful impediment to the formation of the civil partnership,

    (b) that the conditions in subsection (2) are met, and

    (c) that there is sufficient reason why a licence should be granted.

(2) The conditions are that one of the proposed civil partners—

    (a) is seriously ill and not expected to recover, and

    (b) understands the nature and purport of signing a Registrar General's licence.

(3) The certificate of a registered medical practitioner is sufficient evidence of any or all of the matters referred to in subsection (2).

23 Application to be reported to Registrar General

On receiving a notice of proposed civil partnership under section 21 and any evidence under section 22, the registration authority must—

    (a) inform the Registrar General, and

    (b) comply with any directions the Registrar General may give for verifying the evidence given.

24 Objection to issue of Registrar General's licence

(1) Any person may object to the Registrar General giving authority for the issue of his licence by giving the Registrar General or any registration authority notice of his objection.

(2) A notice of objection must—

    (a) state the objector's place of residence and the ground of objection, and

    (b) be signed by or on behalf of the objector.

(3) If a notice of objection is given to a registration authority, it must ensure that the fact that it has been given and the information in it are recorded in the register as soon as possible.

25 Issue of Registrar General's licence

(1) This section applies where a notice of proposed civil partnership is given to a registration authority under section 21.

(2) The registration authority may issue a Registrar General's licence if, and only if, given authority to do so by the Registrar General.

(3) The Registrar General—

(a) may not give his authority unless he is satisfied that one of the proposed civil partners is seriously ill and not expected to recover, but
(b) if so satisfied, must give his authority unless a lawful impediment to the issue of his licence has been shown to his satisfaction to exist.

(4) A licence under this section must state that it is issued on the authority of the Registrar General.

(5) Regulations may (subject to subsection (4)) make provision as to the contents of a licence under this section.

(6) If an objection has been made to the Registrar General giving authority for the issue of his licence, he is not to give that authority until—

(a) he has investigated the objection and decided whether it ought to obstruct the issue of his licence, or
(b) the objection has been withdrawn by the person who made it.

(7) Any decision of the Registrar General under subsection (6)(a) is final.

26 Frivolous objections: liability for costs

(1) This section applies if—

(a) a person objects to the Registrar General giving authority for the issue of his licence, but
(b) the Registrar General declares that the grounds on which the objection is made are frivolous and ought not to obstruct the issue of his licence.

(2) The person who made the objection is liable for—

(a) the costs of the proceedings before the Registrar General, and
(b) damages recoverable by the proposed civil partner to whom the objection relates.

(3) For the purpose of enabling any person to recover any such costs and damages, a copy of a declaration of the Registrar General purporting to be sealed with the seal of the General Register Office is evidence that the Registrar General has made the declaration.

27 Period during which registration may take place

(1) If a Registrar General's licence has been issued under section 25, the proposed civil partners may register as civil partners by signing it at any time within 1 month from the day on which the notice of proposed civil partnership was given.

(2) If they do not register as civil partners by signing the licence within the 1 month period—

(a) the notice of proposed civil partnership and the licence are void, and
(b) no civil partnership registrar may officiate at the signing of the licence by them.

Supplementary

28 Registration authorities

In this Chapter 'registration authority' means—

  (a) in relation to England, a county council, the council of any district comprised in an area for which there is no county council, a London borough council, the Common Council of the City of London or the Council of the Isles of Scilly;
  (b) in relation to Wales, a county council or a county borough council.

29 Civil partnership registrars

(1) A civil partnership registrar is an individual who is designated by a registration authority as a civil partnership registrar for its area.

(2) It is the duty of each registration authority to ensure that there is a sufficient number of civil partnership registrars for its area to carry out in that area the functions of civil partnership registrars.

(3) Each registration authority must inform the Registrar General as soon as is practicable—

  (a) of any designation it has made of a person as a civil partnership registrar, and
  (b) of the ending of any such designation.

(4) The Registrar General must make available to the public a list—

  (a) of civil partnership registrars, and
  (b) of the registration authorities for which they are designated to act.

30 The Registrar General and the register

(1) In this Chapter 'the Registrar General' means the Registrar General for England and Wales.

(2) The Registrar General must provide a system for keeping any records that relate to civil partnerships and are required by this Chapter to be made.

(3) The system may, in particular, enable those records to be kept together with other records kept by the Registrar General.

(4) In this Chapter 'the register' means the system for keeping records provided under subsection (2).

31 Offences relating to civil partnership schedule

(1) A person commits an offence if he issues a civil partnership schedule knowing that he does so—

  (a) before the waiting period in relation to each notice of proposed civil partnership has expired,
  (b) after the end of the applicable period, or
  (c) at a time when its issue has been forbidden under Schedule 2 by a person entitled to forbid its issue.

(2) A person commits an offence if, in his actual or purported capacity as a civil partnership registrar, he officiates at the signing of a civil partnership schedule by proposed civil partners knowing that he does so—

  (a) at a place other than the place specified in the notices of proposed civil partnership and the civil partnership schedule,

   (b) in the absence of a civil partnership registrar,

   (c) before the waiting period in relation to each notice of proposed civil partnership has expired, or

   (d) even though the civil partnership is void under section 49(b) or (c).

(3) A person guilty of an offence under subsection (1) or (2) is liable on conviction on indictment to imprisonment for a term not exceeding 5 years or to a fine (or both).

(4) A prosecution under this section may not be commenced more than 3 years after the commission of the offence.

32 Offences relating to Registrar General's licence

(1) A person commits an offence if—

   (a) he gives information by way of evidence in response to a requirement under section 22(1), knowing that the information is false;

   (b) he gives a certificate as provided for by section 22(3), knowing that the certificate is false.

(2) A person commits an offence if, in his actual or purported capacity as a civil partnership registrar, he officiates at the signing of a Registrar General's licence by proposed civil partners knowing that he does so—

   (a) at a place other than the place specified in the licence,

   (b) in the absence of a civil partnership registrar,

   (c) after the end of 1 month from the day on which the notice of proposed civil partnership was given, or

   (d) even though the civil partnership is void under section 49(b) or (c).

(3) A person guilty of an offence under subsection (1) or (2) is liable—

   (a) on conviction on indictment, to imprisonment not exceeding 3 years or to a fine (or both);

   (b) on summary conviction, to a fine not exceeding the statutory maximum.

(4) A prosecution under this section may not be commenced more than 3 years after the commission of the offence.

33 Offences relating to the recording of civil partnerships

(1) A civil partnership registrar commits an offence if he refuses or fails to comply with the provisions of this Chapter or of any regulations made under section 36.

(2) A civil partnership registrar guilty of an offence under subsection (1) is liable—

   (a) on conviction on indictment, to imprisonment for a term not exceeding 2 years or to a fine (or both);

   (b) on summary conviction, to a fine not exceeding the statutory maximum;

and on conviction shall cease to be a civil partnership registrar.

(3) A person commits an offence if—

   (a) under arrangements made by a registration authority for the purposes of section 2(4), he is under a duty to record information required to be recorded under section 2(4), but

   (b) he refuses or without reasonable cause omits to do so.

(4) A person guilty of an offence under subsection (3) is liable on summary conviction to a fine not exceeding level 3 on the standard scale.

(5) A person commits an offence if he records in the register information relating to the formation of a civil partnership by the signing of a civil partnership schedule, knowing that the civil partnership is void under section 49(b) or (c).

(6) A person guilty of an offence under subsection (5) is liable on conviction on indictment, to imprisonment for a term not exceeding 5 years or to a fine (or both).

(7) A person commits an offence if he records in the register information relating to the formation of a civil partnership by the signing of a Registrar General's licence, knowing that the civil partnership is void under section 49(b) or (c).

(8) A person guilty of an offence under subsection (7) is liable—

  (a) on conviction on indictment, to imprisonment for a term not exceeding 3 years or to a fine (or both);
  (b) on summary conviction, to a fine not exceeding the statutory maximum.

(9) A prosecution under subsection (5) or (7) may not be commenced more than 3 years after the commission of the offence.

34 Fees

(1) The Chancellor of the Exchequer may by order provide for fees, of such amounts as may be specified in the order, to be payable to such persons as may be prescribed by the order in respect of—

  (a) the giving of a notice of proposed civil partnership and the attestation of the necessary declaration;
  (b) the making of an application under section 12(1) (application to reduce waiting period);
  (c) the issue of a Registrar General's licence;
  (d) the attendance of the civil partnership registrar when two people sign the civil partnership document;
  (e) such other services provided in connection with civil partnerships either by registration authorities or by or on behalf of the Registrar General as may be prescribed by the order.

(2) The Registrar General may remit the fee for the issue of his licence in whole or in part in any case where it appears to him that the payment of the fee would cause hardship to the proposed civil partners.

35 Power to assimilate provisions relating to civil registration

(1) The Chancellor of the Exchequer may by order make—

  (a) such amendments of this Act as appear to him appropriate for the purpose of assimilating any provision connected with the formation or recording of civil partnerships in England and Wales to any provision made (whether or not under an order under section 1 of the Regulatory Reform Act 2001 (c 6)) in relation to civil marriage in England and Wales, and
  (b) such amendments of other enactments and of subordinate legislation as appear to him appropriate in consequence of any amendments made under paragraph (a).

(2) 'Civil marriage' means marriage solemnised otherwise than according to the rites of the Church of England or any other religious usages.

(3) 'Amendment' includes repeal or revocation.

(4) 'Subordinate legislation' has the same meaning as in the Interpretation Act 1978 (c 30).

36 Regulations and orders

(1) Regulations may make provision supplementing the provisions of this Chapter.

(2) Regulations may in particular make provision—

    (a) relating to the use of Welsh in documents and records relating to civil partnerships;
    (b) with respect to the retention of documents relating to civil partnerships;
    (c) prescribing the duties of civil partnership registrars;
    (d) prescribing the duties of persons in whose presence any declaration is made for the purposes of this Chapter;
    (e) for the issue by the Registrar General of guidance supplementing any provision made by the regulations.
    (f) for the issue by registration authorities or the Registrar General of certified copies of entries in the register and for such copies to be received in evidence.

(3) In this Chapter 'regulations' means regulations made by the Registrar General with the approval of the Chancellor of the Exchequer.

(4) Any power to make regulations or an order under this Chapter is exercisable by statutory instrument.

(5) A statutory instrument containing an order under section 34 is subject to annulment in pursuance of a resolution of either House of Parliament.

CHAPTER 2
DISSOLUTION, NULLITY AND OTHER PROCEEDINGS

Introduction

37 Powers to make orders and effect of orders

(1) The court may, in accordance with this Chapter—

    (a) make an order (a 'dissolution order') which dissolves a civil partnership on the ground that it has broken down irretrievably;
    (b) make an order (a 'nullity order') which annuls a civil partnership which is void or voidable;
    (c) make an order (a 'presumption of death order') which dissolves a civil partnership on the ground that one of the civil partners is presumed to be dead;
    (d) make an order (a 'separation order') which provides for the separation of the civil partners.

(2) Every dissolution, nullity or presumption of death order—

    (a) is, in the first instance, a conditional order, and
    (b) may not be made final before the end of the prescribed period (see section 38);

and any reference in this Chapter to a conditional order is to be read accordingly.

(3) A nullity order made where a civil partnership is voidable annuls the civil partnership only as respects any time after the order has been made final, and the civil partnership is to be treated (despite the order) as if it had existed up to that time.

(4) In this Chapter, other than in sections 58 to 61, 'the court' means—

    (a) the High Court, or
    (b) if a county court has jurisdiction by virtue of Part 5 of the Matrimonial and Family Proceedings Act 1984 (c 42), a county court.

(5) This Chapter is subject to sections 219 to 224 (jurisdiction of the court).

38 The period before conditional orders may be made final

(1) Subject to subsections (2) to (4), the prescribed period for the purposes of section 37(2)(b) is—

    (a) 6 weeks from the making of the conditional order, or

    (b) if the 6 week period would end on a day on which the office or registry of the court dealing with the case is closed, the period of 6 weeks extended to the end of the first day on which the office or registry is next open.

(2) The Lord Chancellor may by order amend this section so as to substitute a different definition of the prescribed period for the purposes of section 37(2)(b).

(3) But the Lord Chancellor may not under subsection (2) provide for a period longer than 6 months to be the prescribed period.

(4) In a particular case the court dealing with the case may by order shorten the prescribed period.

(5) The power to make an order under subsection (2) is exercisable by statutory instrument.

(6) An instrument containing such an order is subject to annulment in pursuance of a resolution of either House of Parliament.

39 Intervention of the Queen's Proctor

(1) This section applies if an application has been made for a dissolution, nullity or presumption of death order.

(2) The court may, if it thinks fit, direct that all necessary papers in the matter are to be sent to the Queen's Proctor who must under the directions of the Attorney General instruct counsel to argue before the court any question in relation to the matter which the court considers it necessary or expedient to have fully argued.

(3) If any person at any time—

    (a) during the progress of the proceedings, or

    (b) before the conditional order is made final,

gives information to the Queen's Proctor on any matter material to the due decision of the case, the Queen's Proctor may take such steps as the Attorney General considers necessary or expedient.

(4) If the Queen's Proctor intervenes or shows cause against the making of the conditional order in any proceedings relating to its making, the court may make such order as may be just as to—

    (a) the payment by other parties to the proceedings of the costs incurred by him in doing so, or

    (b) the payment by the Queen's Proctor of any costs incurred by any of those parties because of his doing so.

(5) The Queen's Proctor is entitled to charge as part of the expenses of his office—

    (a) the costs of any proceedings under subsection (2);

    (b) if his reasonable costs of intervening or showing cause as mentioned in subsection (4) are not fully satisfied by an order under subsection (4)(a), the amount of the difference;

    (c) if the Treasury so directs, any costs which he pays to any parties under an order made under subsection (4)(b).

40 Proceedings before order has been made final

(1) This section applies if—

(a) a conditional order has been made, and
(b) the Queen's Proctor, or any person who has not been a party to proceedings in which the order was made, shows cause why the order should not be made final on the ground that material facts have not been brought before the court.

(2) This section also applies if—

(a) a conditional order has been made,
(b) 3 months have elapsed since the earliest date on which an application could have been made for the order to be made final,
(c) no such application has been made by the civil partner who applied for the conditional order, and
(d) the other civil partner makes an application to the court under this subsection.

(3) The court may—

(a) make the order final,
(b) rescind the order,
(c) require further inquiry, or
(d) otherwise deal with the case as it thinks fit.

(4) Subsection (3)(a)—

(a) applies despite section 37(2) (period before conditional orders may be made final), but
(b) is subject to section 48(4) (protection for respondent in separation cases) and section 63 (restrictions on making of orders affecting children).

41 Time bar on applications for dissolution orders

(1) No application for a dissolution order may be made to the court before the end of the period of 1 year from the date of the formation of the civil partnership.

(2) Nothing in this section prevents the making of an application based on matters which occurred before the end of the 1 year period.

42 Attempts at reconciliation of civil partners

(1) This section applies in relation to cases where an application is made for a dissolution or separation order.

(2) Rules of court must make provision for requiring the solicitor acting for the applicant to certify whether he has—

(a) discussed with the applicant the possibility of a reconciliation with the other civil partner, and
(b) given the applicant the names and addresses of persons qualified to help effect a reconciliation between civil partners who have become estranged.

(3) If at any stage of proceedings for the order it appears to the court that there is a reasonable possibility of a reconciliation between the civil partners, the court may adjourn the proceedings for such period as it thinks fit to enable attempts to be made to effect a reconciliation between them.

(4) The power to adjourn under subsection (3) is additional to any other power of adjournment.

43 Consideration by the court of certain agreements or arrangements

(1) This section applies in relation to cases where—

    (a) proceedings for a dissolution or separation order are contemplated or have begun, and

    (b) an agreement or arrangement is made or proposed to be made between the civil partners which relates to, arises out of, or is connected with, the proceedings.

(2) Rules of court may make provision for enabling—

    (a) the civil partners, or either of them, to refer the agreement or arrangement to the court, and

    (b) the court—

        (i) to express an opinion, if it thinks it desirable to do so, as to the reasonableness of the agreement or arrangement, and

        (ii) to give such directions, if any, in the matter as it thinks fit.

Dissolution of civil partnership

44 Dissolution of civil partnership which has broken down irretrievably

(1) Subject to section 41, an application for a dissolution order may be made to the court by either civil partner on the ground that the civil partnership has broken down irretrievably.

(2) On an application for a dissolution order the court must inquire, so far as it reasonably can, into—

    (a) the facts alleged by the applicant, and

    (b) any facts alleged by the respondent.

(3) The court hearing an application for a dissolution order must not hold that the civil partnership has broken down irretrievably unless the applicant satisfies the court of one or more of the facts described in subsection (5)(a), (b), (c) or (d).

(4) But if the court is satisfied of any of those facts, it must make a dissolution order unless it is satisfied on all the evidence that the civil partnership has not broken down irretrievably.

(5) The facts referred to in subsections (3) and (4) are—

    (a) that the respondent has behaved in such a way that the applicant cannot reasonably be expected to live with the respondent;

    (b) that—

        (i) the applicant and the respondent have lived apart for a continuous period of at least 2 years immediately preceding the making of the application ('2 years' separation'), and

        (ii) the respondent consents to a dissolution order being made;

    (c) that the applicant and the respondent have lived apart for a continuous period of at least 5 years immediately preceding the making of the application ('5 years' separation');

    (d) that the respondent has deserted the applicant for a continuous period of at least 2 years immediately preceding the making of the application.

45 Supplemental provisions as to facts raising presumption of breakdown

(1) Subsection (2) applies if—

    (a) in any proceedings for a dissolution order the applicant alleges, in reliance on section 44(5)(a), that the respondent has behaved in such a way that the applicant cannot reasonably be expected to live with the respondent, but

(b) after the date of the occurrence of the final incident relied on by the applicant and held by the court to support his allegation, the applicant and the respondent have lived together for a period (or periods) which does not, or which taken together do not, exceed 6 months.

(2) The fact that the applicant and respondent have lived together as mentioned in subsection (1)(b) must be disregarded in determining, for the purposes of section 44(5)(a), whether the applicant cannot reasonably be expected to live with the respondent.

(3) Subsection (4) applies in relation to cases where the applicant alleges, in reliance on section 44(5)(b), that the respondent consents to a dissolution order being made.

(4) Rules of court must make provision for the purpose of ensuring that the respondent has been given such information as will enable him to understand—

(a) the consequences to him of consenting to the making of the order, and
(b) the steps which he must take to indicate his consent.

(5) For the purposes of section 44(5)(d) the court may treat a period of desertion as having continued at a time when the deserting civil partner was incapable of continuing the necessary intention, if the evidence before the court is such that, had he not been so incapable, the court would have inferred that the desertion continued at that time.

(6) In considering for the purposes of section 44(5) whether the period for which the civil partners have lived apart or the period for which the respondent has deserted the applicant has been continuous, no account is to be taken of—

(a) any one period not exceeding 6 months, or
(b) any two or more periods not exceeding 6 months in all,

during which the civil partners resumed living with each other.

(7) But no period during which the civil partners have lived with each other counts as part of the period during which the civil partners have lived apart or as part of the period of desertion.

(8) For the purposes of section 44(5)(b) and (c) and this section civil partners are to be treated as living apart unless they are living with each other in the same household, and references in this section to civil partners living with each other are to be read as references to their living with each other in the same household.

46 Dissolution order not precluded by previous separation order etc

(1) Subsections (2) and (3) apply if any of the following orders has been made in relation to a civil partnership—

(a) a separation order;
(b) an order under Schedule 6 (financial relief in magistrates' courts etc);
(c) an order under section 33 of the Family Law Act 1996 (c 27) (occupation orders);
(d) an order under section 37 of the 1996 Act (orders where neither civil partner entitled to occupy the home).

(2) Nothing prevents—

(a) either civil partner from applying for a dissolution order, or
(b) the court from making a dissolution order,

on the same facts, or substantially the same facts, as those proved in support of the making of the order referred to in subsection (1).

(3) On the application for the dissolution order, the court—

    (a) may treat the order referred to in subsection (1) as sufficient proof of any desertion or other fact by reference to which it was made, but

    (b) must not make the dissolution order without receiving evidence from the applicant.

(4) If—

    (a) the application for the dissolution order follows a separation order or any order requiring the civil partners to live apart,

    (b) there was a period of desertion immediately preceding the institution of the proceedings for the separation order, and

    (c) the civil partners have not resumed living together and the separation order has been continuously in force since it was made,

the period of desertion is to be treated for the purposes of the application for the dissolution order as if it had immediately preceded the making of the application.

(5) For the purposes of section 44(5)(d) the court may treat as a period during which the respondent has deserted the applicant any period during which there is in force—

    (a) an injunction granted by the High Court or a county court which excludes the respondent from the civil partnership home, or

    (b) an order under section 33 or 37 of the 1996 Act which prohibits the respondent from occupying a dwelling-house in which the applicant and the respondent have, or at any time have had, a civil partnership home.

47 Refusal of dissolution in 5 year separation cases on ground of grave hardship

(1) The respondent to an application for a dissolution order in which the applicant alleges 5 years' separation may oppose the making of an order on the ground that—

    (a) the dissolution of the civil partnership will result in grave financial or other hardship to him, and

    (b) it would in all the circumstances be wrong to dissolve the civil partnership.

(2) Subsection (3) applies if—

    (a) the making of a dissolution order is opposed under this section,

    (b) the court finds that the applicant is entitled to rely in support of his application on the fact of 5 years' separation and makes no such finding as to any other fact mentioned in section 44(5), and

    (c) apart from this section, the court would make a dissolution order.

(3) The court must—

    (a) consider all the circumstances, including the conduct of the civil partners and the interests of the civil partners and of any children or other persons concerned, and

    (b) if it is of the opinion that the ground mentioned in subsection (1) is made out, dismiss the application for the dissolution order.

(4) 'Hardship' includes the loss of the chance of acquiring any benefit which the respondent might acquire if the civil partnership were not dissolved.

48 Proceedings before order made final: protection for respondent in separation cases

(1) The court may, on an application made by the respondent, rescind a conditional dissolution order if—

(a) it made the order on the basis of a finding that the applicant was entitled to rely on the fact of 2 years' separation coupled with the respondent's consent to a dissolution order being made,

(b) it made no such finding as to any other fact mentioned in section 44(5), and

(c) it is satisfied that the applicant misled the respondent (whether intentionally or unintentionally) about any matter which the respondent took into account in deciding to give his consent.

(2) Subsections (3) to (5) apply if—

(a) the respondent to an application for a dissolution order in which the applicant alleged—
  (i) 2 years' separation coupled with the respondent's consent to a dissolution order being made, or
  (ii) 5 years' separation,

  has applied to the court for consideration under subsection (3) of his financial position after the dissolution of the civil partnership, and

(b) the court—
  (i) has made a conditional dissolution order on the basis of a finding that the applicant was entitled to rely in support of his application on the fact of 2 years' or 5 years' separation, and
  (ii) has made no such finding as to any other fact mentioned in section 44(5).

(3) The court hearing an application by the respondent under subsection (2) must consider all the circumstances, including—

(a) the age, health, conduct, earning capacity, financial resources and financial obligations of each of the parties, and

(b) the financial position of the respondent as, having regard to the dissolution, it is likely to be after the death of the applicant should the applicant die first.

(4) Subject to subsection (5), the court must not make the order final unless it is satisfied that—

(a) the applicant should not be required to make any financial provision for the respondent, or

(b) the financial provision made by the applicant for the respondent is—
  (i) reasonable and fair, or
  (ii) the best that can be made in the circumstances.

(5) The court may if it thinks fit make the order final if—

(a) it appears that there are circumstances making it desirable that the order should be made final without delay, and

(b) it has obtained a satisfactory undertaking from the applicant that he will make such financial provision for the respondent as it may approve.

Nullity

49 Grounds on which civil partnership is void

Where two people register as civil partners of each other in England and Wales, the civil partnership is void if—

(a) at the time when they do so, they are not eligible to register as civil partners of each other under Chapter 1 (see section 3),

(b) at the time when they do so they both know—
  (i) that due notice of proposed civil partnership has not been given,
  (ii) that the civil partnership document has not been duly issued,

(iii) that the civil partnership document is void under section 17(3) or 27(2) (registration after end of time allowed for registering),

(iv) that the place of registration is a place other than that specified in the notices (or notice) of proposed civil partnership and the civil partnership document, or

(v) that a civil partnership registrar is not present, or

(c) the civil partnership document is void under paragraph 6(5) of Schedule 2 (civil partnership between child and another person forbidden).

50 Grounds on which civil partnership is voidable

(1) Where two people register as civil partners of each other in England and Wales, the civil partnership is voidable if—

(a) either of them did not validly consent to its formation (whether as a result of duress, mistake, unsoundness of mind or otherwise);

(b) at the time of its formation either of them, though capable of giving a valid consent, was suffering (whether continuously or intermittently) from mental disorder of such a kind or to such an extent as to be unfitted for civil partnership;

(c) at the time of its formation, the respondent was pregnant by some person other than the applicant;

(d) an interim gender recognition certificate under the Gender Recognition Act 2004 (c 7) has, after the time of its formation, been issued to either civil partner;

(e) the respondent is a person whose gender at the time of its formation had become the acquired gender under the 2004 Act.

(2) In this section and section 51 'mental disorder' has the same meaning as in the Mental Health Act 1983 (c 20).

51 Bars to relief where civil partnership is voidable

(1) The court must not make a nullity order on the ground that a civil partnership is voidable if the respondent satisfies the court—

(a) that the applicant, with knowledge that it was open to him to obtain a nullity order, conducted himself in relation to the respondent in such a way as to lead the respondent reasonably to believe that he would not seek to do so, and

(b) that it would be unjust to the respondent to make the order.

(2) Without prejudice to subsection (1), the court must not make a nullity order by virtue of section 50(1)(a), (b), (c) or (e) unless—

(a) it is satisfied that proceedings were instituted within 3 years from the date of the formation of the civil partnership, or

(b) leave for the institution of proceedings after the end of that 3 year period has been granted under subsection (3).

(3) A judge of the court may, on an application made to him, grant leave for the institution of proceedings if he—

(a) is satisfied that the applicant has at some time during the 3 year period suffered from mental disorder, and

(b) considers that in all the circumstances of the case it would be just to grant leave for the institution of proceedings.

(4) An application for leave under subsection (3) may be made after the end of the 3 year period.

(5) Without prejudice to subsection (1), the court must not make a nullity order by virtue of section 50(1)(d) unless it is satisfied that proceedings were instituted within the period of 6 months from the date of issue of the interim gender recognition certificate.

(6) Without prejudice to subsections (1) and (2), the court must not make a nullity order by virtue of section 50(1)(c) or (e) unless it is satisfied that the applicant was at the time of the formation of the civil partnership ignorant of the facts alleged.

52 Proof of certain matters not necessary to validity of civil partnership

(1) Where two people have registered as civil partners of each other in England and Wales, it is not necessary in support of the civil partnership to give any proof—

- (a) that any person whose consent to the civil partnership was required by section 4 (parental etc consent) had given his consent, or
- (b) that the civil partnership registrar was designated as such by the registration authority in whose area the registration took place;

and no evidence is to be given to prove the contrary in any proceedings touching the validity of the civil partnership.

(2) Subsection (1)(a) is subject to section 49(c) (civil partnership void if forbidden).

53 Power to validate civil partnership

(1) Where two people have registered as civil partners of each other in England and Wales, the Lord Chancellor may by order validate the civil partnership if it appears to him that it is or may be void under section 49(b).

(2) An order under subsection (1) may include provisions for relieving a person from any liability under section 31(2), 32(2) or 33(5) or (7).

(3) The draft of an order under subsection (1) must be advertised, in such manner as the Lord Chancellor thinks fit, not less than one month before the order is made.

(4) The Lord Chancellor must—

- (a) consider all objections to the order sent to him in writing during that month, and
- (b) if it appears to him necessary, direct a local inquiry into the validity of any such objections.

(5) An order under subsection (1) is subject to special parliamentary procedure.

54 Validity of civil partnerships registered outside England and Wales

(1) Where two people register as civil partners of each other in Scotland, the civil partnership is—

- (a) void, if it would be void in Scotland under section 123, and
- (b) voidable, if the circumstances fall within section 50(1)(d).

(2) Where two people register as civil partners of each other in Northern Ireland, the civil partnership is—

- (a) void, if it would be void in Northern Ireland under section 173, and
- (b) voidable, if the circumstances fall within any paragraph of section 50(1).

(3) Subsection (4) applies where two people register as civil partners of each other under an Order in Council under—

(a) section 210 (registration at British consulates etc), or

(b) section 211 (registration by armed forces personnel),

('the relevant section').

(4) The civil partnership is—

(a) void, if—

    (i)   the condition in subsection (2)(a) or (b) of the relevant section is not met, or

    (ii) a requirement prescribed for the purposes of this paragraph by an Order in Council under the relevant section is not complied with, and

(b) voidable, if—

    (i)   the appropriate part of the United Kingdom is England and Wales or Northern Ireland and the circumstances fall within any paragraph of section 50(1), or

    (ii) the appropriate part of the United Kingdom is Scotland and the circumstances fall within section 50(1)(d).

(5) The appropriate part of the United Kingdom is the part by reference to which the condition in subsection (2)(b) of the relevant section is met.

(6) Subsections (7) and (8) apply where two people have registered an apparent or alleged overseas relationship.

(7) The civil partnership is void if—

(a) the relationship is not an overseas relationship, or

(b) (even though the relationship is an overseas relationship) the parties are not treated under Chapter 2 of Part 5 as having formed a civil partnership.

(8) The civil partnership is voidable if—

(a) the overseas relationship is voidable under the relevant law,

(b) the circumstances fall within section 50(1)(d), or

(c) where either of the parties was domiciled in England and Wales or Northern Ireland at the time when the overseas relationship was registered, the circumstances fall within section 50(1)(a), (b), (c) or (e).

(9) Section 51 applies for the purposes of—

(a) subsections (1)(b), (2)(b) and (4)(b),

(b) subsection (8)(a), in so far as applicable in accordance with the relevant law, and

(c) subsection (8)(b) and (c).

(10) In subsections (8)(a) and (9)(b) 'the relevant law' means the law of the country or territory where the overseas relationship was registered (including its rules of private international law).

(11) For the purposes of subsections (8) and (9)(b) and (c), references in sections 50 and 51 to the formation of the civil partnership are to be read as references to the registration of the overseas relationship.

Presumption of death orders

55 Presumption of death orders

(1) The court may, on an application made by a civil partner, make a presumption of death order if it is satisfied that reasonable grounds exist for supposing that the other civil partner is dead.

(2) In any proceedings under this section the fact that—

(a) for a period of 7 years or more the other civil partner has been continually absent from the applicant, and

(b) the applicant has no reason to believe that the other civil partner has been living within that time,

is evidence that the other civil partner is dead until the contrary is proved.

Separation orders

56 Separation orders

(1) An application for a separation order may be made to the court by either civil partner on the ground that any such fact as is mentioned in section 44(5)(a), (b), (c) or (d) exists.

(2) On an application for a separation order the court must inquire, so far as it reasonably can, into—

(a) the facts alleged by the applicant, and

(b) any facts alleged by the respondent,

but whether the civil partnership has broken down irretrievably is irrelevant.

(3) If the court is satisfied on the evidence of any such fact as is mentioned in section 44(5)(a), (b), (c) or (d) it must, subject to section 63, make a separation order.

(4) Section 45 (supplemental provisions as to facts raising presumption of breakdown) applies for the purposes of an application for a separation order alleging any such fact as it applies in relation to an application for a dissolution order alleging that fact.

57 Effect of separation order

If either civil partner dies intestate as respects all or any of his or her real or personal property while—

(a) a separation order is in force, and

(b) the separation is continuing,

the property as respects which he or she died intestate devolves as if the other civil partner had then been dead.

Declarations

58 Declarations

(1) Any person may apply to the High Court or a county court for one or more of the following declarations in relation to a civil partnership specified in the application—

(a) a declaration that the civil partnership was at its inception a valid civil partnership;

(b) a declaration that the civil partnership subsisted on a date specified in the application;

(c) a declaration that the civil partnership did not subsist on a date so specified;

(d) a declaration that the validity of a dissolution, annulment or legal separation obtained outside England and Wales in respect of the civil partnership is entitled to recognition in England and Wales;

(e) a declaration that the validity of a dissolution, annulment or legal separation so obtained in respect of the civil partnership is not entitled to recognition in England and Wales.

(2) Where an application under subsection (1) is made to a court by a person other than a civil partner in the civil partnership to which the application relates, the court must refuse to hear the

application if it considers that the applicant does not have a sufficient interest in the determination of that application.

59 General provisions as to making and effect of declarations

(1) Where on an application for a declaration under section 58 the truth of the proposition to be declared is proved to the satisfaction of the court, the court must make the declaration unless to do so would be manifestly contrary to public policy.

(2) Any declaration under section 58 binds Her Majesty and all other persons.

(3) The court, on the dismissal of an application for a declaration under section 58, may not make any declaration for which an application has not been made.

(4) No declaration which may be applied for under section 58 may be made otherwise than under section 58 by any court.

(5) No declaration may be made by any court, whether under section 58 or otherwise, that a civil partnership was at its inception void.

(6) Nothing in this section affects the powers of any court to make a nullity order in respect of a civil partnership.

60 The Attorney General and proceedings for declarations

(1) On an application for a declaration under section 58 the court may at any stage of the proceedings, of its own motion or on the application of any party to the proceedings, direct that all necessary papers in the matter be sent to the Attorney General.

(2) The Attorney General, whether or not he is sent papers in relation to an application for a declaration under section 58, may—

(a) intervene in the proceedings on that application in such manner as he thinks necessary or expedient, and
(b) argue before the court dealing with the application any question in relation to the application which the court considers it necessary to have fully argued.

(3) Where any costs are incurred by the Attorney General in connection with any application for a declaration under section 58, the court may make such order as it considers just as to the payment of those costs by parties to the proceedings.

61 Supplementary provisions as to declarations

(1) Any declaration made under section 58, and any application for such a declaration, must be in the form prescribed by rules of court.

(2) Rules of court may make provision—

(a) as to the information required to be given by any applicant for a declaration under section 58;
(b) requiring notice of an application under section 58 to be served on the Attorney General and on persons who may be affected by any declaration applied for.

(3) No proceedings under section 58 affect any final judgment or order already pronounced or made by any court of competent jurisdiction.

(4) The court hearing an application under section 58 may direct that the whole or any part of the proceedings must be heard in private.

(5) An application for a direction under subsection (4) must be heard in private unless the court otherwise directs.

General provisions

62 Relief for respondent in dissolution proceedings

(1) If in any proceedings for a dissolution order the respondent alleges and proves any such fact as is mentioned in section 44(5)(a), (b), (c) or (d) the court may give to the respondent the relief to which he would have been entitled if he had made an application seeking that relief.

(2) When applying subsection (1), treat—

(a) the respondent as the applicant, and
(b) the applicant as the respondent,

for the purposes of section 44(5).

63 Restrictions on making of orders affecting children

(1) In any proceedings for a dissolution, nullity or separation order, the court must consider—

(a) whether there are any children of the family to whom this section applies, and
(b) if there are any such children, whether (in the light of the arrangements which have been, or are proposed to be, made for their upbringing and welfare) it should exercise any of its powers under the Children Act 1989 (c 41) with respect to any of them.

(2) If, in the case of any child to whom this section applies, it appears to the court that—

(a) the circumstances of the case require it, or are likely to require it, to exercise any of its powers under the 1989 Act with respect to any such child,
(b) it is not in a position to exercise the power or (as the case may be) those powers without giving further consideration to the case, and
(c) there are exceptional circumstances which make it desirable in the interests of the child that the court should give a direction under this section,

it may direct that the order is not to be made final, or (in the case of a separation order) is not to be made, until the court orders otherwise.

(3) This section applies to—

(a) any child of the family who has not reached 16 at the date when the court considers the case in accordance with the requirements of this section, and
(b) any child of the family who has reached 16 at that date and in relation to whom the court directs that this section shall apply.

64 Parties to proceedings under this Chapter

(1) Rules of court may make provision with respect to—

(a) the joinder as parties to proceedings under sections 37 to 56 of persons involved in allegations of improper conduct made in those proceedings,
(b) the dismissal from such proceedings of any parties so joined, and
(c) the persons who are to be parties to proceedings on an application under section 58.

(2) Rules of court made under this section may make different provision for different cases.

(3) In every case in which the court considers, in the interest of a person not already a party to the proceedings, that the person should be made a party, the court may if it thinks fit allow the person to intervene upon such terms, if any, as the court thinks just.

(6) No order may be made under section 35 unless a draft of the statutory instrument containing the order has been laid before, and approved by a resolution of, each House of Parliament.

CHAPTER 3
PROPERTY AND FINANCIAL ARRANGEMENTS

65 Contribution by civil partner to property improvement

(1) This section applies if—

  (a) a civil partner contributes in money or money's worth to the improvement of real or personal property in which or in the proceeds of sale of which either or both of the civil partners has or have a beneficial interest, and
  (b) the contribution is of a substantial nature.

(2) The contributing partner is to be treated as having acquired by virtue of the contribution a share or an enlarged share (as the case may be) in the beneficial interest of such an extent—

  (a) as may have been then agreed, or
  (b) in default of such agreement, as may seem in all the circumstances just to any court before which the question of the existence or extent of the beneficial interest of either of the civil partners arises (whether in proceedings between them or in any other proceedings).

(3) Subsection (2) is subject to any agreement (express or implied) between the civil partners to the contrary.

66 Disputes between civil partners about property

(1) In any question between the civil partners in a civil partnership as to title to or possession of property, either civil partner may apply to—

  (a) the High Court, or
  (b) such county court as may be prescribed by rules of court.

(2) On such an application, the court may make such order with respect to the property as it thinks fit (including an order for the sale of the property).

(3) Rules of court made for the purposes of this section may confer jurisdiction on county courts whatever the situation or value of the property in dispute.

67 Applications under section 66 where property not in possession etc

(1) The right of a civil partner ('A') to make an application under section 66 includes the right to make such an application where A claims that the other civil partner ('B') has had in his possession or under his control—

  (a) money to which, or to a share of which, A was beneficially entitled, or
  (b) property (other than money) to which, or to an interest in which, A was beneficially entitled,

and that either the money or other property has ceased to be in B's possession or under B's control or that A does not know whether it is still in B's possession or under B's control.

(2) For the purposes of subsection (1)(a) it does not matter whether A is beneficially entitled to the money or share—

(a) because it represents the proceeds of property to which, or to an interest in which, A was beneficially entitled, or

(b) for any other reason.

(3) Subsections (4) and (5) apply if, on such an application being made, the court is satisfied that B—

(a) has had in his possession or under his control money or other property as mentioned in subsection (1)(a) or (b), and

(b) has not made to A, in respect of that money or other property, such payment or disposition as would have been appropriate in the circumstances.

(4) The power of the court to make orders under section 66 includes power to order B to pay to A—

(a) in a case falling within subsection (1)(a), such sum in respect of the money to which the application relates, or A's s share of it, as the court considers appropriate, or

(b) in a case falling within subsection (1)(b), such sum in respect of the value of the property to which the application relates, or A's interest in it, as the court considers appropriate.

(5) If it appears to the court that there is any property which—

(a) represents the whole or part of the money or property, and

(b) is property in respect of which an order could (apart from this section) have been made under section 66,

the court may (either instead of or as well as making an order in accordance with subsection (4)) make any order which it could (apart from this section) have made under section 66.

(6) Any power of the court which is exercisable on an application under section 66 is exercisable in relation to an application made under that section as extended by this section.

68 Applications under section 66 by former civil partners

(1) This section applies where a civil partnership has been dissolved or annulled.

(2) Subject to subsection (3), an application may be made under section 66 (including that section as extended by section 67) by either former civil partner despite the dissolution or annulment (and references in those sections to a civil partner are to be read accordingly).

(3) The application must be made within the period of 3 years beginning with the date of the dissolution or annulment.

69 Actions in tort between civil partners

(1) This section applies if an action in tort is brought by one civil partner against the other during the subsistence of the civil partnership.

(2) The court may stay the proceedings if it appears—

(a) that no substantial benefit would accrue to either civil partner from the continuation of the proceedings, or

(b) that the question or questions in issue could more conveniently be disposed of on an application under section 66.

(3) Without prejudice to subsection (2)(b), the court may in such an action—

(a) exercise any power which could be exercised on an application under section 66, or

(b) give such directions as it thinks fit for the disposal under that section of any question arising in the proceedings.

70 Assurance policy by civil partner for benefit of other civil partner etc

Section 11 of the Married Women's Property Act 1882 (c 75) (money payable under policy of assurance not to form part of the estate of the insured) applies in relation to a policy of assurance—

(a) effected by a civil partner on his own life, and
(b) expressed to be for the benefit of his civil partner, or of his children, or of his civil partner and children, or any of them,

as it applies in relation to a policy of assurance effected by a husband and expressed to be for the benefit of his wife, or of his children, or of his wife and children, or of any of them.

71 Wills, administration of estates and family provision

Schedule 4 amends enactments relating to wills, administration of estates and family provision so that they apply in relation to civil partnerships as they apply in relation to marriage.

72 Financial relief for civil partners and children of family

(1) Schedule 5 makes provision for financial relief in connection with civil partnerships that corresponds to provision made for financial relief in connection with marriages by Part 2 of the Matrimonial Causes Act 1973 (c 18).

(2) Any rule of law under which any provision of Part 2 of the 1973 Act is interpreted as applying to dissolution of a marriage on the ground of presumed death is to be treated as applying (with any necessary modifications) in relation to the corresponding provision of Schedule 5.

(3) Schedule 6 makes provision for financial relief in connection with civil partnerships that corresponds to provision made for financial relief in connection with marriages by the Domestic Proceedings and Magistrates' Courts Act 1978 (c 22).

(4) Schedule 7 makes provision for financial relief in England and Wales after a civil partnership has been dissolved or annulled, or civil partners have been legally separated, in a country outside the British Islands.

CHAPTER 4
CIVIL PARTNERSHIP AGREEMENTS

73 Civil partnership agreements unenforceable

(1) A civil partnership agreement does not under the law of England and Wales have effect as a contract giving rise to legal rights.

(2) No action lies in England and Wales for breach of a civil partnership agreement, whatever the law applicable to the agreement.

(3) In this section and section 74 'civil partnership agreement' means an agreement between two people—

(a) to register as civil partners of each other—
    (i)   in England and Wales (under this Part),
    (ii) in Scotland (under Part 3),
    (iii) in Northern Ireland (under Part 4), or

    (iv) outside the United Kingdom under an Order in Council made under Chapter 1 of Part 5 (registration at British consulates etc or by armed forces personnel), or

  (b) to enter into an overseas relationship.

(4) This section applies in relation to civil partnership agreements whether entered into before or after this section comes into force, but does not affect any action commenced before it comes into force.

74 Property where civil partnership agreement is terminated

(1) This section applies if a civil partnership agreement is terminated.

(2) Section 65 (contributions by civil partner to property improvement) applies, in relation to any property in which either or both of the parties to the agreement had a beneficial interest while the agreement was in force, as it applies in relation to property in which a civil partner has a beneficial interest.

(3) Sections 66 and 67 (disputes between civil partners about property) apply to any dispute between or claim by one of the parties in relation to property in which either or both had a beneficial interest while the agreement was in force, as if the parties were civil partners of each other.

(4) An application made under section 66 or 67 by virtue of subsection (3) must be made within 3 years of the termination of the agreement.

(5) A party to a civil partnership agreement who makes a gift of property to the other party on the condition (express or implied) that it is to be returned if the agreement is terminated is not prevented from recovering the property merely because of his having terminated the agreement.

CHAPTER 5
CHILDREN

75 Parental responsibility, children of the family and relatives

(1) Amend the Children Act 1989 (c 41) ('the 1989 Act') as follows.

(2) In section 4A(1) (acquisition of parental responsibility by step-parent) after 'is married to' insert ', or a civil partner of,'.

(3) In section 105(1) (interpretation), for the definition of 'child of the family' (in relation to the parties to a marriage) substitute—

    '"child of the family", in relation to parties to a marriage, or to two people who are civil partners of each other, means—

    (a) a child of both of them, and

    (b) any other child, other than a child placed with them as foster parents by a local authority or voluntary organisation, who has been treated by both of them as a child of their family.'

(4) In the definition of 'relative' in section 105(1), for 'by affinity)' substitute 'by marriage or civil partnership)'.

76 Guardianship

In section 6 of the 1989 Act (guardians: revocation and disclaimer) after subsection (3A) insert—

    '(3B) An appointment under section 5(3) or (4) (including one made in an unrevoked will or codicil) is revoked if the person appointed is the civil partner of the person who made the appointment and either—

> (a) an order of a court of civil jurisdiction in England and Wales dissolves or annuls the civil partnership, or
> (b) the civil partnership is dissolved or annulled and the dissolution or annulment is entitled to recognition in England and Wales by virtue of Chapter 3 of Part 5 of the Civil Partnership Act 2004,

unless a contrary intention appears by the appointment.'

77 Entitlement to apply for residence or contact order

In section 10(5) of the 1989 Act (persons entitled to apply for residence or contact order) after paragraph (a) insert—

> '(aa) any civil partner in a civil partnership (whether or not subsisting) in relation to whom the child is a child of the family;'.

78 Financial provision for children

(1) Amend Schedule 1 to the 1989 Act (financial provision for children) as follows.

(2) In paragraph 2(6) (meaning of 'periodical payments order') after paragraph (d) insert—

> '(e) Part 1 or 9 of Schedule 5 to the Civil Partnership Act 2004 (financial relief in the High Court or a county court etc);
> (f) Schedule 6 to the 2004 Act (financial relief in the magistrates' courts etc),'.

(3) In paragraph 15(2) (person with whom a child lives or is to live) after 'husband or wife' insert 'or civil partner'.

(4) For paragraph 16(2) (extended meaning of 'parent') substitute—

> '(2) In this Schedule, except paragraphs 2 and 15, "parent" includes—

> > (a) any party to a marriage (whether or not subsisting) in relation to whom the child concerned is a child of the family, and
> > (b) any civil partner in a civil partnership (whether or not subsisting) in relation to whom the child concerned is a child of the family;

> and for this purpose any reference to either parent or both parents shall be read as a reference to any parent of his and to all of his parents.'

79 Adoption

(1) Amend the Adoption and Children Act 2002 (c 38) as follows.

(2) In section 21 (placement orders), in subsection (4)(c), after 'child marries' insert ', forms a civil partnership'.

(3) In section 47 (conditions for making adoption orders), after subsection (8) insert—

> '(8A) An adoption order may not be made in relation to a person who is or has been a civil partner.'

(4) In section 51 (adoption by one person), in subsection (1), after 'is not married' insert 'or a civil partner'.

(5) After section 51(3) insert—

'(3A) An adoption order may be made on the application of one person who has attained the age of 21 years and is a civil partner if the court is satisfied that—

(a) the person's civil partner cannot be found,

(b) the civil partners have separated and are living apart, and the separation is likely to be permanent, or

(c) the person's civil partner is by reason of ill-health, whether physical or mental, incapable of making an application for an adoption order.'

(6) In section 64 (other provision to be made by regulations), in subsection (5) for 'or marriage' substitute ', marriage or civil partnership'.

(7) In section 74(1) (enactments for whose purposes section 67 does not apply), for paragraph (a) substitute—

'(a) section 1 of and Schedule 1 to the Marriage Act 1949 or Schedule 1 to the Civil Partnership Act 2004 (prohibited degrees of kindred and affinity),'.

(8) In section 79 (connections between the register and birth records), in subsection (7)—

(a) in paragraph (b), after 'intends to be married' insert 'or form a civil partnership', and

(b) for 'the person whom the applicant intends to marry' substitute 'the intended spouse or civil partner'.

(9) In section 81 (Adoption Contact Register: supplementary), in subsection (2) for 'or marriage' substitute ', marriage or civil partnership'.

(10) In section 98 (pre-commencement adoptions: information), in subsection (7), in the definition of 'relative' for 'or marriage' substitute ', marriage or civil partnership'.

(11) In section 144 (interpretation), in the definition of 'relative' in subsection (1), after 'by marriage' insert 'or civil partnership'.

(12) In section 144(4) (meaning of 'couple'), after paragraph (a) insert—

'(aa) two people who are civil partners of each other, or'.

CHAPTER 6
MISCELLANEOUS

80 False statements etc with reference to civil partnerships

(1) A person commits an offence if—

(a) for the purpose of procuring the formation of a civil partnership, or a document mentioned in subsection (2), he—

(i) makes or signs a declaration required under this Part or Part 5, or

(ii) gives a notice or certificate so required,

knowing that the declaration, notice or certificate is false,

(b) for the purpose of a record being made in any register relating to civil partnerships, he—

(i) makes a statement as to any information which is required to be registered under this Part or Part 5, or

(ii) causes such a statement to be made,

knowing that the statement is false,

(c) he forbids the issue of a document mentioned in subsection (2)(a) or (b) by representing himself to be a person whose consent to a civil partnership between a child and another person is required under this Part or Part 5, knowing the representation to be false, or

(d) with respect to a declaration made under paragraph 5(1) of Schedule 1 he makes a statement mentioned in paragraph 6 of that Schedule which he knows to be false in a material particular.

(2) The documents are—

(a) a civil partnership schedule or a Registrar General's licence under Chapter 1;

(b) a document required by an Order in Council under section 210 or 211 as an authority for two people to register as civil partners of each other;

(c) a certificate of no impediment under section 240.

(3) A person guilty of an offence under subsection (1) is liable—

(a) on conviction on indictment, to imprisonment for a term not exceeding 7 years or to a fine (or both);

(b) on summary conviction, to a fine not exceeding the statutory maximum.

(4) The Perjury Act 1911 (c 6) has effect as if this section were contained in it.

81 Housing and tenancies

Schedule 8 amends certain enactments relating to housing and tenancies.

82 Family homes and domestic violence

Schedule 9 amends Part 4 of the Family Law Act 1996 (c 27) and related enactments so that they apply in relation to civil partnerships as they apply in relation to marriages.

83 Fatal accidents claims

(1) Amend the Fatal Accidents Act 1976 (c 30) as follows.

(2) In section 1(3) (meaning of 'dependant' for purposes of right of action for wrongful act causing death), after paragraph (a) insert—

'(aa) the civil partner or former civil partner of the deceased;'.

(3) In paragraph (b)(iii) of section 1(3), after 'wife' insert 'or civil partner'.

(4) After paragraph (f) of section 1(3) insert—

'(fa) any person (not being a child of the deceased) who, in the case of any civil partnership in which the deceased was at any time a civil partner, was treated by the deceased as a child of the family in relation to that civil partnership;'.

(5) After section 1(4) insert—

'(4A) The reference to the former civil partner of the deceased in subsection (3)(aa) above includes a reference to a person whose civil partnership with the deceased has been annulled as well as a person whose civil partnership with the deceased has been dissolved.'

(6) In section 1(5)(a), for 'by affinity' substitute 'by marriage or civil partnership'.

(7) In section 1A(2) (persons for whose benefit claim for bereavement damages may be made)—

(a) in paragraph (a), after 'wife or husband' insert 'or civil partner', and

(b) in paragraph (b), after 'was never married' insert 'or a civil partner'.

(8) In section 3 (assessment of damages), in subsection (4), after 'wife' insert 'or civil partner'.

84 Evidence

(1) Any enactment or rule of law relating to the giving of evidence by a spouse applies in relation to a civil partner as it applies in relation to the spouse.

(2) Subsection (1) is subject to any specific amendment made by or under this Act which relates to the giving of evidence by a civil partner.

(3) For the avoidance of doubt, in any such amendment, references to a person's civil partner do not include a former civil partner.

(4) References in subsections (1) and (2) to giving evidence are to giving evidence in any way (whether by supplying information, making discovery, producing documents or otherwise).

(5) Any rule of law—

    (a) which is preserved by section 7(3) of the Civil Evidence Act 1995 (c 38) or section 118(1) of the Criminal Justice Act 2003 (c 44), and
    (b) under which in any proceedings evidence of reputation or family tradition is admissible for the purpose of proving or disproving the existence of a marriage,

is to be treated as applying in an equivalent way for the purpose of proving or disproving the existence of a civil partnership.

PART 3
CIVIL PARTNERSHIP: SCOTLAND

CHAPTER 1
FORMATION AND ELIGIBILITY

85 Formation of civil partnership by registration

(1) For the purposes of section 1, two people are to be regarded as having registered as civil partners of each other once each of them has signed the civil partnership schedule, in the presence of—

    (a) each other,
    (b) two witnesses both of whom have attained the age of 16, and
    (c) the authorised registrar,

(all being present at a registration office or at a place agreed under section 93).

(2) But the two people must be eligible to be so registered.

(3) Subsection (1) applies regardless of whether subsection (4) is complied with.

(4) After the civil partnership schedule has been signed under subsection (1), it must also be signed, in the presence of the civil partners and each other by—

    (a) each of the two witnesses, and
    (b) the authorised registrar.

86 Eligibility

(1) Two people are not eligible to register in Scotland as civil partners of each other if—

    (a) they are not of the same sex,

(b) they are related in a forbidden degree,

(c) either has not attained the age of 16,

(d) either is married or already in civil partnership, or

(e) either is incapable of—

    (i)   understanding the nature of civil partnership, or

    (ii) validly consenting to its formation.

(2) Subject to subsections (3) and (4), a man is related in a forbidden degree to another man if related to him in a degree specified in column 1 of Schedule 10 and a woman is related in a forbidden degree to another woman if related to her in a degree specified in column 2 of that Schedule.

(3) A man and any man related to him in a degree specified in column 1 of paragraph 2 of Schedule 10, or a woman and any woman related to her in a degree specified in column 2 of that paragraph, are not related in a forbidden degree if—

(a) both persons have attained the age of 21, and

(b) the younger has not at any time before attaining the age of 18 lived in the same household as the elder and been treated by the elder as a child of the elder's family.

(4) A man and any man related to him in a degree specified in column 1 of paragraph 3 of Schedule 10, or a woman and any woman related to her in a degree specified in column 2 of that paragraph, are not related in a forbidden degree if—

(a) both persons have attained the age of 21, and

(b) in the case of—

    (i)   a man entering civil partnership with the father of his former wife, both the former wife and the former wife's mother are dead,

    (ii) a man entering civil partnership with the father of his former civil partner, both the former civil partner and the former civil partner's mother are dead,

    (iii) a man entering civil partnership with the former husband of his daughter, both the daughter and the daughter's mother are dead,

    (iv) a man entering civil partnership with the former civil partner of his son, both the son and the son's mother are dead,

    (v) a woman entering civil partnership with the mother of her former husband, both the former husband and the former husband's father are dead,

    (vi) a woman entering civil partnership with the mother of her former civil partner, both the former civil partner and the former civil partner's father are dead,

    (vii) a woman entering civil partnership with the former wife of her son, both the son and the son's father are dead, or

   (viii)a woman entering civil partnership with the former civil partner of her daughter, both the daughter and the daughter's father are dead.

(5) Subsection (4) and paragraphs 2 and 3 of Schedule 10 have effect subject to the modifications specified in subsections (6) and (7) in the case of a person (here the 'relevant person') whose gender has become the acquired gender under the Gender Recognition Act 2004 (c 7).

(6) Any reference in subsection (4) or those paragraphs to a former wife or former husband of the relevant person includes (respectively) any former husband or former wife of the relevant person.

(7) And the reference—

(a) in sub-paragraph (iii) of subsection (4)(b) to the relevant person's daughter's mother is to the relevant person's daughter's father if the relevant person is the daughter's mother,

(b) in sub-paragraph (iv) of that subsection to the relevant person's son's mother is to the relevant person's son's father if the relevant person is the son's mother,

(c) in sub-paragraph (vii) of that subsection to the relevant person's son's father is to the relevant person's son's mother if the relevant person is the son's father, and

(d) in sub-paragraph (viii) of that subsection to the relevant person's daughter's father is to the relevant person's daughter's mother if the relevant person is the daughter's father.

(8) References in this section and in Schedule 10 to relationships and degrees of relationship are to be construed in accordance with section 1(1) of the Law Reform (Parent and Child) (Scotland) Act 1986 (c 9).

(9) For the purposes of this section, a degree of relationship specified in paragraph 1 of Schedule 10 exists whether it is of the full blood or the half blood.

(10) Amend section 41(1) of the Adoption (Scotland) Act 1978 (c 28) (application to determination of forbidden degrees of provisions of that Act relating to the status conferred by adoption) as follows—

(a) after first 'marriage' insert ', to the eligibility of persons to register as civil partners of each other', and

(b) for 'and incest' substitute ', to such eligibility and to incest'.

CHAPTER 2
REGISTRATION

87 Appointment of authorised registrars

For the purpose of affording reasonable facilities throughout Scotland for registration as civil partners, the Registrar General—

(a) is to appoint such number of district registrars as he thinks necessary, and

(b) may, in respect of any district for which he has made an appointment under paragraph (a), appoint one or more assistant registrars,

as persons who may carry out such registration (in this Part referred to as 'authorised registrars').

88 Notice of proposed civil partnership

(1) In order to register as civil partners, each of the intended civil partners must submit to the district registrar a notice, in the prescribed form and accompanied by the prescribed fee, of intention to enter civil partnership (in this Part referred to as a 'notice of proposed civil partnership').

(2) A notice submitted under subsection (1) must also be accompanied by—

(a) the birth certificate of the person submitting it,

(b) if that person has previously been married or in civil partnership and—

(i) the marriage or civil partnership has been dissolved, a copy of the decree of divorce or dissolution, or

(ii) the other party to that marriage or civil partnership has died, the death certificate of that other party, and

(c) if that person has previously ostensibly been married or in civil partnership but decree of annulment has been obtained, a copy of that decree.

(3) If a person is unable to submit a certificate or decree required by subsection (2) he may instead make a declaration to that effect, stating what the reasons are; and he must provide the district registrar with such—

(a) information in respect of the matters to which the certificate or document would have related, and

(b) documentary evidence in support of that information,

as the district registrar may require.

(4) If a document submitted under subsection (2) or (3) is in a language other than English, the person submitting it must attach to the document a translation of it in English, certified by the translator as a correct translation.

(5) A person submitting a notice under subsection (1) must make and sign the necessary declaration (the form for which must be included in any form prescribed for the notice).

(6) The necessary declaration is a declaration that the person submitting the notice believes that the intended civil partners are eligible to be in civil partnership with each other.

89 Civil partnership notice book

(1) On receipt of a notice of proposed civil partnership, the district registrar is to enter in a book (to be known as 'the civil partnership book') supplied to him for that purpose by the Registrar General such particulars, extracted from the notice, as may be prescribed and the date of receipt by him of that notice.

(2) The form and content of any page of that book is to be prescribed.

90 Publicisation

(1) Where notices of a proposed civil partnership are submitted to a district registrar, he must, as soon as practicable after the day on which they are submitted (or, if the two documents are not submitted on the same day, after the day on which the first is submitted), publicise the relevant information and send it to the Registrar General who must also publicise it.

(2) 'The relevant information' means—

(a) the names of the intended civil partners, and

(b) the date on which it is intended to register them as civil partners of each other, being a date more than 14 days after publicisation by the district registrar under subsection (1).

(3) Paragraph (b) of subsection (2) is subject to section 91.

(4) The manner in which and means by which relevant information is to be publicised are to be prescribed.

91 Early registration

An authorised registrar who receives a request in writing from one or both of two intended civil partners that they should be registered as civil partners of each other on a date specified in the request (being a date 14 days or fewer after publicisation by the district registrar under subsection (1) of section 90) may, provided that he is authorised to do so by the Registrar General, fix that date as the date for registration; and if a date is so fixed, paragraph (b) of subsection (2) of that section is to be construed as if it were a reference to that date.

92 Objections to registration

(1) Any person may at any time before the registration in Scotland of two people as civil partners of each other submit in writing an objection to such registration to the district registrar.

(2) But where the objection is that the intended civil partners are not eligible to be in civil partnership with each other because either is incapable of—

(a) understanding the nature of civil partnership, or
(b) validly consenting to its formation,

it shall be accompanied by a supporting certificate signed by a registered medical practitioner.

(3) A person claiming that he may have reason to submit such an objection may, free of charge and at any time when the registration office at which a notice of proposed civil partnership to which the objection would relate is open for public business, inspect any relevant entry in the civil partnership book.

(4) Where the district registrar receives an objection in accordance with subsection (1) he must—

(a) in any case where he is satisfied that the objection relates to no more than a misdescription or inaccuracy in a notice submitted under section 88(1)—
  (i) notify the intended civil partners of the nature of the objection and make such enquiries into the matter mentioned in it as he thinks fit, and
  (ii) subject to the approval of the Registrar General, make any necessary correction to any document relating to the proposed civil partnership, or
(b) in any other case—
  (i) at once notify the Registrar General of the objection, and
  (ii) pending consideration of the objection by the Registrar General, suspend the completion or issue of the civil partnership schedule in respect of the proposed civil partnership.

(5) If the Registrar General is satisfied, on consideration of an objection of which he has received notification under subsection (4)(b)(i) that—

(a) there is a legal impediment to registration, he must direct the district registrar not to register the intended civil partners and to notify them accordingly, or
(b) there is no such impediment, he must inform the district registrar to that effect.

(6) For the purposes of this section and section 94, there is a legal impediment to registration where the intended civil partners are not eligible to be in civil partnership with each other.

93 Place of registration

(1) Two people may be registered as civil partners of each other at a registration office or any other place which they and the local registration authority agree is to be the place of registration.

(2) The place of registration may, if the approval of the Registrar General is obtained, be outwith the district of the authorised registrar carrying out the registration.

(3) But the place must not be in religious premises, that is to say premises which—

(a) are used solely or mainly for religious purposes, or
(b) have been so used and have not subsequently been used solely or mainly for other purposes.

(4) 'Local registration authority' has the meaning given by section 5(3) of the 1965 Act.

94 The civil partnership schedule

Where—

(a) the district registrar has received a notice of proposed civil partnership in respect of each of the intended civil partners and—

(i)   is satisfied that there is no legal impediment to their registration as civil partners of each other, or

(ii) as the case may be, is informed under section 92(5)(b) that there is no such impediment,

(b) the 14 days mentioned in paragraph (b) of section 90(2) have expired (or as the case may be the date which, by virtue of section 91, that paragraph is to be construed as a reference to has been reached), and

(c) the period which has elapsed since the day of receipt of the notices by him (or, if the two notices were not received on the same day, since the day of receipt of the later) does not exceed 3 months,

he is to complete a civil partnership schedule in the prescribed form.

95 Further provision as to registration

(1) Before the persons present sign in accordance with section 85 the authorised registrar is to require the intended civil partners to confirm that (to the best of their knowledge) the particulars set out in the civil partnership schedule are correct.

(2) As soon as practicable after the civil partnership schedule has been signed, the authorised registrar must cause those particulars to be entered in a register (to be known as the 'civil partnership register') supplied to him for that purpose by the Registrar General.

(3) The form and content of any page of that register is to be prescribed.

(4) A fee payable by the intended civil partners for their registration as civil partners of each other is to be prescribed.

96 Civil partnership with former spouse

(1) Where an intended civil partner has a full gender recognition certificate issued under section 5(1) of the Gender Recognition Act 2004 (c 7) and the other intended civil partner was the other party in the proceedings in which the certificate was issued, the procedures for their registration as civil partners of each other may—

(a) if they so elect, and

(b) if each of them submits a notice under section 88(1) within 30 days after the certificate is issued,

be expedited as follows.

(2) The registration may take place on any of the 30 days immediately following—

(a) that on which the notices are submitted, or

(b) (if the two notices are not submitted on the same day) that on which the later is submitted.

(3) And accordingly there are to be disregarded—

(a) in section 90—
(i)   in subsection (2)(b), the words from 'being' to the end, and
(ii) subsection (3),

(b) section 91, and

(c) in section 94, paragraph (b).

97 Certificates of no impediment for Part 2 purposes

(1) This section applies where—

(a) two people propose to register as civil partners of each other under Chapter 1 of Part 2, and

(b) one of them ('A') resides in Scotland but the other ('B') resides in England or Wales.

(2) A may submit a notice of intention to register under section 88 as if A and B intended to register as civil partners in the district in which A resides.

(3) If the district registrar is satisfied (after consultation, if he considers it necessary, with the Registrar General) that there is no impediment (in terms of section 92(6)) to A registering as B's civil partner, he must issue a certificate to A in the prescribed form that there is not known to be any such impediment.

(4) But the certificate may not be issued to A earlier than 14 days after the receipt (as entered in the civil partnership notice book) of the notice under subsection (2) unless—

(a) the circumstances are as mentioned in section 96(1), and

(b) A makes an election for the certificate to be issued as soon as possible.

(5) Any person may, at any time before a certificate is issued under subsection (3), submit to the district registrar an objection in writing to its issue.

(6) Any objection made under subsection (5) must be taken into account by the district registrar in deciding whether he is satisfied that there is no legal impediment to A registering as B's civil partner.

98 Application of certain sections of 1965 Act to civil partnership register

Sections 34 (examination of registers by district examiners), 37(1) and (2) (search of indexes kept by registrars), 38(1) and (2) (search of indexes kept by Registrar General) and 44 (Register of Corrections etc) of the 1965 Act apply in relation to the civil partnership register as they apply in relation to the registers of births, deaths and marriages.

99 Correction of errors in civil partnership register

(1) No alteration is to be made in the civil partnership register except as authorised by or under this or any other Act ('Act' including an Act of the Scottish Parliament).

(2) Any clerical error in the register or error in it of a kind prescribed may be corrected by the district registrar.

(3) The Registrar General may authorise district examiners ('district examiner' having the meaning given by section 2(1) of the 1965 Act) to correct any error in the register of a type specified by him which they discover during an examination under section 34 of the 1965 Act.

100 Offences

(1) A person ('A') commits an offence who registers in Scotland as the civil partner of another person ('B') knowing that either or both—

(a) A is already married to or in civil partnership with a person other than B, or

(b) B is already married to or in civil partnership with a person other than A.

(2) A person commits an offence who knowingly—

(a) falsifies or forges any civil partnership document (that is to say, any document issued or made, or purporting to be issued or made, or required, under this Part),

(b) uses, or gives or sends to any person as genuine, any false or forged civil partnership document,

(c) being an authorised registrar, purports to register two people as civil partners of each other before any civil partnership schedule available to him at the time of registration has been duly completed,

(d) not being an authorised registrar, conducts himself in such a way as to lead intended civil partners to believe that he is authorised to register them as civil partners of each other,

(e) being an authorised registrar, purports to register two people as civil partners of each other without both of them being present, or

(f) being an authorised registrar, purports to register two people as civil partners of each other in a place other than a registration office or a place agreed under section 93.

(3) A person guilty of an offence under subsection (1) or (2) is liable—

(a) on conviction on indictment, to imprisonment for a term not exceeding 2 years or to a fine (or both);

(b) on summary conviction, to imprisonment for a term not exceeding 3 months or to a fine not exceeding level 3 on the standard scale (or both).

(4) Summary proceedings for an offence under subsection (1) or (2) may be commenced at any time within 3 months after evidence sufficient in the opinion of the Lord Advocate to justify the proceedings comes to his knowledge or within 12 months after the offence is committed (whichever period last expires).

(5) Subsection (3) of section 136 of the Criminal Procedure (Scotland) Act 1995 (c 46) (time limits) has effect for the purposes of this section as it has for the purposes of that section.

CHAPTER 3
OCCUPANCY RIGHTS AND TENANCIES

Occupancy rights

101 Occupancy rights

(1) Where, apart from the provisions of this Chapter, one civil partner in a civil partnership is entitled, or permitted by a third party, to occupy a family home of the civil partnership (that civil partner being referred in this Chapter as an 'entitled partner') and the other civil partner is not so entitled or permitted (a 'non-entitled partner'), the non-entitled partner has, subject to the provisions of this Chapter, the following rights—

(a) if in occupation, a right to continue to occupy the family home;
(b) if not in occupation, a right to enter into and occupy the family home.

(2) The rights conferred by subsection (1) to continue to occupy or, as the case may be, to enter and occupy the family home include, without prejudice to their generality, the right to do so together with any child of the family.

(3) In subsection (1), an 'entitled partner' includes a civil partner who is entitled, or permitted by a third party, to occupy the family home along with an individual who is not the other civil partner only if that individual has waived a right of occupation in favour of the civil partner so entitled or permitted.

(4) If the entitled partner refuses to allow the non-entitled partner to exercise the right conferred by subsection (1)(b), the non-entitled partner may exercise that right only with the leave of the Court of Session or the sheriff under section 103(3) or (4).

(5) A non-entitled partner may renounce in writing the rights mentioned in paragraphs (a) and (b) of subsection (1) only—

(a) in a particular family home, or
(b) in a particular property which it is intended by the civil partners will become their family home.

(6) A renunciation under subsection (5) has effect only if, at the time of making the renunciation, the non-entitled partner swears or affirms before a notary public that it is made freely and without coercion of any kind.

(7) In this Part—

'child of the family' means a child under the age of 16 years who has been accepted by both civil partners as a child of the family, and

'family' means the civil partners in the civil partnership, together with any child so accepted by them.

(8) In subsection (6), 'notary public' includes any person duly authorised, by the law of the country other than Scotland in which the swearing or affirmation takes place, to administer oaths or receive affirmations in that other country.

102 Occupancy: subsidiary and consequential rights

(1) For the purpose of securing the occupancy rights of a non-entitled partner, that partner is, in relation to a family home, entitled without the consent of the entitled partner—

(a) to make any payment due by the entitled partner in respect of rent, rates, secured loan instalments, interest or other outgoings (not being outgoings on repairs or improvements);
(b) to perform any other obligation incumbent on the entitled partner (not being an obligation in respect of non-essential repairs or improvements);
(c) to enforce performance of an obligation by a third party which that third party has undertaken to the entitled partner to the extent that the entitled partner may enforce such performance;
(d) to carry out such essential repairs as the entitled partner may carry out;
(e) to carry out such non-essential repairs or improvements as may be authorised by an order of the court, being such repairs or improvements as the entitled partner may carry out and which the court considers to be appropriate for the reasonable enjoyment of the occupancy rights;
(f) to take such other steps, for the purpose of protecting the occupancy rights of the non-entitled partner, as the entitled partner may take to protect the occupancy rights of the entitled partner.

(2) Any payment made under subsection (1)(a) or any obligation performed under subsection (1)(b) has effect in relation to the rights of a third party as if the payment were made or the obligation were performed by the entitled partner; and the performance of an obligation which has been enforced under subsection (1)(c) has effect as if it had been enforced by the entitled partner.

(3) Where there is an entitled and a non-entitled partner, the court, on the application of either of them, may, having regard in particular to the respective financial circumstances of the partners, make an order apportioning expenditure incurred or to be incurred by either partner—

(a) without the consent of the other partner, on any of the items mentioned in paragraphs (a) and (d) of subsection (1);
(b) with the consent of the other partner, on anything relating to a family home.

(4) Where both partners are entitled, or permitted by a third party, to occupy a family home—

(a) either partner is entitled, without the consent of the other partner, to carry out such non-essential repairs or improvements as may be authorised by an order of the court, being such repairs or improvements as the court considers to be appropriate for the reasonable enjoyment of the occupancy rights;

(b) the court, on the application of either partner, may, having regard in particular to the respective financial circumstances of the partners, make an order apportioning expenditure incurred or to be incurred by either partner, with or without the consent of the other partner, on anything relating to the family home.

(5) Where one partner ('A') owns or hires, or is acquiring under a hire-purchase or conditional sale agreement, furniture and plenishings in a family home—

(a) the other partner may, without the consent of A—

  (i) make any payment due by A which is necessary, or take any other step which A is entitled to take, to secure the possession or use of any such furniture and plenishings (and any such payment is to have effect in relation to the rights of a third party as if it were made by A), or

  (ii) carry out such essential repairs to the furniture and plenishings as A is entitled to carry out;

(b) the court, on the application of either partner, may, having regard in particular to the respective financial circumstances of the partners, make an order apportioning expenditure incurred or to be incurred by either partner—

  (i) without the consent of the other partner, in making payments under a hire, hire-purchase or conditional sale agreement, or in paying interest charges in respect of the furniture and plenishings, or in carrying out essential repairs to the furniture and plenishings, or

  (ii) with the consent of the other partner, on anything relating to the furniture or plenishings.

(6) An order under subsection (3), (4)(b) or (5)(b) may require one partner to make a payment to the other partner in implementation of the apportionment.

(7) Any application under subsection (3), (4)(b) or (5)(b) is to be made within 5 years after the date on which any payment in respect of such incurred expenditure was made.

(8) Where—

(a) the entitled partner is a tenant of a family home,
(b) possession of it is necessary in order to continue the tenancy, and
(c) the entitled partner abandons such possession,

the tenancy is continued by such possession by the non-entitled partner.

(9) In this section 'improvements' includes alterations and enlargement.

103 Regulation by court of rights of occupancy of family home

(1) Where there is an entitled and a non-entitled partner, or where both partners are entitled, or permitted by a third party, to occupy a family home, either partner may apply to the court for an order—

(a) declaring the occupancy rights of the applicant partner;
(b) enforcing the occupancy rights of the applicant partner;
(c) restricting the occupancy rights of the non-applicant partner;
(d) regulating the exercise by either partner of his or her occupancy rights;

(e) protecting the occupancy rights of the applicant partner in relation to the other partner.

(2) Where one partner owns or hires, or is acquiring under a hire-purchase or conditional sale agreement, furniture and plenishings in a family home and the other partner has occupancy rights in that home, that other person may apply to the court for an order granting to the applicant the possession or use in the family home of any such furniture and plenishings; but, subject to section 102, an order under this subsection does not prejudice the rights of any third party in relation to the non-performance of any obligation under such hire-purchase or conditional sale agreement.

(3) The court is to grant an application under subsection (1)(a) if it appears to the court that the application relates to a family home; and, on an application under any of paragraphs (b) to (e) of subsection (1) or under subsection (2), the court may make such order relating to the application as appears to it to be just and reasonable having regard to all the circumstances of the case including—

    (a) the conduct of the partners, whether in relation to each other or otherwise,

    (b) the respective needs and financial resources of the partners,

    (c) the needs of any child of the family,

    (d) the extent (if any) to which—

        (i) the family home, and

        (ii) in relation only to an order under subsection (2), any item of furniture and plenishings referred to in that subsection, is used in connection with a trade, business or profession of either partner, and

    (e) whether the entitled partner offers or has offered to make available to the non-entitled partner any suitable alternative accommodation.

(4) Pending the making of an order under subsection (3), the court, on the application of either partner, may make such interim order as it considers necessary or expedient in relation to—

    (a) the residence of either partner in the home to which the application relates,

    (b) the personal effects of either partner or of any child of the family, or

    (c) the furniture and plenishings,

but an interim order may be made only if the non-applicant partner has been afforded an opportunity of being heard by or represented before the court.

(5) The court is not to make an order under subsection (3) or (4) if it appears that the effect of the order would be to exclude the non-applicant partner from the family home.

(6) If the court makes an order under subsection (3) or (4) which requires the delivery to one partner of anything which has been left in or removed from the family home, it may also grant a warrant authorising a messenger-at-arms or sheriff officer to enter the family home or other premises occupied by the other partner and to search for and take possession of the thing required to be delivered, (if need be by opening shut and lockfast places) and to deliver the thing in accordance with the order.

(7) A warrant granted under subsection (6) is to be executed only after expiry of such period as the court is to specify in the order for delivery.

(8) Where it appears to the court—

    (a) on the application of a non-entitled partner, that the applicant has suffered a loss of occupancy rights or that the quality of the applicant's occupation of a family home has been impaired, or

    (b) on the application of a partner who has been given the possession or use of furniture and plenishings by virtue of an order under subsection (3), that the applicant has suffered a loss of such possession or use or that the quality of the applicant's possession or use of the furniture and plenishings has been impaired, in consequence of any act or default on the part of the other partner which was intended to result in such loss or impairment, it may order that other partner to pay to the applicant such compensation as it considers just and reasonable in respect of that loss or impairment.

(9) A partner may renounce in writing the right to apply under subsection (2) for the possession or use of any item of furniture and plenishings.

104 Exclusion orders

(1) Where there is an entitled and non-entitled partner, or where both partners are entitled, or permitted by a third party, to occupy a family home, either partner, whether or not that partner is in occupation at the time of the application, may apply to the court for an order (in this Chapter referred to as 'an exclusion order') suspending the occupancy rights of the other partner ('the non-applicant partner') in a family home.

(2) Subject to subsection (3), the court is to make an exclusion order if it appears to it that to do so is necessary for the protection of the applicant or any child of the family from any conduct, or threatened or reasonably apprehended conduct, of the non-applicant partner which is or would be injurious to the physical or mental health of the applicant or child.

(3) The court is not to make an exclusion order if it appears to it that to do so would be unjustified or unreasonable—

(a) having regard to all the circumstances of the case including the matters specified in paragraphs (a) to (e) of section 103(3), and
(b) where the family home—
    (i) is, or is part of, an agricultural holding within the meaning of section 1 of the Agricultural Holdings (Scotland) Act 1991 (c 55), or
    (ii) is let, or is a home in respect of which possession is given, to the non-applicant partner or to both partners by an employer as an incident of employment,

having regard to any requirement that the non-applicant partner, or, as the case may be, both partners must reside in the family home and to the likely consequences of the exclusion of the non-applicant partner from the family home.

(4) In making an exclusion order the court is, on the application of the applicant partner—

(a) to grant a warrant for the summary ejection of the non-applicant partner from the family home unless the non-applicant partner satisfies the court that it is unnecessary for it to grant such a remedy,
(b) to grant an interdict prohibiting the non-applicant partner from entering the family home without the express permission of the applicant, and
(c) to grant an interdict prohibiting the removal by the non-applicant partner, except with the written consent of the applicant or by a further order of the court, of any furniture and plenishings in the family home unless the non-applicant partner satisfies the court that it is unnecessary for it to grant such a remedy.

(5) In making an exclusion order the court may—

(a) grant an interdict prohibiting the non-applicant partner from entering or remaining in a specified area in the vicinity of the family home;
(b) where the warrant for the summary ejection of the non-applicant partner has been granted in that partner's absence, give directions as to the preservation of that partner's goods and effects which remain in the family home;
(c) on the application of either partner, make the exclusion order or the warrant or interdict mentioned in paragraph (a), (b) or (c) of subsection (4) or paragraph (a) of this subsection subject to such terms and conditions as the court may prescribe;

(d) on the application of either partner, make such other order as it considers necessary for the proper enforcement of an order made under subsection (4) or paragraph (a), (b) or (c).

(6) Pending the making of an exclusion order, the court may, on the application of the applicant partner, make an interim order suspending the occupancy rights of the non-applicant partner in the family home to which the application for the exclusion order relates; and subsections (4) and (5) apply to such an interim order as they apply to an exclusion order.

(7) But an interim order may be made only if the non-applicant partner has been afforded an opportunity of being heard by or represented before the court.

(8) Without prejudice to subsections (1) and (6), where both partners are entitled, or permitted by a third party, to occupy a family home, it is incompetent for one partner to bring an action of ejection from the family home against the other partner.

105 Duration of orders under sections 103 and 104

(1) The court may, on the application of either partner, vary or recall any order made by it under section 103 or 104.

(2) Subject to subsection (3), any such order, unless previously so varied or recalled, ceases to have effect—

(a) on the dissolution of the civil partnership,
(b) subject to section 106(1), where there is an entitled and non-entitled partner, on the entitled partner ceasing to be an entitled partner in respect of the family home to which the order relates, or
(c) where both partners are entitled, or permitted by a third party, to occupy the family home, on both partners ceasing to be so entitled or permitted.

(3) Without prejudice to the generality of subsection (2), an order under section 103(3) or (4) which grants the possession or use of furniture and plenishings ceases to have effect if the furniture and plenishings cease to be permitted by a third party to be retained in the family home.

106 Continued exercise of occupancy rights after dealing

(1) Subject to subsection (3)—

(a) the continued exercise of the rights conferred on a non-entitled partner by the provisions of this Chapter in respect of a family home are not prejudiced by reason only of any dealing of the entitled partner relating to that home, and
(b) a third party is not by reason only of such a dealing entitled to occupy that home or any part of it.

(2) In this section and section 107—

'dealing' includes the grant of a heritable security and the creation of a trust but does not include a conveyance under section 80 of the Lands Clauses Consolidation Act 1845 (c 18);

'entitled partner' does not include a civil partner who, apart from the provisions of this Chapter—

(a) is permitted by a third party to occupy a family home, or

(b) is entitled to occupy a family home along with an individual who is not the other civil partner whether or not that individual has waived a right of occupation in favour of the civil partner so entitled, ('non-entitled partner' being construed accordingly).

(3) This section does not apply in any case where—

    (a) the non-entitled partner in writing either—
        (i) consents or has consented to the dealing (any consent being in such form as the Scottish Ministers may, by regulations made by statutory instrument, prescribe), or
        (ii) renounces or has renounced occupancy rights in relation to the family home or property to which the dealing relates,
    (b) the court has made an order under section 107 dispensing with the consent of the non-entitled partner to the dealing,
    (c) the dealing occurred, or implements a binding obligation entered into by the entitled partner, before the registration of the civil partnership,
    (d) the dealing occurred, or implements a binding obligation entered into, before the commencement of this section,
    (e) the dealing comprises a sale to a third party who has acted in good faith, if there is produced to the third party by the seller—
        (i) an affidavit sworn or affirmed by the seller declaring that the subjects of sale are not, or were not at the time of the dealing, a family home in relation to which a civil partner of the seller has or had occupancy rights,
        (ii) a renunciation of occupancy rights or consent to the dealing which bears to have been properly made or given by the non-entitled partner, or
    (f) the entitled partner has permanently ceased to be entitled to occupy the family home, and at any time after that a continuous period of 5 years has elapsed during which the non-entitled partner has not occupied the family home.

(4) For the purposes of subsection (3)(e), the time of the dealing, in the case of the sale of an interest in heritable property, is the date of delivery to the purchaser of the deed transferring title to that interest.

107 Dispensation with civil partner's consent to dealing

(1) The court may, on the application of an entitled partner or any other person having an interest, make an order dispensing with the consent of a non-entitled partner to a dealing which has taken place or a proposed dealing, if—

    (a) such consent is unreasonably withheld,
    (b) such consent cannot be given by reason of physical or mental disability, or
    (c) the non-entitled partner cannot be found after reasonable steps have been taken to trace that partner.

(2) For the purposes of subsection (1)(a), a non-entitled partner has unreasonably withheld consent to a dealing which has taken place or a proposed dealing, where it appears to the court either—

    (a) that the non-entitled partner—
        (i) has led the entitled partner to believe that the non-entitled partner would consent to the dealing, and
        (ii) would not be prejudiced by any change in the circumstances of the case since the conduct which gave rise to that belief occurred, or
    (b) that the entitled partner has, having taken all reasonable steps to do so, been unable to obtain an answer to a request for consent.

(3) The court, in considering whether to make an order under subsection (1), is to have regard to all the circumstances of the case including the matters specified in paragraphs (a) to (e) of section 103(3).

(4) Where—

    (a) an application is made for an order under this section, and

    (b) an action is or has been raised by a non-entitled partner to enforce occupancy rights,

the action is to be sisted until the conclusion of the proceedings on the application.

108 Interests of heritable creditors

(1) The rights of a third party with an interest in the family home as a creditor under a secured loan in relation to the non-performance of any obligation under the loan are not prejudiced by reason only of the occupancy rights of the non-entitled partner; but where a non-entitled partner has or obtains occupation of a family home and—

    (a) the entitled partner is not in occupation, and

    (b) there is a third party with such an interest in the family home,

the court may, on the application of the third party, make an order requiring the non-entitled partner to make any payment due by the entitled partner in respect of the loan.

(2) This section does not apply to secured loans in respect of which the security was granted prior to the commencement of section 13 of the Law Reform (Miscellaneous Provisions) (Scotland) Act 1985 (c 73) unless the third party in granting the secured loan acted in good faith and there was produced to the third party by the entitled partner—

    (a) an affidavit sworn or affirmed by the entitled partner declaring that there is no non-entitled partner, or

    (b) a renunciation of occupancy rights or consent to the taking of the loan which bears to have been properly made or given by the non-entitled partner.

(3) This section does not apply to secured loans in respect of which the security was granted after the commencement of section 13 of the Law Reform (Miscellaneous Provisions) (Scotland) Act 1985 (c 73) unless the third party in granting the secured loan acted in good faith and there was produced to the third party by the grantor—

    (a) an affidavit sworn or affirmed by the grantor declaring that the security subjects are not or were not at the time of the granting of the security a family home in relation to which a civil partner of the grantor has or had occupancy rights, or

    (b) a renunciation of occupancy rights or consent to the granting of the security which bears to have been properly made or given by the non-entitled partner.

(4) For the purposes of subsections (2) and (3), the time of granting a security, in the case of a heritable security, is the date of delivery of the deed creating the security.

109 Provisions where both civil partners have title

(1) Subject to subsection (2), where, apart from the provisions of this Chapter, both civil partners are entitled to occupy a family home—

    (a) the rights in that home of one civil partner are not prejudiced by reason only of any dealing of the other civil partner, and

    (b) a third party is not by reason only of such a dealing entitled to occupy that home or any part of it.

(2) Sections 106(3) and 107 and the definition of 'dealing' in section 106(2) apply for the purposes of subsection (1) as they apply for the purposes of section 106(1) but subject to the following modifications—

(a) any reference to the entitled partner and to the non-entitled partner is to be construed as a reference to a civil partner who has entered into, or as the case may be proposes to enter into, a dealing and to the other civil partner respectively, and

(b) in paragraph (b) of section 107(4) the reference to occupancy rights is to be construed as a reference to any rights in the family home.

110 Rights of occupancy in relation to division and sale

Where a civil partner brings an action for the division and sale of a family home owned in common with the other civil partner, the court, after having regard to all the circumstances of the case including—

(a) the matters specified in paragraphs (a) to (d) of section 103(3), and

(b) whether the civil partner bringing the action offers or has offered to make available to the other civil partner any suitable alternative accommodation,

may refuse to grant decree in that action or may postpone the granting of decree for such period as it considers reasonable in the circumstances or may grant decree subject to such conditions as it may prescribe.

111 Adjudication

(1) Where a family home as regards which there is an entitled partner and a non-entitled partner is adjudged, the Court of Session, on the application of the non-entitled partner made within 40 days after the date of the decree of adjudication, may—

(a) order the reduction of the decree, or

(b) make such order as it thinks appropriate to protect the occupancy rights of the non-entitled partner,

if satisfied that the purpose of the diligence was wholly or mainly to defeat the occupancy rights of the non-entitled partner.

(2) Section 106(2) applies in construing 'entitled partner' and 'non-entitled partner' for the purposes of subsection (1).

Transfer of tenancy

112 Transfer of tenancy

(1) The court may, on the application of a non-entitled partner, make an order transferring the tenancy of a family home to that partner and providing, subject to subsection (12), for the payment by the non-entitled partner to the entitled partner of such compensation as seems to it to be just and reasonable in all the circumstances of the case.

(2) In an action—

(a) for dissolution of a civil partnership, the Court of Session or the sheriff,

(b) for declarator of nullity of a civil partnership, the Court of Session,

may, on granting decree or within such period as the court may specify on granting decree, make an order granting an application under subsection (1).

(3) In determining whether to grant an application under subsection (1), the court is to have regard to all the circumstances of the case including the matters specified in paragraphs (a) to (e) of section 103(3) and the suitability of the applicant to become the tenant and the applicant's capacity to perform the obligations under the lease of the family home.

(4) The non-entitled partner is to serve a copy of an application under subsection (1) on the landlord and, before making an order under subsection (1), the court is to give the landlord an opportunity of being heard by it.

(5) On the making of an order granting an application under subsection (1), the tenancy vests in the non-entitled partner without intimation to the landlord, subject to all the liabilities under the lease (other than liability for any arrears of rent for the period before the making of the order).

(6) The arrears mentioned in subsection (5) are to remain the liability of the original entitled partner.

(7) The clerk of court is to notify the landlord of the making of an order granting an application under subsection (1).

(8) It is not competent for a non-entitled partner to apply for an order under subsection (1) where the family home—

(a) is let to the entitled partner by the entitled partner's employer as an incident of employment, and the lease is subject to a requirement that the entitled partner must reside there,
(b) is or is part of an agricultural holding,
(c) is on, or pertains to—
(i) a croft,
(ii) the subject of a cottar, or
(iii) the holding of a landholder or of a statutory small tenant,
(d) is let on a long lease, or
(e) is part of the tenancy land of a tenant-at-will.

(9) In subsection (8)—

'agricultural holding' has the same meaning as in section 1 of the Agricultural Holdings (Scotland) Act 1991 (c 55),

'cottar' has the same meaning as in section 12(5) of the Crofters (Scotland) Act 1993 (c 44),

'croft' has the same meaning as in that Act of 1993,

'holding', in relation to a landholder and a statutory small tenant, 'landholder' and 'statutory small tenant' have the same meanings respectively as in sections 2(1), 2(2) and 32(1) of the Small Landholders (Scotland) Act 1911 (c 49),

'long lease' has the same meaning as in section 28(1) of the Land Registration (Scotland) Act 1979 (c 33), and

'tenant-at-will' has the same meaning as in section 20(8) of that Act of 1979.

(10) Where both civil partners are joint or common tenants of a family home, the court may, on the application of one of the civil partners, make an order vesting the tenancy in that civil partner solely and providing, subject to subsection (12), for the payment by the applicant to the other partner of such compensation as seems just and reasonable in the circumstances of the case.

(11) Subsections (2) to (9) apply for the purposes of an order under subsection (10) as they apply for the purposes of an order under subsection (1) but subject to the following modifications—

(a) in subsection (3), for 'tenant' there is substituted 'sole tenant';
(b) in subsection (4), for 'non-entitled' there is substituted 'applicant';
(c) in subsection (5), for 'non-entitled' there is substituted 'applicant',
(d) in subsection (6), for 'liability of the original entitled partner' there is substituted 'joint and several liability of both partners';
(e) in subsection (8)—

(i) for 'a non-entitled' there is substituted 'an applicant',

(ii) for paragraph (a) there is substituted—

'(a) is let to both partners by their employer as an incident of employment, and the lease is subject to a requirement that both partners must reside there;',

and

(iii) paragraphs (c) and (e) are omitted.

(12) Where the family home is a Scottish secure tenancy within the meaning of the Housing (Scotland) Act 2001 (asp 10), no account is to be taken, in assessing the amount of any compensation to be awarded under subsection (1) or (10), of the loss, by virtue of the transfer of the tenancy of the home, of a right to purchase the home under Part 3 of the Housing (Scotland) Act 1987 (c 26).

CHAPTER 4
INTERDICTS

113 Civil partners: competency of interdict

(1) It shall not be incompetent for the Court of Session or the sheriff to entertain an application by one civil partner in a civil partnership for a relevant interdict by reason only that the civil partners are living together in civil partnership.

(2) In subsection (1) and in section 114, 'relevant interdict' means an interdict, including an interim interdict, which—

(a) restrains or prohibits any conduct of one civil partner towards the other civil partner or a child of the family, or

(b) prohibits a civil partner from entering or remaining in a family home or in a specified area in the vicinity of a family home.

114 Attachment of powers of arrest to relevant interdicts

(1) Subject to subsection (2), the court is, on the application of an applicant civil partner, to attach a power of arrest—

(a) to any relevant interdict which is ancillary to an exclusion order (including an interim order under section 104(6));

(b) to any other relevant interdict where the non-applicant civil partner has had the opportunity of being heard by or represented before the court, unless it appears to the court that in all the circumstances of the case such a power is unnecessary.

(2) The court may attach a power of arrest to an interdict by virtue of subsection (1) only if satisfied that attaching the power would not result in the non-applicant civil partner being subject, in relation to the interdict, to a power of arrest under both this Chapter and the Protection from Abuse (Scotland) Act 2001 (asp 14).

(3) A power of arrest attached to an interdict by virtue of subsection (1) does not have effect until such interdict together with the attached power of arrest is served on the non-applicant civil partner; and such a power of arrest, unless previously recalled, ceases to have effect upon the dissolution of the civil partnership.

(4) If, by virtue of subsection (1), a power of arrest is attached to an interdict, a constable may arrest without warrant the non-applicant civil partner if the constable has reasonable cause for suspecting that civil partner of being in breach of the interdict.

(5) If, by virtue of subsection (1), a power of arrest is attached to an interdict, the applicant civil partner is, as soon as possible after service of the interdict, to ensure that there is delivered—

    (a) to the chief constable of the police area in which the family home is situated, and

    (b) if the applicant civil partner resides in another police area, to the chief constable of that other police area,

a copy of the application for the interdict and of the interlocutor granting the interdict together with a certificate of service of the interdict and, where the application to attach the power of arrest to the interdict was made after the interdict was granted, a copy of that application and of the interlocutor granting it and a certificate of service of the interdict together with the attached power of arrest.

(6) Where any relevant interdict to which, by virtue of subsection (1), there is attached a power of arrest, is varied or recalled, the civil partner who applied for the variation or recall is to ensure that there is delivered—

    (a) to the chief constable of the police area in which the family home is situated, and

    (b) if the applicant civil partner resides in another police area, to the chief constable of that other police area,

a copy of the application for variation or recall and of the interlocutor granting the variation or recall.

(7) In this section and in sections 115 and 116—

    'applicant civil partner' means the civil partner who has applied for the interdict, and

    'non-applicant civil partner' is to be construed accordingly.

115 Police powers after arrest

(1) Where a person has been arrested under section 114(4), the officer in charge of a police station may—

    (a) if satisfied that there is no likelihood of violence to the applicant civil partner or any child of the family, liberate that person unconditionally, or

    (b) refuse to liberate that person.

(2) For such refusal and the detention of that person until appearance in court by virtue of section 116(2) or of any provision of the Criminal Procedure (Scotland) Act 1975 (c 21) the officer is not to be subjected to any claim whatsoever.

(3) Where a person arrested under section 114(4) is liberated under subsection (1), the facts and circumstances which gave rise to the arrest are to be reported forthwith to the procurator fiscal who, if he decides to take no criminal proceedings in respect of those facts and circumstances, is at the earliest opportunity to take all reasonable steps to intimate his decision to the persons mentioned in paragraphs (a) and (b) of section 116(5).

116 Procedure after arrest

(1) The provisions of this section apply only where—

    (a) the non-applicant civil partner has not been liberated under section 115(1), and

    (b) the procurator fiscal decides that no criminal proceedings are to be taken in respect of the facts and circumstances which gave rise to the arrest.

(2) The non-applicant civil partner who has been arrested under section 114(4) is wherever practicable to be brought before the sheriff sitting as a court of summary criminal jurisdiction for

the district in which that civil partner was arrested not later than in the course of the first day after the arrest, such day not being a Saturday, a Sunday or a court holiday prescribed for that court under section 8 of the Criminal Procedure (Scotland) Act 1995 (c 46).

(3) Nothing in subsection (2) prevents the non-applicant civil partner being brought before the sheriff on a Saturday, a Sunday or such a court holiday when the sheriff is, in pursuance of that section of that Act, sitting for the disposal of criminal business.

(4) Subsections (1) to (3) of section 15 of that Act (intimation to a named person) apply to a non-applicant civil partner who has been arrested under section 114(4) as they apply to a person who has been arrested in respect of any offence.

(5) The procurator fiscal is at the earliest opportunity, and in any event prior to the non-applicant civil partner being brought before the sheriff under subsection (2), to take all reasonable steps to intimate—

    (a) to the applicant civil partner, and
    (b) to the solicitor who acted for that civil partner when the interdict was granted or to any other solicitor who the procurator fiscal has reason to believe acts for the time being for that civil partner,

that the criminal proceedings referred to in subsection (1) will not be taken.

(6) On the non-applicant civil partner being brought before the sheriff under subsection (2) (as read with subsection (3)), the following procedures apply—

    (a) the procurator fiscal is to present to the court a petition containing—
        (i)   a statement of the particulars of the non-applicant civil partner,
        (ii)   a statement of the facts and circumstances which gave rise to the arrest, and
        (iii) a request that the non-applicant civil partner be detained for a further period not exceeding 2 days,
    (b) if it appears to the sheriff that—
        (i)   the statement referred to in paragraph (a)(ii) ostensibly discloses a breach of interdict by the non-applicant civil partner,
        (ii)   proceedings for breach of interdict will be taken, and
        (iii) there is a substantial risk of violence by the non-applicant civil partner against the applicant civil partner or any child of the family,

    he may order the non-applicant civil partner to be detained for a further period not exceeding 2 days, and
    (c) in any case to which paragraph (b) does not apply, the non-applicant civil partner is, unless in custody in respect of any other matter, to be released from custody.

(7) In computing the period of 2 days referred to in paragraphs (a) and (b) of subsection (6), no account is to be taken of a Saturday or Sunday or of any holiday in the court in which the proceedings for breach of interdict will require to be raised.

CHAPTER 5
DISSOLUTION, SEPARATION AND NULLITY

Dissolution and separation

117 Dissolution

(1) An action for the dissolution of a civil partnership may be brought in the Court of Session or in the sheriff court.

(2) In such an action the court may grant decree, if, but only if, it is established that—

(a) the civil partnership has broken down irretrievably, or
(b) an interim gender recognition certificate under the Gender Recognition Act 2004 (c 7) has, after the date of registration of the civil partnership, been issued to either of the civil partners.

(3) The irretrievable breakdown of a civil partnership is taken to be established if—

(a) since the date of registration of the civil partnership the defender has at any time behaved (whether or not as a result of mental abnormality and whether such behaviour has been active or passive) in such a way that the pursuer cannot reasonably be expected to cohabit with the defender,
(b) the defender has wilfully and without reasonable cause deserted the pursuer and during a continuous period of two years immediately succeeding the defender's desertion—
  (i) there has been no cohabitation between the parties, and
  (ii) the pursuer has not refused a genuine and reasonable offer by the defender to adhere,
(c) there has been no cohabitation between the civil partners at any time during a continuous period of two years after the date of registration of the civil partnership and immediately preceding the bringing of the action and the defender consents to the granting of decree of dissolution of the civil partnership, or
(d) there has been no cohabitation between the civil partners at any time during a continuous period of 5 years after that date and immediately preceding the bringing of the action.

(4) Provision is to be made by act of sederunt—

(a) for the purpose of ensuring that, in an action to which paragraph (c) of subsection (3) relates, the defender has been given such information as enables that civil partner to understand—
  (i) the consequences of consenting to the granting of decree, and
  (ii) the steps which must be taken to indicate such consent, and
(b) as to the manner in which the defender in such an action is to indicate such consent, and any withdrawal of such consent,

and where the defender has indicated (and not withdrawn) such consent in the prescribed manner, that indication is sufficient evidence of such consent.

(5) Provision is to be made by act of sederunt for the purpose of ensuring that, where in an action for the dissolution of a civil partnership the defender is suffering from mental illness, the court appoints a curator ad litem to the defender.

(6) In an action to which paragraph (d) of subsection (3) relates, even though irretrievable breakdown of the civil partnership is established the court is not bound to grant decree if in its opinion to do so would result in grave financial hardship to the defender.

(7) For the purposes of subsection (6), hardship includes the loss of the chance of acquiring any benefit.

(8) In an action for dissolution of a civil partnership the standard of proof required to establish the ground of action is on balance of probability.

118 Encouragement of reconciliation

(1) At any time before granting decree in an action by virtue of paragraph (a) of section 117(2) for dissolution of a civil partnership, if it appears to the court that there is a reasonable prospect of a reconciliation between the civil partners it must continue, or further continue, the action for such period as it thinks proper to enable attempts to be made to effect such a reconciliation.

(2) If during any such continuation the civil partners cohabit with one another, no account is to be taken of such cohabitation for the purposes of that action.

119 Effect of resumption of cohabitation

(1) In an action to which paragraph (b) of section 117(3) relates, the irretrievable breakdown of a civil partnership is not to be taken to be established if, after the expiry of the period mentioned in that paragraph—

(a) the pursuer resumes cohabitation with the defender, and
(b) cohabits with the defender at any time after the end of a period of 3 months commencing with the date of such resumption.

(2) Subsection (1) is subject to section 118(2).

(3) In considering whether any period mentioned in paragraph (b), (c) or (d) of section 117(3) has been continuous, no account is to be taken of any period or periods not exceeding 6 months in all during which the civil partners cohabited with one another; but no such period or periods during which the civil partners cohabited with one another is to count as part of the period of non-cohabitation required by any of those paragraphs.

120 Separation

(1) An action for the separation of the civil partners in a civil partnership may be brought in the Court of Session or in the sheriff court.

(2) In such an action the court may grant decree if satisfied that the circumstances set out in any of paragraphs (a) to (d) of section 117(3) are established.

121 Dissolution following on decree of separation

(1) The court may grant decree in an action for the dissolution of a civil partnership even though decree of separation has previously been granted to the pursuer on the same, or substantially the same, facts as those averred in support of that action; and in any such action the court may treat an extract decree of separation lodged in process as sufficient proof of the facts under which that decree was granted.

(2) Nothing in this section entitles a court to grant decree of dissolution of a civil partnership without receiving evidence from the pursuer.

122 Registration of dissolution of civil partnership

(1) The Registrar General is to maintain at the General Register Office a register of decrees of dissolution of civil partnership (a register which shall be known as the 'Register of Dissolutions of Civil Partnership').

(2) The Registrar General is to cause to be made and kept at the General Register Office an alphabetical index of the entries in that register.

(3) The register is to be in such form as may be prescribed.

(4) On payment to him of such fee or fees as may be prescribed, the Registrar General must, at any time when the General Register Office is open for that purpose—

(a) cause a search of the index to be made on behalf of any person or permit any person to search the index himself,
(b) issue to any person an extract of any entry in the register which that person may require.

(5) An extract of any entry in the register is to be sufficient evidence of the decree of dissolution to which it relates.

(6) The Registrar General may—

(a) delete,
(b) amend, or
(c) substitute another entry for,

any entry in the register.

Nullity

123 Nullity

Where two people register in Scotland as civil partners of each other, the civil partnership is void if, and only if—

(a) they were not eligible to do so, or
(b) though they were so eligible, either of them did not validly consent to its formation.

124 Validity of civil partnerships registered outside Scotland

(1) Where two people register as civil partners of each other in England and Wales—

(a) the civil partnership is void if it would be void in England and Wales under section 49, and
(b) the civil partnership is voidable if it would be voidable there under section 50(1)(a), (b), (c) or (e).

(2) Where two people register as civil partners of each other in Northern Ireland, the civil partnership is—

(a) void, if it would be void in Northern Ireland under section 173, and
(b) voidable, if it would be voidable there under section 174(1)(a), (b), (c) or (e).

(3) Subsection (4) applies where two people register as civil partners of each other under an Order in Council under—

(a) section 210 (registration at British consulates etc), or
(b) section 211 (registration by armed forces personnel),

('the relevant section').

(4) The civil partnership is—

(a) void, if—
  (i) the condition in subsection (2)(a) or (b) of the relevant section is not met, or
  (ii) a requirement prescribed for the purposes of this paragraph by an Order in Council under the relevant section is not complied with, and
(b) voidable, if—
  (i) the appropriate part of the United Kingdom is England and Wales and the circumstances fall within section 50(1)(a), (b), (c) or (e), or
  (ii) the appropriate part of the United Kingdom is Northern Ireland and the circumstances fall within section 174(1)(a), (b), (c) or (e).

(5) The appropriate part of the United Kingdom is the part by reference to which the condition in subsection (2)(b) of the relevant section is met.

(6) Subsections (7) and (8) apply where two people have registered an apparent or alleged overseas relationship.

(7) The civil partnership is void if—

(a) the relationship is not an overseas relationship, or

(b) (even though the relationship is an overseas relationship), the parties are not treated under Chapter 2 of Part 5 as having formed a civil partnership.

(8) The civil partnership is voidable if—

(a) the overseas relationship is voidable under the relevant law,

(b) where either of the parties was domiciled in England and Wales at the time when the overseas relationship was registered, the circumstances fall within section 50(1)(a), (b), (c) or (e), or

(c) where either of the parties was domiciled in Northern Ireland at the time when the overseas relationship was registered, the circumstances fall within section 174(1)(a), (b), (c) or (e).

(9) Section 51 or (as the case may be) section 175 applies for the purposes of—

(a) subsections (1)(b), (2)(b) and (4)(b),

(b) subsection (8)(a), in so far as applicable in accordance with the relevant law, and

(c) subsection (8)(b) and (c).

(10) In subsections (8)(a) and (9)(b) 'the relevant law' means the law of the country or territory where the overseas relationship was registered (including its rules of private international law).

(11) For the purposes of subsections (8) and (9)(b) and (c), references in sections 50 and 51 or (as the case may be) sections 174 and 175 to the formation of the civil partnership are to be read as references to the registration of the overseas relationship.

Financial provision after overseas proceedings

125 Financial provision after overseas dissolution or annulment

Schedule 11 relates to applications for financial provision in Scotland after a civil partnership has been dissolved or annulled in a country or territory outside the British Islands.

CHAPTER 6
MISCELLANEOUS AND INTERPRETATION

Miscellaneous

126 Regulations

(1) In this Chapter and in Chapters 2 and 5, 'prescribed' means prescribed by regulations made by the Registrar General.

(2) Regulations so made may make provision (including provision as to fees) supplementing, in respect of the provision of services by or on behalf of the Registrar General or by local registration authorities (as defined by section 5(3) of the 1965 Act), the provisions of Chapter 2 of this Part.

(3) Any power to make regulations under subsection (1) or (2) is exercisable by statutory instrument; and no such regulations are to be made except with the approval of the Scottish Ministers.

(4) A statutory instrument containing regulations under subsection (1) or (2), or regulations under section 106(3)(a)(i), is subject to annulment in pursuance of a resolution of the Scottish Parliament.

127 Attachment

Where an attachment has been executed of furniture and plenishings of which the debtor's civil partner has the possession or use by virtue of an order under section 103(3) or (4), the sheriff, on the application of that civil partner made within 40 days after the execution of the attachment, may—

(a) declare the attachment null, or
(b) make such order as he thinks appropriate to protect such possession or use by that civil partner,

if satisfied that the purpose of the attachment was wholly or mainly to prevent such possession or use.

128 Promise or agreement to enter into civil partnership

No promise or agreement to enter into civil partnership creates any rights or obligations under the law of Scotland; and no action for breach of such a promise or agreement may be brought in any court in Scotland, whatever the law applicable to the promise or agreement.

129 Lord Advocate as party to action for nullity or dissolution of civil partnership

(1) The Lord Advocate may enter appearance as a party in any action—

(a) of declarator of nullity of a civil partnership, or
(b) for dissolution of a civil partnership,

and he may lead such proof and maintain such pleas as he thinks fit.

(2) The Court, whenever it considers it necessary for the proper disposal of any such action, is to direct that the action be brought to the notice of the Lord Advocate for him to determine whether to enter appearance.

(3) No expenses are claimable by or against the Lord Advocate in any such action in which he enters appearance.

130 Civil partner of accused a competent witness

(1) The civil partner of an accused may be called as a witness—

(a) by the accused, or
(b) without the consent of the accused, by a co-accused or by the prosecutor.

(2) But the civil partner is not a compellable witness for the co-accused or for the prosecutor and is not compelled to disclose any communication made, while the civil partnership subsists, between the civil partners.

(3) The failure of a civil partner of an accused to give evidence is not to be commented on by the defence or the prosecutor.

131 Succession: legal rights arising by virtue of civil partnership

(1) Where a person dies survived by a civil partner then, unless the circumstance is as mentioned in subsection (2), the civil partner has right to half of the moveable net estate belonging to the deceased at the time of death.

(2) That circumstance is that the person is also survived by issue, in which case the civil partner has right to a third of that moveable net estate and those issue have right to another third of it.

(3) In this section—

'issue' means issue however remote, and

'net estate' has the meaning given by section 36(1) (interpretation) of the Succession (Scotland) Act 1964 (c 41).

(4) Every testamentary disposition executed after the commencement of this section by which provision is made in favour of the civil partner of the testator and which does not contain a declaration to the effect that the provision so made is in full and final satisfaction of the right to any share in the testator's estate to which the civil partner is entitled by virtue of subsection (1) or (2), has effect (unless the disposition contains an express provision to the contrary) as if it contained such a declaration.

(5) In section 36(1) of the Succession (Scotland) Act 1964 (c 41), in the definition of 'legal rights', for 'and legitim' substitute 'legitim and rights under section 131 of the Civil Partnership Act 2004'.

132 Assurance policies

Section 2 of the Married Women's Policies of Assurance (Scotland) Act 1880 (c 26) (which provides that a policy of assurance may be effected in trust for a person's spouse, children or spouse and children) applies in relation to a policy of assurance—

(a) effected by a civil partner (in this section referred to as 'A') on A's own life, and
(b) expressed upon the face of it to be for the benefit of A's civil partner, or of A's children, or of A's civil partner and children,

as it applies in relation to a policy of assurance effected as, and expressed upon the face of it to be for such benefit as, is mentioned in that section.

133 Council Tax: liability of civil partners

After section 77 of the Local Government Finance Act 1992 (c 14), insert—

'77A Liability of civil partners

(1) Where—

(a) a person who is liable to pay council tax in respect of any chargeable dwelling and any day is in civil partnership with another person or living with another person in a relationship which has the characteristics of the relationship between civil partners; and
(b) that other person is also a resident of the dwelling on that day but would not, apart from this section, be so liable,

those persons shall be jointly and severally liable to pay the council tax payable in respect of that dwelling and that day.

(2) Subsection (1) above shall not apply as respects any day on which the other person there mentioned falls to be disregarded for the purposes of discount—

(a) by virtue of paragraph 2 of Schedule 1 to this Act (the severely mentally impaired); or
(b) being a student, by virtue of paragraph 4 of that Schedule.'

134 General provisions as to fees

(1) Subject to such exceptions as may be prescribed, a district registrar may refuse to comply with any application voluntarily made to him under this Part until the appropriate fee, if any, provided for by or under this Part is paid to him; and any such fee, if not prepaid, is recoverable by the registrar to whom it is payable.

(2) Circumstances, of hardship or otherwise, may be prescribed in which fees provided for by or under this Part may be remitted by the Registrar General.

Interpretation

135 Interpretation of this Part

In this Part, unless the context otherwise requires—

'the 1965 Act' means the Registration of Births, Deaths and Marriages (Scotland) Act 1965 (c 49);

'authorised registrar' has the meaning given by section 87;

'caravan' means a caravan which is mobile or affixed to land;

'child of the family' has the meaning given by section 101(7);

'civil partnership book' has the meaning given by section 89;

'civil partnership register' has the meaning given by section 95(2);

'civil partnership schedule' has the meaning given by section 94;

'the court' means the Court of Session or the sheriff;

'district' means a registration district as defined by section 5(1) of the 1965 Act;

'district registrar' has the meaning given by section 7(12) of the 1965 Act;

'entitled partner' and 'non-entitled partner', subject to sections 106(2) and 111(2), have the meanings respectively assigned to them by section 101(1);

'exclusion order' has the meaning given by section 104(1);

'family' has the meaning given by section 101(7);

'family home' means any house, caravan, houseboat or other structure which has been provided or has been made available by one or both of the civil partners as, or has become, a family residence and includes any garden or other ground or building attached to, and usually occupied with, or otherwise required for the amenity or convenience of, the house, caravan, houseboat or other structure but does not include a residence provided or made available by one civil partner for that civil partner to reside in, whether with any child of the family or not, separately from the other civil partner;

'furniture and plenishings' means any article situated in a family home of civil partners which—

(a) is owned or hired by either civil partner or is being acquired by either civil partner under a hire-purchase agreement or conditional sale agreement, and

(b) is reasonably necessary to enable the home to be used as a family residence,

but does not include any vehicle, caravan or houseboat or such other structure as is mentioned in the definition of 'family home';

'notice of proposed civil partnership' has the meaning given by section 88(1);

'occupancy rights' means the rights conferred by section 101(1);

'Registrar General' means the Registrar General of Births, Deaths and Marriages for Scotland;

'registration office' means a registration office provided under section 8(1) of the 1965 Act;

'tenant' includes—

    (a) a sub-tenant,

    (b) a statutory tenant as defined in section 3 of the Rent (Scotland) Act 1984 (c 58), and

    (c) a statutory assured tenant as defined in section 16(1) of the Housing (Scotland) Act 1988 (c 43),

and 'tenancy' is to be construed accordingly.

136 The expression 'relative' in the 1965 Act

In section 56(1) of the 1965 Act (interpretation), in the definition of 'relative', at the end insert ', a civil partner and anyone related to the civil partner of the person as regards whom the expression is being construed'.

PART 4
CIVIL PARTNERSHIP: NORTHERN IRELAND
CHAPTER 1
REGISTRATION

Formation and eligibility

137 Formation of civil partnership by registration

(1) For the purposes of section 1, two people are to be regarded as having registered as civil partners of each other once each of them has signed the civil partnership schedule in the presence of—

    (a) each other,
    (b) two witnesses both of whom profess to be 16 or over, and
    (c) the registrar.

(2) Subsection (1) applies regardless of whether subsections (3) and (4) are complied with.

(3) After the civil partnership schedule has been signed under subsection (1), it must also be signed, in the presence of the civil partners and each other, by—

    (a) each of the two witnesses, and
    (b) the registrar.

(4) After the witnesses and the registrar have signed the civil partnership schedule, the registrar must cause the registration of the civil partnership to be recorded as soon as practicable.

(5) No religious service is to be used while the registrar is officiating at the signing of a civil partnership schedule.

138 Eligibility

(1) Two people are not eligible to register as civil partners of each other if—

    (a) they are not of the same sex,
    (b) either of them is already a civil partner or lawfully married,
    (c) either of them is under 16,
    (d) they are within prohibited degrees of relationship, or
    (e) either of them is incapable of understanding the nature of civil partnership.

(2) Schedule 12 contains provisions for determining when two people are within prohibited degrees of relationship.

Preliminaries to registration

139 Notice of proposed civil partnership

(1) For two people to register as civil partners of each other under this Chapter, each of them must give the registrar a notice of proposed civil partnership (a 'civil partnership notice').

(2) A civil partnership notice must be—

    (a) in the prescribed form, and
    (b) accompanied by the prescribed fee and such documents and other information as may be prescribed.

(3) In prescribed cases a civil partnership notice must be given to the registrar by each party in person.

140 Civil partnership notice book and list of intended civil partnerships

(1) The registrar must keep a record of—

    (a) such particulars as may be prescribed, taken from each civil partnership notice received by him, and
    (b) the date on which each civil partnership notice is received by him.

(2) In this Chapter 'civil partnership notice book' means the record kept under subsection (1).

(3) The registrar must, in accordance with any guidance issued by the Registrar General, place on public display a list containing in relation to each proposed civil partnership in respect of which the registrar has received a civil partnership notice—

    (a) the names of the proposed civil partners, and
    (b) the date on which it is intended to register them as civil partners of each other.

(4) As soon as practicable after the date mentioned in subsection (3) the registrar must remove from the list the names and the date mentioned in that subsection.

(5) Any person claiming that he may have reason to make an objection to a proposed civil partnership may inspect any entry relating to the civil partnership in the civil partnership notice book without charge.

141 Power to require evidence of name etc

(1) A registrar to whom a civil partnership notice is given may require the person giving it to provide him with specified evidence relating to each proposed civil partner.

(2) Such a requirement may be imposed at any time before the registrar issues the civil partnership schedule under section 143.

(3) 'Specified evidence', in relation to a person, means such evidence as may be specified in guidance issued by the Registrar General—

(a) of the person's name and surname,
(b) of the person's age,
(c) as to whether the person is or has been a civil partner or lawfully married, and
(d) of the person's nationality.

142 Objections

(1) Any person may at any time before the formation of a civil partnership in Northern Ireland make an objection in writing to the registrar.

(2) An objection on the ground that one of the proposed civil partners is incapable of understanding the nature of civil partnership must be accompanied by a supporting certificate signed by a medical practitioner.

(3) If the registrar is satisfied that the objection relates to no more than a misdescription or inaccuracy in the civil partnership notice, he must—

(a) notify the proposed civil partners,
(b) make such inquiries as he thinks fit, and
(c) subject to the approval of the Registrar General, make any necessary correction to any document relating to the proposed civil partnership.

(4) In any other case the registrar must notify the Registrar General of the objection.

(5) If the Registrar General is satisfied that there is a legal impediment to the formation of the civil partnership, he must direct the registrar to—

(a) notify the parties, and
(b) take all reasonable steps to ensure that the formation of the civil partnership does not take place.

(6) If subsection (5) does not apply, the Registrar General must direct the registrar to proceed under section 143.

(7) For the purposes of this section and section 143 there is a legal impediment to the formation of a civil partnership where the proposed civil partners are not eligible to be registered as civil partners of each other.

(8) A person who has submitted an objection may withdraw it at any time, but the Registrar General may have regard to an objection which has been withdrawn.

143 Civil partnership schedule

After the registrar receives a civil partnership notice from each of the proposed civil partners, he must complete a civil partnership schedule in the prescribed form, if—

(a) he is satisfied that there is no legal impediment to the formation of the civil partnership, or
(b) the Registrar General has directed him under section 142(6) to proceed under this section.

144 Place of registration

(1) The place at which two people may register as civil partners of each other must be—

(a) a registration office, or
(b) a place approved under subsection (3).

(2) Subsection (1) is subject to subsections (5) and (7).

(3) A local registration authority may, in accordance with regulations under subsection (4), approve places where civil partnerships may be registered in its district.

(4) Regulations under section 159 may make provision for or in connection with the approval of places under subsection (3), including provision as to—

(a) the kinds of place in respect of which approvals may be granted,
(b) the procedure to be followed in relation to applications for approval,
(c) the considerations to be taken into account in determining whether to approve any places,
(d) the duration and renewal of approvals (whether for one occasion or for a period),
(e) the conditions that must or may be imposed on granting or renewing an approval,
(f) the determination and charging of fees in respect of[en rule]
   (i)   applications for the approval of places,
   (ii) the renewal of approvals, and
   (iii) the attendance by registrars at places approved under the regulations,
(g) the circumstances in which a local registration authority must or may revoke or suspend an approval or vary any of the conditions imposed in relation to an approval,
(h) the renewal of decisions made by virtue of the regulations,
(i) appeals to a county court from decisions made by virtue of the regulations,
(j) the notification to the Registrar General of all approvals granted, renewed, revoked, suspended or varied,
(k) the notification to the registrar for the district in which a place approved under the regulations is situated of all approvals relating to such a place which are granted, renewed, revoked, suspended or varied,
(l) the keeping by the Registrar General, registrars and local registration authorities of registers of places approved under the regulations, and
(m) the issue by the Registrar General of guidance supplementing the provision made by the regulations.

(5) If either of the parties to a proposed civil partnership gives the registrar a medical statement, the civil partnership may, with the approval of the Registrar General, be registered at any place where that party is.

(6) In subsection (5) 'medical statement', in relation to any person, means a statement made in the prescribed form by a registered medical practitioner that in his opinion at the time the statement is made—

(a) by reason of serious illness or serious bodily injury, that person ought not to move or be moved from the place where he is at that time, and
(b) it is likely that it will be the case for at least the following 3 months that by reason of illness or disability the person ought not to move or be moved from that place.

(7) If the Registrar General so directs, a registrar must register a civil partnership in a place specified in the direction.

Young persons

145 Parental etc consent where proposed civil partner under 18

(1) The consent of the appropriate persons is required before a young person and another person may register as civil partners of each other.

(2) Schedule 13 contains provisions—

    (a) for determining who are the appropriate persons for the purposes of this section (see Part 1 of the Schedule);

    (b) for orders dispensing with consent and for recording consents and orders (see Parts 2 and 3 of the Schedule).

(3) Each consent required by subsection (1) must be—

    (a) in the prescribed form; and

    (b) produced to the registrar before the issue of the civil partnership schedule.

(4) Nothing in this section affects any need to obtain the consent of the High Court before a ward of court and another person may register as civil partners of each other.

(5) In this section and Schedule 13 'young person' means a person who is under 18.

Supplementary

146 Validity of registration

(1) This section applies to any legal proceedings commenced at any time after the registration of a civil partnership is recorded under section 137.

(2) The validity of the civil partnership must not be questioned in any such proceedings on the ground of any contravention of a provision of, or made under, this Act.

147 Corrections and cancellations

(1) Regulations under section 159 may make provision for the making of corrections by the Registrar General or any registrar.

(2) The Registrar General must cancel the registration of a void civil partnership or direct the registrar to do so.

148 Interpreters

(1) If the registrar considers it necessary or desirable, he may use the services of an interpreter (not being one of the civil partners or a witness).

(2) The interpreter must—

    (a) before the registration of the civil partnership, sign a statement in English that he understands, and is able to converse in, any language in respect of which he is to act as an interpreter, and

    (b) immediately after the registration of the civil partnership, give the registrar a certificate written in English and signed by the interpreter that he has faithfully acted as the interpreter.

149 Detained persons

(1) If—

- (a) one of the parties to a proposed civil partnership is detained in a prison or as a patient in a hospital, and
- (b) the civil partnership is to be registered in that prison or hospital,

the civil partnership notice given by that party must be accompanied by a statement to which subsection (2) applies.

(2) This subsection applies to a statement which—

- (a) is made in the prescribed form by the responsible authority not more than 21 days before the date on which the civil partnership notice is given,
- (b) identifies the establishment where the person is detained, and
- (c) states that the responsible authority has no objection to that establishment being the place of registration for that civil partnership.

(3) In subsection (2) 'responsible authority' means—

- (a) if the person named in the statement is detained in a prison, the governor or other officer in charge of that prison;
- (b) if the person named in the statement is detained in a hospital or special accommodation, the Health and Social Services Board administering that hospital or the Department of Health, Social Services and Public Safety, respectively;
- (c) if the person named in the statement is detained in a private hospital, the person in charge of that hospital.

(4) After the registrar receives a civil partnership notice accompanied by a statement to which subsection (2) applies, he must notify the Registrar General and not complete a civil partnership schedule unless the Registrar General directs him to proceed under section 143.

(5) In this section—

- (a) 'prison' includes a remand centre and a young offenders centre, and
- (b) 'hospital', 'patient', 'private hospital' and 'special accommodation' have the same meaning as in the Mental Health (Northern Ireland) Order 1986 (SI 1986/595 (NI 4)).

150 Certificates of no impediment for Part 2 purposes

(1) This section applies where—

- (a) two people propose to register as civil partners of each other under Chapter 1 of Part 2, and
- (b) one of them ('A') resides in Northern Ireland but the other ('B') resides in England or Wales.

(2) A may give a civil partnership notice under section 139 as if A and B intended to register as civil partners under this Chapter.

(3) If the registrar is satisfied that there is no legal impediment (in the sense given in section 142(7)) to A registering as B's civil partner, he must issue a certificate in the prescribed form that there is not known to be any such impediment.

(4) But the certificate may not be issued before the expiration of such period from the date recorded under section 140(3)(b) as may be prescribed.

(5) Any person may, at any time before a certificate is issued under subsection (3), submit to the registrar an objection in writing to its issue.

(6) Any objection made under subsection (5) must be taken into account by the registrar in deciding whether he is satisfied that there is no legal impediment to A registering as B's civil partner.

151 Registration districts and registration authorities

(1) Each local government district shall be a registration district and the district council shall be the local registration authority for the purposes of this Part.

(2) A district council shall, in the exercise of functions conferred on it as a local registration authority—

    (a) act as agent for the Department of Finance and Personnel, and

    (b) act in accordance with such directions as that Department may give to the council.

(3) Any expenditure to be incurred by the district council in the exercise of functions conferred on it as a local registration authority shall be subject to the approval of the Registrar General.

(4) The Department of Finance and Personnel shall retain or, as the case may be, defray in respect of each financial year the amount of the difference between—

    (a) the aggregate of the amounts of salaries, pension provision and other expenses payable by virtue of this Part in respect of any registration district, and

    (b) the aggregate of the amounts received in that registration district under any statutory provision or otherwise by way of fees or other expenses.

152 Registrars and other staff

(1) A local registration authority shall, with the approval of the Registrar General, appoint—

    (a) a registrar of civil partnerships, and

    (b) one or more deputy registrars of civil partnerships.

(2) A person holding an appointment under subsection (1) may with the approval of, and shall at the direction of, the Registrar General be removed from his office of registrar or deputy registrar by the local registration authority.

(3) A local registration authority shall, at the direction of the Registrar General, appoint additional persons to register civil partnerships and carry out other functions for the purposes of this Part.

(4) A person shall not be appointed under subsection (1) or (3) if he is under the age of 21.

(5) Regulations under section 159 may confer additional functions on a person holding an appointment under subsection (1).

(6) A person holding an appointment under subsection (1) shall, in exercising his functions under this Part or any other statutory provision, be subject to such instructions or directions as the Registrar General may give.

153 Records and documents to be sent to Registrar General

If the Registrar General directs him to do so, a person must send to the Registrar General any record or document relating to civil partnerships in accordance with the Registrar General's directions.

154 Annual report

(1) The Registrar General must send to the Department of Finance and Personnel an annual report of the number of civil partnerships registered during each year, together with such other information as he considers it appropriate to include.

(2) The Department of Finance and Personnel must lay the report before the Northern Ireland Assembly.

155 Searches

(1) The Registrar General must provide indexes to civil partnership registration records in his custody for inspection by the public.

(2) A registrar must provide indexes to civil partnership registration records in his custody for inspection by the public.

(3) Any person may, on payment of the prescribed fee—

  (a) search any index mentioned in subsection (1) or (2), and
  (b) require the Registrar General or, as the case may be, the registrar to give him a document in the prescribed form relating to the registration of a civil partnership.

(4) The Registrar General must cause any document given by him under this section or section 156 to be stamped with the seal of the General Register Office.

(5) Judicial notice shall be taken of any document so stamped.

156 Proof of civil partnership for purposes of certain statutory provisions

(1) Where the civil partnership of a person is required to be proved for the purposes of any prescribed statutory provision, any person—

  (a) on application to the Registrar General, and
  (b) on payment of the prescribed fee,

is entitled to a document in the prescribed form relating to the registration of the civil partnership of that person.

(2) An application under subsection (1) must be in such form and accompanied by such particulars as the Registrar General may require.

(3) The Registrar General or any registrar may, on payment of the prescribed fee, issue such information (including a document as mentioned in subsection (1)) as may be required for the purposes of any prescribed statutory provision.

157 Fees

(1) The Department of Finance and Personnel may by order prescribe—

  (a) any fee which is required to be prescribed for the purposes of this Chapter;
  (b) fees for such other matters as that Department considers necessary or expedient for the purposes of this Chapter.

(2) The power to make an order under subsection (1) is exercisable by statutory rule for the purposes of the Statutory Rules (Northern Ireland) Order 1979 (SI 1979/1573 (NI 12)).

(3) An order under subsection (1) may only be made if a draft has been laid before and approved by resolution of the Northern Ireland Assembly.

158 Offences

(1) Any registrar who signs a civil partnership schedule in the absence of the civil partners is guilty of an offence.

(2) Any person who is not a registrar but officiates at the signing of a civil partnership schedule in such a way as to lead the civil partners to believe that he is a registrar is guilty of an offence.

(3) A person who is guilty of an offence under this section is liable on summary conviction to a fine not exceeding level 5 on the standard scale or to imprisonment for a term not exceeding 6 months or to both.

(4) Notwithstanding anything in Article 19(1) of the Magistrates' Courts (Northern Ireland) Order 1981 (SI 1981/1675 (NI 26)) (limitation of time for taking proceedings), proceedings for an offence under this section may be instituted at any time within 3 years after the commission of the offence.

159 Regulations

(1) The Department of Finance and Personnel may by regulations make such provision as appears to it necessary or expedient for the registration of civil partnerships in Northern Ireland.

(2) The power to make regulations under subsection (1) is exercisable by statutory rule for the purposes of the Statutory Rules (Northern Ireland) Order 1979 (SI 1979/1573 (NI 12)).

(3) Regulations under subsection (1) shall be subject to negative resolution (within the meaning of section 41(6) of the Interpretation Act (Northern Ireland) 1954 (1954 c 33 (NI))).

160 Interpretation

In this Chapter—

'civil partnership notice' means a notice of proposed civil partnership under section 139;

'civil partnership notice book' has the meaning given by section 140;

'prescribed', except in relation to a fee, means prescribed by regulations under section 159 and, in relation to a fee, means prescribed by order under section 157;

'registrar' means such person appointed under section 152(1)(a) or (b) or (3) as may be prescribed;

'Registrar General' means the Registrar General for Northern Ireland;

'statutory provision' has the meaning given by section 1(f) of the Interpretation Act (Northern Ireland) 1954 (1954 c 33 (NI)).

CHAPTER 2
DISSOLUTION, NULLITY AND OTHER PROCEEDINGS

Introduction

161 Powers to make orders and effect of orders

(1) The court may, in accordance with this Chapter—

   (a) make an order (a 'dissolution order') which dissolves a civil partnership on the ground that it has broken down irretrievably;
   (b) make an order (a 'nullity order') which annuls a civil partnership which is void or voidable;
   (c) make an order (a 'presumption of death order') which dissolves a civil partnership on the ground that one of the civil partners is presumed to be dead;

(d) make an order (a 'separation order') which provides for the separation of the civil partners.

(2) Every dissolution, nullity or presumption of death order—

(a) is, in the first instance, a conditional order, and
(b) may not be made final before the end of the prescribed period (see section 162);

and any reference in this Chapter to a conditional order is to be read accordingly.

(3) A nullity order made where a civil partnership is voidable annuls the civil partnership only as respects any time after the order has been made final, and the civil partnership is to be treated (despite the order) as if it had existed up to that time.

(4) In this Chapter 'the court' has the meaning given by section 188.

(5) This Chapter is subject to section 219 and sections 228 to 232 (jurisdiction of the court).

162 The period before conditional orders may be made final

(1) Subject to subsection (2), the prescribed period for the purposes of section 161(2)(b) is 6 weeks from the making of the conditional order.

(2) In a particular case the court dealing with the case may by order shorten the prescribed period.

163 Intervention by the Crown Solicitor

(1) This section applies if an application has been made for a dissolution, nullity or presumption of death order.

(2) The court may, if it thinks fit, direct that all necessary papers in the matter are to be sent to the Crown Solicitor who must under the directions of the Attorney General instruct counsel to argue before the court any question in relation to the matter which the court considers it necessary or expedient to have fully argued.

(3) If any person at any time—

(a) during the progress of the proceedings, or
(b) before the conditional order is made final,

gives information to the Crown Solicitor on any matter material to the due decision of the case, the Crown Solicitor may take such steps as the Attorney General considers necessary or expedient.

(4) If the Crown Solicitor intervenes or shows cause against the making of the conditional order in any proceedings relating to its making, the court may make such order as may be just as to—

(a) the payment by other parties to the proceedings of the costs incurred by him in doing so, or
(b) the payment by the Crown Solicitor of any costs incurred by any of those parties because of his doing so.

(5) In this Chapter—

'the Attorney General' means the Attorney General for Northern Ireland; and

'the Crown Solicitor' means the Crown Solicitor for Northern Ireland.

164 Proceedings before order has been made final

(1) This section applies if—

(a) a conditional order has been made, and

(b) the Crown Solicitor, or any person who has not been a party to proceedings in which the order was made, shows cause why the order should not be made final on the ground that material facts have not been brought before the court.

(2) This section also applies if—

(a) a conditional order has been made,
(b) 3 months have elapsed since the earliest date on which an application could have been made for the order to be made final,
(c) no such application has been made by the civil partner who applied for the conditional order, and
(d) the other civil partner makes an application to the court under this subsection.

(3) The court may—

(a) make the order final,
(b) rescind the order,
(c) require further inquiry, or
(d) otherwise deal with the case as it thinks fit.

(4) Subsection (3)(a)—

(a) applies despite section 161(2) (period before conditional orders may be made final), but
(b) is subject to section 172(4) (protection for respondent in separation cases) and section 186 (restrictions on making of orders affecting children).

165 Time bar on applications for dissolution orders

(1) No application for a dissolution order may be made to the court before the end of the period of 2 years from the date of the formation of the civil partnership.

(2) Nothing in this section prevents the making of an application based on matters which occurred before the end of the 2 year period.

166 Attempts at reconciliation of civil partners

(1) This section applies in relation to cases where an application is made for a dissolution or separation order.

(2) If at any stage of proceedings for the order it appears to the court that there is a reasonable possibility of a reconciliation between the civil partners, the court may adjourn the proceedings for such period as it thinks fit to enable attempts to be made to effect a reconciliation between them.

(3) If during any such adjournment the parties resume living with each other in the same household, no account is to be taken of the fact for the purposes of the proceedings.

(4) The power to adjourn under subsection (2) is additional to any other power of adjournment.

167 Consideration by the court of certain agreements or arrangements

(1) This section applies to cases where—

(a) proceedings for a dissolution or separation order are contemplated or have begun, and
(b) an agreement or arrangement is made or proposed to be made between the civil partners which relates to, arises out of, or is connected with, the proceedings.

(2) Rules of court may make provision for enabling—

   (a) the civil partners, or either of them, on application made either before or after the making of the application for a dissolution or separation order, to refer the agreement or arrangement to the court, and

   (b) the court—

      (i) to express an opinion, if it thinks it desirable to do so, as to the reasonableness of the agreement or arrangement, and

     (ii) to give such directions, if any, in the matter as it thinks fit.

Dissolution of civil partnership

168 Dissolution of civil partnership which has broken down irretrievably

(1) Subject to section 165, an application for a dissolution order may be made to the court by either civil partner on the ground that the civil partnership has broken down irretrievably.

(2) On an application for a dissolution order the court must inquire, so far as it reasonably can, into—

   (a) the facts alleged by the applicant, and

   (b) any facts alleged by the respondent.

(3) The court hearing an application for a dissolution order must not hold that the civil partnership has broken down irretrievably unless the applicant satisfies the court of one or more of the facts described in subsection (5)(a), (b), (c) or (d).

(4) But if the court is satisfied of any of those facts, it must make a dissolution order unless it is satisfied on all the evidence that the civil partnership has not broken down irretrievably.

(5) The facts referred to in subsections (3) and (4) are—

   (a) that the respondent has behaved in such a way that the applicant cannot reasonably be expected to live with the respondent;

   (b) that—

      (i) the applicant and the respondent have lived apart for a continuous period of at least 2 years immediately preceding the making of the application ('2 years' separation'), and

     (ii) the respondent consents to a dissolution order being made;

   (c) that the applicant and the respondent have lived apart for a continuous period of at least 5 years immediately preceding the making of the application ('5 years' separation');

   (d) that the respondent has deserted the applicant for a continuous period of at least 2 years immediately preceding the making of the application.

(6) The court must not make a dissolution order without considering the oral testimony of the applicant unless for special reasons it orders that such testimony be dispensed with.

169 Supplemental provisions as to facts raising presumption of breakdown

(1) Subsection (2) applies if—

   (a) in any proceedings for a dissolution order the applicant alleges, in reliance on section 168(5)(a), that the respondent has behaved in such a way that the applicant cannot reasonably be expected to live with the respondent, but

   (b) after the date of the occurrence of the final incident relied on by the applicant and held by the court to support his allegation, the applicant and the respondent have lived together for a period (or periods) which does not, or which taken together do not, exceed 6 months.

(2) The fact that the applicant and respondent have lived together as mentioned in subsection (1)(b) must be disregarded in determining, for the purposes of section 168(5)(a), whether the applicant cannot reasonably be expected to live with the respondent.

(3) Subsection (4) applies in relation to cases where the applicant alleges, in reliance on section 168(5)(b), that the respondent consents to a dissolution order being made.

(4) Rules of court must make provision for the purpose of ensuring that the respondent has been given such information as will enable him to understand—

(a) the consequences to him of consenting to the order, and
(b) the steps which he must take to indicate his consent.

(5) For the purposes of section 168(5)(d) the court may treat a period of desertion as having continued at a time when the deserting civil partner was incapable of continuing the necessary intention, if the evidence before the court is such that, had he not been so incapable, the court would have inferred that the desertion continued at that time.

(6) In considering for the purposes of section 168(5) whether the period for which the civil partners have lived apart or the period for which the respondent has deserted the applicant has been continuous, no account is to be taken of—

(a) any one period not exceeding 6 months, or
(b) any two or more periods not exceeding 6 months in all,

during which the civil partners resumed living together.

(7) But no period during which the civil partners have lived with each other counts as part of the period during which the civil partners have lived apart or as part of the period of desertion.

(8) For the purposes of section 168(5)(b) and (c) and this section civil partners are to be treated as living apart unless they are living with each other in the same household, and references in this section to civil partners living with each other are to be read as references to their living with each other in the same household.

170 Dissolution order not precluded by previous separation order etc

(1) Subsections (2) and (3) apply if any of the following orders has been made in relation to a civil partnership—

(a) a separation order;
(b) an order under Schedule 16 (financial relief in court of summary jurisdiction etc);
(c) an occupation order under Article 11 of the Family Homes and Domestic Violence (Northern Ireland) Order 1998 (SI 1998/1071 (NI 6) (occupation orders));
(d) an order under Article 15 of that Order (orders where neither civil partner entitled to occupy the home).

(2) Nothing prevents—

(a) either civil partner from applying for a dissolution order, or
(b) the court from making a dissolution order,

on the same facts, or substantially the same facts, as those proved in support of the making of the order referred to in subsection (1).

(3) On the application for the dissolution order, the court—

(a) may treat the order referred to in subsection (1) as sufficient proof of any desertion or other fact by reference to which it was made, but

(b) must not make the dissolution order without receiving evidence from the applicant.

(4) If—

(a) the application for the dissolution order follows a separation order or any order requiring the civil partners to live apart,

(b) there was a period of desertion immediately preceding the institution of the proceedings for the separation order, and

(c) the civil partners have not resumed living together and the separation order has been continuously in force since it was made,

the period of desertion is to be treated for the purposes of the application for the dissolution order as if it had immediately preceded the making of the application.

(5) For the purposes of section 168(5)(d) the court may treat as a period during which the respondent has deserted the applicant any period during which there is in force—

(a) an injunction granted by the High Court or a county court which excludes the respondent from the civil partnership home, or

(b) an order under Article 11 or 15 of the Family Homes and Domestic Violence (Northern Ireland) Order 1998 (SI 1998/1071 (NI 6)) which prohibits the respondent from occupying a dwelling-house in which the applicant and the respondent have, or at any time have had, a civil partnership home.

171 Refusal of dissolution in 5 year separation cases on ground of grave hardship

(1) The respondent to an application for a dissolution order in which the applicant alleges 5 years' separation may oppose the making of an order on the ground that—

(a) the dissolution of the civil partnership will result in grave financial or other hardship to him, and

(b) it would in all the circumstances be wrong to dissolve the civil partnership.

(2) Subsection (3) applies if—

(a) the making of a dissolution order is opposed under this section,

(b) the court finds that the applicant is entitled to rely in support of his application on the fact of 5 years' separation and makes no such finding as to any other fact mentioned in section 168(5), and

(c) apart from this section, the court would make a dissolution order.

(3) The court must—

(a) consider all the circumstances, including the conduct of the civil partners and the interests of the civil partners and of any children or other persons concerned, and

(b) if it is of the opinion that the ground mentioned in subsection (1) is made out, dismiss the application for the dissolution order.

(4) 'Hardship' includes the loss of the chance of acquiring any benefit which the respondent might acquire if the civil partnership were not dissolved.

172 Proceedings before order made final: protection for respondent in separation cases

(1) The court may, on an application made by the respondent, rescind a conditional dissolution order if—

(a) it made the order on the basis of a finding that the applicant was entitled to rely on the fact of 2 years' separation coupled with the respondent's consent to a dissolution order being made,

(b) it made no such finding as to any other fact mentioned in section 168(5), and

(c) it is satisfied that the applicant misled the respondent (whether intentionally or unintentionally) about any matter which the respondent took into account in deciding to give his consent.

(2) Subsections (3) to (5) apply if—

(a) the respondent to an application for a dissolution order in which the applicant alleged—
  (i) 2 years' separation coupled with the respondent's consent to a dissolution order being made, or
  (ii) 5 years' separation,

has applied to the court for consideration under subsection (3) of his financial position after the dissolution of the civil partnership, and

(b) the court—
  (i) has made a conditional dissolution order on the basis of a finding that the applicant was entitled to rely in support of his application on the fact of 2 years' or 5 years' separation, and
  (ii) has made no such finding as to any other fact mentioned in section 168(5).

(3) The court hearing an application by the respondent under subsection (2) must consider all the circumstances, including—

(a) the age, health, conduct, earning capacity, financial resources and financial obligations of each of the parties, and

(b) the financial position of the respondent as, having regard to the dissolution, it is likely to be after the death of the applicant should the applicant die first.

(4) The court must not make the order final unless it has, by order, declared that it is satisfied that—

(a) the applicant should not be required to make any financial provision for the respondent,

(b) the financial provision made by the applicant for the respondent is—
  (i) reasonable and fair, or
  (ii) the best that can be made in the circumstances, or

(c) there are circumstances making it desirable that the order should be made final without delay.

(5) The court must not make an order declaring that it is satisfied as mentioned in subsection (4)(c) unless it has obtained a satisfactory undertaking from the applicant that he will bring the question of financial provision for the respondent before the court within a specified time.

(6) Subsection (7) applies if, following an application under subsection (2) which is not withdrawn, the court makes the order final without making an order under subsection (4).

(7) The final order is voidable at the instance of the respondent or of the court but no person is entitled to challenge the validity of the order after it is made final on the ground that subsections (4) and (5) were not satisfied.

(8) If the court refuses to make an order under subsection (4), it must, on an application by the applicant, make an order declaring that it is not satisfied as mentioned in that subsection.

Nullity

173 Grounds on which civil partnership is void

Where two people register as civil partners of each other in Northern Ireland, the civil partnership is void if—

    (a) at the time when they do so, they are not eligible to register as civil partners of each other under Chapter 1 (see section 138), or

    (b) at the time when they do so they both know—

        (i) that due notice of proposed civil partnership has not been given,

        (ii) that the civil partnership schedule has not been duly issued,

        (iii) that the place of registration is a place other than that specified in the civil partnership schedule, or

        (iv) that a registrar is not present.

174 Grounds on which civil partnership is voidable

(1) Where two people register as civil partners of each other in Northern Ireland, the civil partnership is voidable if—

    (a) either of them did not validly consent to its formation (whether as a result of duress, mistake, unsoundness of mind or otherwise);

    (b) at the time of its formation either of them, though capable of giving a valid consent, was suffering (whether continuously or intermittently) from mental disorder of such a kind or to such an extent as to be unfitted for civil partnership;

    (c) at the time of its formation, the respondent was pregnant by some person other than the applicant;

    (d) an interim gender recognition certificate under the Gender Recognition Act 2004 (c 7) has, after the time of its formation, been issued to either civil partner;

    (e) the respondent is a person whose gender at the time of its formation had become the acquired gender under the 2004 Act.

(2) In this section and section 175 'mental disorder' has the same meaning as in the Mental Health (Northern Ireland) Order 1986 (SI 1986/595 (NI 4)).

175 Bars to relief where civil partnership is voidable

(1) The court must not make a nullity order on the ground that a civil partnership is voidable if the respondent satisfies the court—

    (a) that the applicant, with knowledge that it was open to him to obtain a nullity order, conducted himself in relation to the respondent in such a way as to lead the respondent reasonably to believe that he would not seek to do so, and

    (b) that it would be unjust to the respondent to make the order.

(2) Without prejudice to subsection (1), the court must not make a nullity order by virtue of section 174(1)(a), (b), (c) or (e) unless—

    (a) it is satisfied that proceedings were instituted within 3 years from the date of the formation of the civil partnership, or

    (b) leave for the institution of proceedings after the end of that 3 year period has been granted under subsection (3).

(3) A judge of the court may, on an application made to him, grant leave for the institution of proceedings if he—

(a) is satisfied that the applicant has at some time during the 3 year period suffered from mental disorder, and

(b) considers that in all the circumstances of the case it would be just to grant leave for the institution of proceedings.

(4) An application for leave under subsection (3) may be made after the end of the 3 year period.

(5) Without prejudice to subsection (1), the court must not make a nullity order by virtue of section 174(1)(d) unless it is satisfied that proceedings were instituted within the period of 6 months from the date of issue of the interim gender recognition certificate.

(6) Without prejudice to subsections (1) and (2), the court must not make a nullity order by virtue of section 174(1)(c) or (e) unless it is satisfied that the applicant was at the time of the formation of the civil partnership ignorant of the facts alleged.

176 Proof of certain matters not necessary to validity of civil partnership

Where two people have registered as civil partners of each other in Northern Ireland, it is not necessary in support of the civil partnership to give any proof—

(a) that any person whose consent to the civil partnership was required by section 145 (parental etc consent) had given his consent;

(b) that the registrar was properly appointed under section 152;

and no evidence is to be given to prove the contrary in any proceedings touching the validity of the civil partnership.

177 Validity of civil partnerships registered outside Northern Ireland

(1) Where two people register as civil partners of each other in England or Wales, the civil partnership is—

(a) void, if it would be void in England and Wales under section 49, and

(b) voidable, if the circumstances fall within any paragraph of section 174(1).

(2) Where two people register as civil partners of each other in Scotland, the civil partnership is—

(a) void, if it would be void in Scotland under section 123, and

(b) voidable, if the circumstances fall within section 174(1)(d).

(3) Subsection (4) applies where two people register as civil partners of each other under an Order in Council under—

(a) section 210 (registration at British consulates etc), or

(b) section 211 (registration by armed forces personnel),

('the relevant section').

(4) The civil partnership is—

(a) void, if—

(i) the condition in subsection (2)(a) or (b) of the relevant section is not met, or

(ii) a requirement prescribed for the purposes of this paragraph by an Order in Council under the relevant section is not complied with, and

(b) voidable, if—

(i) the appropriate part of the United Kingdom is Northern Ireland or England and Wales and the circumstances fall within any paragraph of section 174(1), or

(ii) the appropriate part of the United Kingdom is Scotland and the circumstances fall within section 174(1)(d).

(5) The appropriate part of the United Kingdom is the part by reference to which the condition in subsection (2)(b) of the relevant section is met.

(6) Subsections (7) and (8) apply where two people have registered an apparent or alleged overseas relationship.

(7) The civil partnership is void if—

(a) the relationship is not an overseas relationship, or
(b) (even though the relationship is an overseas relationship) the parties are not treated under Chapter 2 of Part 5 as having formed a civil partnership.

(8) The civil partnership is voidable if—

(a) the overseas relationship is voidable under the relevant law,
(b) the circumstances fall within section 174(1)(d), or
(c) where either of the parties was domiciled in Northern Ireland or England and Wales at the time when the overseas relationship was registered, the circumstances fall within section 174(1)(a), (b), (c) or (e).

(9) Section 175 applies for the purposes of—

(a) subsections (1)(b), (2)(b) and (4)(b),
(b) subsection (8)(a), in so far as applicable in accordance with the relevant law, and
(c) subsection (8)(b) and (c).

(10) In subsections (8)(a) and (9)(b) 'the relevant law' means the law of the country or territory where the overseas relationship was registered (including its rules of private international law).

(11) For the purposes of subsections (8) and (9)(b) and (c), references in sections 174 and 175 to the formation of a civil partnership are to be read as references to the registration of the overseas relationship.

Presumption of death orders

178 Presumption of death orders

(1) The High Court may, on an application made by a civil partner, make a presumption of death order if it is satisfied that reasonable grounds exist for supposing that the other civil partner is dead.

(2) In any proceedings under this section the fact that—

(a) for a period of 7 years or more the other civil partner has been continually absent from the applicant, and
(b) the applicant has no reason to believe that the other civil partner has been living within that time,

is evidence that the other civil partner is dead until the contrary is proved.

Separation orders

179 Separation orders

(1) An application for a separation order may be made to the court by either civil partner on the ground that any such fact as is mentioned in section 168(5)(a), (b), (c) or (d) exists.

(2) On an application for a separation order the court must inquire, so far as it reasonably can, into—

(a) the facts alleged by the applicant, and

(b) any facts alleged by the respondent,

but whether the civil partnership has broken down irretrievably is irrelevant.

(3) If the court is satisfied on the evidence of any such fact as is mentioned in section 168(5)(a), (b), (c) or (d) it must, subject to section 186, make a separation order.

(4) Section 169 (supplemental provisions as to facts raising presumption of breakdown) applies for the purposes of an application for a separation order alleging any such fact as it applies in relation to an application for a dissolution order alleging that fact.

180 Effect of separation order

If either civil partner dies intestate as respects all or any of his or her real or personal property while—

(a) a separation order is in force, and
(b) the separation order is continuing,

the property as respects which he or she died intestate devolves as if the other civil partner had then been dead.

Declarations

181 Declarations

(1) Any person may apply to the court for one or more of the following declarations in relation to a civil partnership specified in the application—

(a) a declaration that the civil partnership was at its inception a valid civil partnership;
(b) a declaration that the civil partnership subsisted on a date specified in the application;
(c) a declaration that the civil partnership did not subsist on a date so specified;
(d) a declaration that the validity of a dissolution, annulment or legal separation obtained in any country outside Northern Ireland in respect of the civil partnership is entitled to recognition in Northern Ireland;
(e) a declaration that the validity of a dissolution, annulment or legal separation so obtained in respect of the civil partnership is not entitled to recognition in Northern Ireland.

(2) Where an application under subsection (1) is made to the court by a person other than a civil partner in the civil partnership to which the application relates, the court must refuse to hear the application if it considers that the applicant does not have a sufficient interest in the determination of that application.

182 General provisions as to making and effect of declarations

(1) Where on an application for a declaration under section 181 the truth of the proposition to be declared is proved to the satisfaction of the court, the court must make the declaration unless to do so would be manifestly contrary to public policy.

(2) Any declaration under section 181 binds Her Majesty and all other persons.

(3) The court, on the dismissal of an application for a declaration under section 181, may not make any declaration for which an application has not been made.

(4) No declaration which may be applied for under section 181 may be made otherwise than under section 181 by any court.

(5) No declaration may be made by any court, whether under section 181 or otherwise, that a civil partnership was at its inception void.

(6) Nothing in this section affects the powers of any court to annul a civil partnership.

183 The Attorney General and proceedings for declarations

(1) On an application for a declaration under section 181 the court may at any stage of the proceedings, of its own motion or on the application of any party to the proceedings, direct that all necessary papers in the matter be sent to the Attorney General.

(2) The Attorney General, whether or not he is sent papers in relation to an application for a declaration under section 181, may—

(a) intervene in the proceedings on that application in such manner as he thinks necessary or expedient, and

(b) argue before the court any question in relation to the application which the court considers it necessary to have fully argued.

(3) Where any costs are incurred by the Attorney General in connection with any application for a declaration under section 181, the court may make such order as it considers just as to the payment of those costs by parties to the proceedings.

184 Supplementary provisions as to declarations

(1) Any declaration made under section 181, and any application for such a declaration, must be in the form prescribed by family proceedings rules.

(2) Family proceedings rules may make provision—

(a) as to the information required to be given by any applicant for a declaration under section 181;

(b) requiring notice of an application under section 181 to be served on the Attorney General and on persons who may be affected by any declaration applied for.

(3) No proceedings under section 181 affects any final judgment or order already pronounced or made by any court of competent jurisdiction.

(4) The court hearing an application under section 181 may direct that the whole or any part of the proceedings must be heard in private.

(5) An application for a direction under subsection (4) must be heard in private unless the court otherwise directs.

(6) Family proceedings rules must make provision for an appeal to the Court of Appeal from any declaration made by a county court under section 181 or from the dismissal of an application under that section, upon a point of law, a question of fact or the admission or rejection of any evidence.

(7) Subsection (6) does not affect Article 61 of the County Courts (Northern Ireland) Order 1980 (SI 1980/397 (NI 3)) (cases stated).

(8) In this section 'family proceedings rules' means family proceedings rules made under Article 12 of the Family Law (Northern Ireland) Order 1993 (SI 1993/1576 (NI 6)).

General provisions

185 Relief for respondent in dissolution proceedings

(1) If in any proceedings for a dissolution or separation order the respondent alleges and proves any such fact as is mentioned in section 168(5)(a), (b), (c) or (d) the court may give to the respondent the relief to which he would have been entitled if he had made an application seeking that relief.

(2) When applying subsection (1), treat—

    (a) the respondent as the applicant, and
    (b) the applicant as the respondent,

for the purposes of section 168(5).

186 Restrictions on making of orders affecting children

(1) In any proceedings for a dissolution, nullity or separation order, the court must consider—

    (a) whether there are any children of the family to whom this section applies, and
    (b) if there are any such children, whether (in the light of the arrangements which have been, or are proposed to be, made for their upbringing and welfare) it should exercise any of its powers under the Children (Northern Ireland) Order 1995 (SI 1995/755 (NI 2)) with respect to any of them.

(2) If, in any case to which this section applies, it appears to the court that—

    (a) the circumstances of the case require it, or are likely to require it, to exercise any of its powers under the 1995 Order with respect to any such child,
    (b) it is not in a position to exercise the power or (as the case may be) those powers without giving further consideration to the case, and
    (c) there are exceptional circumstances which make it desirable in the interests of the child that the court should give a direction under this section,

it may direct that the order is not to be made final, or (in the case of a separation order) is not to be made, until the court orders otherwise.

(3) This section applies to—

    (a) any child of the family who has not reached 16 at the date when the court considers the case in accordance with the requirements of this section, and
    (b) any child of the family who has reached 16 at that date and in relation to whom the court directs that this section shall apply.

187 Parties to proceedings under this Chapter

(1) Rules of court may make provision with respect to—

    (a) the joinder as parties to proceedings under sections 161 to 179 of persons involved in allegations of improper conduct made in those proceedings,
    (b) the dismissal from such proceedings of any parties so joined, and
    (c) the persons who are to be parties to proceedings on an application under section 181.

(2) Rules of court made under this section may make different provision for different cases.

(3) In every case in which the court considers, in the interest of a person not already a party to the proceedings, that the person should be made a party, the court may if it thinks fit allow the person to intervene upon such terms, if any, as the court thinks just.

The court

188 The court

(1) In this Chapter 'the court' means—

(a) the High Court, or
(b) where an order made by the Lord Chancellor is in force designating a county court sitting for any division as a civil partnership proceedings county court, a county court sitting for that division.

(2) Subsection (1) is subject to the following provisions of this section.

(3) Subsection (1) does not apply where the context shows that 'the court' means some particular court.

(4) The Lord Chancellor may make an order such as is mentioned in subsection (1)(b).

(5) In this Part 'civil partnership proceedings county court' means, where an order made by the Lord Chancellor under subsection (4) is in force designating a county court sitting for any division as a civil partnership proceedings county court, a county court sitting for that division.

(6) Except to the extent that rules of court otherwise provide, the jurisdiction conferred by virtue of this section and section 190 on a civil partnership proceedings county court is exercisable throughout Northern Ireland, but rules of court may provide for a civil partnership cause (within the meaning of section 190) pending in one such court to be heard and determined—

(a) partly in that court and partly in another, or
(b) in another.

(7) Any jurisdiction conferred on a civil partnership proceedings county court is exercisable even though by reason of any amount claimed the jurisdiction would not but for this subsection be exercisable by a county court.

(8) The jurisdiction of a civil partnership proceedings county court to exercise any power under Schedule 15 (except a power under Part 8 of or paragraph 62 of that Schedule or a power under paragraph 57, 58 or 66 of that Schedule which is exercisable by county courts generally) shall, except to the extent that rules of court otherwise permit and, in particular, without prejudice to section 190(4) and (6), be exercisable only in connection with an application or order pending in or made by such a court.

(9) The power to make an order under subsection (4) is exercisable by statutory rule for the purposes of the Statutory Rules (Northern Ireland) Order 1979 (SI 1979/1573 (NI 12)).

189 Appeals

(1) Rules of court shall make provision for an appeal upon a point of law, a question of fact or the admission or rejection of any evidence to the Court of Appeal from—

(a) any order made by a judge of a civil partnership proceedings county court in the exercise of the jurisdiction conferred by a relevant provision, or
(b) the dismissal by a judge of a civil partnership proceedings county court of any application under a relevant provision.

(2) 'Relevant provision' means any provision of—

(a) this Chapter or Schedule 15 (except paragraphs 56 to 58 and 66);
(b) the Children (Northern Ireland) Order 1995 (SI 1995/755 (NI 2)).

(3) A person dissatisfied with—

(a) an order made by any county court in exercise of the jurisdiction conferred by paragraph 57, 58 or 66 of Schedule 15, or

(b) with the dismissal of any application made by him under any of those paragraphs,

is entitled to appeal from the order or dismissal as if the order or dismissal had been made in exercise of the jurisdiction conferred by Part 3 of the County Courts (Northern Ireland) Order 1980 (SI 1980/397 (NI 3)) and the appeal brought under Part 6 of that Order and Articles 61 (cases stated by county court judge) and 62 (cases stated by High Court on appeal from county court) of that Order apply accordingly.

190 Transfer of proceedings

(1) This section applies if an order is made under section 188.

(2) Rules of court—

(a) must provide for the transfer to the High Court—
   (i) of any civil partnership cause pending in a civil partnership proceedings county court which ceases to be undefended, and
   (ii) of any civil partnership cause so pending, where the transfer appears to the civil partnership proceedings county court to be desirable;

(b) may provide for the transfer to the High Court of any civil partnership cause which remains undefended;

(c) may provide for the transfer or retransfer from the High Court to a civil partnership proceedings county court of any civil partnership cause which is, or again becomes, undefended;

(d) must define the circumstances in which any civil partnership cause is to be treated for the purposes of this subsection as undefended.

(3) 'Civil partnership cause' means an action for the dissolution or annulment of a civil partnership or for the legal separation of civil partners.

(4) Rules of court may provide for the transfer or retransfer—

(a) from a civil partnership proceedings county court to the High Court, or

(b) from the High Court to a civil partnership proceedings county court,

of any proceedings for the exercise of a power under this Chapter or Schedule 15 (except proceedings on an application under paragraph 57, 58 or 66).

(5) The power conferred by subsections (2) and (4) includes power to provide for the removal of proceedings at the direction of the High Court; but nothing in this section affects—

(a) any other power of the High Court to remove proceedings to that court from a county court, or

(b) any power to remit proceedings from that court to a county court.

(6) A court has jurisdiction to entertain any proceedings transferred to the court by virtue of rules made in pursuance of subsection (4).

CHAPTER 3
PROPERTY AND FINANCIAL ARRANGEMENTS

191 Disputes between civil partners about property

(1) In any question between the civil partners in a civil partnership as to title to or possession of property, either civil partner may apply by summons or otherwise in a summary way to—

(a) the High Court, or

(b) a county court.

(2) On such an application, the court may make such order with respect to the property as it thinks fit (including an order for the sale of the property).

(3) Rules of court made for the purposes of this section may confer jurisdiction on county courts whatever the situation or value of the property in dispute.

192 Applications under section 191 where property not in possession etc

(1) The right of a civil partner ('A') to make an application under section 191 includes the right to make such an application where A claims that the other civil partner ('B') has had in his possession or under his control—

(a) money to which, or to a share of which, A was beneficially entitled, or

(b) property (other than money) to which, or to an interest in which, A was beneficially entitled,

and that either the money or other property has ceased to be in B's possession or under B's control or that A does not know whether it is still in B's possession or under B's control.

(2) For the purposes of subsection (1)(a) it does not matter whether A is beneficially entitled to the money or share—

(a) because it represents the proceeds of property to which, or to an interest in which, A was beneficially entitled, or

(b) for any other reason.

(3) Subsections (4) and (5) apply if, on such an application being made, the court is satisfied that B—

(a) has had in his possession or under his control money or other property as mentioned in subsection (1)(a) or (b), and

(b) has not made to A, in respect of that money or other property, such payment or disposition as would have been just and equitable in the circumstances.

(4) The power of the court to make orders under section 191 includes power to order B to pay to A—

(a) in a case falling within subsection (1)(a), such sum in respect of the money to which the application relates, or A's share of it, as the court considers appropriate, or

(b) in a case falling within subsection (1)(b), such sum in respect of the value of the property to which the application relates, or A's interest in it, as the court considers appropriate.

(5) If it appears to the court that there is any property which—

(a) represents the whole or part of the money or property, and

(b) is property in respect of which an order could (apart from this section) have been made under section 191,

the court may (either instead of or as well as making an order in accordance with subsection (4)) make any order which it could (apart from this section) have made under section 191.

(6) Any power of the court which is exercisable on an application under section 191 is exercisable in relation to an application made under that section as extended by this section.

193 Applications under section 191 by former civil partners

(1) Where a civil partnership has been dissolved or annulled or is void (whether or not it has been annulled), either party may make an application under section 191 (or under that section as extended by section 192) and references in those sections to a civil partner are to be read accordingly.

(2) An application under subsection (1) must—

  (a) where the civil partnership has been dissolved or annulled, be made within the period of 3 years beginning with the date of the dissolution or annulment, and
  (b) where a civil partnership is void but has not been annulled and the parties have ceased to live together in the same household, be made within the period of 3 years beginning with the date on which they ceased so to live together.

194 Assurance policy by civil partner for benefit of other civil partner etc

Section 4 of the Law Reform (Husband and Wife) Act (Northern Ireland) 1964 (c 23 (NI)) (money payable under policy of life assurance or endowment not to form part of the estate of the insured) applies in relation to a policy of life assurance or endowment—

  (a) effected by a civil partner on his own life, and
  (b) expressed to be for the benefit of his civil partner, or of his children, or of his civil partner and children, or any of them,

as it applies in relation to a policy of life assurance or endowment effected by a husband and expressed to be for the benefit of his wife, or of his children, or of his wife and children, or of any of them.

195 Wills, administration of estates and family provision

Schedule 14 amends enactments relating to wills, administration of estates and family provision so that they apply in relation to civil partnerships as they apply in relation to marriage.

196 Financial relief for civil partners and children of family

(1) Schedule 15 makes provision for financial relief in connection with civil partnerships that corresponds to the provision made for financial relief in connection with marriages by Part 3 of the Matrimonial Causes (Northern Ireland) Order 1978 (SI 1978/1045 (NI 15)).

(2) Any rule of law under which any provision of Part 3 of the 1978 Order is interpreted as applying to dissolution of a marriage on the ground of presumed death is to be treated as applying (with any necessary modifications) in relation to the corresponding provision of Schedule 15.

(3) Schedule 16 makes provision for financial relief in connection with civil partnerships that corresponds to provision made for financial relief in connection with marriages by the Domestic Proceedings (Northern Ireland) Order 1980 (SI 1980/563 (NI 5)).

(4) Schedule 17 makes provision for financial relief in Northern Ireland after a civil partnership has been dissolved or annulled, or civil partners have been legally separated, in a country outside the British Islands.

CHAPTER 4
CIVIL PARTNERSHIP AGREEMENTS

197 Civil partnership agreements unenforceable

(1) A civil partnership agreement does not under the law of Northern Ireland have effect as a contract giving rise to legal rights.

(2) No action lies in Northern Ireland for breach of a civil partnership agreement, whatever the law applicable to the agreement.

(3) In this section and section 198 'civil partnership agreement' means an agreement between two people—

- (a) to register as civil partners of each other—
    - (i) in Northern Ireland (under Part 4),
    - (ii) in England and Wales (under Part 2),
    - (iii) in Scotland (under Part 3), or
    - (iv) outside the United Kingdom under an Order in Council made under Chapter 1 of Part 5 (registration at British consulates etc or by armed forces personnel), or
- (b) to enter into an overseas relationship.

(4) This section applies in relation to civil partnership agreements whether entered into before or after this section comes into force, but does not affect any action commenced before it comes into force.

198 Property where civil partnership agreement is terminated

(1) This section applies if a civil partnership agreement is terminated.

(2) Sections 191 and 192 (disputes between civil partners about property) apply to any dispute between, or claim by, one of the parties in relation to property in which either or both had a beneficial interest while the agreement was in force, as if the parties were civil partners of each other.

(3) An application made under section 191 or 192 by virtue of subsection (2) must be made within 3 years of the termination of the agreement.

(4) A party to a civil partnership agreement who makes a gift of property to the other party on the condition (express or implied) that it is to be returned if the agreement is terminated is not prevented from recovering the property merely because of his having terminated the agreement.

CHAPTER 5
CHILDREN

199 Parental responsibility, children of the family and relatives

(1) Amend the Children (Northern Ireland) Order 1995 (SI 1995/755 (NI 2)) ('the 1995 Order') as follows.

(2) In Article 2(2) (interpretation), for the definition of 'child of the family' in relation to the parties to a marriage, substitute—

'"child of the family", in relation to parties to a marriage, or to two people who are civil partners of each other, means—

(a) a child of both of them, and

(b) any other child, other than a child placed with them as foster parents by an authority or voluntary organisation, who has been treated by both of them as a child of their family.'

(3) In the definition of 'relative' in Article 2(2), for 'by affinity)' substitute 'by marriage or civil partnership)'.

(4) In Article 7(1C) (acquisition of parental responsibility by step-parent), after 'is married to' insert ', or a civil partner of,'.

200 Guardianship

In Article 161 of the 1995 Order (revocation of appointment), after paragraph (7) insert—

'(8) An appointment under paragraph (1) or (2) of Article 160 (including one made in an unrevoked will) is revoked if—

(a) the civil partnership of the person who made the appointment is dissolved or annulled, and
(b) the person appointed is his former civil partner.

(9) Paragraph (8) is subject to a contrary intention appearing from the appointment.

(10) In paragraph (8) "dissolved or annulled" means—

(a) dissolved by a dissolution order or annulled by a nullity order under Part 4 of the Civil Partnership Act 2004, or
(b) dissolved or annulled in any country or territory outside Northern Ireland by a dissolution or annulment which is entitled to recognition in Northern Ireland by virtue of Chapter 3 of Part 5 of that Act.'

201 Entitlement to apply for residence or contact order

In Article 10(5) of the 1995 Order (persons entitled to apply for residence or contact order), after sub-paragraph (a) insert—

'(aa) any civil partner in a civil partnership (whether or not subsisting) in relation to whom the child is a child of the family;'.

202 Financial provision for children

(1) Amend Schedule 1 to the 1995 Order (financial provision for children) as follows.

(2) For paragraph 1(2) (extended meaning of 'parent') substitute—

'(2) In this Schedule, except paragraphs 3 and 17, "parent" includes—

(a) any party to a marriage (whether or not subsisting) in relation to whom the child concerned is a child of the family, and
(b) any civil partner in a civil partnership (whether or not subsisting) in relation to whom the child concerned is a child of the family;

and for this purpose any reference to either parent or both parents shall be read as a reference to any parent of his and to all of his parents.'

(3) In paragraph 3(6) (meaning of 'periodical payments order'), after paragraph (d) insert—

'(e) Part 1 or 8 of Schedule 15 to the Civil Partnership Act 2004 (financial relief in the High Court or county court etc);

(f) Schedule 16 to the 2004 Act (financial relief in court of summary jurisdiction etc);'.

(4) In paragraph 17(2) (person with whom a child lives or is to live), after 'husband or wife' insert 'or civil partner'.

203 Adoption

(1) Amend the Adoption (Northern Ireland) Order 1987 (SI 1987/2203 (NI 22)) as follows.

(2) In Article 2 (interpretation), in the definition of 'relative' in paragraph (2), for 'affinity' substitute 'marriage or civil partnership'.

(3) In Article 12 (adoption orders), in paragraph (5), after 'married' insert 'or who is or has been a civil partner'.

(4) In Article 15 (adoption by one person), in paragraph (1)(a), after 'is not married' insert 'or a civil partner'.

(5) In Article 33 (meaning of 'protected child'), in paragraph (3)(g), after 'marriage' insert 'or forming a civil partnership'.

(6) In Article 40 (status conferred by adoption), in paragraph (3)(a), after '1984' insert 'or for the purposes of Schedule 12 to the Civil Partnership Act 2004'.

(7) In Article 54 (disclosure of birth records of adopted children), in paragraph (2)—

  (a) after 'intending to be married' insert 'or to form a civil partnership';
  (b) for 'the person whom he intends to marry' substitute 'the intended spouse or civil partner';
  (c) after '1984' insert 'or Schedule 12 to the Civil Partnership Act 2004'.

(8) In Article 54A (Adoption Contact Register), in paragraph (13)(a), for 'or marriage' substitute ', marriage or civil partnership'.

CHAPTER 6
MISCELLANEOUS

204 False statements etc with reference to civil partnerships

(1) Amend Article 8 of the Perjury (Northern Ireland) Order 1979 (SI 1979/1714 (NI 19)) (false statements etc with reference to marriage) as follows.

(2) After paragraph (1) insert—

  '(1A) Any person who—

  (a) for the purpose of procuring the formation of a civil partnership or a document mentioned in paragraph (1B)—
    (i) makes or signs a declaration required under Part 4 or 5 of the Civil Partnership Act 2004; or
    (ii) gives a notice or certificate required under Part 4 or 5 of the Civil Partnership Act 2004,

    knowing that the declaration, notice or certificate is false;
  (b) for the purpose of a record being made in any register relating to civil partnerships—
    (i) makes a statement as to any information which is required to be registered under Part 4 or 5 of the Civil Partnership Act 2004; or
    (ii) causes such a statement to be made,

knowing that the statement is false;

(c) forbids the issue of a document mentioned in paragraph (1B)(a) or (b) by representing himself to be a person whose consent to a civil partnership between a child and another person is required under Part 4 or 5 of the Civil Partnership Act 2004, knowing the representation to be false,

shall be guilty of an offence.

(1B) The documents are—

(a) a civil partnership schedule;

(b) a document required by an Order in Council under section 210 or 211 of the Civil Partnership Act 2004 as an authority for two people to register as civil partners of each other;

(c) a certificate of no impediment under section 240 of the Civil Partnership Act 2004.'

(3) In paragraph (2), after 'paragraph (1)' insert 'or (1A)'.

(4) In the heading to Article 8, after 'marriage' insert 'or civil partnership'.

205 Housing and tenancies

Schedule 18 amends certain enactments relating to housing and tenancies.

206 Family homes and domestic violence

Schedule 19 amends the Family Homes and Domestic Violence (Northern Ireland) Order 1998 (SI 1998/1071 (NI 6)) and related enactments so that they apply in relation to civil partnerships as they apply in relation to marriages.

207 Fatal accidents claims

(1) Amend the Fatal Accidents (Northern Ireland) Order 1977 (SI 1977/1251 (NI 18)) as follows.

(2) In Article 2(2) (meaning of 'dependant'), after sub-paragraph (a) insert—

'(aa) the civil partner or former civil partner of the deceased;'.

(3) In sub-paragraph (b)(iii) of Article 2(2), after 'wife' insert 'or civil partner'.

(4) After sub-paragraph (f) of Article 2(2) insert—

'(fa) any person (not being a child of the deceased) who, in the case of any civil partnership in which the deceased was at any time a civil partner, was treated by the deceased as a child of the family in relation to that civil partnership;'.

(5) After Article 2(2A) insert—

'(2B) The reference to the former civil partner of the deceased in paragraph (2)(aa) includes a reference to a person whose civil partnership with the deceased has been annulled as well as a person whose civil partnership with the deceased has been dissolved.'

(6) In Article 2(3)(b), for 'by affinity' substitute 'by marriage or civil partnership'.

(7) In Article 3A(2) (persons for whose benefit claim for bereavement damages may be made)—

(a) in sub-paragraph (a), after 'wife or husband' insert 'or civil partner', and

(b) in sub-paragraph (b), after 'was never married' insert 'or a civil partner'.

(8) In Article 5 (assessment of damages), in paragraph (3A), after 'wife' insert 'or civil partner'.

208 Evidence

(1) Any enactment or rule of law relating to the giving of evidence by a spouse applies in relation to a civil partner as it applies in relation to the spouse.

(2) Subsection (1) is subject to any specific amendment made by or under this Act which relates to the giving of evidence by a civil partner.

(3) For the avoidance of doubt, in any such amendment, references to a person's civil partner do not include a former civil partner.

(4) References in subsections (1) and (2) to giving evidence are to giving evidence in any way (whether by supplying information, making discovery, producing documents or otherwise).

(5) Any rule of law—

    (a) which is preserved by Article 22(1) of the Criminal Justice (Evidence) (Northern Ireland) Order 2004 (SI 2004/1501 (NI 10)), and

    (b) under which in any proceedings evidence of reputation or family tradition is admissible for the purpose of proving or disproving the existence of a marriage,

is to be treated as applying in an equivalent way for the purpose of proving or disproving the existence of a civil partnership.

209 Restriction on publicity of reports of proceedings

Section 1 of the Matrimonial Causes (Reports) Act (Northern Ireland) 1966 (c 29 (NI)) (restriction on publication of reports of proceedings) shall extend to proceedings—

    (a) for the dissolution or annulment of a civil partnership or for the legal separation of civil partners,

    (b) under section 181,

    (c) under Part 8 of Schedule 15, or

    (d) under Part 10 of Schedule 15 in relation to an order under Part 8 of that Schedule.

PART 5
CIVIL PARTNERSHIP FORMED OR DISSOLVED ABROAD ETC

CHAPTER 1
REGISTRATION OUTSIDE UK UNDER ORDER IN COUNCIL

210 Registration at British consulates etc

(1) Her Majesty may by Order in Council make provision for two people to register as civil partners of each other—

    (a) in prescribed countries or territories outside the United Kingdom, and

    (b) in the presence of a prescribed officer of Her Majesty's Diplomatic Service,

in cases where the officer is satisfied that the conditions in subsection (2) are met.

(2) The conditions are that—

    (a) at least one of the proposed civil partners is a United Kingdom national,

    (b) the proposed civil partners would have been eligible to register as civil partners of each other in such part of the United Kingdom as is determined in accordance with the Order,

    (c) the authorities of the country or territory in which it is proposed that they register as civil partners will not object to the registration, and

    (d) insufficient facilities exist for them to enter into an overseas relationship under the law of that country or territory.

(3) An officer is not required to allow two people to register as civil partners of each other if in his opinion the formation of a civil partnership between them would be inconsistent with international law or the comity of nations.

(4) An Order in Council under this section may make provision for appeals against a refusal, in reliance on subsection (3), to allow two people to register as civil partners of each other.

(5) An Order in Council under this section may provide that two people who register as civil partners of each other under such an Order are to be treated for the purposes of sections 221(1)(c)(i) and (2)(c)(i), 222(c), 224(b), 225(1)(c)(i) and (3)(c)(i), 229(1)(c)(i) and (2)(c)(i), 230(c) and 232(b) and section 1(3)(c)(i) of the Presumption of Death (Scotland) Act 1977 (c 27) as if they had done so in the part of the United Kingdom determined as mentioned in subsection (2)(b).

211 Registration by armed forces personnel

(1) Her Majesty may by Order in Council make provision for two people to register as civil partners of each other—

    (a) in prescribed countries or territories outside the United Kingdom, and

    (b) in the presence of an officer appointed by virtue of the Registration of Births, Deaths and Marriages (Special Provisions) Act 1957 (c 58),

in cases where the officer is satisfied that the conditions in subsection (2) are met.

(2) The conditions are that—

    (a) at least one of the proposed civil partners—

        (i) is a member of a part of Her Majesty's forces serving in the country or territory,

        (ii) is employed in the country or territory in such other capacity as may be prescribed, or

        (iii) is a child of a person falling within sub-paragraph (i) or (ii) and has his home with that person in that country or territory,

    (b) the proposed civil partners would have been eligible to register as civil partners of each other in such part of the United Kingdom as is determined in accordance with the Order, and

    (c) such other requirements as may be prescribed are complied with.

(3) In determining for the purposes of subsection (2) whether one person is the child of another, a person who is or was treated by another as a child of the family in relation to—

    (a) a marriage to which the other is or was a party, or

    (b) a civil partnership in which the other is or was a civil partner,

is to be regarded as the other's child.

(4) An Order in Council under this section may provide that two people who register as civil partners of each other under such an Order are to be treated for the purposes of section 221(1)(c)(i) and (2)(c)(i), 222(c), 224(b), 225(1)(c)(i) and (3)(c)(i), 229(1)(c)(i) and (2)(c)(i), 230(c) and 232(b) and section 1(3)(c)(i) of the Presumption of Death (Scotland) Act 1977 (c 27) as if they had done so in the part of the United Kingdom determined in accordance with subsection (2)(b).

(5) Any references in this section—

(a) to a country or territory outside the United Kingdom,

(b) to forces serving in such a country or territory, and

(c) to persons employed in such a country or territory,

include references to ships which are for the time being in the waters of a country or territory outside the United Kingdom, to forces serving in any such ship and to persons employed in any such ship.

CHAPTER 2
OVERSEAS RELATIONSHIPS TREATED AS CIVIL PARTNERSHIPS

212 Meaning of 'overseas relationship'

(1) For the purposes of this Act an overseas relationship is a relationship which—

(a) is either a specified relationship or a relationship which meets the general conditions, and

(b) is registered (whether before or after the passing of this Act) with a responsible authority in a country or territory outside the United Kingdom, by two people—

(i) who under the relevant law are of the same sex at the time when they do so, and

(ii) neither of whom is already a civil partner or lawfully married.

(2) In this Chapter, 'the relevant law' means the law of the country or territory where the relationship is registered (including its rules of private international law).

213 Specified relationships

(1) A specified relationship is a relationship which is specified for the purposes of section 212 by Schedule 20.

(2) The Secretary of State may by order amend Schedule 20 by—

(a) adding a relationship,

(b) amending the description of a relationship, or

(c) omitting a relationship.

(3) No order may be made under this section without the consent of the Scottish Ministers and the Department of Finance and Personnel.

(4) The power to make an order under this section is exercisable by statutory instrument.

(5) An order which contains any provision (whether alone or with other provisions) amending Schedule 20 by—

(a) amending the description of a relationship, or

(b) omitting a relationship,

may not be made unless a draft of the statutory instrument containing the order is laid before, and approved by a resolution of, each House of Parliament.

(6) A statutory instrument containing any other order under this section is subject to annulment in pursuance of a resolution of either House of Parliament.

214 The general conditions

The general conditions are that, under the relevant law—

(a) the relationship may not be entered into if either of the parties is already a party to a relationship of that kind or lawfully married,

(b) the relationship is of indeterminate duration, and
(c) the effect of entering into it is that the parties are—
    (i)   treated as a couple either generally or for specified purposes, or
    (ii) treated as married.

215 Overseas relationships treated as civil partnerships: the general rule

(1) Two people are to be treated as having formed a civil partnership as a result of having registered an overseas relationship if, under the relevant law, they—

(a) had capacity to enter into the relationship, and
(b) met all requirements necessary to ensure the formal validity of the relationship.

(2) Subject to subsection (3), the time when they are to be treated as having formed the civil partnership is the time when the overseas relationship is registered (under the relevant law) as having been entered into.

(3) If the overseas relationship is registered (under the relevant law) as having been entered into before this section comes into force, the time when they are to be treated as having formed a civil partnership is the time when this section comes into force.

(4) But if—

(a) before this section comes into force, a dissolution or annulment of the overseas relationship was obtained outside the United Kingdom, and
(b) the dissolution or annulment would be recognised under Chapter 3 if the overseas relationship had been treated as a civil partnership at the time of the dissolution or annulment,

subsection (3) does not apply and subsections (1) and (2) have effect subject to subsection (5).

(5) The overseas relationship is not to be treated as having been a civil partnership for the purposes of any provisions except—

(a) Schedules 7, 11 and 17 (financial relief in United Kingdom after dissolution or annulment obtained outside the United Kingdom);
(b) such provisions as are specified (with or without modifications) in an order under section 259;
(c) Chapter 3 (so far as necessary for the purposes of paragraphs (a) and (b)).

(6) This section is subject to sections 216, 217 and 218.

216 The same-sex requirement

(1) Two people are not to be treated as having formed a civil partnership as a result of having registered an overseas relationship if, at the critical time, they were not of the same sex under United Kingdom law.

(2) But if a full gender recognition certificate is issued under the 2004 Act to a person who has registered an overseas relationship which is within subsection (4), after the issue of the certificate the relationship is no longer prevented from being treated as a civil partnership on the ground that, at the critical time, the parties were not of the same sex.

(3) However, subsection (2) does not apply to an overseas relationship which is within subsection (4) if either of the parties has formed a subsequent civil partnership or lawful marriage.

(4) An overseas relationship is within this subsection if (and only if), at the time mentioned in section 215(2)—

(a) one of the parties ('A') was regarded under the relevant law as having changed gender (but was not regarded under United Kingdom law as having done so), and

(b) the other party was (under United Kingdom law) of the gender to which A had changed under the relevant law.

(5) In this section—

'the critical time' means the time determined in accordance with section 215(2) or (as the case may be) (3);

'the 2004 Act' means the Gender Recognition Act 2004 (c 7);

'United Kingdom law' means any enactment or rule of law applying in England and Wales, Scotland and Northern Ireland.

(6) Nothing in this section prevents the exercise of any enforceable Community right.

217 Person domiciled in a part of the United Kingdom

(1) Subsection (2) applies if an overseas relationship has been registered by a person who was at the time mentioned in section 215(2) domiciled in England and Wales.

(2) The two people concerned are not to be treated as having formed a civil partnership if, at the time mentioned in section 215(2)—

(a) either of them was under 16, or

(b) they would have been within prohibited degrees of relationship under Part 1 of Schedule 1 if they had been registering as civil partners of each other in England and Wales.

(3) Subsection (4) applies if an overseas relationship has been registered by a person who at the time mentioned in section 215(2) was domiciled in Scotland.

(4) The two people concerned are not to be treated as having formed a civil partnership if, at the time mentioned in section 215(2), they were not eligible by virtue of paragraph (b), (c) or (e) of section 86(1) to register in Scotland as civil partners of each other.

(5) Subsection (6) applies if an overseas relationship has been registered by a person who at the time mentioned in section 215(2) was domiciled in Northern Ireland.

(6) The two people concerned are not to be treated as having formed a civil partnership if, at the time mentioned in section 215(2)—

(a) either of them was under 16, or

(b) they would have been within prohibited degrees of relationship under Schedule 12 if they had been registering as civil partners of each other in Northern Ireland.

218 The public policy exception

Two people are not to be treated as having formed a civil partnership as a result of having entered into an overseas relationship if it would be manifestly contrary to public policy to recognise the capacity, under the relevant law, of one or both of them to enter into the relationship.

CHAPTER 3
DISSOLUTION ETC: JURISDICTION AND RECOGNITION

Introduction

219 Power to make provision corresponding to EC Regulation 2201/2003

(1) The Lord Chancellor may by regulations make provision—

  (a) as to the jurisdiction of courts in England and Wales or Northern Ireland in proceedings for the dissolution or annulment of a civil partnership or for legal separation of the civil partners in cases where a civil partner—
  (i)   is or has been habitually resident in a member State,
  (ii) is a national of a member State, or
  (iii) is domiciled in a part of the United Kingdom or the Republic of Ireland, and
  (b) as to the recognition in England and Wales or Northern Ireland of any judgment of a court of another member State which orders the dissolution or annulment of a civil partnership or the legal separation of the civil partners.

(2) The Scottish Ministers may by regulations make provision—

  (a) as to the jurisdiction of courts in Scotland in proceedings for the dissolution or annulment of a civil partnership or for legal separation of the civil partners in such cases as are mentioned in subsection (1)(a), and
  (b) as to the recognition in Scotland of any such judgment as is mentioned in subsection (1)(b).

(3) The regulations may in particular make provision corresponding to that made by Council Regulation (EC) No 2201/2003 of 27th November 2003 in relation to jurisdiction and the recognition and enforcement of judgments in matrimonial matters.

(4) The regulations may provide that for the purposes of this Part and the regulations 'member State' means—

  (a) all member States with the exception of such member States as are specified in the regulations, or
  (b) such member States as are specified in the regulations.

(5) The regulations may make provision under subsections (1)(b) and (2)(b) which applies even if the date of the dissolution, annulment or legal separation is earlier than the date on which this section comes into force.

(6) Regulations under subsection (1) are to be made by statutory instrument and may only be made if a draft has been laid before and approved by resolution of each House of Parliament.

(7) Regulations under subsection (2) are to be made by statutory instrument and may only be made if a draft has been laid before and approved by resolution of the Scottish Parliament.

(8) In this Part 'section 219 regulations' means regulations made under this section.

Jurisdiction of courts in England and Wales

220 Meaning of 'the court'

In sections 221 to 224 'the court' means—

  (a) the High Court, or
  (b) if a county court has jurisdiction by virtue of Part 5 of the Matrimonial and Family Proceedings Act 1984 (c 42), a county court.

221 Proceedings for dissolution, separation or nullity order

(1) The court has jurisdiction to entertain proceedings for a dissolution order or a separation order if (and only if)—

- (a) the court has jurisdiction under section 219 regulations,
- (b) no court has, or is recognised as having, jurisdiction under section 219 regulations and either civil partner is domiciled in England and Wales on the date when the proceedings are begun, or
- (c) the following conditions are met—
    - (i) the two people concerned registered as civil partners of each other in England or Wales,
    - (ii) no court has, or is recognised as having, jurisdiction under section 219 regulations, and
    - (iii) it appears to the court to be in the interests of justice to assume jurisdiction in the case.

(2) The court has jurisdiction to entertain proceedings for a nullity order if (and only if)—

- (a) the court has jurisdiction under section 219 regulations,
- (b) no court has, or is recognised as having, jurisdiction under section 219 regulations and either civil partner—
    - (i) is domiciled in England and Wales on the date when the proceedings are begun, or
    - (ii) died before that date and either was at death domiciled in England and Wales or had been habitually resident in England and Wales throughout the period of 1 year ending with the date of death, or
- (c) the following conditions are met—
    - (i) the two people concerned registered as civil partners of each other in England or Wales,
    - (ii) no court has, or is recognised as having, jurisdiction under section 219 regulations, and
    - (iii) it appears to the court to be in the interests of justice to assume jurisdiction in the case.

(3) At any time when proceedings are pending in respect of which the court has jurisdiction by virtue of subsection (1) or (2) (or this subsection), the court also has jurisdiction to entertain other proceedings, in respect of the same civil partnership, for a dissolution, separation or nullity order, even though that jurisdiction would not be exercisable under subsection (1) or (2).

222 Proceedings for presumption of death order

The court has jurisdiction to entertain proceedings for a presumption of death order if (and only if)—

- (a) the applicant is domiciled in England and Wales on the date when the proceedings are begun,
- (b) the applicant was habitually resident in England and Wales throughout the period of 1 year ending with that date, or
- (c) the two people concerned registered as civil partners of each other in England and Wales and it appears to the court to be in the interests of justice to assume jurisdiction in the case.

223 Proceedings for dissolution, nullity or separation order: supplementary

(1) Rules of court may make provision in relation to civil partnerships corresponding to the provision made in relation to marriages by Schedule 1 to the Domicile and Matrimonial Proceedings Act 1973 (c 45).

(2) The rules may in particular make provision—

- (a) for the provision of information by applicants and respondents in proceedings for dissolution, nullity or separation orders where proceedings relating to the same civil partnership are continuing in another jurisdiction, and

(b) for proceedings before the court to be stayed by the court where there are concurrent proceedings elsewhere in respect of the same civil partnership.

224 Applications for declarations as to validity etc

The court has jurisdiction to entertain an application under section 58 if (and only if)—

(a) either of the civil partners in the civil partnership to which the application relates—
   (i)   is domiciled in England and Wales on the date of the application,
   (ii) has been habitually resident in England and Wales throughout the period of 1 year ending with that date, or
   (iii) died before that date and either was at death domiciled in England and Wales or had been habitually resident in England and Wales throughout the period of 1 year ending with the date of death, or
(b) the two people concerned registered as civil partners of each other in England and Wales and it appears to the court to be in the interests of justice to assume jurisdiction in the case.

Jurisdiction of Scottish courts

225 Jurisdiction of Scottish courts

(1) The Court of Session has jurisdiction to entertain an action for the dissolution of a civil partnership or for separation of civil partners if (and only if)—

(a) the court has jurisdiction under section 219 regulations,
(b) no court has, or is recognised as having, jurisdiction under section 219 regulations and either civil partner is domiciled in Scotland on the date when the proceedings are begun, or
(c) the following conditions are met—
   (i)   the two people concerned registered as civil partners of each other in Scotland,
   (ii) no court has, or is recognised as having, jurisdiction under section 219 regulations, and
   (iii) it appears to the court to be in the interests of justice to assume jurisdiction in the case.

(2) The sheriff has jurisdiction to entertain an action for the dissolution of a civil partnership or for separation of civil partners if (and only if) the requirements of paragraph (a) or (b) of subsection (1) are met and either civil partner—

(a) was resident in the sheriffdom for a period of 40 days ending with the date when the action is begun, or
(b) had been resident in the sheriffdom for a period of not less than 40 days ending not more than 40 days before that date and has no known residence in Scotland at that date.

(3) The Court of Session has jurisdiction to entertain an action for declarator of nullity of a civil partnership if (and only if)—

(a) the Court has jurisdiction under section 219 regulations,
(b) no court has, or is recognised as having, jurisdiction under section 219 regulations and either of the ostensible civil partners—
   (i)   is domiciled in Scotland on the date when the proceedings are begun, or
   (ii) died before that date and either was at death domiciled in Scotland or had been habitually resident in Scotland throughout the period of 1 year ending with the date of death, or
(c) the following conditions are met—
   (i)   the two people concerned registered as civil partners of each other in Scotland,
   (ii) no court has, or is recognised as having, jurisdiction under section 219 regulations, and
   (iii) it appears to the court to be in the interests of justice to assume jurisdiction in the case.

(4) At any time when proceedings are pending in respect of which a court has jurisdiction by virtue of any of subsections (1) to (3) (or this subsection) it also has jurisdiction to entertain other proceedings, in respect of the same civil partnership (or ostensible civil partnership), for dissolution, separation or (but only where the court is the Court of Session) declarator of nullity, even though that jurisdiction would not be exercisable under any of subsections (1) to (3).

226 Sisting of proceedings

(1) Rules of court may make provision in relation to civil partnerships corresponding to the provision made in relation to marriages by Schedule 3 to the Domicile and Matrimonial Proceedings Act 1973 (c 45) (sisting of Scottish consistorial actions).

(2) The rules may in particular make provision—

(a) for the provision of information by the pursuer and by any other person who has entered appearance in an action where proceedings relating to the same civil partnership (or ostensible civil partnership) are continuing in another jurisdiction, and
(b) for an action to be sisted where there are concurrent proceedings elsewhere in respect of the same civil partnership (or ostensible civil partnership).

227 Scottish ancillary and collateral orders

(1) This section applies where after the commencement of this Act an application is competently made to the Court of Session or the sheriff for the making, or the variation or recall, of an order which is ancillary or collateral to an action for—

(a) the dissolution of a civil partnership,
(b) the separation of civil partners, or
(c) declarator of nullity of a civil partnership.

(2) And the section applies whether the application is made in the same proceedings or in other proceedings and whether it is made before or after the pronouncement of a final decree in the action.

(3) If the court has or, as the case may be, had jurisdiction to entertain the action, it has jurisdiction to entertain the application unless—

(a) jurisdiction to entertain the action was under section 219 regulations, and
(b) to make, vary or recall the order to which the application relates would contravene the regulations.

(4) Where the Court of Session has jurisdiction by virtue of this section to entertain an application for the variation or recall, as respects any person, of an order made by it and the order is one to which section 8 (variation and recall by the sheriff of certain orders made by the Court of Session) of the Law Reform (Miscellaneous Provisions) (Scotland) Act 1966 (c 19) applies, then for the purposes of any application under that section for the variation or recall of the order in so far as it relates to the person, the sheriff (as defined in that section) has jurisdiction to exercise the power conferred on him by that section.

(5) The reference in subsection (1) to an order which is ancillary or collateral is to an order relating to children, aliment, financial provision or expenses.

Jurisdiction of courts in Northern Ireland

228 Meaning of 'the court'

In sections 229 to 232 'the court' has the meaning given by section 188.

229 Proceedings for dissolution, separation or nullity order

(1) The court has jurisdiction to entertain proceedings for a dissolution order or a separation order if (and only if)—

- (a) the court has jurisdiction under section 219 regulations,
- (b) no court has, or is recognised as having, jurisdiction under section 219 regulations and either civil partner is domiciled in Northern Ireland on the date when the proceedings are begun, or
- (c) the following conditions are met—
  - (i) the two people concerned registered as civil partners of each other in Northern Ireland,
  - (ii) no court has, or is recognised as having, jurisdiction under section 219 regulations, and
  - (iii) it appears to the court to be in the interests of justice to assume jurisdiction in the case.

(2) The court has jurisdiction to entertain proceedings for a nullity order if (and only if)—

- (a) the court has jurisdiction under section 219 regulations,
- (b) no court has, or is recognised as having, jurisdiction under section 219 regulations and either civil partner—
  - (i) is domiciled in Northern Ireland on the date when the proceedings are begun, or
  - (ii) died before that date and either was at death domiciled in Northern Ireland or had been habitually resident in Northern Ireland throughout the period of 1 year ending with the date of death, or
- (c) the following conditions are met—
  - (i) the two people concerned registered as civil partners of each other in Northern Ireland,
  - (ii) no court has, or is recognised as having, jurisdiction under section 219 regulations, and
  - (iii) it appears to the court to be in the interests of justice to assume jurisdiction in the case.

(3) At any time when proceedings are pending in respect of which the court has jurisdiction by virtue of subsection (1) or (2) (or this subsection), the court also has jurisdiction to entertain other proceedings, in respect of the same civil partnership, for a dissolution, separation or nullity order, even though that jurisdiction would not be exercisable under subsection (1) or (2).

230 Proceedings for presumption of death order

The High Court has jurisdiction to entertain proceedings for a presumption of death order if (and only if)—

- (a) the applicant is domiciled in Northern Ireland on the date when the proceedings are begun,
- (b) the applicant was habitually resident in Northern Ireland throughout the period of 1 year ending with that date, or
- (c) the two people concerned registered as civil partners of each other in Northern Ireland and it appears to the High Court to be in the interests of justice to assume jurisdiction in the case.

231 Proceedings for dissolution, nullity or separation order: supplementary

(1) Rules of court may make provision in relation to civil partnerships corresponding to the provision made in relation to marriages by Schedule 1 to the Matrimonial Causes (Northern Ireland) Order 1978 (SI 1978/1045 (NI 15)).

(2) The rules may in particular make provision—

- (a) for the provision of information by applicants and respondents in proceedings for dissolution, nullity or separation orders where proceedings relating to the same civil partnership are continuing in another jurisdiction, and

(b) for proceedings before the court to be stayed by the court where there are concurrent proceedings elsewhere in respect of the same civil partnership.

232 Applications for declarations as to validity etc

The court has jurisdiction to entertain an application under section 181 if (and only if)—

(a) either of the civil partners in the civil partnership to which the application relates—
  (i) is domiciled in Northern Ireland on the date of the application,
  (ii) has been habitually resident in Northern Ireland throughout the period of 1 year ending with that date, or
  (iii) died before that date and either was at death domiciled in Northern Ireland or had been habitually resident in Northern Ireland throughout the period of 1 year ending with the date of death, or
(b) the two people concerned registered as civil partners of each other in Northern Ireland and it appears to the court to be in the interests of justice to assume jurisdiction in the case.

Recognition of dissolution, annulment and separation

233 Effect of dissolution, annulment or separation obtained in the UK

(1) No dissolution or annulment of a civil partnership obtained in one part of the United Kingdom is effective in any part of the United Kingdom unless obtained from a court of civil jurisdiction.

(2) Subject to subsections (3) and (4), the validity of a dissolution or annulment of a civil partnership or a legal separation of civil partners which has been obtained from a court of civil jurisdiction in one part of the United Kingdom is to be recognised throughout the United Kingdom.

(3) Recognition of the validity of a dissolution, annulment or legal separation obtained from a court of civil jurisdiction in one part of the United Kingdom may be refused in any other part if the dissolution, annulment or separation was obtained at a time when it was irreconcilable with a decision determining the question of the subsistence or validity of the civil partnership—

(a) previously given by a court of civil jurisdiction in the other part, or
(b) previously given by a court elsewhere and recognised or entitled to be recognised in the other part.

(4) Recognition of the validity of a dissolution or legal separation obtained from a court of civil jurisdiction in one part of the United Kingdom may be refused in any other part if the dissolution or separation was obtained at a time when, according to the law of the other part, there was no subsisting civil partnership.

234 Recognition in the UK of overseas dissolution, annulment or separation

(1) Subject to subsection (2), the validity of an overseas dissolution, annulment or legal separation is to be recognised in the United Kingdom if, and only if, it is entitled to recognition by virtue of sections 235 to 237.

(2) This section and sections 235 to 237 do not apply to an overseas dissolution, annulment or legal separation as regards which provision as to recognition is made by section 219 regulations.

(3) For the purposes of subsections (1) and (2) and sections 235 to 237, an overseas dissolution, annulment or legal separation is a dissolution or annulment of a civil partnership or a legal separation of civil partners which has been obtained outside the United Kingdom (whether before or after this section comes into force).

235 Grounds for recognition

(1) The validity of an overseas dissolution, annulment or legal separation obtained by means of proceedings is to be recognised if—

    (a) the dissolution, annulment or legal separation is effective under the law of the country in which it was obtained, and

    (b) at the relevant date either civil partner—

        (i) was habitually resident in the country in which the dissolution, annulment or legal separation was obtained,

        (ii) was domiciled in that country, or

        (iii) was a national of that country.

(2) The validity of an overseas dissolution, annulment or legal separation obtained otherwise than by means of proceedings is to be recognised if—

    (a) the dissolution, annulment or legal separation is effective under the law of the country in which it was obtained,

    (b) at the relevant date—

        (i) each civil partner was domiciled in that country, or

        (ii) either civil partner was domiciled in that country and the other was domiciled in a country under whose law the dissolution, annulment or legal separation is recognised as valid, and

    (c) neither civil partner was habitually resident in the United Kingdom throughout the period of 1 year immediately preceding that date.

(3) In this section 'the relevant date' means—

    (a) in the case of an overseas dissolution, annulment or legal separation obtained by means of proceedings, the date of the commencement of the proceedings;

    (b) in the case of an overseas dissolution, annulment or legal separation obtained otherwise than by means of proceedings, the date on which it was obtained.

(4) Where in the case of an overseas annulment the relevant date fell after the death of either civil partner, any reference in subsection (1) or (2) to that date is to be read in relation to that civil partner as a reference to the date of death.

236 Refusal of recognition

(1) Recognition of the validity of an overseas dissolution, annulment or legal separation may be refused in any part of the United Kingdom if the dissolution, annulment or separation was obtained at a time when it was irreconcilable with a decision determining the question of the subsistence or validity of the civil partnership—

    (a) previously given by a court of civil jurisdiction in that part of the United Kingdom, or

    (b) previously given by a court elsewhere and recognised or entitled to be recognised in that part of the United Kingdom.

(2) Recognition of the validity of an overseas dissolution or legal separation may be refused in any part of the United Kingdom if the dissolution or separation was obtained at a time when, according to the law of that part of the United Kingdom, there was no subsisting civil partnership.

(3) Recognition of the validity of an overseas dissolution, annulment or legal separation may be refused if—

    (a) in the case of a dissolution, annulment or legal separation obtained by means of proceedings, it was obtained—

   (i)   without such steps having been taken for giving notice of the proceedings to a civil partner as, having regard to the nature of the proceedings and all the circumstances, should reasonably have been taken, or

   (ii) without a civil partner having been given (for any reason other than lack of notice) such opportunity to take part in the proceedings as, having regard to those matters, he should reasonably have been given, or

(b) in the case of a dissolution, annulment or legal separation obtained otherwise than by means of proceedings—

   (i)   there is no official document certifying that the dissolution, annulment or legal separation is effective under the law of the country in which it was obtained, or

   (ii) where either civil partner was domiciled in another country at the relevant date, there is no official document certifying that the dissolution, annulment or legal separation is recognised as valid under the law of that other country, or

(c) in either case, recognition of the dissolution, annulment or legal separation would be manifestly contrary to public policy.

(4) In this section—

    'official', in relation to a document certifying that a dissolution, annulment or legal separation is effective, or is recognised as valid, under the law of any country, means issued by a person or body appointed or recognised for the purpose under that law;

    'the relevant date' has the same meaning as in section 235.

237 Supplementary provisions relating to recognition of dissolution etc

(1) For the purposes of sections 235 and 236, a civil partner is to be treated as domiciled in a country if he was domiciled in that country—

(a) according to the law of that country in family matters, or

(b) according to the law of the part of the United Kingdom in which the question of recognition arises.

(2) The Lord Chancellor or the Scottish Ministers may by regulations make provision—

(a) applying sections 235 and 236 and subsection (1) with modifications in relation to any country whose territories have different systems of law in force in matters of dissolution, annulment or legal separation;

(b) applying sections 235 and 236 with modifications in relation to—

   (i)   an overseas dissolution, annulment or legal separation in the case of an overseas relationship (or an apparent or alleged overseas relationship);

   (ii) any case where a civil partner is domiciled in a country or territory whose law does not recognise legal relationships between two people of the same sex;

(c) with respect to recognition of the validity of an overseas dissolution, annulment or legal separation in cases where there are cross-proceedings;

(d) with respect to cases where a legal separation is converted under the law of the country or territory in which it is obtained into a dissolution which is effective under the law of that country or territory;

(e) with respect to proof of findings of fact made in proceedings in any country or territory outside the United Kingdom.

(3) The power to make regulations under subsection (2) is exercisable by statutory instrument.

(4) A statutory instrument containing such regulations—

(a) if made by the Lord Chancellor, is subject to annulment in pursuance of a resolution of either House of Parliament;

(b) if made by the Scottish Ministers, is subject to annulment in pursuance of a resolution of the Scottish Parliament.

(5) In this section (except subsection (4)) and sections 233 to 236 and 238—

'annulment' includes any order annulling a civil partnership, however expressed;

'part of the United Kingdom' means England and Wales, Scotland or Northern Ireland;

'proceedings' means judicial or other proceedings.

(6) Nothing in this Chapter is to be read as requiring the recognition of any finding of fault made in proceedings for dissolution, annulment or legal separation or of any maintenance, custody or other ancillary order made in any such proceedings.

238 Non-recognition elsewhere of dissolution or annulment

(1) This section applies where, in any part of the United Kingdom—

(a) a dissolution or annulment of a civil partnership has been granted by a court of civil jurisdiction, or
(b) the validity of a dissolution or annulment of a civil partnership is recognised by virtue of this Chapter.

(2) The fact that the dissolution or annulment would not be recognised outside the United Kingdom does not—

(a) preclude either party from forming a subsequent civil partnership or marriage in that part of the United Kingdom, or
(b) cause the subsequent civil partnership or marriage of either party (wherever it takes place) to be treated as invalid in that part.

CHAPTER 4
MISCELLANEOUS AND SUPPLEMENTARY

239 Commanding officers' certificates for Part 2 purposes

(1) Her Majesty may by Order in Council make provision in relation to cases where—

(a) two people wish to register as civil partners of each other in England and Wales (under Chapter 1 of Part 2), and
(b) one of them ('A') is a member of Her Majesty's forces serving outside the United Kingdom and the other is resident in England and Wales,

for the issue by A's commanding officer to A of a certificate of no impediment.

(2) The Order may provide for the issue of the certificate to be subject to the giving of such notice and the making of such declarations as may be prescribed.

(3) A certificate of no impediment is a certificate that no legal impediment to the formation of the civil partnership has been shown to the commanding officer issuing the certificate to exist.

(4) 'Commanding officer'—

(a) in relation to a person subject to military law, means the officer who would be that person's commanding officer for the purposes of section 82 of the Army Act 1955 (3 & 4 Eliz. 2 c 18) if he were charged with an offence;

(b) in relation to a person subject to air-force law, means the officer who would be that person's commanding officer for the purposes of section 82 of the Air Force Act 1955 (3 & 4 Eliz. 2 c 19) if he were charged with an offence;

(c) in relation to a person subject to the Naval Discipline Act 1957 (c 53), means the officer in command of the ship or naval establishment to which he belongs.

240 Certificates of no impediment to overseas relationships

(1) Her Majesty may by Order in Council make provision for the issue of certificates of no impediment to—

(a) United Kingdom nationals, and

(b) such other persons falling within subsection (2) as may be prescribed,

who wish to enter into overseas relationships in prescribed countries or territories outside the United Kingdom with persons who are not United Kingdom nationals and who do not fall within subsection (2).

(2) A person falls within this subsection if under any enactment for the time being in force in any country mentioned in Schedule 3 to the British Nationality Act 1981 (c 61) (Commonwealth countries) that person is a citizen of that country.

(3) A certificate of no impediment is a certificate that, after proper notices have been given, no legal impediment to the recipient entering into the overseas relationship has been shown to the person issuing the certificate to exist.

241 Transmission of certificates of registration of overseas relationships

(1) Her Majesty may by Order in Council provide—

(a) for the transmission to the Registrar General, by such persons or in such manner as may be prescribed, of certificates of the registration of overseas relationships entered into by United Kingdom nationals in prescribed countries or territories outside the United Kingdom,

(b) for the issue by the Registrar General of a certified copy of such a certificate received by him, and

(c) for such certified copies to be received in evidence.

(2) 'The Registrar General' means—

(a) in relation to England and Wales, the Registrar General for England and Wales,

(b) in relation to Scotland, the Registrar General of Births, Deaths and Marriages for Scotland, and

(c) in relation to Northern Ireland, the Registrar General for Northern Ireland.

242 Power to make provision relating to certain Commonwealth forces

(1) This section applies if it appears to Her Majesty that any law in force in Canada, the Commonwealth of Australia or New Zealand (or in a territory of either of the former two countries) makes, in relation to forces raised there, provision similar to that made by section 211 (registration by armed forces personnel).

(2) Her Majesty may by Order in Council make provision for securing that the law in question has effect as part of the law of the United Kingdom.

243 Fees

(1) The power to make an order under section 34(1) (fees) includes power to make an order prescribing fees in respect of anything which, by virtue of an Order in Council under this Part, is required to be done by registration authorities in England and Wales or by or on behalf of the Registrar General for England and Wales.

(2) Regulations made by the Registrar General of Births, Deaths and Marriages for Scotland may prescribe fees in respect of anything which, by virtue of an Order in Council under this Part, is required to be done by him or on his behalf.

(3) Subsections (3) and (4) of section 126 apply to regulations made under subsection (2) as they apply to regulations under Part 3.

(4) The power to make an order under section 157(1) includes power to make an order prescribing fees in respect of anything which, by virtue of an Order in Council under this Part, is required to be done by or on behalf of the Registrar General for Northern Ireland.

244 Orders in Council: supplementary

(1) An Order in Council under section 210, 211, 239, 240, 241 or 242 may make—

    (a) different provision for different cases, and
    (b) such supplementary, incidental, consequential, transitional, transitory or saving provision as appears to Her Majesty to be appropriate.

(2) The provision that may be made by virtue of subsection (1)(b) includes in particular provision corresponding to or applying with modifications any provision made by or under—

    (a) this Act, or
    (b) any Act relating to marriage outside the United Kingdom.

(3) A statutory instrument containing an Order in Council under section 210, 211, 239, 240, 241 or 242 is subject to annulment in pursuance of a resolution of either House of Parliament.

(4) Subsection (3) applies whether or not the Order also contains other provisions made by Order in Council under—

    the Foreign Marriage Act 1892 (c 23),

    section 3 of the Foreign Marriage Act 1947 (c 33), or

    section 39 of the Marriage Act 1949 (c 76).

    (5) In sections 210, 211, 239, 240 and 241 'prescribed' means prescribed by an Order in Council under the section in question.

245 Interpretation

(1) In this Part 'United Kingdom national' means a person who is—

    (a) a British citizen, a British overseas territories citizen, a British Overseas citizen or a British National (Overseas),
    (b) a British subject under the British Nationality Act 1981 (c 61), or
    (c) a British protected person, within the meaning of that Act.

(2) In this Part 'Her Majesty's forces' has the same meaning as in the Army Act 1955 (3 & 4 Eliz. 2 c 18).

PART 6
RELATIONSHIPS ARISING THROUGH CIVIL PARTNERSHIP

246 Interpretation of statutory references to stepchildren etc

(1) In any provision to which this section applies, references to a stepchild or step-parent of a person (here, 'A'), and cognate expressions, are to be read as follows—

A's stepchild includes a person who is the child of A's civil partner (but is not A's child);

A's step-parent includes a person who is the civil partner of A's parent (but is not A's parent);

A's stepdaughter includes a person who is the daughter of A's civil partner (but is not A's daughter);

A's stepson includes a person who is the son of A's civil partner (but is not A's son);

A's stepfather includes a person who is the civil partner of A's father (but is not A's parent);

A's stepmother includes a person who is the civil partner of A's mother (but is not A's parent);

A's stepbrother includes a person who is the son of the civil partner of A's parent (but is not the son of either of A's parents);

A's stepsister includes a person who is the daughter of the civil partner of A's parent (but is not the daughter of either of A's parents).

(2) For the purposes of any provision to which this section applies—

'brother-in-law' includes civil partner's brother,

'daughter-in-law' includes daughter's civil partner,

'father-in-law' includes civil partner's father,

'mother-in-law' includes civil partner's mother,

'parent-in-law' includes civil partner's parent,

'sister-in-law' includes civil partner's sister, and

'son-in-law' includes son's civil partner.

247 Provisions to which section 246 applies: Acts of Parliament etc

(1) Section 246 applies to—

(a) any provision listed in Schedule 21 (references to stepchildren, in-laws etc in existing Acts),
(b) except in so far as otherwise provided, any provision made by a future Act, and
(c) except in so far as otherwise provided, any provision made by future subordinate legislation.

(2) A Minister of the Crown may by order—

(a) amend Schedule 21 by adding to it any provision of an existing Act;
(b) provide for section 246 to apply to prescribed provisions of existing subordinate legislation.

(3) The power conferred by subsection (2) is also exercisable—

(a) by the Scottish Ministers, in relation to a relevant Scottish provision;

    (b) by a Northern Ireland department, in relation to a provision which deals with a transferred matter;

    (c) by the National Assembly for Wales, if the order is made by virtue of subsection (2)(b) and deals with matters with respect to which functions are exercisable by the Assembly.

(4) Subject to subsection (5), the power to make an order under subsection (2) is exercisable by statutory instrument.

(5) Any power of a Northern Ireland department to make an order under subsection (2) is exercisable by statutory rule for the purposes of the Statutory Rules (Northern Ireland) Order 1979 (SI 1979/1573 (NI 12)).

(6) A statutory instrument containing an order under subsection (2) made by a Minister of the Crown is subject to annulment in pursuance of a resolution of either House of Parliament.

(7) A statutory instrument containing an order under subsection (2) made by the Scottish Ministers is subject to annulment in pursuance of a resolution of the Scottish Parliament.

(8) A statutory rule containing an order under subsection (2) made by a Northern Ireland department is subject to negative resolution (within the meaning of section 41(6) of the Interpretation Act (Northern Ireland) 1954 (c 33 (NI))).

(9) In this section—

    'Act' includes an Act of the Scottish Parliament;

    'existing Act' means an Act passed on or before the last day of the Session in which this Act is passed;

    'existing subordinate legislation' means subordinate legislation made before the day on which this section comes into force;

    'future Act' means an Act passed after the last day of the Session in which this Act is passed;

    'future subordinate legislation' means subordinate legislation made on or after the day on which this section comes into force;

    'Minister of the Crown' has the same meaning as in the Ministers of the Crown Act 1975 (c 26);

    'prescribed' means prescribed by the order;

    'relevant Scottish provision' means a provision that would be within the legislative competence of the Scottish Parliament if it were included in an Act of that Parliament;

    'subordinate legislation' has the same meaning as in the Interpretation Act 1978 (c 30) except that it includes an instrument made under an Act of the Scottish Parliament;

    'transferred matter' has the meaning given by section 4(1) of the Northern Ireland Act 1998 (c 47) and 'deals with' in relation to a transferred matter is to be construed in accordance with section 98(2) and (3) of the 1998 Act.

248 Provisions to which section 246 applies: Northern Ireland

(1) Section 246 applies to—

    (a) any provision listed in Schedule 22 (references to stepchildren, etc in Northern Ireland legislation),

    (b) except in so far as otherwise provided, any provision made by any future Northern Ireland legislation, and

(c) except in so far as otherwise provided, any provision made by any future subordinate legislation.

(2) The Department of Finance and Personnel may by order—

(a) amend Schedule 22 by adding to it any provision of existing Northern Ireland legislation;
(b) provide for section 246 to apply to prescribed provisions of existing subordinate legislation.

(3) The power to make an order under subsection (2) is exercisable by statutory rule for the purposes of the Statutory Rules (Northern Ireland) Order 1979 (SI 1979/1573 (NI 12)).

(4) An order under subsection (2) is subject to negative resolution (within the meaning of section 41(6) of the Interpretation Act (Northern Ireland) 1954 (1954 c 33 (NI))).

(5) In this section—

'existing Northern Ireland legislation' means Northern Ireland legislation passed or made on or before the last day of the Session in which this Act is passed;

'existing subordinate legislation' means subordinate legislation made before the day on which this section comes into force;

'future Northern Ireland legislation' means Northern Ireland legislation passed or made after the last day of the Session in which this Act is passed;

'future subordinate legislation' means subordinate legislation made on or after the day on which this section comes into force;

'prescribed' means prescribed by the order;

'subordinate legislation' means any instrument (within the meaning of section 1(c) of the Interpretation Act (Northern Ireland) 1954 (1954 c 33 (NI))).

PART 7
MISCELLANEOUS

249 Immigration control and formation of civil partnerships

Schedule 23 contains provisions relating to the formation of civil partnerships in the United Kingdom by persons subject to immigration control.

250 Gender recognition where applicant a civil partner

(1) Amend the Gender Recognition Act 2004 (c 7) as follows.

(2) In—

(a) section 3 (evidence), in subsection (6)(a), and
(b) section 4 (successful applications), in subsections (2) and (3),

after 'is married' insert 'or a civil partner'.

(3) In section 5 (subsequent issue of full certificates)—

(a) in subsection (2), after 'is again married' insert 'or is a civil partner',
(b) in subsection (6)(a), for 'is not married' substitute 'is neither married nor a civil partner', and
(c) for the heading substitute 'Issue of full certificates where applicant has been married'.

(4) After section 5 insert—

'5A Issue of full certificates where applicant has been a civil partner

(1) A court which—

    (a) makes final a nullity order made on the ground that an interim gender recognition certificate has been issued to a civil partner, or

    (b) (in Scotland) grants a decree of dissolution on that ground,

must, on doing so, issue a full gender recognition certificate to that civil partner and send a copy to the Secretary of State.

(2) If an interim gender recognition certificate has been issued to a person and either—

    (a) the person's civil partnership is dissolved or annulled (otherwise than on the ground mentioned in subsection (1)) in proceedings instituted during the period of six months beginning with the day on which it was issued, or

    (b) the person's civil partner dies within that period,

the person may make an application for a full gender recognition certificate at any time within the period specified in subsection (3) (unless the person is again a civil partner or is married).

(3) That period is the period of six months beginning with the day on which the civil partnership is dissolved or annulled or the death occurs.

(4) An application under subsection (2) must include evidence of the dissolution or annulment of the civil partnership and the date on which proceedings for it were instituted, or of the death of the civil partner and the date on which it occurred.

(5) An application under subsection (2) is to be determined by a Gender Recognition Panel.

(6) The Panel—

    (a) must grant the application if satisfied that the applicant is neither a civil partner nor married, and

    (b) otherwise must reject it.

(7) If the Panel grants the application it must issue a full gender recognition certificate to the applicant.'

(5) In—

    (a) section 7 (applications: supplementary), in subsection (1),

    (b) section 8 (appeals etc), in subsections (1) and (5), and

    (c) section 22 (prohibition on disclosure of information), in subsection (2)(a),

after '5(2)' insert ', 5A(2)'.

(6) In section 21 (foreign gender change and marriage), in subsection (4), after 'entered into a later (valid) marriage' insert 'or civil partnership'.

(7) In section 25 (interpretation), in the definition of 'full gender recognition certificate' and 'interim gender recognition certificate', for 'or 5' substitute ', 5 or 5A'.

(8) In Schedule 1 (Gender Recognition Panels), in paragraph 5, after '5(2)' insert ', 5A(2)'.

(9) In Schedule 3 (registration), in paragraphs 9(1), 19(1) and 29(1), for 'or 5(2)' substitute ', 5(2) or 5A(2)'.

251 Discrimination against civil partners in employment field

(1) Amend the Sex Discrimination Act 1975 (c 65) as follows.

(2) For section 3 (discrimination against married persons in employment field) substitute—

'3 Discrimination against married persons and civil partners in employment field

(1) In any circumstances relevant for the purposes of any provision of Part 2, a person discriminates against a person ("A") who fulfils the condition in subsection (2) if—

    (a) on the ground of the fulfilment of the condition, he treats A less favourably than he treats or would treat a person who does not fulfil the condition, or

    (b) he applies to A a provision, criterion or practice which he applies or would apply equally to a person who does not fulfil the condition, but—

        (i) which puts or would put persons fulfilling the condition at a particular disadvantage when compared with persons not fulfilling the condition, and

        (ii) which puts A at that disadvantage, and

        (iii) which he cannot show to be a proportionate means of achieving a legitimate aim.

(2) The condition is that the person is—

    (a) married, or

    (b) a civil partner.

(3) For the purposes of subsection (1), a provision of Part 2 framed with reference to discrimination against women is to be treated as applying equally to the treatment of men, and for that purpose has effect with such modifications as are requisite.'

(3) In section 5 (interpretation), for subsection (3) substitute—

'(3) Each of the following comparisons, that is—

    (a) a comparison of the cases of persons of different sex under section 1(1) or (2),

    (b) a comparison of the cases of persons required for the purposes of section 2A, and

    (c) a comparison of the cases of persons who do and who do not fulfil the condition in section 3(2),

must be such that the relevant circumstances in the one case are the same, or not materially different, in the other.';

and omit section 1(4).

(4) In section 7 (exception where sex is a genuine occupational qualification), in subsection (2)(h) for 'by a married couple' substitute—

    '(i) by a married couple,

    (ii) by a couple who are civil partners of each other, or

    (iii) by a married couple or a couple who are civil partners of each other'.

(5) In section 65 (remedies on complaint under section 63), in subsection (1B) for 'or marital status as the case may be' substitute 'or (as the case may be) fulfilment of the condition in section 3(2)'.

252 Discrimination against civil partners in employment field: Northern Ireland

(1) Amend the Sex Discrimination (Northern Ireland) Order 1976 (SI 1976/1042 (NI 15)) as follows.

(2) For Article 5 (discrimination against married persons in employment field) substitute—

'5 Discrimination against married persons and civil partners in employment field

(1) In any circumstances relevant for the purposes of any provision of Part 3, a person discriminates against a person ("A") who fulfils the condition in paragraph (2) if—

  (a) on the ground of the fulfilment of the condition, he treats A less favourably than he treats or would treat a person who does not fulfil the condition, or
  (b) he applies to A a provision, criterion or practice which he applies or would apply equally to a person who does not fulfil the condition, but—
     (i) which puts or would put persons fulfilling the condition at a particular disadvantage when compared with persons not fulfilling the condition, and
     (ii) which puts A at that disadvantage, and
     (iii) which he cannot show to be a proportionate means of achieving a legitimate aim.

(2) The condition is that the person is—

  (a) married, or
  (b) a civil partner.

(3) For the purposes of paragraph (1), a provision of Part 3 framed with reference to discrimination against women is to be treated as applying equally to the treatment of men, and for that purpose has effect with such modifications as are requisite.'

(3) For Article 7 (basis of comparison) substitute—

'7 Basis of comparison

Each of the following comparisons, that is—

  (a) a comparison of the cases of persons of different sex under Article 3(1) or (2),
  (b) a comparison of the cases of persons required for the purposes of Article 4A, and
  (c) a comparison of the cases of persons who do and who do not fulfil the condition in Article 5(2),

must be such that the relevant circumstances in the one case are the same, or not materially different, in the other.';

and omit Article 3(4).

(4) In Article 10 (exception where sex is a genuine occupational qualification), in paragraph (2)(h) for 'by a married couple' substitute—

     '(i) by a married couple,
     (ii) by a couple who are civil partners of each other, or
     (iii) by a married couple or a couple who are civil partners of each other'.

(5) In Article 65 (remedies on complaint under Article 63), in paragraph (1B) for 'or marital status as the case may be' substitute 'or (as the case may be) fulfilment of the condition in Article 5(2)'.

253 Civil partners to have unlimited insurable interest in each other

(1) Where two people are civil partners, each of them is to be presumed for the purposes of section 1 of the Life Assurance Act 1774 (c 48) to have an interest in the life of the other.

(2) For the purposes of section 3 of the 1774 Act, there is no limit on the amount of value of the interest.

254 Social security, child support and tax credits

(1) Schedule 24 contains amendments relating to social security, child support and tax credits.

(2) Subsection (3) applies in relation to any provision of any Act, Northern Ireland legislation or subordinate legislation which—

(a) relates to social security, child support or tax credits, and
(b) contains references (however expressed) to persons who are living or have lived together as husband and wife.

(3) The power under section 259 to make orders amending enactments, Northern Ireland legislation and subordinate legislation is to be treated as including power to amend the provision to refer to persons who are living or have lived together as if they were civil partners.

(4) Subject to subsection (5), section 175(3), (5) and (6) of the Social Security Contributions and Benefits Act 1992 (c 4) applies to the exercise of the power under section 259 in relation to social security, child support or tax credits as it applies to any power under that Act to make an order (there being disregarded for the purposes of this subsection the exceptions in section 175(3) and (5) of that Act).

(5) Section 171(3), (5) and (6) of the Social Security Contributions and Benefits (Northern Ireland) Act 1992 (c 7) applies to the exercise by a Northern Ireland department of the power under section 259 in relation to social security and child support as it applies to any power under that Act to make an order (there being disregarded for the purposes of this subsection the exceptions in section 171(3) and (5) of that Act).

(6) The reference in subsection (2) to an Act or Northern Ireland legislation relating to social security is to be read as including a reference to—

(a) the Pneumoconiosis etc (Workers' Compensation) Act 1979 (c 41), and
(b) the Pneumoconiosis, etc, (Workers' Compensation) (Northern Ireland) Order 1979 (SI 1979/925 (NI 9));

and the references in subsections (4) and (5) to social security are to be construed accordingly.

255 Power to amend enactments relating to pensions

(1) A Minister of the Crown may by order make such amendments, repeals or revocations in any enactment, Northern Ireland legislation, subordinate legislation or Church legislation relating to pensions, allowances or gratuities as he considers appropriate for the purpose of, or in connection with, making provision with respect to pensions, allowances or gratuities for the surviving civil partners or dependants of deceased civil partners.

(2) The power conferred by subsection (1) is also exercisable—

(a) by the Scottish Ministers, if the provision making the amendment, repeal or revocation is a relevant Scottish provision;
(b) by a Northern Ireland department, if the provision making the amendment, repeal or revocation deals with a transferred matter.

(3) In the case of judicial pensions, allowances or gratuities, the power conferred by subsection (1) is exercisable—

(a) in relation to any judicial office whose jurisdiction is exercised exclusively in relation to Scotland, by the Secretary of State, or
(b) subject to paragraph (a), by the Lord Chancellor.

(4) The provision which may be made by virtue of subsection (1)—

(a) may be the same as, or different to, the provision made with respect to widows, widowers or the dependants of persons who are not civil partners, and

(b) may be made with a view to ensuring that pensions, allowances or gratuities take account of rights which accrued, service which occurred or any other circumstances which existed before the passing of this Act.

(5) The power conferred by subsection (1) is not restricted by any provision of this Act.

(6) Before the appropriate person makes an order under subsection (1) he must consult such persons as he considers appropriate.

(7) Subsection (6) does not apply—

(a) to an order in the case of which the appropriate person considers that consultation is inexpedient because of urgency, or

(b) to an order made before the end of the period of 6 months beginning with the coming into force of this section.

(8) Subject to subsection (9), the power to make an order under subsection (1) is exercisable by statutory instrument.

(9) Any power of a Northern Ireland department to make an order under this section is exercisable by statutory rule for the purposes of the Statutory Rules (Northern Ireland) Order 1979 (SI 1979/1573 (NI 12)).

(10) An order under subsection (1) may not be made—

(a) by a Minister of the Crown, unless a draft of the statutory instrument containing the order has been laid before, and approved by a resolution of, each House of Parliament;

(b) by the Scottish Ministers, unless a draft of the statutory instrument containing the order has been laid before, and approved by a resolution of, the Scottish Parliament;

(c) by a Northern Ireland department, unless a draft of the statutory rule containing the order has been laid before, and approved by a resolution of, the Northern Ireland Assembly.

(11) In this section—

'the appropriate person', in relation to an order under this section, means the person making the order;

'Church legislation' means—

(a) any Measure of the Church Assembly or of the General Synod of the Church of England, or

(b) any order, regulation or other instrument made under or by virtue of such a Measure;

'enactment' includes an enactment comprised in an Act of the Scottish Parliament;

'Minister of the Crown' has the same meaning as in the Ministers of the Crown Act 1975 (c 26);

'relevant Scottish provision' means a provision that would be within the legislative competence of the Scottish Parliament if it were included in an Act of that Parliament;

'subordinate legislation' has the same meaning as in the Interpretation Act 1978 (c 30) except that it includes any instrument made under an Act of the Scottish Parliament and any instrument within the meaning of section 1(c) of the Interpretation Act (Northern Ireland) 1954 (1954 c 33 (NI));

'transferred matter' has the meaning given by section 4(1) of the Northern Ireland Act 1998 (c 47) and 'deals with' in relation to a transferred matter is to be construed in accordance with section 98(2) and (3) of the 1998 Act.

256 Amendment of certain enactments relating to pensions

Schedule 25 amends certain enactments relating to pensions.

257 Amendment of certain enactments relating to the armed forces

Schedule 26 amends certain enactments relating to the armed forces.

PART 8
SUPPLEMENTARY

258 Regulations and orders

(1) This section applies to any power conferred by this Act to make regulations or an order (except a power of a court to make an order).

(2) The power may be exercised so as to make different provision for different cases and different purposes.

(3) The power includes power to make any supplementary, incidental, consequential, transitional, transitory or saving provision which the person making the regulations or order considers expedient.

259 Power to make further provision in connection with civil partnership

(1) A Minister of the Crown may by order make such further provision (including supplementary, incidental, consequential, transitory, transitional or saving provision) as he considers appropriate—

   (a) for the general purposes, or any particular purpose, of this Act,
   (b) in consequence of any provision made by or under this Act, or
   (c) for giving full effect to this Act or any provision of it.

(2) The power conferred by subsection (1) is also exercisable—

   (a) by the Scottish Ministers, in relation to a relevant Scottish provision;
   (b) by a Northern Ireland department, in relation to a provision which deals with a transferred matter;
   (c) by the National Assembly for Wales, in relation to a provision which is made otherwise than by virtue of subsection (3) and deals with matters with respect to which functions are exercisable by the Assembly.

(3) An order under subsection (1) may—

   (a) amend or repeal any enactment contained in an Act passed on or before the last day of the Session in which this Act is passed, including an enactment conferring power to make subordinate legislation where the power is limited by reference to persons who are or have been parties to a marriage;
   (b) amend, repeal or (as the case may be) revoke any provision contained in Northern Ireland legislation passed or made on or before the last day of the Session in which this Act is passed, including a provision conferring power to make subordinate legislation where the power is limited by reference to persons who are or have been parties to a marriage;

(c) amend, repeal or (as the case may be) revoke any Church legislation.

(4) An order under subsection (1) may—

  (a) provide for any provision of this Act which comes into force before another such provision has come into force to have effect, until that other provision has come into force, with such modifications as are specified in the order;
  (b) amend or revoke any subordinate legislation.

(5) The power to make an order under subsection (1) is not restricted by any other provision of this Act.

(6) Subject to subsection (7), the power to make an order under subsection (1) is exercisable by statutory instrument.

(7) Any power of a Northern Ireland department to make an order under this section is exercisable by statutory rule for the purposes of the Statutory Rules (Northern Ireland) Order 1979 (SI 1979/1573 (NI 12)).

(8) An order under subsection (1) which contains any provision (whether alone or with other provisions) made by virtue of subsection (3) may not be made—

  (a) by a Minister of the Crown, unless a draft of the statutory instrument containing the order has been laid before, and approved by a resolution of, each House of Parliament;
  (b) by the Scottish Ministers, unless a draft of the statutory instrument containing the order has been laid before, and approved by a resolution of, the Scottish Parliament;
  (c) by a Northern Ireland department, unless a draft of the statutory rule containing the order has been laid before, and approved by a resolution of, the Northern Ireland Assembly.

(9) A statutory instrument containing an order under subsection (1) to which subsection (8) does not apply—

  (a) if made by a Minister of the Crown, is subject to annulment in pursuance of a resolution of either House of Parliament;
  (b) if made by the Scottish Ministers, is subject to annulment in pursuance of a resolution of the Scottish Parliament.

(10) A statutory rule made by a Northern Ireland department and containing an order to which subsection (8) does not apply is subject to negative resolution (within the meaning of section 41(6) of the Interpretation Act (Northern Ireland) 1954 (c 33 (NI))).

(11) In this section—

  'Act' includes an Act of the Scottish Parliament;

  'Church legislation' has the same meaning as in section 255;

  'Minister of the Crown' has the same meaning as in the Ministers of the Crown Act 1975 (c 26);

  'relevant Scottish provision' means a provision that would be within the legislative competence of the Scottish Parliament if it were included in an Act of that Parliament;

  'subordinate legislation' has the same meaning as in the Interpretation Act 1978 (c 30) except that it includes any instrument made under an Act of the Scottish Parliament and any instrument within the meaning of section 1(c) of the Interpretation Act (Northern Ireland) 1954 (c 33 (NI));

'transferred matter' has the meaning given by section 4(1) of the Northern Ireland Act 1998 (c 47) and 'deals with' in relation to a transferred matter is to be construed in accordance with section 98(2) and (3) of the 1998 Act.

260 Community obligations and civil partners

(1) Subsection (2) applies where any person, by Order in Council or regulations under section 2(2) of the European Communities Act 1972 (c 68) (general implementation of Treaties)—

(a) is making provision for the purpose of implementing, or for a purpose concerning, a Community obligation of the United Kingdom which relates to persons who are or have been parties to a marriage, or
(b) has made such provision and it has not been revoked.

(2) The appropriate person may by Order in Council or (as the case may be) by regulations make provision in relation to persons who are or have been civil partners in a civil partnership that is the same or similar to the provision referred to in subsection (1).

(3) 'Marriage' and 'civil partnership' include a void marriage and a void civil partnership respectively.

(4) 'The appropriate person' means—

(a) if subsection (1)(a) applies, the person making the provision referred to there;
(b) if subsection (1)(b) applies, any person who would have power to make the provision referred to there if it were being made at the time of the exercise of the power under subsection (2).

(5) The following provisions apply in relation to the power conferred by subsection (2) to make an Order in Council or regulations as they apply in relation to the power conferred by section 2(2) of the 1972 Act to make an Order in Council or regulations—

(a) paragraph 2 of Schedule 2 to the 1972 Act (procedure etc in relation to making of Orders in Council and regulations: general);
(b) paragraph 15(3)(c) of Schedule 8 to the Scotland Act 1998 (c 46) (modifications of paragraph 2 in relation to Scottish Ministers and to Orders in Council made on the recommendation of the First Minister);
(c) paragraph 3 of Schedule 2 to the 1972 Act (modifications of paragraph 2 in relation to Northern Ireland departments etc) and the Statutory Rules (Northern Ireland) Order 1979 (SI 1979/1573 (NI 12)) (treating the power conferred by subsection (2) as conferred by an Act passed before 1st January 1974 for the purposes of the application of that Order);
(d) section 29(3) of the Government of Wales Act 1998 (c 38) (modifications of paragraph 2 in relation to the National Assembly for Wales).

261 Minor and consequential amendments, repeals and revocations

(1) Schedule 27 contains minor and consequential amendments.

(2) Schedule 28 contains consequential amendments of enactments relating to Scotland.

(3) Schedule 29 contains minor and consequential amendments relating to Northern Ireland.

(4) Schedule 30 contains repeals and revocations.

262 Extent

(1) Part 2 (civil partnership: England and Wales), excluding section 35 but including Schedules 1 to 9, extends to England and Wales only.

(2) Part 3 (civil partnership: Scotland), including Schedules 10 and 11, extends to Scotland only.

(3) Part 4 (civil partnership: Northern Ireland), including Schedules 12 to 19, extends to Northern Ireland only.

(4) In Part 5 (civil partnerships formed or dissolved abroad etc)—

    (a) sections 220 to 224 extend to England and Wales only;
    (b) sections 225 to 227 extend to Scotland only;
    (c) sections 228 to 232 extend to Northern Ireland only.

(5) In Part 6—

    (a) any amendment made by virtue of section 247(1)(a) and Schedule 21 has the same extent as the provision subject to the amendment;
    (b) section 248 and Schedule 22 extend to Northern Ireland only.

(6) Section 251 extends to England and Wales and Scotland only.

(7) Section 252 extends to Northern Ireland only.

(8) Schedule 28 extends to Scotland only.

(9) Schedule 29 extends to Northern Ireland only.

(10) Any amendment, repeal or revocation made by Schedules 24 to 27 and 30 has the same extent as the provision subject to the amendment, repeal or revocation.

263 Commencement

(1) Part 1 comes into force in accordance with provision made by order by the Secretary of State, after consulting the Scottish Ministers and the Department of Finance and Personnel.

(2) Part 2, including Schedules 1 to 9, comes into force in accordance with provision made by order by the Secretary of State.

(3) Part 3, including Schedules 10 and 11, comes into force in accordance with provision made by order by the Scottish Ministers, after consulting the Secretary of State.

(4) Part 4, including Schedules 12 to 19, comes into force in accordance with provision made by order by the Department of Finance and Personnel, after consulting the Secretary of State.

(5) Part 5, excluding section 213(2) to (6) but including Schedule 20, comes into force in accordance with provision made by order by the Secretary of State, after consulting the Scottish Ministers and the Department of Finance and Personnel.

(6) Section 213(2) to (6) comes into force on the day on which this Act is passed.

(7) In Part 6 —

    (a) sections 246 and 247(1) and Schedule 21 come into force in accordance with provision made by order by the Secretary of State, after consulting the Scottish Ministers and the Department of Finance and Personnel,
    (b) section 248(1) and Schedule 22 come into force in accordance with provision made by order by the Department of Finance and Personnel, after consulting the Secretary of State, and

    (c) sections 247(2) to (7) and 248(2) to (5) come into force on the day on which this Act is passed.

(8) In Part 7—

    (a) sections 249, 251, 253, 256 and 257 and Schedules 23, 25 and 26 come into force in accordance with provision made by order by the Secretary of State,

    (b) section 250 comes into force in accordance with provision made by order by the Secretary of State, after consulting the Scottish Ministers and the Department of Finance and Personnel,

    (c) section 252 comes into force in accordance with provision made by the Department of Finance and Personnel, after consulting the Secretary of State,

    (d) subject to paragraph (e), section 254(1) and Schedule 24 come into force in accordance with provision made by order by the Secretary of State,

    (e) the provisions of Schedule 24 listed in subsection (9), and section 254(1) so far as relating to those provisions, come into force in accordance with provision made by the Department of Finance and Personnel, after consulting the Secretary of State, and

    (f) sections 254(2) to (6) and 255 come into force on the day on which this Act is passed.

(9) The provisions are—

    (a) Part 2;

    (b) in Part 5, paragraphs 67 to 85, 87, 89 to 99 and 102 to 105;

    (c) Part 6;

    (d) Parts 9 and 10;

    (e) Part 15.

(10) In this Part—

    (a) sections 258, 259, 260 and 262, this section and section 264 come into force on the day on which this Act is passed,

    (b) section 261(1) and Schedule 27 and, except so far as relating to any Acts of the Scottish Parliament or any provision which extends to Northern Ireland only, section 261(4) and Schedule 30 come into force in accordance with provision made by order by the Secretary of State,

    (c) section 261(2) and Schedule 28 and, so far as relating to any Acts of the Scottish Parliament, section 261(4) and Schedule 30 come into force in accordance with provision made by order by the Scottish Ministers, after consulting the Secretary of State,

    (d) section 261(3) and Schedule 29 and, so far as relating to any provision which extends to Northern Ireland only, section 261(4) and Schedule 30 come into force in accordance with provision made by order by the Department of Finance and Personnel, after consulting the Secretary of State.

(11) The power to make an order under this section is exercisable by statutory instrument.

264 Short title

This Act may be cited as the Civil Partnership Act 2004.

SCHEDULES

SCHEDULE 1

SECTIONS 3(2) AND 5(3)

PROHIBITED DEGREES OF RELATIONSHIP: ENGLAND AND WALES

PART 1
THE PROHIBITIONS

Absolute prohibitions

1(1) Two people are within prohibited degrees of relationship if one falls within the list below in relation to the other.

Adoptive child

Adoptive parent

Child

Former adoptive child

Former adoptive parent

Grandparent

Grandchild

Parent

Parent's sibling

Sibling

Sibling's child

(2) In the list 'sibling' means a brother, sister, half-brother or half-sister.

Qualified prohibitions

2(1) Two people are within prohibited degrees of relationship if one of them falls within the list below in relation to the other, unless—

   (a) both of them have reached 21 at the time when they register as civil partners of each other, and
   (b) the younger has not at any time before reaching 18 been a child of the family in relation to the other.

   Child of former civil partner

   Child of former spouse

   Former civil partner of grandparent

   Former civil partner of parent

   Former spouse of grandparent

Former spouse of parent

Grandchild of former civil partner

Grandchild of former spouse

(2) 'Child of the family', in relation to another person, means a person who—

(a) has lived in the same household as that other person, and
(b) has been treated by that other person as a child of his family.

3 Two people are within prohibited degrees of relationship if one falls within column 1 of the table below in relation to the other, unless—

(a) both of them have reached 21 at the time when they register as civil partners of each other, and
(b) the persons who fall within column 2 are dead.

Relationship	Relevant deaths
Former civil partner of child	The child The child's other parent
Former spouse of child	The child The child's other parent
Parent of former civil partner	The former civil partner The former civil partner's other parent
Parent of former spouse	The former spouse The former spouse's other parent

PART 2
SPECIAL PROVISIONS RELATING TO QUALIFIED PROHIBITIONS

Provisions relating to paragraph 2

4 Paragraphs 5 to 7 apply where two people are subject to paragraph 2 but intend to register as civil partners of each other by signing a civil partnership schedule.

5(1) The fact that a notice of proposed civil partnership has been given must not be recorded in the register unless the registration authority—

(a) is satisfied by the production of evidence that both the proposed civil partners have reached 21, and
(b) has received a declaration made by each of the proposed civil partners—
    (i) specifying their affinal relationship, and
    (ii) declaring that the younger of them has not at any time before reaching 18 been a child of the family in relation to the other.

(2) Sub-paragraph (1) does not apply if a declaration is obtained under paragraph 7.

(3) A declaration under sub-paragraph (1)(b) must contain such information and must be signed and attested in such manner as may be prescribed by regulations.

(4) The fact that a registration authority has received a declaration under sub-paragraph (1)(b) must be recorded in the register.

(5) A declaration under sub-paragraph (1)(b) must be filed and kept by the registration authority.

6(1) Sub-paragraph (2) applies if—

(a) a registration authority receives from a person who is not one of the proposed civil partners a written statement signed by that person which alleges that a declaration made under paragraph 5 is false in a material particular, and

(b) the register shows that such a statement has been received.

(2) The registration authority in whose area it is proposed that the registration take place must not issue a civil partnership schedule unless a High Court declaration is obtained under paragraph 7.

7(1) Either of the proposed civil partners may apply to the High Court for a declaration that, given that—

(a) both of them have reached 21, and

(b) the younger of those persons has not at any time before reaching 18 been a child of the family in relation to the other,

there is no impediment of affinity to the formation of the civil partnership.

(2) Such an application may be made whether or not any statement has been received by the registration authority under paragraph 6.

8 Section 13 (objection to proposed civil partnership) does not apply in relation to a civil partnership to which paragraphs 5 to 7 apply, except so far as an objection to the issue of a civil partnership schedule is made under that section on a ground other than the affinity between the proposed civil partners.

Provisions relating to paragraph 3

9(1) This paragraph applies where two people are subject to paragraph 3 but intend to register as civil partners of each other by signing a civil partnership schedule.

(2) The fact that a notice of proposed civil partnership has been given must not be recorded in the register unless the registration authority is satisfied by the production of evidence—

(a) that both the proposed civil partners have reached 21, and

(b) that the persons referred to in paragraph 3(b) are dead.

SCHEDULE 2

SECTION 4(2) AND 5(3)

CIVIL PARTNERSHIPS OF PERSONS UNDER 18: ENGLAND AND WALES

PART 1
APPROPRIATE PERSONS

1 Column 2 of the table specifies the appropriate persons (or person) to give consent to a child whose circumstances fall within column 1 and who intends to register as the civil partner of another—

Case	*Appropriate persons*
1 The circumstances do not fall within any of items 2 to 8.	Each of the following— (a) any parent of the child who has parental responsibility for him, and (b) any guardian of the child.

Case	Appropriate persons
2 A special guardianship order is in force with respect to the child and the circumstances do not fall within any of items 3 to 7.	Each of the child's special guardians.
3 A care order has effect with respect to the child and the circumstances do not fall within item 5.	Each of the following— (a) the local authority designated in the order, and (b) each parent, guardian or special guardian (in so far as their parental responsibility has not been restricted under section 33(3) of the 1989 Act).
4 A residence order has effect with respect to the child and the circumstances do not fall within item 5.	Each of the persons with whom the child lives, or is to live, as a result of the order.
5 An adoption agency is authorised to place the child for adoption under section 19 of the 2002 Act.	Either— (a) the adoption agency, or (b) if a care order has effect with respect to the child, the local authority designated in the order.
6 A placement order is in force with respect to the child.	The local authority authorised by the placement order to place the child for adoption.
7 The child has been placed for adoption with prospective adopters.	The prospective adopters (in so far as their parental responsibility has not been restricted under section 25(4) of the 2002 Act), in addition to any person specified in relation to item 5 or 6.
8 The circumstances do not fall within any of items 2 to 7, but a residence order was in force with respect to the child immediately before he reached 16.	The persons with whom the child lived, or was to live, as a result of the order.

2 In the table—

    'the 1989 Act' means the Children Act 1989 (c 41) and 'guardian of a child', 'parental responsibility', 'residence order', 'special guardian', 'special guardianship order' and 'care order' have the same meaning as in that Act;

    'the 2002 Act' means the Adoption and Children Act 2002 (c 38) and 'adoption agency', 'placed for adoption', 'placement order' and 'local authority' have the same meaning as in that Act;

    'appropriate local authority' means the local authority authorised by the placement order to place the child for adoption.

PART 2
OBTAINING CONSENT: GENERAL

Consent of appropriate person unobtainable

3(1) This paragraph applies if—

    (a) a child and another person intend to register as civil partners of each other under any procedure other than the special procedure, and

    (b) the registration authority to whom the child gives a notice of proposed civil partnership is satisfied that the consent of a person whose consent is required ('A') cannot be obtained because A is absent, inaccessible or under a disability.

(2) If there is any other person whose consent is also required, the registration authority must dispense with the need for A's consent.

(3) If no other person's consent is required—

(a) the Registrar General may dispense with the need for any consent, or
(b) the court may, on an application being made to it, consent to the child registering as the civil partner of the person mentioned in sub-paragraph (1)(a).

(4) The consent of the court under sub-paragraph (3)(b) has the same effect as if it had been given by A.

Consent of appropriate person refused

4(1) This paragraph applies if—

(a) a child and another person intend to register as civil partners of each other under any procedure other than the special procedure, and
(b) any person whose consent is required refuses his consent.

(2) The court may, on an application being made to it, consent to the child registering as the civil partner of the person mentioned in sub-paragraph (1)(a).

(3) The consent of the court under sub-paragraph (2) has the same effect as if it had been given by the person who has refused his consent.

Declaration

5 If one of the proposed civil partners is a child and is not a surviving civil partner, the necessary declaration under section 8 must also—

(a) state in relation to each appropriate person—
  (i) that that person's consent has been obtained,
  (ii) that the need to obtain that person's consent has been dispensed with under paragraph 3, or
  (iii) that the court has given consent under paragraph 3 or 4, or
(b) state that no person exists whose consent is required to a civil partnership between the child and another person.

Forbidding proposed civil partnership

6(1) This paragraph applies if it has been recorded in the register that a notice of proposed civil partnership between a child and another person has been given.

(2) Any person whose consent is required to a child and another person registering as civil partners of each other may forbid the issue of a civil partnership schedule by giving any registration authority written notice that he forbids it.

(3) A notice under sub-paragraph (2) must specify—

(a) the name of the person giving it,
(b) his place of residence, and
(c) the capacity, in relation to either of the proposed civil partners, in which he forbids the issue of the civil partnership schedule.

(4) On receiving the notice, the registration authority must as soon as is practicable record in the register the fact that the issue of a civil partnership schedule has been forbidden.

(5) If the issue of a civil partnership schedule has been forbidden under this paragraph, the notice of proposed civil partnership and all proceedings on it are void.

(6) Sub-paragraphs (2) and (5) do not apply if the court has given its consent under paragraph 3 or 4.

Evidence

7(1) This paragraph applies if, for the purpose of obtaining a civil partnership schedule, a person declares that the consent of any person or persons whose consent is required under section 4 has been given.

(2) The registration authority may refuse to issue the civil partnership schedule unless satisfied by the production of written evidence that the consent of that person or those persons has in fact been given.

Issue of civil partnership schedule

8 The duty in section 14(1) to issue a civil partnership schedule does not apply if its issue has been forbidden under paragraph 6.

9 If a proposed civil partnership is between a child and another person, the civil partnership schedule must contain a statement that the issue of the civil partnership schedule has not been forbidden under paragraph 6.

PART 3
OBTAINING CONSENT: SPECIAL PROCEDURE

Consent of appropriate person unobtainable or refused

10(1) Sub-paragraph (2) applies if—

(a) a child and another person intend to register as civil partners of each other under the special procedure, and
(b) the Registrar General is satisfied that the consent of a person ('A') whose consent is required cannot be obtained because A is absent, inaccessible, or under a disability.

(2) If this sub-paragraph applies—

(a) the Registrar General may dispense with the need for A's consent (whether or not there is any other person whose consent is also required), or
(b) the court may, on application being made, consent to the child registering as the civil partner of the person mentioned in sub-paragraph (1)(a).

(3) The consent of the court under sub-paragraph (2)(b) has the same effect as if it had been given by A.

(4) Sub-paragraph (5) applies if—

(a) a child and another person intend to register as civil partners of each other under the special procedure, and
(b) any person whose consent is required refuses his consent.

(5) The court may, on application being made, consent to the child registering as the civil partner of the person mentioned in sub-paragraph (4)(a).

(6) The consent of the court under sub-paragraph (5) has the same effect as if it had been given by the person who has refused his consent.

Declaration

11 If one of the proposed civil partners is a child and is not a surviving civil partner, the necessary declaration under section 8 must also—

(a) state in relation to each appropriate person—
   (i) that that person's consent has been obtained,
   (ii) that the need to obtain that person's consent has been dispensed with under paragraph 10(2), or
   (iii) that the court has given consent under paragraph 10(2) or (5), or
(b) state that no person exists whose consent is required to a civil partnership between the child and another person.

Forbidding proposed civil partnership

12 Paragraph 6 applies in relation to the special procedure as if—

(a) any reference to forbidding the issue of a civil partnership schedule were a reference to forbidding the Registrar General to give authority for the issue of his licence, and
(b) sub-paragraph (6) referred to the court giving its consent under paragraph 10(2) or (5).

Evidence

13(1) This paragraph applies—

(a) if a child and another person intend to register as civil partners of each other under the special procedure, and
(b) the consent of any person ('A') is required to the child registering as the civil partner of that person.

(2) The person giving the notice (under section 21) of proposed civil partnership to the registration authority must produce to the authority such evidence as the Registrar General may require to satisfy him that A's consent has in fact been given.

(3) The power to require evidence under sub-paragraph (2) is in addition to the power to require evidence under section 22.

Issue of Registrar General's licence

14 The duty of the Registrar General under section 25(3)(b) to give authority for the issue of his licence does not apply if he has been forbidden to do so by virtue of paragraph 12.

PART 4
PROVISIONS RELATING TO THE COURT

15(1) For the purposes of Parts 2 and 3 of this Schedule, 'the court' means—

(a) the High Court,
(b) the county court of the district in which any applicant or respondent resides, or
(c) a magistrates' court acting in the local justice area in which any applicant or respondent resides.

(2) Rules of court may be made for enabling applications under Part 2 or 3 of this Schedule—

(a) if made to the High Court, to be heard in chambers;
(b) if made to the county court, to be heard and determined by the district judge subject to appeal to the judge;

(c) if made to a magistrates' court, to be heard and determined otherwise than in open court.

(3) Rules of court must provide that, where an application is made in consequence of a refusal to give consent, notice of the application is to be served on the person who has refused consent.

SCHEDULE 3

SECTION 5(2)

REGISTRATION BY FORMER SPOUSES ONE OF WHOM HAS CHANGED SEX

Application of Schedule

1 This Schedule applies if—

(a) a court—
  (i) makes absolute a decree of nullity granted on the ground that an interim gender recognition certificate has been issued to a party to the marriage, or
  (ii) (in Scotland) grants a decree of divorce on that ground,

and, on doing so, issues a full gender recognition certificate (under section 5(1) of the Gender Recognition Act 2004 (c 7)) to that party, and
(b) the parties wish to register in England or Wales as civil partners of each other without being delayed by the waiting period.

The relevant period

2 For the purposes of this Schedule the relevant period is the period—

(a) beginning with the issue of the full gender recognition certificate, and
(b) ending at the end of 1 month from the day on which it is issued.

Modifications of standard procedure and procedures for house-bound and detained persons

3 If—

(a) each of the parties gives a notice of proposed civil partnership during the relevant period, and
(b) on doing so, each makes an election under this paragraph,

Chapter 1 of Part 2 applies with the modifications given in paragraphs 4 to 6.

4(1) Omit—

(a) section 10 (proposed civil partnership to be publicised);
(b) section 11 (meaning of 'the waiting period');
(c) section 12 (power to shorten the waiting period).

(2) In section 14 (issue of civil partnership schedule), for subsection (1) substitute—

'(1) As soon as the notices of proposed civil partnership have been given, the registration authority in whose area it is proposed that the registration take place must, at the request of one or both of the proposed civil partners, issue a document to be known as a "civil partnership schedule".'

(3) For section 17 (period during which registration may take place) substitute—

'17 Period during which registration may take place

(1) The proposed civil partners may register as civil partners by signing the civil partnership schedule at any time during the applicable period.

(2) If they do not register as civil partners by signing the civil partnership schedule before the end of the applicable period—

(a) the notices of proposed civil partnership and the civil partnership schedule are void, and

(b) no civil partnership registrar may officiate at the signing of the civil partnership schedule by them.

(3) The applicable period, in relation to two people registering as civil partners of each other, is the period of 1 month beginning with—

(a) the day on which the notices of proposed civil partnership are given, or

(b) if the notices are not given on the same day, the earlier of those days.'

5 In section 18 (house-bound persons), in subsection (3)—

(a) treat the reference to the standard procedure as a reference to the standard procedure as modified by this Schedule, and

(b) omit paragraph (c) (which provides for a 3 month registration period).

6 In section 19 (detained persons), in subsection (3)—

(a) treat the reference to the standard procedure as a reference to the standard procedure as modified by this Schedule, and

(b) omit paragraph (c) (which provides for a 3 month registration period).

Modified procedures for certain non-residents

7(1) Sub-paragraphs (5) to (8) apply (in place of section 20) in the following three cases.

(2) The first is where—

(a) two people wish to register as civil partners of each other in England and Wales, and

(b) one of them ('A') resides in Scotland and the other ('B') resides in England or Wales.

(3) The second is where—

(a) two people wish to register as civil partners of each other in England and Wales, and

(b) one of them ('A') resides in Northern Ireland and the other ('B') resides in England or Wales.

(4) The third is where—

(a) two people wish to register as civil partners of each other in England and Wales, and

(b) one of them ('A') is a member of Her Majesty's forces who is serving outside the United Kingdom and the other ('B') resides in England or Wales.

(5) A is not required to give a notice of proposed civil partnership to a registration authority in England or Wales in order to register in England or Wales as B's civil partner.

(6) B may give a notice of proposed civil partnership and make the necessary declaration without regard to the requirement that would otherwise apply that A must reside in England or Wales.

(7) If, on giving such notice, B makes an election under this paragraph, Chapter 1 of Part 2 applies with the modifications given in paragraphs 4 to 6 and the further modifications in sub-paragraph (8).

(8) The further modifications are that—

    (a) the civil partnership schedule is not to be issued by a registration authority unless A or B produces to that registration authority a certificate of no impediment issued to A under the relevant provision;

    (b) the applicable period is the period of one month beginning with the day on which B's notice is given;

    (c) section 31 applies as if in subsections (1)(a) and (2)(c) for 'each notice' there were substituted 'B's notice'.

(9) 'The relevant provision' means—

    (a) if A resides in Scotland, section 97;

    (b) if A resides in Northern Ireland, section 150;

    (c) if A is a member of Her Majesty's forces who is serving outside the United Kingdom, section 239.

(10) 'Her Majesty's forces' has the same meaning as in the Army Act 1955 (3 & 4 Eliz. 2 c 18).

SCHEDULE 4

SECTION 71

WILLS, ADMINISTRATION OF ESTATES AND FAMILY PROVISION

PART 1
WILLS

1 Amend the Wills Act 1837 (c 26) as follows.

2 After section 18A insert—

'18B Will to be revoked by civil partnership

(1) Subject to subsections (2) to (6), a will is revoked by the formation of a civil partnership between the testator and another person.

(2) A disposition in a will in exercise of a power of appointment takes effect despite the formation of a subsequent civil partnership between the testator and another person unless the property so appointed would in default of appointment pass to the testator's personal representatives.

(3) If it appears from a will—

    (a) that at the time it was made the testator was expecting to form a civil partnership with a particular person, and

    (b) that he intended that the will should not be revoked by the formation of the civil partnership,

the will is not revoked by its formation.

(4) Subsections (5) and (6) apply if it appears from a will—

    (a) that at the time it was made the testator was expecting to form a civil partnership with a particular person, and

    (b) that he intended that a disposition in the will should not be revoked by the formation of the civil partnership.

(5) The disposition takes effect despite the formation of the civil partnership.

(6) Any other disposition in the will also takes effect, unless it appears from the will that the testator intended the disposition to be revoked by the formation of the civil partnership.

18C Effect of dissolution or annulment of civil partnership on wills

(1) This section applies if, after a testator has made a will—

- (a) a court of civil jurisdiction in England and Wales dissolves his civil partnership or makes a nullity order in respect of it, or
- (b) his civil partnership is dissolved or annulled and the dissolution or annulment is entitled to recognition in England and Wales by virtue of Chapter 3 of Part 5 of the Civil Partnership Act 2004.

(2) Except in so far as a contrary intention appears by the will—

- (a) provisions of the will appointing executors or trustees or conferring a power of appointment, if they appoint or confer the power on the former civil partner, take effect as if the former civil partner had died on the date on which the civil partnership is dissolved or annulled, and
- (b) any property which, or an interest in which, is devised or bequeathed to the former civil partner shall pass as if the former civil partner had died on that date.

(3) Subsection (2)(b) does not affect any right of the former civil partner to apply for financial provision under the Inheritance (Provision for Family and Dependants) Act 1975.'

3 The following provisions—

- (a) section 15 of the Wills Act 1837 (c 26) (avoidance of gifts to attesting witnesses and their spouses), and
- (b) section 1 of the Wills Act 1968 (c 28) (restriction of operation of section 15),

apply in relation to the attestation of a will by a person to whose civil partner there is given or made any such disposition as is described in section 15 of the 1837 Act as they apply in relation to a person to whose spouse there is given or made any such disposition.

4 In section 16 of the 1837 Act, after 'wife or husband' insert 'or civil partner'.

5 Except where a contrary intention is shown, it is presumed that if a testator—

- (a) devises or bequeaths property to his civil partner in terms which in themselves would give an absolute interest to the civil partner, but
- (b) by the same instrument purports to give his issue an interest in the same property,

the gift to the civil partner is absolute despite the purported gift to the issue.

PART 2
ADMINISTRATION OF ESTATES AND FAMILY PROVISION

Public Trustee Act 1906 (c 55)

6 In section 6(1), after 'widower, widow' (in both places) insert ', surviving civil partner'.

Administration of Estates Act 1925 (c 23)

7 In section 46 (succession to real and personal estate on intestacy), for 'husband or wife' (in each place) substitute 'spouse or civil partner'.

8(1) Amend section 47(1) (meaning of 'the statutory trusts') as follows.

(2) In paragraph (i), after 'or marry under that age' (in the first place) insert 'or form a civil partnership under that age'.

(3) In that paragraph, after 'or marry' (in the second place) insert ', or form a civil partnership,'.

(4) In paragraph (ii), after 'marries' insert ', or forms a civil partnership,'.

9 In section 47A, in subsection (1) and in the proviso to subsection (5), for 'husband or wife' substitute 'spouse or civil partner'.

10 In section 48(2), for 'husband or wife' (in each place) substitute 'spouse or civil partner'.

11 In section 51(3) (devolution of certain estates vested in infant who dies without having married and without issue), after 'without having been married' insert 'or having formed a civil partnership,'.

12 In section 55(1)(xviii) (which defines 'valuable consideration' as including marriage), after 'includes marriage,' insert 'and formation of a civil partnership,'.

Intestates' Estates Act 1952 (c 64)

13(1) Amend section 5 and Schedule 2 (rights of surviving spouse as respects the matrimonial home) as follows.

(2) For 'husband or wife' (in each place) substitute 'spouse or civil partner'.

(3) In section 5, after 'matrimonial' insert 'or civil partnership'.

(4) In the heading of each—

    (a) after 'spouse' insert 'or civil partner', and
    (b) after 'matrimonial' insert 'or civil partnership'.

Family Provision Act 1966 (c 35)

14 In section 1(1) (fixed net sum payable to surviving spouse of person dying intestate), for 'husband or wife' substitute 'spouse or civil partner'.

Inheritance (Provision for Family and Dependants) Act 1975 (c 63)

15(1) Amend section 1 (application for financial provision from deceased person's estate) as follows.

(2) For subsection (1)(a) and (b) (application may be made by spouse or by former spouse who has not remarried) substitute—

    '(a) the spouse or civil partner of the deceased;
    (b) a former spouse or former civil partner of the deceased, but not one who has formed a subsequent marriage or civil partnership;'.

(3) In subsection (1)(ba) (application may be made by person living as husband or wife of the deceased), after 'subsection (1A)' insert 'or (1B)'.

(4) In subsection (1)(d) (application may be made by child of the family), after 'marriage' (in each place) insert 'or civil partnership'.

(5) After subsection (1A) insert—

'(1B) This subsection applies to a person if for the whole of the period of two years ending immediately before the date when the deceased died the person was living—

(a) in the same household as the deceased, and
(b) as the civil partner of the deceased.'

(6) In subsection (2) (meaning of 'reasonable financial provision'), after paragraph (a) insert—

'(aa) in the case of an application made by virtue of subsection (1)(a) above by the civil partner of the deceased (except where, at the date of death, a separation order under Chapter 2 of Part 2 of the Civil Partnership Act 2004 was in force in relation to the civil partnership and the separation was continuing), means such financial provision as it would be reasonable in all the circumstances of the case for a civil partner to receive, whether or not that provision is required for his or her maintenance;'.

16 In section 2(1) (orders which may be made on an application), after paragraph (f) insert—

'(g) an order varying any settlement made—
    (i)   during the subsistence of a civil partnership formed by the deceased, or
    (ii) in anticipation of the formation of a civil partnership by the deceased,

on the civil partners (including such a settlement made by will), the variation being for the benefit of the surviving civil partner, or any child of both the civil partners, or any person who was treated by the deceased as a child of the family in relation to that civil partnership.'

17(1) Amend section 3(2) (application by spouse or former spouse: matters to which court is to have regard) as follows.

(2) For the words from the beginning to '1(1)(b) of this Act' substitute—

'This subsection applies, without prejudice to the generality of paragraph (g) of subsection (1) above, where an application for an order under section 2 of this Act is made by virtue of section 1(1)(a) or (b) of this Act.'

(3) The words from 'the court shall, in addition' to the end of paragraph (b) shall become a second sentence of the subsection and, in paragraph (a) of the sentence so formed, after 'duration of the marriage' insert 'or civil partnership'.

(4) The words from 'in the case of an application by the wife or husband' to the end shall become a third sentence of the subsection.

(5) At the end insert the following sentence—

'In the case of an application by the civil partner of the deceased, the court shall also, unless at the date of the death a separation order under Chapter 2 of Part 2 of the Civil Partnership Act 2004 was in force and the separation was continuing, have regard to the provision which the applicant might reasonably have expected to receive if on the day on which the deceased died the civil partnership, instead of being terminated by death, had been terminated by a dissolution order.'

18 In section 3(2A) (application by person living as husband or wife of deceased: matters to which court is to have regard), in paragraph (a), after 'wife' insert 'or civil partner'.

19 In section 6(3) and (10) (variation etc of orders which cease on occurrence of specified event other than remarriage of former spouse), for '(other than the remarriage of a former wife or former husband)' substitute '(other than the formation of a subsequent marriage or civil partnership by a former spouse or former civil partner)'.

20 After section 14 insert—

'14A Provision as to cases where no financial relief was granted in proceedings for the dissolution etc of a civil partnership

(1) Subsection (2) below applies where—

  (a) a dissolution order, nullity order, separation order or presumption of death order has been made under Chapter 2 of Part 2 of the Civil Partnership Act 2004 in relation to a civil partnership,

  (b) one of the civil partners dies within twelve months from the date on which the order is made, and

  (c) either—

    (i) an application for a financial provision order under Part 1 of Schedule 5 to that Act or a property adjustment order under Part 2 of that Schedule has not been made by the other civil partner, or

    (ii) such an application has been made but the proceedings on the application have not been determined at the time of the death of the deceased.

(2) If an application for an order under section 2 of this Act is made by the surviving civil partner, the court shall, notwithstanding anything in section 1 or section 3 of this Act, have power, if it thinks it just to do so, to treat the surviving civil partner as if the order mentioned in subsection (1)(a) above had not been made.

(3) This section shall not apply in relation to a separation order unless at the date of the death of the deceased the separation order was in force and the separation was continuing.'

21 After section 15 insert—

'15ZA Restriction imposed in proceedings for the dissolution etc of a civil partnership on application under this Act

(1) On making a dissolution order, nullity order, separation order or presumption of death order under Chapter 2 of Part 2 of the Civil Partnership Act 2004, or at any time after making such an order, the court, if it considers it just to do so, may, on the application of either of the civil partners, order that the other civil partner shall not on the death of the applicant be entitled to apply for an order under section 2 of this Act.

(2) In subsection (1) above "the court" means the High Court or, where a county court has jurisdiction by virtue of Part 5 of the Matrimonial and Family Proceedings Act 1984, a county court.

(3) In the case of a dissolution order, nullity order or presumption of death order ("the main order") an order may be made under subsection (1) above before (as well as after) the main order is made final, but if made before the main order is made final it shall not take effect unless the main order is made final.

(4) Where an order under subsection (1) above made in connection with a dissolution order, nullity order or presumption of death order has come into force with respect to a civil partner,

then, on the death of the other civil partner, the court shall not entertain any application for an order under section 2 of this Act made by the surviving civil partner.

(5) Where an order under subsection (1) above made in connection with a separation order has come into force with respect to a civil partner, then, if the other civil partner dies while the separation order is in force and the separation is continuing, the court shall not entertain any application for an order under section 2 of this Act made by the surviving civil partner.'

22 After section 15A insert—

'15B Restriction imposed in proceedings under Schedule 7 to the Civil Partnership Act 2004 on application under this Act

(1) On making an order under paragraph 9 of Schedule 7 to the Civil Partnership Act 2004 (orders for financial provision, property adjustment and pension-sharing following overseas dissolution etc of civil partnership) the court, if it considers it just to do so, may, on the application of either of the civil partners, order that the other civil partner shall not on the death of the applicant be entitled to apply for an order under section 2 of this Act.

(2) In subsection (1) above "the court" means the High Court or, where a county court has jurisdiction by virtue of Part 5 of the Matrimonial and Family Proceedings Act 1984, a county court.

(3) Where an order under subsection (1) above has been made with respect to one of the civil partners in a case where a civil partnership has been dissolved or annulled, then, on the death of the other civil partner, the court shall not entertain an application under section 2 of this Act made by the surviving civil partner.

(4) Where an order under subsection (1) above has been made with respect to one of the civil partners in a case where civil partners have been legally separated, then, if the other civil partner dies while the legal separation is in force, the court shall not entertain an application under section 2 of this Act made by the surviving civil partner.'

23 In section 16(1) (power to vary secured periodical payments orders)—

  (a) after 'the Matrimonial Causes Act 1973' insert 'or Schedule 5 to the Civil Partnership Act 2004', and
  (b) after 'that Act' insert 'of 1973 or Part 11 of that Schedule'.

24 In section 17(4) (meaning of 'maintenance agreement')—

  (a) for 'entered into a marriage' substitute 'formed a marriage or civil partnership',
  (b) after 'of the parties to that marriage' insert 'or of the civil partners', and
  (c) after 'marriage' (in the third and fourth places) insert 'or civil partnership'.

25 After section 18 insert—

'18A Availability of court's powers under this Act in applications under paragraphs 60 and 73 of Schedule 5 to the Civil Partnership Act 2004

(1) Where—

  (a) a person against whom a secured periodical payments order was made under Schedule 5 to the Civil Partnership Act 2004 has died and an application is made under paragraph 60 of that Schedule for the variation or discharge of that order or for the revival of the operation of any suspended provision of the order, or

(b) a party to a maintenance agreement within the meaning of Part 13 of that Schedule has died, the agreement being one which provides for the continuation of payments under the agreement after the death of one of the parties, and an application is made under paragraph 73 of that Schedule for the alteration of the agreement under paragraph 69 of that Schedule,

the court shall have power to direct that the application made under paragraph 60 or 73 of that Schedule shall be deemed to have been accompanied by an application for an order under section 2 of this Act.

(2) Where the court gives a direction under subsection (1) above it shall have power, in the proceedings on the application under paragraph 60 or 73 of that Schedule, to make any order which the court would have had power to make under the provisions of this Act if the application under that paragraph had been made jointly with an application for an order under section 2 of this Act; and the court shall have power to give such consequential directions as may be necessary for enabling the court to exercise any of the powers available to the court under this Act in the case of an application for an order under section 2.

(3) Where an order made under section 15ZA(1) of this Act is in force with respect to a civil partner, the court shall not give a direction under subsection (1) above with respect to any application made under paragraph 60 or 73 of that Schedule by that civil partner on the death of the other civil partner.'

26(1) Amend section 19 (effect, duration and form of orders) as follows.

(2) In subsection (2)(a), for 'former husband or former wife' substitute 'former spouse or former civil partner'.

(3) In subsection (2), after paragraph (b) insert

'or

(c) an applicant who was the civil partner of the deceased in a case where, at the date of death, a separation order under Chapter 2 of Part 2 of the Civil Partnership Act 2004 was in force in relation to their civil partnership and the separation was continuing,'.

(4) In that subsection, in the words after paragraph (b), for 'on the remarriage of the applicant' onwards substitute 'on the formation by the applicant of a subsequent marriage or civil partnership, except in relation to any arrears due under the order on the date of the formation of the subsequent marriage or civil partnership.'

(5) In subsection (3), after 'section 15(1)' insert 'or 15ZA(1)'.

27(1) Amend section 25 (interpretation) as follows.

(2) In subsection (1), in the definition of 'former wife' and 'former husband', for 'former wife' or 'former husband' substitute 'former spouse'.

(3) In that subsection, before that definition insert—

'"former civil partner" means a person whose civil partnership with the deceased was during the lifetime of the deceased either—

(a) dissolved or annulled by an order made under the law of any part of the British Islands, or

(b) dissolved or annulled in any country or territory outside the British Islands by a dissolution or annulment which is entitled to be recognised as valid by the law of England and Wales;'.

(4) In subsection (4)—

(a) before 'wife' insert 'spouse,' and

(b) in paragraph (b), for 'entered into a later marriage' substitute 'formed a subsequent marriage or civil partnership'.

(5) For subsection (5) substitute—

'(4A) For the purposes of this Act any reference to a civil partner shall be treated as including a reference to a person who in good faith formed a void civil partnership with the deceased unless either—

(a) the civil partnership between the deceased and that person was dissolved or annulled during the lifetime of the deceased and the dissolution or annulment is recognised by the law of England and Wales, or

(b) that person has during the lifetime of the deceased formed a subsequent civil partnership or marriage.

(5) Any reference in this Act to the formation of, or to a person who has formed, a subsequent marriage or civil partnership includes (as the case may be) a reference to the formation of, or to a person who has formed, a marriage or civil partnership which is by law void or voidable.

(5A) The formation of a marriage or civil partnership shall be treated for the purposes of this Act as the formation of a subsequent marriage or civil partnership, in relation to either of the spouses or civil partners, notwithstanding that the previous marriage or civil partnership of that spouse or civil partner was void or voidable.'

(6) After subsection (6) insert—

'(6A) Any reference in this Act to an order made under, or under any provision of, the Civil Partnership Act 2004 shall be construed as including a reference to anything which is deemed to be an order made (as the case may be) under that Act or provision.'

SCHEDULE 5

SECTION 72(1)

FINANCIAL RELIEF IN THE HIGH COURT OR A COUNTY COURT ETC

PART 1
FINANCIAL PROVISION IN CONNECTION WITH DISSOLUTION, NULLITY OR SEPARATION

Circumstances in which orders under this Part may be made

1(1) The court may make any one or more of the orders set out in paragraph 2(1)—

(a) on making a dissolution, nullity or separation order, or

(b) at any time afterwards.

(2) The court may make any one or more of the orders set out in paragraph 2(1)(d), (e) and (f)—

(a) in proceedings for a dissolution, nullity or separation order, before making the order;

(b) if proceedings for a dissolution, nullity or separation order are dismissed after the beginning of the trial, either straightaway or within a reasonable period after the dismissal.

(3) The power of the court to make an order under sub-paragraph (1) or (2)(a) in favour of a child of the family is exercisable from time to time.

(4) If the court makes an order in favour of a child under sub-paragraph (2)(b), it may from time to time make a further order in the child's favour of any of the kinds set out in paragraph 2(1)(d), (e) or (f).

The orders: periodical and secured periodical payments and lump sums

2(1) The orders are—

    (a) an order that either civil partner must make to the other such periodical payments for such term as may be specified;

    (b) an order that either civil partner must secure to the other, to the satisfaction of the court, such periodical payments for such term as may be specified;

    (c) an order that either civil partner must pay to the other such lump sum or sums as may be specified;

    (d) an order that one of the civil partners must make —

        (i) to such person as may be specified for the benefit of a child of the family, or

        (ii) to a child of the family,

    such periodical payments for such term as may be specified;

    (e) an order that one of the civil partners must secure—

        (i) to such person as may be specified for the benefit of a child of the family, or

        (ii) to a child of the family,

    to the satisfaction of the court, such periodical payments for such term as may be specified;

    (f) an order that one of the civil partners must pay such lump sum as may be specified—

        (i) to such person as may be specified for the benefit of a child of the family, or

        (ii) to a child of the family.

(2) 'Specified' means specified in the order.

Particular provision that may be made by lump sum orders

3(1) An order under this Part requiring one civil partner to pay the other a lump sum may be made for the purpose of enabling the other civil partner to meet any liabilities or expenses reasonably incurred by the other in maintaining—

    (a) himself or herself, or

    (b) a child of the family,

before making an application for an order under this Part in his or her favour.

(2) An order under this Part requiring a lump sum to be paid to or for the benefit of a child of the family may be made for the purpose of enabling any liabilities or expenses reasonably incurred by or for the benefit of the child before making an application for an order under this Part to be met.

(3) An order under this Part for the payment of a lump sum may—

    (a) provide for its payment by instalments of such amount as may be specified, and

    (b) require the payment of the instalments to be secured to the satisfaction of the court.

(4) Sub-paragraphs (1) to (3) do not restrict the powers to make the orders set out in paragraph 2(1)(c) and (f).

(5) If the court—

    (a) makes an order under this Part for the payment of a lump sum, and

    (b) directs that—

        (i) payment of the sum or any part of it is to be deferred, or

(ii) the sum or any part of it is to be paid by instalments,

it may provide for the deferred amount or the instalments to carry interest at such rate as may be specified from such date as may be specified until the date when payment of it is due.

(6) A date specified under sub-paragraph (5) must not be earlier than the date of the order.

(7) 'Specified' means specified in the order.

When orders under this Part may take effect

4(1) If an order is made under paragraph 2(1)(a), (b) or (c) on or after making a dissolution or nullity order, neither the order nor any settlement made in pursuance of it takes effect unless the dissolution or nullity order has been made final.

(2) This paragraph does not affect the power of the court to give a direction under paragraph 76 (settlement of instrument by conveyancing counsel).

Restrictions on making of orders under this Part

5 The power to make an order under paragraph 2(1)(d), (e) or (f) is subject to paragraph 49(1) and (5) (restrictions on orders in favour of children who have reached 18).

PART 2
PROPERTY ADJUSTMENT ON OR AFTER DISSOLUTION, NULLITY OR SEPARATION

Circumstances in which property adjustment orders may be made

6(1) The court may make one or more property adjustment orders—

(a) on making a dissolution, nullity or separation order, or
(b) at any time afterwards.

(2) In this Schedule 'property adjustment order' means a property adjustment order under this Part.

Property adjustment orders

7(1) The property adjustment orders are—

(a) an order that one of the civil partners must transfer such property as may be specified, being property to which he is entitled—
    (i) to the other civil partner,
    (ii) to a child of the family, or
    (iii) to such person as may be specified for the benefit of a child of the family;
(b) an order that a settlement of such property as may be specified, being property to which one of the civil partners is entitled, be made to the satisfaction of the court for the benefit of—
    (i) the other civil partner and the children of the family, or
    (ii) either or any of them;
(c) an order varying for the benefit of—
    (i) the civil partners and the children of the family, or
    (ii) either or any of them,

a relevant settlement;

(d) an order extinguishing or reducing the interest of either of the civil partners under a relevant settlement.

(2) The court may make a property adjustment order under sub-paragraph (1)(c) even though there are no children of the family.

(3) In this paragraph—

'entitled' means entitled in possession or reversion,

'relevant settlement' means, in relation to a civil partnership, a settlement made, during its subsistence or in anticipation of its formation, on the civil partners including one made by will or codicil, but not including one in the form of a pension arrangement (within the meaning of Part 4), and

'specified' means specified in the order.

When property adjustment orders may take effect

8(1) If a property adjustment order is made on or after making a dissolution or nullity order, neither the property adjustment order nor any settlement made under it takes effect unless the dissolution or nullity order has been made final.

(2) This paragraph does not affect the power to give a direction under paragraph 76 (settlement of instrument by conveyancing counsel).

Restrictions on making property adjustment orders

9 The power to make a property adjustment order under paragraph 7(1)(a) is subject to paragraph 49(1) and (5) (restrictions on making orders in favour of children who have reached 18).

PART 3
SALE OF PROPERTY ORDERS

Circumstances in which sale of property orders may be made

10(1) The court may make a sale of property order—

(a) on making —
 (i) under Part 1, a secured periodical payments order or an order for the payment of a lump sum, or
 (ii) a property adjustment order, or
(b) at any time afterwards.

(2) In this Schedule 'sale of property order' means a sale of property order under this Part.

Sale of property orders

11(1) A sale of property order is an order for the sale of such property as may be specified, being property in which, or in the proceeds of sale of which, either or both of the civil partners has or have a beneficial interest, either in possession or reversion.

(2) A sale of property order may contain such consequential or supplementary provisions as the court thinks fit.

(3) A sale of property order may in particular include—

(a) provision requiring the making of a payment out of the proceeds of sale of the property to which the order relates, and

(b) provision requiring any property to which the order relates to be offered for sale to a specified person, or class of persons.

(4) 'Specified' means specified in the order.

When sale of property orders may take effect

12(1) If a sale of property order is made on or after the making of a dissolution or nullity order, it does not take effect unless the dissolution or nullity order has been made final.

(2) Where a sale of property order is made, the court may direct that—

(a) the order, or

(b) such provision of it as the court may specify,

is not to take effect until the occurrence of an event specified by the court or the end of a period so specified.

When sale of property orders cease to have effect

13 If a sale of property order contains a provision requiring the proceeds of sale of the property to which the order relates to be used to secure periodical payments to a civil partner, the order ceases to have effect—

(a) on the death of the civil partner, or

(b) on the formation of a subsequent civil partnership or marriage by the civil partner.

Protection of third parties

14(1) Sub-paragraphs (2) and (3) apply if—

(a) a civil partner has a beneficial interest in any property, or in the proceeds of sale of any property, and

(b) another person ('A') who is not the other civil partner also has a beneficial interest in the property or the proceeds.

(2) Before deciding whether to make a sale of property order in relation to the property, the court must give A an opportunity to make representations with respect to the order.

(3) Any representations made by A are included among the circumstances to which the court is required to have regard under paragraph 20.

PART 4
PENSION SHARING ORDERS ON OR AFTER DISSOLUTION OR NULLITY ORDER

Circumstances in which pension sharing orders may be made

15(1) The court may make a pension sharing order—

(a) on making a dissolution or nullity order, or

(b) at any time afterwards.

(2) In this Schedule 'pension sharing order' means a pension sharing order under this Part.

Pension sharing orders

16(1) A pension sharing order is an order which—

    (a) provides that one civil partner's—
        (i)   shareable rights under a specified pension arrangement, or
        (ii) shareable state scheme rights,

are to be subject to pension sharing for the benefit of the other civil partner, and
    (b) specifies the percentage value to be transferred.

(2) Shareable rights under a pension arrangement are rights in relation to which pension sharing is available under—

    (a) Chapter 1 of Part 4 of the Welfare Reform and Pensions Act 1999 (c 30), or
    (b) corresponding Northern Ireland legislation.

(3) Shareable state scheme rights are rights in relation to which pension sharing is available under—

    (a) Chapter 2 of Part 4 of the 1999 Act, or
    (b) corresponding Northern Ireland legislation.

(4) In this Part 'pension arrangement' means—

    (a) an occupational pension scheme,
    (b) a personal pension scheme,
    (c) a retirement annuity contract,
    (d) an annuity or insurance policy purchased, or transferred, for the purpose of giving effect to rights under—
        (i)   an occupational pension scheme, or
        (ii) a personal pension scheme, and
    (e) an annuity purchased, or entered into, for the purpose of discharging liability in respect of a pension credit under—
        (i)   section 29(1)(b) of the 1999 Act, or
        (ii) corresponding Northern Ireland legislation.

(5) In sub-paragraph (4)—

    'occupational pension scheme' has the same meaning as in the Pension Schemes Act 1993 (c 48);

    'personal pension scheme' has the same meaning as in the 1993 Act;

    'retirement annuity contract' means a contract or scheme approved under Chapter 3 of Part 14 of the Income and Corporation Taxes Act 1988 (c 1).

Pension sharing orders: apportionment of charges

17 If a pension sharing order relates to rights under a pension arrangement, the court may include in the order provision about the apportionment between the civil partners of any charge under—

    (a) section 41 of the 1999 Act (charges in respect of pension sharing costs), or
    (b) corresponding Northern Ireland legislation.

Restrictions on making of pension sharing orders

18(1) A pension sharing order may not be made in relation to a pension arrangement which—

    (a) is the subject of a pension sharing order in relation to the civil partnership, or

(b) has been the subject of pension sharing between the civil partners.

(2) A pension sharing order may not be made in relation to shareable state scheme rights if—

(a) such rights are the subject of a pension sharing order in relation to the civil partnership, or
(b) such rights have been the subject of pension sharing between the civil partners.

(3) A pension sharing order may not be made in relation to the rights of a person under a pension arrangement if there is in force a requirement imposed by virtue of Part 6 which relates to benefits or future benefits to which that person is entitled under the pension arrangement.

When pension sharing orders may take effect

19(1) A pension sharing order is not to take effect unless the dissolution or nullity order on or after which it is made has been made final.

(2) No pension sharing order may be made so as to take effect before the end of such period after the making of the order as may be prescribed by regulations made by the Lord Chancellor.

(3) The power to make regulations under sub-paragraph (2) is exercisable by statutory instrument which is subject to annulment in pursuance of a resolution of either House of Parliament.

PART 5
MATTERS TO WHICH COURT IS TO HAVE REGARD UNDER PARTS 1 TO 4

General

20 The court in deciding—

(a) whether to exercise its powers under—
 (i) Part 1 (financial provision on dissolution etc),
 (ii) Part 2 (property adjustment orders),
 (iii) Part 3 (sale of property orders), or
 (iv) any provision of Part 4 (pension sharing orders) other than paragraph 17 (apportionment of charges), and
(b) if so, in what way,

must have regard to all the circumstances of the case, giving first consideration to the welfare, while under 18, of any child of the family who has not reached 18.

Particular matters to be taken into account when exercising powers in relation to civil partners

21(1) This paragraph applies to the exercise by the court in relation to a civil partner of its powers under—

(a) Part 1 (financial provision on dissolution etc) by virtue of paragraph 2(1)(a), (b) or (c),
(b) Part 2 (property adjustment orders),
(c) Part 3 (sale of property orders), or
(d) Part 4 (pension sharing orders).

(2) The court must in particular have regard to—

(a) the income, earning capacity, property and other financial resources which each civil partner—

    (i)   has, or

    (ii) is likely to have in the foreseeable future,

including, in the case of earning capacity, any increase in that capacity which it would in the opinion of the court be reasonable to expect a civil partner in the civil partnership to take steps to acquire;

    (b) the financial needs, obligations and responsibilities which each civil partner has or is likely to have in the foreseeable future;

    (c) the standard of living enjoyed by the family before the breakdown of the civil partnership;

    (d) the age of each civil partner and the duration of the civil partnership;

    (e) any physical or mental disability of either of the civil partners;

    (f) the contributions which each civil partner has made or is likely in the foreseeable future to make to the welfare of the family, including any contribution by looking after the home or caring for the family;

    (g) the conduct of each civil partner, if that conduct is such that it would in the opinion of the court be inequitable to disregard it;

    (h) in the case of proceedings for a dissolution or nullity order, the value to each civil partner of any benefit which, because of the dissolution or annulment of the civil partnership, that civil partner will lose the chance of acquiring.

Particular matters to be taken into account when exercising powers in relation to children

22(1) This paragraph applies to the exercise by the court in relation to a child of the family of its powers under—

    (a) Part 1 (financial provision on dissolution etc) by virtue of paragraph 2(1)(d), (e) or (f)),

    (b) Part 2 (property adjustment orders), or

    (c) Part 3 (sale of property orders).

(2) The court must in particular have regard to—

    (a) the financial needs of the child;

    (b) the income, earning capacity (if any), property and other financial resources of the child;

    (c) any physical or mental disability of the child;

    (d) the way in which the child was being and in which the civil partners expected the child to be educated or trained;

    (e) the considerations mentioned in relation to the civil partners in paragraph 21(2)(a), (b), (c) and (e).

(3) In relation to the exercise of any of those powers against a civil partner ('A') in favour of a child of the family who is not A's child, the court must also have regard to—

    (a) whether A has assumed any responsibility for the child's maintenance;

    (b) if so, the extent to which, and the basis upon which, A assumed such responsibility and the length of time for which A discharged such responsibility;

    (c) whether in assuming and discharging such responsibility A did so knowing that the child was not A's child;

    (d) the liability of any other person to maintain the child.

Terminating financial obligations

23(1) Sub-paragraphs (2) and (3) apply if, on or after the making of a dissolution or nullity order, the court decides to exercise its powers under—

    (a) Part 1 (financial provision on dissolution etc) by virtue of paragraph 2(1)(a), (b) or (c),

(b) Part 2 (property adjustment orders),

(c) Part 3 (sale of property orders), or

(d) Part 4 (pension sharing orders),

in favour of one of the civil partners.

(2) The court must consider whether it would be appropriate to exercise those powers in such a way that the financial obligations of each civil partner towards the other will be terminated as soon after the making of the dissolution or nullity order as the court considers just and reasonable.

(3) If the court decides to make—

(a) a periodical payments order, or

(b) a secured periodical payments order,

in favour of one of the civil partners ('A'), it must in particular consider whether it would be appropriate to require the payments to be made or secured only for such term as would in its opinion be sufficient to enable A to adjust without undue hardship to the termination of A's financial dependence on the other civil partner.

(4) If—

(a) on or after the making of a dissolution or nullity order, an application is made by one of the civil partners for a periodical payments or secured periodical payments order in that civil partner's favour, but

(b) the court considers that no continuing obligation should be imposed on either civil partner to make or secure periodical payments in favour of the other,

the court may dismiss the application with a direction that the applicant is not entitled to make any future application in relation to that civil partnership for an order under Part 1 by virtue of paragraph 2(1)(a) or (b).

PART 6
MAKING OF PART 1 ORDERS HAVING REGARD TO PENSION BENEFITS

Pension benefits to be included in matters to which court is to have regard

24(1) The matters to which the court is to have regard under paragraph 21(2)(a) include any pension benefits under a pension arrangement or by way of pension which a civil partner has or is likely to have; and, accordingly, in relation to any pension benefits paragraph 21(2)(a)(ii) has effect as if 'in the foreseeable future' were omitted.

(2) The matters to which the court is to have regard under paragraph 21(2)(h) include any pension benefits which, because of the making of a dissolution or nullity order, a civil partner will lose the chance of acquiring.

(3) 'Pension benefits' means—

(a) benefits under a pension arrangement, or

(b) benefits by way of pension (whether under a pension arrangement or not).

Provisions applying where pension benefits taken into account in decision to make Part 1 order

25(1) This paragraph applies if, having regard to any benefits under a pension arrangement, the court decides to make an order under Part 1.

(2) To the extent to which the Part 1 order is made having regard to any benefits under a pension arrangement, it may require the person responsible for the pension arrangement, if at any time any payment in respect of any benefits under the arrangement becomes due to the civil partner with pension rights, to make a payment for the benefit of the other civil partner.

(3) The Part 1 order must express the amount of any payment required to be made by virtue of sub-paragraph (2) as a percentage of the payment which becomes due to the civil partner with pension rights.

(4) Any such payment by the person responsible for the arrangement—

(a) discharges so much of his liability to the civil partner with pension rights as corresponds to the amount of the payment, and

(b) is to be treated for all purposes as a payment made by the civil partner with pension rights in or towards the discharge of that civil partner's liability under the order.

(5) If the civil partner with pension rights has a right of commutation under the arrangement, the Part 1 order may require that civil partner to exercise it to any extent.

(6) This paragraph applies to any payment due in consequence of commutation in pursuance of the Part 1 order as it applies to other payments in respect of benefits under the arrangement.

(7) The power conferred by sub-paragraph (5) may not be exercised for the purpose of commuting a benefit payable to the civil partner with pension rights to a benefit payable to the other civil partner.

(8) The powers conferred by sub-paragraphs (2) and (5) may not be exercised in relation to a pension arrangement which—

(a) is the subject of a pension sharing order in relation to the civil partnership, or

(b) has been the subject of pension sharing between the civil partners.

Pensions: lump sums

26(1) This paragraph applies if the benefits which the civil partner with pension rights has or is likely to have under a pension arrangement include any lump sum payable in respect of that civil partner's death.

(2) The court's power under Part 1 to order a civil partner to pay a lump sum to the other civil partner includes the power to make by the order any provision in sub-paragraph (3) to (5).

(3) If the person responsible for the pension arrangement has power to determine the person to whom the sum, or any part of it, is to be paid, the court may require him to pay the whole or part of that sum, when it becomes due, to the other civil partner.

(4) If the civil partner with pension rights has power to nominate the person to whom the sum, or any part of it, is to be paid, the court may require the civil partner with pension rights to nominate the other civil partner in respect of the whole or part of that sum.

(5) In any other case, the court may require the person responsible for the pension arrangement in question to pay the whole or part of that sum, when it becomes due, for the benefit of the other civil partner instead of to the person to whom, apart from the order, it would be paid.

(6) Any payment by the person responsible for the arrangement under an order made under Part 1 made by virtue of this paragraph discharges so much of his liability in respect of the civil partner with pension rights as corresponds to the amount of the payment.

(7) The powers conferred by this paragraph may not be exercised in relation to a pension arrangement which—

(a) is the subject of a pension sharing order in relation to the civil partnership, or

(b) has been the subject of pension sharing between the civil partners.

Pensions: supplementary

27 If—

(a) a Part 1 order made by virtue of paragraph 25 or 26 imposes any requirement on the person responsible for a pension arrangement ('the first arrangement'),

(b) the civil partner with pension rights acquires rights under another pension arrangement ('the new arrangement') which are derived (directly or indirectly) from the whole of that civil partner's rights under the first arrangement, and

(c) the person responsible for the new arrangement has been given notice in accordance with regulations made by the Lord Chancellor,

the Part 1 order has effect as if it had been made instead in respect of the person responsible for the new arrangement.

Regulations

28(1) The Lord Chancellor may by regulations—

(a) make provision, in relation to any provision of paragraph 25 or 26 which authorises the court making a Part 1 order to require the person responsible for a pension arrangement to make a payment for the benefit of the other civil partner, as to—
(i) the person to whom, and
(ii) the terms on which,

the payment is to be made;

(b) make provision, in relation to payment under a mistaken belief as to the continuation in force of a provision included by virtue of paragraph 25 or 26 in a Part 1 order, about the rights or liabilities of the payer, the payee or the person to whom the payment was due;

(c) require notices to be given in respect of changes of circumstances relevant to Part 1 orders which include provision made by virtue of paragraphs 25 and 26;

(d) make provision for the person responsible for a pension arrangement to be discharged in prescribed circumstances from a requirement imposed by virtue of paragraph 25 or 26;

(e) make provision about calculation and verification in relation to the valuation of—
(i) benefits under a pension arrangement, or
(ii) shareable state scheme rights (within the meaning of paragraph 16(3)),

for the purposes of the court's functions in connection with the exercise of any of its powers under this Schedule.

(2) Regulations under sub-paragraph (1)(e) may include—

(a) provision for calculation or verification in accordance with guidance from time to time prepared by a prescribed person, and

(b) provision by reference to regulations under section 30 or 49(4) of the 1999 Act.

(3) The power to make regulations under paragraph 27 or this paragraph is exercisable by statutory instrument which is subject to annulment in pursuance of a resolution of either House of Parliament.

(4) 'Prescribed' means prescribed by regulations.

Interpretation of provisions relating to pensions

29(1) In this Part 'the civil partner with pension rights' means the civil partner who has or is likely to have benefits under a pension arrangement.

(2) In this Part 'pension arrangement' has the same meaning as in Part 4.

(3) In this Part, references to the person responsible for a pension arrangement are to be read in accordance with section 26 of the Welfare Reform and Pensions Act 1999 (c 30).

PART 7
PENSION PROTECTION FUND COMPENSATION ETC

PPF compensation to be included in matters to which court is to have regard

30(1) The matters to which a court is to have regard under paragraph 21(2)(a) include any PPF compensation to which a civil partner is or is likely to be entitled; and, accordingly, in relation to any PPF compensation paragraph 21(2)(a)(ii) has effect as if 'in the foreseeable future' were omitted.

(2) The matters to which a court is to have regard under paragraph 21(2)(h) include any PPF compensation which, because of the making of a dissolution or nullity order, a civil partner will lose the chance of acquiring entitlement to.

(3) In this Part 'PPF compensation' means compensation payable under—

(a) Chapter 3 of Part 2 of the Pensions Act 2004 (pension protection), or
(b) corresponding Northern Ireland legislation.

Assumption of responsibility by PPF Board in paragraph 25(2) cases

31(1) This paragraph applies to an order under Part 1 so far as it includes provision made by virtue of paragraph 25(2) which—

(a) imposed requirements on the trustees or managers of an occupational pension scheme for which the Board has assumed responsibility, and
(b) was made before the trustees or managers received the transfer notice.

(2) From the time the trustees or managers of the scheme receive the transfer notice, the order has effect—

(a) except in descriptions of case prescribed by regulations, with the modifications set out in sub-paragraph (3), and
(b) with such other modifications as may be prescribed by regulations.

(3) The modifications are that—

(a) references in the order to the trustees or managers of the scheme have effect as references to the Board, and
(b) references in the order to any pension or lump sum to which the civil partner with pension rights is or may become entitled under the scheme have effect as references to any PPF compensation to which that person is or may become entitled in respect of the pension or lump sum.

Assumption of responsibility by PPF Board in paragraph 25(5) cases

32(1) This paragraph applies to an order under Part 1 if—

(a) it includes provision made by virtue of paragraph 25(5) which requires the civil partner with pension rights to exercise his right of commutation under an occupational pension scheme to any extent, and

(b) before the requirement is complied with the Board has assumed responsibility for the scheme.

(2) From the time the trustees or managers of the scheme receive the transfer notice, the order has effect with such modifications as may be prescribed by regulations.

Lump sums: power to modify paragraph 26 in respect of assessment period

33 Regulations may modify paragraph 26 in its application to an occupational pension scheme during an assessment period in relation to the scheme.

Assumption of responsibility by the Board not to affect power of court to vary order etc

34(1) This paragraph applies where the court makes, in relation to an occupational pension scheme—

(a) a pension sharing order, or

(b) an order including provision made by virtue of paragraph 25(2) or (5).

(2) If the Board subsequently assumes responsibility for the scheme, that does not affect—

(a) the powers of the court under paragraph 51 to vary or discharge the order or to suspend or revive any provision of it;

(b) on an appeal, the powers of the appeal court to affirm, reinstate, set aside or vary the order.

Regulations

35 Regulations may make such consequential modifications of any provision of, or made by virtue of, this Schedule as appear to the Lord Chancellor necessary or expedient to give effect to the provisions of this Part.

36(1) In this Part 'regulations' means regulations made by the Lord Chancellor.

(2) A power to make regulations under this Part is exercisable by statutory instrument which is subject to annulment in pursuance of a resolution of either House of Parliament.

Interpretation

37(1) In this Part—

'assessment period' means—

(a) an assessment period within the meaning of Part 2 of the Pensions Act 2004 (pension protection), or

(b) an equivalent period under corresponding Northern Ireland legislation;

'the Board' means the Board of the Pension Protection Fund;

'the civil partner with pension rights' has the meaning given by paragraph 29(1);

'occupational pension scheme' has the same meaning as in the Pension Schemes Act 1993 (c 48);

'transfer notice' has the same meaning as in—

  (a) Chapter 3 of Part 2 of the 2004 Act, or
  (b) corresponding Northern Ireland legislation.

(2) References in this Part to the Board assuming responsibility for a scheme are to the Board assuming responsibility for the scheme in accordance with—

  (a) Chapter 3 of Part 2 of the 2004 Act (pension protection), or
  (b) corresponding Northern Ireland legislation.

PART 8
MAINTENANCE PENDING OUTCOME OF DISSOLUTION, NULLITY OR SEPARATION PROCEEDINGS

38 On an application for a dissolution, nullity or separation order, the court may make an order requiring either civil partner to make to the other for the other's maintenance such periodical payments for such term—

  (a) beginning no earlier than the date on which the application was made, and
  (b) ending with the date on which the proceedings are determined,

as the court thinks reasonable.

PART 9
FAILURE TO MAINTAIN: FINANCIAL PROVISION (AND INTERIM ORDERS)

Circumstances in which orders under this Part may be made

39(1) Either civil partner in a subsisting civil partnership may apply to the court for an order under this Part on the ground that the other civil partner ('the respondent')—

  (a) has failed to provide reasonable maintenance for the applicant, or
  (b) has failed to provide, or to make a proper contribution towards, reasonable maintenance for any child of the family.

(2) The court must not entertain an application under this paragraph unless—

  (a) the applicant or the respondent is domiciled in England and Wales on the date of the application,
  (b) the applicant has been habitually resident there throughout the period of 1 year ending with that date, or
  (c) the respondent is resident there on that date.

(3) If, on an application under this paragraph, it appears to the court that—

  (a) the applicant or any child of the family to whom the application relates is in immediate need of financial assistance, but
  (b) it is not yet possible to determine what order, if any, should be made on the application,

the court may make an interim order.

(4) If, on an application under this paragraph, the applicant satisfies the court of a ground mentioned in sub-paragraph (1), the court may make one or more of the orders set out in paragraph 41.

Interim orders

40 An interim order is an order requiring the respondent to make to the applicant, until the determination of the application, such periodical payments as the court thinks reasonable.

Orders that may be made where failure to maintain established

41(1) The orders are—

(a) an order that the respondent must make to the applicant such periodical payments for such term as may be specified;
(b) an order that the respondent must secure to the applicant, to the satisfaction of the court, such periodical payments for such term as may be specified;
(c) an order that the respondent must pay to the applicant such lump sum as may be specified;
(d) an order that the respondent must make such periodical payments for such term as may be specified—
  (i) to such person as may be specified, for the benefit of the child to whom the application relates, or
  (ii) to the child to whom the application relates;
(e) an order that the respondent must secure—
  (i) to such person as may be specified for the benefit of the child to whom the application relates, or
  (ii) to the child to whom the application relates,

to the satisfaction of the court, such periodical payments for such term as may be specified;
(f) an order that the respondent must pay such lump sum as may be specified—
  (i) to such person as may be specified for the benefit of the child to whom the application relates, or
  (ii) to the child to whom the application relates.

(2) In this Part 'specified' means specified in the order.

Particular provision that may be made by lump sum orders

42(1) An order under this Part for the payment of a lump sum may be made for the purpose of enabling any liabilities or expenses reasonably incurred in maintaining the applicant or any child of the family to whom the application relates before the making of the application to be met.

(2) An order under this Part for the payment of a lump sum may—

(a) provide for its payment by instalments of such amount as may be specified, and
(b) require the payment of the instalments to be secured to the satisfaction of the court.

(3) Sub-paragraphs (1) and (2) do not restrict the power to make an order by virtue of paragraph 41(1)(c) or (f).

Matters to which the court is to have regard on application under paragraph 39(1)(a)

43(1) This paragraph applies if an application under paragraph 39 is made on the ground mentioned in paragraph 39(1)(a).

(2) In deciding—

(a) whether the respondent has failed to provide reasonable maintenance for the applicant, and
(b) what order, if any, to make under this Part in favour of the applicant,

the court must have regard to all the circumstances of the case including the matters mentioned in paragraph 21(2).

(3) If an application is also made under paragraph 39 in respect of a child of the family who has not reached 18, the court must give first consideration to the welfare of the child while under 18.

(4) Paragraph 21(2)(c) has effect as if for the reference in it to the breakdown of the civil partnership there were substituted a reference to the failure to provide reasonable maintenance for the applicant.

Matters to which the court is to have regard on application under paragraph 39(1)(b)

44(1) This paragraph applies if an application under paragraph 39 is made on the ground mentioned in paragraph 39(1)(b).

(2) In deciding—

(a) whether the respondent has failed to provide, or to make a proper contribution towards, reasonable maintenance for the child of the family to whom the application relates, and
(b) what order, if any, to make under this Part in favour of the child,

the court must have regard to all the circumstances of the case.

(3) Those circumstances include—

(a) the matters mentioned in paragraph 22(2)(a) to (e), and
(b) if the child of the family to whom the application relates is not the child of the respondent, the matters mentioned in paragraph 22(3).

(4) Paragraph 21(2)(c) (as it applies by virtue of paragraph 22(2)(e)) has effect as if for the reference in it to the breakdown of the civil partnership there were substituted a reference to—

(a) the failure to provide, or
(b) the failure to make a proper contribution towards,

reasonable maintenance for the child of the family to whom the application relates.

Restrictions on making orders under this Part

45 The power to make an order under paragraph 41(1)(d), (e) or (f) is subject to paragraph 49(1) and (5) (restrictions on orders in favour of children who have reached 18).

PART 10
COMMENCEMENT OF CERTAIN PROCEEDINGS AND DURATION OF CERTAIN ORDERS

Commencement of proceedings for ancillary relief, etc

46(1) Sub-paragraph (2) applies if an application for a dissolution, nullity or separation order has been made.

(2) Subject to sub-paragraph (3), proceedings for—

(a) an order under Part 1 (financial provision on dissolution etc),

(b) a property adjustment order, or

(c) an order under Part 8 (maintenance pending outcome of dissolution, nullity or separation proceedings),

may be begun (subject to and in accordance with rules of court) at any time after the presentation of the application.

(3) Rules of court may provide, in such cases as may be prescribed by the rules, that—

(a) an application for any such relief as is mentioned in sub-paragraph (2) must be made in the application or response, and

(b) an application for any such relief which—
(i) is not so made, or
(ii) is not made until after the end of such period following the presentation of the application or filing of the response as may be so prescribed,

may be made only with the leave of the court.

Duration of periodical and secured periodical payments orders for a civil partner

47(1) The court may specify in a periodical payments or secured periodical payments order in favour of a civil partner such term as it thinks fit, except that the term must not—

(a) begin before the date of the making of an application for the order, or

(b) extend beyond the limits given in sub-paragraphs (2) and (3).

(2) The limits in the case of a periodical payments order are—

(a) the death of either civil partner;

(b) where the order is made on or after the making of a dissolution or nullity order, the formation of a subsequent civil partnership or marriage by the civil partner in whose favour the order is made.

(3) The limits in the case of a secured periodical payments order are—

(a) the death of the civil partner in whose favour the order is made;

(b) where the order is made on or after the making of a dissolution or nullity order, the formation of a subsequent civil partnership or marriage by the civil partner in whose favour the order is made.

(4) In the case of an order made on or after the making of a dissolution or nullity order, sub-paragraphs (1) to (3) are subject to paragraphs 23(3) and 59(4).

(5) If a periodical payments or secured periodical payments order in favour of a civil partner is made on or after the making of a dissolution or nullity order, the court may direct that that civil partner is not entitled to apply under paragraph 51 for the extension of the term specified in the order.

(6) If—

(a) a periodical payments or secured periodical payments order in favour of a civil partner is made otherwise than on or after the making of a dissolution or nullity order, and

(b) the civil partnership is subsequently dissolved or annulled but the order continues in force,

the order ceases to have effect (regardless of anything in it) on the formation of a subsequent civil partnership or marriage by that civil partner, except in relation to any arrears due under it on the date of its formation.

Subsequent civil partnership or marriage

48 If after the making of a dissolution or nullity order one of the civil partners forms a subsequent civil partnership or marriage, that civil partner is not entitled to apply, by reference to the dissolution or nullity order, for—

(a) an order under Part 1 in that civil partner's favour, or
(b) a property adjustment order,

against the other civil partner in the dissolved or annulled civil partnership.

Duration of continuing orders in favour of children, and age limit on making certain orders in their favour

49(1) Subject to sub-paragraph (5)—

(a) no order under Part 1,
(b) no property adjustment order made by virtue of paragraph 7(1)(a) (transfer of property), and
(c) no order made under Part 9 (failure to maintain) by virtue of paragraph 41,

is to be made in favour of a child who has reached 18.

(2) The term to be specified in a periodical payments or secured periodical payments order in favour of a child may begin with—

(a) the date of the making of an application for the order or a later date, or
(b) a date ascertained in accordance with sub-paragraph (7) or (8).

(3) The term to be specified in such an order—

(a) must not in the first instance extend beyond the date of the birthday of the child next following the child's reaching the upper limit of the compulsory school age unless the court considers that in the circumstances of the case the welfare of the child requires that it should extend to a later date, and
(b) must not in any event, subject to sub-paragraph (5), extend beyond the date of the child's 18th birthday.

(4) Sub-paragraph (3)(a) must be read with section 8 of the Education Act 1996 (c 56) (which applies to determine for the purposes of any enactment whether a person is of compulsory school age).

(5) Sub-paragraphs (1) and (3)(b) do not apply in the case of a child if it appears to the court that—

(a) the child is, or will be, or, if an order were made without complying with either or both of those provisions, would be—
   (i) receiving instruction at an educational establishment, or
   (ii) undergoing training for a trade, profession or vocation,

whether or not the child also is, will be or would be in gainful employment, or
(b) there are special circumstances which justify the making of an order without complying with either or both of sub-paragraphs (1) and (3)(b).

(6) A periodical payments order in favour of a child, regardless of anything in the order, ceases to have effect on the death of the person liable to make payments under the order, except in relation to any arrears due under the order on the date of the death.

(7) If—

(a) a maintenance calculation ('the current calculation') is in force with respect to a child, and
(b) an application is made under this Schedule for a periodical payments or secured periodical payments order in favour of that child—
    (i)   in accordance with section 8 of the Child Support Act 1991 (c 48), and
    (ii) before the end of 6 months beginning with the making of the current calculation,

the term to be specified in any such order made on that application may be expressed to begin on, or at any time after, the earliest permitted date.

(8) 'The earliest permitted date' is whichever is the later of—

(a) the date 6 months before the application is made, or
(b) the date on which the current calculation took effect or, where successive maintenance calculations have been continuously in force with respect to a child, on which the first of those calculations took effect.

(9) If—

(a) a maintenance calculation ceases to have effect by or under any provision of the 1991 Act, and
(b) an application is made, before the end of 6 months beginning with the relevant date, for a periodical payments or secured periodical payments order in favour of a child with respect to whom that maintenance calculation was in force immediately before it ceased to have effect,

the term to be specified in any such order made on that application may begin with the date on which that maintenance calculation ceased to have effect or any later date.

(10) 'The relevant date' means the date on which the maintenance calculation ceased to have effect.

(11) In this paragraph 'maintenance calculation' has the same meaning as it has in the 1991 Act by virtue of section 54 of the 1991 Act as read with any regulations in force under that section.

PART 11
VARIATION, DISCHARGE ETC OF CERTAIN ORDERS FOR FINANCIAL RELIEF

Orders etc to which this Part applies

50(1) This Part applies to the following orders—

(a) a periodical payments order under Part 1 (financial provision on dissolution etc) or Part 9 (failure to maintain);
(b) a secured periodical payments order under Part 1 or 9;
(c) an order under Part 8 (maintenance pending outcome of dissolution proceedings etc);
(d) an interim order under Part 9;
(e) an order made under Part 1 by virtue of paragraph 3(3) or under Part 9 by virtue of paragraph 42(2) (lump sum by instalments);
(f) a deferred order made under Part 1 by virtue of paragraph 2(1)(c) (lump sum for civil partner) which includes provision made by virtue of—
    (i)   paragraph 25(2), or
    (ii) paragraph 26,

(provision in respect of pension rights);
(g) a property adjustment order made on or after the making of a separation order by virtue of paragraph 7(1)(b), (c) or (d) (order for settlement or variation of settlement);
(h) a sale of property order;

(i)   a pension sharing order made before the dissolution or nullity order has been made final.

(2) If the court has made an order referred to in sub-paragraph (1)(f)(ii), this Part ceases to apply to the order on the death of either of the civil partners.

(3) The powers exercisable by the court under this Part in relation to an order are also exercisable in relation to any instrument executed in pursuance of the order.

Powers to vary, discharge, suspend or revive order

51(1) If the court has made an order to which this Part applies, it may—

(a)   vary or discharge the order,
(b)   suspend any provision of it temporarily, or
(c)   revive the operation of any provision so suspended.

(2) Sub-paragraph (1) is subject to the provisions of this Part and paragraph 47(5).

Power to remit arrears

52(1) If the court has made an order referred to in paragraph 50(1)(a), (b), (c) or (d), it may remit the payment of any arrears due under the order or under any part of the order.

(2) Sub-paragraph (1) is subject to the provisions of this Part.

Additional powers on discharging or varying a periodical or secured periodical payments order after dissolution of civil partnership

53(1) Sub-paragraph (2) applies if, after the dissolution of a civil partnership, the court—

(a)   discharges a periodical payments order or secured periodical payments order made in favour of a civil partner, or
(b)   varies such an order so that payments under the order are required to be made or secured only for such further period as is determined by the court.

(2) The court may make supplemental provision consisting of any of the following—

(a)   an order for the payment of a lump sum in favour of one of the civil partners;
(b)   one or more property adjustment orders in favour of one of the civil partners;
(c)   one or more pension sharing orders;
(d)   a direction that the civil partner in whose favour the original order discharged or varied was made is not entitled to make any further application for—
    (i)   a periodical payments or secured periodical payments order, or
    (ii)   an extension of the period to which the original order is limited by any variation made by the court.

(3) The power under sub-paragraph (2) is in addition to any power the court has apart from that sub-paragraph.

54(1) An order for the payment of a lump sum under paragraph 53 may—

(a)   provide for the payment of it by instalments of such amount as may be specified, and
(b)   require the payment of the instalments to be secured to the satisfaction of the court.

(2) Sub-paragraphs (5) and (6) of paragraph 3 (interest on deferred instalments) apply where the court makes an order for the payment of a lump sum under paragraph 53 as they apply where it makes such an order under Part 1.

(3) If under paragraph 53 the court makes more than one property adjustment order in favour of the same civil partner, each of those orders must fall within a different paragraph of paragraph 7(1) (types of property adjustment orders).

(4) Part 3 (orders for the sale of property) and paragraph 76 (direction for settlement of instrument) apply where the court makes a property adjustment order under paragraph 53 as they apply where it makes any other property adjustment order.

(5) Paragraph 18 (restrictions on making of pension sharing order) applies in relation to a pension sharing order under paragraph 53 as it applies in relation to any other pension sharing order.

Variation etc of periodical or secured periodical payments orders made in cases of failure to maintain

55(1) An application for the variation under paragraph 51 of a periodical payments order or secured periodical payments order made under Part 9 in favour of a child may, if the child has reached 16, be made by the child himself.

(2) Sub-paragraph (3) applies if a periodical payments order made in favour of a child under Part 9 ceases to have effect—

(a) on the date on which the child reaches 16, or
(b) at any time after that date but before or on the date on which the child reaches 18.

(3) If, on an application made to the court for an order under this sub-paragraph, it appears to the court that—

(a) the child is, will be or, if an order were made under this sub-paragraph, would be—
   (i) receiving instruction at an educational establishment, or
   (ii) undergoing training for a trade, profession or vocation,

whether or not the child also is, will be or would be in gainful employment, or
(b) there are special circumstances which justify the making of an order under this sub-paragraph,

the court may by order revive the order mentioned in sub-paragraph (2) from such date as it may specify.

(4) A date specified under sub-paragraph (3) must not be earlier than the date of the application under that sub-paragraph.

(5) If under sub-paragraph (3) the court revives an order it may exercise its power under paragraph 51 in relation to the revived order.

Variation etc of property adjustment and pension sharing orders

56 The court must not exercise the powers conferred by this Part in relation to a property adjustment order falling within paragraph 7(1)(b), (c) or (d) (order for settlement or for variation of settlement) except on an application made in proceedings—

(a) for the rescission of the separation order by reference to which the property adjustment order was made, or
(b) for a dissolution order in relation to the civil partnership.

57(1) In relation to a pension sharing order which is made at a time before the dissolution or nullity order has been made final—

(a) the powers conferred by this Part (by virtue of paragraph 50(1)(i)) may be exercised—

    (i)   only on an application made before the pension sharing order has or, but for paragraph (b), would have taken effect, and

    (ii) only if, at the time when the application is made, the dissolution or nullity order has not been made final, and

(b) an application made in accordance with paragraph (a) prevents the pension sharing order from taking effect before the application has been dealt with.

(2) No variation of a pension sharing order is to be made so as to take effect before the order is made final.

(3) The variation of a pension sharing order prevents the order taking effect before the end of such period after the making of the variation as may be prescribed by regulations made by the Lord Chancellor.

(4) The power to make regulations under sub-paragraph (3) is exercisable by statutory instrument which is subject to annulment in pursuance of a resolution of either House of Parliament.

58(1) Sub-paragraphs (2) and (3)—

(a) are subject to paragraphs 53 and 54, and

(b) do not affect any power exercisable by virtue of paragraph 50(e), (f), (g) or (i) or otherwise than by virtue of this Part.

(2) No property adjustment order or pension sharing order may be made on an application for the variation of a periodical payments or secured periodical payments order made (whether in favour of a civil partner or in favour of a child of the family) under Part 1.

(3) No order for the payment of a lump sum may be made on an application for the variation of a periodical payments or secured periodical payments order in favour of a civil partner (whether made under Part 1 or 9).

Matters to which court is to have regard in exercising powers under this Part

59(1) In exercising the powers conferred by this Part the court must have regard to all the circumstances of the case, giving first consideration to the welfare, while under 18, of any child of the family who has not reached 18.

(2) The circumstances of the case include, in particular, any change in any of the matters to which the court was required to have regard when making the order to which the application relates.

(3) Sub-paragraph (4) applies in the case of—

(a) a periodical payments order, or

(b) a secured periodical payments order,

made on or after the making of a dissolution or nullity order.

(4) The court must consider whether in all the circumstances, and after having regard to any such change, it would be appropriate to vary the order so that payments under the order are required—

(a) to be made, or

(b) to be secured,

only for such further period as will in the opinion of the court be sufficient to enable the civil partner in whose favour the order was made to adjust without undue hardship to the termination of those payments.

(5) In considering what further period will be sufficient, the court must, if the civil partnership has been dissolved, take into account any proposed exercise by it of its powers under paragraph 53.

(6) If the civil partner against whom the order was made has died, the circumstances of the case also include the changed circumstances resulting from that civil partner's death.

Variation of secured periodical payments order where person liable has died

60(1) This paragraph applies if the person liable to make payments under a secured periodical payments order has died.

(2) Subject to sub-paragraph (3), an application under this Part relating to the order (and to any sale of property order which requires the proceeds of sale of property to be used for securing those payments) may be made by—

(a) the person entitled to payments under the periodical payments order, or
(b) the personal representatives of the deceased person.

(3) No such application may be made without the leave of the court after the end of 6 months from the date on which representation in regard to the estate of that person is first taken out.

(4) The personal representatives of the person who has died are not liable for having distributed any part of the estate of the deceased after the end of the 6 month period on the ground that they ought to have taken into account the possibility that the court might allow an application under this paragraph to be made after that period by the person entitled to payments under the order.

(5) Sub-paragraph (4) does not affect any power to recover any part of the estate so distributed arising by virtue of the making of an order in pursuance of this paragraph.

(6) In considering for the purposes of sub-paragraph (3) the question when representation was first taken out—

(a) a grant limited to settled land or to trust property is to be disregarded, and
(b) a grant limited to real estate or to personal estate is to be disregarded unless a grant limited to the remainder of the estate has previously been made or is made at the same time.

Power to direct when variation etc is to take effect

61(1) If the court, in exercise of its powers under this Part, decides—

(a) to vary, or
(b) to discharge,

a periodical payments or secured periodical payments order, it may direct that the variation or discharge is not to take effect until the end of such period as may be specified in the order.

(2) Sub-paragraph (1) is subject to paragraph 47(1) and (6).

62(1) If—

(a) a periodical payments or secured periodical payments order in favour of more than one child ('the order') is in force,
(b) the order requires payments specified in it to be made to or for the benefit of more than one child without apportioning those payments between them,
(c) a maintenance calculation ('the calculation') is made with respect to one or more, but not all, of the children with respect to whom those payments are to be made, and
(d) an application is made, before the end of the period of 6 months beginning with the date on which the calculation was made, for the variation or discharge of the order,

the court may, in exercise of its powers under this Part to vary or discharge the order, direct that the variation or discharge is to take effect from the date on which the calculation took effect or any later date.

(2) If—

(a) an order ('the child order') of a kind prescribed for the purposes of section 10(1) of the Child Support Act 1991 (c 48) is affected by a maintenance calculation,

(b) on the date on which the child order became so affected there was in force a periodical payments or secured periodical payments order ('the civil partner's order') in favour of a civil partner having the care of the child in whose favour the child order was made, and

(c) an application is made, before the end of the period of 6 months beginning with the date on which the maintenance calculation was made, for the civil partner's order to be varied or discharged,

the court may, in exercise of its powers under this Part to vary or discharge the civil partner's order, direct that the variation or discharge is to take effect from the date on which the child order became so affected or any later date.

(3) For the purposes of sub-paragraph (2), an order is affected if it ceases to have effect or is modified by or under section 10 of the 1991 Act.

(4) Sub-paragraphs (1) and (2) do not affect any other power of the court to direct that the variation of discharge of an order under this Part is to take effect from a date earlier than that on which the order for variation or discharge was made.

(5) In this paragraph 'maintenance calculation' has the same meaning as it has in the 1991 Act by virtue of section 54 of the 1991 Act as read with any regulations in force under that section.

PART 12
ARREARS AND REPAYMENTS

Payment of certain arrears unenforceable without the leave of the court

63(1) This paragraph applies if any arrears are due under—

(a) an order under Part 1 (financial provision on dissolution etc),

(b) an order under Part 8 (maintenance pending outcome of dissolution, nullity or separation proceedings), or

(c) an order under Part 9 (failure to maintain),

and the arrears became due more than 12 months before proceedings to enforce the payment of them are begun.

(2) A person is not entitled to enforce through the High Court or any county court the payment of the arrears without the leave of that court.

(3) The court hearing an application for the grant of leave under this paragraph may—

(a) refuse leave,

(b) grant leave subject to such restrictions and conditions (including conditions as to the allowing of time for payment or the making of payment by instalments) as that court thinks proper, or

(c) remit the payment of the arrears or of any part of them.

(4) An application for the grant of leave under this paragraph must be made in such manner as may be prescribed by rules of court.

Orders for repayment in certain cases of sums paid under certain orders

64(1) This paragraph applies if—

(a) a person ('R') is entitled to receive payments under an order listed in sub-paragraph (2), and
(b) R's circumstances or the circumstances of the person ('P') liable to make payments under the order have changed since the order was made, or the circumstances have changed as a result of P's death.

(2) The orders are—

(a) any order under Part 8 (maintenance pending outcome of dissolution, nullity or separation proceedings);
(b) any interim order under Part 9;
(c) any periodical payments order;
(d) any secured periodical payments order.

(3) P or P's personal representatives may (subject to sub-paragraph (7)) apply for an order under this paragraph against R or R's personal representatives.

(4) If it appears to the court that, because of the changed circumstances or P's death, the amount received by R in respect of a relevant period exceeds the amount which P or P's personal representatives should have been required to pay, it may order the respondent to the application to pay to the applicant such sum, not exceeding the amount of the excess, as it thinks just.

(5) 'Relevant period' means a period after the circumstances changed or (as the case may be) after P's death.

(6) An order under this paragraph for the payment of any sum may provide for the payment of that sum by instalments of such amount as may be specified in the order.

(7) An application under this paragraph—

(a) may be made in proceedings in the High Court or a county court for—
    (i) the variation or discharge of the order listed in sub-paragraph (2), or
    (ii) leave to enforce, or the enforcement of, the payment of arrears under that order, but
(b) if not made in such proceedings, must be made to a county court;

and accordingly references in this paragraph to the court are references to the High Court or a county court, as the circumstances require.

(8) The jurisdiction conferred on a county court by this paragraph is exercisable even though, because of the amount claimed in the application, the jurisdiction would not but for this sub-paragraph be exercisable by a county court.

Orders for repayment after cessation of order because of subsequent civil partnership etc

65(1) Sub-paragraphs (3) and (4) apply if—

(a) a periodical payments or secured periodical payments order in favour of a civil partner ('R') has ceased to have effect because of the formation of a subsequent civil partnership or marriage by R, and
(b) the person liable to make payments under the order ('P') (or P's personal representatives) has made payments in accordance with it in respect of a relevant period in the mistaken belief that the order was still subsisting.

(2) 'Relevant period' means a period after the date of the formation of the subsequent civil partnership or marriage.

(3) P (or P's personal representatives) is not entitled to bring proceedings in respect of a cause of action arising out of the circumstances mentioned in sub-paragraph (1)(a) and (b) against R (or R's personal representatives).

(4) But, on an application under this paragraph by P (or P's personal representatives) against R (or R's personal representatives), the court—

- (a) may order the respondent to pay to the applicant a sum equal to the amount of the payments made in respect of the relevant period, or
- (b) if it appears to the court that it would be unjust to make that order, may—
  - (i) order the respondent to pay to the applicant such lesser sum as it thinks fit, or
  - (ii) dismiss the application.

(5) An order under this paragraph for the payment of any sum may provide for the payment of that sum by instalments of such amount as may be specified in the order.

(6) An application under this paragraph—

- (a) may be made in proceedings in the High Court or a county court for leave to enforce, or the enforcement of, payment of arrears under the order in question, but
- (b) if not made in such proceedings, must be made to a county court;

and accordingly references in this paragraph to the court are references to the High Court or a county court, as the circumstances require.

(7) The jurisdiction conferred on a county court by this paragraph is exercisable even though, because of the amount claimed in the application, the jurisdiction would not but for this sub-paragraph be exercisable by a county court.

(8) Subject to sub-paragraph (9)—

- (a) the designated officer for a magistrates' court to whom any payments under a payments order are required to be made is not liable for any act done by him in pursuance of the payments order after the date on which that order ceased to have effect because of the formation of a subsequent civil partnership or marriage by the person entitled to payments under it, and
- (b) the collecting officer under an attachment of earnings order made to secure payments under a payments order is not liable for any act done by him after that date in accordance with any enactment or rule of court specifying how payments made to him in compliance with the attachment of earnings order are to be dealt with.

(9) Sub-paragraph (8) applies if (and only if) the act—

- (a) was one which the officer would have been under a duty to do had the payments order not ceased to have effect, and
- (b) was done before notice in writing of the formation of the subsequent civil partnership or marriage was given to him by or on behalf of—
  - (i) the person entitled to payments under the payments order,
  - (ii) the person liable to make payments under it, or
  - (iii) the personal representatives of either of them.

(10) In sub-paragraphs (8) and (9) 'payments order' means a periodical payments order or secured periodical payments order and 'collecting officer', in relation to an attachment of earnings order, means—

- (a) the officer of the High Court,
- (b) the district judge of a county court, or

(c) the designated officer for a magistrates' court,

to whom a person makes payments in compliance with the order.

PART 13
CONSENT ORDERS AND MAINTENANCE AGREEMENTS

Consent orders for financial relief

66(1) Regardless of anything in the preceding provisions of this Schedule, on an application for a consent order for financial relief, the court may, unless it has reason to think that there are other circumstances into which it ought to inquire, make an order in the terms agreed on the basis only of such information supplied with the application as is required by rules of court.

(2) Sub-paragraph (1) applies to an application for a consent order varying or discharging an order for financial relief as it applies to an application for an order for financial relief.

(3) In this paragraph—

'consent order', in relation to an application for an order, means an order in the terms applied for to which the respondent agrees;

'order for financial relief' means an order under any of Parts 1, 2, 3, 4 and 9.

Meaning of 'maintenance agreement' and 'financial arrangements'

67(1) In this Part 'maintenance agreement' means any agreement in writing between the civil partners in a civil partnership which—

(a) is made during the continuance or after the dissolution or annulment of the civil partnership and contains financial arrangements, or

(b) is a separation agreement which contains no financial arrangements but is made in a case where no other agreement in writing between the civil partners contains financial arrangements.

(2) In this Part 'financial arrangements' means provisions governing the rights and liabilities towards one another when living separately of the civil partners in a civil partnership (including a civil partnership which has been dissolved or annulled) in respect of—

(a) the making or securing of payments, or

(b) the disposition or use of any property,

including such rights and liabilities with respect to the maintenance or education of a child (whether or not a child of the family).

(3) 'Education' includes training.

Validity of maintenance agreements

68 If a maintenance agreement includes a provision purporting to restrict any right to apply to a court for an order containing financial arrangements—

(a) that provision is void, but

(b) any other financial arrangements contained in the agreement—

(i) are not void or unenforceable as a result, and

(ii)   unless void or unenforceable for any other reason, are (subject to paragraphs 69 and 73) binding on the parties to the agreement.

Alteration of agreements by court during lives of parties

69(1) Either party to a maintenance agreement may apply to the court or, subject to sub-paragraph (6), to a magistrates' court for an order under this paragraph if—

(a) the maintenance agreement is for the time being subsisting, and
(b) each of the parties to the agreement is for the time being domiciled or resident in England and Wales.

(2) The court may make an order under this paragraph if it is satisfied that—

(a) because of a change in the circumstances in the light of which—
   (i)   any financial arrangements contained in the agreement were made, or
   (ii) financial arrangements were omitted from it,

the agreement should be altered so as to make different financial arrangements or so as to contain financial arrangements, or
(b) that the agreement does not contain proper financial arrangements with respect to any child of the family.

(3) In sub-paragraph (2)(a) the reference to a change in the circumstances includes a change foreseen by the parties when making the agreement.

(4) An order under this paragraph may make such alterations in the agreement—

(a) by varying or revoking any financial arrangements contained in it, or
(b) by inserting in it financial arrangements for the benefit of one of the parties to the agreement or of a child of the family,

as appear to the court to be just having regard to all the circumstances, including, if relevant, the matters mentioned in paragraph 22(3).

(5) The effect of the order is that the agreement is to be treated as if any alteration made by the order had been made by agreement between the partners and for valuable consideration.

(6) The power to make an order under this paragraph is subject to paragraphs 70 and 71.

Restrictions on applications to and orders by magistrates' courts under paragraph 69

70(1) A magistrates' court must not entertain an application under paragraph 69(1) unless—

(a) both the parties to the agreement are resident in England and Wales, and
(b) the court acts in, or is authorised by the Lord Chancellor to act for, a local justice area in which at least one of the parties is resident.

(2) A magistrates' court must not make any order on such an application other than—

(a) if the agreement includes no provision for periodical payments by either of the parties, an order inserting provision for the making by one of the parties of periodical payments for the maintenance of—
   (i)   the other party, or
   (ii) any child of the family;
(b) if the agreement includes provision for the making by one of the parties of periodical payments, an order increasing or reducing the rate of, or terminating, any of those payments.

Provisions relating to periodical and secured periodical payments: duration

71(1) If a court decides to make an order under paragraph 69 altering an agreement—

(a) by inserting provision for the making or securing by one of the parties to the agreement of periodical payments for the maintenance of the other party, or
(b) by increasing the rate of the periodical payments which the agreement provides shall be made by one of the parties for the maintenance of the other,

it may specify such term as it thinks fit as the term for which the payments or, as the case may be, the additional payments attributable to the increase are to be made under the altered agreement, except that the term must not extend beyond the limits in sub-paragraphs (2) and (3).

(2) The limits if the payments are not to be secured are—

(a) the death of either of the parties to the agreement, or
(b) the formation of a subsequent civil partnership or marriage by the party to whom the payments are to be made.

(3) The limits if the payments are to be secured are—

(a) the death of the party to whom the payments are to be made, or
(b) the formation of a subsequent civil partnership or marriage by that party.

(4) Sub-paragraph (5) applies if a court decides to make an order under paragraph 69 altering an agreement by—

(a) inserting provision for the making or securing by one of the parties to the agreement of periodical payments for the maintenance of a child of the family, or
(b) increasing the rate of the periodical payments which the agreement provides shall be made or secured by one of the parties for the maintenance of such a child.

(5) The court, in deciding the term for which under the agreement as altered by the order—

(a) the payments are to be made or secured for the benefit of the child, or
(b) the additional payments attributable to the increase are to be made or secured for the benefit of the child,

must apply paragraph 49(2) to (5) (age limits) as if the order in question were a periodical payments or secured periodical payments order in favour of the child.

Saving

72 Nothing in paragraphs 68 to 71 affects—

(a) any power of a court before which any proceedings between the parties to a maintenance agreement are brought under any other enactment (including a provision of this Schedule) to make an order containing financial arrangements, or
(b) any right of either party to apply for such an order in such proceedings.

Alteration of agreements by court after death of one party

73(1) This paragraph applies if—

(a) a maintenance agreement provides for the continuation of payments under the agreement after the death of one of the parties, and
(b) that party ('A') dies domiciled in England and Wales.

(2) Subject to sub-paragraph (4), the surviving party or A's personal representatives may apply to the High Court or a county court for an order under paragraph 69.

(3) If a maintenance agreement is altered by a court on an application made under sub-paragraph (2), the same consequences follow as if the alteration had been made immediately before the death by agreement between the parties and for valuable consideration.

(4) An application under this paragraph may not, without the leave of the High Court or a county court, be made after the end of 6 months from the date on which representation in regard to A's estate is first taken out.

(5) A's personal representatives are not liable for having distributed any part of A's estate after the end of the 6 month period on the ground that they ought to have taken into account the possibility that a court might allow an application by virtue of this paragraph to be made by the surviving party after that period.

(6) Sub-paragraph (5) does not affect any power to recover any part of the estate so distributed arising by virtue of the making of an order in pursuance of this paragraph.

(7) Paragraph 60(6) applies for the purposes of sub-paragraph (4) as it applies for the purposes of paragraph 60(3).

PART 14
MISCELLANEOUS AND SUPPLEMENTARY

Avoidance of transactions intended to prevent or reduce financial relief

74(1) This paragraph applies if proceedings for relief ('financial relief') are brought by one person ('A') against another ('B') under Part 1, 2, 4, 8, 9, or 11 (other than paragraph 60(2)), or paragraph 69.

(2) If the court is satisfied, on an application by A, that B is, with the intention of defeating A's claim for financial relief, about to—

    (a) make any disposition, or
    (b) transfer out of the jurisdiction or otherwise deal with any property,

it may make such order as it thinks fit for restraining B from doing so or otherwise for protecting the claim.

(3) If the court is satisfied, on an application by A, that—

    (a) B has, with the intention of defeating A's claim for financial relief, made a reviewable disposition, and
    (b) if the disposition were set aside, financial relief or different financial relief would be granted to A,

it make an order setting aside the disposition.

(4) If the court is satisfied, on an application by A in a case where an order has been obtained by A against B under any of the provisions mentioned in sub-paragraph (1), that B has, with the intention of defeating A's claim for financial relief, made a reviewable disposition, it may make an order setting aside the disposition.

(5) An application for the purposes of sub-paragraph (3) must be made in the proceedings for the financial relief in question.

(6) If the court makes an order under sub-paragraph (3) or (4) setting aside a disposition it must give such consequential directions as it thinks fit for giving effect to the order (including directions requiring the making of any payments or the disposal of any property).

75(1) Any reference in paragraph 74 to defeating A's claim for financial relief is to—

(a) preventing financial relief from being granted to A, or to A for the benefit of a child of the family,
(b) reducing the amount of any financial relief which might be so granted, or
(c) frustrating or impeding the enforcement of any order which might be or has been made at A's instance under any of those provisions.

(2) In paragraph 74 and this paragraph 'disposition'—

(a) does not include any provision contained in a will or codicil, but
(b) subject to paragraph (a), includes any conveyance, assurance or gift of property of any description (whether made by an instrument or otherwise).

(3) Any disposition made by B (whether before or after the commencement of the proceedings for financial relief) is a reviewable disposition for the purposes of paragraphs 74(3) and (4) unless it was made—

(a) for valuable consideration (other than formation of a civil partnership), and
(b) to a person who, at the time of the disposition, acted in relation to it in good faith and without notice of any intention on B's part to defeat A's claim for financial relief.

(4) If an application is made under paragraph 74 with respect to a disposition which took place less than 3 years before the date of the application or with respect to a disposition or other dealing with property which is about to take place and the court is satisfied—

(a) in a case falling within paragraph 74(2) or (3), that the disposition or other dealing would (apart from paragraph 74) have the consequence of defeating A's claim for financial relief, or
(b) in a case falling within paragraph 74(4), that the disposition has had the consequence of defeating A's claim for financial relief,

it is presumed, unless the contrary is shown, that the person who disposed of or is about to dispose of or deal with the property did so or, as the case may be, is about to do so, with the intention of defeating A's claim for financial relief.

Direction for settlement of instrument for securing payments or effecting property adjustment

76(1) This paragraph applies if the court decides to make—

(a) an order under Part 1 or 9 requiring any payments to be secured, or
(b) a property adjustment order.

(2) The court may direct that the matter be referred to one of the conveyancing counsel of the court for him to settle a proper instrument to be executed by all necessary parties.

(3) If the order referred to in sub-paragraph (1) is to be made in proceedings for a dissolution, nullity or separation order, the court may, if it thinks fit, defer the making of the dissolution, nullity or separation order until the instrument has been duly executed.

Settlement, etc, made in compliance with a property adjustment order may be avoided on bankruptcy of settlor

77 The fact that—

(a) a settlement, or
(b) a transfer of property,

had to be made in order to comply with a property adjustment order does not prevent the settlement or transfer from being a transaction in respect of which an order may be made under section 339 or 340 of the Insolvency Act 1986 (c 45) (transfers at an undervalue and preferences).

Payments, etc, under order made in favour of person suffering from mental disorder

78(1) This paragraph applies if—

    (a) the court makes an order under this Schedule requiring—
        (i)   payments (including a lump sum payment) to be made, or
        (ii) property to be transferred,

        to a civil partner, and
    (b) the court is satisfied that the person in whose favour the order is made is incapable, because of mental disorder, of managing and administering his or her property and affairs.

(2) 'Mental disorder' has the same meaning as in the Mental Health Act 1983 (c 20).

(3) Subject to any order, direction or authority made or given in relation to that person under Part 8 of the 1983 Act, the court may order the payments to be made or, as the case may be, the property to be transferred to such persons having charge of that person as the court may direct.

Appeals relating to pension sharing orders which have taken effect

79(1) Sub-paragraphs (2) and (3) apply if an appeal against a pension sharing order is begun on or after the day on which the order takes effect.

(2) If the pension sharing order relates to a person's rights under a pension arrangement, the appeal court may not set aside or vary the order if the person responsible for the pension arrangement has acted to his detriment in reliance on the order taking effect.

(3) If the pension sharing order relates to a person's shareable state scheme rights, the appeal court may not set aside or vary the order if the Secretary of State has acted to his detriment in reliance on the taking effect of the order.

(4) In determining for the purposes of sub-paragraph (2) or (3) whether a person has acted to his detriment in reliance on the taking effect of the order, the appeal court may disregard any detriment which in its opinion is insignificant.

(5) Where sub-paragraph (2) or (3) applies, the appeal court may make such further orders (including one or more pension sharing orders) as it thinks fit for the purpose of putting the parties in the position it considers appropriate.

(6) Paragraph 19 only applies to a pension sharing order under this paragraph if the decision of the appeal court can itself be the subject of an appeal.

(7) In sub-paragraph (2), the reference to the person responsible for the pension arrangement is to be read in accordance with paragraph 29(3).

Interpretation

80(1) References in this Schedule to—

    (a) periodical payments orders,
    (b) secured periodical payments orders, and
    (c) orders for the payment of a lump sum,

are references to such of the orders that may be made under Parts 1 and 9 (other than interim orders) as are relevant in the context of the reference in question.

(2) In this Schedule 'child of the family', in relation to two people who are civil partners of each other, means—

(a) a child of both of them, and
(b) any other child, other than a child placed with them as foster parents by a local authority or voluntary organisation, who has been treated by both the civil partners as a child of their family.

(3) In this Schedule 'the court' (except where the context otherwise requires) means—

(a) the High Court, or
(b) where a county court has jurisdiction by virtue of Part 5 of the Matrimonial and Family Proceedings Act 1984 (c 42), a county court.

(4) References in this Schedule to a subsequent civil partnership include a civil partnership which is by law void or voidable.

(5) References in this Schedule to a subsequent marriage include a marriage which is by law void or voidable.

SCHEDULE 6

SECTION 72(3)

FINANCIAL RELIEF IN MAGISTRATES' COURTS ETC

PART 1
FAILURE TO MAINTAIN ETC: FINANCIAL PROVISION

Circumstances in which orders under this Part may be made

1(1) On an application to it by one of the civil partners, a magistrates' court may make any one or more of the orders set out in paragraph 2 if it is satisfied that the other civil partner—

(a) has failed to provide reasonable maintenance for the applicant,
(b) has failed to provide, or to make a proper contribution towards, reasonable maintenance for any child of the family,
(c) has behaved in such a way that the applicant cannot reasonably be expected to live with the respondent, or
(d) has deserted the applicant.

(2) The power of the court under sub-paragraph (1) is subject to the following provisions of this Schedule.

The orders: periodical and secured periodical payments and lump sums

2(1) The orders are—

(a) an order that the respondent must make to the applicant such periodical payments for such term as may be specified;
(b) an order that the respondent must pay to the applicant such lump sum as may be specified;
(c) an order that the respondent must make—
    (i) to the applicant for the benefit of a child of the family to whom the application relates, or

(ii) to a child of the family to whom the application relates;

such periodical payments for such term as may be specified;

(d) an order that the respondent must pay such lump sum as may be specified—
   (i) to the applicant for the benefit of a child of the family to whom the application relates, or
   (ii) to such a child of the family to whom the application relates.

(2) The amount of a lump sum required to be paid under sub-paragraph (1)(b) or (d) must not exceed—

(a) £1,000, or
(b) such larger amount as the Lord Chancellor may from time to time by order fix for the purposes of this sub-paragraph.

(3) The power to make an order under sub-paragraph (2) is exercisable by statutory instrument which is subject to annulment in pursuance of a resolution of either House of Parliament.

(4) 'Specified' means specified in the order.

Particular provision that may be made by lump sum orders

3(1) An order under this Part for the payment of a lump sum may be made for the purpose of enabling any liability or expenses reasonably incurred in maintaining the applicant or any child of the family to whom the application relates before the making of the order to be met.

(2) Sub-paragraph (1) does not restrict the power to make the orders set out in paragraph 2(1)(b) and (d).

Matters to which court is to have regard in exercising its powers under this Part – general

4 If an application is made for an order under this Part, the court, in deciding—

(a) whether to exercise its powers under this Part, and
(b) if so, in what way,

must have regard to all the circumstances of the case, giving first consideration to the welfare while under 18 of any child of the family who has not reached 18.

Particular matters to be taken into account when exercising powers in relation to civil partners

5(1) This paragraph applies in relation to the exercise by the court of its power to make an order by virtue of paragraph 2(1)(a) or (b).

(2) The court must in particular have regard to—

(a) the income, earning capacity, property and other financial resources which each civil partner—
   (i) has, or
   (ii) is likely to have in the foreseeable future,

   including, in the case of earning capacity, any increase in that capacity which it would in the opinion of the court be reasonable to expect a civil partner in the civil partnership to take steps to acquire;
(b) the financial needs, obligations and responsibilities which each civil partner has or is likely to have in the foreseeable future;

(c) the standard of living enjoyed by the civil partners before the occurrence of the conduct which is alleged as the ground of the application;

(d) the age of each civil partner and the duration of the civil partnership;

(e) any physical or mental disability of either civil partner;

(f) the contributions which each civil partner has made or is likely in the foreseeable future to make to the welfare of the family, including any contribution by looking after the home or caring for the family;

(g) the conduct of each civil partner, if that conduct is such that it would in the opinion of the court be inequitable to disregard it.

Particular matters to be taken into account when exercising powers in relation to children

6(1) This paragraph applies in relation to the exercise by the court of its power to make an order by virtue of paragraph 2(1)(c) or (d).

(2) The court must in particular have regard to—

(a) the financial needs of the child;

(b) the income, earning capacity (if any), property and other financial resources of the child;

(c) any physical or mental disability of the child;

(d) the standard of living enjoyed by the family before the occurrence of the conduct which is alleged as the ground of the application;

(e) the way in which the child was being and in which the civil partners expected the child to be educated or trained;

(f) the considerations mentioned in relation to the civil partners in paragraph 5(2)(a) and (b).

(3) In relation to the exercise of its power to make an order in favour of a child of the family who is not the respondent's child, the court must also have regard to—

(a) whether the respondent has assumed any responsibility for the child's maintenance;

(b) if so, the extent to which, and the basis on which, the respondent assumed that responsibility and the length of time during which the respondent discharged that responsibility;

(c) whether in assuming and discharging that responsibility the respondent did so knowing that the child was not the respondent's child;

(d) the liability of any other person to maintain the child.

Reconciliation

7(1) If an application is made for an order under this Part—

(a) the court, before deciding whether to exercise its powers under this Part, must consider whether there is any possibility of reconciliation between the civil partners, and

(b) if at any stage of the proceedings on that application it appears to the court that there is a reasonable possibility of such a reconciliation, the court may adjourn the proceedings for such period as it thinks fit to enable attempts to be made to effect a reconciliation.

(2) If the court adjourns any proceedings under sub-paragraph (1), it may request—

(a) an officer of the Children and Family Court Advisory and Support Service, or

(b) any other person,

to attempt to effect a reconciliation between the civil partners.

(3) If any such request is made, the officer or other person—

(a) must report in writing to the court whether the attempt has been successful, but

(b) must not include in the report any other information.

Refusal of order in case more suitable for High Court

8(1) If on hearing an application for an order under this Part a magistrates' court is of the opinion that any of the matters in question between the civil partners would be more conveniently dealt with by the High Court, the magistrates' court must refuse to make any order on the application.

(2) No appeal lies from a refusal under sub-paragraph (1).

(3) But, in any proceedings in the High Court relating to or comprising the same subject matter as an application in respect of which a magistrates' court has refused to make any order, the High Court may order the application to be reheard and determined by a magistrates' court acting for the same local justice area as the court which refused to make any order.

PART 2
ORDERS FOR AGREED FINANCIAL PROVISION

Orders for payments which have been agreed by the parties

9(1) Either civil partner may apply to a magistrates' court for an order under this Part on the ground that that civil partner or the other civil partner has agreed to make such financial provision as may be specified in the application.

(2) On such an application, the court may order that the applicant or the respondent (as the case may be) is to make the financial provision specified in the application, if—

   (a) it is satisfied that the applicant or the respondent (as the case may be) has agreed to make that provision, and
   (b) it has no reason to think that it would be contrary to the interests of justice to do so.

(3) Sub-paragraph (2) is subject to paragraph 12.

Meaning of 'financial provision' and of references to specified financial provision

10(1) In this Part 'financial provision' means any one or more of the following—

   (a) the making of periodical payments by one civil partner to the other;
   (b) the payment of a lump sum by one civil partner to the other;
   (c) the making of periodical payments by one civil partner to a child of the family or to the other civil partner for the benefit of such a child;
   (d) the payment by one party of a lump sum to a child of the family or to the other civil partner for the benefit of such a child.

(2) Any reference in this Part to the financial provision specified in an application or specified by the court is a reference—

   (a) to the type of provision specified in the application or by the court,
   (b) to the amount so specified as the amount of any payment to be made under the application or order, and
   (c) in the case of periodical payments, to the term so specified as the term for which the payments are to be made.

Evidence to be produced where respondent not present etc

11(1) This paragraph applies if—

   (a) the respondent is not present, or

(b) is not represented by counsel or a solicitor,

at the hearing of an application for an order under this Part.

(2) The court must not make an order under this Part unless there is produced to it such evidence as may be prescribed by rules of court of—

(a) the consent of the respondent to the making of the order,

(b) the financial resources of the respondent, and

(c) if the financial provision specified in the application includes or consists of provision in respect of a child of the family to be made by the applicant to the respondent for the benefit of the child or to the child, the financial resources of the child.

Exercise of powers in relation to children

12(1) This paragraph applies if the financial provision specified in an application under this Part—

(a) includes, or

(b) consists of,

provision in respect of a child of the family.

(2) The court must not make an order under this Part unless it considers that the provision which the applicant or the respondent (as the case may be) has agreed to make in respect of the child provides for, or makes a proper contribution towards, the financial needs of the child.

Power to make alternative orders

13(1) This paragraph applies if on an application under this Part the court decides—

(a) that it would be contrary to the interests of justice to make an order for the making of the financial provision specified in the application, or

(b) that any financial provision which the applicant or the respondent (as the case may be) has agreed to make in respect of a child of the family does not provide for, or make a proper contribution towards, the financial needs of that child.

(2) If the court is of the opinion—

(a) that it would not be contrary to the interests of justice to make an order for the making of some other financial provision specified by the court, and

(b) that, in so far as that other financial provision contains any provision for a child of the family, it provides for, or makes a proper contribution towards, the financial needs of that child,

then, if both the civil partners agree, the court may order that the applicant or the respondent (as the case may be) is to make that other financial provision.

Relationship between this Part and Part 1

14(1) A civil partner who has applied for an order under Part 1 is not precluded at any time before the determination of the application from applying for an order under this Part.

(2) If—

(a) an order is made under this Part on the application of either civil partner, and

(b) either of them has also made an application for a Part 1 order,

the application for the Part 1 order is to be treated as if it had been withdrawn.

PART 3
ORDERS OF COURT WHERE CIVIL PARTNERS LIVING APART BY AGREEMENT

Powers of court where civil partners are living apart by agreement

15(1) If—

    (a) the civil partners have been living apart for a continuous period exceeding 3 months, neither civil partner having deserted the other, and

    (b) one of the civil partners has been making periodical payments for the benefit of the other civil partner or of a child of the family,

the other civil partner may apply to a magistrates' court for an order under this Part.

(2) An application made under sub-paragraph (1) must specify the total amount of the payments made by the respondent during the period of 3 months immediately preceding the date of the making of the application.

(3) If on an application for an order under this Part the court is satisfied that the respondent has made the payments specified in the application, the court may make one or both of the orders set out in paragraph 16.

(4) Sub-paragraph (3) is subject to the provisions of this Schedule.

The orders that may be made under this Part

16(1) The orders are—

    (a) an order that the respondent is to make to the applicant such periodical payments for such term as may be specified;

    (b) an order that the respondent is to make—

        (i)   to the applicant for the benefit of a child of the family to whom the application relates, or

        (ii) to a child of the family to whom the application relates.

    such periodical payments for such term as may be specified.

(2) 'Specified' means specified in the order.

Restrictions on orders under this Part

17 The court in the exercise of its powers under this Part must not require—

    (a) the respondent to make payments whose total amount during any period of 3 months exceeds the total amount paid by him for the benefit of—

        (i)   the applicant, or

        (ii) a child of the family,

    during the period of 3 months immediately preceding the date of the making of the application;

    (b) the respondent to make payments to or for the benefit of any person which exceed in amount the payments which the court considers that it would have required the respondent to make to or for the benefit of that person on an application under Part 1;

    (c) payments to be made to or for the benefit of a child of the family who is not the respondent's child, unless the court considers that it would have made an order in favour of that child on an application under Part 1.

Relationship with powers under Part 1

18(1) Sub-paragraph (2) applies if on an application under this Part the court considers that the orders which it has the power to make under this Part—

(a) would not provide reasonable maintenance for the applicant, or
(b) if the application relates to a child of the family, would not provide, or make a proper contribution towards, reasonable maintenance for that child.

(2) The court—

(a) must refuse to make an order under this Part, but
(b) may treat the application as if it were an application for an order under Part 1.

Matters to be taken into consideration

19 Paragraphs 4 to 6 apply in relation to an application for an order under this Part as they apply in relation to an application for an order under Part 1, subject to the modification that for the reference in paragraph 5(2)(c) to the occurrence of the conduct which is alleged as the ground of the application substitute a reference to the living apart of the civil partners.

PART 4
INTERIM ORDERS

Circumstances in which interim orders may be made

20(1) This paragraph applies if an application has been made for an order under Part 1, 2 or 3.

(2) A magistrates' court may make an interim order—

(a) at any time before making a final order on, or dismissing, the application, or
(b) on refusing (under paragraph 8) to make on order on the application.

(3) The High Court may make an interim order on ordering the application to be reheard by a magistrates' court (either after the refusal of an order under paragraph 8 or on an appeal made by virtue of paragraph 46).

(4) Not more than one interim order may be made with respect to an application for an order under Part 1, 2 or 3.

(5) Sub-paragraph (4) does not affect the power of a court to make an interim order on a further application under Part 1, 2 or 3.

Meaning of interim order

21(1) An interim order is an order requiring the respondent to make such periodical payments as the court thinks reasonable—

(a) to the applicant,
(b) to any child of the family who is under 18, or
(c) to the applicant for the benefit of such a child.

(2) In relation to an interim order in respect of an application for an order under Part 2 by the civil partner who has agreed to make the financial provision specified in the application, sub-paragraph (1) applies as if—

(a) the reference to the respondent were a reference to the applicant, and
(b) the references to the applicant were references to the respondent.

When interim order may start

22(1) An interim order may provide for payments to be made from such date as the court may specify, except that the date must not be earlier than the date of the making of the application for an order under Part 1, 2 or 3.

(2) Sub-paragraph (1) is subject to paragraph 27(7) and (8).

Payments which can be treated as having been paid on account

23(1) If an interim order made by the High Court on an appeal made by virtue of paragraph 46 provides for payments to be made from a date earlier than the date of the making of the order, the interim order may provide that payments made by the respondent under an order made by a magistrates' court are to be treated, to such extent and in such manner as may be provided by the interim order, as having been paid on account of any payment provided for by the interim order.

(2) In relation to an interim order in respect of an application for an order under Part 2 by the civil partner who has agreed to make the financial provision specified in the application, sub-paragraph (1) applies as if the reference to the respondent were a reference to the applicant.

When interim order ceases to have effect

24(1) Subject to sub-paragraphs (2) and (3), an interim order made on an application for an order under Part 1, 2 or 3 ceases to have effect on the earliest of the following dates—

(a) the date, if any, specified for the purpose in the interim order;
(b) the date on which the period of 3 months beginning with the date of the making of the interim order ends;
(c) the date on which a magistrates' court either makes a final order on, or dismisses, the application.

(2) If an interim order made under this Part would, but for this sub-paragraph, cease to have effect under sub-paragraph (1)(a) or (b)—

(a) the magistrates' court which made the order, or
(b) in the case of an interim order made by the High Court, the magistrates' court by which the application for an order under Part 1, 2 or 3 is to be reheard,

may by order provide that the interim order is to continue in force for a further period.

(3) An order continued in force under sub-paragraph (2) ceases to have effect on the earliest of the following dates—

(a) the date, if any, specified for the purpose in the order continuing it;
(b) the date on which ends the period of 3 months beginning with—
    (i) the date of the making of the order continuing it, or
    (ii) if more than one such order has been made with respect to the application, the date of the making of the first such order;
(c) the date on which the court either makes a final order on, or dismisses, the application.

Supplementary

25(1) An interim order made by the High Court under paragraph 20(3) on ordering an application to be reheard by a magistrates' court is to be treated for the purposes of—

(a) its enforcement, and
(b) Part 6 (variation etc of orders),

as if it were an order of that magistrates' court (and not of the High Court).

(2) No appeal lies from the making of or refusal to make, the variation of or refusal to vary, or the revocation of or refusal to revoke, an interim order.

PART 5
COMMENCEMENT AND DURATION OF ORDERS UNDER PARTS 1, 2 AND 3

Duration of periodical payments order for a civil partner

26(1) The court may specify in a periodical payments order made under paragraph 2(1)(a) or Part 3 in favour of a civil partner such term as it thinks fit, except that the term must not—

(a) begin before the date of the making of the application for the order, or
(b) extend beyond the death of either of the civil partners.

(2) If—

(a) a periodical payments order is made under paragraph 2(1)(a) or Part 3 in favour of one of the civil partners, and
(b) the civil partnership is subsequently dissolved or annulled but the order continues in force,

the periodical payments order ceases to have effect (regardless of anything in it) on the formation of a subsequent civil partnership or marriage by that civil partner, except in relation to any arrears due under the order on the date of that event.

Age limit on making orders for financial provision for children and duration of such orders

27(1) Subject to sub-paragraph (5), no order is to be made under paragraph 2(1)(c) or (d) or Part 3 in favour of a child who has reached 18.

(2) The term to be specified in a periodical payments order made under paragraph 2(1)(c) or Part 3 in favour of a child may begin with—

(a) the date of the making of an application for the order or a later date, or
(b) a date ascertained in accordance with sub-paragraph (7) or (8).

(3) The term to be specified in such an order—

(a) must not in the first instance extend beyond the date of the birthday of the child next following his reaching the upper limit of the compulsory school age unless the court considers that in the circumstances of the case the welfare of the child requires that it should extend to a later date, and
(b) must not in any event, subject to sub-paragraph (5), extend beyond the date of the child's 18th birthday.

(4) Sub-paragraph (3)(a) must be read with section 8 of the Education Act 1996 (c 56) (which applies to determine for the purposes of any enactment whether a person is of compulsory school age).

(5) Sub-paragraphs (1) and (3)(b) do not apply in the case of a child if it appears to the court that—

(a) the child is, or will be, or, if such an order were made without complying with either or both of those provisions, would be—
(i) receiving instruction at an educational establishment, or

    (ii) undergoing training for a trade, profession or vocation,

whether or not also the child is, will be or would be, in gainful employment, or

(b) there are special circumstances which justify the making of the order without complying with either or both of sub-paragraphs (1) and (3)(b).

(6) Any order made under paragraph 2(1)(c) or Part 3 in favour of a child, regardless of anything in the order, ceases to have effect on the death of the person liable to make payments under the order.

(7) If—

(a) a maintenance calculation ('current calculation') is in force with respect to a child, and
(b) an application is made for an order under paragraph 2(1)(c) or Part 3—
    (i)   in accordance with section 8 of the Child Support Act 1991 (c 48), and
    (ii) before the end of 6 months beginning with the making of the current calculation,

the term to be specified in any such order made on that application may be expressed to begin on, or at any time after, the earliest permitted date.

(8) 'The earliest permitted date' is whichever is the later of—

(a) the date 6 months before the application is made, or
(b) the date on which the current calculation took effect or, where successive maintenance calculations have been continuously in force with respect to a child, on which the first of those calculations took effect.

(9) If—

(a) a maintenance calculation ceases to have effect by or under any provision of the 1991 Act, and
(b) an application is made, before the end of 6 months beginning with the relevant date, for a periodical payments order under paragraph 2(1)(c) or Part 3 in favour of a child with respect to whom that maintenance calculation was in force immediately before it ceased to have effect,

the term to be specified in any such order, or in any interim order under Part 4, made on that application, may begin with the date on which that maintenance calculation ceased to have effect or any later date.

(10) 'The relevant date' means the date on which the maintenance calculation ceased to have effect.

(11) In this Schedule 'maintenance calculation' has the same meaning as it has in the 1991 Act by virtue of section 54 of the 1991 Act as read with any regulations in force under that section.

Application of paragraphs 26 and 27 to Part 2 orders

28(1) Subject to sub-paragraph (3), paragraph 26 applies in relation to an order under Part 2 which requires periodical payments to be made to a civil partner for his own benefit as it applies in relation to an order under paragraph 2(1)(a).

(2) Subject to sub-paragraph (3), paragraph 27 applies in relation to an order under Part 2 for the making of financial provision in respect of a child of the family as it applies in relation to an order under paragraph 2(1)(c) or (d).

(3) If—

(a) the court makes an order under Part 2 which contains provision for the making of periodical payments, and

(b) by virtue of paragraph 14, an application for an order under Part 1 is treated as if it had been withdrawn,

the term which may be specified under Part 2 as the term for which the payments are to be made may begin with the date of the making of the application for the order under Part 1 or any later date.

Effect on certain orders of parties living together

29(1) Sub-paragraph (2) applies if periodical payments are required to be made to a civil partner (whether for the civil partner's own benefit or for the benefit of a child of the family)—

(a) by an order made under Part 1 or 2, or
(b) by an interim order made under Part 4 (otherwise than on an application under Part 3).

(2) The order is enforceable even though—

(a) the civil partners are living with each other at the date of the making of the order, or
(b) if they are not living with each other at that date, they subsequently resume living with each other;

but the order ceases to have effect if after that date the parties continue to live with each other, or resume living with each other, for a continuous period exceeding 6 months.

(3) Sub-paragraph (4) applies if—

(a) an order is made under Part 1 or 2 which requires periodical payments to be made to a child of the family, or
(b) an interim order is made under Part 4 (otherwise than on an application under Part 3) which requires periodical payments to be made to a child of the family.

(4) Unless the court otherwise directs, the order continues to have effect and is enforceable even if—

(a) the civil partners are living with each other at the date of the making of the order, or
(b) if they are not living with each other at that date, they subsequently resume living with each other.

(5) An order made under Part 3, and any interim order made on an application for an order under that Part, ceases to have effect if the civil partners resume living with each other.

(6) If an order made under this Schedule ceases to have effect under—

(a) sub-paragraph (2) or (5), or
(b) a direction given under sub-paragraph (4),

a magistrates' court may, on an application made by either civil partner, make an order declaring that the order ceased to have effect from such date as the court may specify.

PART 6
VARIATION ETC OF ORDERS

Power to vary, revoke, suspend or revive order

30(1) If a magistrates' court has made an order for the making of periodical payments under Part 1, 2 or 3, the court may, on an application made under this Part—

(a) vary or revoke the order,

    (b) suspend any provision of it temporarily, or

    (c) revive any provision so suspended.

(2) If a magistrates' court has made an interim order under Part 4, the court may, on an application made under this Part—

    (a) vary or revoke the order,

    (b) suspend any provision of it temporarily, or

    (c) revive any provision so suspended,

except that it may not by virtue of this sub-paragraph extend the period for which the order is in force.

Powers to order lump sum on variation

31(1) If a magistrates' court has made an order under paragraph 2(1)(a) or (c) for the making of periodical payments, the court may, on an application made under this Part, make an order for the payment of a lump sum under paragraph 2(1)(b) or (d).

(2) If a magistrates' court has made an order under Part 2 for the making of periodical payments by a civil partner the court may, on an application made under this Part, make an order for the payment of a lump sum by that civil partner—

    (a) to the other civil partner, or

    (b) to a child of the family or to that other civil partner for the benefit of that child.

(3) Where the court has power by virtue of this paragraph to make an order for the payment of a lump sum—

    (a) the amount of the lump sum must not exceed the maximum amount that may at that time be required to be paid under Part 1, but

    (b) the court may make an order for the payment of a lump sum not exceeding that amount even if the person required to pay it was required to pay a lump sum by a previous order under this Schedule.

(4) Where—

    (a) the court has power by virtue of this paragraph to make an order for the payment of a lump sum, and

    (b) the respondent or the applicant (as the case may be) has agreed to pay a lump sum of an amount exceeding the maximum amount that may at that time be required to be paid under Part 1,

the court may, regardless of sub-paragraph (3), make an order for the payment of a lump sum of that amount.

Power to specify when order as varied is to take effect

32 An order made under this Part which varies an order for the making of periodical payments may provide that the payments as so varied are to be made from such date as the court may specify, except that, subject to paragraph 33, the date must not be earlier than the date of the making of the application under this Part.

33(1) If—

    (a) there is in force an order ('the order')—

    (i)   under paragraph 2(1)(c),

    (ii) under Part 2 making provision of a kind set out in paragraph 10(1)(c) (regardless of whether it makes provision of any other kind mentioned in paragraph 10(1)(c)),

    (iii) under paragraph 16(1)(b), or

    (iv) which is an interim order under Part 4 under which the payments are to be made to a child or to the applicant for the benefit of a child,

  (b) the order requires payments specified in it to be made to or for the benefit of more than one child without apportioning those payments between them,

  (c) a maintenance calculation ('the calculation') is made with respect to one or more, but not all, of the children with respect to whom those payments are to be made, and

  (d) an application is made, before the end of 6 months beginning with the date on which the calculation was made, for the variation or revocation of the order,

the court may, in exercise of its powers under this Part to vary or revoke the order, direct that the variation or revocation is to take effect from the date on which the calculation took effect or any later date.

(2) If—

  (a) an order ('the child order') of a kind prescribed for the purposes of section 10(1) of the Child Support Act 1991 is affected by a maintenance calculation,

  (b) on the date on which the child order became so affected there was in force an order ('the civil partner's order')—

    (i)   under paragraph 2(1)(a),

    (ii) under Part 2 making provision of a kind set out in paragraph 10(1)(a) (regardless of whether it makes provision of any other kind mentioned in paragraph 10(1)(a)),

    (iii) under paragraph 16(1)(a), or

    (iv) which is an interim order under Part 4 under which the payments are to be made to the applicant (otherwise than for the benefit of a child), and

  (c) an application is made, before the end of 6 months beginning with the date on which the maintenance calculation was made, for the civil partner's order to be varied or revoked,

the court may, in exercise of its powers under this Part to vary or revoke the civil partner's order, direct that the variation or revocation is to take effect from the date on which the child order became so affected or any later date.

(3) For the purposes of sub-paragraph (2), an order is affected if it ceases to have effect or is modified by or under section 10 of the 1991 Act.

Matters to which court is to have regard in exercising powers under this Part

34(1) In exercising the powers conferred by this Part the court must, so far as it appears to the court just to do so, give effect to any agreement which has been reached between the civil partners in relation to the application.

(2) If—

  (a) there is no such agreement, or

  (b) if the court decides not to give effect to the agreement,

the court must have regard to all the circumstances of the case, giving first consideration to the welfare while under 18 of any child of the family who has not reached 18.

(3) Those circumstances include any change in any of the matters—

  (a) to which the court was required to have regard when making the order to which the application relates, or

(b) in the case of an application for the variation or revocation of an order made under Part 2 or on an appeal made by virtue of paragraph 46, to which the court would have been required to have regard if that order had been made under Part 1.

Variation of orders for periodical payments: further provisions

35(1) The power of the court under paragraphs 30 to 34 to vary an order for the making of periodical payments includes power, if the court is satisfied that payment has not been made in accordance with the order, to exercise one of its powers under section 59(3)(a) to (d) of the Magistrates' Courts Act 1980 (c 43).

(2) Sub-paragraph (1) is subject to paragraph 37.

36(1) If—

(a) a magistrates' court has made an order under this Schedule for the making of periodical payments, and
(b) payments under the order are required to be made by any method of payment falling within section 59(6) of the 1980 Act (standing order, etc),

an application may be made under this sub-paragraph to the court for the order to be varied as mentioned in sub-paragraph (2).

(2) Subject to sub-paragraph (4), if an application is made under sub-paragraph (1), a justices' clerk, after—

(a) giving written notice (by post or otherwise) of the application to the respondent, and
(b) allowing the respondent, within the period of 14 days beginning with the date of the giving of that notice, an opportunity to make written representations,

may vary the order to provide that payments under the order are to be made to the designated officer for the court.

(3) The clerk may proceed with an application under sub-paragraph (1) even if the respondent has not received written notice of the application.

(4) If an application has been made under sub-paragraph (1), the clerk may, if he considers it inappropriate to exercise his power under sub-paragraph (2), refer the matter to the court which, subject to paragraph 37, may vary the order by exercising one of its powers under section 59(3)(a) to (d) of the 1980 Act.

37(1) Before varying the order by exercising one of its powers under section 59(3)(a) to (d) of the 1980 Act, the court must have regard to any representations made by the parties to the application.

(2) If the court does not propose to exercise its power under section 59(3)(c), (cc) or (d) of the 1980 Act, the court must, unless upon representations expressly made in that behalf by the person to whom payments under the order are required to be made it is satisfied that it is undesirable to do so, exercise its power under section 59(3)(b).

38(1) Section 59(4) of the 1980 Act (power of court to order that account be opened) applies for the purposes of paragraphs 35 and 36(4) as it applies for the purposes of section 59.

(2) None of the powers of the court, or of a justices' clerk, conferred by paragraphs 35 to 37 and sub-paragraph (1) is exercisable in relation to an order under this Schedule for the making of periodical payments which is not a qualifying maintenance order (within the meaning of section 59 of the 1980 Act).

Persons who may apply under this Part

39 An application under paragraph 30, 31 or 36 may be made—

(a) if it is for the variation or revocation of an order under Part 1, 2, 3 or 4 for periodical payments, by either civil partner, and

(b) if it is for the variation of an order under paragraph 2(1)(c) or Part 2 or 3 for periodical payments to or in respect of a child, also by the child himself, if he has reached 16.

Revival of orders for periodical payments

40(1) If an order made by a magistrates' court under this Schedule for the making of periodical payments to or in respect of a child (other than an interim order) ceases to have effect—

(a) on the date on which the child reaches 16, or

(b) at any time after that date but before or on the date on which he reaches 18,

the child may apply to the court which made the order for an order for its revival.

(2) If on such an application it appears to the court that—

(a) the child is, will be or (if an order were made under this sub-paragraph) would be receiving instruction at an educational establishment or undergoing training for a trade, profession or vocation, whether or not while in gainful employment, or

(b) there are special circumstances which justify the making of an order under this sub-paragraph,

the court may by order revive the order from such date as the court may specify, not being earlier than the date of the making of the application.

(3) Any order revived under this paragraph may be varied or revoked under paragraphs 30 to 34 in the same way as it could have been varied or revoked had it continued in being.

Variation of instalments of lump sum

41 If in the exercise of its powers under section 75 of the 1980 Act a magistrates' court orders that a lump sum required to be paid under this Schedule is to be paid by instalments, the court, on an application made by either the person liable to pay or the person entitled to receive that sum, may vary that order by varying—

(a) the number of instalments payable,

(b) the amount of any instalment payable, and

(c) the date on which any instalment becomes payable.

Supplementary provisions with respect to variation and revocation of orders

42 None of the following powers apply in relation to an order made under this Schedule—

(a) the powers of a magistrates' court to revoke, revive or vary an order for the periodical payment of money and the power of a justices' clerk to vary such an order under section 60 of the 1980 Act;

(b) the power of a magistrates' court to suspend or rescind certain other orders under section 63(2) of the 1980 Act.

PART 7
ARREARS AND REPAYMENTS

Enforcement etc of orders for payment of money

43 Section 32 of the Domestic Proceedings and Magistrates' Courts Act 1978 (c 22) applies in relation to orders under this Schedule as it applies in relation to orders under Part 1 of that Act.

Orders for repayment after cessation of order because of subsequent civil partnership etc

44(1) Sub-paragraphs (3) and (4) apply if—

    (a) an order made under paragraph 2(1)(a) or Part 2 or 3 has, under paragraph 26(2), ceased to have effect because of the formation of a subsequent civil partnership or marriage by the party ('R') in whose favour it was made, and

    (b) the person liable to make payments under the order ('P') made payments in accordance with it in respect of a relevant period in the mistaken belief that the order was still subsisting.

(2) 'Relevant period' means a period after the date of the formation of the subsequent civil partnership or marriage.

(3) No proceedings in respect of a cause of action arising out of the circumstances mentioned in sub-paragraph (1)(a) and (b) is maintainable by P (or P's personal representatives) against R (or R's personal representatives).

(4) But on an application made under this paragraph by P (or P's personal representatives) against R (or R's personal representatives) the court—

    (a) may order the respondent to pay to the applicant a sum equal to the amount of the payments made in respect of the relevant period, or

    (b) if it appears to the court that it would be unjust to make that order, may—

        (i) order the respondent to pay to the applicant such lesser sum as it thinks fit, or

        (ii) dismiss the application.

(5) An order under this paragraph for the payment of any sum may provide for the payment of that sum by instalments of such amount as may be specified in the order.

(6) An application under this paragraph—

    (a) may be made in proceedings in the High Court or a county court for leave to enforce, or the enforcement of, the payment of arrears under an order made under paragraph 2(1)(a) or Part 2 or 3, but

    (b) if not made in such proceedings, must be made to a county court,

and accordingly references in this paragraph to the court are references to the High Court or a county court, as the circumstances require.

(7) The jurisdiction conferred on a county court by this paragraph is exercisable by a county court even though, because of the amount claimed in an application under this paragraph, the jurisdiction would not but for this sub-paragraph be exercisable by a county court.

(8) Subject to sub-paragraph (9)—

    (a) the designated officer for a magistrates' court to whom any payments under an order made under paragraph 2(1)(a), or Part 2 or 3, are required to be made is not liable for any act done by him in pursuance of the order after the date on which that order ceased to have effect because of the formation of a subsequent civil partnership or marriage by the person entitled to payments under it, and

(b) the collecting officer under an attachment of earnings order made to secure payments under the order under paragraph 2(1)(a), or Part 2 or 3, is not liable for any act done by him after that date in accordance with any enactment or rule of court specifying how payments made to him in compliance with the attachment of earnings order are to be dealt with.

(9) Sub-paragraph (8) applies if (but only if) the act—

(a) was one which he would have been under a duty to do had the order under paragraph 2(1)(a) or Part 2 or 3 not ceased to have effect, and

(b) was done before notice in writing of the formation of the subsequent civil partnership or marriage was given to him by or on behalf of—

(i)   the person entitled to payments under the order,

(ii)   the person liable to make payments under it, or

(iii) the personal representatives of either of them.

(10) In this paragraph 'collecting officer', in relation to an attachment of earnings order, means—

(a) the officer of the High Court, or

(b) the officer designated by the Lord Chancellor,

to whom a person makes payments in compliance with the order.

PART 8
SUPPLEMENTARY

Restrictions on making of orders under this Schedule: welfare of children

45 If—

(a) an application is made by a civil partner for an order under Part 1, 2 or 3, and

(b) there is a child of the family who is under 18,

the court must not dismiss or make a final order on the application until it has decided whether to exercise any of its powers under the Children Act 1989 (c 41) with respect to the child.

Constitution of courts, powers of High Court and county court in relation to orders and appeals

46 The following provisions of the Domestic Proceedings and Magistrates' Courts Act 1978 (c 22) apply in relation to an order under this Schedule relating to a civil partnership as they apply in relation to an order under Part 1 of that Act relating to a marriage—

(a) section 28 (powers of the High Court and a county court in relation to certain orders),

(b) section 29 (appeals), and

(c) section 31 (constitution of courts).

Provisions as to jurisdiction and procedure

47(1) Subject to section 2 of the Family Law Act 1986 (c 55) and section 70 of the Magistrates' Courts Act 1980 (c 43) and any determination of the Lord Chancellor, a magistrates' court has jurisdiction to hear an application for an order under this Schedule if it acts in, or is authorised by the Lord Chancellor to act for, a local justice area in which either the applicant or the respondent ordinarily resides at the date of the making of the application.

(2) Any jurisdiction conferred on a magistrates' court by this Schedule is exercisable even if any party to the proceedings is not domiciled in England and Wales.

Meaning of 'child of the family'

48 In this Schedule 'child of the family', in relation to two people who are civil partners of each other, means—

(a) a child of both of them, and

(b) any other child, other than a child placed with them as foster parents by a local authority or voluntary organisation, who has been treated by both the civil partners as a child of their family.

SCHEDULE 7

SECTION 72(4)

FINANCIAL RELIEF IN ENGLAND AND WALES AFTER OVERSEAS DISSOLUTION ETC OF A CIVIL PARTNERSHIP

PART 1
FINANCIAL RELIEF

Part applies where civil partnership has been dissolved etc overseas

1(1) This Part of this Schedule applies where—

(a) a civil partnership has been dissolved or annulled, or the civil partners have been legally separated, by means of judicial or other proceedings in an overseas country, and

(b) the dissolution, annulment or legal separation is entitled to be recognised as valid in England and Wales.

(2) This Part of this Schedule applies even if the date of the dissolution, annulment or legal separation is earlier than the date on which the Part comes into force.

(3) In this Schedule 'overseas country' means a country or territory outside the British Islands.

(4) In this Part of this Schedule 'child of the family' means—

(a) a child of both of the civil partners, and

(b) any other child, other than a child placed with them as foster parents or by a local authority or voluntary organisation, who has been treated by both the civil partners as a child of their family.

Either civil partner may make application for financial relief

2(1) Either of the civil partners may make an application to the court for an order under paragraph 9 or 13.

(2) The rights conferred by sub-paragraph (1) are subject to—

(a) paragraph 3 (civil partner may not apply after forming subsequent civil partnership etc), and

(b) paragraph 4 (application may not be made until leave to make it has been granted).

(3) An application for an order under paragraph 9 or 13 must be made in a manner prescribed by rules of court.

No application after formation of subsequent civil partnership or marriage

3(1) If—

(a) the civil partnership has been dissolved or annulled, and

(b) after the dissolution or annulment, one of the civil partners forms a subsequent civil partnership or marriage,

that civil partner shall not be entitled to make, in relation to the civil partnership, an application for an order under paragraph 9 or 13.

(2) The reference in sub-paragraph (1) to the forming of a subsequent civil partnership or marriage includes a reference to the forming of a civil partnership or marriage which is by law void or voidable.

Leave of court required for making of application

4(1) No application for an order under paragraph 9 or 13 shall be made unless the leave of the court has been obtained in accordance with rules of court.

(2) The court shall not grant leave under this paragraph unless it considers that there is substantial ground for the making of an application for such an order.

(3) The court may grant leave under this paragraph notwithstanding that an order has been made by a court in a country outside England and Wales requiring the other civil partner to make any payment, or transfer any property, to the applicant or to a child of the family.

(4) Leave under this paragraph may be granted subject to such conditions as the court thinks fit.

Interim orders for maintenance

5(1) Where—

(a) leave is granted under paragraph 4, and

(b) it appears to the court that the civil partner who applied for leave, or any child of the family, is in immediate need of financial assistance,

the court may, subject to sub-paragraph (4), make an interim order for maintenance.

(2) An interim order for maintenance is one requiring the other civil partner to make—

(a) to the applicant, or

(b) to the child,

such periodical payments as the court thinks reasonable for such term as the court thinks reasonable.

(3) The term must be one—

(a) beginning not earlier than the date of the grant of leave, and

(b) ending with the date of the determination of the application made under the leave.

(4) If it appears to the court that the court will, in the event of an application being made under the leave, have jurisdiction to entertain the application only under paragraph 7(4), the court shall not make an interim order under this paragraph.

(5) An interim order under this paragraph may be made subject to such conditions as the court thinks fit.

Paragraphs 7 and 8 apply where application made for relief under paragraph 9 or 13

6 Paragraphs 7 and 8 apply where—

    (a) one of the civil partners has been granted leave under paragraph 4, and

    (b) acting under the leave, that civil partner makes an application for an order under paragraph 9 or 13.

Jurisdiction of the court

7(1) The court shall have jurisdiction to entertain the application only if one or more of the following jurisdictional requirements is satisfied.

(2) The first requirement is that either of the civil partners—

    (a) was domiciled in England and Wales on the date when the leave was applied for, or

    (b) was domiciled in England and Wales on the date when the dissolution, annulment or legal separation took effect in the overseas country in which it was obtained.

(3) The second is that either of the civil partners—

    (a) was habitually resident in England and Wales throughout the period of one year ending with the date when the leave was applied for, or

    (b) was habitually resident in England and Wales throughout the period of one year ending with the date on which the dissolution, annulment or legal separation took effect in the overseas country in which it was obtained.

(4) The third is that either or both of the civil partners had, at the date when the leave was applied for, a beneficial interest in possession in a dwelling-house situated in England or Wales which was at some time during the civil partnership a civil partnership home of the civil partners.

(5) In sub-paragraph (4) 'possession' includes receipt of, or the right to receive, rents and profits, but here 'rent' does not include mortgage interest.

Duty of the court to consider whether England and Wales is appropriate venue for application

8(1) Before deciding the application, the court must consider whether in all the circumstances of the case it would be appropriate for an order of the kind applied for to be made by a court in England and Wales.

(2) If the court is not satisfied that it would be appropriate, the court shall dismiss the application.

(3) The court must, in particular, have regard to the following matters—

    (a) the connection which the civil partners have with England and Wales;

    (b) the connection which the civil partners have with the country in which the civil partnership was dissolved or annulled or in which they were legally separated;

    (c) the connection which the civil partners have with any other country outside England and Wales;

    (d) any financial benefit which, in consequence of the dissolution, annulment or legal separation—

        (i) the applicant, or

        (ii) a child of the family,

    has received, or is likely to receive, by virtue of any agreement or the operation of the law of a country outside England and Wales;

(e) in a case where an order has been made by a court in a country outside England and Wales requiring the other civil partner—

    (i)   to make any payment, or

    (ii) to transfer any property,

for the benefit of the applicant or a child of the family, the financial relief given by the order and the extent to which the order has been complied with or is likely to be complied with;

(f) any right which the applicant has, or has had, to apply for financial relief from the other civil partner under the law of any country outside England and Wales and, if the applicant has omitted to exercise that right, the reason for that omission;

(g) the availability in England and Wales of any property in respect of which an order under this Schedule in favour of the applicant could be made;

(h) the extent to which any order made under this Schedule is likely to be enforceable;

(i) the length of time which has elapsed since the date of the dissolution, annulment or legal separation.

Orders for financial provision, property adjustment and pension sharing

9(1) Sub-paragraphs (2) and (3) apply where one of the civil partners has made an application for an order under this paragraph.

(2) If the civil partnership has been dissolved or annulled, the court may on the application make any one or more of the orders which it could make under Part 1, 2 or 4 of Schedule 5 (financial provision, property adjustment and pension sharing) if a dissolution order or nullity order had been made in respect of the civil partnership under Chapter 2 of Part 2 of this Act.

(3) If the civil partners have been legally separated, the court may on the application make any one or more of the orders which it could make under Part 1 or 2 of Schedule 5 (financial provision and property adjustment) if a separation order had been made in respect of the civil partners under Chapter 2 of Part 2 of this Act.

(4) Where under sub-paragraph (2) or (3) the court makes—

(a) an order which, if made under Schedule 5, would be a secured periodical payments order,

(b) an order for the payment of a lump sum, or

(c) an order which, if made under that Schedule, would be a property adjustment order,

then, on making that order or at any time afterwards, the court may make any order which it could make under Part 3 of Schedule 5 (sale of property) if the order under sub-paragraph (2) or (3) had been made under that Schedule.

(5) The powers under sub-paragraphs (2) to (4) are subject to paragraph 11.

Matters to which court is to have regard in exercising its powers under paragraph 9

10(1) The court, in deciding—

(a) whether to exercise its powers under paragraph 9, and

(b) if so, in what way,

must act in accordance with this paragraph.

(2) The court must have regard to all the circumstances of the case, giving first consideration to the welfare, while under 18, of any child of the family who has not reached 18.

(3) The court, in exercising its powers under paragraph 9 in relation to one of the civil partners—

(a) must in particular have regard to the matters mentioned in paragraph 21(2) of Schedule 5, and

(b) shall be under duties corresponding to those imposed by sub-paragraphs (2) and (3) of paragraph 23 of that Schedule (duties to consider termination of financial obligations) where it decides to exercise under paragraph 9 powers corresponding to the powers referred to in those sub-paragraphs.

(4) The matters to which the court is to have regard under sub-paragraph (3)(a), so far as relating to paragraph 21(2)(a) of Schedule 5 (regard to be had to financial resources), include—

(a) any benefits under a pension arrangement which either of the civil partners has or is likely to have, and

(b) any PPF compensation to which a civil partner is or is likely to be entitled,

(whether or not in the foreseeable future).

(5) The matters to which the court is to have regard under sub-paragraph (3)(a), so far as relating to paragraph 21(2)(h) of Schedule 5 (regard to be had to benefits that cease to be acquirable), include—

(a) any benefits under a pension arrangement which, because of the dissolution or annulment of the civil partnership, one of the civil partners will lose the chance of acquiring, and

(b) any PPF compensation which, because of the making of the dissolution or nullity order, a civil partner will lose the chance of acquiring entitlement to.

(6) The court, in exercising its powers under paragraph 9 in relation to a child of the family, must in particular have regard to the matters mentioned in paragraph 22(2) of Schedule 5.

(7) The court, in exercising its powers under paragraph 9 against a civil partner ('A') in favour of a child of the family who is not A's child, must also have regard to the matters mentioned in paragraph 22(3) of Schedule 5.

(8) Where an order has been made by a court outside England and Wales for—

(a) the making of payments, or

(b) the transfer of property,

by one of the civil partners, the court in considering in accordance with this paragraph the financial resources of the other civil partner, or of a child of the family, shall have regard to the extent to which that order has been complied with or is likely to be complied with.

(9) In this paragraph—

(a) 'pension arrangement' has the same meaning as in Part 4 of Schedule 5,

(b) references to benefits under a pension arrangement include any benefits by way of pension, whether under a pension arrangement or not, and

(c) 'PPF compensation' has the same meaning as in Part 7 of Schedule 5.

Restriction of powers under paragraph 9 where jurisdiction depends on civil partnership home in England or Wales

11(1) Sub-paragraphs (2) to (4) apply where the court has jurisdiction to entertain an application for an order under paragraph 9 only because a dwelling-house which was a civil partnership home of the civil partners is situated in England or Wales.

(2) The court may make under paragraph 9 any one or more of the following orders (but no other)—

(a) an order that one of the civil partners shall pay to the other a specified lump sum;

(b) an order that one of the civil partners shall pay to a child of the family, or to a specified person for the benefit of a child of the family, a specified lump sum;

(c) an order that one of the civil partners shall transfer that civil partner's interest in the dwelling-house, or a specified part of that interest—

    (i) to the other,

    (ii) to a child of the family, or

    (iii) to a specified person for the benefit of a child of the family;

(d) an order that a settlement of the interest of one of the civil partners in the dwelling-house, or a specified part of that interest, be made to the satisfaction of the court for the benefit of any one or more of—

    (i) the other civil partner and the children of the family, or

    (ii) either or any of them;

(e) an order varying for the benefit of any one or more of—

    (i) the civil partners and the children of the family, or

    (ii) either or any of them,

a relevant settlement so far as that settlement relates to an interest in the dwelling-house;

(f) an order extinguishing or reducing the interest of either of the civil partners under a relevant settlement so far as that interest is an interest in the dwelling-house;

(g) an order for the sale of the interest of one of the civil partners in the dwelling-house.

(3) Where under paragraph 9 the court makes just one order for the payment of a lump sum by one of the civil partners, the amount of the lump sum must not exceed the amount specified in sub-paragraph (5).

(4) Where under paragraph 9 the court makes two or more orders each of which is an order for the payment of a lump sum by the same civil partner, the total of the amounts of the lump sums must not exceed the amount specified in sub-paragraph (5).

(5) That amount is—

(a) if the interest of the paying civil partner in the dwelling-house is sold in pursuance of an order made under sub-paragraph (2)(g), the amount of the proceeds of sale of that interest after deducting from those proceeds any costs incurred in the sale of that interest;

(b) if that interest is not so sold, the amount which in the opinion of the court represents the value of that interest.

(6) Where the interest of one of the civil partners in the dwelling-house is held jointly or in common with any other person or persons—

(a) the reference in sub-paragraph (2)(g) to the interest of one of the civil partners shall be construed as including a reference to the interest of that other person, or the interest of those other persons, in the dwelling-house, and

(b) the reference in sub-paragraph (5)(a) to the amount of the proceeds of a sale ordered under sub-paragraph (2)(g) shall be construed as a reference to that part of those proceeds which is attributable to the interest of that civil partner in the dwelling-house.

(7) In sub-paragraph (2)—

'relevant settlement' means a settlement made, during the subsistence of the civil partnership or in anticipation of its formation, on the civil partners, including one made by will or codicil;

'specified' means specified in the order.

Consent orders under paragraph 9

12(1) On an application for a consent order under paragraph 9, the court may make an order in the terms agreed on the basis only of the prescribed information furnished with the application.

(2) Sub-paragraph (1) does not apply if the court has reason to think that there are other circumstances into which it ought to inquire.

(3) Sub-paragraph (1) applies to an application for a consent order varying or discharging an order under paragraph 9 as it applies to an application for such an order.

(4) Sub-paragraph (1) applies despite paragraph 10.

(5) In this paragraph—

'consent order', in relation to an application for an order, means an order in the terms applied for to which the respondent agrees;

'prescribed' means prescribed by rules of court.

Orders for transfers of tenancies of dwelling-houses

13(1) This paragraph applies if—

(a) an application is made by one of the civil partners for an order under this paragraph, and
(b) one of the civil partners is entitled, either in his own right or jointly with the other civil partner, to occupy a dwelling-house in England or Wales by virtue of a tenancy which is a relevant tenancy within the meaning of Schedule 7 to the Family Law Act 1996 (c 27).

(2) The court may make in relation to that dwelling-house any order which it could make under Part 2 of that Schedule (order transferring tenancy or switching statutory tenants) if it had power to make a property adjustment order under Part 2 of Schedule 5 to this Act with respect to the civil partnership.

(3) The provisions of paragraphs 10, 11 and 14(1) of Schedule 7 to the Family Law Act 1996 (payments by transferee, pre-transfer liabilities and right of landlord to be heard) apply in relation to any order under this paragraph as they apply to any order under Part 2 of that Schedule.

Application to orders under paragraphs 5 and 9 of provisions of Schedule 5

14(1) The following provisions of Schedule 5 apply in relation to an order made under paragraph 5 or 9 of this Schedule as they apply in relation to a like order made under that Schedule—

(a) paragraph 3(1) to (3) and (7) (lump sums);
(b) paragraph 11(2) to (4), 12(2), 13 and 14 (orders for sale);
(c) paragraphs 17, 18 and 19(2) and (3) (pension sharing);
(d) paragraphs 25 and 26 (orders under Part 1 relating to pensions);
(e) paragraphs 31 to 37 (orders under Part 1 relating to pensions where Board has assumed responsibility for scheme);
(f) paragraphs 47(1) to (4) and (6) and 49 (duration of orders);
(g) paragraphs 50 to 54 and 57 to 62, except paragraph 50(1)(g) (variation etc of orders);
(h) paragraphs 63 to 65 (arrears and repayments);
(i) paragraphs 76 to 79 (drafting of instruments, bankruptcy, mental disorder, and pension-sharing appeals).

(2) Sub-paragraph (1)(d) does not apply where the court has jurisdiction to entertain an application for an order under paragraph 9 only because a dwelling-house which was a civil partnership home of the civil partners is situated in England or Wales.

(3) Paragraph 27 of Schedule 5 (change of pension arrangement under which rights are shared) applies in relation to an order made under paragraph 9 of this Schedule by virtue of sub-paragraph (1)(d) above as it applies to an order made under Part 1 of Schedule 5 by virtue of paragraph 25 or 26 of that Schedule.

(4) The Lord Chancellor may by regulations make for the purposes of this Schedule provision corresponding to any provision which may be made by him under paragraph 28(1) to (3) of Schedule 5 (supplementary provision about orders relating to pensions under Part 1 of that Schedule).

(5) The power to make regulations under this paragraph is exercisable by statutory instrument which is subject to annulment in pursuance of a resolution of either House of Parliament.

Avoidance of transactions designed to defeat claims under paragraphs 5 and 9

15(1) Sub-paragraphs (2) and (3) apply where one of the civil partners ('A') is granted leave under paragraph 4 to make an application for an order under paragraph 9.

(2) If the court is satisfied, on application by A, that the other civil partner ('B') is, with the intention of defeating a claim by A, about to—

(a) make any disposition, or
(b) transfer out of the jurisdiction, or otherwise deal with, any property,

it may make such order as it thinks fit for restraining B from doing so or otherwise for protecting the claim.

(3) If the court is satisfied, on application by A—

(a) that the other civil partner ('B') has, with the intention of defeating a claim by A, made a reviewable disposition, and
(b) that, if the disposition were set aside—
    (i) financial relief under paragraph 5 or 9, or
    (ii) different financial relief under paragraph 5 or 9,

    would be granted to A,

it may make an order setting aside the disposition.

(4) If—

(a) an order under paragraph 5 or 9 has been made by the court at the instance of one of the civil partners ('A'), and
(b) the court is satisfied, on application by A, that the other civil partner ('B') has, with the intention of defeating a claim by A, made a reviewable disposition,

the court may make an order setting aside the disposition.

(5) Where the court has jurisdiction to entertain an application for an order under paragraph 9 only under paragraph 7(4), it shall not make any order under sub-paragraph (2), (3) or (4) in respect of any property other than the dwelling-house concerned.

(6) Where the court makes an order under sub-paragraph (3) or (4) setting aside a disposition, it shall give such consequential directions as it thinks fit for giving effect to the order (including directions requiring the making of any payments or the disposal of any property).

(7) For the purposes of sub-paragraphs (3) and (4), but subject to sub-paragraph (8), any disposition made by B is a 'reviewable disposition' (whether made before or after the commencement of A's application under that sub-paragraph).

(8) A disposition made by B is not a reviewable disposition for those purposes if made for valuable consideration (other than formation of a civil partnership) to a person who, at the time of the disposition, acted in relation to it in good faith and without notice of any intention on the part of B to defeat A's claim.

(9) A reference in this paragraph to defeating a claim by one of the civil partners is a reference to—

    (a) preventing financial relief being granted, or reducing the amount of financial relief which might be granted, under paragraph 5 or 9 at the instance of that civil partner, or

    (b) frustrating or impeding the enforcement of any order which might be, or has been, made under paragraph 5 or 9 at the instance of that civil partner.

Presumptions for the purposes of paragraph 15

16(1) Sub-paragraph (3) applies where—

    (a) an application is made under paragraph 15(2) or (3) by one of the civil partners with respect to—

        (i) a disposition which took place less than 3 years before the date of the application, or

        (ii) a disposition or other dealing with property which is about to take place, and

    (b) the court is satisfied that the disposition or other dealing would (apart from paragraph 15 and this paragraph of this Schedule) have the consequence of defeating a claim by the applicant.

(2) Sub-paragraph (3) also applies where—

    (a) an application is made under paragraph 15(4) by one of the civil partners with respect to a disposition which took place less than 3 years before the date of the application, and

    (b) the court is satisfied that the disposition has had the consequence of defeating a claim by the applicant.

(3) It shall be presumed, unless the contrary is shown, that the person who—

    (a) disposed of, or

    (b) is about to dispose of or deal with the property,

did so, or (as the case may be) is about to do so, with the intention of defeating the applicant's claim.

(4) A reference in this paragraph to defeating a claim by one of the civil partners has the meaning given by paragraph 15(9).

PART 2
STEPS TO PREVENT AVOIDANCE PRIOR TO APPLICATION FOR LEAVE UNDER PARAGRAPH 4

Prevention of transactions intended to defeat prospective claims under paragraphs 5 and 9

17(1) If it appears to the court, on application by one of the persons ('A') who formed a civil partnership—

    (a) that the civil partnership has been dissolved or annulled, or that the civil partners have been legally separated, by means of judicial or other proceedings in an overseas country,

    (b) that A intends to apply for leave to make an application for an order under paragraph 9 as soon as he or she has been habitually resident in England and Wales for the period of one year, and

(c) that the other civil partner ('B') is, with the intention of defeating A's claim, about to—

    (i)   make any disposition, or

    (ii) transfer out of the jurisdiction, or otherwise deal with, any property,

the court may make such order as it thinks fit for restraining B from taking such action as is mentioned in paragraph (c).

(2) Sub-paragraph (1) applies even if the date of the dissolution, annulment or legal separation is earlier than the date on which that sub-paragraph comes into force.

(3) Sub-paragraph (4) applies where—

  (a) an application is made under sub-paragraph (1) with respect to—

    (i)   a disposition which took place less than 3 years before the date of the application, or

    (ii) a disposition or other dealing with property which is about to take place, and

  (b) the court is satisfied that the disposition or other dealing would (apart from this paragraph of this Schedule) have the consequence of defeating a claim by the applicant.

(4) It shall be presumed, unless the contrary is shown, that the person who—

  (a) disposed of, or

  (b) is about to dispose of or deal with the property,

did so, or (as the case may be) is about to do so, with the intention of defeating the applicant's claim.

(5) A reference in this paragraph to defeating a person's claim is a reference to preventing financial relief being granted, or reducing the amount of financial relief which might be granted, under paragraph 5 or 9 at the instance of that person.

PART 3
SUPPLEMENTARY

Paragraphs 15 to 17: meaning of 'disposition' and saving

18(1) In paragraphs 15 to 17 'disposition' does not include any provision contained in a will or codicil but, with that exception, includes any conveyance, assurance or gift of property of any description, whether made by an instrument or otherwise.

(2) The provisions of paragraphs 15 to 17 are without prejudice to any power of the High Court to grant injunctions under section 37 of the Supreme Court Act 1981 (c 54).

Interpretation of Schedule

19 In this Schedule—

  'the court' means the High Court or, where a county court has jurisdiction by virtue of Part 5 of the Matrimonial and Family Proceedings Act 1984 (c 42), a county court;

  'dwelling-house' includes—

    (a) any building, or part of a building, which is occupied as a dwelling, and

    (b) any yard, garden, garage or outhouse belonging to, and occupied with, the dwelling-house;

  'overseas country' has the meaning given by paragraph 1(3).

SCHEDULE 8

SECTION 81

HOUSING AND TENANCIES

Law of Property Act 1925 (c 20)

1(1) Amend section 149(6) (which includes provision for a lease determinable on marriage of the lessee to take effect as a lease for 90 years determinable by notice after the lessee's marriage) as follows.

(2) After 'or on the marriage of the lessee,' insert 'or on the formation of a civil partnership between the lessee and another person,'.

(3) For 'after the death or marriage (as the case may be) of the original lessee, or of the survivor of the original lessees,' substitute 'after (as the case may be) the death or marriage of, or the formation of a civil partnership by, the original lessee or the survivor of the original lessees,'.

Landlord and Tenant Act 1954 (c 56)

2 In paragraph 1(e) of Schedule 3 (grounds for possession: premises required as residence for landlord or family member), for the words from 'as a residence' to 'spouse, and' substitute

'as a residence for—
  (i)   himself,

  (ii) any son or daughter of his over eighteen years of age,

  (iii) his father or mother, or

  (iv) the father, or mother, of his spouse or civil partner,

and'.

Leasehold Reform Act 1967 (c 88)

3 In section 1(1ZC)(c) (which refers to section 149(6) of the Law of Property Act 1925), after 'terminable after a death or marriage' insert 'or the formation of a civil partnership'.

4 In section 1B (which refers to a tenancy granted so as to become terminable by notice after a death or marriage), for 'a death or marriage' substitute 'a death, a marriage or the formation of a civil partnership'.

5(1) Amend section 3(1) (meaning of 'long tenancy') as follows.

(2) In the words describing section 149(6) of the Law of Property Act 1925, after 'terminable after a death or marriage' insert 'or the formation of a civil partnership'.

(3) In the proviso (exclusion of certain tenancies terminable by notice after death or marriage)—

  (a) for 'a death or marriage' substitute 'a death, a marriage or the formation of a civil partnership', and
  (b) in paragraph (a), after 'marriage of' insert ', or the formation of a civil partnership by,'.

6(1) Amend section 7 (rights of members of family succeeding to tenancy on death) as follows.

(2) In subsection (7) ('family member'), for 'wife or husband' (in each place) substitute 'spouse or civil partner'.

(3) In subsection (8) (surviving spouse's rights on intestacy)—

    (a) in paragraph (a), for 'wife or husband' substitute 'spouse or civil partner', and
    (b) in paragraph (b), for 'husband or wife' substitute 'spouse or civil partner'.

7 In section 18(3) (members of landlord's family whose residential rights exclude enfranchisement or extension), for 'wife or husband' (in each place) substitute 'spouse or civil partner'.

Caravan Sites Act 1968 (c 52)

8 In section 3(2) ('occupier' includes surviving spouse of deceased occupier), for 'or widower' (in each place) substitute ', widower or surviving civil partner'.

Rent (Agriculture) Act 1976 (c 80)

9(1) Amend section 3 (protected occupiers by succession) as follows.

(2) For subsection (2) (succession by surviving spouse) substitute—

    '(2) Where the original occupier was a person who died leaving a surviving partner who was residing in the dwelling-house immediately before the original occupier's death then, after the original occupier's death, if the surviving partner has, in relation to the dwelling-house, a relevant licence or tenancy, the surviving partner shall be a protected occupier of the dwelling-house.'

    (3) In subsection (3) (succession by other family members)—

        (a) for 'surviving spouse' substitute 'surviving partner',
        (b) for 'his' (in each place) substitute 'the original occupier's', and
        (c) for 'him' substitute 'the original occupier'.

    (4) After subsection (3) insert—

    '(3A) In subsections (2) and (3) above "surviving partner" means surviving spouse or surviving civil partner.'

10(1) Amend section 4 (statutory tenants and tenancies) as follows.

(2) For subsection (3) (surviving spouse's statutory tenancy) substitute—

    '(3) If the original occupier was a person who died leaving a surviving partner who was residing in the dwelling-house immediately before the original occupier's death then, after the original occupier's death, unless the surviving partner is a protected occupier of the dwelling-house by virtue of section 3(2) above, the surviving partner shall be the statutory tenant if and so long as he occupies the dwelling-house as his residence.'

(3) In subsection (4) (statutory tenancy for other family members)—

    (a) for 'surviving spouse' substitute 'surviving partner',
    (b) for 'his' (in each place) substitute 'the original occupier's', and
    (c) for 'him' substitute 'the original occupier'.

(4) For subsection (5A) (references to original occupier's spouse include person living with occupier as his or her wife or husband) substitute—

    '(5ZA) In subsections (3) and (4) above "surviving partner" means surviving spouse or surviving civil partner.

    (5A) For the purposes of subsection (3) above—

    (a) a person who was living with the original occupier as his or her husband or wife shall be treated as the spouse of the original occupier, and

    (b) a person who was living with the original occupier as if they were civil partners shall be treated as the civil partner of the original occupier,

and, subject to subsection (5B) below, "surviving spouse" and "surviving civil partner" in subsection (5ZA) above shall be construed accordingly.'

11 In section 31(3)(c) (power of Secretary of State and National Assembly for Wales to require information about occupiers of housing accommodation associated with agricultural or forestry land), after 'who has been married to' insert ', or has been the civil partner of,'.

12 In paragraph 1 of Case 9 in Part 1 of Schedule 4 (discretionary grounds for possession: dwelling required as residence for member of landlord's family), after 'husband' (in each place) insert 'or civil partner'.

Rent Act 1977 (c 42)

13(1) In Part 1 of Schedule 1 (statutory tenants by succession), amend paragraph 2 (succession by surviving spouse) as follows.

(2) In sub-paragraph (1), after 'surviving spouse' insert ', or surviving civil partner,'.

(3) For sub-paragraph (2) substitute—

    '(2) For the purposes of this paragraph—

        (a) a person who was living with the original tenant as his or her wife or husband shall be treated as the spouse of the original tenant, and

        (b) a person who was living with the original tenant as if they were civil partners shall be treated as the civil partner of the original tenant.'

(4) In sub-paragraph (3), for the words after 'the county court' substitute 'shall for the purposes of this paragraph be treated (according to whether that one of them is of the opposite sex to, or of the same sex as, the original tenant) as the surviving spouse or the surviving civil partner.'

14 In Schedule 15 (grounds for possession), in Case 9 in Part 1 (dwelling required as residence for landlord or member of his family), for 'wife or husband' substitute 'spouse or civil partner'.

Protection from Eviction Act 1977 (c 43)

15 In section 4(2)(b) (special provisions for agricultural employees: 'occupier' includes surviving spouse of former tenant), for 'widow or widower' (in each place) substitute 'surviving spouse or surviving civil partner'.

Housing Act 1980 (c 51)

16 In section 54(2) (protected shorthold tenancy etc may not be assigned except in pursuance of certain orders), after paragraph (c) insert

    ', or

        (d) Part 2 of Schedule 5, or paragraph 9(2) or (3) of Schedule 7, to the Civil Partnership Act 2004 (property adjustment orders in connection with civil partnership proceedings or after overseas dissolution of civil partnership, etc).'

17 In section 76(3) (which amends provisions of the Rent (Agriculture) Act 1976 replaced by this Schedule), for 'sections 3(2) and (3)(a) and 4(3) and (4)(a)' substitute 'sections 3(3)(a) and 4(4)(a)'.

Housing Act 1985 (c 68)

18 In sections 39(2)(b) and 160(2)(b) (meaning of 'qualifying person' in definition of 'exempted disposal'), after 'the spouse or a former spouse' insert ', or the civil partner or a former civil partner,'.

19 In section 39(3) (disposals exempt if in pursuance of certain orders), after paragraph (d) insert

', or
> (e) Part 2 or 3 of Schedule 5, or paragraph 9 of Schedule 7, to the Civil Partnership Act 2004 (property adjustment orders, or orders for the sale of property, in connection with civil partnership proceedings or after overseas dissolution of civil partnership, etc).'

20 In section 87(a) (entitlement of tenant's spouse to succeed to secure tenancy), after 'spouse' insert 'or civil partner'.

21(1) Amend section 88 (cases where secure tenant is a successor) as follows.

(2) In subsection (1)(d), for '(2) and (3)' substitute '(2) to (3)'.

(3) After subsection (2) insert—

> '(2A) A tenant to whom the tenancy was assigned in pursuance of an order under Part 2 of Schedule 5, or paragraph 9(2) or (3) of Schedule 7, to the Civil Partnership Act 2004 (property adjustment orders in connection with civil partnership proceedings or after overseas dissolution of civil partnership, etc) is a successor only if the other civil partner was a successor.'

22(1) Amend section 89 (succession to periodic secured tenancy) as follows.

(2) In subsection (2)(a) (tenant's spouse is preferred successor), after 'spouse' insert 'or civil partner'.

(3) In subsection (3)(a), after 'parents)' in sub-paragraph (iii) insert

', or
> (iv) Part 2 of Schedule 5, or paragraph 9(2) or (3) of Schedule 7, to the Civil Partnership Act 2004 (property adjustment orders in connection with civil partnership proceedings or after overseas dissolution of civil partnership, etc)'.

23 In section 90(3)(a) (secure tenancy for term certain does not cease to be secure tenancy if vested under certain orders), after sub-paragraph (iii) insert—

> '(iv) Part 2 of Schedule 5, or paragraph 9(2) or (3) of Schedule 7, to the Civil Partnership Act 2004 (property adjustment orders in connection with civil partnership proceedings or after overseas dissolution of civil partnership, etc), or'.

24 In section 91(3)(b) (assignments not prohibited if in pursuance of certain orders), after 'parents)' in sub-paragraph (iii) insert

', or
> (iv) Part 2 of Schedule 5, or paragraph 9(2) or (3) of Schedule 7, to the Civil Partnership Act 2004 (property adjustment orders in connection with civil partnership proceedings or after overseas dissolution of civil partnership, etc)'.

25 In section 99B(2)(e) (subsection applies to assignees in pursuance of certain orders), after 'parents)' in sub-paragraph (iii) insert

', or

(iv) Part 2 of Schedule 5, or paragraph 9(2) or (3) of Schedule 7, to the Civil Partnership Act 2004 (property adjustment orders in connection with civil partnership proceedings or after overseas dissolution of civil partnership, etc)'.

26 In section 101(3)(c) (assignees in pursuance of certain orders are qualifying successors), after 'parents)' in sub-paragraph (iii) insert

', or

(iv) Part 2 of Schedule 5, or paragraph 9(2) or (3) of Schedule 7, to the Civil Partnership Act 2004 (property adjustment orders in connection with civil partnership proceedings or after overseas dissolution of civil partnership, etc)'.

27(1) Amend sections 113 and 186 (meaning of 'member of a person's family' in Parts 3 and 4) as follows.

(2) In subsection (1)(a)—

(a) after 'spouse' insert 'or civil partner', and
(b) after 'live together as husband and wife' insert 'or as if they were civil partners'.

(3) In subsection (2)(a), after 'a relationship by marriage' insert 'or civil partnership'.

28 In section 123(2)(a) (family members with whom right to buy may be exercised), after 'is his spouse' insert ', is his civil partner'.

29 In section 130(3) (persons whose receipt of discount results in reduction of subsequent discount)—

(a) in paragraph (b), after 'spouse' insert ', or civil partner,' and
(b) in paragraph (c), after 'deceased spouse' insert ', or deceased civil partner,'.

30 In section 160(3) (right to buy: disposals in pursuance of certain orders are exempted), after paragraph (d) insert

', or

(e) Part 2 or 3 of Schedule 5, or paragraph 9 of Schedule 7, to the Civil Partnership Act 2004 (property adjustment orders, or orders for the sale of property, in connection with civil partnership proceedings or after overseas dissolution of civil partnership, etc).'

31 In section 171B(4)(b) (persons who become tenants in pursuance of certain orders are qualifying successors), after sub-paragraph (iv) insert

'or

(v) an order under Part 2 of Schedule 5, or a property adjustment order under paragraph 9(2) or (3) of Schedule 7, to the Civil Partnership Act 2004 (property adjustment orders in connection with civil partnership proceedings or after overseas dissolution of civil partnership, etc),'.

32 In section 554(2A) (grant by registered social landlords to former owner-occupier of defective dwelling), for paragraph (b) substitute—

'(b) is the spouse or civil partner, or a former spouse or former civil partner, or the surviving spouse or surviving civil partner, of a person falling within paragraph (a); or'.

33 In Part 1 of Schedule 2 (secure tenancies: grounds for possession if court considers possession reasonable), in ground 2A (violence by member of a couple)—

(a) for 'a married couple or' substitute 'a married couple, a couple who are civil partners of each other,' and

(b) after 'as husband or wife' insert 'or a couple living together as if they were civil partners'.

34 In paragraphs 2, 5 and 5A of Schedule 4 (qualifying period for right to buy and discount)—

(a) after 'deceased spouse' in paragraph (c) of each of those paragraphs insert ', or deceased civil partner,' and

(b) after 'spouse' (in each other place) insert 'or civil partner'.

35(1) Amend Schedule 6A (redemption of landlord's share) as follows.

(2) In paragraph 1(2)(a) (meaning of 'excluded disposal'), after 'spouse' insert 'or civil partner'.

(3) In paragraph 1(2)(c) (disposals excluded if in pursuance of certain orders), after sub-paragraph (iv) insert

'or

 (v) Part 2 or 3 of Schedule 5, or paragraph 9 of Schedule 7, to the Civil Partnership Act 2004 (property adjustment orders, or orders for the sale of property, in connection with civil partnership proceedings or after overseas dissolution of civil partnership, etc),'.

(4) In paragraphs 4(3)(b) and 12(1), (2) and (3)(d), for 'qualifying spouse' substitute 'qualifying partner'.

(5) In paragraph 12(2) (which will define 'qualifying partner'), for paragraph (c) and the words after that paragraph substitute—

'(c) he—
 (i) is the spouse, the civil partner, a former spouse, a former civil partner, the surviving spouse, the surviving civil partner, a surviving former spouse or a surviving former civil partner of the person who immediately before that time was entitled to the interest to which this paragraph applies or, as the case may be, the last remaining such interest, or
 (ii) is the surviving spouse, the surviving civil partner, a surviving former spouse or a surviving former civil partner of a person who immediately before his death was entitled to such an interest.'

Agricultural Holdings Act 1986 (c 5)

36(1) In sections 35(2) and 49(3) (interpretation respectively of sections 36 to 48, and sections 49 to 58, etc), amend the definition of 'close relative' as follows.

(2) In paragraph (a), for 'or husband' substitute ', husband or civil partner'.

(3) In paragraph (d), after 'marriage' (in each place) insert 'or civil partnership'.

37 In section 36 (eligible person may apply for new tenancy on death of tenant), after subsection (4) insert—

'(4A) In the case of the deceased's civil partner the reference in subsection (3)(a) above to the relative's agricultural work shall be read as a reference to agricultural work carried out by either the civil partner or the deceased (or both of them).'

38 In section 50 (eligible person may apply for new tenancy on retirement of tenant), after subsection (3) insert—

'(3A) In the case of the civil partner of the retiring tenant the reference in subsection (2)(a) above to the relative's agricultural work shall be read as a reference to agricultural work carried out by either the civil partner or the retiring tenant (or both of them).'

39(1) Amend Schedule 6 (eligibility to apply for new tenancy under Part 4) as follows.

(2) In paragraph 1(2) (control of body corporate by deceased's close relative)—

(a) after 'or his spouse' insert 'or his civil partner', and
(b) after 'together' insert 'or he and his civil partner together'.

(3) In paragraph 1 (preliminary), after sub-paragraph (3) insert—

'(4) Any reference in this Schedule to the civil partner of a close relative of the deceased does not apply in relation to any time when the relative's civil partnership is subject to—

(a) a separation order under Chapter 2 of Part 2 of the Civil Partnership Act 2004, or
(b) a dissolution order, nullity order or presumption of death order that is a conditional order under that Chapter.'

(4) In paragraph 6(2) (no disregard of occupation by relative under tenancy granted by his spouse), after 'spouse' insert 'or civil partner'.

(5) In paragraph 9(1)(a) (occupation by spouse of relative treated as occupation by relative), after 'spouse' insert ', or civil partner,'.

(6) In paragraph 9(2) (cases involving joint occupation by spouse, or controlled body, and another)—

(a) for the words from 'joint occupation of land' to 'sub-paragraphs' substitute

'joint occupation of land by—
(a) his spouse or civil partner or a body corporate, and
(b) any other person or persons,

sub-paragraphs',

and
(b) after 'spouse' (in the second place) insert 'or civil partner,'.

(7) In paragraph 10(3)(a) (meaning of 'connected person'), after 'spouse' insert 'or civil partner'.

(8) In the italic heading before each of paragraphs 9 and 10, after 'spouse' insert ', civil partner'.

Landlord and Tenant Act 1987 (c 31)

40(1) Amend section 4 (meaning of 'relevant disposal' for purposes of tenants' rights of first refusal) as follows.

(2) In subsection (2)(c) (disposals in pursuance of certain orders not relevant disposals), after sub-paragraph (vi) insert—

'(vii) Part 2 of Schedule 5, or paragraph 9(2) or (3) of Schedule 7, to the Civil Partnership Act 2004 (property adjustment orders in connection with civil partnership proceedings or after overseas dissolution of a civil partnership, etc), or

(viii) Part 3 of Schedule 5, or paragraph 9(4) of Schedule 7, to the Civil Partnership Act 2004 (orders for the sale of property in connection with civil partnership proceedings or after overseas dissolution of a civil partnership, etc) where the order includes provision requiring the property concerned to be offered for sale to a person or class of persons specified in the order;'.

(3) In subsection (5)(a)—

(a) after 'spouse' insert 'or civil partner', and
(b) after 'live together as husband and wife' insert 'or as if they were civil partners'.

(4) In subsection (6)(a), after 'a relationship by marriage' insert 'or civil partnership'.

Housing Act 1988 (c 50)

41(1) Amend section 17 (succession to assured periodic tenancy by spouse) as follows.

(2) In subsection (1), after 'spouse' (in each place) insert 'or civil partner'.

(3) For subsection (4) substitute—

'(4) For the purposes of this section—

(a) a person who was living with the tenant as his or her wife or husband shall be treated as the tenant's spouse, and
(b) a person who was living with the tenant as if they were civil partners shall be treated as the tenant's civil partner.'

(4) In subsection (5), for the words after 'the county court' substitute 'shall for the purposes of this section be treated (according to whether that one of them is of the opposite sex to, or of the same sex as, the tenant) as the tenant's spouse or the tenant's civil partner.'

42 In section 82(1)(b) (after disposal by housing action trust, legal assistance may be given to surviving spouse of pre-disposal tenant), for 'or widower' substitute ', widower or surviving civil partner'.

43(1) Amend Schedule 2 (assured tenancies: grounds for possession) as follows.

(2) In Part 1 (cases where court must order possession), in paragraph (b) of Ground 1 (landlord previously resident or requiring premises as residence for himself or his spouse), for 'his or his spouse's' substitute 'his, his spouse's or his civil partner's'.

(3) In Part 2 (cases where court may order possession), in Ground 14A (violence by member of a couple)—

(a) for 'a married couple or' substitute 'a married couple, a couple who are civil partners of each other,' and
(b) after 'as husband or wife' insert 'or a couple living together as if they were civil partners'.

44(1) Amend paragraph 3 of Schedule 3 (agricultural worker condition where dwelling occupied by surviving spouse or family member of previous qualifying occupier) as follows.

(2) In sub-paragraphs (1)(c)(i), (3)(a) and (6), for 'widow or widower' substitute 'surviving partner'.

(3) For sub-paragraph (2) substitute—

'(2) For the purposes of sub-paragraph (1)(c)(i) above and sub-paragraph (3) below—

(a) "surviving partner" means widow, widower or surviving civil partner; and
(b) a surviving partner of the previous qualifying occupier of the dwelling-house is a qualifying surviving partner if that surviving partner was residing in the dwelling-house immediately before the previous qualifying occupier's death.'

(4) For sub-paragraph (5) (person living as wife or husband with previous occupier) substitute—

'(5) For the purposes of sub-paragraph (2)(a) above—

(a) a person who, immediately before the previous qualifying occupier's death, was living with the previous occupier as his or her wife or husband shall be treated as the widow or widower of the previous occupier, and

(b) a person who, immediately before the previous qualifying occupier's death, was living with the previous occupier as if they were civil partners shall be treated as the surviving civil partner of the previous occupier.'

45(1) Amend paragraph 4 of Schedule 11 (exempted disposals by housing action trusts) as follows.

(2) In sub-paragraph (2)(b) (meaning of 'qualifying person' in definition of 'exempted disposal'), after 'the spouse or a former spouse' insert ', or the civil partner or a former civil partner,'.

(3) In sub-paragraph (4) (disposals in pursuance of certain orders), after paragraph (d) insert

', or

(e) Part 2 or 3 of Schedule 5, or paragraph 9 of Schedule 7, to the Civil Partnership Act 2004 (property adjustment orders, or orders for the sale of property, in connection with civil partnership proceedings or after overseas dissolution of civil partnership, etc).'

Local Government and Housing Act 1989 (c 42)

46 In paragraph 5(1)(c) of Schedule 10 (long residential tenancies: grounds for possession: premises required as residence for landlord or family member), for the words from 'as a residence' to 'mother and,' substitute

'as a residence for—
(i) himself,

(ii) any son or daughter of his over eighteen years of age,

(iii) his father or mother, or

(iv) the father, or mother, of his spouse or civil partner,

and,'.

Leasehold Reform, Housing and Urban Development Act 1993 (c 28)

47(1) Amend section 7 (meaning of 'long lease') as follows.

(2) In subsection (1)(b) (which refers to section 149(6) of the Law of Property Act 1925), after 'terminable after a death or marriage' insert 'or the formation of a civil partnership'.

(3) In subsection (2) (exclusion of certain leases terminable by notice after death or marriage)—

(a) for 'a death or marriage' substitute 'a death, a marriage or the formation of a civil partnership', and

(b) in paragraph (a), after 'marriage of' insert ', or the formation of a civil partnership by,'.

48 In section 10(5) (members of family of resident landlord), for 'wife or husband' (in each place) substitute 'spouse or civil partner'.

Agricultural Tenancies Act 1995 (c 8)

49 In section 7(3) (which refers to section 149(6) of the Law of Property Act 1925), after 'marriage of' insert ', or formation of a civil partnership by,'.

Housing Act 1996 (c 52)

50(1) Amend section 15 (relevant and exempted disposals) as follows.

(2) In subsection (5)(b) (meaning of 'qualifying person' in the definition of 'exempted disposal'), after 'the spouse or a former spouse' insert ', or the civil partner or a former civil partner,'.

(3) In subsection (6) (disposals in pursuance of certain orders are exempt), after paragraph (d) insert

'; or

(e) Part 2 or 3 of Schedule 5, or paragraph 9 of Schedule 7, to the Civil Partnership Act 2004 (property adjustment orders, or orders for the sale of property, in connection with civil partnership proceedings or after overseas dissolution of civil partnership, etc).'

51(1) Amend sections 62 and 140 (meaning of 'member of a person's family' in Part 1 and in Chapter 1 of Part 5) as follows.

(2) In subsection (1)(a)—

(a) after 'spouse' insert 'or civil partner', and
(b) after 'live together as husband and wife' insert 'or as if they were civil partners'.

(3) In subsection (2)(a), after 'a relationship by marriage' insert 'or civil partnership'.

52 In section 132 (introductory tenancies: cases where tenant is successor), after subsection (2) insert—

'(2A) A tenant to whom the tenancy was assigned in pursuance of an order under Part 2 of Schedule 5, or paragraph 9(2) or (3) of Schedule 7, to the Civil Partnership Act 2004 (property adjustment orders in connection with civil partnership proceedings or after overseas dissolution of civil partnership, etc) is a successor only if the other civil partner was a successor.'

53(1) Amend section 133 (succession to introductory tenancy) as follows.

(2) In subsection (2)(a) (spouse of deceased tenant is preferred successor), after 'spouse' insert 'or civil partner'.

(3) In subsection (3)(a) (tenancy ceases to be introductory on vesting otherwise than in pursuance of certain orders), after 'parents)' in sub-paragraph (iii) insert

', or

(iv) Part 2 of Schedule 5, or paragraph 9(2) or (3) of Schedule 7, to the Civil Partnership Act 2004 (property adjustment orders in connection with civil partnership proceedings or after overseas dissolution of civil partnership, etc)'.

54 In section 134(2)(a) (introductory tenancy may not be assigned except in pursuance of certain orders), after 'parents)' in sub-paragraph (iii) insert

', or

(iv) Part 2 of Schedule 5, or paragraph 9(2) or (3) of Schedule 7, to the Civil Partnership Act 2004 (property adjustment orders in connection with civil partnership proceedings or after overseas dissolution of civil partnership, etc)'.

55 In section 143H(5)(a) (two or more successors to demoted tenancy), for 'spouse or (if the tenant has no spouse)' substitute 'spouse or civil partner or (if the tenant has neither spouse nor civil partner)'.

56 In section 143I(3) (tenancy does not cease to be demoted tenancy if vested pursuant to certain orders), after paragraph (c) insert—

> '(d) Part 2 of Schedule 5, or paragraph 9(2) or (3) of Schedule 7, to the Civil Partnership Act 2004 (property adjustment orders in connection with civil partnership proceedings or after overseas dissolution of civil partnership, etc).'

57 For paragraphs (a) and (b) of section 143J(5) (successor by assignment to secure tenancy terminated by demotion order) substitute—

> '(a) the tenancy was assigned—
>> (i) in proceedings under section 24 of the Matrimonial Causes Act 1973 (property adjustment orders in connection with matrimonial proceedings) or section 17(1) of the Matrimonial and Family Proceedings Act 1984 (property adjustment orders after overseas divorce, etc), or
>> (ii) in proceedings under Part 2 of Schedule 5, or paragraph 9(2) or (3) of Schedule 7, to the Civil Partnership Act 2004 (property adjustment orders in connection with civil partnership proceedings or after overseas dissolution of civil partnership, etc),
> (b) where the tenancy was assigned as mentioned in paragraph (a)(i), neither he nor the other party to the marriage was a successor, and
> (c) where the tenancy was assigned as mentioned in paragraph (a)(ii), neither he nor the other civil partner was a successor.'

58 In section 143K(2) (demoted tenancy may be assigned only in pursuance of certain orders), after paragraph (c) insert—

> '(d) Part 2 of Schedule 5, or paragraph 9(2) or (3) of Schedule 7, to the Civil Partnership Act 2004 (property adjustment orders in connection with civil partnership proceedings or after overseas dissolution of civil partnership, etc).'

59(1) Amend section 143P (meaning of 'member of another's family') as follows.

(2) In subsection (1)(a), after 'spouse' insert 'or civil partner'.

(3) In subsection (3)(a), after 'marriage' insert 'or civil partnership'.

60 In section 160 (cases where provisions about allocations do not apply), in each of subsections (2)(e) and (3)(d) (cases where secure or introductory tenancy vests etc in pursuance of certain orders), after sub-paragraph (iii) insert

> ', or
>> (iv) Part 2 of Schedule 5, or paragraph 9(2) or (3) of Schedule 7, to the Civil Partnership Act 2004 (property adjustment orders in connection with civil partnership proceedings or after overseas dissolution of civil partnership, etc).'

61(1) Amend section 178 (meaning of 'associated person' in Part 7) as follows.

(2) In subsection (1), after paragraph (a) insert—

> '(aa) they are or have been civil partners of each other;'.

(3) In subsection (1), after paragraph (e) insert—

> '(ea) they have entered into a civil partnership agreement between them (whether or not that agreement has been terminated);'.

(4) In subsection (3), after the definition of 'child' insert—

'"civil partnership agreement" has the meaning given by section 73 of the Civil Partnership Act 2004;'.

(5) In subsection (3), for the definition of 'cohabitants' substitute—

'"cohabitants" means—

(a) a man and a woman who, although not married to each other, are living together as husband and wife, or

(b) two people of the same sex who, although not civil partners of each other, are living together as if they were civil partners;

and "former cohabitants" shall be construed accordingly;'.

(6) In subsection (3), in each of paragraphs (a) and (b) of the definition of 'relative', for 'spouse or former spouse' substitute 'spouse, civil partner, former spouse or former civil partner'.

(7) In paragraph (b) of that definition, for 'affinity' substitute 'marriage or civil partnership'.

Housing Grants, Construction and Regeneration Act 1996 (c 53)

62 In section 30(6)(a) (power to provide for financial position of others to be taken into account in means-testing applicant for grant), after 'his spouse,' insert 'his civil partner,'.

63(1) In section 54(3) (disposals in pursuance of certain orders are exempt) as it has effect by virtue of article 11(2) of the 2002 Order (saving for certain purposes of repealed provisions), after paragraph (d) insert

'; or
(e) Part 2 or 3 of Schedule 5, or paragraph 9 of Schedule 7, to the Civil Partnership Act 2004 (property adjustment orders, or orders for the sale of property, in connection with civil partnership proceedings or after overseas dissolution of civil partnership, etc).'

(2) In sub-paragraph (1) 'the 2002 Order' means the Regulatory Reform (Housing Assistance) (England and Wales) Order 2002 (SI 2002/1860).

Commonhold and Leasehold Reform Act 2002 (c 15)

64 In section 76(2)(c) (which refers to section 149(6) of the Law of Property Act 1925), after 'terminable after a death or marriage' insert 'or the formation of a civil partnership'.

65 In section 77(1) ('long lease': exclusion of certain leases terminable by notice after death or marriage)—

(a) for 'a death or marriage' substitute 'a death, a marriage or the formation of a civil partnership', and
(b) in paragraph (a), after 'marriage of' insert ', or the formation of a civil partnership by,'.

66 In paragraph 3(8) of Schedule 6 (members of freeholder's family whose occupation of premises excludes premises from right to manage), after 'spouse' (in each place) insert 'or civil partner'.

SCHEDULE 9

FAMILY HOMES AND DOMESTIC VIOLENCE

PART 1
AMENDMENTS OF THE FAMILY LAW ACT 1996 (C 27)

1(1) Amend section 30 (rights concerning matrimonial home where one spouse has no estate, etc) as follows.

(2) In subsection (1)—

    (a) in paragraph (a)—
        (i) after 'one spouse' insert 'or civil partner ('A')', and
        (ii) for 'that spouse' substitute 'A'.
    (b) in paragraph (b), after 'other spouse' insert 'or civil partner ('B')'.

(3) In subsection (2)—

    (a) for 'the spouse not so entitled' substitute 'B',
    (b) for '('matrimonial home rights')' substitute '('home rights')', and
    (c) in paragraph (a), for 'the other spouse' substitute 'A'.

(4) In subsection (3)—

    (a) for 'a spouse' and for 'that spouse' substitute 'B', and
    (b) for 'the other spouse' (in both places) substitute 'A'.

(5) In subsection (4)—

    (a) for 'A spouse's' substitute 'B's',
    (b) in paragraph (a), for 'by the other spouse as the other spouse's' substitute 'by A as A's', and
    (c) in paragraph (b)—
        (i) for 'the spouse occupies the dwelling-house as that spouse's' substitute 'B occupies the dwelling-house as B's', and
        (ii) for 'by the other spouse as the other spouse's' substitute 'by A as A's'.

(6) In subsection (5)—

    (a) for 'a spouse ('the first spouse')' substitute 'B', and
    (b) in paragraph (b), for 'the other spouse ('the second spouse')' substitute 'A',
    (c) for 'the second spouse' substitute 'A', and
    (d) for 'the first spouse against the second spouse' substitute 'B against A'.

(7) In subsection (6)—

    (a) for 'a spouse' substitute 'B', and
    (b) for 'the other spouse' (in both places) substitute 'A'.

(8) In subsection (7), for the words from first 'which' to the end substitute

    'which—

        (a) in the case of spouses, has at no time been, and was at no time intended by them to be, a matrimonial home of theirs; and
        (b) in the case of civil partners, has at no time been, and was at no time intended by them to be, a civil partnership home of theirs.'

(9) In subsection (8)—

    (a) for 'A spouse's matrimonial home rights' substitute 'B's home rights',

    (b) in paragraph (a), after 'marriage' insert 'or civil partnership', and

    (c) in paragraph (b), for 'the other spouse' substitute 'A'.

(10) In subsection (9)—

    (a) for 'a spouse' (in both places) substitute 'a person', and

    (b) for 'matrimonial home rights' substitute 'home rights'.

(11) In the heading to section 30, for 'matrimonial home where one spouse' substitute 'home where one spouse or civil partner' and, in the preceding cross-heading, after 'matrimonial' insert 'or civil partnership'.

2(1) Amend section 31 (effect of matrimonial home rights as charge on dwelling-house) as follows.

(2) In subsection (1) for 'marriage, one spouse' substitute 'marriage or civil partnership, A'.

(3) In subsection (2) for 'The other spouse's matrimonial home rights' substitute 'B's home rights'.

(4) In subsection (3)—

    (a) in paragraph (a), for 'the spouse so entitled' substitute 'A', and

    (b) in paragraph (b), after 'marriage' insert 'or of the formation of the civil partnership'.

(5) In subsection (4)—

    (a) for 'a spouse's matrimonial home rights' substitute 'B's home rights',

    (b) for 'the other spouse' substitute 'A', and

    (c) for 'either of the spouses' substitute 'A or B'.

(6) In subsection (5) for 'the other spouse' substitute 'A'.

(7) In subsection (7) for 'the spouses' substitute 'A and B'.

(8) In subsection (8)—

    (a) for 'a spouse's matrimonial home rights' substitute 'B's home rights',

    (b) in paragraph (a), for 'the other spouse' substitute 'A', and

    (c) in paragraph (b), after 'marriage' insert 'or civil partnership'.

(9) In subsection (9)—

    (a) in paragraph (a), for 'a spouse's matrimonial home rights' substitute 'B's home rights', and

    (b) for 'the other spouse' (in both places) substitute 'A'.

(10) In subsection (10)—

    (a) for 'a spouse' and for 'that spouse' substitute 'A', and

    (b) in paragraph (b), for 'a spouse's matrimonial home rights' substitute 'B's home rights'.

(11) For subsection (12)(a) substitute—

    '(a) B's home rights are a charge on the estate of A or of trustees of A, and'.

(12) In the heading to section 31, for 'matrimonial home rights' substitute 'home rights'.

3 For section 32 (further provisions relating to matrimonial home rights) substitute—

'32 Further provisions relating to home rights

Schedule 4 (provisions supplementary to sections 30 and 31) has effect.'

4(1) Amend section 33 (occupation orders where applicant has estate or interest etc or has matrimonial home rights) as follows.

(2) In subsection (1)(a)(ii), for 'matrimonial home rights' substitute 'home rights'.

(3) After subsection (2) insert—

'(2A) If a civil partnership agreement (as defined by section 73 of the Civil Partnership Act 2004) is terminated, no application under this section may be made by virtue of section 62(3)(eza) by reference to that agreement after the end of the period of three years beginning with the day on which it is terminated.'

(4) In subsection (3)(e)—

(a) for 'matrimonial home rights' substitute 'home rights', and
(b) after 'spouse' insert 'or civil partner'.

(5) In subsection (4), for 'matrimonial home rights' substitute 'home rights'.

(6) In subsection (5)—

(a) for 'matrimonial home rights' substitute 'home rights',
(b) after 'is the other spouse' insert 'or civil partner',
(c) after 'during the marriage' insert 'or civil partnership',
(d) in paragraph (a), after 'spouse' insert 'or civil partner', and
(e) in paragraph (b), after 'marriage' insert 'or civil partnership'.

(7) In the heading to section 33, for 'matrimonial home rights' substitute 'home rights'.

5 In section 34 (effect of order under section 33 where rights are charge on dwelling-house), in subsection (1)—

(a) for 'a spouse's matrimonial home rights' substitute 'B's home rights', and
(b) for 'the other spouse' (in each place) substitute 'A'.

6(1) Amend section 35 (one former spouse with no existing right to occupy) as follows.

(2) In subsection (1)(a) and (b), after 'former spouse' insert 'or former civil partner'.

(3) For subsection (1)(c) substitute—

'(c) the dwelling-house—
(i)   in the case of former spouses, was at any time their matrimonial home or was at any time intended by them to be their matrimonial home, or
(ii) in the case of former civil partners, was at any time their civil partnership home or was at any time intended by them to be their civil partnership home.'

(4) In subsection (2), after 'former spouse' (in both places) insert 'or former civil partner'.

(5) In subsection (6)(f), after 'marriage' insert 'or civil partnership'.

(6) After subsection (6)(g)(i), insert—

'(ia) for a property adjustment order under Part 2 of Schedule 5 to the Civil Partnership Act 2004;'.

(7) In subsection (9)(a), after 'former spouses' insert 'or former civil partners'.

(8) In subsections (11) and (12), after 'former spouse' insert 'or former civil partner'.

(9) For subsection (13)(a) and (b) substitute—

> '(a) as if he were B (the person entitled to occupy the dwelling-house by virtue of that section); and
> (b) as if the respondent were A (the person entitled as mentioned in subsection (1)(a) of that section).'

(10) In the heading to section 35, after 'former spouse' insert 'or former civil partner'.

7 In section 36 (one cohabitant or former cohabitant with no existing right to occupy), for subsection (13)(a) and (b) substitute—

> '(a) as if he were B (the person entitled to occupy the dwelling-house by virtue of that section); and
> (b) as if the respondent were A (the person entitled as mentioned in subsection (1)(a) of that section).'

8(1) Amend section 37 (neither spouse entitled to occupy) as follows.

(2) After subsection (1) insert—

> '(1A) This section also applies if—
>
> (a) one civil partner or former civil partner and the other civil partner or former civil partner occupy a dwelling-house which is or was the civil partnership home; but
> (b) neither of them is entitled to remain in occupation—
>> (i) by virtue of a beneficial estate or interest or contract; or
>> (ii) by virtue of any enactment giving him the right to remain in occupation.'

(3) In subsection (3)(b), for 'spouses' substitute 'parties'.

(4) In the heading to section 37, after 'spouse' insert 'or civil partner'.

9 In section 42 (non-molestation orders), after subsection (4) insert—

> '(4ZA) If a civil partnership agreement (as defined by section 73 of the Civil Partnership Act 2004) is terminated, no application under this section may be made by virtue of section 62(3)(eza) by reference to that agreement after the end of the period of three years beginning with the day on which it is terminated.'

10(1) In section 44 (evidence of agreement to marry), after subsection (2) insert—

> '(3) Subject to subsection (4), the court shall not make an order under section 33 or 42 by virtue of section 62(3)(eza) unless there is produced to it evidence in writing of the existence of the civil partnership agreement (as defined by section 73 of the Civil Partnership Act 2004).
>
> (4) Subsection (3) does not apply if the court is satisfied that the civil partnership agreement was evidenced by—
>
> (a) a gift by one party to the agreement to the other as a token of the agreement, or
> (b) a ceremony entered into by the parties in the presence of one or more other persons assembled for the purpose of witnessing the ceremony.'

(2) In the heading to section 44, after 'marry' insert 'or form a civil partnership'.

11 In section 49 (variation and discharge of orders), in subsection (3)—

> (a) for 'a spouse's matrimonial home rights' substitute 'B's home rights are, under section 31,', and

(b) for 'the other spouse' (in each place) substitute 'A'.

12(1) Amend section 54 (dwelling-house subject to mortgage) as follows.

(2) In subsections (3)(a) and (4), for 'matrimonial home rights' substitute 'home rights'.

(3) In subsection (5), after 'spouse, former spouse' insert ', civil partner, former civil partner'.

13(1) Amend section 62 (meaning of 'cohabitants', 'relevant child' and 'associated persons') as follows.

(2) In subsection (1)—

(a) in paragraph (a), for 'two persons who, although not married to each other, are living together as husband and wife or (if of the same sex) in an equivalent relationship;' substitute 'two persons who are neither married to each other nor civil partners of each other but are living together as husband and wife or as if they were civil partners;', and

(b) in paragraph (b), after 'have subsequently married each other' insert 'or become civil partners of each other'.

(3) After subsection (3)(a) insert—

'(aa) they are or have been civil partners of each other;'.

(4) After subsection (3)(e) insert—

'(eza) they have entered into a civil partnership agreement (as defined by section 73 of the Civil Partnership Act 2004) (whether or not that agreement has been terminated);'.

14(1) Amend section 63 (interpretation of Part 4) as follows.

(2) In subsection (1), after the definition of 'health' insert—

'"home rights" has the meaning given by section 30;'.

(3) Omit the definition of 'matrimonial home rights' in that subsection.

(4) In the definition of relative in that subsection—

(a) in paragraphs (a) and (b), for 'spouse or former spouse' substitute 'spouse, former spouse, civil partner or former civil partner',

(b) in paragraph (b), for 'by affinity)' substitute 'by marriage or civil partnership)', and

(c) after 'were married to each other' insert 'or were civil partners of each other'.

(5) After subsection (2)(i) insert—

'(j) Schedules 5 to 7 to the Civil Partnership Act 2004.'

15(1) Amend Schedule 4 (provisions supplementary to sections 30 and 31) as follows.

(2) In paragraph 2, after 'spouse' (in both places) insert 'or civil partner'.

(3) In paragraph 3(1) and (3), after 'spouse' insert 'or civil partner'.

(4) In paragraph 4(1), for 'spouse's matrimonial home rights' substitute 'spouse's or civil partner's home rights'.

(5) For paragraphs 4(1)(a) to (c) substitute—

'(a) in the case of a marriage—
    (i) by the production of a certificate or other sufficient evidence, that either spouse is dead,

    (ii) by the production of an official copy of a decree or order of a court, that the marriage has been terminated otherwise than by death, or

    (iii) by the production of an order of the court, that the spouse's home rights constituting the charge have been terminated by the order, and

  (b) in the case of a civil partnership—

    (i) by the production of a certificate or other sufficient evidence, that either civil partner is dead,

    (ii) by the production of an official copy of an order or decree of a court, that the civil partnership has been terminated otherwise than by death, or

    (iii) by the production of an order of the court, that the civil partner's home rights constituting the charge have been terminated by the order.'

(6) In paragraph 4(2)—

  (a) in paragraph (a)—
    (i) after 'marriage' insert 'or civil partnership', and
    (ii) after 'spouse' insert 'or civil partner', and
  (b) in paragraph (b), after 'spouse' insert 'or civil partner'.

(7) In paragraph 4(3), after 'spouse' insert 'or civil partner'.

(8) In the heading to paragraph 4, after 'marriage' insert 'or civil partnership'.

(9) In paragraph 5(1), for 'spouse entitled to matrimonial home rights' substitute 'spouse or civil partner entitled to home rights'.

(10) In paragraph 5(2)—

  (a) for 'matrimonial home rights' substitute 'home rights', and
  (b) in paragraph (a), after 'spouse' insert 'or civil partner'.

(11) In the heading to paragraph 5, for 'matrimonial home rights' substitute 'home rights'.

(12) In paragraph 6, after 'spouse' (in both places) insert 'or civil partner'.

16(1) Amend Schedule 7 (transfer of certain tenancies on divorce etc or on separation of cohabitants) as follows.

(2) In paragraph 1, before the definition of 'cohabitant' insert—

    '"civil partner", except in paragraph 2, includes (where the context requires) former civil partner;'.

(3) In paragraph 2(1), after 'spouse' (in both places) insert 'or civil partner'.

(4) For paragraph 2(2) substitute—

    '(2) The court may make a Part II order—

    (a) on granting a decree of divorce, a decree of nullity of marriage or a decree of judicial separation or at any time thereafter (whether, in the case of a decree of divorce or nullity of marriage, before or after the decree is made absolute), or

    (b) at any time when it has power to make a property adjustment order under Part 2 of Schedule 5 to the Civil Partnership Act 2004 with respect to the civil partnership.'

  (5) Omit 'or' at the end of paragraph 4(a) and insert—

    '(aa) in the case of civil partners, a civil partnership home; or'.

(6) In paragraph 5(a), after 'spouses' insert ', civil partners'.

(7) In paragraph 6—

    (a) after 'spouse' (in the first place) insert ', a civil partner', and
    (b) after 'spouse' (in the second place) insert ', civil partner'.

(8) In paragraph 7(1) and (2), after 'spouse' (in each place) insert ', civil partner'.

(9) For paragraph 7(3) to (4) substitute—

'(3) If the spouse, civil partner or cohabitant so entitled is a successor within the meaning of Part 4 of the Housing Act 1985—

    (a) his former spouse (or, in the case of judicial separation, his spouse),
    (b) his former civil partner (or, if a separation order is in force, his civil partner), or
    (c) his former cohabitant,

is to be deemed also to be a successor within the meaning of that Part.

(3A) If the spouse, civil partner or cohabitant so entitled is a successor within the meaning of section 132 of the Housing Act 1996—

    (a) his former spouse (or, in the case of judicial separation, his spouse),
    (b) his former civil partner (or, if a separation order is in force, his civil partner), or
    (c) his former cohabitant,

is to be deemed also to be a successor within the meaning of that section.

(4) If the spouse, civil partner or cohabitant so entitled is for the purposes of section 17 of the Housing Act 1988 a successor in relation to the tenancy or occupancy—

    (a) his former spouse (or, in the case of judicial separation, his spouse),
    (b) his former civil partner (or, if a separation order is in force, his civil partner), or
    (c) his former cohabitant,

is to be deemed to be a successor in relation to the tenancy or occupancy for the purposes of that section.'

(10) In paragraph 7(5)(a), after 'spouse' insert ', civil partner'.

(11) Omit paragraph 7(6).

(12) In paragraph 8(1) and (2)(a) and (b), after 'spouse' insert ', civil partner'.

(13) In paragraph 8(3), after 'surviving spouse' insert 'or surviving civil partner'.

(14) In paragraphs 9(1), (2)(a) and (b) and (3) (in both places) and 10(1) (in both places), after 'spouse' insert ', civil partner'.

(15) In paragraph 11(1), after 'spouses' insert ', civil partners'.

(16) In paragraph 11(2), after 'spouse' insert ', civil partner'.

(17) For paragraph 12 and the heading preceding it, substitute—

'Date when order made between spouses or civil partners takes effect

12 The date specified in a Part II order as the date on which the order is to take effect must not be earlier than—

    (a) in the case of a marriage in respect of which a decree of divorce or nullity has been granted, the date on which the decree is made absolute;

(b) in the case of a civil partnership in respect of which a dissolution or nullity order has been made, the date on which the order is made final.'

(18) For paragraph 13 and the heading preceding it substitute—

'Effect of remarriage or subsequent civil partnership

13(1) If after the grant of a decree dissolving or annulling a marriage either spouse remarries or forms a civil partnership, that spouse is not entitled to apply, by reference to the grant of that decree, for a Part II order.

(2) If after the making of a dissolution or nullity order either civil partner forms a subsequent civil partnership or marries, that civil partner is not entitled to apply, by reference to the making of that order, for a Part II order.

(3) In sub-paragraphs (1) and (2)—

(a) the references to remarrying and marrying include references to cases where the marriage is by law void or voidable, and
(b) the references to forming a civil partnership include references to cases where the civil partnership is by law void or voidable.'

(19) In paragraph 15(1)—

(a) after 'spouse' insert 'or civil partner', and
(b) for 'spouse's matrimonial home rights' substitute 'spouse's or civil partner's home rights'.

(20) In paragraph 15(2), after 'spouse' insert ', civil partner'.

PART 2
CONSEQUENTIAL AMENDMENTS

Land Compensation Act 1973 (c 26)

17(1) Amend section 29A (spouses having statutory rights of occupation) as follows.

(2) In subsection (1)—

(a) for 'one spouse ('A')' substitute 'one spouse or civil partner ('A')', and
(b) for 'the other spouse ('B') acquires matrimonial home rights' substitute 'the other spouse or civil partner ('B') acquires home rights'.

(3) In subsection (2) for 'matrimonial home rights' substitute 'home rights'.

(4) In the heading to section 29A, after 'spouses' insert 'and civil partners'.

Housing Act 1985 (c 68)

18(1) Amend section 85 (extended discretion of court in certain proceedings for possession) as follows.

(2) In subsection (5)—

(a) in paragraph (a) for 'tenant's spouse or former spouse, having matrimonial home rights' substitute 'tenant's spouse or former spouse, or civil partner or former civil partner, having home rights',

(b) after 'the spouse or former spouse' insert ', or the civil partner or former civil partner,', and

(c) for 'those matrimonial home rights' substitute 'those home rights'.

(3) In subsection (5A)—

(a) in paragraph (a), for 'former spouse of the tenant' substitute 'former spouse or former civil partner of the tenant', and

(b) in paragraph (b) and in the words following paragraph (c) after 'former spouse,' insert 'former civil partner,'.

19 In section 99B (persons qualifying for compensation) in subsection (2)(f), after 'spouse, former spouse,' insert 'civil partner, former civil partner,'.

20 In section 101 (rent not to be increased on account of tenant's improvements) in subsection (3)(d), after 'spouse, former spouse,' insert 'civil partner, former civil partner,'.

Insolvency Act 1986 (c 45)

21(1) Amend section 336 (rights of occupation etc of bankrupt's spouse) as follows.

(2) In subsection (1), for 'matrimonial home rights' substitute 'home rights'.

(3) In subsection (2)—

(a) for 'a spouse's matrimonial home rights' substitute 'a spouse's or civil partner's home rights', and

(b) after 'the other spouse' (in each place) insert 'or civil partner'.

(4) In subsection (4)(b) and (c) after 'spouse or former spouse' insert 'or civil partner or former civil partner'.

(5) In the heading to section 336 after 'spouse' insert 'or civil partner'.

22(1) Amend section 337 (rights of occupation of bankrupt) as follows.

(2) In subsection (2), for 'spouse (if any) has matrimonial home rights' substitute 'spouse or civil partner (if any) has home rights'.

(3) In subsection (3)—

(a) in paragraph (a), for 'matrimonial home rights' substitute 'home rights', and

(b) in paragraph (c), after 'spouse' insert 'or civil partner'.

Housing Act 1988 (c 50)

23(1) Amend section 9 (extended discretion of court in possession claims) as follows.

(2) In subsection (5)—

(a) for 'tenant's spouse or former spouse, having matrimonial home rights' substitute 'tenant's spouse or former spouse, or civil partner or former civil partner, having home rights',

(b) after 'the spouse or former spouse' insert ', or the civil partner or former civil partner', and

(c) for 'those matrimonial home rights' substitute 'those home rights'.

(3) In subsection (5A)—

(a) for 'former spouse of the tenant' substitute 'former spouse or former civil partner of the tenant',

(b) for 'cohabitant, former cohabitant or former spouse' (in both places) substitute 'former spouse, former civil partner, cohabitant or former cohabitant'.

Commonhold and Leasehold Reform Act 2002 (c 15)

24(1) Amend section 61 (matrimonial rights) as follows.

(2) For 'matrimonial home rights (within the meaning of section 30(2) of the Family Law Act 1996 (c 27) (matrimonial home))' substitute 'home rights (within the meaning of section 30(2) of the Family Law Act 1996 (c 27) (rights in respect of matrimonial or civil partnership home))'.

(3) In the heading to section 61 for 'Matrimonial' substitute 'Home'.

PART 3
TRANSISTIONAL PROVISION

25(1) Any reference (however expressed) in any enactment, instrument or document (whether passed or made before or after the passing of this Act)—

(a) to rights of occupation under, or within the meaning of, the Matrimonial Homes Act 1983 (c 19), or

(b) to matrimonial home rights under, or within the meaning of, Part 4 of the Family Law Act 1996 (c 27),

is to be construed, so far as is required for continuing the effect of the enactment, instrument or document, as being or as the case requires including a reference to home rights under, or within the meaning of, Part 4 of the 1996 Act as amended by this Schedule.

(2) Any reference (however expressed) in Part 4 of the 1996 Act or in any other enactment, instrument or document (including any enactment amended by this Schedule) to home rights under, or within the meaning of, Part 4 of the 1996 Act is to be construed as including, in relation to times, circumstances and purposes before the commencement of this Schedule, references to rights of occupation under, or within the meaning of, the 1983 Act and to matrimonial home rights under, or within the meaning of, Part 4 of the 1996 Act without the amendments made by this Schedule.

SCHEDULE 10

SECTION 86

FORBIDDEN DEGREES OF RELATIONSHIP: SCOTLAND

Column 1	Column 2
1.— Relationships by consanguinity	
Father	Mother
Son	Daughter
Father's father	Father's mother
Mother's father	Mother's mother
Son's son	Son's daughter
Daughter's son	Daughter's daughter
Brother	Sister
Father's brother	Father's sister
Mother's brother	Mother's sister

Column 1	Column 2
Brother's son	Brother's daughter
Sister's son	Sister's daughter
Father's father's father	Father's father's mother
Father's mother's father	Father's mother's mother
Mother's father's father	Mother's father's mother
Mother's mother's father	Mother's mother's mother
Son's son's son	Son's son's daughter
Son's daughter's son	Son's daughter's daughter
Daughter's son's son	Daughter's son's daughter
Daughter's daughter's son	Daughter's daughter's daughter

2.– Relationships by affinity

Column 1	Column 2
Son of former wife	Daughter of former husband
Son of former civil partner	Daughter of former civil partner
Former husband of mother	Former wife of father
Former civil partner of father	Former civil partner of mother
Former husband of father's mother	Former wife of father's father
Former civil partner of father's father	Former civil partner of father's mother
Former husband of mother's mother	Former wife of mother's father
Former civil partner of mother's father	Former civil partner of mother's mother
Son of son of former wife	Daughter of son of former husband
Son of son of former civil partner	Daughter of son of former civil partner
Son of daughter of former wife	Daughter of daughter of former husband
Son of daughter of former civil partner	Daughter of daughter of former civil partner

3.– Further relationships by affinity

Column 1	Column 2
Father of former wife	Mother of former husband
Father of former civil partner	Mother of former civil partner
Former husband of daughter	Former wife of son
Former civil partner of son	Former civil partner of daughter

SCHEDULE 11

SECTION 125

FINANCIAL PROVISION IN SCOTLAND AFTER OVERSEAS
PROCEEDINGS

PART 1
INTRODUCTORY

1(1) This Schedule applies where—

(a) a civil partnership has been dissolved or annulled in a country or territory outside the British Islands by means of judicial or other proceedings (here the 'overseas proceedings'), and
(b) the dissolution or annulment (here the 'overseas determination') is entitled to be recognised as valid in Scotland.

(2) This Schedule applies even if the date of the overseas determination is earlier than the date on which this Schedule comes into force.

PART 2
CIRCUMSTANCES IN WHICH COURT MAY ENTERTAIN APPLICATION
FOR FINANCIAL PROVISION

2(1) Subject to sub-paragraph (4), if the jurisdictional requirements and the conditions set out in sub-paragraphs (2) and (3), respectively, are satisfied, the court may entertain an application by one of the former civil partners or former ostensible civil partners, (here 'A') for an order for financial provision.

(2) The jurisdictional requirements are—

(a) that A is domiciled or habitually resident in Scotland when the application is made,
(b) that the other former civil partner, or former ostensible civil partner, (here 'B')—
    (i) is domiciled or habitually resident in Scotland when the application is made,
    (ii) was domiciled or habitually resident in Scotland when A and B last lived together in civil partnership, or
    (iii) when the application is made is an owner or tenant of, or has a beneficial interest in, property in Scotland which has at some time been a family home of A and B, and
(c) where the court is the sheriff, that when the application is made either—
    (i) A or B is habitually resident in the sheriffdom, or
    (ii) property mentioned in sub-paragraph (2)(b)(iii) is wholly or partially in the sheriffdom.

(3) The conditions are that—

(a) B initiated the overseas proceedings,
(b) the application is made within 5 years after the overseas determination takes effect,
(c) the civil partnership (or ostensible civil partnership) had a substantial connection with Scotland,
(d) A and B are alive when the application is made, and
(e) (taking Part 3 of this Act to have been in force) a court in Scotland would have had jurisdiction to entertain an action for dissolution or annulment of the civil partnership, if such an action had been brought immediately before the overseas determination took effect.

(4) Where the jurisdiction of the court to entertain proceedings under this Schedule would fall to be determined by reference to the jurisdictional requirements imposed by virtue of Part 1 of the Civil

Jurisdiction and Judgments Act 1982 (c 27) (implementation of certain European conventions) or by virtue of Council Regulation (EC) No. 44/2001 of 22nd December 2000 on jurisdiction and the recognition and enforcement of judgments in civil and commercial matters, then—

(a) satisfaction of the jurisdictional requirements set out in sub-paragraph (2) does not obviate the need to satisfy those so imposed, and

(b) satisfaction of those so imposed obviates the need to satisfy those set out in sub-paragraph (2).

PART 3
DISPOSAL OF APPLICATIONS

3(1) Subject to sub-paragraphs (2) to (5), Scots law applies in relation to an application made under paragraph 2 as it would apply were the application made in an action in Scotland for, as the case may be, dissolution or annulment of a civil partnership.

(2) In disposing of an application made under paragraph 2 the court must exercise its powers so as to place A and B, in so far as it is reasonable and practicable to do so, in the financial position in which they would have been had that application been disposed of, in such an action in Scotland, on the date when the overseas determination took effect.

(3) In determining what is reasonable and practicable for the purposes of sub-paragraph (2), the court must have regard in particular to—

(a) A and B's respective resources, both present and foreseeable, at the date the application is disposed of,

(b) any order made by a foreign court in or in connection with the overseas proceedings, being an order—
   (i) for the making of financial provision, in whatever form, by A for B or by B for A, or
   (ii) for the transfer of property from A to B or from B to A.

(4) Subject to sub-paragraph (5), the court may make an order for an interim award of a periodical allowance where—

(a) it appears from A's averments that in the disposal of the application an order for financial provision is likely to be made, and

(b) the court considers that such an interim award is necessary to avoid hardship to A.

(5) Where but for paragraph 2(2)(b)(iii) the court would not have jurisdiction to entertain the application, the court may make no order for financial provision other than an order—

(a) relating to the former family home or its furniture and plenishings, or

(b) that B must pay A a capital sum not exceeding the value of B's interest in the former family home and its furniture and plenishings.

PART 4
THE EXPRESSION 'ORDER FOR FINANCIAL PROVISION'

4 In this Schedule, 'order for financial provision' means any one or more of the orders specified in section 8(1) of the Family Law (Scotland) Act 1985 (c 37) or an order under section 111.

SCHEDULE 12

PROHIBITED DEGREES OF RELATIONSHIP: NORTHERN IRELAND

Absolute prohibitions

1(1) Two people are within prohibited degrees of relationship if one falls within the list below in relation to the other.

Adoptive child

Adoptive parent

Child

Former adoptive child

Former adoptive parent

Grandparent

Grandchild

Parent

Parent's sibling

Sibling

Sibling's child

(2) In the list 'sibling' means a brother, sister, half-brother or half-sister.

Qualified prohibitions

2(1) Two people are within prohibited degrees of relationship if one of them falls within the list below in relation to the other, unless—

    (a) both of them have reached 21 at the time when they register as civil partners of each other, and

    (b) the younger has not at any time before reaching 18 been a child of the family in relation to the other.

        Child of former civil partner

        Child of former spouse

        Former civil partner of grandparent

        Former civil partner of parent

        Former spouse of grandparent

        Former spouse of parent

        Grandchild of former civil partner

        Grandchild of former spouse

(2) 'Child of the family', in relation to another person, means a person who—

    (a) has lived in the same household as that other person, and

(b) has been treated by that other person as a child of his family.

3 Two people are within prohibited degrees of relationship if one falls within column 1 of the table below in relation to the other, unless—

(a) both of them have reached 21 at the time when they register as civil partners of each other, and

(b) the persons who fall within column 2 are dead.

Relationship	Relevant deaths
Former civil partner of child	The child The child's other parent
Former spouse of child	The child The child's other parent
Parent of former civil partner	The former civil partner The former civil partner's other parent
Parent of former spouse	The former spouse The former spouse's other parent

SCHEDULE 13

SECTION 145(2)

CIVIL PARTNERSHIPS OF PERSONS UNDER 18: NORTHERN IRELAND

PART 1
APPROPRIATE PERSONS

1 Column 2 of the table specifies the appropriate persons (or person) to give consent to a young person whose circumstances fall within column 1 and who intends to register as the civil partner of another—

Case	Appropriate persons
1 The circumstances do not fall within any of items 2 to 4.	Each of the following— (a) any parent of the young person who has parental responsibility for him, and (b) any guardian of the young person.
2 A care order has effect with respect to the young person.	Each of the following— (a) the Health and Social Services Board or Health and Social Services trust designated in the order, and (b) any parent or guardian mentioned in item 1.
3 A residence order has effect with respect to the young person.	Each of the persons with whom the young person lives, or is to live, as a result of the order.
4 The circumstances do not fall within item 2 or 3, but a residence order had effect with respect to the young person immediately before he reached 16.	The persons with whom the young person lived, or was to live, as a result of the order.

2 In the table the following expressions have the same meaning as in the Children (Northern Ireland) Order 1995 (SI 1995/755 (NI 2))—

'care order';

'Health and Social Services trust';

'parental responsibility';

'residence order';

and in item 1 'any guardian of the young person' means any person falling within the definition of 'guardian of a child' in Article 2(2) of that Order.

PART 2
DISPENSING WITH CONSENT

Order dispensing with consent

3(1) This paragraph applies if—

   (a) a young person and another person intend to register as civil partners of each other, and
   (b) a county court is satisfied as mentioned in sub-paragraphs (3) and (4).

(2) A county court may make an order dispensing with the consent of any person whose consent is required.

(3) The court must be satisfied that the registration of the civil partnership is in the best interests of the young person.

(4) The court must be satisfied that—

   (a) it is not reasonably practicable to obtain the consent of any person whose consent is required,
   (b) any person whose consent is required withholds or refuses that consent, or
   (c) there is uncertainty as to whose consent is required.

(5) An application for an order under this paragraph may be made—

   (a) by or on behalf of the young person, or
   (b) by or on behalf of the other person (who may be another young person) mentioned in sub-paragraph (1)(a),

and without the intervention of a next friend.

(6) The decision of the county court on any application made under this paragraph is final and conclusive.

PART 3
RECORDING CONSENTS AND ORDERS

4 Any consent required by section 145(1) must be sent to the registrar.

5 Any order made under paragraph 3, or a certified copy of it, must be sent to the registrar.

6 The registrar must keep a record of—

   (a) such particulars as may be prescribed, taken from each consent or order received by him, and
   (b) the date on which each consent or order is received by him.

7 The record kept under paragraph 6 must be kept with the civil partnership notice book and section 140(5) (right of inspection) applies accordingly.

SCHEDULE 14

SECTION 195

WILLS, ADMINISTRATION OF ESTATES AND FAMILY PROVISION: NORTHERN IRELAND

PART 1
WILLS

1 Amend the Wills and Administration Proceedings (Northern Ireland) Order 1994 (SI 1994/1899 (NI 13)) as follows.

2 In Article 4(1) (will made by person under 18 invalid unless he is or has been married), for 'married' substitute 'a spouse or civil partner'.

3 In Article 8(1) and (3) (avoidance of gifts to attesting witnesses and their spouses), after 'spouse' (in each place) insert 'or civil partner'.

4 In Article 9 (witnessing by creditor), after 'spouse' insert 'or civil partner'.

5 After Article 13 insert—

'13A Effect of civil partnership

(1) Subject to paragraphs (2) to (6), a will is revoked by the formation of a civil partnership between the testator and another person.

(2) A disposition in a will in exercise of a power of appointment takes effect despite the formation of a subsequent civil partnership between the testator and another person unless the property so appointed would in default of appointment pass to the testator's personal representatives.

(3) If it appears from a will—

(a) that at the time it was made the testator was expecting to form a civil partnership with a particular person, and
(b) that he intended that the will should not be revoked by the formation of the civil partnership,

the will is not revoked by its formation.

(4) Paragraphs (5) and (6) apply if it appears from a will—

(a) that at the time it was made the testator was expecting to form a civil partnership with a particular person, and
(b) that he intended that a gift in the will should not be revoked by the formation of the civil partnership.

(5) The gift takes effect despite the formation of the civil partnership.

(6) Any other gift in the will also takes effect, unless it appears from the will that the testator intended the gift to be revoked by the formation of the civil partnership.

13B Effect of dissolution or annulment of civil partnership

(1) This Article applies if, after a testator has made a will—

- (a) a court of civil jurisdiction in Northern Ireland dissolves his civil partnership or makes a nullity order in respect of it, or
- (b) his civil partnership is dissolved or annulled and the dissolution or annulment is entitled to recognition in Northern Ireland under Chapter 3 of Part 5 of the Civil Partnership Act 2004.

(2) Subject to any contrary intention appearing from the will—

- (a) provisions of the will appointing executors or trustees or conferring a power of appointment, if they appoint or confer the power on the former civil partner, take effect as if the former civil partner had died on the date on which the civil partnership is dissolved or annulled, and
- (b) except as provided in paragraph (3), any property comprising or included in a gift to the former civil partner passes as if the former civil partner had died on that date.

(3) Where property comprising or included in a gift to the former civil partner is a share of residue, the will takes effect as if the gift of the residue were to the other person or persons entitled to it (and, if more than one, in such shares as to preserve the ratio of their former shares), to the exclusion of the former civil partner.

(4) Paragraph (2)(b) does not affect any right of the former civil partner to apply for financial provision under the Inheritance (Provision for Family and Dependants) (Northern Ireland) Order 1979 (SI 1979/ 924 (NI 8)).'

6 In Article 14 (revocation), in paragraph (1)(a), after 'Article 12 (marriage)' insert 'or Article 13A (civil partnership)'.

7(1) Amend Article 23 (presumption as to effect of gift to spouses) as follows.

(2) After 'spouse' (in each place) insert 'or civil partner'.

(3) In the heading to Article 23, after 'spouses' insert 'or civil partners'.

8 In Article 27(3) (construction and effect of references to failure of issue), after 'married' insert 'or formed a civil partnership'.

PART 2
ADMINISTRATION OF ESTATES AND FAMILY PROVISION

Administration of Estates Act (Northern Ireland) 1955 (c 24 (NI))

9(1) Amend section 6A (spouse dying within 28 days of intestate) as follows.

(2) After 'spouse' (in each place) insert 'or civil partner'.

(3) In the sidenote to section 6A, after 'Spouse' insert 'or civil partner'.

10(1) Amend section 7 (rights of surviving spouse) as follows.

(2) After 'spouse' (in each place) insert 'or civil partner'.

(3) In subsection (7), after 'husband' insert ', or of section 180 of the Civil Partnership Act 2004'.

(4) In the sidenote to section 7, after 'spouse' insert 'or civil partner'.

11 In section 8 (rights of issue), after 'spouse' insert 'or civil partner'.

12 In section 9 (rights of parents), after 'spouse' insert 'or civil partner'.

13 In section 10 (rights of brothers and sisters and their issue), after 'spouse' (in both places) insert 'or civil partner'.

14 In section 11 (rights of next-of-kin), in subsection (1) after 'neither spouse' insert 'nor civil partner'.

15 In section 38 (power to appoint trustees of infant's property), in subsection (5) after 'marries' insert ', or forms a civil partnership,'.

Inheritance (Provision for Family and Dependants) (Northern Ireland) Order 1979 (SI 1979/ 924 (NI 8))

16(1) Amend Article 2 (interpretation) as follows.

(2) In paragraph (2), after the definition of 'child' insert—

"'civil partnership proceedings county court" has the same meaning as in the Civil Partnership Act 2004;'.

(3) In that paragraph, in the definition of 'former wife' and 'former husband', for "former wife' or 'former husband" substitute "former spouse".

(4) In that paragraph, before that definition insert—

"'former civil partner" means a person whose civil partnership with the deceased was during the lifetime of the deceased either—

    (a) dissolved or annulled by an order made under the law of any part of the United Kingdom or the Channel Islands or the Isle of Man, or

    (b) dissolved or annulled in any country or territory outside the United Kingdom, the Channel Islands and the Isle of Man by a dissolution or annulment which is entitled to be recognised as valid by the law of Northern Ireland;'.

(5) In that paragraph, in the definition of 'reasonable financial provision', after paragraph (a) insert—

'(aa) in the case of an application made by virtue of Article 3(1)(a) by the civil partner of the deceased (except where, at the date of death, a separation order under Chapter 2 of Part 4 of the Civil Partnership Act 2004 was in force in relation to the civil partnership and the separation was continuing), means such financial provision as it would be reasonable in all the circumstances of the case for a civil partner to receive, whether or not that provision is required for his or her maintenance;'.

(6) In paragraph (5)—

    (a) before 'wife' insert 'spouse,', and

    (b) in sub-paragraph (b), for 'entered into a later marriage' substitute 'formed a subsequent marriage or civil partnership'.

(7) For paragraph (6) substitute—

'(5A) For the purposes of this Order any reference to a civil partner shall be treated as including a reference to a person who in good faith formed a void civil partnership with the deceased unless either—

(a) the civil partnership between the deceased and that person was dissolved or annulled during the lifetime of the deceased and the dissolution or annulment is recognised by the law of Northern Ireland, or

(b) that person has during the lifetime of the deceased formed a subsequent civil partnership or marriage.

(6) Any reference in this Order to the formation of, or to a person who has formed, a subsequent marriage or civil partnership includes (as the case may be) a reference to the formation of, or to a person who has formed, a marriage or civil partnership which is by law void or voidable.

(6A) The formation of a marriage or civil partnership shall be treated for the purposes of this Order as the formation of a subsequent marriage or civil partnership, in relation to either of the spouses or civil partners, notwithstanding that the previous marriage or civil partnership of that spouse or civil partner was void or voidable.'

17(1) Amend Article 3 (application for financial provision from deceased person's estate) as follows.

(2) For paragraph (1)(a) and (b) (application may be made by spouse or by former spouse who has not remarried) substitute—

'(a) the spouse or civil partner of the deceased;

(b) a former spouse or former civil partner of the deceased, but not one who has formed a subsequent marriage or civil partnership;'.

(3) In paragraph (1)(ba) (application may be made by person living as husband or wife of the deceased), after 'paragraph (1A)' insert 'or (1B)'.

(4) In paragraph (1)(d) (application may be made by child of the family), after 'marriage' (in each place) insert 'or civil partnership'.

(5) After paragraph (1A) insert—

'(1B) This paragraph applies to a person if for the whole of the period of two years ending immediately before the date when the deceased died the person was living—

(a) in the same household as the deceased, and

(b) as the civil partner of the deceased.'

18 In Article 4(1) (orders which may be made on an application), after sub-paragraph (f) insert—

'(g) an order varying any settlement made—
   (i)   during the subsistence of a civil partnership formed by the deceased, or
   (ii) in anticipation of the formation of a civil partnership by the deceased,

on the civil partners (including such a settlement made by will), the variation being for the benefit of the surviving civil partner, or any child of both the civil partners, or any person who was treated by the deceased as a child of the family in relation to that civil partnership.'

19(1) Amend Article 5(2) (application by spouse or former spouse: matters to which court is to have regard) as follows.

(2) For the words from the beginning to 'or (b)' substitute—

'This paragraph applies, without prejudice to the generality of sub-paragraph (g) of paragraph (1), where an application for an order under Article 4 is made by virtue of Article 3(1)(a) or (b).'

(3) The words from 'the court shall, in addition' to the end of sub-paragraph (b) shall become a second sentence of the paragraph and, in sub-paragraph (a) of the sentence so formed, after 'duration of the marriage' insert 'or civil partnership'.

(4) The words from 'in the case of an application by the wife or husband' to the end shall become a third sentence of the paragraph, omitting the immediately preceding 'and'.

(5) At the end insert the following sentence—

'In the case of an application by the civil partner of the deceased, the court shall also, unless at the date of the death a separation order under Chapter 2 of Part 4 of the Civil Partnership Act 2004 was in force and the separation was continuing, have regard to the provision which the applicant might reasonably have expected to receive if on the day on which the deceased died the civil partnership, instead of being terminated by death, had been terminated by a dissolution order.'

20 In Article 5(2A) (application by person living as husband or wife of deceased: matters to which court is to have regard), in sub-paragraph (a), after 'wife' insert 'or civil partner'.

21(1) In Article 8(3) and (10) (variation etc of orders which cease on occurrence of specified event other than remarriage of former spouse), for '(other than the remarriage of a former wife or former husband)' substitute '(other than the formation of a subsequent marriage or civil partnership by a former spouse or former civil partner)'.

(2) In Article 8(9), for 'or (f)' substitute '(f) or (g)'.

22 After Article 16 insert—

'16A Provision as to cases where no financial relief was granted in proceedings for the dissolution etc of a civil partnership

(1) Paragraph (2) applies where—

    (a) a dissolution order, nullity order, separation order or presumption of death order has been made under Chapter 2 of Part 4 of the Civil Partnership Act 2004 in relation to a civil partnership,

    (b) one of the civil partners dies within twelve months from the date on which the order is made, and

    (c) either—

        (i) an application for a financial provision order under Part 1 of Schedule 15 to that Act or a property adjustment order under Part 2 of that Schedule has not been made by the other civil partner, or

        (ii) such an application has been made but the proceedings on the application have not been determined at the time of the death of the deceased.

(2) If an application for an order under Article 4 is made by the surviving civil partner, the court shall, notwithstanding anything in Article 3 or 5, have power, if it thinks it just to do so, to treat the surviving civil partner as if the order mentioned in paragraph (1)(a) had not been made.

(3) This Article shall not apply in relation to a separation order unless at the date of the death of the deceased the separation order was in force and the separation was continuing.'

23 After Article 17 insert—

'17ZA Restriction imposed in proceedings for the dissolution etc of a civil partnership on application under this Order

(1) On making a dissolution order, nullity order, separation order or presumption of death order under Chapter 2 of Part 4 of the Civil Partnership Act 2004, or at any time after making such an order, the High Court or a civil partnership proceedings county court, if it considers it just to do so, may, on the application of either of the civil partners, order that the other civil partner shall not on the death of the applicant be entitled to apply for an order under Article 4.

(2) In the case of a dissolution order, nullity order or presumption of death order ("the main order") an order may be made under paragraph (1) before (as well as after) the main order is made final, but if made before the main order is made final it shall not take effect unless the main order is made final.

(3) Where an order under paragraph (1) made in connection with a dissolution order, nullity order or presumption of death order has come into force with respect to a civil partner, then, on the death of the other civil partner, the court shall not entertain any application for an order under Article 4 made by the surviving civil partner.

(4) Where an order under paragraph (1) made in connection with a separation order has come into force with respect to a civil partner, then, if the other civil partner dies while the separation order is in force and the separation is continuing, the court shall not entertain any application for an order under Article 4 made by the surviving civil partner.'

24 After Article 17A insert—

'17B Restriction imposed in proceedings under Schedule 17 to the Civil Partnership Act 2004 on application under this Order

(1) On making an order under paragraph 9 of Schedule 17 to the Civil Partnership Act 2004 (orders for financial provision, property adjustment and pension-sharing following overseas dissolution etc of civil partnership) the High Court, if it considers it just to do so, may, on the application of either of the civil partners, order that the other civil partner shall not on the death of the applicant be entitled to apply for an order under Article 4.

(2) Where an order under paragraph (1) has been made with respect to one of the civil partners in a case where a civil partnership has been dissolved or annulled, then, on the death of the other civil partner, the court shall not entertain an application under Article 4 made by the surviving civil partner.

(3) Where an order under paragraph (1) has been made with respect to one of the civil partners in a case where civil partners have been legally separated, then, if the other civil partner dies while the legal separation is in force, the court shall not entertain an application under Article 4 made by the surviving civil partner.'

25 In Article 18(1) (power to vary secured periodical payments orders)—

(a) after 'Matrimonial Causes (Northern Ireland) Order 1978' insert 'or Schedule 15 to the Civil Partnership Act 2004', and
(b) after 'that Order' insert 'or Part 10 of that Schedule'.

26 In Article 19(4) (meaning of 'maintenance agreement')—

(a) for 'entered into a marriage' substitute 'formed a marriage or civil partnership',
(b) after 'of the parties to that marriage' insert 'or of the civil partners', and

(c) after 'marriage' (in the third and fourth places) insert 'or civil partnership'.

27 After Article 20 insert—

'20A Availability of court's powers under this Order in applications under paragraphs 53 and 66 of Schedule 15 to the Civil Partnership Act 2004

(1) Where—

(a) a person against whom a secured periodical payments order was made under Schedule 15 to the Civil Partnership Act 2004 has died and an application is made under paragraph 53 of that Schedule for the variation or discharge of that order or for the revival of the operation of any suspended provision of the order, or

(b) a party to a maintenance agreement within the meaning of Part 12 of that Schedule has died, the agreement being one which provides for the continuation of payments under the agreement after the death of one of the parties, and an application is made under paragraph 66 of that Schedule for the alteration of the agreement under paragraph 62 of that Schedule,

the court to which the application is made under paragraph 53 or 66 shall have power to direct that the application shall be deemed to have been accompanied by an application for an order under Article 4.

(2) Where the court to which an application is made under paragraph 53 or 66 gives a direction under paragraph (1), that court shall have power—

(a) to make any order which the court would have had power to make under the provisions of this Order if the application under paragraph 53 or 66 had been made jointly with an application for an order under Article 4; and

(b) to give such consequential directions as may be necessary for enabling it to exercise any of the powers available to it under this Order in the case of an application for an order under Article 4.

(3) Where an order made under Article 17ZA(1) is in force with respect to a civil partner, a direction shall not be given under paragraph (1) with respect to any application made under paragraph 53 or 66 by that civil partner on the death of the other civil partner.'

28(1) Amend Article 21 (effect, duration and form of orders) as follows.

(2) In paragraph (2)(a), for 'former husband or former wife' substitute 'former spouse or former civil partner'.

(3) In paragraph (2), after sub-paragraph (b) insert

'or

(c) an applicant who was the civil partner of the deceased in a case where, at the date of death, a separation order under Chapter 2 of Part 4 of the Civil Partnership Act 2004 was in force in relation to their civil partnership and the separation was continuing,'.

(4) In that paragraph, in the words after sub-paragraph (b), for 'on the remarriage of the applicant' onwards substitute 'on the formation by the applicant of a subsequent marriage or civil partnership, except in relation to any arrears due under the order on the date of the formation of the subsequent marriage or civil partnership.'

SCHEDULE 15

SECTION 196(1)

FINANCIAL RELIEF IN THE HIGH COURT OR A COUNTY COURT ETC: NORTHERN IRELAND

PART 1
FINANCIAL PROVISION IN CONNECTION WITH DISSOLUTION, NULLITY OR SEPARATION

Circumstances in which orders under this Part may be made

1(1) The court may make any one or more of the orders set out in paragraph 2(1)—

(a) on making a dissolution, nullity or separation order, or
(b) at any time afterwards.

(2) The court may make any one or more of the orders set out in paragraph 2(1)(d), (e) and (f)—

(a) in proceedings for a dissolution, nullity or separation order, before making the order;
(b) if proceedings for a dissolution, nullity or separation order are dismissed after the beginning of the trial, either straightaway or within a reasonable period after the dismissal.

(3) The power of the court to make an order under sub-paragraph (1) or (2)(a) in favour of a child of the family is exercisable from time to time.

(4) If the court makes an order in favour of a child under sub-paragraph (2)(b), it may from time to time make a further order in the child's favour of any of the kinds set out in paragraph 2(1)(d), (e) or (f).

(5) If the court makes an order under sub-paragraph (1), (2) or (4), it may give such consequential directions as it thinks fit for giving effect to the order (including directions requiring the disposal of any property).

The orders: periodical and secured periodical payments and lump sums

2(1) The orders are—

(a) an order that either civil partner must make to the other such periodical payments for such term as may be specified;
(b) an order that either civil partner must secure to the other, to the satisfaction of the court, such periodical payments for such term as may be specified;
(c) an order that either civil partner must pay to the other such lump sum or sums as may be specified;
(d) an order that one of the civil partners must make—
    (i) to such person as may be specified for the benefit of a child of the family, or
    (ii) to a child of the family,

    such periodical payments for such term as may be specified;
(e) an order that one of the civil partners must secure—
    (i) to such person as may be specified for the benefit of a child of the family, or
    (ii) to a child of the family,

    to the satisfaction of the court, such periodical payments for such term as may be specified;
(f) an order that one of the civil partners must pay such lump sum as may be specified—

(i)   to such person as may be specified for the benefit of a child of the family, or

(ii)   to a child of the family.

(2) 'Specified' means specified in the order.

Particular provision that may be made by lump sum orders

3(1) An order under this Part requiring one civil partner to pay the other a lump sum may be made for the purpose of enabling the other civil partner to meet any liabilities or expenses reasonably incurred by the other in maintaining—

(a) himself or herself, or

(b) a child of the family,

before making an application for an order under this Part in his or her favour.

(2) An order under this Part requiring a lump sum to be paid to or for the benefit of a child of the family may be made for the purpose of enabling any liabilities or expenses reasonably incurred by or for the benefit of the child before making an application for an order under this Part to be met.

(3) An order under this Part for the payment of a lump sum may—

(a) provide for its payment by instalments of such amount as may be specified, and

(b) require the payment of the instalments to be secured to the satisfaction of the court.

(4) Sub-paragraphs (1) to (3) do not restrict the powers to make the orders set out in paragraph 2(1)(c) and (f).

(5) If the court—

(a) makes an order under this Part for the payment of a lump sum, and

(b) directs that—

(i)   payment of the sum or any part of it is to be deferred, or

(ii)   the sum or any part of it is to be paid by instalments,

it may provide for the deferred amount or the instalments to carry interest at such rate as may be specified from such date as may be specified until the date when payment of it is due

(6) A date specified under sub-paragraph (5) must not be earlier than the date of the order.

(7) 'Specified' means specified in the order.

When orders under this Part may take effect

4(1) If an order is made under paragraph 2(1)(a), (b) or (c) on or after making a dissolution or nullity order, neither the order nor any settlement made in pursuance of it takes effect unless the dissolution or nullity order has been made final.

(2) This paragraph does not affect the power of the court to give a direction under paragraph 71 (settlement of instrument by conveyancing counsel).

Restrictions on making of orders under this Part

5 The power to make an order under paragraph 2(1)(d), (e) or (f) is subject to paragraph 44(1) and (5) (restrictions on orders in favour of children who have reached 18).

PART 2
PROPERTY ADJUSTMENT ON OR AFTER DISSOLUTION, NULLITY OR SEPARATION

Circumstances in which property adjustment orders may be made

6(1) The court may make one or more property adjustment orders—

(a) on making a dissolution, nullity or separation order, or
(b) at any time afterwards.

(2) In this Schedule 'property adjustment order' means a property adjustment order under this Part.

Property adjustment orders

7(1) The property adjustment orders are—

(a) an order that one of the civil partners must transfer such property as may be specified, being property to which he is entitled—
   (i)   to the other civil partner,
   (ii) to a child of the family, or
   (iii) to such person as may be specified for the benefit of a child of the family;
(b) an order that a settlement of such property as may be specified, being property to which one of the civil partners is entitled, be made to the satisfaction of the court for the benefit of—
   (i) the other civil partner and the children of the family, or
   (ii) either or any of them;
(c) an order varying for the benefit of—
   (i) the civil partners and the children of the family, or
   (ii) either or any of them,

   a relevant settlement;
(d) an order extinguishing or reducing the interest of either of the civil partners under a relevant settlement.

(2) The court may make a property adjustment order under sub-paragraph (1)(c) even though there are no children of the family.

(3) If the court makes a property adjustment order, it may give such consequential directions as it thinks fit for giving effect to the order (including directions requiring the making of any payments or the disposal of any property).

(4) In this paragraph—

'entitled' means entitled in possession or reversion,

'relevant settlement' means, in relation to a civil partnership, a settlement made, during its subsistence or in anticipation of its formation, on the civil partners including one made by will or codicil, but not including one in the form of a pension arrangement (within the meaning of Part 3), and

'specified' means specified in the order.

When property adjustment orders may take effect

8(1) If a property adjustment order is made on or after making a dissolution or nullity order, neither the property adjustment order nor any settlement made under it takes effect unless the dissolution or nullity order has been made final.

(2) This paragraph does not affect the power to give a direction under paragraph 71 (settlement of instrument by conveyancing counsel).

Restrictions on making property adjustment orders

9 The power to make a property adjustment order under paragraph 7(1)(a) is subject to paragraph 44(1) and (5) (restrictions on making orders in favour of children who have reached 18).

PART 3
PENSION SHARING ORDERS ON OR AFTER DISSOLUTION OR NULLITY ORDER

Circumstances in which pension sharing orders may be made

10(1) The court may make a pension sharing order—

    (a) on making a dissolution or nullity order, or
    (b) at any time afterwards.

(2) In this Schedule 'pension sharing order' means a pension sharing order under this Part.

Pension sharing orders

11(1) A pension sharing order is an order which—

    (a) provides that one civil partner's—
        (i)   shareable rights under a specified pension arrangement, or
        (ii) shareable state scheme rights,

    are to be subject to pension sharing for the benefit of the other civil partner, and
    (b) specifies the percentage value to be transferred.

(2) Shareable rights under a pension arrangement are rights in relation to which pension sharing is available under—

    (a) Chapter 1 of Part 5 of the Welfare Reform and Pensions (Northern Ireland) Order 1999 (SI 1999/3147 (NI 11)), or
    (b) Chapter 1 of Part 4 of the Welfare Reform and Pensions Act 1999 (c 30).

(3) Shareable state scheme rights are rights in relation to which pension sharing is available under—

    (a) Chapter 2 of Part 5 of the 1999 Order, or
    (b) Chapter 2 of Part 4 of the 1999 Act.

(4) In this Part 'pension arrangement' means—

    (a) an occupational pension scheme,
    (b) a personal pension scheme,
    (c) a retirement annuity contract,
    (d) an annuity or insurance policy purchased, or transferred, for the purpose of giving effect to rights under—

    (i)   an occupational pension scheme, or

    (ii) a personal pension scheme, and

(e) an annuity purchased, or entered into, for the purpose of discharging liability in respect of a pension credit under—

    (i)   Article 26(1)(b) of the 1999 Order, or

    (ii) section 29(1)(b) of the 1999 Act.

(5) In sub-paragraph (4)—

    'occupational pension scheme' has the same meaning as in the Pension Schemes (Northern Ireland) Act 1993 (c 49);

    'personal pension scheme' has the same meaning as in the 1993 Act;

    'retirement annuity contract' means a contract or scheme approved under Chapter 3 of Part 14 of the Income and Corporation Taxes Act 1988 (c 1).

Pension sharing orders: apportionment of charges

12 If a pension sharing order relates to rights under a pension arrangement, the court may include in the order provision about the apportionment between the civil partners of any charge under—

(a) Article 38 of the 1999 Order (charges in respect of pension sharing costs), or

(b) section 41 of the 1999 Act.

Restrictions on making of pension sharing orders

13(1) A pension sharing order may not be made in relation to a pension arrangement which—

(a) is the subject of a pension sharing order in relation to the civil partnership, or

(b) has been the subject of pension sharing between the civil partners.

(2) A pension sharing order may not be made in relation to shareable state scheme rights if—

(a) such rights are the subject of a pension sharing order in relation to the civil partnership, or

(b) such rights have been the subject of pension sharing between the civil partners.

(3) A pension sharing order may not be made in relation to the rights of a person under a pension arrangement if there is in force a requirement imposed by virtue of Part 5 which relates to benefits or future benefits to which that person is entitled under the pension arrangement.

When pension sharing orders may take effect

14(1) A pension sharing order is not to take effect unless the dissolution or nullity order on or after which it is made has been made final.

(2) No pension sharing order may be made so as to take effect before the end of such period after the making of the order as may be prescribed by regulations made by the Lord Chancellor.

(3) The power to make regulations under sub-paragraph (2) is exercisable by statutory rule for the purposes of the Statutory Rules (Northern Ireland) Order 1979 (SI 1979/1573 (NI 12)).

(4) Regulations under sub-paragraph (2) are subject to annulment in pursuance of a resolution of either House of Parliament in the same manner as a statutory instrument; and section 5 of the Statutory Instruments Act 1946 (c 36) applies accordingly.

PART 4
MATTERS TO WHICH COURT IS TO HAVE REGARD UNDER PARTS 1 TO 3

General

15 The court in deciding—

    (a) whether to exercise its powers under—

        (i)   Part 1 (financial provision on dissolution etc),

        (ii) Part 2 (property adjustment orders), or

        (iii) any provision of Part 3 (pension sharing orders) other than paragraph 12 (apportionment of charges), and

    (b) if so, in what way,

must have regard to all the circumstances of the case, giving first consideration to the welfare, while under 18, of any child of the family who has not reached 18.

Particular matters to be taken into account when exercising powers in relation to civil partners

16(1) This paragraph applies to the exercise by the court in relation to a civil partner of its powers under—

    (a) Part 1 (financial provision on dissolution etc) by virtue of paragraph 2(1)(a), (b) or (c),

    (b) Part 2 (property adjustment orders), or

    (c) Part 3 (pension sharing orders).

(2) The court must in particular have regard to—

    (a) the income, earning capacity, property and other financial resources which each civil partner—

        (i)   has, or

        (ii) is likely to have in the foreseeable future,

        including, in the case of earning capacity, any increase in that capacity which it would in the opinion of the court be reasonable to expect the civil partner to take steps to acquire;

    (b) the financial needs, obligations and responsibilities which each civil partner has or is likely to have in the foreseeable future;

    (c) the standard of living enjoyed by the family before the breakdown of the civil partnership;

    (d) the age of each civil partner and the duration of the civil partnership;

    (e) any physical or mental disability of either of the civil partners;

    (f) the contributions which each civil partner has made or is likely in the foreseeable future to make to the welfare of the family, including any contribution by looking after the home or caring for the family;

    (g) the conduct of each civil partner, if that conduct is such that it would in the opinion of the court be inequitable to disregard it;

    (h) in the case of proceedings for a dissolution or nullity order, the value to each civil partner of any benefit which, because of the dissolution or annulment of the civil partnership, that civil partner will lose the chance of acquiring.

Particular matters to be taken into account when exercising powers in relation to children

17(1) This paragraph applies to the exercise by the court in relation to a child of the family of its powers under—

(a) Part 1 (financial provision on dissolution etc) by virtue of paragraph 2(1)(d), (e) or (f), or

(b) Part 2 (property adjustment orders).

(2) The court must in particular have regard to—

(a) the financial needs of the child;

(b) the income, earning capacity (if any), property and other financial resources of the child;

(c) any physical or mental disability of the child;

(d) the way in which the child was being and in which the civil partners expected the child to be educated or trained;

(e) the considerations mentioned in relation to the civil partners in paragraph 16(2)(a), (b), (c) and (e).

(3) In relation to the exercise of any of those powers against a civil partner ('A') in favour of a child of the family who is not A's child, the court must also have regard to—

(a) whether A has assumed any responsibility for the child's maintenance,

(b) if so, the extent to which, and the basis upon which, A assumed such responsibility and the length of time for which A discharged such responsibility;

(c) whether in assuming and discharging such responsibility A did so knowing that the child was not A's child;

(d) the liability of any other person to maintain the child.

Terminating considerations

18(1) Sub-paragraphs (2) and (3) apply if, on or after the making of a dissolution or nullity order, the court decides to exercise its powers under—

(a) Part 1 (financial provision on dissolution etc) by virtue of paragraph 2(1)(a), (b) or (c),

(b) Part 2 (property adjustment orders), or

(c) Part 3 (pension sharing orders),

in favour of one of the civil partners.

(2) The court must consider whether it would be appropriate to exercise those powers in such a way that the financial obligations of each civil partner towards the other will be terminated as soon after the making of the dissolution or nullity order as the court considers just and reasonable.

(3) If the court decides to make—

(a) a periodical payments order, or

(b) a secured periodical payments order,

in favour of one of the civil partners ('A'), it must in particular consider whether it would be appropriate to require the payments to be made or secured only for such term as would in its opinion be sufficient to enable A to adjust without undue hardship to the termination of A's financial dependence on the other civil partner.

(4) If—

(a) on or after the making of a dissolution or nullity order, an application is made by one of the civil partners for a periodical payments or secured periodical payments order in that civil partner's favour, but

(b) the court considers that no continuing obligation should be imposed on either civil partner to make or secure periodical payments in favour of the other, the court may dismiss the application with a direction that the applicant is not entitled to make any future application in relation to that civil partnership for an order under Part 1 by virtue of paragraph 2(1)(a) or (b).

PART 5
MAKING OF PART 1 ORDERS HAVING REGARD TO PENSION BENEFITS

Pension benefits to be included in matters to which court is to have regard

19(1) The matters to which the court is to have regard under paragraph 16(2)(a) include any pension benefits under a pension arrangement or by way of pension which a civil partner has or is likely to have; and, accordingly, in relation to any pension benefits paragraph 16(2)(a)(ii) has effect as if 'in the foreseeable future' were omitted.

(2) The matters to which the court is to have regard under paragraph 16(2)(h) include any pension benefits which, because of the making of a dissolution or nullity order, a civil partner will lose the chance of acquiring.

(3) 'Pension benefits' means—

  (a) benefits under a pension arrangement, or
  (b) benefits by way of pension (whether under a pension arrangement or not).

Provisions applying where pension benefits taken into account in decision to make Part 1 order

20(1) This paragraph applies if, having regard to any benefits under a pension arrangement, the court decides to make an order under Part 1.

(2) To the extent to which the Part 1 order is made having regard to any benefits under a pension arrangement, it may require the person responsible for the pension arrangement, if at any time any payment in respect of any benefits under the arrangement becomes due to the civil partner with pension rights, to make a payment for the benefit of the other civil partner.

(3) The Part 1 order must express the amount of any payment required to be made by virtue of sub-paragraph (2) as a percentage of the payment which becomes due to the civil partner with pension rights.

(4) Any such payment by the person responsible for the arrangement—

  (a) discharges so much of his liability to the civil partner with pension rights as corresponds to the amount of the payment, and
  (b) is to be treated for all purposes as a payment made by the civil partner with pension rights in or towards the discharge of that civil partner's liability under the order.

(5) If the civil partner with pension rights has a right of commutation under the arrangement, the Part 1 order may require that civil partner to exercise it to any extent.

(6) This paragraph applies to any payment due in consequence of commutation in pursuance of the Part 1 order as it applies to other payments in respect of benefits under the arrangement.

(7) The power conferred by sub-paragraph (5) may not be exercised for the purpose of commuting a benefit payable to the civil partner with pension rights to a benefit payable to the other civil partner.

(8) The powers conferred by sub-paragraphs (2) and (5) may not be exercised in relation to a pension arrangement which—

(a) is the subject of a pension sharing order in relation to the civil partnership, or

(b) has been the subject of pension sharing between the civil partners.

Pensions: lump sums

21(1) This paragraph applies if the benefits which the civil partner with pension rights has or is likely to have under a pension arrangement include any lump sum payable in respect of that civil partner's death.

(2) The court's power under Part 1 to order a civil partner to pay a lump sum to the other civil partner includes the power to make by the order any of the provision in sub-paragraphs (3) to (5).

(3) If the person responsible for the pension arrangement has power to determine the person to whom the sum, or any part of it, is to be paid, the court may require him to pay the whole or part of that sum, when it becomes due, to the other civil partner.

(4) If the civil partner with pension rights has power to nominate the person to whom the sum, or any part of it, is to be paid, the court may require the civil partner with pension rights to nominate the other civil partner in respect of the whole or part of that sum.

(5) In any other case, the court may require the person responsible for the pension arrangement in question to pay the whole or part of that sum, when it becomes due, for the benefit of the other civil partner instead of to the person to whom, apart from the order, it would be paid.

(6) Any payment by the person responsible for the arrangement under an order made under Part 1 made by virtue of this paragraph discharges so much of his liability in respect of the civil partner with pension rights as corresponds to the amount of the payment.

(7) The powers conferred by this paragraph may not be exercised in relation to a pension arrangement which—

(a) is the subject of a pension sharing order in relation to the civil partnership, or

(b) has been the subject of pension sharing between the civil partners.

Pensions: supplementary

22 If—

(a) a Part 1 order made by virtue of paragraph 20 or 21 imposes any requirement on the person responsible for a pension arrangement ('the first arrangement'),

(b) the civil partner with pension rights acquires rights under another pension arrangement ('the new arrangement') which are derived (directly or indirectly) from the whole of that civil partner's rights under the first arrangement, and

(c) the person responsible for the new arrangement has been given notice in accordance with regulations made by the Lord Chancellor,

the Part 1 order has effect as if it had been made instead in respect of the person responsible for the new arrangement.

Regulations

23(1) The Lord Chancellor may by regulations—

(a) make provision, in relation to any provision of paragraphs 20 or 21 which authorises the court making a Part 1 order to require the person responsible for a pension arrangement to make a payment for the benefit of the other civil partner, as to—

(i) the person to whom, and

    (ii)   the terms on which,

the payment is to be made;

(b) make provision, in relation to payment under a mistaken belief as to the continuation in force of a provision included by virtue of paragraph 20 or 21 in a Part 1 order, about the rights or liabilities of the payer, the payee or the person to whom the payment was due;

(c) require notices to be given in respect of changes of circumstances relevant to Part 1 orders which include provision made by virtue of paragraphs 20 and 21;

(d) make provision for the person responsible for a pension arrangement to be discharged in prescribed circumstances from a requirement imposed by virtue of paragraph 20 or 21;

(e) make provision about calculation and verification in relation to the valuation of—

    (i)   benefits under a pension arrangement, or

    (ii)   shareable state scheme rights (within the meaning of paragraph 11(3)),

for the purposes of the court's functions in connection with the exercise of any of its powers under this Schedule.

(2) Regulations under sub-paragraph (1)(e) may include—

(a) provision for calculation or verification in accordance with guidance from time to time prepared by a prescribed person, and

(b) provision by reference to regulations under Article 27 or 46(4) of the Welfare Reform and Pensions (Northern Ireland) Order 1999 (SI 1999/3147 (NI 11)).

(3) The power to make regulations under paragraph 22 or this paragraph is exercisable by statutory rule for the purposes of the Statutory Rules (Northern Ireland) Order 1979 (SI 1979/1573 (NI 12)).

(4) Regulations under paragraph 22 or this paragraph are subject to annulment in pursuance of a resolution of either House of Parliament in the same manner as a statutory instrument; and section 5 of the Statutory Instruments Act 1946 (c 36) applies accordingly.

(5) 'Prescribed' means prescribed by regulations.

Interpretation of provisions relating to pensions

24(1) In this Part 'the civil partner with pension rights' means the civil partner who has or is likely to have benefits under a pension arrangement.

(2) In this Part 'pension arrangement' has the same meaning as in Part 3.

(3) In this Part, references to the person responsible for a pension arrangement are to be read in accordance with Article 23 of the 1999 Order.

PART 6
PENSION PROTECTION FUND COMPENSATION ETC

PPF compensation to be included in matters to which court is to have regard

25(1) The matters to which a court is to have regard under paragraph 16(2)(a) include any PPF compensation to which a civil partner is or is likely to be entitled; and, accordingly, in relation to any PPF compensation paragraph 16(2)(a)(ii) has effect as if 'in the foreseeable future' were omitted.

(2) The matters to which a court is to have regard under paragraph 16(2)(h) include any PPF compensation which, because of the making of a dissolution or nullity order, a civil partner will lose the chance of acquiring entitlement to.

(3) In this Part 'PPF compensation' means compensation payable under—

    (a) Chapter 3 of Part 2 of the Pensions Act 2004 (pension protection), or

    (b) corresponding Northern Ireland legislation.

Assumption of responsibility by PPF Board in paragraph 20(2) cases

26(1) This paragraph applies to an order under Part 1 so far as it includes provision made by virtue of paragraph 20(2) which—

    (a) imposed requirements on the trustees or managers of an occupational pension scheme for which the Board has assumed responsibility, and

    (b) was made before the trustees or managers received the transfer notice.

(2) From the time the trustees or managers of the scheme receive the transfer notice, the order has effect—

    (a) except in descriptions of case prescribed by regulations, with the modifications set out in sub-paragraph (3), and

    (b) with such other modifications as may be prescribed by regulations.

(3) The modifications are that—

    (a) references in the order to the trustees or managers of the scheme have effect as references to the Board, and

    (b) references in the order to any pension or lump sum to which the civil partner with pension rights is or may become entitled under the scheme have effect as references to any PPF compensation to which that person is or may become entitled in respect of the pension or lump sum.

Assumption of responsibility by PPF Board in paragraph 20(5) cases

27(1) This paragraph applies to an order under Part 1 if—

    (a) it includes provision made by virtue of paragraph 20(5) which requires the civil partner with pension rights to exercise his right of commutation under an occupational pension scheme to any extent, and

    (b) before the requirement is complied with the Board has assumed responsibility for the scheme.

(2) From the time the trustees or managers of the scheme receive the transfer notice, the order has effect with such modifications as may be prescribed by regulations.

Lump sums: power to modify paragraph 21 in respect of assessment period

28 Regulations may modify paragraph 21 in its application to an occupational pension scheme during an assessment period in relation to the scheme.

Assumption of responsibility by the Board not to affect power of court to vary order etc

29(1) This paragraph applies where the court makes, in relation to an occupational pension scheme—

    (a) a pension sharing order, or

    (b) an order including provision made by virtue of paragraph 20(2) or (5).

(2) If the Board subsequently assumes responsibility for the scheme, that does not affect—

(a) the powers of the court under paragraph 46 to vary or discharge the order or to suspend or revive any provision of it;

(b) on an appeal, the powers of the appeal court to affirm, reinstate, set aside or vary the order.

Regulations

30 Regulations may make such consequential modifications of any provision of, or made by virtue of, this Schedule as appear to the Lord Chancellor necessary or expedient to give effect to the provisions of this Part.

31(1) In this Part 'regulations' means regulations made by the Lord Chancellor.

(2) A power to make regulations under this Part is exercisable by statutory rule for the purposes of the Statutory Rules (Northern Ireland) Order 1979 (SI 1979/1573 (NI 12)).

(3) Regulations under this Part are subject to annulment in pursuance of a resolution of either House of Parliament in the same manner as a statutory instrument; and section 5 of the Statutory Instruments Act 1946 (c 36) applies accordingly.

Interpretation

32(1) In this Part—

'assessment period' means—

(a) an assessment period within the meaning of Part 2 of the Pensions Act 2004 (pension protection), or

(b) an equivalent period under corresponding Northern Ireland legislation;

'the Board' means the Board of the Pension Protection Fund;

'the civil partner with pension rights' has the meaning given by paragraph 24(1);

'occupational pension scheme' has the same meaning as in the Pension Schemes (Northern Ireland) Act 1993 (c 49);

'transfer notice' has the same meaning as in—

(a) Chapter 3 of Part 2 of the 2004 Act, or

(b) corresponding Northern Ireland legislation.

(2) References in this Part to the Board assuming responsibility for a scheme are to the Board assuming responsibility for the scheme in accordance with—

(a) Chapter 3 of Part 2 of the 2004 Act (pension protection), or
(b) corresponding Northern Ireland legislation.

PART 7
MAINTENANCE PENDING OUTCOME OF DISSOLUTION, NULLITY OR SEPARATION PROCEEDINGS

33 On an application for a dissolution, nullity or separation order, the court may make an order requiring either civil partner to make to the other for the other's maintenance such periodical payments for such term—

(a) beginning no earlier than the date on which the application was made, and
(b) ending with the date on which the proceedings are determined,

as the court thinks reasonable.

PART 8
FAILURE TO MAINTAIN: FINANCIAL PROVISION (AND INTERIM ORDERS)

Circumstances in which orders under this Part may be made

34(1) Either civil partner in a subsisting civil partnership may apply to the court for an order under this Part on the ground that the other civil partner ('the respondent')—

(a) has failed to provide reasonable maintenance for the applicant, or
(b) has failed to provide, or to make a proper contribution towards, reasonable maintenance for any child of the family.

(2) The court must not entertain an application under this paragraph unless—

(a) the applicant or the respondent is domiciled in Northern Ireland on the date of the application,
(b) the applicant has been habitually resident there throughout the period of 1 year ending with that date, or
(c) the respondent is resident there on that date.

(3) If, on an application under this paragraph, it appears to the court that—

(a) the applicant or any child of the family to whom the application relates is in immediate need of financial assistance, but
(b) it is not yet possible to determine what order, if any, should be made on the application,

the court may make an interim order.

(4) If, on an application under this paragraph, the applicant satisfies the court of a ground mentioned in sub-paragraph (1), the court may make one or more of the orders set out in paragraph 36.

Interim orders

35 An interim order is an order requiring the respondent to make to the applicant, until the determination of the application, such periodical payments as the court thinks reasonable.

Orders that may be made where failure to maintain established

36(1) The orders are—

(a) an order that the respondent must make to the applicant such periodical payments for such term as may be specified;
(b) an order that the respondent must secure to the applicant, to the satisfaction of the court, such periodical payments for such term as may be specified;
(c) an order that the respondent must pay to the applicant such lump sum as may be specified;
(d) an order that the respondent must make such periodical payments for such term as may be specified—
    (i) to such person as may be specified, for the benefit of the child to whom the application relates, or
    (ii) to the child to whom the application relates;
(e) an order that the respondent must secure—

> (i)   to such person as may be specified for the benefit of the child to whom the application relates, or
> (ii) to the child to whom the application relates,

to the satisfaction of the court, such periodical payments for such term as may be specified;
 (f) an order that the respondent must pay such lump sum as may be specified—
> (i)   to such person as may be specified for the benefit of the child to whom the application relates, or
> (ii) to the child to whom the application relates.

(2) In this Part 'specified' means specified in the order.

Particular provision that may be made by lump sum orders

37(1) An order under this Part for the payment of a lump sum may be made for the purpose of enabling any liabilities or expenses reasonably incurred in maintaining the applicant or any child of the family to whom the application relates before the making of the application to be met.

(2) An order under this Part for the payment of a lump sum may—

> (a) provide for its payment by instalments of such amount as may be specified, and
> (b) require the payment of the instalments to be secured to the satisfaction of the court.

(3) Sub-paragraphs (1) and (2) do not restrict the power to make an order by virtue of paragraph 36(1)(c) or (f).

Matters to which the court is to have regard on application under paragraph 34(1)(a)

38(1) This paragraph applies if an application under paragraph 34 is made on the ground mentioned in paragraph 34(1)(a).

(2) In deciding—

> (a) whether the respondent has failed to provide reasonable maintenance for the applicant, and
> (b) what order, if any, to make under this Part in favour of the applicant,

the court must have regard to all the circumstances of the case including the matters mentioned in paragraph 16(2).

(3) If an application is also made under paragraph 34 in respect of a child of the family who has not reached 18, the court must give first consideration to the welfare of the child while under 18.

(4) Paragraph 16(2)(c) has effect as if for the reference in it to the breakdown of the civil partnership there were substituted a reference to the failure to provide reasonable maintenance for the applicant.

Matters to which the court is to have regard on application under paragraph 34(1)(b)

39(1) This paragraph applies if an application under paragraph 34 is made on the ground mentioned in paragraph 34(1)(b).

(2) In deciding—

> (a) whether the respondent has failed to provide, or to make a proper contribution towards, reasonable maintenance for the child of the family to whom the application relates, and
> (b) what order, if any, to make under this Part in favour of the child,

the court must have regard to all the circumstances of the case.

(3) Those circumstances include—

(a) the matters mentioned in paragraph 17(2)(a) to (e), and
(b) if the child of the family to whom the application relates is not the child of the respondent, the matters mentioned in paragraph 17(3).

(4) Paragraph 16(2)(c) (as it applies by virtue of paragraph 17(2)(e)) has effect as if for the reference in it to the breakdown of the civil partnership there were substituted a reference to—

(a) the failure to provide, or
(b) the failure to make a proper contribution towards,

reasonable maintenance for the child of the family to whom the application relates.

Restrictions on making orders under this Part

40 The power to make an order under paragraph 36(1)(d), (e) or (f) is subject to paragraph 44(1) and (5) (restrictions on orders in favour of children who have reached 18).

PART 9
COMMENCEMENT OF CERTAIN PROCEEDINGS AND DURATION OF CERTAIN ORDERS

Commencement of proceedings for ancillary relief, etc

41(1) Sub-paragraph (2) applies if an application for a dissolution, nullity or separation order has been made.

(2) Subject to sub-paragraph (3), proceedings for—

(a) an order under Part 1 (financial provision on dissolution etc),
(b) a property adjustment order, or
(c) an order under Part 7 (maintenance pending outcome of dissolution, nullity or separation proceedings),

may be begun (subject to and in accordance with rules of court), at any time after the presentation of the application.

(3) Rules of court may provide, in such cases as may be prescribed by the rules that—

(a) an application for any such relief as is mentioned in sub-paragraph (2) must be made in the application or defence, and
(b) an application for any such relief which—
  (i) is not so made, or
  (ii) is not made until after the end of such period following the presentation of the application or filing of the defence as may be so prescribed,

  may be made only with the leave of the court.

Duration of periodical and secured periodical payments orders for a civil partner

42(1) The court may specify in a periodical payments or secured periodical payments order in favour of a civil partner such term as it thinks fit, except that the term must not—

(a) begin before the date of the making of an application for the order, or

(b) extend beyond the limits given in sub-paragraphs (2) and (3).

(2) The limits in the case of a periodical payments order are—

   (a) the death of either civil partner;
   (b) where the order is made on or after the making of a dissolution or nullity order, the formation of a subsequent civil partnership or marriage by the civil partner in whose favour the order is made.

(3) The limits in the case of a secured periodical payments order are—

   (a) the death of the civil partner in whose favour the order is made;
   (b) where the order is made on or after the making of a dissolution or nullity order, the formation of a subsequent civil partnership or marriage by the civil partner in whose favour the order is made.

(4) In the case of an order made on or after the making of a dissolution or nullity order, sub-paragraphs (1) to (3) are subject to paragraphs 18(3) and 52(4).

(5) If a periodical payments or secured periodical payments order in favour of a civil partner is made on or after the making of a dissolution or nullity order, the court may direct that that civil partner is not entitled to apply under paragraph 46 for the extension of the term specified in the order.

(6) If—

   (a) a periodical payments or secured periodical payments order in favour of a civil partner is made otherwise than on or after the making of a dissolution or nullity order, and
   (b) the civil partnership is subsequently dissolved or annulled but the order continues in force,

the order ceases to have effect (regardless of anything in it) on the formation of a subsequent civil partnership or marriage by that civil partner, except in relation to any arrears due under it on the date of its formation.

Subsequent civil partnership or marriage

43 If after the making of a dissolution or nullity order one of the civil partners forms a subsequent civil partnership or marriage, that civil partner is not entitled to apply, by reference to the dissolution or nullity order, for—

   (a) an order under Part 1 in that civil partner's favour, or
   (b) a property adjustment order,

against the other civil partner in the dissolved or annulled civil partnership.

Duration of continuing orders in favour of children, and age limit on making certain orders in their favour

44(1) Subject to sub-paragraph (5)—

   (a) no order under Part 1,
   (b) no property adjustment order made by virtue of paragraph 7(1)(a) (transfer of property), and
   (c) no order made under Part 8 (failure to maintain) by virtue of paragraph 36,

is to be made in favour of a child who has reached 18.

(2) The term to be specified in a periodical payments or secured periodical payments order in favour of a child may begin with—

(a) the date of the making of an application for the order or a later date, or
(b) a date ascertained in accordance with sub-paragraph (7) or (8).

(3) The term to be specified in such an order—

(a) must not in the first instance extend beyond the date of the birthday of the child next following the child's reaching the upper limit of the compulsory school age unless the court considers that in the circumstances of the case the welfare of the child requires that it should extend to a later date, and
(b) must not in any event, subject to sub-paragraph (5), extend beyond the date of the child's 18th birthday.

(4) In sub-paragraph (3)(a) 'compulsory school age' has the meaning given in Article 46 of the Education and Libraries (Northern Ireland) Order 1986 (SI 1986/594 (NI 3)).

(5) Sub-paragraphs (1) and (3)(b) do not apply in the case of a child, if it appears to the court that—

(a) the child is, or will be, or, if an order were made without complying with either or both of those provisions, would be—
(i) receiving instruction at an educational establishment, or
(ii) undergoing training for a trade, profession or vocation,

whether or not the child also is, will be or would be in gainful employment, or
(b) there are special circumstances which justify the making of an order without complying with either or both of sub-paragraphs (1) and (3)(b).

(6) A periodical payments order in favour of a child, regardless of anything in the order, ceases to have effect on the death of the person liable to make payments under the order, except in relation to any arrears due under the order on the date of the death.

(7) If—

(a) a maintenance calculation ('the current calculation') is in force with respect to a child, and
(b) an application is made under this Schedule for a periodical payments or secured periodical payments order in favour of that child before the end of 6 months beginning with the making of the current calculation,

the term to be specified in any such order made on that application may be expressed to begin on, or at any time after, the earliest permitted date.

(8) 'The earliest permitted date' is whichever is the later of—

(a) the date 6 months before the application is made, or
(b) the date on which the current calculation took effect or, where successive maintenance calculations have been continuously in force with respect to a child, on which the first of those calculations took effect.

(9) If—

(a) a maintenance calculation ceases to have effect by or under any provision of the Child Support (Northern Ireland) Order 1991 (SI 1991/2628 (NI 23)), and
(b) an application is made, before the end of 6 months beginning with the relevant date, for a periodical payments or secured periodical payments order in favour of a child with respect to whom that maintenance calculation was in force immediately before it ceased to have effect,

the term to be specified in any such order made on that application may begin with the date on which that maintenance calculation ceased to have effect or any later date.

(10) 'The relevant date' means the date on which the maintenance calculation ceased to have effect.

(11) In this Schedule 'maintenance calculation' has the same meaning as it has in the 1991 Order.

PART 10
VARIATION, DISCHARGE ETC OF CERTAIN ORDERS FOR FINANCIAL RELIEF

Orders etc to which this Part applies

45(1) This Part applies to the following orders—

(a) a periodical payments order under Part 1 (financial provision on dissolution etc) or Part 8 (failure to maintain);

(b) a secured periodical payments order under Part 1 or 8;

(c) an order under Part 7 (maintenance pending outcome of dissolution proceedings etc);

(d) an interim order under Part 8;

(e) an order made under Part 1 by virtue of paragraph 3(3) or under Part 8 by virtue of paragraph 37(2) (lump sum by instalments);

(f) a deferred order made under Part 1 by virtue of paragraph 2(1)(c) (lump sum for civil partner) which includes provision made by virtue of—

    (i) paragraph 20(2), or

    (ii) paragraph 21,

(provision in respect of pension rights);

(g) a property adjustment order made on or after the making of a separation order by virtue of paragraph 7(1)(b), (c) or (d) (order for settlement or variation of settlement);

(h) a pension sharing order made before the dissolution or nullity order has been made final.

(2) If the court has made an order referred to in sub-paragraph (1)(f)(ii), this Part ceases to apply to the order on the death of either of the civil partners.

(3) The powers exercisable by the court under this Part in relation to an order are also exercisable in relation to any instrument executed in pursuance of the order.

Powers to vary, discharge, suspend or revive order

46(1) If the court has made an order to which this Part applies, it may—

(a) vary or discharge the order,

(b) suspend any provision of it temporarily, or

(c) revive the operation of any provision so suspended.

(2) Sub-paragraph (1) is subject to the provisions of this Part and paragraph 42(5).

Power to remit arrears

47(1) If the court has made an order referred to in paragraph 45(1)(a), (b), (c) or (d), it may remit the payment of any arrears due under the order or under any part of the order.

(2) Sub-paragraph (1) is subject to the provisions of this Part.

Variation etc of periodical or secured periodical payments orders made in cases of failure to maintain

48(1) An application for the variation under paragraph 46 of a periodical payments order or secured periodical payments order made under Part 8 in favour of a child may, if the child has reached 16, be made by the child himself.

(2) Sub-paragraph (3) applies if a periodical payments order made in favour of a child under Part 8 ceases to have effect—

    (a) on the date on which the child reaches 16, or
    (b) at any time after that date but before or on the date on which the child reaches 18.

(3) If, on an application made to the court for an order under this sub-paragraph, it appears to the court that—

    (a) the child is, will be or, if an order were made under this sub-paragraph, would be—
        (i)   receiving instruction at an educational establishment, or
        (ii) undergoing training for a trade, profession or vocation,

        whether or not the child also is, will be or would be in gainful employment, or
    (b) there are special circumstances which justify the making of an order under this sub-paragraph,

the court may by order revive the order mentioned in sub-paragraph (2) from a date specified by it.

(4) The date specified under sub-paragraph (3) must not be earlier than the date of the application under that sub-paragraph.

(5) If under sub-paragraph (3) the court revives an order it may exercise its power under paragraph 46 in relation to the revived order.

Variation etc of property adjustment and pension sharing orders

49 The court must not exercise the powers conferred by this Part in relation to a property adjustment order falling within paragraph 7(1)(b), (c) or (d) (order for settlement or for variation of settlement) except on an application made in proceedings—

    (a) for the rescission of the separation order by reference to which the property adjustment order was made, or
    (b) for a dissolution order in relation to the civil partnership.

50(1) In relation to a pension sharing order which is made at a time before the dissolution or nullity order has been made final—

    (a) the powers conferred by this Part (by virtue of paragraph 45(1)(h)) may be exercised—
        (i)   only on an application made before the pension sharing order has or, but for paragraph (b), would have taken effect, and
        (ii) only if, at the time when the application is made, the dissolution or nullity order has not been made final, and
    (b) an application made in accordance with paragraph (a) prevents the pension sharing order from taking effect before the application has been dealt with.

(2) No variation of a pension sharing order is to be made so as to take effect before the order is made final.

(3) The variation of a pension sharing order prevents the order taking effect before the end of such period after the making of the variation as may be prescribed by regulations made by the Lord Chancellor.

(4) The power to make regulations under sub-paragraph (3) is exercisable by statutory rule for the purposes of the Statutory Rules (Northern Ireland) Order 1979 (SI 1979/1573 (NI 12)).

(5) Regulations under sub-paragraph (3) are subject to annulment in pursuance of a resolution of either House of Parliament in the same manner as a statutory instrument; and section 5 of the Statutory Instruments Act 1946 (c 36) applies accordingly.

51(1) No property adjustment order or pension sharing order may be made on an application for the variation of a periodical payments or secured periodical payments order made (whether in favour of a civil partner or in favour of a child of the family) under Part 1.

(2) No order for the payment of a lump sum may be made on an application for the variation of a periodical payments or secured periodical payments order in favour of a civil partner (whether made under Part 1 or 8).

Matters to which court is to have regard in exercising powers under this Part

52(1) In exercising the powers conferred by this Part the court must have regard to all the circumstances of the case, giving first consideration to the welfare, while under 18, of any child of the family who has not reached 18.

(2) The circumstances of the case include, in particular, any change in any of the matters to which the court was required to have regard when making the order to which the application relates.

(3) Sub-paragraph (4) applies in the case of—

(a) a periodical payments order, or
(b) a secured periodical payments order,

made on or after the making of a dissolution or nullity order.

(4) The court must consider whether in all the circumstances, and after having regard to any such change, it would be appropriate to vary the order so that payments under the order are required—

(a) to be made, or
(b) to be secured,

only for such further period as will in the opinion of the court be sufficient to enable the civil partner in whose favour the order was made to adjust without undue hardship to the termination of those payments.

(5) If the civil partner against whom the order was made has died, the circumstances of the case also include the changed circumstances resulting from that civil partner's death.

Variation of secured periodical payments order where person liable has died

53(1) This paragraph applies if the person liable to make payments under a secured periodical payments order has died.

(2) Subject to sub-paragraph (3), an application under this Part relating to the order may be made by—

(a) the person entitled to payments under the periodical payments order, or
(b) the personal representatives of the deceased person.

(3) No such application may be made without the leave of the court after the end of 6 months from the date on which representation in regard to the estate of that person is first taken out.

(4) The personal representatives of the person who has died are not liable for having distributed any part of the estate of the deceased after the end of the 6 month period on the ground that they ought to have taken into account the possibility that the court might allow an application under this paragraph to be made after that period by the person entitled to payments under the order.

(5) Sub-paragraph (4) does not affect any power to recover any part of the estate so distributed arising by virtue of the making of an order in pursuance of this paragraph.

(6) In considering for the purposes of sub-paragraph (3) the question when representation was first taken out a grant limited to part of the estate is to be disregarded unless a grant limited to the remainder of the estate has previously been made or is made at the same time.

Power to direct when variation etc is to take effect

54(1) If the court, in exercise of its powers under this Part, decides—

  (a) to vary, or
  (b) to discharge,

a periodical payments or secured periodical payments order, it may direct that the variation or discharge is not to take effect until the end of such period as may be specified.

(2) Sub-paragraph (1) is subject to paragraph 42(1) and (6).

55(1) If—

  (a) a periodical payments or secured periodical payments order in favour of more than one child ('the order') is in force,
  (b) the order requires payments specified in it to be made to or for the benefit of more than one child without apportioning those payments between them,
  (c) a maintenance calculation ('the calculation') is made with respect to one or more, but not all, of the children with respect to whom those payments are to be made, and
  (d) an application is made, before the end of the period of 6 months beginning with the date on which the calculation was made, for the variation or discharge of the order,

the court may, in exercise of its powers under this Part to vary or discharge the order, direct that the variation or discharge is to take effect from the date on which the calculation took effect or any later date.

(2) If—

  (a) an order ('the child order') of a kind prescribed for the purposes of Article 12(1) of the Child Support (Northern Ireland) Order 1991 (SI 1991/2628 (NI 23)) is affected by a maintenance calculation,
  (b) on the date on which the child order became so affected there was in force a periodical payments or secured periodical payments order ('the civil partner's order') in favour of a civil partner having the care of the child in whose favour the child order was made, and
  (c) an application is made, before the end of the period of 6 months beginning with the date on which the maintenance calculation was made, for the civil partner's order to be varied or discharged,

the court may, in exercise of its powers under this Part to vary or discharge the civil partner's order, direct that the variation or discharge is to take effect from the date on which the child order became so affected or any later date.

(3) For the purposes of sub-paragraph (2), an order is affected if it ceases to have effect or is modified by or under Article 12 of the 1991 Order.

(4) Sub-paragraphs (1) and (2) do not affect any other power of the court to direct that the variation or discharge of an order under this Part is to take effect from a date earlier than that on which the order for variation or discharge was made.

PART 11
ARREARS AND REPAYMENTS

Payment of certain arrears unenforceable without the leave of the court

56(1) This paragraph applies if any arrears are due under—

(a) an order under Part 1 (financial provision on dissolution etc),
(b) an order under Part 7 (maintenance pending outcome of dissolution, nullity or separation proceedings), or
(c) an interim order under Part 8 (failure to maintain),

and the arrears became due more than 12 months before proceedings to enforce the payment of them are begun.

(2) A person is not entitled to enforce through the court the payment of the arrears without the leave of that court.

(3) The court hearing an application for the grant of leave under this paragraph may—

(a) refuse leave,
(b) grant leave subject to such restrictions and conditions (including conditions as to the allowing of time for payment or the making of payment by instalments) as that court thinks proper, or
(c) remit the payment of the arrears or of any part of them.

Orders for repayment in certain cases of sums paid under certain orders

57(1) This paragraph applies if—

(a) a person ('R') is entitled to receive payments under an order listed in sub-paragraph (4), and
(b) R's circumstances or the circumstances of the person ('P') liable to make payments under the order have changed since the order was made, or the circumstances have changed as a result of P's death.

(2) The orders are—

(a) any order under Part 7 (maintenance pending outcome of dissolution, nullity or separation proceedings);
(b) any interim order under Part 8;
(c) any periodical payments order;
(d) any secured periodical payments order.

(3) P or P's personal representatives may (subject to sub-paragraph (7)) apply for an order under this paragraph against R or R's personal representatives.

(4) If it appears to the court that, because of the changed circumstances or P's death, the amount received by R in respect of a relevant period exceeds the amount which P or P's personal representatives should have been required to pay, it may order the respondent to the application to pay to the applicant such sum, not exceeding the amount of the excess, as it thinks just.

(5) 'Relevant period' means a period after the circumstances changed or (as the case may be) after P's death.

(6) An order under this paragraph for the payment of any sum may provide for the payment of that sum by instalments of an amount specified in the order.

(7) An application under this paragraph—

(a) may be made in proceedings in the High Court for—
  (i) the variation or discharge of the order listed in sub-paragraph (2), or
  (ii) leave to enforce, or the enforcement of, the payment of arrears under that order, but
(b) if not made in such proceedings, must be made to a county court;

and accordingly references in this paragraph to the court are references to the High Court or a county court (whether a civil partnership proceedings county court or not), as the circumstances require.

(8) The jurisdiction conferred on a county court by this paragraph is exercisable even though, because of the amount claimed in the application, the jurisdiction would not but for this sub-paragraph be exercisable by a county court.

Orders for repayment after cessation of order because of subsequent civil partnership etc

58(1) Sub-paragraphs (3) and (4) apply if—

(a) a periodical payments or secured periodical payments order in favour of a civil partner ('R') has ceased to have effect because of the formation of a subsequent civil partnership or marriage by R, and
(b) the person liable to make payments under the order ('P') (or P's personal representatives) has made payments in accordance with it in respect of a relevant period in the mistaken belief that the order was still subsisting.

(2) 'Relevant period' means a period after the date of the formation of the civil partnership or marriage.

(3) P (or P's personal representatives) is not entitled to bring proceedings in respect of a cause of action arising out of the circumstances mentioned in sub-paragraph (1)(a) and (b) against R (or R's personal representatives).

(4) But, on an application under this paragraph by P (or P's personal representatives) against R (or R's personal representatives), the court—

(a) may order the respondent to pay to the applicant a sum equal to the amount of the payments made in respect of the relevant period, or
(b) if it appears to the court that it would be unjust to make that order, may—
  (i) order the respondent to pay to the applicant such lesser sum as it thinks fit, or
  (ii) dismiss the application.

(5) An order under this paragraph for the payment of any sum may provide for the payment of that sum by instalments of such amount as may be specified in the order.

(6) An application under this paragraph—

(a) may be made in proceedings in the High Court for leave to enforce, or the enforcement of, payment of arrears under the order in question, but
(b) if not made in such proceedings, must be made to a county court;

and accordingly references in this paragraph to the court are references to the High Court or a county court (whether a civil partnership proceedings county court or not), as the circumstances require.

(7) The jurisdiction conferred on a county court by this paragraph is exercisable even though, because of the amount claimed in the application, the jurisdiction would not but for this sub-paragraph be exercisable by a county court.

(8) Subject to sub-paragraph (9), the collecting officer of a court of summary jurisdiction to whom any payments under a payments order, or under an attachment of earnings order made to secure payments under a payments order, are required to be made is not liable—

(a) for any act done by him in pursuance of the payments order after the date on which that order ceased to have effect because of the formation of a subsequent civil partnership or marriage by R, or

(b) for any act done by him after that date in accordance with any statutory provision specifying how payments made to him in compliance with the attachment of earnings order are to be dealt with.

(9) Sub-paragraph (8) applies if (and only if) the act—

(a) was one which the officer would have been under a duty to do had the payments order not ceased to have effect, and

(b) was done before notice in writing of the formation of the civil partnership or marriage, was given to him by or on behalf of R, P, or R or P's personal representatives.

(10) In this paragraph—

'collecting officer' means the officer mentioned in section 15(2) of the Maintenance and Affiliation Orders Act (Northern Ireland) 1966 (c 35) or Article 85(2) of the Magistrates' Courts (Northern Ireland) Order 1981 (SI 1981/1675 (NI 26));

'statutory provision' has the meaning given by section 1(f) of the Interpretation Act (Northern Ireland) 1954 (1954 c 33 (NI)).

PART 12
CONSENT ORDERS AND MAINTAINENCE AGREEMENTS

Consent orders for financial relief

59(1) Regardless of anything in the preceding provisions of this Schedule, on an application for a consent order for financial relief, the court may, unless it has reason to think that there are other circumstances into which it ought to inquire, make an order in the terms agreed on the basis only of such information supplied with the application as is required by rules of court.

(2) Sub-paragraph (1) applies to an application for a consent order varying or discharging an order for financial relief as it applies to an application for an order for financial relief.

(3) In this paragraph—

'consent order', in relation to an application for an order, means an order in the terms applied for to which the respondent agrees;

'order for financial relief' means an order under any of Parts 1, 2, 3 and 8.

Meaning of 'maintenance agreement' and 'financial arrangements'

60(1) In this Part 'maintenance agreement' means any written agreement between the civil partners in a civil partnership which—

(a) is made during the continuance or after the dissolution or annulment of the civil partnership and contains financial arrangements, or

(b) is a separation agreement which contains no financial arrangements but is made in a case where no other agreement in writing between the civil partners contains financial arrangements.

(2) In this Part 'financial arrangements' means provisions governing the rights and liabilities towards one another when living separately of the civil partners in a civil partnership (including a civil partnership which has been dissolved or annulled) in respect of—

(a) the making or securing of payments, or

(b) the disposition or use of any property,

including such rights and liabilities with respect to the maintenance or education of a child (whether or not a child of the family).

(3) 'Education' includes training.

Validity of maintenance agreements

61 If a maintenance agreement includes a provision purporting to restrict any right to apply to a court for an order containing financial arrangements—

(a) that provision is void, but

(b) any other financial arrangements contained in the agreement—
   (i) are not void or unenforceable as a result, and
   (ii) unless void or unenforceable for any other reason, are (subject to paragraphs 62 and 66) binding on the parties to the agreement.

Alteration of agreements by court during lives of parties

62(1) Either party to a maintenance agreement may apply to the court or, subject to sub-paragraph (6), to a court of summary jurisdiction for an order under this paragraph if—

(a) the maintenance agreement is for the time being subsisting, and

(b) each of the parties to the agreement is for the time being domiciled or resident in Northern Ireland.

(2) The court may make an order under this paragraph if it is satisfied that—

(a) because of a change in the circumstances in the light of which—
   (i) any financial arrangements contained in the agreement were made, or
   (ii) financial arrangements were omitted from it,

   the agreement should be altered so as to make different financial arrangements or so as to contain financial arrangements, or

(b) that the agreement does not contain proper financial arrangements with respect to any child of the family.

(3) In sub-paragraph (2)(a) the reference to a change in the circumstances includes a change foreseen by the parties when making the agreement.

(4) An order under this paragraph may make such alterations in the agreement—

(a) by varying or revoking any financial arrangements contained in it, or

(b) by inserting in it financial arrangements for the benefit of one of the parties to the agreement or of a child of the family, as appear to the court to be just having regard to all the circumstances, including, if relevant, the matters mentioned in paragraph 17(3).

(5) The effect of the order is that the agreement is to be treated as if any alteration made by the order had been made by agreement between the partners and for valuable consideration.

(6) The power to make an order under this paragraph is subject to paragraphs 63 and 64.

Restrictions on applications to and orders by courts of summary jurisdiction under paragraph 62

63(1) A court of summary jurisdiction must not entertain an application under paragraph 62(1) unless—

(a) both the parties to the agreement are resident in Northern Ireland, and
(b) the court acts for a petty sessions district included in the county court division in which at least one of the parties is resident.

(2) A court of summary jurisdiction must not make any order on such an application other than—

(a) if the agreement includes no provision for periodical payments by either of the parties, an order inserting provision for the making by one of the parties of periodical payments for the maintenance of—
    (i)   the other party, or
    (ii) any child of the family;
(b) if the agreement includes provision for the making by one of the parties of periodical payments, an order increasing or reducing the rate of, or terminating, any of those payments.

Provisions relating to periodical and secured periodical payments: duration

64(1) If a court decides to make an order under paragraph 62 altering an agreement—

(a) by inserting provision for the making or securing by one of the parties to the agreement of periodical payments for the maintenance of the other party, or
(b) by increasing the rate of the periodical payments which the agreement provides shall be made by one of the parties for the maintenance of the other,

it may specify such term as it thinks fit as the term for which the payments or, as the case may be, the additional payments attributable to the increase are to be made under the altered agreement, except that the term must not extend beyond the limits in sub-paragraphs (2) and (3).

(2) The limits if the payments are not to be secured are—

(a) the death of either of the parties to the agreement, or
(b) the formation of a subsequent civil partnership or marriage by the party to whom the payments are to be made.

(3) The limits if the payments are to be secured are—

(a) the death of the party to whom the payments are to be made, or
(b) the formation of a subsequent civil partnership or marriage by that party.

(4) Sub-paragraph (5) applies if a court decides to make an order under paragraph 62 altering an agreement by—

(a) inserting provision for the making or securing by one of the parties to the agreement of periodical payments for the maintenance of a child of the family, or

(b) increasing the rate of the periodical payments which the agreement provides shall be made or secured by one of the parties for the maintenance of such a child.

(5) The court, in deciding the term for which under the agreement as altered by the order the payments, or the additional payments attributable to the increase, are to be made or secured for the benefit of the child, must apply paragraph 44(2) to (5) (age limits) as if the order in question were a periodical payments or secured periodical payments order in favour of the child.

Saving

65 Nothing in paragraphs 61 or 64 affects—

(a) any power of a court before which any proceedings between the parties to a maintenance agreement are brought under any other enactment (including a provision of this Schedule) to make an order containing financial arrangements, or
(b) any right of either party to apply for such an order in such proceedings.

Alteration of agreements by court after death of one party

66(1) This paragraph applies if—

(a) a maintenance agreement provides for the continuation of payments under the agreement after the death of one of the parties, and
(b) that party ('A') dies domiciled in Northern Ireland.

(2) Subject to sub-paragraphs (4) and (5), the surviving party or A's personal representatives may apply to the High Court or a county court for an order under paragraph 62 and accordingly, for the purposes of this paragraph, any reference in that paragraph to the court includes a reference to a county court (whether a civil partnership proceedings county court or not).

(3) If a maintenance agreement is altered by a court on an application made under sub-paragraph (2), the same consequences follow as if the alteration had been made immediately before the death by agreement between the parties and for valuable consideration.

(4) An application under this paragraph may not, without the leave of the High Court or a county court, be made after the end of 6 months from the date on which representation in regard to A's estate is first taken out.

(5) A county court has jurisdiction under this paragraph only if it is shown to the satisfaction of the court that, at the relevant date, the property included in A's net estate did not exceed £15,000 in value.

(6) A's personal representatives are not liable for having distributed any part of A's estate after the end of the 6 month period on the ground that they ought to have taken into account the possibility that a court might allow an application by virtue of this paragraph to be made by the surviving party after that period.

(7) Sub-paragraph (6) does not affect any power to recover any part of the estate so distributed arising by virtue of the making of an order in pursuance of this paragraph.

(8) Paragraph 53(6) applies for the purposes of sub-paragraph (4) as it applies for the purposes of paragraph 53(3).

(9) In sub-paragraph (5)—

'the property included in A's net estate' means all property of which A had power to dispose by will, otherwise than by virtue of a special power of appointment, less the amount of A's funeral, testamentary and administration expenses, debts and liabilities, including any inheritance tax payable out of A's estate on A's death;

'relevant date' means the date of A's death.

PART 13
MISCELLANEOUS AND SUPPLEMENTARY

Avoidance of transactions intended to prevent or reduce financial relief

67(1) This paragraph applies if proceedings for relief ('financial relief') are brought by one person ('A') against another ('B') under Part 1, 2, 3, 7, 8 or 9 (other than paragraph 53(2)), or paragraph 62.

(2) If the court is satisfied, on an application by A, that B is, with the intention of defeating A's claim for financial relief, about to—

(a) make any disposition, or
(b) transfer out of the jurisdiction or otherwise deal with any property,

it may make such order as it thinks fit for restraining B from doing so or otherwise for protecting the claim.

(3) If the court is satisfied, on an application by A, that—

(a) B has, with the intention of defeating A's claim for financial relief, made a reviewable disposition, and
(b) if the disposition were set aside, financial relief or different financial relief would be granted to A,

it may make an order setting aside the disposition.

(4) If the court is satisfied, on an application by A in a case where an order has been obtained by A against B under any of the provisions mentioned in sub-paragraph (1), that B has, with the intention of defeating A's claim for financial relief, made a reviewable disposition, it may make an order setting aside the disposition.

(5) An application for the purposes of sub-paragraph (3) must be made in the proceedings for the financial relief in question.

(6) If the court makes an order under sub-paragraph (3) or (4) setting aside a disposition it must give such consequential directions as it thinks fit for giving effect to the order (including directions requiring the making of any payments or the disposal of any property).

68(1) Any reference in paragraph 67 to defeating A's claim for financial relief is to—

(a) preventing financial relief from being granted to A, or to A for the benefit of a child of the family,
(b) reducing the amount of any financial relief which might be so granted, or
(c) frustrating or impeding the enforcement of any order which might be or has been made at A's instance under any of the provisions mentioned in paragraph 67(1).

(2) In paragraph 67 and this paragraph 'disposition'—

(a) does not include any provision contained in a will or codicil, but
(b) subject to paragraph (a), includes any conveyance, assurance or gift of property of any description (whether made by an instrument or otherwise).

(3) Any disposition made by B (whether before or after the commencement of the proceedings for financial relief) is a reviewable disposition for the purposes of paragraph 67(3) and (4) unless it was made—

  (a) for valuable consideration (other than formation of a civil partnership), and
  (b) to a person who, at the time of the disposition, acted in relation to it in good faith and without notice of any intention on B's part to defeat A's claim for financial relief.

(4) If an application is made under paragraph 67 with respect to a disposition which took place less than 3 years before the date of the application or with respect to a disposition or other dealing with property which is about to take place and the court is satisfied—

  (a) in a case falling within paragraph 67(2) or (3), that the disposition or other dealing would (apart from paragraph 67) have the consequence of defeating A's claim for financial relief, or
  (b) in a case falling within paragraph 67(4), that the disposition has had the consequence of defeating A's claim for financial relief,

it is presumed, unless the contrary is shown, that the person who disposed of or is about to dispose of or deal with the property did so or, as the case may be, is about to do so, with the intention of defeating A's claim for financial relief.

69(1) An order under paragraph 67(2), to the extent that it restrains B from making a disposition of any land in Northern Ireland which is specified in the order—

  (a) creates on the land a statutory charge, and
  (b) subject to section 88 of the 1970 Act (statutory charge to be void against purchaser in certain circumstances), renders liable to be set aside by the court at the instance of A any disposition of the land in contravention of the order.

(2) In this paragraph and paragraph 70—

  'disposition' has the same meaning as in paragraphs 67 and 68;

  '1970 Act' means the Land Registration Act (Northern Ireland) 1970 (c 18 (NI));

  'statutory charge' has the same meaning as in the 1970 Act.

(3) Nothing in sub-paragraph (1)(b) or section 88(1) of the 1970 Act affects any power of the court to set aside a disposition under paragraph 67(3) or (4).

70(1) The registration of a statutory charge created under paragraph 69(1)(a) shall be effective until—

  (a) the expiration of 1 year from the date of its registration or of the last renewal of its registration, unless the registration is renewed or further renewed before the expiration of that period, or
  (b) the court orders that it is to cease to have effect.

(2) When the registration ceases to have effect the Registrar of Titles may cancel it.

(3) Nothing in this paragraph affects any provision of section 91 of the 1970 Act (cancellation and modification of statutory charges).

(4) An application for the renewal, under sub-paragraph (1)(a), of the registration of a charge may be made in the same manner as the application for the original registration.

Direction for settlement of instrument for securing payments or effecting property adjustment

71(1) This paragraph applies if the court decides to make—

(a) an order under Parts 1 or 8 requiring any payments to be secured, or
(b) a property adjustment order,

or if it gives directions for the disposal of any property.

(2) The court may direct that the matter be referred to a conveyancing counsel appointed by the court for him to settle a proper instrument to be executed by all necessary parties.

(3) If the order referred to in sub-paragraph (1) is to be made in proceedings for a dissolution, nullity or separation order, the court may, if it thinks fit, defer the making of the dissolution, nullity or separation order until the instrument has been duly executed.

Settlement, etc, made in compliance with a property adjustment order may be avoided on bankruptcy of settlor

72 The fact that—

(a) a settlement, or
(b) a transfer of property,

had to be made in order to comply with a property adjustment order does not prevent the settlement or transfer from being a transaction in respect of which an order may be made under Article 312 or 313 of the Insolvency (Northern Ireland) Order 1989 (SI 1989/2405 (NI 19)) (transfers at an undervalue and preferences).

Payments, etc, under order made in favour of person suffering from mental disorder

73(1) This paragraph applies if—

(a) the court makes an order under this Schedule requiring—
    (i) payments (including a lump sum payment) to be made, or
    (ii) property to be transferred,

    to a civil partner, and
(b) the court is satisfied that the person in whose favour the order is made is incapable, because of mental disorder, of managing and administering his or her property and affairs.

(2) 'Mental disorder' has the same meaning as in the Mental Health (Northern Ireland) Order 1986 (SI 1986/595 (NI 4)).

(3) Subject to any order, direction or authority made or given in relation to that person under Part 8 of the 1986 Order, the court may order the payments to be made, or as the case may be, the property to be transferred, to such persons having charge of that person as the court may direct.

Appeals relating to pension sharing orders which have taken effect

74(1) Sub-paragraphs (2) and (3) apply if an appeal against a pension sharing order is begun on or after the day on which the order takes effect.

(2) If the pension sharing order relates to a person's rights under a pension arrangement, the appeal court may not set aside or vary the order if the person responsible for the pension arrangement has acted to his detriment in reliance on the order taking effect.

(3) If the pension sharing order relates to a person's shareable state scheme rights, the appeal court may not set aside or vary the order if the Department for Social Development has acted to its detriment in reliance on the taking effect of the order.

(4) In determining for the purposes of sub-paragraph (2) or (3) whether a person or the Department has acted to his or its detriment in reliance on the taking effect of the order, the appeal court may disregard any detriment which in its opinion is insignificant.

(5) Where sub-paragraph (2) or (3) applies, the appeal court may make such further orders (including one or more pension sharing orders) as it thinks fit for the purpose of putting the parties in the position it considers appropriate.

(6) Paragraph 14 only applies to a pension sharing order under this paragraph if the decision of the appeal court can itself be the subject of an appeal.

(7) In sub-paragraph (2), the reference to the person responsible for the pension arrangement is to be read in accordance with paragraph 24(3).

Interpretation

75(1) References in this Schedule to—

    (a) periodical payments orders,
    (b) secured periodical payments orders, and
    (c) orders for the payment of a lump sum,

are references to such of the orders that may be made under Parts 1 and 8 (other than interim orders) as are relevant in the context of the reference in question.

(2) In this Schedule 'child of the family', in relation to two people who are the civil partners of each other, means—

    (a) a child of both of them, and
    (b) any other child, other than a child placed with the civil partners as foster parents by an authority or a voluntary organisation, who has been treated by both the civil partners as a child of their family.

(3) In sub-paragraph (2) 'authority' and 'voluntary organisation' have the same meaning as in the Children (Northern Ireland) Order 1995 (SI 1995/ 755 (NI 2)).

(4) In this Schedule 'the court' has the meaning given by section 188.

(5) References in this Schedule to a subsequent civil partnership include a civil partnership which is by law void or voidable.

(6) References in this Schedule to a subsequent marriage include a marriage which is by law void or voidable.

SCHEDULE 16

SECTION 196(3)

FINANCIAL RELIEF IN COURT OF SUMMARY JURISDICTION ETC: NORTHERN IRELAND

PART 1
FAILURE TO MAINTAIN ETC: FINANCIAL PROVISION

Circumstances in which orders under this Part may be made

1(1) On an application to it by one of the civil partners, the court may make any one or more of the orders set out in paragraph 2 if it is satisfied that the other civil partner—

(a) has failed to provide reasonable maintenance for the applicant,

(b) has failed to provide, or to make a proper contribution towards, reasonable maintenance for any child of the family,

(c) has behaved in such a way that the applicant cannot reasonably be expected to live with the respondent, or

(d) has deserted the applicant.

(2) The power of the court under sub-paragraph (1) is subject to the following provisions of this Schedule.

The orders: periodical and secured periodical payments and lump sums

2(1) The orders are—

(a) an order that the respondent must make to the applicant such periodical payments for such term as may be specified;

(b) an order that the respondent must pay to the applicant such lump sum as may be specified;

(c) an order that the respondent must make—
   (i) to the applicant for the benefit of a child of the family to whom the application relates, or
   (ii) to a child of the family to whom the application relates, such periodical payments for such term as may be specified;

(d) an order that the respondent must pay such lump sum as may be specified—
   (i) to the applicant for the benefit of a child of the family to whom the application relates, or
   (ii) to a child of the family to whom the application relates.

(2) The amount of a lump sum specified under sub-paragraph (1)(b) or (d) must not exceed—

(a) £1,000, or

(b) such larger amount as the Lord Chancellor may from time to time by order fix for the purposes of this sub-paragraph.

(3) The power to make an order under sub-paragraph (2) is exercisable by statutory rule for the purposes of the Statutory Rules (Northern Ireland) Order 1979 (SI 1979/1573 (NI 12)).

(4) An order under sub-paragraph (2) is subject to annulment in pursuance of a resolution of either House of Parliament in the same manner as a statutory instrument; and section 5 of the Statutory Instruments Act 1946 (c 36) applies accordingly.

(5) 'Specified' means specified in the order.

Particular provision that may be made by lump sum orders

3(1) An order under this Part for the payment of a lump sum may be made for the purpose of enabling any liability or expenses reasonably incurred in maintaining the applicant or any child of the family to whom the application relates before the making of the order to be met.

(2) Sub-paragraph (1) does not restrict the power to make the orders set out in paragraph 2(1)(b) and (d).

Matters to which court is to have regard in exercising its powers under this Part – general

4 If an application is made for an order under this Part, the court, in deciding—

(a) whether to exercise its powers under this Part, and
(b) if so, in what way,

must have regard to all the circumstances of the case, giving first consideration to the welfare while under 18 of any child of the family who has not reached 18.

Particular matters to be taken into account when exercising powers in relation to civil partners

5(1) This paragraph applies in relation to the exercise by the court of its power to make an order by virtue of paragraph 2(1)(a) or (b).

(2) The court must in particular have regard to—

(a) the income, earning capacity, property and other financial resources which each civil partner—
  (i) has, or
  (ii) is likely to have in the foreseeable future,

  including, in the case of earning capacity, any increase in that capacity which it would in the opinion of the court be reasonable to expect the civil partner to take steps to acquire;
(b) the financial needs, obligations and responsibilities which each civil partner has or is likely to have in the foreseeable future;
(c) the standard of living enjoyed by the civil partners before the occurrence of the conduct which is alleged as the ground of the application;
(d) the age of each civil partner and the duration of the civil partnership;
(e) any physical or mental disability of either civil partner;
(f) the contributions which each civil partner has made or is likely in the foreseeable future to make to the welfare of the family, including any contribution by looking after the home or caring for the family;
(g) the conduct of each civil partner, if that conduct is such that it would in the opinion of the court be inequitable to disregard it.

Particular matters to be taken into account when exercising powers in relation to children

6(1) This paragraph applies in relation to the exercise by the court of its power to make an order by virtue of paragraph 2(1)(c) or (d).

(2) The court must in particular have regard to—

(a) the financial needs of the child;
(b) the income, earning capacity (if any), property and other financial resources of the child;
(c) any physical or mental disability of the child;

(d) the standard of living enjoyed by the family before the occurrence of the conduct which is alleged as the ground of the application;

(e) the way in which the child was being and in which the civil partners expected the child to be educated or trained;

(f) the considerations mentioned in relation to the civil partners in paragraph 5(2)(a) and (b).

(3) In relation to the exercise of its power to make an order in favour of a child of the family who is not the respondent's child, the court must also have regard to—

(a) whether the respondent has assumed any responsibility for the child's maintenance,

(b) if so, the extent to which, and the basis on which, the respondent assumed that responsibility and the length of time during which the respondent discharged that responsibility;

(c) whether in assuming and discharging that responsibility the respondent did so knowing that the child was not the respondent's child;

(d) the liability of any other person to maintain the child.

Reconciliation

7(1) If before the hearing of any evidence in proceedings on an application for an order under this Part a statement is made to the court by or on behalf of the civil partners showing a possibility of reconciliation between them, the court must adjourn the proceedings for such period as it thinks fit.

(2) If at any stage of the proceedings on an application for an order under this Part it appears to the court that there is a reasonable possibility of a reconciliation between the civil partners, the court may adjourn the proceedings for such period as it thinks fit to enable attempts to be made to effect a reconciliation.

(3) If the court adjourns any proceedings under sub-paragraph (1) or (2), it may request that—

(a) a suitably qualified person acting under arrangements made by the Department of Health, Social Services and Public Safety, or

(b) any other person, willing and able to do so and acceptable to both parties, whom the court may appoint,

should attempt to effect a reconciliation between the civil partners.

(4) If any such request is made, the person—

(a) must report in writing to the court whether the attempt has been successful, but

(b) must not include in the report any other information.

(5) The powers conferred by this paragraph are additional to any other power of the court to adjourn proceedings.

Refusal of order in case more suitable for High Court

8(1) If on hearing an application for an order under this Part a court of summary jurisdiction is of the opinion that any of the matters in question between the civil partners would be more suitably dealt with by the High Court, the court of summary jurisdiction must refuse to make any order on the application.

(2) No appeal lies from a refusal under sub-paragraph (1).

(3) But, in any proceedings in the High Court relating to or comprising the same subject matter as an application in respect of which a court of summary jurisdiction has refused to make any order, the High Court may order the application to be reheard and determined by a court of summary jurisdiction acting for the same petty sessions district as the court which refused to make any order.

PART 2
ORDERS FOR AGREED FINANCIAL PROVISION

Orders for payments which have been agreed by the parties

9(1) Either civil partner may apply to the court for an order under this Part on the ground that that civil partner or the other civil partner has agreed to make such financial provision as may be specified in the application.

(2) On such an application or on a request under paragraph 14, the court may order that the applicant or the respondent (as the case may be) is to make the financial provision specified in the application or request, if—

(a) it is satisfied that the applicant or the respondent (as the case may be) has agreed in writing to make that provision, and
(b) it has no reason to think that it would be contrary to the interests of justice to do so.

(3) Sub-paragraph (2) is subject to paragraph 12.

(4) The making of an order under this Part ('Part 2 order') does not prevent the making of an order under Part 1 ('Part 1 order') on a subsequent application for a Part 1 order.

(5) On the making of a Part 2 order, the Part 1 order ceases to have effect.

(6) Sub-paragraph (5) does not affect the power of the court under Part 6 to revoke the Part 1 order.

Meaning of 'financial provision' and of references to specified financial provision

10(1) In this Part 'financial provision' means any one or more of the following—

(a) the making of periodical payments by one civil partner to the other;
(b) the payment of a lump sum by one civil partner to the other;
(c) the making of periodical payments by one civil partner to a child of the family or to the other civil partner for the benefit of such a child;
(d) the payment by one party of a lump sum to a child of the family or to the other civil partner for the benefit of such a child.

(2) Any reference in this Part to the financial provision specified in an application under this Part or a request under paragraph 14 or specified by the court is a reference—

(a) to the type of provision specified in the application or request or by the court,
(b) to the amount so specified as the amount of any payment to be made under the application or order, and
(c) in the case of periodical payments, to the term so specified as the term for which the payments are to be made.

Evidence to be produced where respondent not present etc

11(1) This paragraph applies if the respondent—

(a) is not present, or
(b) is not represented by counsel or a solicitor,

at the hearing of an application for an order under this Part.

(2) The court must not make an order under this Part unless there is produced to it such evidence as may be prescribed by rules of court of—

(a) the consent of the respondent to the making of the order,

(b) the financial resources of the respondent, and

(c) if the financial provision specified in the application includes or consists of provision in respect of a child of the family to be made by the applicant to the respondent for the benefit of the child or to the child, the financial resources of the child.

Exercise of powers in relation to children

12(1) This paragraph applies if the financial provision specified in an application under this Part or a request under paragraph 14—

(a) includes, or

(b) consists of,

provision in respect of a child of the family.

(2) The court must not make an order under this Part unless it considers that the provision which the applicant or the respondent (as the case may be) has agreed to make in respect of the child provides for, or makes a proper contribution towards, the financial needs of the child.

Power to make alternative orders

13(1) This paragraph applies if on an application under this Part or a request under paragraph 14 the court decides—

(a) that it would be contrary to the interests of justice to make an order for the making of the financial provision specified in the application or request, or

(b) that any financial provision which the applicant or the respondent (as the case may be) has agreed to make in respect of a child of the family does not provide for, or make a proper contribution towards, the financial needs of that child.

(2) If the court is of the opinion—

(a) that it would not be contrary to the interests of justice to make an order for the making of some other financial provision specified by the court, and

(b) that, in so far as that other financial provision contains any provision for a child of the family, it provides for, or makes a proper contribution towards, the financial needs of that child,

then, if both the civil partners agree, the court may order the applicant or the respondent (as the case may be) is to make that other financial provision.

Request for order under this Part in proceedings under Part 1

14(1) On an application for an order under Part 1, both civil partners may, before the determination of the application, request the court to make an order under this Part that the applicant or the respondent (as the case may be) is to make the financial provision specified in the request.

(2) If an order is made under this Part on a request under this paragraph the application for the Part 1 order is to be treated as if it had been withdrawn.

(3) In any of the following provisions of this Schedule —

(a) references to an application for an order under this Part include a request under this paragraph, and

(b) references to an applicant or respondent, in relation to any such request, are to the applicant or respondent in relation to the pending application under Part 1.

PART 3
ORDERS OF COURT WHERE CIVIL PARTNERS LIVING APART BY AGREEMENT

Powers of court where civil partners are living apart by agreement

15(1) If—

(a) the civil partners have been living apart for a continuous period exceeding 3 months, neither civil partner having deserted the other, and

(b) one of the civil partners has been making periodical payments for the benefit of the other civil partner or of a child of the family,

the other civil partner may apply to the court for an order under this Part.

(2) An application made under sub-paragraph (1) must specify the total amount of the payments made by the respondent during the period of 3 months immediately preceding the date of the making of the application.

(3) If on an application for an order under this Part the court is satisfied that the respondent has made the payments specified in the application, the court may make one or both of the orders set out in paragraph 16.

(4) Sub-paragraph (3) is subject to the provisions of this Schedule.

The orders that may be made under this Part

16(1) The orders are—

(a) an order that the respondent is to make to the applicant such periodical payments for such term as may be specified;

(b) an order that the respondent is to make—
   (i)   to the applicant for the benefit of a child of the family to whom the application relates, or
   (ii) to a child of the family to whom the application relates,

such periodical payments for such term as may be specified.

(2) 'Specified' means specified in the order.

Restrictions on orders under this Part

17 The court in the exercise of its powers under this Part must not require—

(a) the respondent to make payments whose total amount during any period of 3 months exceeds the total amount paid by him for the benefit of—
   (i)   the applicant, or
   (ii) a child of the family,

during the period of 3 months immediately preceding the date of the making of the application;

(b) the respondent to make payments to or for the benefit of any person which exceed in amount the payments which the court considers that it would have required the respondent to make to or for the benefit of that person on an application under Part 1;

(c) payments to be made to or for the benefit of a child of the family who is not the respondent's child, unless the court considers that it would have made an order in favour of that child on an application under Part 1.

Relationship with powers under Part 1

18(1) Sub-paragraph (2) applies if on an application under this Part the court considers that the orders which it has the power to make under this Part—

(a) would not provide reasonable maintenance for the applicant, or

(b) if the application relates to a child of the family, would not provide, or make a proper contribution towards, reasonable maintenance for that child.

(2) The court—

(a) must refuse to make an order under this Part, but

(b) may treat the application as if it were an application for an order under Part 1.

Matters to be taken into consideration

19 Paragraphs 4 to 6 apply in relation to an application for an order under this Part as they apply in relation to an application for an order under Part 1, subject to the modification that for the reference in paragraph 5(2)(c) to the occurrence of the conduct which is alleged as the ground of the application substitute a reference to the living apart of the civil partners.

PART 4
INTERIM ORDERS

Circumstances in which interim orders may be made

20(1) This paragraph applies if an application has been made for an order under Part 1, 2 or 3.

(2) The court may make an interim order—

(a) at any time before making a final order on, or dismissing, the application, or

(b) on refusing (under paragraph 8) to make an order on the application.

(3) The High Court may make an interim order on ordering the application to be reheard by a court (after the refusal of an order under paragraph 8).

(4) The county court may make an interim order on an appeal from the order made by the court on the application at any time before making a final order on, or dismissing, an appeal made by virtue of paragraph 46.

(5) Not more than one interim order may be made with respect to an application for an order under Part 1, 2 or 3.

(6) Sub-paragraph (5) does not affect the power of a court to make an interim order on a further application under Part 1, 2 or 3.

Meaning of interim order

21(1) An interim order is an order requiring the respondent to make such periodical payments as the court thinks reasonable—

(a) to the applicant,

(b) to any child of the family who is under 18, or

(c) to the applicant for the benefit of such a child.

(2) In relation to an interim order in respect of an application for an order under Part 2 by the civil partner who has agreed to make the financial provision specified in the application, sub-paragraph (1) applies as if—

(a) the reference to the respondent were a reference to the applicant, and

(b) the references to the applicant were references to the respondent.

When interim order may start

22(1) An interim order may provide for payments to be made from such date as the court may specify, except that the date must not be earlier than the date of the making of the application for an order under Part 1, 2 or 3.

(2) Sub-paragraph (1) is subject to paragraph 27(10) and (11).

Payments which can be treated as having been paid on account

23(1) If an order under Part 1, 2 or 3 made by the county court on an appeal from the court provides for payments to be made from a date earlier than the date of the making of the order, the interim order may provide that payments made by the respondent under an order made by the court are to be treated, to such extent and in such manner as may be provided by the interim order, as having been paid on account of any payment provided for by the interim order.

(2) In relation to an interim order in respect of an application for an order under Part 2 by the civil partner who has agreed to make the financial provision specified in the application, sub-paragraph (1) applies as if the reference to the respondent were a reference to the applicant.

When interim order ceases to have effect

24(1) Subject to sub-paragraphs (2) and (3), an interim order made on an application for an order under Part 1, 2 or 3 ceases to have effect on the earliest of the following dates—

(a) the date, if any, specified for the purpose in the interim order;

(b) the date on which the period of 14 weeks from the date of the making of the interim order ends;

(c) the date on which the court either makes a final order on, or dismisses, the application, or, where the interim order was made by a county court on an appeal, the date on which that court either makes a final order on, or dismisses, the appeal.

(2) If an interim order made under this Part would, but for this sub-paragraph, cease to have effect under sub-paragraph (1)(a) or (b)—

(a) the court which made the order, or

(b) in the case of an interim order made by the High Court, the court by which the application for an order under Part 1, 2 or 3 is to be reheard,

may by order provide that the interim order is to continue in force for a further period.

(3) An order continued in force under sub-paragraph (2) ceases to have effect on the earliest of the following dates—

(a) the date, if any, specified for the purpose in the order continuing it;

(b) the date on which ends the period of 14 weeks from—

    (i) the date of the making of the order continuing it, or

    (ii) if more than one such order has been made with respect to the application, the date of the making of the first such order;

(c) the date on which the court either makes a final order on, or dismisses, the application, or, where the interim order was made by a county court on an appeal, the date on which that court either makes a final order on, or dismisses, the appeal.

Supplementary

25 An interim order made by the High Court under paragraph 20(3) on ordering an application to be reheard by the court is to be treated for the purposes of—

(a) its enforcement, and
(b) Part 6 (variation etc of orders),

as if it were an order of the court (and not of the High Court).

PART 5
COMMENCEMENT AND DURATION OF ORDERS UNDER PARTS 1, 2 AND 3

Duration of periodical payments order for a civil partner

26(1) The court may specify in a periodical payments order made under paragraph 2(1)(a) or Part 3 in favour of a civil partner such term as it thinks fit, except that the term must not—

(a) begin before the date of the making of the application for the order, or
(b) extend beyond the death of either of the civil partners.

(2) If—

(a) a periodical payments order is made under paragraph 2(1)(a) or Part 3 in favour of one of the civil partners, and
(b) the civil partnership is subsequently dissolved or annulled but the order continues in force,

the periodical payments order ceases to have effect (regardless of anything in it) on the formation of a subsequent civil partnership or marriage by that civil partner, except in relation to any arrears due under the order on the date of that event.

(3) If a periodical payments order ceases to have effect by virtue of sub-paragraph (2) on the formation of a subsequent civil partnership or marriage by a person, that person must give notice of the subsequent civil partnership or marriage to the court.

(4) Any person who without reasonable excuse fails to give notice as required by sub-paragraph (3) is guilty of an offence and liable on summary conviction to a fine not exceeding level 3 on the standard scale.

Age limit on making orders for financial provision for children and duration of such orders

27(1) Subject to sub-paragraph (5), no order is to be made under paragraph 2(1)(c) or (d) or Part 3 in favour of a child who has reached 18.

(2) The term to be specified in a periodical payments order made under paragraph 2(1)(c) or Part 3 in favour of a child may begin with—

(a) the date of the making of an application for the order or a later date, or
(b) a date ascertained in accordance with sub-paragraph (7) or (8).

(3) The term to be specified in such an order—

(a) must not in the first instance extend beyond the date of the birthday of the child next following his reaching the upper limit of the compulsory school age unless the court considers that in the circumstances of the case the welfare of the child requires that it should extend to a later date, and

(b) must not in any event, subject to sub-paragraph (5), extend beyond the date of the child's 18th birthday.

(4) In sub-paragraph (3)(a) 'compulsory school age' has the meaning given in Article 46 of the Education and Libraries (Northern Ireland) Order 1986 (SI 1986/594 (NI 3)).

(5) Sub-paragraphs (1) and (3)(b) do not apply in the case of a child if it appears to the court that—

(a) the child is, or will be, or, if such an order were made without complying with either or both of those provisions, would be—
  (i) receiving instruction at an educational establishment, or
  (ii) undergoing training for a trade, profession or vocation,

  whether or not also the child is, will be or would be, in gainful employment, or
(b) there are special circumstances which justify the making of the order without complying with either or both of sub-paragraphs (1) and (3)(b).

(6) Any order made under paragraph 2(1)(c) or Part 3 in favour of a child, regardless of anything in the order, ceases to have effect on the death of the person liable to make payments under the order.

(7) An order made under paragraph 2(1)(c) or Part 3 in favour of a child to whom sub-paragraph (5)(a) applies ceases to have effect if the child ceases to receive instruction or undergo training as mentioned in sub-paragraph (5)(a).

(8) If an order made under paragraph 2(1)(c) or Part 3 ceases to have effect by virtue of an event mentioned in sub-paragraph (7), the person to whom the periodical payments are directed by the order to be made must give notice of the event to the court.

(9) A person who without reasonable excuse fails to give notice as required by sub-paragraph (8) is guilty of an offence and liable on summary conviction to a fine not exceeding level 3 on the standard scale.

(10) If—

(a) a maintenance calculation ('current calculation') is in force with respect to a child, and
(b) an application is made for an order under paragraph 2(1)(c) or Part 3 before the end of 6 months beginning with the making of the current calculation,

the term to be specified in any such order made on that application may be expressed to begin on, or at any time after, the earliest permitted date.

(11) 'The earliest permitted date' is whichever is the later of—

(a) the date 6 months before the application is made, or
(b) the date on which the current calculation took effect or, where successive maintenance calculations have been continuously in force with respect to a child, on which the first of those calculations took effect.

(12) If—

(a) a maintenance calculation ceases to have effect by or under any provision of the Child Support (Northern Ireland) Order 1991 (SI 1991/2628 (NI 23)), and
(b) an application is made, before the end of 6 months beginning with the relevant date, for a periodical payments order under paragraph 2(1)(c) or Part 3 in favour of a child with respect to whom that maintenance calculation was in force immediately before it ceased to have effect,

the term to be specified in any such order, or in any interim order under Part 4, made on that application, may begin with the relevant date or any later date.

(13) 'The relevant date' means the date on which the maintenance calculation ceased to have effect.

(14) In this Schedule 'maintenance calculation' means a calculation of maintenance made under the Child Support (Northern Ireland) Order 1991 and includes, except in circumstances prescribed for the purposes of the definition of that expression in Article 2(2) of that Order, a default or interim maintenance decision within the meaning of that Order.

Application of paragraphs 26 and 27 to Part 2 orders

28(1) Subject to sub-paragraph (3), paragraph 26 applies in relation to an order under Part 2 which requires periodical payments to be made to a civil partner for his own benefit as it applies in relation to an order under paragraph 2(1)(a).

(2) Subject to sub-paragraph (3), paragraph 27 applies in relation to an order under Part 2 for the making of financial provision in respect of a child of the family as it applies in relation to an order under paragraph 2(1)(c) or (d).

(3) If—

- (a) the court makes an order under Part 2 which contains provision for the making of periodical payments, and
- (b) by virtue of paragraph 14, an application for an order under Part 1 is treated as if it had been withdrawn,

the term which may be specified under Part 2 as the term for which the payments are to be made may begin with the date of the making of the application for the order under Part 1 or any later date.

Effect on certain orders of parties living together

29(1) Sub-paragraph (2) applies if periodical payments are required to be made to a civil partner (whether for the civil partner's own benefit or for the benefit of a child of the family)—

- (a) by an order made under Part 1 or 2, or
- (b) by an interim order made under Part 4 (otherwise than on an application under Part 3).

(2) The order is enforceable even if—

- (a) the civil partners are living with each other at the date of the making of the order, or
- (b) if they are not living with each other at that date, they subsequently resume living with each other;

but the order ceases to have effect if after that date the civil partners continue to live with each other, or resume living with each other, for a continuous period exceeding 6 months.

(3) Sub-paragraph (4) applies if—

- (a) an order is made under Part 1 or 2 which requires periodical payments to be made to a child of the family, or
- (b) an interim order is made under Part 4 (otherwise than on an application under Part 3) which requires periodical payments to be made to a child of the family.

(4) Unless the court otherwise directs, the order continues to have effect and is enforceable even if—

- (a) the civil partners are living with each other at the date of the making of the order, or
- (b) if they are not living with each other at that date, they subsequently resume living with each other.

(5) An order made under Part 3, and any interim order made on an application for an order under that Part, ceases to have effect if the civil partners resume living with each other.

(6) If an order made under this Schedule ceases to have effect under—

(a) sub-paragraph (2) or (5), or
(b) a direction given under sub-paragraph (4),

the court may, on an application made by either civil partner, make an order declaring that the order ceased to have effect from such date as the court may specify.

(7) If an order made under this Schedule ceases to have effect under sub-paragraph (2) or (5), the civil partners shall give notice of that fact to the court straight away.

PART 6
VARIATION ETC OF ORDERS

Power to vary, revoke, suspend or revive order

30(1) If the court has made an order for the making of periodical payments under Part 2 or 3, it may, on an application made under this Part—

(a) vary or revoke the order,
(b) suspend any provision of it temporarily, or
(c) revive any provision so suspended.

(2) If the court has made an order under Part 4, it may, on an application made under this Part—

(a) vary or revoke the order,
(b) suspend any provision of it temporarily, or
(c) revive any provision so suspended,

except that it may not by virtue of this sub-paragraph extend the period for which the order is in force.

Powers to order lump sum on variation

31(1) If the court has made an order under paragraph 2(1)(a) or (c) for the making of periodical payments, it may, on an application made under this Part, make an order for the payment of a lump sum under paragraph 2(1)(b) or (d).

(2) If the court has made an order under Part 2 for the making of periodical payments by a civil partner, it may, on an application made under this Part, make an order for the payment of a lump sum by that civil partner—

(a) to the other civil partner, or
(b) to a child of the family or to that other civil partner for the benefit of that child.

(3) Where the court has power by virtue of this paragraph to make an order for the payment of a lump sum—

(a) the amount of the lump sum must not exceed the maximum amount that may at that time be required to be paid under Part 1, but
(b) the court may make an order for the payment of a lump sum not exceeding that amount even if the person required to pay it was required to pay a lump sum by a previous order under this Schedule.

(4) Where—

(a) the court has power by virtue of this paragraph to make an order for the payment of a lump sum, and

(b) the respondent or the applicant (as the case may be) has agreed to pay a lump sum of an amount exceeding the maximum amount that may at that time be required to be paid under Part 1,

the court may, regardless of sub-paragraph (3), make an order for the payment of a lump sum of that amount.

Power to specify when order as varied is to take effect

32 An order made under this Part which varies an order for the making of periodical payments may provide that the payments as so varied are to be made from such date as the court may specify, except that, subject to paragraph 33, the date must not be earlier than the date of the making of the application under this Part.

33(1) If—

(a) there is in force an order ('the order')—
   (i) under paragraph 2(1)(c),
   (ii) under Part 2 making provision of a kind set out in paragraph 10(1)(c) (regardless of whether it makes provision of any other kind mentioned in paragraph 10(1)(c)),
   (iii) under paragraph 16(1)(b), or
   (iv) which is an interim order under Part 4 under which the payments are to be made to a child or to the applicant for the benefit of a child,
(b) the order requires payments specified in it to be made to or for the benefit of more than one child without apportioning those payments between them,
(c) a maintenance calculation ('the calculation') is made with respect to one or more, but not all, of the children with respect to whom those payments are to be made, and
(d) an application is made, before the end of 6 months beginning with the date on which the calculation was made, for the variation or revocation of the order,

the court may, in exercise of its powers under this Part to vary or revoke the order, direct that the variation or revocation is to take effect from the date on which the calculation took effect or any later date.

(2) If—

(a) an order ('the child order') of a kind prescribed for the purposes of Article 12(1) of the Child Support (Northern Ireland) Order 1991 (SI 1991/2628 (NI 23)) is affected by a maintenance calculation,
(b) on the date on which the child order became so affected there was in force an order ('the civil partner's order')—
   (i) under paragraph 2(1)(a),
   (ii) under Part 2 making provision of a kind set out in paragraph 10(1)(a) (regardless of whether it makes provision of any other kind mentioned in paragraph 10(1)(a)),
   (iii) under paragraph 16(1)(a), or
   (iv) which is an interim order under Part 4 under which the payments are to be made to the applicant (otherwise than for the benefit of a child), and
(c) an application is made, before the end of 6 months beginning with the date on which the maintenance calculation was made, for the civil partner's order to be varied or revoked,

the court may, in exercise of its powers under this Part to vary or revoke the civil partner's order, direct that the variation or revocation is to take effect from the date on which the child order became so affected or any later date.

(3) For the purposes of sub-paragraph (2), an order is affected if it ceases to have effect or is modified by or under Article 12 of the 1991 Order.

Matters to which court is to have regard in exercising powers under this Part

34(1) In exercising the powers conferred by this Part the court must, so far as it appears to the court just to do so, give effect to any agreement which has been reached between the civil partners in relation to the application.

(2) If—

    (a) there is no such agreement, or
    (b) the court decides not to give effect to the agreement,

the court must have regard to all the circumstances of the case, giving first consideration to the welfare while under 18 of any child of the family who has not reached 18.

(3) Those circumstances include any change in any of the matters—

    (a) to which the court was required to have regard when making the order to which the application relates, or
    (b) in the case of an application for the variation or revocation of an order made under Part 2 or on an appeal, to which the court would have been required to have regard if that order had been made under Part 1.

Variation of orders for periodical payments: further provisions

35(1) The power of the court under paragraphs 30 to 34 to vary an order for the making of periodical payments includes power, if the court is satisfied that payment has not been made in accordance with the order, to exercise one of its powers under Article 85(3)(a) to (d) of the Magistrates' Courts (Northern Ireland) Order 1981 (SI 1981/1675 (NI 26)).

(2) Sub-paragraph (1) is subject to paragraph 37.

36(1) If—

    (a) a court of summary jurisdiction has made an order under this Schedule for the making of periodical payments, and
    (b) payments under the order are required to be made by any method of payment falling within Article 85(7) of the 1981 Order (standing order, etc),

an application may be made under this sub-paragraph to the clerk of petty sessions for the order to be varied as mentioned in sub-paragraph (2).

(2) Subject to sub-paragraph (4), if an application is made under sub-paragraph (1), the clerk, after—

    (a) serving written notice of the application on the respondent, and
    (b) allowing the respondent, within the period of 14 days from the date of the serving of that notice, an opportunity to make written representations,

may vary the order to provide that payments under the order are to be made to the collecting officer.

(3) The clerk may proceed with an application under sub-paragraph (1) even if the respondent has not received written notice of the application.

(4) If an application has been made under sub-paragraph (1), the clerk may, if he considers it inappropriate to exercise his power under sub-paragraph (2), refer the matter to the court which,

subject to paragraph 37, may vary the order by exercising one of its powers under Article 85(3)(a) to (d) of the 1981 Order.

37(1) Before varying the order by exercising one of its powers under Article 85(3)(a) to (d) of the 1981 Order, the court must have regard to any representations made by the parties to the application.

(2) If the court does not propose to exercise its power under Article 85(3)(c) or (d) of the 1981 Order, the court must, unless upon representations expressly made in that behalf by the person to whom payments under the order are required to be made it is satisfied that it is undesirable to do so, exercise its power under Article 85(5)(b).

38(1) Article 85(5) of the 1981 Order (power of court to order that account be opened) applies for the purposes of paragraphs 35 and 36(4) as it applies for the purposes of Article 85.

(2) None of the powers of the court, or of the clerk of petty sessions, conferred by paragraphs 35 to 37 and sub-paragraph (1) is exercisable in relation to an order under this Schedule for the making of periodical payments which is not a qualifying maintenance order (within the meaning of Article 85 of the 1981 Order).

Persons who may apply under this Part

39 An application under paragraph 30, 31 or 36 may be made—

- (a) if it is for the variation or revocation of an order under Part 1, 2, 3 or 4 for periodical payments, by either civil partner, and
- (b) if it is for the variation of an order under paragraph 2(1)(c) or Part 2 or 3 for periodical payments to or in respect of a child, also by the child himself, if he has reached 16.

Revival of orders for periodical payments

40(1) If an order made by the court under this Schedule for the making of periodical payments to or in respect of a child (other than an interim order) ceases to have effect—

- (a) on the date on which the child reaches 16, or
- (b) at any time after that date but before or on the date on which he reaches 18,

the child may apply to the court for an order for its revival.

(2) If on such an application it appears to the court that—

- (a) the child is, will be or (if an order were made under this sub-paragraph) would be receiving instruction at an educational establishment or undergoing training for a trade, profession or vocation, whether or not while in gainful employment, or
- (b) there are special circumstances which justify the making of an order under this sub-paragraph,

the court may by order to revive the order from such date as the court may specify, not being earlier than the date of the making of the application.

(3) Any order revived under this paragraph may be varied or revoked under paragraphs 30 to 34 in the same way as it could have been varied or revoked had it continued in being.

Variation of instalments or remission of lump sum

41(1) If in the exercise of its powers under Article 97 of the 1981 Order the court orders that a lump sum required to be paid under this Schedule is to be paid by instalments, the court, on an application made by either the person liable to pay or the person entitled to receive that sum, may vary that order by varying—

(a) the number of instalments payable,

(b) the amount of any instalment payable, and

(c) the date on which any instalment becomes payable.

(2) On the hearing of a complaint for the enforcement, revocation, suspension or variation of an order under this Schedule which provides for the payment of a lump sum the court may remit the whole or any part of that sum.

Supplementary provisions with respect to variation and revocation of orders

42 The powers of a court of summary jurisdiction to revoke, suspend, revive or vary an order for the periodical payment of money and the power of the clerk of petty sessions to vary such an order under Article 86 of the 1981 Order do not apply in relation to an order made under this Schedule.

PART 7
ARREARS AND REPAYMENTS

Enforcement etc of orders for payment of money

43 Article 36 of the Domestic Proceedings (Northern Ireland) Order 1980 (SI 1980/563 (NI 5)) applies in relation to orders under this Schedule as it applies in relation to orders under that Order.

Orders for repayment after cessation of order because of subsequent civil partnership etc

44(1) Sub-paragraphs (3) and (4) apply if—

(a) an order made under paragraph 2(1)(a) or Part 2 or 3 has, under paragraph 26(2), ceased to have effect because of the formation of a subsequent civil partnership or marriage by the party ('R') in whose favour it was made, and

(b) the person liable to make payments under the order ('P') made payments in accordance with it in respect of a relevant period in the mistaken belief that the order was still subsisting.

(2) 'Relevant period' means a period after the date of the formation of the subsequent civil partnership or marriage.

(3) No proceedings in respect of a cause of action arising out of the circumstances mentioned in sub-paragraph (1)(a) and (b) is maintainable by P (or P's personal representatives) against R (or R's personal representatives).

(4) But on an application made under this paragraph by P (or P's personal representatives) against R (or R's personal representatives) the court—

(a) may order the respondent to an application made under this paragraph to pay to the applicant a sum equal to the amount of the payments made in respect of the relevant period, or

(b) if it appears to the court that it would be unjust to make that order, may—

(i) order the respondent to pay to the applicant such lesser sum as it thinks fit, or

(ii) dismiss the application.

(5) An order under this paragraph for the payment of any sum may provide for the payment of that sum by instalments of such amount as may be specified in the order.

(6) An application under this paragraph—

(a) may be made in proceedings in the High Court for leave to enforce, or in proceedings in the High Court or a court of summary jurisdiction for the enforcement of, the payment of arrears under an order made under paragraph 2(1)(a) or Part 2 or 3, but

(b) if not made in such proceedings, must be made to a county court,

and accordingly references in this paragraph to the court are references to the High Court or a county court or a court of summary jurisdiction, as the circumstances require.

(7) The jurisdiction conferred on a county court by this paragraph is exercisable by a county court even though, because of the amount claimed in an application under this paragraph, the jurisdiction would not but for this sub-paragraph be exercisable by a county court.

(8) A person dissatisfied with an order made by a county court in the exercise of the jurisdiction conferred by this paragraph or with the dismissal of any application instituted by him under the provisions of this paragraph shall be entitled to appeal from the order or from the dismissal as if the order or dismissal had been made in exercise of the jurisdiction conferred by Part 3 of the County Courts (Northern Ireland) Order 1980 (SI 1980/397 (NI 3)) and the appeal brought under Part 6 of that Order, and Articles 61 (cases stated by county court judge) and 62 (cases stated by High Court on appeal from county court) of that Order shall apply accordingly.

(9) Subject to sub-paragraph (10), the collecting officer of a court of summary jurisdiction to whom any payments under an order made under paragraph 2(1)(a) or Part 2 or 3, or under an attachment of earnings order made to secure payments under the first-mentioned order, are required to be made is not liable—

(a) for any act done by him in pursuance of the first-mentioned order after the date on which that order or a provision of it ceased to have effect because of the formation of a subsequent civil partnership or marriage by the person entitled to payments under it, and

(b) for any act done by him after that date in accordance with any statutory provision specifying how payments made to him in compliance with the attachment of earnings order are to be dealt with.

(10) Sub-paragraph (9) applies if (but only if) the act—

(a) was one which he would have been under a duty to do had the order under paragraph 2(1)(a) or Part 2 or 3 not ceased to have effect, and

(b) was done before notice in writing of the formation of the subsequent civil partnership or marriage was given to him by or on behalf of—

(i)   the person entitled to payments under the order,

(ii) the person liable to make payments under it, or

(iii) the personal representatives of either of them.

(11) In this paragraph—

'collecting officer' means the officer mentioned in Article 85(2) or (3) of the Magistrates' Courts (Northern Ireland) Order 1981 (SI 1981/ 1675 (NI 26)), and

'statutory provision' has the meaning given by section 1(f) of the Interpretation Act (Northern Ireland) 1954 (c 33(NI)).

PART 8
SUPPLEMENTARY

Restrictions on making of orders under this Schedule: welfare of children

45 If—

(a) an application is made by a civil partner for an order under Part 1, 2 or 3, and

(b) there is a child of the family who is under 18,

the court must not dismiss or make a final order on the application until it has decided whether to exercise any of its powers under the Children (Northern Ireland) Order 1995 (SI 1995/755 (NI 2)) with respect to the child.

Application of certain provisions of the Domestic Proceedings (Northern Ireland) Order 1980

46 Articles 30 to 35 of the Domestic Proceedings (Northern Ireland) Order 1980 (SI 1980/563 (NI 5)) apply for the purposes of this Schedule as they apply for the purposes of that Order.

Interpretation

47(1) In this Schedule 'child of the family', in relation to two people who are civil partners of each other, means—

(a) a child of both of them, and

(b) any other child, other than a child placed with them as foster parents by an authority or a voluntary organisation, who has been treated by both the civil partners as a child of their family.

(2) In sub-paragraph (1) 'authority' and 'voluntary organisation' have the same meaning as in the Children (Northern Ireland) Order 1995 (SI 1995/ 755 (NI 2)).

(3) In any provision of this Schedule 'the court' (except where the context otherwise requires) means a court of summary jurisdiction which by virtue of this Schedule or of rules of court has jurisdiction for the purposes of that provision.

(4) References in this Schedule to a subsequent civil partnership include a civil partnership which is by law void or voidable.

(5) References in this Schedule to a subsequent marriage include a marriage which is by law void or voidable.

SCHEDULE 17

SECTION 196(4)

FINANCIAL RELIEF IN NORTHERN IRELAND AFTER OVERSEAS DISSOLUTION ETC OF A CIVIL PARTNERSHIP

PART 1
FINANCIAL RELIEF

Part applies where civil partnership has been dissolved etc overseas

1(1) This Part of this Schedule applies where—

- (a) a civil partnership has been dissolved or annulled, or the civil partners have been legally separated, by means of judicial or other proceedings in an overseas country, and
- (b) the dissolution, annulment or legal separation is entitled to be recognised as valid in Northern Ireland.

(2) This Part of this Schedule applies even if the date of the dissolution, annulment or legal separation is earlier than the date on which the Part comes into force.

(3) In this Schedule 'overseas country' means a country or territory outside the United Kingdom, the Channel Islands and the Isle of Man.

(4) In this Part of this Schedule 'child of the family' means—

- (a) a child of both of the civil partners, and
- (b) any other child, other than a child placed with them as foster parents or by an authority or voluntary organisation, who has been treated by both the civil partners as a child of their family.

(5) In sub-paragraph (4) 'authority' and 'voluntary organisation' have the same meaning as in the Children (Northern Ireland) Order 1995 (SI 1995/ 755 (NI 2)).

Either civil partner may make application for financial relief

2(1) Either of the civil partners may make an application to the court for an order under paragraph 9 or 13.

(2) The rights conferred by sub-paragraph (1) are subject to—

- (a) paragraph 3 (civil partner may not apply after forming subsequent civil partnership etc), and
- (b) paragraph 4 (application may not be made until leave to make it has been granted).

(3) An application for an order under paragraph 9 or 13 must be made in a manner prescribed by rules of court.

No application after formation of subsequent civil partnership or marriage

3(1) If—

- (a) the civil partnership has been dissolved or annulled, and
- (b) after the dissolution or annulment, one of the civil partners forms a subsequent civil partnership or marriage,

that civil partner shall not be entitled to make, in relation to the civil partnership, an application for an order under paragraph 9 or 13.

(2) The reference in sub-paragraph (1) to the forming of a subsequent civil partnership or marriage includes a reference to the forming of a civil partnership or marriage which is by law void or voidable.

Leave of court required for making of application

4(1) No application for an order under paragraph 9 or 13 shall be made unless the leave of the court has been obtained in accordance with rules of court.

(2) The court shall not grant leave under this paragraph unless it considers that there is substantial ground for the making of an application for such an order.

(3) The court may grant leave under this paragraph notwithstanding that an order has been made by a court in a country outside Northern Ireland requiring the other civil partner to make any payment, or transfer any property, to the applicant or to a child of the family.

(4) Leave under this paragraph may be granted subject to such conditions as the court thinks fit.

Interim orders for maintenance

5(1) Where—

(a) leave is granted under paragraph 4, and
(b) it appears to the court that the civil partner who applied for leave, or any child of the family, is in immediate need of financial assistance,

the court may, subject to sub-paragraph (4), make an interim order for maintenance.

(2) An interim order for maintenance is one requiring the other civil partner to make—

(a) to the applicant, or
(b) to the child,

such periodical payments as the court thinks reasonable for such term as the court thinks reasonable.

(3) The term must be one—

(a) beginning not earlier than the date of the grant of leave, and
(b) ending with the date of the determination of the application made under the leave.

(4) If it appears to the court that the court will, in the event of an application being made under the leave, have jurisdiction to entertain the application only under paragraph 7(4), the court shall not make an interim order under this paragraph.

(5) An interim order under this paragraph may be made subject to such conditions as the court thinks fit.

Paragraphs 7 and 8 apply where application made for relief under paragraph 9 or 13

6 Paragraphs 7 and 8 apply where—

(a) one of the civil partners has been granted leave under paragraph 4, and
(b) acting under the leave, that civil partner makes an application for an order under paragraph 9 or 13.

Jurisdiction of the court

7(1) The court shall have jurisdiction to entertain the application only if one or more of the following jurisdictional requirements is satisfied.

(2) The first requirement is that either of the civil partners—

(a) was domiciled in Northern Ireland on the date when the leave was applied for, or
(b) was domiciled in Northern Ireland on the date when the dissolution, annulment or legal separation took effect in the overseas country in which it was obtained.

(3) The second is that either of the civil partners—

(a) was habitually resident in Northern Ireland throughout the period of one year ending with the date when the leave was applied for, or
(b) was habitually resident in Northern Ireland throughout the period of one year ending with the date on which the dissolution, annulment or legal separation took effect in the overseas country in which it was obtained.

(4) The third is that either or both of the civil partners had, at the date when the leave was applied for, a beneficial interest in possession in a dwelling-house situated in Northern Ireland which was at some time during the civil partnership a civil partnership home of the civil partners.

(5) In sub-paragraph (4) 'possession' includes receipt of, or the right to receive, rents and profits, but here 'rent' does not include mortgage interest.

Duty of the court to consider whether Northern Ireland is appropriate venue for application

8(1) Before deciding the application, the court must consider whether in all the circumstances of the case it would be appropriate for an order of the kind applied for to be made by a court in Northern Ireland.

(2) If the court is not satisfied that it would be appropriate, the court shall dismiss the application.

(3) The court must, in particular, have regard to the following matters—

(a) the connection which the civil partners have with Northern Ireland;
(b) the connection which the civil partners have with the country in which the civil partnership was dissolved or annulled or in which they were legally separated;
(c) the connection which the civil partners have with any other country outside Northern Ireland;
(d) any financial benefit which, in consequence of the dissolution, annulment or legal separation—
   (i)   the applicant, or
   (ii) a child of the family,

   has received, or is likely to receive, by virtue of any agreement or the operation of the law of a country outside Northern Ireland;
(e) in a case where an order has been made by a court in a country outside Northern Ireland requiring the other civil partner—
   (i)   to make any payment, or
   (ii) to transfer any property,

   for the benefit of the applicant or a child of the family, the financial relief given by the order and the extent to which the order has been complied with or is likely to be complied with;

(f) any right which the applicant has, or has had, to apply for financial relief from the other civil partner under the law of any country outside Northern Ireland and, if the applicant has omitted to exercise that right, the reason for that omission;

(g) the availability in Northern Ireland of any property in respect of which an order under this Schedule in favour of the applicant could be made;

(h) the extent to which any order made under this Schedule is likely to be enforceable;

(i) the length of time which has elapsed since the date of the dissolution, annulment or legal separation.

Orders for financial provision, property adjustment and pension sharing

9(1) Sub-paragraphs (2) and (3) apply where one of the civil partners has made an application for an order under this paragraph.

(2) If the civil partnership has been dissolved or annulled, the court may on the application make any one or more of the orders which it could make under Part 1, 2 or 3 of Schedule 15 (financial provision, property adjustment and pension sharing) if a dissolution order or nullity order had been made in respect of the civil partnership under Chapter 2 of Part 4 of this Act.

(3) If the civil partners have been legally separated, the court may on the application make any one or more of the orders which it could make under Part 1 or 2 of Schedule 15 (financial provision and property adjustment) if a separation order had been made in respect of the civil partners under Chapter 2 of Part 4 of this Act.

(4) The powers under sub-paragraphs (2) and (3) are subject to paragraph 11.

Matters to which court is to have regard in exercising its powers under paragraph 9

10(1) The court, in deciding—

(a) whether to exercise its powers under paragraph 9, and

(b) if so, in what way,

must act in accordance with this paragraph.

(2) The court must have regard to all the circumstances of the case, giving first consideration to the welfare, while under 18, of any child of the family who has not reached 18.

(3) The court, in exercising its powers under paragraph 9 in relation to one of the civil partners—

(a) must in particular have regard to the matters mentioned in paragraph 16(2) of Schedule 15, and

(b) shall be under duties corresponding to those imposed by sub-paragraphs (2) and (3) of paragraph 18 of that Schedule (duties to consider termination of financial obligations) where it decides to exercise under paragraph 9 powers corresponding to the powers referred to in those sub-paragraphs.

(4) The matters to which the court is to have regard under sub-paragraph (3)(a), so far as relating to paragraph 16(2)(a) of Schedule 15 (regard to be had to financial resources), include—

(a) any benefits under a pension arrangement which either of the civil partners has or is likely to have, and

(b) any PPF compensation to which a civil partner is or is likely to be entitled,

(whether or not in the foreseeable future).

(5) The matters to which the court is to have regard under sub-paragraph (3)(a), so far as relating to paragraph 16(2)(h) of Schedule 15 (regard to be had to benefits that cease to be acquirable), include—

(a) any benefits under a pension arrangement which, because of the dissolution or annulment of the civil partnership, one of the civil partners will lose the chance of acquiring, and

(b) any PPF compensation which, because of the making of the dissolution or nullity order, a civil partner will lose the chance of acquiring entitlement to.

(6) The court, in exercising its powers under paragraph 9 in relation to a child of the family, must in particular have regard to the matters mentioned in paragraph 17(2) of Schedule 15.

(7) The court, in exercising its powers under paragraph 9 against a civil partner ('A') in favour of a child of the family who is not A's child, must also have regard to the matters mentioned in paragraph 17(3) of Schedule 15.

(8) Where an order has been made by a court outside Northern Ireland for—

(a) the making of payments, or

(b) the transfer of property,

by one of the civil partners, the court in considering in accordance with this paragraph the financial resources of the other civil partner, or of a child of the family, shall have regard to the extent to which that order has been complied with or is likely to be complied with.

(9) In this paragraph—

(a) 'pension arrangement' has the same meaning as in Part 3 of Schedule 15,

(b) references to benefits under a pension arrangement include any benefits by way of pension, whether under a pension arrangement or not, and

(c) 'PPF compensation' has the same meaning as in Part 6 of Schedule 15.

Restriction of powers under paragraph 9 where jurisdiction depends on civil partnership home in Northern Ireland

11(1) Sub-paragraphs (2) to (4) apply where the court has jurisdiction to entertain an application for an order under paragraph 9 only because a dwelling-house which was a civil partnership home of the civil partners is situated in Northern Ireland.

(2) The court may make under paragraph 9 any one or more of the following orders (but no other)—

(a) an order that one of the civil partners shall pay to the other a specified lump sum;

(b) an order that one of the civil partners shall pay to a child of the family, or to a specified person for the benefit of a child of the family, a specified lump sum;

(c) an order that one of the civil partners shall transfer that civil partner's interest in the dwelling-house, or a specified part of that interest—

(i) to the other,

(ii) to a child of the family, or

(iii) to a specified person for the benefit of a child of the family;

(d) an order that a settlement of the interest of one of the civil partners in the dwelling-house, or a specified part of that interest, be made to the satisfaction of the court for the benefit of any one or more of—

(i) the other civil partner and the children of the family, or

(ii) either or any of them;

    (e) an order varying for the benefit of any one or more of—
        (i) the civil partners and the children of the family, or
        (ii) either or any of them,

    a relevant settlement so far as that settlement relates to an interest in the dwelling-house;
    (f) an order extinguishing or reducing the interest of either of the civil partners under a relevant settlement so far as that interest is an interest in the dwelling-house;
    (g) an order for the sale of the interest of one of the civil partners in the dwelling-house.

(3) Where under paragraph 9 the court makes just one order for the payment of a lump sum by one of the civil partners, the amount of the lump sum must not exceed the amount specified in sub-paragraph (5).

(4) Where under paragraph 9 the court makes two or more orders each of which is an order for the payment of a lump sum by the same civil partner, the total of the amounts of the lump sums must not exceed the amount specified in sub-paragraph (5).

(5) That amount is—

    (a) if the interest of the paying civil partner in the dwelling-house is sold in pursuance of an order made under sub-paragraph (2)(g), the amount of the proceeds of sale of that interest after deducting from those proceeds any costs incurred in the sale of that interest;
    (b) if that interest is not so sold, the amount which in the opinion of the court represents the value of that interest.

(6) Where the interest of one of the civil partners in the dwelling-house is held jointly or in common with any other person or persons—

    (a) the reference in sub-paragraph (2)(g) to the interest of one of the civil partners shall be construed as including a reference to the interest of that other person, or the interest of those other persons, in the dwelling-house, and
    (b) the reference in sub-paragraph (5)(a) to the amount of the proceeds of a sale ordered under sub-paragraph (2)(g) shall be construed as a reference to that part of those proceeds which is attributable to the interest of that civil partner in the dwelling-house.

(7) In sub-paragraph (2)—

    'relevant settlement' means a settlement made, during the subsistence of the civil partnership or in anticipation of its formation, on the civil partners, including one made by will or codicil;

    'specified' means specified in the order.

Consent orders under paragraph 9

12(1) On an application for a consent order under paragraph 9, the court may make an order in the terms agreed on the basis only of the prescribed information furnished with the application.

(2) Sub-paragraph (1) does not apply if the court has reason to think that there are other circumstances into which it ought to inquire.

(3) Sub-paragraph (1) applies to an application for a consent order varying or discharging an order under paragraph 9 as it applies to an application for such an order.

(4) Sub-paragraph (1) applies despite paragraph 10.

(5) In this paragraph—

'consent order', in relation to an application for an order, means an order in the terms applied for to which the respondent agrees;

'prescribed' means prescribed by rules of court.

Orders for transfers of tenancies of dwelling-houses

13(1) This paragraph applies if—

(a) an application is made by one of the civil partners for an order under this paragraph, and
(b) one of the civil partners is entitled, either in his own right or jointly with the other civil partner, to occupy a dwelling-house in Northern Ireland by virtue of a tenancy which is a tenancy mentioned in Schedule 2 to the Family Homes and Domestic Violence (Northern Ireland) Order 1998 (SI 1998/1071 (NI 6)).

(2) The court may make in relation to that dwelling-house any order which it could make under Part 2 of that Schedule (order transferring tenancy or switching statutory tenants) if it had power to make a property adjustment order under Part 2 of Schedule 15 to this Act with respect to the civil partnership.

(3) The provisions of paragraphs 9, 10 and 13(1) of Schedule 2 to the Family Homes and Domestic Violence (Northern Ireland) Order 1998 (payments by transferee, pre-transfer liabilities and right of landlord to be heard) apply in relation to any order under this paragraph as they apply to any order under Part 2 of that Schedule.

Application to orders under paragraphs 5 and 9 of provisions of Schedule 15

14(1) The following provisions of Schedule 15 apply in relation to an order made under paragraph 5 or 9 of this Schedule as they apply in relation to a like order made under that Schedule—

(a) paragraph 3(1) to (3) and (7) (lump sums);
(b) paragraphs 12, 13 and 14(2) to (4) (pension sharing);
(c) paragraphs 20 and 21 (orders under Part 1 relating to pensions);
(d) paragraphs 26 to 32 (orders under Part 1 relating to pensions where Board has assumed responsibility for scheme);
(e) paragraphs 42(1) to (4) and (6) and 44 (duration of orders);
(f) paragraphs 45 to 47, and 50 to 55, except paragraph 45(1)(g) (variation etc of orders);
(g) paragraphs 56 to 58 (arrears and repayments);
(h) paragraphs 71 to 74 (drafting of instruments, bankruptcy, mental disorder, and pension-sharing appeals).

(2) Sub-paragraph (1)(d) does not apply where the court has jurisdiction to entertain an application for an order under paragraph 9 only because a dwelling-house which was a civil partnership home of the civil partners is situated in Northern Ireland.

(3) Paragraph 22 of Schedule 15 (change of pension arrangement under which rights are shared) applies in relation to an order made under paragraph 9 of this Schedule by virtue of sub-paragraph (1)(d) as it applies to an order made under Part 1 of Schedule 15 by virtue of paragraph 20 or 21 of that Schedule.

(4) The Lord Chancellor may by regulations make for the purposes of this Schedule provision corresponding to any provision which may be made by him under paragraph 23(1) to (3) of Schedule 15 (supplementary provision about orders relating to pensions under Part 1 of that Schedule).

(5) The power to make regulations under this paragraph is exercisable by statutory rule for the purposes of the Statutory Rules (Northern Ireland) Order 1979 (SI 1979/1573 (NI 12)).

(6) Regulations under this paragraph are subject to annulment in pursuance of a resolution of either House of Parliament in the same manner as a statutory instrument; and section 5 of the Statutory Instruments Act 1946 (c 36) applies accordingly.

Avoidance of transactions designed to defeat claims under paragraphs 5 and 9

15(1) Sub-paragraphs (2) and (3) apply where one of the civil partners ('A') is granted leave under paragraph 4 to make an application for an order under paragraph 9.

(2) If the court is satisfied, on application by A, that the other civil partner ('B') is, with the intention of defeating a claim by A, about to—

    (a) make any disposition, or

    (b) transfer out of the jurisdiction, or otherwise deal with, any property,

it may make such order as it thinks fit for restraining B from doing so or otherwise for protecting the claim.

(3) If the court is satisfied, on application by A—

    (a) that the other civil partner ('B') has, with the intention of defeating a claim by A, made a reviewable disposition, and

    (b) that, if the disposition were set aside—

        (i) financial relief under paragraph 5 or 9, or

        (ii) different financial relief under paragraph 5 or 9,

    would be granted to A,

it may make an order setting aside the disposition.

(4) If—

    (a) an order under paragraph 5 or 9 has been made by the court at the instance of one of the civil partners ('A'), and

    (b) the court is satisfied, on application by A, that the other civil partner ('B') has, with the intention of defeating a claim by A, made a reviewable disposition,

the court may make an order setting aside the disposition.

(5) Where the court has jurisdiction to entertain an application for an order under paragraph 9 only under paragraph 7(4), it shall not make any order under sub-paragraph (2), (3) or (4) in respect of any property other than the dwelling-house concerned.

(6) Where the court makes an order under sub-paragraph (3) or (4) setting aside a disposition, it shall give such consequential directions as it thinks fit for giving effect to the order (including directions requiring the making of any payments or the disposal of any property).

(7) For the purposes of sub-paragraphs (3) and (4), but subject to sub-paragraph (8), any disposition made by B is a 'reviewable disposition' (whether made before or after the commencement of A's application under that sub-paragraph).

(8) A disposition made by B is not a reviewable disposition for those purposes if made for valuable consideration (other than formation of a civil partnership) to a person who, at the time of the disposition, acted in relation to it in good faith and without notice of any intention on the part of B to defeat A's claim.

(9) A reference in this paragraph to defeating a claim by one of the civil partners is a reference to—

    (a) preventing financial relief being granted, or reducing the amount of financial relief which might be granted, under paragraph 5 or 9 at the instance of that civil partner, or

(b) frustrating or impeding the enforcement of any order which might be, or has been, made under paragraph 5 or 9 at the instance of that civil partner.

Presumptions for the purposes of paragraph 15

16(1) Sub-paragraph (3) applies where—

    (a) an application is made under paragraph 15(2) or (3) by one of the civil partners with respect to—

        (i) a disposition which took place less than 3 years before the date of the application, or

        (ii) a disposition or other dealing with property which is about to take place, and

    (b) the court is satisfied that the disposition or other dealing would (apart from paragraph 15 and this paragraph of this Schedule) have the consequence of defeating a claim by the applicant.

(2) Sub-paragraph (3) also applies where—

    (a) an application is made under paragraph 15(4) by one of the civil partners with respect to a disposition which took place less than 3 years before the date of the application, and

    (b) the court is satisfied that the disposition has had the consequence of defeating a claim by the applicant.

(3) It shall be presumed, unless the contrary is shown, that the person who—

    (a) disposed of, or

    (b) is about to dispose of or deal with the property,

did so, or (as the case may be) is about to do so, with the intention of defeating the applicant's claim.

(4) A reference in this paragraph to defeating a claim by one of the civil partners has the meaning given by paragraph 15(9).

PART 2
STEPS TO PREVENT AVIODANCE PRIOR TO APPLICATION FOR LEAVE UNDER PARAGRAPH 4

Prevention of transactions intended to defeat prospective claims under paragraphs 5 and 9

17(1) If it appears to the court, on application by one of the persons ('A') who formed a civil partnership—

    (a) that the civil partnership has been dissolved or annulled, or that the civil partners have been legally separated, by means of judicial or other proceedings in an overseas country,

    (b) that A intends to apply for leave to make an application for an order under paragraph 9 as soon as he or she has been habitually resident in Northern Ireland for the period of one year, and

    (c) that the other civil partner ('B') is, with the intention of defeating A's claim, about to—

        (i) make any disposition, or

        (ii) transfer out of the jurisdiction, or otherwise deal with, any property,

the court may make such order as it thinks fit for restraining B from taking such action as is mentioned in paragraph (c).

(2) Sub-paragraph (1) applies even if the date of the dissolution, annulment or legal separation is earlier than the date on which that sub-paragraph comes into force.

(3) Sub-paragraph (4) applies where—

(a) an application is made under sub-paragraph (1) with respect to—
    (i) a disposition which took place less than 3 years before the date of the application, or
    (ii) a disposition or other dealing with property which is about to take place, and
(b) the court is satisfied that the disposition or other dealing would (apart from this paragraph of this Schedule) have the consequence of defeating a claim by the applicant.

(4) It shall be presumed, unless the contrary is shown, that the person who—

(a) disposed of, or
(b) is about to dispose of or deal with the property,

did so, or (as the case may be) is about to do so, with the intention of defeating the applicant's claim.

(5) A reference in this paragraph to defeating a person's claim is a reference to preventing financial relief being granted, or reducing the amount of financial relief which might be granted, under paragraph 5 or 9 at the instance of that person.

PART 3
SUPPLEMENTARY

Paragraphs 15 to 17: meaning of 'disposition' and saving

18(1) In paragraphs 15 to 17 'disposition' does not include any provision contained in a will or codicil but, with that exception, includes any conveyance, assurance or gift of property of any description, whether made by an instrument or otherwise.

(2) The provisions of paragraphs 15 to 17 are without prejudice to any power of the court to grant injunctions under section 91 of the Judicature (Northern Ireland) Act 1978 (c 23).

Interpretation of Schedule

19 In this Schedule—

'the court' means the High Court;

'dwelling-house' includes—

(a) any building, or part of a building, which is occupied as a dwelling, and
(b) any yard, garden, garage or outhouse belonging to, and occupied with, the dwelling-house;

'overseas country' has the meaning given by paragraph 1(3).

SCHEDULE 18

SECTION 205

HOUSING AND TENANCIES: NORTHERN IRELAND

Rent (Northern Ireland) Order 1978 (SI 1978/1050 (NI 20))

1 In Article 14 (extended discretion of court), in paragraph (2), after 'spouse' (in both places) insert 'or civil partner'.

2(1) Amend Schedule 1 (statutory tenants by succession) as follows.

(2) In paragraph 2, after 'surviving spouse' insert ', or surviving civil partner,'.

(3) In paragraph 7, after 'surviving spouse' insert ', or surviving civil partner,'.

3 In Schedule 4 (grounds for possession), in Case 3 in Part 1 (dwelling-house required as residence for landlord or member of his family), in paragraph (d), for 'wife or husband' substitute 'spouse or civil partner'.

Housing (Northern Ireland) Order 1981 (SI 1981/156 (NI 3))

4(1) Amend Article 2A (meaning of member of a person's family) as follows.

(2) In paragraph (1)(a)—

(a) after 'spouse' insert 'or civil partner', and
(b) after 'live together as husband and wife' insert 'or as if they were civil partners'.

(3) In paragraph (2)(a), after 'a relationship by marriage' insert 'or civil partnership'.

Housing (Northern Ireland) Order 1983 (SI 1983/1118 (NI 15))

5(1) In Article 24 (interpretation), amend paragraph (3) (meaning of member of another's family) as follows.

(2) After 'spouse' insert ', civil partner'.

(3) After 'marriage' insert 'or civil partnership'.

(4) After 'live together as husband and wife' insert 'or as if they were civil partners'.

6(1) Amend Article 26 (succession on death of tenant) as follows.

(2) In paragraph (2)(a), after 'spouse' insert 'or civil partner'.

(3) In paragraph (3)(a), after 'spouse' insert 'or civil partner'.

(4) In paragraph (4), for 'paragraph (4A)' substitute 'paragraphs (4A) and (4B)'.

(5) After paragraph (4A) insert—

'(4B) A tenant to whom the tenancy was assigned in pursuance of an order under any of the following provisions of the Civil Partnership Act 2004—

(a) Part 2 of Schedule 15; or
(b) paragraph 9(2) or (3) of Schedule 17,

is a successor only if the other civil partner was a successor.'

7 In Article 32 (assignments), in paragraph (1), after sub-paragraph (a) insert—

'(aa) the assignment is made in pursuance of an order made under Part 2 of Schedule 15, or paragraph 9(2) or (3) of Schedule 17, to the Civil Partnership Act 2004; or'.

8 In Article 33 (other disposals), in paragraph (2), after sub-paragraph (a) insert—

'(aa) the vesting or other disposal is in pursuance of an order made under Part 2 of Schedule 15, or paragraph 9(2) or (3) of Schedule 17, to the Civil Partnership Act 2004; or'.

9 In Article 94 (subletting or assignment), in paragraph (2), after '1978' insert 'or Part 2 of Schedule 15, or paragraph 9(2) or (3) of Schedule 17, to the Civil Partnership Act 2004'.

10 In Schedule 3 (grounds for possession of dwelling-houses let under secure tenancies), in Ground 2A—

(a) for 'a married couple or' substitute 'a married couple, a couple who are civil partners of each other', and

(b) after 'as husband and wife' insert 'or a couple living together as if they were civil partners'.

Housing (Northern Ireland) Order 2003 (SI 2003/412 (NI 2))

11(1) Amend Article 3 (meaning of a person's family) as follows.

(2) In paragraph (1)(a)—

(a) after 'spouse' insert 'or civil partner', and

(b) after 'live together as husband and wife' insert 'or as if they were civil partners'.

(3) In paragraph (2)(a), after 'a relationship by marriage' insert 'or civil partnership'.

12 In Article 13 (persons qualified to succeed tenant under an introductory tenancy), in paragraph (a), after 'spouse' insert 'or civil partner'.

13 Article 14 (cases where tenant is a successor), in paragraph (2), after sub-paragraph (c) insert—

'(d) Part 2 of Schedule 15, or paragraph 9(2) or (3) of Schedule 17, to the Civil Partnership Act 2004 (property adjustment orders in connection with civil partnership proceedings or after overseas dissolution of civil partnership, etc),'.

14(1) Amend Article 15 (persons qualified to succeed tenant under an introductory tenancy) as follows.

(2) In paragraph (2)(a), after 'spouse' insert 'or civil partner'.

(3) In paragraph (3)(a), after head (iv) insert—

'(v) Part 2 of Schedule 15, or paragraph 9(2) or (3) of Schedule 17, to the Civil Partnership Act 2004 (property adjustment orders in connection with civil partnership proceedings or after overseas dissolution of civil partnership, etc),'.

15 Article 16 (assignment in general prohibited), in paragraph (2)(a), after head (iv) insert—

'(v) Part 2 of Schedule 15, or paragraph 9(2) or (3) of Schedule 17, to the Civil Partnership Act 2004 (property adjustment orders in connection with civil partnership proceedings or after overseas dissolution of civil partnership, etc),'.

16 In Article 28 (interpretation of Part 3), in the definition of 'partner'—

(a) after 'spouse' (in both places) insert 'or civil partner', and

(b) after 'husband or wife' insert 'or as if they were civil partners'.

SCHEDULE 19

SECTION 206

FAMILY HOMES AND DOMESTIC VIOLENCE: NORTHERN IRELAND

PART 1
AMENDMENTS OF THE FAMILY HOMES AND DOMESTIC VIOLENCE (NORTHERN IRELAND) ORDER (SI 1998/1071 (NI 6))

1(1) Amend Article 2 (interpretation) as follows.

(2) In paragraph (2), after the definition of 'health' insert—

'"home rights" has the meaning given by Article 4;'.

(3) In the definition of 'matrimonial charge' in that paragraph, after 'matrimonial' insert 'or civil partnership'.

(4) Omit the definition of 'matrimonial home rights' in that paragraph.

(5) In the definition of 'relative' in that paragraph—

  (a) in paragraphs (a) and (b) for 'spouse or former spouse' substitute 'spouse, former spouse, civil partner or former civil partner', and
  (b) after 'were married to each other' insert 'or were civil partners of each other'.

(6) After paragraph (3)(g) insert—

  '(h) the Civil Partnership Act 2004.'

(7) In paragraph (7), after 'matrimonial' insert 'or civil partnership'.

2(1) Amend Article 3 (meaning of 'cohabitees', 'relevant child' and 'associated persons') as follows.

(2) For paragraph (1)(a) substitute—

  '(a) "cohabitees" are two persons who are neither married to each other nor civil partners of each other but are living together as husband and wife or as if they were civil partners;'.

(3) In paragraph (1)(b), after 'have subsequently married each other' insert 'or become civil partners of each other'.

(4) After paragraph (3)(a) insert—

  '(aa) they are or have been civil partners of each other;'.

  (5) After paragraph (3)(e) insert—

  '(eza) they have entered into a civil partnership agreement (as defined by section 197 of the Civil Partnership Act 2004) (whether or not that agreement has been terminated);'.

3(1) Amend Article 4 (rights concerning matrimonial home where one spouse has no estate, etc) as follows.

(2) In paragraph (1)—

  (a) in sub-paragraph (a)—
    (i) after 'one spouse' insert 'or civil partner ('A')', and
    (ii) for 'that spouse' substitute 'A',
  (b) in sub-paragraph (b), after 'other spouse' insert 'or civil partner ('B')'.

(3) In paragraph (2)—

  (a) for 'the spouse not so entitled' substitute 'B',
  (b) for '('matrimonial home rights')' substitute '('home rights')', and
  (c) in sub-paragraph (a), for 'the other spouse' substitute 'A'.

(4) In paragraph (3)—

  (a) for 'a spouse' and for 'that spouse' substitute 'B', and
  (b) for 'the other spouse' (in both places) substitute 'A'.

(5) In paragraph (4)—

  (a) for 'A spouse's' substitute 'B's',

(b) in sub-paragraph (a), for 'by the other spouse as the other spouse's' substitute 'by A as A's', and

(c) in sub-paragraph (b)—

    (i) for 'the spouse occupies the dwelling-house as that spouse's' substitute 'B occupies the dwelling-house as B's', and

    (ii) for 'by the other spouse as the other spouse's' substitute 'by A as A's'.

(6) In paragraph (5)—

(a) for 'a spouse ('the first spouse')' substitute 'B', and

(b) in sub-paragraph (b), for 'the other spouse ('the second spouse')' substitute 'A',

(c) for 'the second spouse' (in both places) substitute 'A', and

(d) for 'the first spouse' substitute 'B'.

(7) In paragraph (6)—

(a) for 'a spouse' substitute 'B', and

(b) for 'the other spouse' (in both places) substitute 'A'.

(8) In paragraph (7), for the words from first 'which' to the end substitute

'which—

    (a) in the case of spouses, has at no time been, and was at no time intended by them to be, a matrimonial home of theirs; and

    (b) in the case of civil partners, has at no time been, and was at no time intended by them to be, a civil partnership home of theirs.'

(9) In paragraph (8)—

(a) for 'A spouse's matrimonial home rights' substitute 'B's home rights',

(b) in sub-paragraph (a), after 'marriage' insert 'or civil partnership', and

(c) in sub-paragraph (b), for 'the other spouse' substitute 'A'.

(10) In paragraph (9)—

(a) for 'a spouse' substitute 'a person',

(b) for 'matrimonial home rights' substitute 'home rights', and

(c) after 'spouses' insert 'or civil partners'.

(11) In the heading to Article 4, for 'matrimonial home where one spouse' substitute 'home where one spouse or civil partner' and, in the preceding cross-heading, after 'matrimonial' insert 'or civil partnership'.

4(1) Amend Article 5 (effect of matrimonial home rights as charge on dwelling-house) as follows.

(2) In paragraph (1), for 'marriage, one spouse' substitute 'marriage or civil partnership, A'.

(3) In paragraph (2), for 'The other spouse's matrimonial home rights' substitute 'B's home rights'.

(4) In paragraph (3)—

(a) in sub-paragraph (a), for 'the spouse so entitled' substitute 'A', and

(b) in sub-paragraph (b), after 'marriage' insert 'or of the formation of the civil partnership'.

(5) In paragraph (4)—

(a) for 'a spouse's matrimonial home rights' substitute 'B's home rights',

(b) for 'the other spouse' substitute 'A', and

(c) for 'either of the spouses' substitute 'A or B'.

(6) In paragraph (5), for 'the other spouse' substitute 'A'.

(7) In paragraph (6), for 'the spouses' substitute 'A and B'.

(8) In paragraph (7)—

    (a) for 'a spouse's matrimonial home rights' substitute 'B's home rights',

    (b) in sub-paragraph (a), for 'the other spouse' substitute 'A', and

    (c) in sub-paragraph (b), after 'marriage' insert 'or civil partnership'.

(9) In paragraph (8)—

    (a) in sub-paragraph (a), for 'a spouse's matrimonial home rights' substitute 'B's home rights', and

    (b) for 'the other spouse' (in both places) substitute 'A'.

(10) In the heading to Article 5, for 'matrimonial home rights' substitute 'home rights'.

5(1) Amend Article 6 (registration, etc of matrimonial charge) as follows.

(2) In paragraphs (1), (3), (4), (5) and (6), after 'matrimonial' insert 'or civil partnership'.

(3) In the heading to Article 6, after 'matrimonial' insert 'or civil partnership'.

6(1) Amend Article 7 (restriction on registration where spouse entitled to more than one matrimonial charge) as follows.

(2) In paragraphs (1), (2) and (3), after 'spouse' (in each place) insert 'or civil partner'.

(3) In paragraphs (1), (2), (3) and (4), after 'matrimonial' (in each place) insert 'or civil partnership'.

(4) In paragraph (3), for 'matrimonial home rights' substitute 'home rights'.

(5) In the heading to Article 7, after 'matrimonial' insert 'or civil partnership'.

7(1) Amend Article 8 (cancellation of registration of matrimonial charge before completion of disposal of dwelling-house) as follows.

(2) In paragraphs (1) and (2), after 'matrimonial' insert 'or civil partnership'.

(3) In the heading to Article 8, after 'matrimonial' insert 'or civil partnership'.

8(1) Amend Article 9 (cancellation of registration after termination of marriage, etc) as follows.

(2) In paragraph (1), for 'matrimonial charge' substitute 'matrimonial or civil partnership charge'.

(3) In paragraphs (1)(a), (2)(a) and (b) and (3), after 'spouse' insert 'or civil partner'.

(4) In paragraphs (1)(b), (2)(a) and (4), after 'marriage' (in each place) insert 'or civil partnership'.

(5) In paragraphs (1)(c), (2), (3) and (4), after 'matrimonial' (in each place) insert 'or civil partnership'.

(6) In paragraph (1)(c), for 'spouse's matrimonial home rights' substitute 'spouse's or civil partner's home rights'.

(7) In the heading to Article 9, after 'marriage' insert 'or civil partnership'.

9(1) Amend Article 10 (release of matrimonial home rights and postponement of priority of matrimonial charge) as follows.

(2) In paragraph (1), for 'spouse entitled to matrimonial home rights' substitute 'spouse or civil partner entitled to home rights'.

(3) In paragraphs (2) and (3), for 'matrimonial charge' (in each place) substitute 'matrimonial or civil partnership charge'.

(4) In paragraph (2), for 'matrimonial home rights' substitute 'home rights'.

(5) In paragraph (3), after 'spouse' insert 'or civil partner'.

(6) In the heading to Article 10, after 'matrimonial' (in each place) insert 'or civil partnership'.

10(1) Amend Article 11 (occupation orders where applicant has estate or interest etc or has matrimonial home rights) as follows.

(2) In paragraph (1)(a)(ii), for 'matrimonial home rights' substitute 'home rights'.

(3) After paragraph (2) insert—

'(2A) If a civil partnership agreement (within the meaning of the Civil Partnership Act 2004) is terminated, no application under this Article may be made by virtue of Article 3(3)(eza) by reference to that agreement after the end of the period of three years beginning with the day on which it is terminated.'

(4) In paragraph (3)(f)—

(a) for 'matrimonial home rights' substitute 'home rights', and
(b) after 'spouse' insert 'or civil partner'.

(5) In paragraph (4), for 'matrimonial home rights' substitute 'home rights'.

(6) In paragraph (5)—

(a) for 'matrimonial home rights' substitute 'home rights',
(b) after 'is the other spouse' insert 'or civil partner',
(c) after 'during the marriage' insert 'or civil partnership',
(d) in sub-paragraph (a), after 'spouse' insert 'or civil partner', and
(e) in sub-paragraph (b), after 'marriage' insert 'or civil partnership'.

(7) In the heading to Article 11, for 'matrimonial home rights' substitute 'home rights'.

11 In Article 12 (effect of order under Article 11 where rights are charge on dwelling-house), in paragraph (1)—

(a) for 'a spouse's matrimonial home rights' substitute 'B's home rights', and
(b) for 'the other spouse' (in each place) substitute 'A'.

12(1) Amend Article 13 (one former spouse with no existing right to occupy) as follows.

(2) In paragraph (1)(a) and (b), after 'former spouse' insert 'or former civil partner'.

(3) For paragraph (1)(c) substitute—

'(c) the dwelling house—
(i) in the case of former spouses, was at any time their matrimonial home or was at any time intended by them to be their matrimonial home, or
(ii) in the case of former civil partners, was at any time their civil partnership home or was at any time intended by them to be their civil partnership home.'

(4) In paragraph (2), after 'former spouse' (in both places) insert 'or former civil partner'.

(5) In paragraph (6)(f), after 'marriage' insert 'or civil partnership'.

(6) After paragraph (6)(g)(i), insert—

'(ia) for a property adjustment order under Part 2 of Schedule 15 to the Civil Partnership Act 2004;'.

(7) In paragraph (9)(a), after 'former spouses' insert 'or former civil partners'.

(8) In paragraphs (11) and (12), after 'former spouse' insert 'or former civil partner'.

(9) For paragraph (13)(a) and (b) substitute—

'(a) as if he were B (the person entitled to occupy the dwelling-house by virtue of that Article); and
(b) as if the respondent were A (the person entitled as mentioned in paragraph (1)(a) of that Article).'

(10) In the heading to Article 13, after 'former spouse' insert 'or former civil partner'.

13 In Article 14 (one cohabitee or former cohabitee with no existing right to occupy), for paragraph (13)(a) and (b) substitute—

'(a) as if he were B (the person entitled to occupy the dwelling-house by virtue of that Article); and
(b) as if the respondent were A (the person entitled as mentioned in paragraph (1)(a) of that Article).'

14(1) Amend Article 15 (neither spouse entitled to occupy) as follows.

(2) After paragraph (1) insert—

'(1A) This Article also applies if—

(a) one civil partner or former civil partner and the other civil partner or former civil partner occupy a dwelling-house which is or was the civil partnership home; but
(b) neither of them is entitled to remain in occupation—
(i) by virtue of a beneficial estate or contract; or
(ii) by virtue of any statutory provision giving him the right to remain in occupation.'

(3) In paragraph (3)(c), for 'spouses' substitute 'parties'.

(4) In the heading to Article 15, after 'spouse' insert 'or civil partner'.

15 In Article 20 (non-molestation orders), after paragraph (4) insert—

'(4ZA) If a civil partnership agreement (within the meaning of the Civil Partnership Act 2004) is terminated, no application under this Article may be made by virtue of Article 3(3)(eza) by reference to that agreement after the end of the period of three years beginning with the day on which it is terminated.'

16(1) In Article 22 (evidence of agreement to marry), after paragraph (2) insert—

'(3) Subject to paragraph (4), the court shall not make an order under Article 11 or 20 by virtue of Article 3(3)(eza) unless there is produced to it evidence in writing of the existence of the civil partnership agreement (within the meaning of the Civil Partnership Act 2004).

(4) Paragraph (3) does not apply if the court is satisfied that the civil partnership agreement was evidenced by—

(a) a gift by one party to the agreement to the other as a token of the agreement, or
(b) a ceremony entered into by the parties in the presence of one or more other persons assembled for the purpose of witnessing the ceremony.'

(2) In the heading to Article 22, after 'marry' insert 'or form a civil partnership'.

17 In Article 24 (variation and discharge of orders), in paragraph (3)—

    (a) for 'a spouse's matrimonial home rights are' substitute 'B's home rights are, under Article 12,', and

    (b) for 'the other spouse' (in each place) substitute 'A'.

18(1) Amend Article 31 (dwelling-house subject to mortgage) as follows.

(2) In paragraphs (3)(a) and (4), for 'matrimonial home rights' substitute 'home rights'.

(3) In paragraph (5), after 'spouse, former spouse' insert ', civil partner, former civil partner'.

19(1) Amend Article 33 (actions by mortgagees: service of notice on certain persons) as follows.

(2) In paragraphs (1) and (2), after 'matrimonial' insert 'or civil partnership'.

20(1) Amend Article 39 (appeals) as follows.

(2) At the end of paragraph (2)(b) insert

    'or

        (c) where the county court is a civil partnership proceedings county court exercising jurisdiction under the Civil Partnership Act 2004.'

(3) At the end of paragraph (6) insert 'or a civil partnership proceedings county court exercising jurisdiction under the Civil Partnership Act 2004 in the same proceedings'.

21(1) Amend Schedule 2 (transfer of certain tenancies on divorce etc or on separation of cohabitees) as follows.

(2) In paragraph 1(2), before the definition of 'cohabitee' insert—

    '"civil partner", except in paragraph 2, includes (where the context requires) former civil partner;'.

(3) In paragraph 2(1), after 'spouse' (in both places) insert 'or civil partner'.

(4) For paragraph 2(2) substitute—

    '(2) The court may make a Part II order—

        (a) on granting a decree of divorce, a decree of nullity of marriage or a decree of judicial separation or at any time thereafter (whether, in the case of a decree of divorce or nullity of marriage, before or after the decree is made absolute), or

        (b) at any time when it has power to make a property adjustment order under Part 2 of Schedule 15 to the Civil Partnership Act 2004 with respect to the civil partnership.'

(5) In paragraph 2(3), after 'spouse' insert 'or civil partner'.

(6) Omit 'or' at the end of paragraph 4(1)(a) and insert—

    '(aa) in the case of civil partners, a civil partnership home; or'.

(7) In paragraph 5(a), after 'spouses' insert ', civil partners'.

(8) In paragraph 6, after 'spouse' (in both places) insert ', civil partner'.

(9) In paragraph 7(1) and (2), after 'spouse' (in each place) insert ', civil partner'.

(10) For paragraph 7(3) substitute—

'(3) If the spouse, civil partner or cohabitee so entitled is a successor within the meaning of Chapter 2 of Part 2 of the Housing (Northern Ireland) Order 1983 (SI 1983/1118 (NI 15))—

(a) his former spouse (or, in the case of judicial separation, his spouse),
(b) his former civil partner (or, if a separation order is in force, his civil partner), or
(c) his former cohabitee,

is to be deemed also to be a successor within the meaning of that Chapter.'

(11) In paragraph 8(1) and (2)(a) and (b), after 'spouse' insert ', civil partner'.

(12) In paragraph 8(3), after 'widower' insert 'or surviving civil partner'.

(13) In paragraph 9(1) (in both places), after 'spouse' insert ', civil partner'.

(14) In paragraph 10(1), after 'spouses' insert ', civil partners'.

(15) In paragraph 10(2), after 'spouse' insert ', civil partner'.

(16) For paragraph 11 and the heading preceding it, substitute—

'Date when order made between spouses or civil partners takes effect

11 The date specified in a Part II order as the date on which the order is to take effect must not be earlier than—

(a) in the case of a marriage in respect of which a decree of divorce or nullity has been granted, the date on which the decree is made absolute;
(b) in the case of a civil partnership in respect of which a dissolution or nullity order has been made, the date on which the order is made final.'

(17) For paragraph 12 and the heading preceding it substitute—

'Effect of remarriage or subsequent civil partnership

12(1) If after the grant of a decree dissolving or annulling a marriage either spouse remarries or forms a civil partnership, that spouse is not entitled to apply, by reference to the grant of that decree, for a Part II order.

(2) If after the making of a dissolution or nullity order either civil partner forms a subsequent civil partnership or marries, that civil partner is not entitled to apply, by reference to the making of that order, for a Part II order.

(3) In sub-paragraphs (1) and (2)—

(a) the references to remarrying and marrying, include references to cases where the marriage is by law void or voidable, and
(b) the references to forming a civil partnership, include references to cases where the civil partnership is by law void or voidable.'

(18) In paragraph 14(1)—

(a) after 'spouse' insert 'or civil partner', and
(b) for 'spouse's matrimonial home rights' substitute 'spouse's or civil partner's home rights'.

(19) In paragraph 14(2), after 'spouse' insert ', civil partner'.

PART 2
CONSEQUENTIAL AMENDMENTS

Land Registration Act (Northern Ireland) 1970 (c 18)

22 In Part 1 of Schedule 6 (registration of certain burdens), in paragraph 14A for 'matrimonial charge (within the meaning of Article 5(1) of the Family Law (Miscellaneous Provisions) (Northern Ireland) Order 1984 or' substitute 'matrimonial or civil partnership charge ('.

Registration of Deeds Act (Northern Ireland) 1970 (c 25)

23 In section 4(4A), for 'matrimonial charge (within the meaning of Article 5(1) of the Family Law (Miscellaneous Provisions) (Northern Ireland) Order 1984 or' substitute 'matrimonial or civil partnership charge ('.

Land Acquisition and Compensation (Northern Ireland) Order 1973 (SI 1973/1896 (NI 21))

24(1) Amend Article 30A (spouses having statutory rights of occupation) as follows.

(2) In paragraph (1)—

(a) for 'one spouse ('A')' substitute 'one spouse or civil partner ('A')', and
(b) for 'the other spouse ('B') acquires matrimonial home rights' substitute 'the other spouse or civil partner ('B') acquires home rights'.

(3) In paragraph (2), for 'matrimonial home rights' substitute 'home rights'.

(4) In the heading to Article 30A, after 'spouses' insert 'and civil partners'.

Rent (Northern Ireland) Order 1978 (SI 1978/1050 (NI 20))

25(1) Amend Article 14 (extended discretion of court in certain proceedings for possession) as follows.

(2) In paragraph (4A)(b), for 'tenant's spouse or former spouse, having matrimonial home rights' substitute 'tenant's spouse or former spouse, or civil partner or former civil partner, having home rights'.

(3) In paragraph (4B)—

(a) after 'the spouse or former spouse' insert ', or the civil partner or former civil partner,', and
(b) for 'those matrimonial home rights' substitute 'those home rights'.

(4) In paragraph (4C)—

(a) in sub-paragraph (b), for 'former spouse of the tenant' substitute 'former spouse or former civil partner of the tenant', and
(b) in sub-paragraph (c) after 'former spouse,' insert 'former civil partner,'.

(5) In paragraph (4D), after 'former spouse,' insert 'former civil partner,'.

Housing (Northern Ireland) Order 1983 (SI 1983/1118 (NI 15))

26 In Article 36(1)(d) (rent not to be increased on account of tenant's improvements), after 'former spouse' insert 'civil partner, former civil partner,'.

27(1) Amend Article 47 (extended discretion of court in possession claims) as follows.

(2) In paragraph (5), for 'tenant's spouse or former spouse, having matrimonial home rights' substitute 'tenant's spouse or former spouse, or civil partner or former civil partner, having home rights'.

(3) In paragraph (6)—

    (a) after 'the spouse or former spouse' insert ', or the civil partner or former civil partner', and
    (b) for 'those matrimonial home rights' substitute 'those home rights'.

(4) In paragraph (7)—

    (a) in sub-paragraph (b), for 'former spouse of the tenant' substitute 'former spouse or former civil partner of the tenant',
    (b) in sub-paragraph (c), after 'former spouse' insert 'former civil partner'.

(5) In paragraph (8) after 'former spouse,' insert 'former civil partner,'.

Insolvency (Northern Ireland) Order 1989 (SI 1989/2405 (NI 19))

28(1) Amend Article 309 (rights of occupation etc of bankrupt's spouse) as follows.

(2) In paragraph (1), for 'matrimonial home rights' substitute 'home rights'.

(3) In paragraph (2)—

    (a) for 'a spouse's matrimonial home rights' substitute 'a spouse's or civil partner's home rights', and
    (b) after 'the other spouse' (in each place) insert 'or civil partner'.

(4) In paragraph (3) after 'spouse or former spouse' insert 'or civil partner or former civil partner'.

29(1) Amend Article 310 (rights of occupation of bankrupt) as follows.

(2) In paragraph (2), for 'spouse (if any) has matrimonial home rights' substitute 'spouse or civil partner (if any) has home rights'.

(3) In paragraph (3)—

    (a) in sub-paragraph (a), for 'matrimonial home rights' substitute 'home rights', and
    (b) in sub-paragraph (c), after 'spouse' insert or 'civil partner'.

PART 3
TRANSITIONAL PROVISION

30(1) Any reference (however expressed) in any enactment, instrument or document (whether passed or made before or after the passing of this Act)—

    (a) to rights of occupation under, or within the meaning of, Part II of the Family Law (Miscellaneous Provisions) (Northern Ireland) Order 1984 (SI 1984/1984 (NI 14)), or
    (b) to matrimonial home rights under, or within the meaning of, the Family Homes and Domestic Violence (Northern Ireland) Order 1998 (SI 1998/1071 (NI 6)),

is to be construed, so far as is required for continuing the effect of the instrument or document, as being or as the case requires including a reference to home rights under, or within the meaning of, the 1998 Order as amended by this Schedule.

(2) Any reference (however expressed) in the 1998 Order or in any other enactment, instrument or document (including any enactment amended by this Schedule) to home rights under, or within

the meaning of, the 1998 Order is to be construed as including, in relation to times, circumstances and purposes before the commencement of this Schedule, references to rights of occupation under, or within the meaning of, Part II of the 1984 Order and to matrimonial home rights under, or within the meaning of, the 1998 Order without the amendments made by this Schedule.

(3) Any reference (however expressed) in any enactment, instrument or document (whether passed or made before or after the passing of this Act) to a matrimonial charge under, or within the meaning of—

(a) Article 5(1) of the 1984 Order, or

(b) the 1998 Order,

is to be construed, so far as is required for continuing the effect of the instrument or document, as being or as the case requires including a reference to a matrimonial or civil partnership charge under, or within the meaning of, the 1998 Order as amended by this Schedule.

(4) Any reference (however expressed) in the 1998 Order or in any other enactment, instrument or document (including any enactment amended by this Schedule) to a matrimonial or civil partnership charge under, or within the meaning of, the 1998 Order is to be construed as including, in relation to times, circumstances and purposes before the commencement of this Schedule, references to a matrimonial charge under, or within the meaning of—

(a) Article 5(1) of the 1984 Order, or

(b) the 1998 Order.

SCHEDULE 20

SECTION 213

MEANING OF OVERSEAS RELATIONSHIP: SPECIFIED RELATIONSHIPS

A relationship is specified for the purposes of section 213 (meaning of 'overseas relationship') if it is registered in a country or territory given in the first column of the table and fits the description given in relation to that country or territory in the second column—

Country or territory	Description
Belgium	cohabitation légale (statutory cohabitation)
Belgium	marriage
Canada: Nova Scotia	domestic partnership
Canada: Quebec	civil union
Denmark	registreret partnerskab (registered partnership)
Finland	rekisteröity parisuhde (registered partnership)
France	pacte civile de solidarité (civil solidarity pact)
Germany	Lebenspartnerschaft (life partnership)
Iceland	staðfesta samvist (confirmed cohabitation)
Netherlands	geregistreerde partnerschap (registered partnership)
Netherlands	marriage
Norway	registrert partnerskap (registered partnership)
Sweden	registrerat partnerskap (registered partnership)

Country or territory	Description
United States of America: Vermont	civil union

SCHEDULE 21

SECTION 247

REFERENCES TO STEPCHILDREN ETC IN EXISTING ACTS

1 The Declinature Act 1681 (c 79) (Senators of College of Justice not to sit in causes of persons related to them).

2 Section 21 of the Small Landholders (Scotland) Act 1911 (c 49) (assignment of holding).

3 Section 68(2)(e) of the Marriage Act 1949 (c 76) (solemnisation of marriages of stepchildren of servicemen in naval, military and air force chapels etc).

4 Section 7(7) of the Leasehold Reform Act 1967 (c 88) (rights of members of family succeeding to tenancy on death: member of another's family).

5 Section 18(3) of that Act (residential rights and exclusion of enfranchisement or extension: adult member of another's family).

6 Section 2(2) of the Employers' Liability (Compulsory Insurance) Act 1969 (c 57) (employees to be covered).

7 Section 27(5) of the Parliamentary and other Pensions Act 1972 (c 48) (pensions for dependants of Prime Minister or Speaker).

8 Section 184(5) of the Consumer Credit Act 1974 (c 39) (associates).

9 Section 1(5) of the Fatal Accidents Act 1976 (c 30) (right of action for wrongful act causing death: who are dependants).

10 The definition of 'relative' in section 31(1) of the Credit Unions Act 1979 (c 34) (interpretation, etc).

11 Section 32(3) of the Estate Agents Act 1979 (c 38) ('associate': meaning of relative).

12 Section 13(1) of the Administration of Justice Act 1982 (c 53) (deduction of relationships).

13 Section 12(5) of the Mental Health Act 1983 (c 20) (general provisions as to medical recommendations: persons who may not give recommendations).

14 Section 25C(10) of that Act (supervision applications: meaning of 'close relative').

15 Section 5(3) of the Mobile Homes Act 1983 (c 34) (interpretation: member of another's family).

16 Section 153(4) of the Companies Act 1985 (c 6) (transactions not prohibited by section 151).

17 Section 203(1) of that Act (notification of family and corporate interests: person interested in shares).

18 Section 327(2) of that Act (extension of section 323 to spouses and children).

19 Section 328(8) of that Act (extension of section 324 to spouses and children).

20 Section 346(2) of that Act ('connected persons').

21 Section 430E(8) of that Act (associates).

22 Section 742A(6) of that Act (meaning of 'offer to the public').

23 Section 74(4)(a) of the Bankruptcy (Scotland) Act 1985 (c 66) (meaning of 'associate').

24 Section 113(2) of the Housing Act 1985 (c 68) (members of a person's family).

25 Section 186(2) of that Act (members of a person's family).

26 Section 105(2) of the Housing Associations Act 1985 (c 69) (members of a person's family).

27 Section 20(6) of the Airports Act 1986 (c 31) (powers of investment and disposal in relation to public airport companies).

28 Section 435(8) of the Insolvency Act 1986 (c 45) (meaning of 'associate').

29 Section 70(2)(a) and (c), (3)(a) and (4) of the Building Societies Act 1986 (c 53) (interpretation).

30 Section 83(2)(c) of the Housing (Scotland) Act 1987 (c 26) (members of a person's family).

31 Section 4(6) of the Landlord and Tenant Act 1987 (c 31) (relevant disposals).

32 Section 52(2)(a) of the Companies Act 1989 (c 40) (meaning of 'associate').

33 The definition of 'relative' in section 105(1) of the Children Act 1989 (c 41) (interpretation).

34 Paragraph 1(2) of Schedule 2 to the Broadcasting Act 1990 (c 42) (restrictions on the holding of licences).

35 Section 11(1) of the Agricultural Holdings (Scotland) Act 1991 (c 55) (bequest of lease).

36 Section 77(3)(c) of the Friendly Societies Act 1992 (c 40) (information on appointed actuary to be annexed to balance sheet).

37 The definitions of 'son' and 'daughter' in section 119A(2) of that Act (meaning of 'associate').

38 Paragraph 2(1) of Schedule 5 to the Charities Act 1993 (c 10) (meaning of 'connected person' for purposes of section 36(2)).

39 Section 10(5) of the Leasehold Reform, Housing and Urban Development Act 1993 (c 28) (premises with a resident landlord: adult member of another's family).

40 Section 61(2) of the Crofters (Scotland) Act 1993 (c 44) (member of family).

41 Section 2 of the Criminal Law (Consolidation) (Scotland) Act 1995 (c 39) (intercourse with stepchild).

42 Section 161(1) of the Employment Rights Act 1996 (c 18) (domestic servants).

43 The definition of 'relative' in section 63(1) of the Family Law Act 1996 (c 27) (interpretation of Part 4 of the 1996 Act).

44 Section 62(2) of the Housing Act 1996 (c 52) (members of a person's family: Part 1).

45 Section 140(2) of that Act (members of a person's family: Chapter 1).

46 Section 143P(3) of that Act (members of a person's family: Chapter 1A).

47 The definition of 'relative' in section 178(3) of that Act (meaning of associated person).

48 Section 422(4)(b) of the Financial Services and Markets Act 2000 (c 8) (controller).

49 Paragraph 16(2) of Schedule 11 to that Act (offers of securities).

50 Section 108(2)(c) of the Housing (Scotland) Act 2001 (asp 10) (meaning of certain terms).

51 Section 1(3) of the Mortgage Rights (Scotland) Act 2001 (asp 11) (application to suspend enforcement of standard security).

52 Paragraph 3(8) of Schedule 6 to the Commonhold and Leasehold Reform Act 2002 (c 15) (premises excluded from right to manage).

53 Section 127(6) of the Enterprise Act 2002 (c 40) (associated persons).

SCHEDULE 22

SECTION 248

REFERENCES TO STEPCHILDREN ETC IN EXISTING NORTHERN IRELAND LEGISLATION

1 The definition of 'member of the family' in section 101 of the Industrial and Provident Societies Act (Northern Ireland) 1969 (c 24 (NI)) (interpretation).

2 Section 1(3)(f) of the Leasehold (Enlargement and Extension) Act (Northern Ireland) 1971 (c 7 (NI)) (persons to have rights to acquire a fee simple or to obtain extension of a lease).

3 Section 19(1)(a) of that Act (family of a person).

4 Section 3(7) of the Pensions (Increase) Act (Northern Ireland) 1971 (c 35 (NI)) (dependants).

5 Article 6 of the Employers' Liability (Defective Equipment and Compulsory Insurance) (Northern Ireland) Order 1972 (SI 1972/963 (NI 6)) (employees to be exempted).

6 Article 2(2) of the Fatal Accidents (Northern Ireland) Order 1977 (SI 1977/ 1251 (NI 18)) (dependants).

7 Article 2(5) of the Housing (Northern Ireland) Order 1981 (SI 1981/156 (NI 3)) (interpretation).

8 Article 24(3) of the Housing (Northern Ireland) Order 1983 (SI 1983/1118 (NI 15)) (interpretation).

9 The definition of 'member of the family' in Article 2(2) of the Credit Unions (Northern Ireland) Order 1985 (SI 1985/1205 (NI 12)) (interpretation).

10 Schedule 1 to the Mental Health (Northern Ireland) Order 1986 (SI 1986/ 595 (NI 4)) (general provisions as to medical recommendations: persons who may not give recommendations).

11 Article 10A of the Companies (Northern Ireland) Order 1986 (SI 1986/1032 (NI 6)) (meaning of 'offer to the public').

12 Article 211(1) of that Order (notification of family and corporate interests: person interested in shares).

13 Article 335(2) of that Order (extension of Article 331 to spouses and children).

14 Article 336(8) of that Order (extension of Article 332 to spouses and children).

15 Article 354(2) of that Order ('connected persons').

16 Article 423(8) of that Order (associates).

17 Article 4(8) of the Insolvency (Northern Ireland) Order 1989 (SI 1989/2405 (NI 19)) (meaning of 'associate').

18 Article 54(2)(a) of the Companies (Northern Ireland) Order 1990 (SI 1990/ 593 (NI 5)) (meaning of 'associate').

19 Article 2(4) of the Registered Homes (Northern Ireland) Order 1992 (SI 1992/3204 (NI 20)) (meaning of 'relative').

20 The definition of 'relative' in Article 2(2) of the Children (Northern Ireland) Order 1995 (SI 1995/755 (NI 2)).

21 Article 196(1) of the Employment Rights (Northern Ireland) Order 1996 (SI 1996/1919 (NI 16)) (domestic servants).

22 The definition of 'relative' in Article 2(2) of the Family Homes and Domestic Violence (Northern Ireland) Order 1998 (SI 1998/1071 (NI 6)) (interpretation).

23 Article 3(2) of the Housing (Northern Ireland) Order 2003 (SI 2003/412 (NI 2)) (members of a person's family).

24 The definition of 'relative' in Article 2(2) of the Firearms (Northern Ireland) Order 2004 (SI 2004/702 (NI 3)) (interpretation).

SCHEDULE 23

SECTION 249

IMMIGRATION CONTROL AND FORMATION OF CIVIL PARTNERSHIPS
PART 1
INTRODUCTION

Application of Schedule

1(1) This Schedule applies if—

(a) two people wish to register as civil partners of each other, and
(b) one of them is subject to immigration control.

(2) For the purposes of this Schedule a person is subject to immigration control if—

(a) he is not an EEA national, and
(b) under the Immigration Act 1971 (c 77) he requires leave to enter or remain in the United Kingdom (whether or not leave has been given).

(3) 'EEA national' means a national of a State which is a contracting party to the Agreement on the European Economic Area signed at Oporto on 2nd May 1992 (as it has effect from time to time).

The qualifying condition

2(1) For the purposes of this Schedule the qualifying condition, in relation to a person subject to immigration control, is that the person—

(a) has an entry clearance granted expressly for the purpose of enabling him to form a civil partnership in the United Kingdom,
(b) has the written permission of the Secretary of State to form a civil partnership in the United Kingdom, or

(c) falls within a class specified for the purpose of this paragraph by regulations made by the Secretary of State.

(2) 'Entry clearance' has the meaning given by section 33(1) of the Immigration Act 1971.

(3) Section 25 of the Asylum and Immigration (Treatment of Claimants, etc) Act 2004 (c 19) (regulations about applications for permission to marry) applies in relation to the permission referred to in sub-paragraph (1)(b) as it applies in relation to permission to marry under sections 19(3)(b), 21(3)(b) and 23(3)(b) of that Act.

PART 2
ENGLAND AND WALES

Application of this Part

3 This Part of this Schedule applies if the civil partnership is to be formed in England and Wales by signing a civil partnership schedule.

Procedure for giving notice of proposed civil partnership

4(1) Each notice of proposed civil partnership under Chapter 1 of Part 2 of this Act—

    (a) must be given to a registration authority specified for the purposes of this paragraph by regulations made by the Secretary of State, and

    (b) must be delivered to the relevant individual in person by the two proposed civil partners.

(2) 'The relevant individual' means such employee or officer or other person provided by the specified registration authority as is determined in accordance with regulations made by the Secretary of State for the purposes of this sub-paragraph.

(3) Regulations under sub-paragraph (2) may, in particular, describe a person by reference to the location or office where he works.

(4) Before making any regulations under this paragraph the Secretary of State must consult the Registrar General.

Declaration

5 The necessary declaration under section 8 must include a statement that the person subject to immigration control fulfils the qualifying condition (and the reason why).

Recording of notice

6(1) The fact that a notice of proposed civil partnership has been given must not be recorded in the register unless the registration authority is satisfied by the production of specified evidence that the person fulfils the qualifying condition.

(2) 'Specified evidence' means such evidence as may be specified in guidance issued by the Registrar General.

Supplementary

7(1) Part 2 of this Act has effect in any case where this Part of this Schedule applies subject to any necessary modification.

(2) In particular section 52 has effect as if the matters proof of which is not necessary in support of the civil partnership included compliance with this Part of this Schedule.

(3) An expression used in this Part of this Schedule and in Chapter 1 of Part 2 of this Act has the same meaning as in that Chapter.

PART 3
SCOTLAND

Application of this Part

8 This Part of this Schedule applies if the civil partnership is to be formed in Scotland.

Procedure for giving notice of proposed civil partnership

9(1) Notice under section 88—

(a) may be submitted to the district registrar of a district specified for the purposes of this paragraph by regulations made by the Secretary of State, and

(b) may not be submitted to the district registrar of any other registration district.

(2) Before making any regulations under this paragraph the Secretary of State must consult the Registrar General.

Pre-condition for making entry in civil partnership notice book etc

10(1) Where the district registrar to whom notice is submitted by virtue of paragraph 9(1) is the district registrar for the proposed place of registration, he shall neither—

(a) make an entry under section 89, nor

(b) complete a civil partnership schedule under section 94,

in respect of the proposed civil partnership unless satisfied, by the provision of specified evidence, that the intended civil partner subject to immigration control fulfils the qualifying condition.

(2) Where the district registrar to whom notice is so submitted (here the 'notified registrar') is not the district registrar for the proposed place of registration (here the 'second registrar')—

(a) the notified registrar shall, if satisfied as is mentioned in sub-paragraph (1), send the notices and any fee, certificate or declaration which accompanied them, to the second registrar, and

(b) the second registrar shall be treated as having received the notices from the intended partners on the dates on which the notified registrar received them.

(3) 'Specified evidence' means such evidence as may be specified in guidance issued by the Secretary of State after consultation with the Registrar General.

Supplementary

11(1) Part 3 of this Act has effect in any case where this Part of this Schedule applies subject to any necessary modification.

(2) An expression used in this Part of this Schedule and in Part 3 of this Act has the same meaning as in that Part.

PART 4
NORTHERN IRELAND

Application of this Part

12 This Part of this Schedule applies if the civil partnership is to be formed in Northern Ireland.

Procedure for giving civil partnership notices

13(1) The civil partnership notices must be given—

  (a) only to a prescribed registrar, and
  (b) in prescribed cases by both parties together in person at a prescribed register office.

(2) Before making any regulations under this paragraph the Secretary of State must consult the Registrar General.

Accompanying statement as to the qualifying condition

14 A civil partnership notice given by a person subject to immigration control must be accompanied by a statement that the person fulfils the qualifying condition (and the reason why).

Civil partnership notice book and civil partnership schedule

15(1) No action must be taken under section 140(1) or 143 (civil partnership notice book and civil partnership schedule) unless the prescribed registrar is satisfied by the production of specified evidence that the person fulfils the qualifying condition.

(2) If the prescribed registrar is satisfied as mentioned in sub-paragraph (1) but is not the registrar for the purposes of section 140(1), the prescribed registrar must send him the civil partnership notices and he is to be treated as having received them when the prescribed registrar received them.

(3) 'Specified evidence' means such evidence as may be specified in guidance issued by the Secretary of State after consultation with the Registrar General.

Supplementary

16(1) Part 4 of this Act has effect in any case where this Part of this Schedule applies subject to any necessary modification.

(2) In particular, section 176 has effect as if the matters proof of which is not necessary in support of the civil partnership included compliance with this Part of this Schedule.

(3) In this Part of this Schedule—

  (a) 'prescribed' means prescribed by regulations made by the Secretary of State;
  (b) 'registrar' means a person appointed under section 152(1)(a) or (b) or (3);
  (c) other expressions have the same meaning as in Chapter 1 of Part 4 of this Act.

(4) Section 18(3) of the Interpretation Act (Northern Ireland) 1954 (c 33 (NI)) (provisions as to holders of offices) shall apply to this Part of this Schedule as if it were an enactment within the meaning of that Act.

PART 5
REGULATIONS

17 Any power to make regulations under this Schedule is exercisable by statutory instrument which is subject to annulment in pursuance of a resolution of either House of Parliament.

SCHEDULE 24

SECTION 254

SOCIAL SECURITY, CHILD SUPPORT AND TAX CREDITS
PART 1
AMENDMENTS OF THE CHILD SUPPORT ACT 1991 (C 48)

1 In section 8 (role of the courts with respect to maintenance for children), after subsection (11)(e) insert—

'(ea) Schedule 5, 6 or 7 to the Civil Partnership Act 2004; or'.

2 In section 15 (powers of inspectors), in subsection (7)—

(a) after 'married' insert 'or is a civil partner', and
(b) after 'spouse' insert 'or civil partner'.

3 In section 55 (meaning of 'child'), in subsection (2)—

(a) in paragraph (a), after 'married' insert 'or a civil partner',
(b) in paragraph (b), after 'marriage' insert ', or been a party to a civil partnership,', and
(c) in paragraph (c), after 'granted' insert 'or has been a party to a civil partnership in respect of which a nullity order has been made'.

4 For paragraph 6(5)(b) (as originally enacted) of Schedule 1 (maintenance assessments) substitute—

'(b) where the absent parent—
  (i)   is living together in the same household with another adult of the opposite sex (regardless of whether or not they are married),
  (ii) is living together in the same household with another adult of the same sex who is his civil partner, or
  (iii) is living together in the same household with another adult of the same sex as if they were civil partners,

income of that other adult,'.

5 After paragraph 6(5) (as originally enacted) of that Schedule insert—

'(5A) For the purposes of this paragraph, two adults of the same sex are to be regarded as living together in the same household as if they were civil partners if, but only if, they would be regarded as living together as husband and wife were they instead two adults of the opposite sex.'

6 In paragraph 10C of that Schedule (as substituted by section 1(3) of, and Schedule 1 to, the Child Support, Pensions and Social Security Act 2000 (c 19)), for sub-paragraph (5) substitute—

'(5) In sub-paragraph (4)(a), "couple" means—

(a) a man and a woman who are married to each other and are members of the same household,

(b) a man and a woman who are not married to each other but are living together as husband and wife,

(c) two people of the same sex who are civil partners of each other and are members of the same household, or

(d) two people of the same sex who are not civil partners of each other but are living together as if they were civil partners.

(6) For the purposes of this paragraph, two people of the same sex are to be regarded as living together as if they were civil partners if, but only if, they would be regarded as living together as husband and wife were they instead two people of the opposite sex.'

PART 2
AMENDMENTS OF THE CHILD SUPPORT (NORTHERN IRELAND) ORDER 1991 (SI 1991/2628 (NI 23))

7 In Article 3 (meaning of 'child'), in paragraph (2)—

(a) in sub-paragraph (a), after 'married' insert 'or a civil partner',

(b) in sub-paragraph (b), after 'marriage' insert ', or been a party to a civil partnership,', and

(c) in sub-paragraph (c), after 'granted' insert 'or has been a party to a civil partnership in respect of which a nullity order has been made'.

8 In Article 10 (role of the courts with respect to maintenance for children), after paragraph (11)(d) insert—

'(da) Schedule 15, 16 or 17 to the Civil Partnership Act 2004; or'.

9 In Article 17 (powers of inspectors), in paragraph (7)—

(a) after 'married' insert 'or is a civil partner', and

(b) after 'spouse' insert 'or civil partner'.

10 For paragraph 6(5)(b) (as originally enacted) of Schedule 1 (maintenance assessments) substitute—

'(b) where the absent parent—
(i) is living together in the same household with another adult of the opposite sex (regardless of whether or not they are married),
(ii) is living together in the same household with another adult of the same sex who is his civil partner, or
(iii) is living together in the same household with another adult of the same sex as if they were civil partners,

income of that other adult,'.

11 After paragraph 6(5) (as originally enacted) of that Schedule insert—

'(5A) For the purposes of this paragraph, two adults of the same sex are to be regarded as living together in the same household as if they were civil partners if, but only if, they would be regarded as living together as husband and wife were they instead two adults of the opposite sex.'

12 In paragraph 10C of that Schedule (as substituted by section 1(3) of, and Schedule 1 to, the Child Support, Pensions and Social Security Act (Northern Ireland) 2000 (c 4 (NI))), for sub-paragraph (5) substitute—

'(5) In sub-paragraph (4)(a), "couple" means—

(a) a man and a woman who are married to each other and are members of the same household,

(b) a man and a woman who are not married to each other but are living together as husband and wife,

(c) two people of the same sex who are civil partners of each other and are members of the same household, or

(d) two people of the same sex who are not civil partners of each other but are living together as if they were civil partners.

(6) For the purposes of this paragraph, two people of the same sex are to be regarded as living together as if they were civil partners if, but only if, they would be regarded as living together as husband and wife were they instead two people of the opposite sex.'

PART 3
AMENDMENTS OF THE SOCIAL SECURITY CONTRIBUTIONS AND BENEFITS ACT 1992 (C 4)

13 In section 20 (descriptions of contributory benefits), in subsection (1)(f)(ii), after 'spouse' insert 'or civil partner'.

14 In section 30A (incapacity benefit: entitlement), in subsection (2)(b)(ii), after 'spouse' insert 'or deceased civil partner'.

15 In section 30B (incapacity benefit: rate), in subsection (3)(a), after 'people' insert 'or civil partners'.

16(1) Amend section 36 (bereavement payment) as follows.

(2) In subsection (1), after 'spouse' (in each place) insert 'or civil partner'.

(3) For subsection (2) substitute—

'(2) A bereavement payment shall not be payable to a person if—

(a) that person and a person of the opposite sex to whom that person was not married were living together as husband and wife at the time of the spouse's or civil partner's death, or

(b) that person and a person of the same sex who was not his or her civil partner were living together as if they were civil partners at the time of the spouse's or civil partner's death.'

17 In section 36A (cases in which sections 37 to 41 apply), in subsection (2), after 'spouse' insert 'or civil partner'.

18(1) Amend section 37 (widowed mother's allowance) as follows.

(2) In subsection (3), after 'remarries' insert 'or forms a civil partnership'.

(3) After subsection (4)(b) insert

'or
(c) for any period during which she and a woman who is not her civil partner are living together as if they were civil partners.'

19(1) Amend section 38 (widow's pension) as follows.

(2) In subsection (2), after 'remarries' insert 'or forms a civil partnership'.

(3) After subsection (3)(c) insert

'or
  (d) for any period during which she and a woman who is not her civil partner are living together as if they were civil partners.'

20(1) Amend section 39A (widowed parent's allowance) as follows.

(2) After 'spouse' (in each place other than subsections (2)(b) and (4)), insert 'or civil partner'.

(3) After 'spouse's' (in each place) insert 'or civil partner's'.

(4) In subsection (2), after paragraph (b) insert

'or
  (c) the surviving civil partner is a woman who—
    (i) was residing together with the deceased civil partner immediately before the time of the death, and
    (ii) is pregnant as the result of being artificially inseminated before that time with the semen of some person, or as a result of the placing in her before that time of an embryo, of an egg in the process of fertilisation, or of sperm and eggs.'

(5) In subsection (4), after 'remarries' insert 'or forms a civil partnership'.

(6) After subsection (4) insert—

'(4A) The surviving civil partner shall not be entitled to the allowance for any period after she or he forms a subsequent civil partnership or marries, but, subject to that, the surviving civil partner shall continue to be entitled to it for any period throughout which she or he—

  (a) satisfies the requirements of subsection (2)(a) or (b) above; and
  (b) is under pensionable age.'

(7) After subsection (5)(b) insert

'or
  (c) for any period during which the surviving spouse or civil partner and a person of the same sex who is not his or her civil partner are living together as if they were civil partners.'

21(1) Amend section 39B (bereavement allowance where no dependent children) as follows.

(2) After 'spouse' (in each place) other than subsection (4), insert 'or civil partner'.

(3) After 'spouse's' (in each place) insert 'or civil partner's'.

(4) In subsection (4), after 'remarries' insert 'or forms a civil partnership'.

(5) After subsection (4) insert—

'(4A) The surviving civil partner shall not be entitled to the allowance for any period after she or he forms a subsequent civil partnership or marries, but, subject to that, the surviving civil partner shall continue to be entitled to it until—

  (a) she or he attains pensionable age, or
  (b) the period of 52 weeks mentioned in subsection (3) above expires,

whichever happens first.'

(6) After subsection (5)(b) insert

'or

    (c) for any period during which the surviving spouse or civil partner and a person of the same sex who is not his or her civil partner are living together as if they were civil partners.'

22 In section 39C (rate of widowed parent's allowance and bereavement allowance)—

    (a) after 'spouse' (in each place) insert 'or civil partner', and
    (b) in subsection (5), after 'spouse's' insert 'or civil partner's'.

23 In section 46 (modifications of section 45 for calculating the additional pension in certain benefits)—

    (a) after 'under pensionable age', in subsection (2), insert 'or by virtue of section 39C(1) above or section 48A(4), 48B(2) or 48BB(5) below in a case where the deceased civil partner died under pensionable age',
    (b) after 'spouse', in paragraph (b)(i) of the definition of 'N' in subsection (2), insert 'or civil partner', and
    (c) after 'spouse' (in each place) in subsection (3), insert 'or civil partner'.

24(1) Amend section 48 (use of former spouse's contributions) as follows.

(2) In subsection (1)—

    (a) for 'married' substitute 'in a relevant relationship',
    (b) for 'marriage' substitute 'relationship', and
    (c) after 'spouse' insert 'or civil partner'.

(3) In subsection (2), for 'marriage' substitute 'relevant relationship'.

(4) For subsection (3) substitute—

    '(3) Where a person has been in a relevant relationship more than once, this section applies only to the last relevant relationship and the references to his relevant relationship and his former spouse or civil partner shall be construed accordingly.

    (4) In this section, 'relevant relationship' means a marriage or civil partnership.'

25(1) Amend section 48A (category B retirement pension for married person) as follows.

(2) After subsection (2) insert—

    '(2A) A person who—

        (a) has attained pensionable age, and
        (b) on attaining that age was a civil partner or forms a civil partnership after attaining that age,

    shall be entitled to a Category B retirement pension by virtue of the contributions of the other party to the civil partnership ('the contributing civil partner') if the following requirement is met.

    (2B) The requirement is that the contributing civil partner—

        (a) has attained pensionable age and become entitled to a Category A retirement pension, and
        (b) satisfies the conditions specified in Schedule 3, Part 1, paragraph 5.'

(3) In subsections (3) and (4), after 'spouse' insert 'or contributing civil partner'.

(4) In subsection (4A), for 'widow or widower' substitute 'widow, widower or surviving civil partner'.

(5) In subsection (5), after 'spouse's' insert 'or contributing civil partner's'.

(6) Section 48A (as amended by this paragraph) does not confer a right to a Category B retirement pension on a person by reason of his or her forming a civil partnership with a person who was born before 6th April 1950.

26(1) Amend section 48B (category B retirement pension for widows and widowers) as follows.

(2) After subsection (1) insert—

'(1A) A person ("the pensioner") who attains pensionable age on or after 6th April 2010 and whose civil partner died—

(a) while they were civil partners of each other, and
(b) after the pensioner attained pensionable age,

shall be entitled to a Category B retirement pension by virtue of the contributions of the civil partner if the civil partner satisfied the conditions specified in Schedule 3, Part 1, paragraph 5.'

(3) In subsection (2), after 'subsection (1)' insert 'or (1A)'.

(4) In subsection (3), after 'spouse' (in each place) insert 'or civil partner'.

27(1) Amend section 48BB (category B retirement pension: entitlement by reference to benefits under section 39A or 39B) as follows.

(2) After 'spouse' (in each place) insert 'or civil partner'.

(3) After 'spouse's' (in each place) insert 'or civil partner's'.

(4) In subsections (1)(b) and (3)(b), for 'remarried' substitute 'following that death married or formed a civil partnership'.

28(1) Amend section 51 (category B retirement pension for widowers) as follows.

(2) After subsection (1) insert—

'(1A) A civil partner shall be entitled to a Category B retirement pension if—

(a) his or her civil partner has died and they were civil partners of each other at the time of that death,
(b) they were both over pensionable age at the time of that death, and
(c) before that death the deceased civil partner satisfied the contribution conditions for a Category A retirement pension in Schedule 3, Part 1, paragraph 5.'

(3) In subsection (2)—

(a) for 'man's' substitute 'person's', and
(b) after 'wife' insert 'or deceased civil partner'.

(4) In subsection (3), after '2002' insert 'or a surviving civil partner'.

(5) In subsection (4)—

(a) for 'man' substitute 'person', and
(b) after 'pension' insert 'under this section'.

(6) Section 51 (as amended by this paragraph) does not confer a right to a Category B retirement pension on a person who attains pensionable age on or after 6th April 2010.

29 In section 51A (special provision for married people), in subsection (1)—

(a) after 'person' insert 'or civil partner', and

(b) after 'marriage' insert 'or civil partnership'.

30 In section 52 (special provision for surviving spouses), in subsection (1), after 'spouse' insert 'or civil partner'.

31 In section 60 (complete or partial failure to satisfy contributions conditions), in subsection (2)—

(a) after 'married' insert 'or a civil partner', and

(b) for 'widow or widower' substitute 'widow, widower or surviving civil partner'.

32 In section 61A (contributions paid in error), in subsection (3)—

(a) after 'spouse' insert 'or civil partner', and

(b) in paragraph (b), for 'widows or widowers' substitute 'widows, widowers or surviving civil partners'.

33 In section 62 (graduated retirement benefit), after subsection (1)(aa) insert—

'(ab) for extending section 37 of that Act (increase of woman's retirement pension by reference to her late husband's graduated retirement benefit) to civil partners and their late civil partners and for that section (except subsection (5)) so to apply as it applies to women and their late husbands;'.

34 In section 77 (guardian's allowance)—

(a) in subsection (6)(a)(ii), after 'spouses' insert 'or civil partners', and

(b) in subsection (8)(a), after 'divorce' insert 'or the civil partnership of the child's parents has been dissolved'.

35 In section 82 (short-term benefit: increase for adult dependants)—

(a) in subsection (3)(a) and (b), after 'husband' insert 'or civil partner',

(b) in subsection (3)(b), for 'his' substitute 'her husband's or civil partner's', and

(c) in subsection (4)(a), after 'spouse' insert 'or civil partner'.

36 In section 83A (pension increase for spouse)—

(a) in subsection (1), for 'married pensioner' substitute 'pensioner who is married or a civil partner', and

(b) in subsections (2) and (3), after 'spouse' (in each place) insert 'or civil partner'.

37(1) Amend section 85 (pension increase: person with care of children) as follows.

(2) Omit subsection (1).

(3) After subsection (1) insert—

'(1A) Subject to subsections (2A) and (4) below, the weekly rate of a Category A retirement pension shall be increased by the amount specified in relation to that pension in Schedule 4, Part 4, column (3) for any period during which a person who is neither the spouse or civil partner of the pensioner nor a child has the care of a child or children in respect of whom the pensioner is entitled to child benefit.'

(4) In subsection (2)—

(a) for 'the following provisions' substitute 'subsections (3) and (4) below', and

(b) for 'pension to which this section applies' substitute 'Category C retirement pension payable by virtue of section 78(1) above'.

(5) After subsection (2) insert—

'(2A) Subsection (1A) above does not apply if the pensioner is a person whose spouse or civil partner is entitled to a Category B retirement pension, or to a Category C retirement pension by virtue of section 78(2) above or in such other cases as may be prescribed.'

(6) In subsection (4), after 'subsection' insert '(1A) or'.

38 In section 113 (general provisions as to disqualification and suspension), in subsection (1), for 'wife or husband,' substitute 'wife, husband or civil partner,'.

39 In section 114 (persons maintaining dependants etc)—

(a) in subsection (2), for 'wife' substitute 'wife, civil partner', and
(b) in subsection (3)(a), after 'spouse' insert 'or civil partner'.

40 After subsection (1)(a) of section 121 (treatment of certain marriages) insert—

'(aa) for a voidable civil partnership which has been annulled, whether before or after the date when the regulations come into force, to be treated for the purposes of the provisions to which this subsection applies as if it had been a valid civil partnership which was dissolved at the date of annulment;'.

41(1) Amend section 122 (interpretation of Parts 1 to 6 and supplementary provisions) as follows.

(2) In subsection (1), in the definition of 'relative' after 'by marriage' insert 'or civil partnership'.

(3) After subsection (1) insert—

'(1A) For the purposes of Parts 1 to 5 and this Part of this Act, two people of the same sex are to be regarded as living together as if they were civil partners if, but only if, they would be regarded as living together as husband and wife were they instead two people of the opposite sex.'

42 In section 124 (income support), in subsection (1)(c), (f) and (g), for 'married or unmarried couple' substitute 'couple'.

43 In section 126 (trade disputes), in subsection (3)(b), (c) and (d), for 'married or unmarried couple' substitute 'couple'.

44 In section 127 (effect of return to work), for 'married or unmarried couple' (in each place) substitute 'couple'.

45 In section 132 (couples), in subsection (1), for 'married or unmarried couple' substitute 'couple'.

46(1) Amend section 137 (interpretation of Part 7 and supplementary provisions) as follows.

(2) In paragraphs (a), (b) and (c) of the definition of 'family' in subsection (1), for 'married or unmarried couple' substitute 'couple'.

(3) After the definition of 'child' in subsection (1) insert—

'"couple" means—

(a) a man and woman who are married to each other and are members of the same household;
(b) a man and woman who are not married to each other but are living together as husband and wife otherwise than in prescribed circumstances;
(c) two people of the same sex who are civil partners of each other and are members of the same household; or

(d) two people of the same sex who are not civil partners of each other but are living together as if they were civil partners otherwise than in prescribed circumstances;'.

(4) Omit the definitions of 'married couple' and 'unmarried couple' in subsection (1).

(5) After subsection (1) insert—

'(1A) For the purposes of this Part, two people of the same sex are to be regarded as living together as if they were civil partners if, but only if, they would be regarded as living together as husband and wife were they instead two people of the opposite sex.'

47 In section 143 (meaning of 'person responsible for child'), in subsection (5), after 'spouses' insert 'or civil partners'.

48(1) Amend section 145A (entitlement after death of child) as follows.

(2) In subsection (2)—

(a) in paragraph (a), after 'couple' insert 'or civil partnership' and after 'to whom he was married' insert 'or who was his civil partner',
(b) in paragraph (b), after 'couple' insert 'or a cohabiting same-sex couple', and
(c) for 'married couple or unmarried couple' substitute 'couple or partnership'.

(3) Before the definition of 'married couple' in subsection (5) insert—

'"civil partnership" means two people of the same sex who are civil partners of each other and are neither—

(a) separated under a court order, nor

(b) separated in circumstances in which the separation is likely to be permanent,

"cohabiting same-sex couple" means two people of the same sex who are not civil partners of each other but are living together as if they were civil partners,'.

(4) After subsection (5) insert—

'(6) For the purposes of this section, two people of the same sex are to be regarded as living together as if they were civil partners if, but only if, they would be regarded as living together as husband and wife were they instead two people of the opposite sex.'

49(1) Amend section 150 (interpretation of Part 10) as follows.

(2) In the definition of 'war widow's pension' in subsection (2)—

(a) after 'any widow's' insert 'or surviving civil partner's', and
(b) after 'widow' insert 'or surviving civil partner'.

(3) For subsection (3) substitute—

'(3) In this Part of this Act, 'couple' has the meaning given by section 137(1) above.'

50 In section 171ZL (entitlement to statutory adoption pay), in subsection (4)(b)—

(a) after 'married couple' insert 'or civil partnership', and
(b) after 'spouse' (in each place) insert 'or civil partner'.

51(1) Amend Schedule 4A (additional pension) as follows.

(2) In paragraph 1(2), after 'under pensionable age,' insert 'or by virtue of section 39C(1), 48A(4) or 48B(2) above, in a case where the deceased civil partner died under pensionable age,'.

(3) In paragraph 1(4)(a) and (b), (5), (6) and (7)(a) and (b), after 'spouse' insert 'or civil partner'.

52(1) Amend Schedule 7 (industrial injuries benefits) as follows.

(2) For paragraph 4(3)(a) of Part 1 substitute—

'(a) a beneficiary is one of two persons who are—
   (i)   spouses or civil partners residing together,
   (ii) a man and woman who are not married to each other but are living together as if they were husband and wife, or
   (iii) two people of the same sex who are not civil partners of each other but are living together as if they were civil partners, and'.

(3) In paragraph 5(2)(a)(ii) of Part 1, after 'spouses' insert 'or civil partners'.

(4) In Part 1—

(a) in paragraph 6(1), (3) and (4), after 'spouse' (in each place) insert 'or civil partner', and
(b) in paragraph 6(4)(a), after 'spouse's' insert 'or civil partner's'.

(5) In paragraph 15 of Part 6—

(a) in sub-paragraph (2), after 'remarries' insert 'or forms a civil partnership', and
(b) at the end of sub-paragraph (3), insert 'or is living together with a person of the same sex as if they were civil partners'.

53(1) Amend Schedule 8 (industrial injuries and diseases: old cases) as follows.

(2) In paragraph 6(4)(d), and the substituted paragraph (d) in paragraph 6(5), after 'spouse' (in each place) insert 'or civil partner'.

(3) After paragraph 8(1) insert—

'(1A) Any reference in this Schedule to a member of a person's family within the meaning of the Workmen's Compensation Act 1925 is to be read as including a civil partner of his.'

54 In Schedule 9 (exclusions from entitlement to child benefit), in paragraph 3, after 'married' insert 'or is a civil partner'.

PART 4
AMENDMENTS OF THE SOCIAL SECURITY ADMINISTRATION ACT 1992
(C 5)

55 In section 2AA (full entitlement to certain benefits conditional on work-focused interview for partner), in subsection (7), for the definition of 'couple' substitute—

'"couple" has the meaning given by section 137(1) of the Contributions and Benefits Act;'.

56 In section 3 (late claims for bereavement benefit where death is difficult to establish)—

(a) after 'spouse' (in each place) insert 'or civil partner', and
(b) after 'spouse's' (in each place) insert 'or civil partner's'.

57(1) Amend section 15A (payment out of benefit of sums in respect of mortgage interest etc) as follows.

(2) In subsection (4)—

(a) in paragraph (a) of the definition of 'partner', for 'to whom the borrower is married' substitute 'who is married to, or a civil partner of, the borrower', and

(b) in paragraph (b) of that definition, for 'to whom the borrower is not married but who lives together with the borrower as husband and wife' substitute 'who is neither married to, nor a civil partner of, the borrower but who lives together with the borrower as husband and wife or as if they were civil partners'.

(3) After subsection (4A) insert—

'(4B) For the purposes of this section, two people of the same sex are to be regarded as living together as if they were civil partners if, but only if, they would be regarded as living together as husband and wife were they instead two people of the opposite sex.'

58(1) Amend section 71 (overpayments – general) as follows.

(2) In subsection (9), for 'married or unmarried couple' substitute 'couple'.

(3) After subsection (11) insert—

'(12) In this section, "couple" has the meaning given by section 137(1) of the Contributions and Benefits Act.'

59 In section 73 (overlapping benefits – general), in subsections (2)(b) and (d) and (5)(b) and (d), for 'wife or husband' substitute 'wife, husband or civil partner'.

60 In section 74A (payment of benefit where maintenance payments collected by Secretary of State), in subsection (5)—

(a) after the definition of 'child maintenance' insert—

'"couple" has the meaning given by section 137(1) of the Contributions and Benefits Act;',

(b) in the definition of 'family', for 'married or unmarried couple' (in each place) substitute 'couple', and

(c) omit the definitions of 'married couple' and 'unmarried couple'.

61(1) Amend section 78 (recovery of social fund awards) as follows.

(2) In subsection (3)(b), for 'married or unmarried couple' substitute 'couple'.

(3) For subsection (5) substitute—

'(5) In this section "couple" has the meaning given by section 137(1) of the Contributions and Benefits Act.'

(4) In subsection (6)—

(a) in paragraph (a), after 'wife' insert 'or civil partner', and

(b) in paragraph (b), after 'husband' insert 'or civil partner'.

62 In section 105 (failure to maintain – general), in subsection (4), after 'spouse' insert 'or civil partner'.

63(1) Amend section 107 (recovery of expenditure on income support: additional amounts and transfer of orders) as follows.

(2) In subsection (1)(b), after 'wife' insert 'or civil partner'.

(3) In subsection (15), after paragraph (a)(ii) of the definition of 'maintenance order' insert—

'(iii) any order under Schedule 7 to the Civil Partnership Act 2004 for the making of periodical payments or for the payment of a lump sum;'.

64 In section 109B (power to require information), in subsection (5)(a), for 'married, his spouse' substitute 'married or is a civil partner, his spouse or civil partner'.

65 In section 139 (arrangement for community charge benefits), in subsection (11), in the definition of 'war widow's pension'—

(a) after 'any widow's' insert 'or surviving civil partner's', and
(b) after 'widow' insert 'or surviving civil partner'.

66 In section 156 (up-rating under section 150 of pensions increased under section 52(3) of the Contributions and Benefits Act)—

(a) in subsection (1), after 'spouse' insert 'or civil partner', and
(b) in subsections (2) and (3), after 'spouse's' (in each place) insert 'or civil partner's'.

PART 5
AMENDMENTS OF THE SOCIAL SECURITY CONTRIBUTIONS AND BENEFITS (NORTHERN IRELAND) ACT 1992 (C 7)

67 In section 20 (descriptions of contributory benefits), in subsection (1)(f)(ii), after 'spouse' insert 'or civil partner'.

68 In section 30A (incapacity benefit: entitlement), in subsection (2)(b)(ii), after 'spouse' insert 'or deceased civil partner'.

69 In section 30B (incapacity benefit: rate), in subsection (3)(a), after 'people' insert 'or civil partners'.

70(1) Amend section 36 (bereavement payment) as follows.

(2) In subsection (1), after 'spouse' (in each place) insert 'or civil partner'.

(3) For subsection (2) substitute—

  '(2) A bereavement payment shall not be payable to a person if—

    (a) that person and a person of the opposite sex to whom that person was not married were living together as husband and wife at the time of the spouse's or civil partner's death, or
    (b) that person and a person of the same sex who was not his or her civil partner were living together as if they were civil partners at the time of the spouse's or civil partner's death.'

71 In section 36A (cases in which sections 37 to 41 apply), in subsection (2), after 'spouse' insert 'or civil partner'.

72(1) Amend section 37 (widowed mother's allowance) as follows.

(2) In subsection (3), after 'remarries' insert 'or forms a civil partnership'.

(3) After subsection (4)(b) insert

  'or
    (c) for any period during which she and a woman who is not her civil partner are living together as if they were civil partners.'

73(1) Amend section 38 (widow's pension) as follows.

(2) In subsection (2), after 'remarries' insert 'or forms a civil partnership'.

(3) After subsection (3)(c) insert

'or
    (d) for any period during which she and a woman who is not her civil partner are living together as if they were civil partners.'

74(1) Amend section 39A (widowed parent's allowance) as follows.

(2) After 'spouse' (in each place other than subsections (2)(b) and (4)), insert 'or civil partner'.

(3) After 'spouse's' (in each place) insert 'or civil partner's'.

(4) In subsection (2), after paragraph (b) insert

'or
    (c) the surviving civil partner is a woman who—
        (i) was residing together with the deceased civil partner immediately before the time of the death, and
        (ii) is pregnant as the result of being artificially inseminated before that time with the semen of some person, or as a result of the placing in her before that time of an embryo, of an egg in the process of fertilisation, or of sperm and eggs.'

(5) In subsection (4), after 'remarries' insert 'or forms a civil partnership'.

(6) After subsection (4) insert—

'(4A) The surviving civil partner shall not be entitled to the allowance for any period after she or he forms a subsequent civil partnership or marries, but, subject to that, the surviving civil partner shall continue to be entitled to it for any period throughout which she or he—

    (a) satisfies the requirements of subsection (2)(a) or (b) above; and
    (b) is under pensionable age.'

(7) After subsection (5)(b) insert

'or
    (c) for any period during which the surviving spouse or civil partner and a person of the same sex who is not his or her civil partner are living together as if they were civil partners.'

75(1) Amend section 39B (bereavement allowance where no dependent children) as follows.

(2) After 'spouse' (in each place other than subsection (4)), insert 'or civil partner'.

(3) After 'spouse's' (in each place) insert 'or civil partner's'.

(4) In subsection (4), after 'remarries' insert 'or forms a civil partnership'.

(5) After subsection (4) insert—

'(4A) The surviving civil partner shall not be entitled to the allowance for any period after she or he forms a subsequent civil partnership or marries, but, subject to that, the surviving civil partner shall continue to be entitled to it until—

    (a) she or he attains pensionable age, or
    (b) the period of 52 weeks mentioned in subsection (3) above expires,

whichever happens first.'

(6) After subsection (5)(b) insert

'or

    (c) for any period during which the surviving spouse or civil partner and a person of the same sex who is not his or her civil partner are living together as if they were civil partners.'

76 In section 39C (rate of widowed parent's allowance and bereavement allowance)—

    (a) after 'spouse' (in each place) insert 'or civil partner', and
    (b) in subsection (5), after 'spouse's' insert 'or civil partner's'.

77 In section 46 (modifications of section 45 for calculating the additional pension in certain benefits)—

    (a) after 'under pensionable age', in subsection (2), insert 'or by virtue of section 39C(1) above or section 48A(4), 48B(2) or 48BB(5) below in a case where the deceased civil partner died under pensionable age',
    (b) after 'spouse', in paragraph (b)(i) of the definition of 'N' in subsection (2), insert 'or civil partner', and
    (c) after 'spouse' (in each place) in subsection (3), insert 'or civil partner'.

78(1) Amend section 48 (use of former spouse's contributions) as follows.

(2) In subsection (1)—

    (a) for 'married' substitute 'in a relevant relationship',
    (b) for 'marriage' substitute 'relationship', and
    (c) after 'spouse' insert 'or civil partner'.

(3) In subsection (2), for 'marriage' substitute 'relevant relationship'.

(4) For subsection (3) substitute—

    '(3) Where a person has been in a relevant relationship more than once, this section applies only to the last relevant relationship and the references to his relevant relationship and his former spouse or civil partner shall be construed accordingly.

    (4) In this section, 'relevant relationship' means a marriage or civil partnership.'

79(1) Amend section 48A (category B retirement pension for married person) as follows.

(2) After subsection (2) insert—

    '(2A) A person who—

        (a) has attained pensionable age, and
        (b) on attaining that age was a civil partner or forms a civil partnership after attaining that age,

    shall be entitled to a Category B retirement pension by virtue of the contributions of the other party to the civil partnership ("the contributing civil partner") if the following requirement is met.

    (2B) The requirement is that the contributing civil partner—

        (a) has attained pensionable age and become entitled to a Category A retirement pension, and
        (b) satisfies the conditions specified in Schedule 3, Part 1, paragraph 5.'

(3) In subsections (3) and (4), after 'spouse' insert 'or contributing civil partner'.

(4) In subsection (4A), for 'widow or widower' substitute 'widow, widower or surviving civil partner'.

(5) In subsection (5), after 'spouse's' insert 'or contributing civil partner's'.

(6) Section 48A (as amended by this paragraph) does not confer a right to a Category B retirement pension on a person by reason of his or her forming a civil partnership with a person who was born before 6th April 1950.

80(1) Amend section 48B (category B retirement pension for widows and widowers) as follows.

(2) After subsection (1) insert—

'(1A) A person ("the pensioner") who attains pensionable age on or after 6th April 2010 and whose civil partner died—

(a) while they were civil partners of each other, and
(b) after the pensioner attained pensionable age,

shall be entitled to a Category B retirement pension by virtue of the contributions of the civil partner if the civil partner satisfied the conditions specified in Schedule 3, Part 1, paragraph 5.'

(3) In subsection (2), after 'subsection (1)' insert 'or (1A)'.

(4) In subsection (3), after 'spouse' (in each place) insert 'or civil partner'.

81(1) Amend section 48BB (category B retirement pension: entitlement by reference to benefits under section 39A or 39B) as follows.

(2) After 'spouse' (in each place) insert 'or civil partner'.

(3) After 'spouse's' (in each place) insert 'or civil partner's'.

(4) In subsections (1)(b) and (3)(b), for 'remarried' substitute 'following that death married or formed a civil partnership'.

82(1) Amend section 51 (category B retirement pension for widowers) as follows.

(2) After subsection (1) insert—

'(1A) A civil partner shall be entitled to a Category B retirement pension if—

(a) his or her civil partner has died and they were civil partners of each other at the time of that death,
(b) they were both over pensionable age at the time of that death, and
(c) before that death the deceased civil partner satisfied the contribution conditions for a Category A retirement pension in Schedule 3, Part 1, paragraph 5.'

(3) In subsection (2)—

(a) for 'man's' substitute 'person's', and
(b) after 'wife' insert 'or deceased civil partner'.

(4) In subsection (3), after '2002' insert 'or a surviving civil partner'.

(5) In subsection (4)—

(a) for 'man' substitute 'person', and
(b) after 'pension' insert 'under this section'.

(6) Section 51 (as amended by this paragraph) does not confer a right to a Category B retirement pension on a person who attains pensionable age on or after 6th April 2010.

83 In section 51A (special provision for married people), in subsection (1)—

    (a) after 'person' insert 'or civil partner', and
    (b) after 'marriage' insert 'or civil partnership'.

84 In section 52 (special provision for surviving spouses), in subsection (1), after 'spouse' insert 'or civil partner'.

85 In section 60 (complete or partial failure to satisfy contribution conditions), in subsection (2)—

    (a) after 'married' insert 'or a civil partner', and
    (b) for 'widow or widower' substitute 'widow, widower or surviving civil partner'.

86 In section 61A (contributions paid in error), in subsection (3)—

    (a) after 'spouse' insert 'or civil partner', and
    (b) in paragraph (b), for 'widows or widowers' substitute 'widows, widowers or surviving civil partners'.

87 In section 62 (graduated retirement benefit), after subsection (1)(aa) insert—

    '(ab) for extending section 36 of that Act (increase of woman's retirement pension by reference to her late husband's graduated retirement benefit) to civil partners and their late civil partners and for that section (except subsection (5)) so to apply as it applies to women and their late husbands;'.

88 In section 77 (guardian's allowance)—

    (a) in subsection (6)(a)(ii), after 'spouses' insert 'or civil partners', and
    (b) in subsection (8)(a), after 'divorce' insert 'or the civil partnership of the child's parents has been dissolved'.

89 In section 82 (short-term benefit: increase for adult dependants)—

    (a) in subsection (3)(a) and (b), after 'husband' insert 'or civil partner',
    (b) in subsection (3)(b), for 'his' substitute 'her husband's or civil partner's', and
    (c) in subsection (4)(a), after 'spouse' insert 'or civil partner'.

90 In section 83A (pension increase for spouse)—

    (a) in subsection (1), for 'married pensioner' substitute 'pensioner who is married or a civil partner', and
    (b) in subsections (2) and (3), after 'spouse' (in each place) insert 'or civil partner'.

91(1) Amend section 85 (pension increase (person with care of children)) as follows.

(2) Omit subsection (1).

(3) After subsection (1) insert—

    '(1A) Subject to subsections (2A) and (4) below, the weekly rate of a Category A retirement pension shall be increased by the amount specified in relation to that pension in Schedule 4, Part 4, column (3) for any period during which a person who is neither the spouse or civil partner of the pensioner nor a child has the care of a child or children in respect of whom the pensioner is entitled to child benefit.'

(4) In subsection (2)—

    (a) for 'the following provisions' substitute 'subsections (3) and (4) below', and
    (b) for 'pension to which this section applies' substitute 'Category C retirement pension payable by virtue of section 78(1) above'.

(5) After subsection (2) insert—

'(2A) Subsection (1A) above does not apply if the pensioner is a person whose spouse or civil partner is entitled to a Category B retirement pension, or to a Category C retirement pension by virtue of section 78(2) above or in such other cases as may be prescribed.'

(6) In subsection (4), after 'subsection' insert '(1A) or'.

92 In section 113 (general provisions as to disqualification and suspension), in subsection (1), for 'wife or husband,' substitute 'wife, husband or civil partner,'.

93 In section 114 (persons maintaining dependants etc)—

(a) in subsection (2), for 'wife' substitute 'wife, civil partner', and
(b) in subsection (3)(a), after 'spouse' insert 'or civil partner'.

94 In section 120 (treatment of certain marriages), after subsection (1)(a) insert—

'(aa) for a voidable civil partnership which has been annulled, whether before or after the date when the regulations come into force, to be treated for the purposes of the provisions to which this subsection applies as if it had been a valid civil partnership which was dissolved at the date of annulment;'.

95(1) Amend section 121 (interpretation of Parts 1 to 6 and supplementary provisions) as follows.

(2) In subsection (1), in the definition of 'relative' after 'by marriage' insert 'or civil partnership'.

(3) After subsection (1) insert—

'(1A) For the purposes of Parts 1 to 5 and this Part of this Act, two people of the same sex are to be regarded as living together as if they were civil partners if, but only if, they would be regarded as living together as husband and wife were they instead two people of the opposite sex.'

96 In section 123 (income support), in subsection (1)(c), (f) and (g), for 'married or unmarried couple' substitute 'couple'.

97 In section 125 (trade disputes), in subsection (3)(b), (c) and (d), for 'married or unmarried couple' substitute 'couple'.

98 In section 126 (effect of return to work), for 'married or unmarried couple' (in each place) substitute 'couple'.

99(1) Amend section 133 (interpretation of Part 7 and supplementary provisions) as follows.

(2) In paragraphs (a), (b) and (c) of the definition of 'family' in subsection (1), for 'married or unmarried couple' substitute 'couple'.

(3) After the definition of 'child' in subsection (1) insert—

' "couple" means—

(a) a man and woman who are married to each other and are members of the same household;
(b) a man and woman who are not married to each other but are living together as husband and wife otherwise than in prescribed circumstances;
(c) two people of the same sex who are civil partners of each other and are members of the same household; or
(d) two people of the same sex who are not civil partners of each other but are living together as if they were civil partners otherwise than in prescribed circumstances;'.

(4) Omit the definitions of 'married couple' and 'unmarried couple' in subsection (1).

(5) After subsection (1) insert—

'(1A) For the purposes of this Part, two people of the same sex are to be regarded as living together as if they were civil partners if, but only if, they would be regarded as living together as husband and wife were they instead two people of the opposite sex.'

100 In section 139 (meaning of 'person responsible for child'), in subsection (5), after 'spouses' insert 'or civil partners'.

101(1) Amend section 141A (entitlement after death of child) as follows.

(2) In subsection (2)—

   (a) in paragraph (a), after 'couple' insert 'or civil partnership' and after 'to whom he was married' insert 'or who was his civil partner',
   (b) in paragraph (b), after 'couple' insert 'or a cohabiting same-sex couple', and
   (c) for 'married couple or unmarried couple' substitute 'couple or partnership'.

(3) Before the definition of 'married couple' in subsection (5) insert—

   ' "civil partnership" means two people of the same sex who are civil partners of each other and are neither—

   (a) separated under a court order, nor

   (b) separated in circumstances in which the separation is likely to be permanent,

   "cohabiting same-sex couple" means two people of the same sex who are not civil partners of each other but are living together as if they were civil partners,'.

(4) After subsection (5) insert—

'(6) For the purposes of this section, two people of the same sex are to be regarded as living together as if they were civil partners if, but only if, they would be regarded as living together as husband and wife were they instead two people of the opposite sex.'

102(1) Amend section 146 (interpretation of Part 10) as follows.

(2) In the definition of 'war widow's pension' in subsection (2)—

   (a) after 'any widow's' insert 'or surviving civil partner's', and
   (b) after 'widow' insert 'or surviving civil partner'.

(3) For subsection (3) substitute—

'(3) In this Part of this Act, "couple" has the meaning given by section 133(1) above.'

103 In section 167ZL (entitlement to statutory adoption pay), in subsection (4)(b)—

   (a) after 'married couple' insert 'or civil partnership', and
   (b) after 'spouse' (in each place) insert 'or civil partner'.

104(1) Amend Schedule 4A (additional pension) as follows.

(2) In paragraph 1(2), after 'under pensionable age,' insert 'or by virtue of section 39C(1), 48A(4) or 48B(2) above, in a case where the deceased civil partner died under pensionable age,'.

(3) In paragraph 1(4)(a) and (b), (5), (6) and (7)(a) and (b), after 'spouse' insert 'or civil partner'.

105(1) Amend Schedule 7 (industrial injuries benefits) as follows.

(2) For paragraph 4(3)(a) of Part 1 substitute—

'(a) a beneficiary is one of two persons who are—
  (i)   spouses or civil partners residing together,
  (ii) a man and woman who are not married to each other but are living together as if they were husband and wife, or
  (iii) two people of the same sex who are not civil partners of each other but are living together as if they were civil partners, and'.

(3) In paragraph 5(2)(a)(ii) of Part 1, after 'spouses' insert 'or civil partners'.

(4) In Part 1—

(a) in paragraph 6(1), (3) and (4), after 'spouse' (in each place) insert 'or civil partner', and
(b) in paragraph 6(4)(a), after 'spouse's' insert 'or civil partner's'.

(5) In paragraph 15 of Part 6—

(a) in sub-paragraph (2), after 'remarries' insert 'or forms a civil partnership', and
(b) at the end of sub-paragraph (3), insert 'or is living together with a person of the same sex as if they were civil partners'.

106 In Schedule 9 (exclusions from entitlement to child benefit), in paragraph 3, after 'married' insert 'or is a civil partner'.

PART 6
AMENDMENTS OF THE SOCIAL SECURITY ADMINISTRATION (NORTHERN IRELAND) ACT 1992 (C 8)

107 In section 2AA (full entitlement to certain benefits conditional on work-focused interview for partner), in subsection (7), for the definition of 'couple' substitute—

'"couple" has the meaning given by section 133(1) of the Contributions and Benefits Act;'.

108 In section 3 (late claims for bereavement benefit where death is difficult to establish)—

(a) after 'spouse' (in each place) insert 'or civil partner', and
(b) after 'spouse's' (in each place) insert 'or civil partner's'.

109(1) Amend section 13A (payment out of benefit of sums in respect of mortgage interest etc) as follows.

(2) In subsection (4)—

(a) in paragraph (a) of the definition of 'partner', for 'to whom the borrower is married' substitute 'who is married to, or a civil partner of, the borrower', and
(b) in paragraph (b) of that definition, for 'to whom the borrower is not married but who lives together with the borrower as husband and wife' substitute 'who is neither married to, nor a civil partner of, the borrower but who lives together with the borrower as husband and wife or as if they were civil partners'.

(3) After subsection (4A) insert—

'(4B) For the purposes of this section, two people of the same sex are to be regarded as living together as if they were civil partners if, but only if, they would be regarded as living together as husband and wife were they instead two people of the opposite sex.'

110(1) Amend section 69 (overpayments – general) as follows.

(2) In subsection (9), for 'married or unmarried couple' substitute 'couple'.

(3) After subsection (11) insert—

'(12) In this section, "couple" has the meaning given by section 133(1) of the Contributions and Benefits Act.'

111 In section 71 (overlapping benefits – general), in subsections (2)(b) and (d) and (5)(b) and (d), for 'wife or husband' substitute 'wife, husband or civil partner'.

112 In section 72A (payment of benefit where maintenance payments collected by Department), in subsection (5)—

(a) after the definition of 'child maintenance' insert—

'"couple" has the meaning given by section 133(1) of the Contributions and Benefits Act;',

(b) in the definition of 'family', for 'married or unmarried couple' (in each place) substitute 'couple', and

(c) omit the definitions of 'married couple' and 'unmarried couple'.

113(1) Amend section 74 (recovery of social fund awards) as follows.

(2) In subsection (3)(b), for 'married or unmarried couple' substitute 'couple'.

(3) For subsection (5) substitute—

'(5) In this section, "couple" has the meaning given by section 133(1) of the Contributions and Benefits Act.'

(4) In subsection (6)—

(a) in paragraph (a), after 'wife' insert 'or civil partner', and

(b) in paragraph (b), after 'husband' insert 'or civil partner'.

114 In section 100 (failure to maintain – general), in subsection (4), after 'spouse' insert 'or civil partner'.

115 In section 102 (recovery of expenditure on income support: additional amounts and transfer of orders), in subsection (1)(b), after 'wife' insert 'or civil partner'.

116 In section 103B (power to require information), in subsection (5)(a), for 'married, his spouse' substitute 'married or is a civil partner, his spouse or civil partner'.

117 In section 136 (up-rating under section 132 of pensions increased under section 52(3) of the Contributions and Benefits Act)—

(a) in subsection (1), after 'spouse' insert 'or civil partner', and

(b) in subsections (2) and (3), after 'spouse's' (in each place) insert 'or civil partner's'.

PART 7
AMENDMENTS OF THE JOBSEEKERS ACT 1995 (C 18)

118 In section 1 (the jobseeker's allowance), in subsection (4), in the definition of 'a joint-claim couple', for 'married or unmarried couple' substitute 'couple'.

119 In section 3 (the income-based conditions), in subsection (1)(dd) and (e), for 'married or unmarried couple' substitute 'couple'.

120 In section 15 (effect on other claimants), in subsection (2)(b), for 'married or unmarried couple' substitute 'couple'.

121 In section 15A (trade disputes: joint-claim couples), in subsection (5)(c), for 'married or unmarried couple' substitute 'couple'.

122 In section 23 (recovery of sums in respect of maintenance), in subsection (1), after 'spouse' insert 'or civil partner'.

123 In section 31 (termination of awards), in subsections (1) and (2), for 'married or unmarried couple' substitute 'couple'.

124(1) Amend section 35 (interpretation) as follows.

(2) After the definition of 'contribution-based jobseeker's allowance' in subsection (1) insert—

'"couple" means—

    (a) a man and woman who are married to each other and are members of the same household;

    (b) a man and woman who are not married to each other but are living together as husband and wife otherwise than in prescribed circumstances;

    (c) two people of the same sex who are civil partners of each other and are members of the same household; or

    (d) two people of the same sex who are not civil partners of each other but are living together as if they were civil partners otherwise than in prescribed circumstances;'.

(3) In paragraphs (a), (b) and (c) of the definition of 'family' in subsection (1), for 'married or unmarried couple' substitute 'couple'.

(4) Omit the definitions of 'married couple' and 'unmarried couple' in subsection (1).

(5) After subsection (1) insert—

'(1A) For the purposes of this Act, two people of the same sex are to be regarded as living together as if they were civil partners if, but only if, they would be regarded as living together as husband and wife were they instead two people of the opposite sex.'

125 In Schedule 1 (supplementary provisions), in paragraph 9C(1), for 'married or unmarried couple' substitute 'couple'.

PART 8
AMENDMENTS OF THE CHILD SUPPORT ACT 1995 (C 34)

126(1) Amend subsection (7) of section 10 (the child maintenance bonus) as follows.

(2) After the definition of 'child maintenance' insert—

'"couple" means—

    (a) a man and woman who are married to each other and are members of the same household;

    (b) a man and woman who are not married to each other but are living together as husband and wife otherwise than in prescribed circumstances;

    (c) two people of the same sex who are civil partners of each other and are members of the same household; or

(d) two people of the same sex who are not civil partners of each other but are living together as if they were civil partners otherwise than in prescribed circumstances;'.

(3) In the definition of 'family' for 'married or unmarried couple' (in each place) substitute 'couple'.

(4) Omit the definitions of 'married couple' and 'unmarried couple'.

127 After section 10(7) insert—

'(7A) For the purposes of this section, two people of the same sex are to be regarded as living together as if they were civil partners if, but only if, they would be regarded as living together as husband and wife were they instead two people of the opposite sex.'

PART 9
AMENDMENTS OF THE CHILD SUPPORT (NORTHERN IRELAND) ORDER 1995 (SI 1995/2702 (NI 13))

128(1) Amend paragraph (7) of Article 4 (the child maintenance bonus) as follows.

(2) After the definition of 'child maintenance' insert—

' "couple" means—

(a) a man and woman who are married to each other and are members of the same household;
(b) a man and woman who are not married to each other but are living together as husband and wife otherwise than in prescribed circumstances;
(c) two people of the same sex who are civil partners of each other and are members of the same household; or
(d) two people of the same sex who are not civil partners of each other but are living together as if they were civil partners otherwise than in prescribed circumstances;'.

(3) In the definition of 'family' for 'married or unmarried couple' (in each place) substitute 'couple'.

(4) Omit the definitions of 'married couple' and 'unmarried couple'.

129 After that paragraph insert—

'(7A) For the purposes of this Article, two people of the same sex are to be regarded as living together as if they were civil partners if, but only if, they would be regarded as living together as husband and wife were they instead two people of the opposite sex.'

PART 10
AMENDMENTS OF THE JOBSEEKERS (NORTHERN IRELAND) ORDER 1995 (SI 1995/2705 (NI 15))

130(1) Amend Article 2 (interpretation) as follows.

(2) After the definition of 'contribution-based jobseeker's allowance' in paragraph (2) insert—

' "couple" means—

(a) a man and woman who are married to each other and are members of the same household;

> (b) a man and woman who are not married to each other but are living together as husband and wife otherwise than in prescribed circumstances;
>
> (c) two people of the same sex who are civil partners of each other and are members of the same household; or
>
> (d) two people of the same sex who are not civil partners of each other but are living together as if they were civil partners otherwise than in prescribed circumstances;'.

(3) In paragraphs (a), (b) and (c) of the definition of 'family' in paragraph (2), for 'married or unmarried couple' substitute 'couple'.

(4) Omit the definitions of 'married couple' and 'unmarried couple' in paragraph (2).

(5) After paragraph (2) insert—

> '(2A) For the purposes of this Order, two people of the same sex are to be regarded as living together as if they were civil partners if, but only if, they would be regarded as living together as husband and wife were they instead two people of the opposite sex.'

131 In Article 3 (the jobseeker's allowance), in paragraph (4), in the definition of 'a joint-claim couple', for 'married or unmarried couple' substitute 'couple'.

132 In Article 5 (the income-based conditions), in paragraphs (1)(dd) and (e), for 'married or unmarried couple' substitute 'couple'.

133 In Article 17 (effect on other claimants), in paragraph (2)(b), for 'married or unmarried couple' substitute 'couple'.

134 In Article 17A (trade disputes: joint-claim couples), in paragraph (5)(c), for 'married or unmarried couple' substitute 'couple'.

135 In Article 25 (recovery of sums in respect of maintenance), in paragraph (1), after 'spouse' insert 'or civil partner'.

136 In Article 32 (termination of awards), in paragraphs (1) and (2), for 'married or unmarried couple' substitute 'couple'.

137 In Schedule 1 (supplementary provisions), in paragraph 9C(1), for 'married or unmarried couple' substitute 'couple'.

PART 11
AMENDMENTS OF THE SOCIAL SECURITY ACT 1998 (C 14)

138(1) Amend section 72 (power to reduce child benefit for lone parents) as follows.

(2) In subsection (2), after 'spouse' (in each place) insert 'or civil partner'.

(3) After subsection (2) insert—

> '(3) For the purpose of this section, a parent is to be regarded as living with another person as his civil partner if, but only if, he would be regarded as living with the other person as his spouse, were they instead two people of the opposite sex.'

PART 12
AMENDMENTS OF THE SOCIAL SECURITY (NORTHERN IRELAND) ORDER 1998 (SI 1998/1506 (NI 10))

139(1) Amend Article 68 (power to reduce child benefit for lone parents) as follows.

(2) In paragraph (2), after 'spouse' (in each place) insert 'or civil partner'.

(3) After paragraph (2) insert—

'(3) For the purpose of this Article, a parent is to be regarded as living with another person as his civil partner if, but only if, he would be regarded as living with the other person as his spouse, were they instead two people of the opposite sex.'.

PART 13
AMENDMENTS OF THE STATE PENSION CREDIT ACT 2002 (C 16)

140 In sections 2(5)(a) and (8)(b), 3(1)(b), 4(1), 5, 6(3)(c)(ii) and 9(4)(a), (b) and (d), for 'married or unmarried couple' substitute 'couple'.

141 In section 2(5)(b), for 'such a couple' substitute 'a couple'.

142(1) Amend subsection (1) of section 17 (other interpretation provisions) as follows.

(2) After the definition of 'the Contributions and Benefits Act' insert—

'"couple" means—

(a) a man and woman who are married to each other and are members of the same household;
(b) a man and woman who are not married to each other but are living together as husband and wife otherwise than in prescribed circumstances;
(c) two people of the same sex who are civil partners of each other and are members of the same household; or
(d) two people of the same sex who are not civil partners of each other but are living together as if they were civil partners otherwise than in prescribed circumstances;'.

(3) In the definition of 'foreign war widow's or widower's pension' for 'widow or widower' (in each place) substitute 'widow, widower or surviving civil partner'.

(4) Omit the definitions of 'married couple' and 'unmarried couple'.

(5) In the definition of 'war widow's or widower's pension'—

(a) in paragraph (a), for 'any widow's or widower's' substitute 'any widow's, widower's or surviving civil partner's', and
(b) in paragraph (b), for 'widow or widower' substitute 'widow, widower or surviving civil partner'.

143 After section 17(1) insert—

'(1A) For the purposes of this Act, two people of the same sex are to be regarded as living together as if they were civil partners if, but only if, they would be regarded as living together as husband and wife were they instead two people of the opposite sex.'

PART 14
AMENDMENTS OF THE TAX CREDITS ACT 2002 (C 21)

144(1) Amend section 3 (claims) as follows.

(2) In subsection (3)(a), for 'married couple or unmarried couple' substitute 'couple'.

(3) For subsections (5) and (6) substitute—

'(5A) In this Part "couple" means—

(a) a man and woman who are married to each other and are neither—
  (i) separated under a court order, nor
  (ii) separated in circumstances in which the separation is likely to be permanent,
(b) a man and woman who are not married to each other but are living together as husband and wife,
(c) two people of the same sex who are civil partners of each other and are neither—
  (i) separated under a court order, nor
  (ii) separated in circumstances in which the separation is likely to be permanent, or
(d) two people of the same sex who are not civil partners of each other but are living together as if they were civil partners.'

145 In sections 4(1)(g), 11(6)(b) and (c), 17(10)(b), 24(2) and 32(6), for 'married couple or an unmarried couple' (in each place) substitute 'couple'.

146 In sections 4(1)(g) and 17(10)(b), for 'the married couple or unmarried couple' substitute 'the couple'.

147(1) Renumber section 48 (interpretation) as subsection (1) of that section.

(2) In subsection (1), after the definition of 'child' insert—

' "couple" has the meaning given by section 3(5A),',

and omit the definitions of 'married couple' and 'unmarried couple'.

(3) After subsection (1) insert—

'(2) For the purposes of this Part, two people of the same sex are to be regarded as living together as if they were civil partners if, but only if, they would be regarded as living together as husband and wife were they instead two people of the opposite sex.'

PART 15
AMENDMENTS OF THE STATE PENSION CREDIT ACT (NORTHERN IRELAND) 2002 (C 14 (NI))

148 In sections 2(5)(a) and (8)(b), 3(1)(b), 4(1), 5, 6(3)(c)(ii) and 9(4)(a), (b) and (d), for 'married or unmarried couple' substitute 'couple'.

149 In section 2(5)(b), for 'such a couple' substitute 'a couple'.

150(1) Amend subsection (1) of section 17 (other interpretation provisions) as follows.

(2) After the definition of 'the Contributions and Benefits Act' insert—

' "couple" means—

(a) a man and woman who are married to each other and are members of the same household;

(b) a man and woman who are not married to each other but are living together as husband and wife otherwise than in prescribed circumstances;

(c) two people of the same sex who are civil partners of each other and are members of the same household; or

(d) two people of the same sex who are not civil partners of each other but are living together as if they were civil partners otherwise than in prescribed circumstances;'.

(3) In the definition of 'foreign war widow's or widower's pension' for 'widow or widower' (in each place) substitute 'widow, widower or surviving civil partner'.

(4) Omit the definitions of 'married couple' and 'unmarried couple'.

(5) In the definition of 'war widow's or widower's pension'—

(a) in paragraph (a), for 'any widow's or widower's' substitute 'any widow's, widower's or surviving civil partner's', and

(b) in paragraph (b), for 'widow or widower' substitute 'widow, widower or surviving civil partner'.

151 After section 17(1) insert—

'(1A) For the purposes of this Act, two people of the same sex are to be regarded as living together as if they were civil partners if, but only if, they would be regarded as living together as husband and wife were they instead two people of the opposite sex.'

SCHEDULE 25

SECTION 256

AMENDMENT OF CERTAIN ENACTMENTS RELATING TO PENSIONS

Fire Services Act 1947 (c 41)

1 In section 26 (firemen's pension scheme), in subsections (1) and (2A), for 'widows,' substitute 'surviving spouses, surviving civil partners,'.

House of Commons Members' Fund Act 1948 (c 36)

2 In section 4 (provision for cases of special hardship), in subsection (1)(b), for 'widowers' substitute 'widowers, surviving civil partners'.

Parliamentary and other Pensions Act 1972 (c 48)

3 In section 27 (pensions for dependants of Prime Minister or Speaker), in subsection (2)(a)(i), for 'widow or widower' substitute 'widow, widower or surviving civil partner'.

Theatres Trust Act 1976 (c 27)

4 In section 3 (employment of staff), in subsection (d)(iii) (power to secure pensions and gratuities payable to or in respect of officers and servants), for 'widow,' substitute 'surviving spouse, surviving civil partner,'.

SCHEDULE 26

SECTION 257

AMENDMENT OF CERTAIN ENACTMENTS RELATING TO THE ARMED FORCES

Greenwich Hospital Act 1865 (c 89)

1 In section 5 (power to appoint pensions to officers, etc), after 'widows' insert 'or surviving civil partners'.

Navy and Marines (Property of Deceased) Act 1865 (c 111)

2 In section 4 (disposal of residue belonging to deceased person in civil service of navy), after 'widow' insert 'or surviving civil partner'.

Pensions Commutation Act 1871 (c 36)

3(1) In section 4 (power to Treasury to commute pensions), in subsection (2) —

  (a) after 'marries' insert 'or forms a civil partnership', and
  (b) after 'widow' insert 'or surviving civil partner'.

(2) In section 4(3), for 'wife' substitute 'wife, civil partner'.

Greenwich Hospital Act 1883 (c 32)

4 In section 2 (power to grant pensions, allowances, and gratuities), in subsection (1), after 'widows' insert 'or surviving civil partners'.

Pensions and Yeomanry Pay Act 1884 (c 55)

5 In section 4 (distribution of money not exceeding £5,000 without requiring probate), after 'widower' insert 'surviving civil partner'.

Regimental Debts Act 1893 (c 5)

6 In section 10 (application of residue undisposed of), in subsection (2), for 'widows' substitute 'widows, surviving civil partners'.

7 In section 24 (application of Act to cases of insanity), in paragraph (a), for 'wife or husband' substitute 'wife, husband or civil partner'.

Naval Medical Compassionate Fund Act 1915 (c 28)

8 In section 1 (power by Order in Council to regulate fund), in subsection (1)(f), for 'widows, widowers' substitute 'widows, widowers, surviving civil partners'.

Naval and Military War Pensions, &c, (Administrative Expenses) Act 1917 (c 14)

9(1) In section 5 (alteration of purposes for which voluntary funds may be applied in certain cases)—

  (a) after 'wives,' (in each place) insert 'civil partners,', and
  (b) after 'widows,' (in each place) insert 'surviving civil partners,'.

(2) In section 6 (power of Secretary of State to accept and administer gifts for assisting disabled officers and men), after 'widows,' insert 'surviving civil partners,'.

War Pensions (Administrative Provisions) Act 1919 (c 53)

10 In section 8 (appeals to Pensions Appeal Tribunals), in subsection (1), for 'the motherless child or' substitute 'surviving civil partner or the orphan,'.

War Pensions Act 1920 (c 23)

11 In section 7 (restoration of forfeited pensions), in subsection (2), after 'wife,' insert 'civil partner,'.

12 In section 8 (statutory right of widow or dependant to a pension), for 'widow' substitute 'widow, surviving civil partner'.

Admiralty Pensions Act 1921 (c 39)

13 In section 2 (restoration of forfeited pension), in subsection (2), after 'wife,' insert 'civil partner,'.

Greenwich Hospital Act 1942 (c 35)

14(1) In section 1 (extension of powers to grant pensions to persons employed for the purposes of Greenwich Hospital), in subsection (1)(a) and (b) for 'widows' substitute 'widows, surviving civil partners'.

(2) In section 1(2), for 'spouses' substitute 'spouses, civil partners'.

Pensions Appeal Tribunals Act 1943 (c 39)

15 In section 1 (appeals against rejection of war pension claims made in respect of members of the naval, military or air forces), in subsection (4)(ii) —

  (a) after 'widower,' insert 'surviving civil partner,',
  (b) for 'husband' substitute 'husband, civil partner',
  (c) after 'marriage' insert 'or civil partnership', and
  (d) after 'place' insert 'or been formed'.

Greenwich Hospital Act 1947 (10 & 11 Geo. 6 c 5)

16 In section 2 (extension of power to grant pensions, etc), in subsection (1), after 'widows' insert 'and surviving civil partners'.

Polish Resettlement Act 1947 (c 19)

17 In section 1 (power to apply Royal Warrant as to pensions etc to certain Polish forces), in subsection (1), after 'widows,' insert 'surviving civil partners,'.

18 In section 2 (allowances from the Assistance Board), in subsection (2)(c)—

  (a) for 'of men' substitute 'or civil partners of persons',
  (b) for 'woman' substitute 'person',
  (c) for 'of a man' substitute 'or civil partner of a person', and
  (d) for 're-married' substitute 'subsequently married or formed a civil partnership'.

Naval Forces (Enforcement of Maintenance Liabilities) Act 1947 (c 24)

19(1) Amend section 1 (deduction from pay in respect of liabilities for maintenance, etc) as follows.

(2) In subsection (1), in paragraphs (a), (aa) and (b) after 'wife' insert 'or civil partner'.

(3) In subsection (2A), after paragraph (a) insert—

'(aa) if, in proceedings in connection with the dissolution or annulment of a civil partnership, an order has been made for the payment of any periodical or other sum in respect of the maintenance of the person who, if the civil partnership had subsisted, would have been the civil partner of any such person as is mentioned in subsection (1) above, references in this section to that person's civil partner include references to the person in whose favour the order was made; and'.

Royal Patriotic Fund Corporation Act 1950 (c 10)

20 In section 1 (extension of objects of soldiers' effects fund), in subsection (1)—

(a) for 'widows or children' substitute 'widows, surviving civil partners or children', and
(b) after 'widows,' insert 'surviving civil partners,'.

Reserve and Auxiliary Forces (Protection of Civil Interests) Act 1951 (c 65)

21 In section 23(1) (interpretation of Part 2)—

(a) in paragraph (a) of the definition of 'dependant', for 'wife' substitute 'spouse or civil partner', and
(b) in the definition of 'statutory tenancy', for 'widow' substitute 'surviving spouse or surviving civil partner'.

22 In paragraph (a) of section 25(6) (meaning of 'dependant'), for 'wife' substitute 'spouse or civil partner'.

23 In section 27(5) (interpretation of section), for 'wife' (in each place) substitute 'spouse or civil partner'.

24 In section 38(5) (interpretation of section), for 'wife' (in each place) substitute 'spouse or civil partner'.

25(1) Amend section 46 (general provisions as to payments to make up civil remuneration) as follows.

(2) In subsection (2), for 'wife' substitute 'spouse or civil partner'.

(3) In subsection (3)—

(a) the words from 'a widow entitled to a widow's pension' to the end of paragraph (iv) become paragraph (a) of the subsection (so that paragraphs (i) to (iv) become sub-paragraphs of that paragraph (a)),
(b) in that paragraph (a), for 'widow entitled to a widow's pension' substitute 'surviving spouse entitled to a surviving spouse's pension',
(c) in sub-paragraph (iv) of that paragraph (a), at the end insert 'or', and
(d) before 'there may' insert the following paragraph—

'(b) a surviving civil partner entitled to a surviving civil partner's pension by virtue of any of those provisions,'.

26 In section 52(2)(a) ('service pay' includes marriage etc allowances), after 'marriage,' insert 'civil partnership,'.

27(1) Amend Schedule 3 (financial provisions consequential on treating a person dying on service as alive and the converse) as follows.

(2) In paragraph 1(3), for 'widow' substitute 'surviving spouse, surviving civil partner'.

(3) In paragraph 2(4), for 'wife' (in each place) substitute 'spouse, civil partner'.

Army Act 1955 (3 & 4 Eliz. 2 c 18)

28(1) Section 150 (enforcement of maintenance and affiliation orders by deduction from pay) is amended as follows.

(2) In subsection (1)(a) and (aa), after 'wife' insert 'or civil partner'.

(3) In subsection (5), after 'marriage had subsisted;' insert—

'references to a civil partner include, in relation to an order made in proceedings in connection with the dissolution or annulment of a civil partnership, references to a person who would have been the civil partner of the defendant if the civil partnership had subsisted.'

29 In section 151 (deductions from pay for maintenance of wife or child), in subsection (1)—

(a) after 'wife' (in the first place) insert 'or civil partner', and
(b) for 'wife' (in the second place) substitute 'wife, civil partner'.

Air Force Act 1955 (3 & 4 Eliz. 2 c 19)

30(1) Section 150 (enforcement of maintenance and affiliation orders by deduction from pay) is amended as follows.

(2) In subsection (1)(a) and (aa), after 'wife' insert 'or civil partner'.

(3) In subsection (5), after 'marriage had subsisted;' insert—

'references to a civil partner include, in relation to an order made in proceedings in connection with the dissolution or annulment of a civil partnership, references to a person who would have been the civil partner of the defendant if the civil partnership had subsisted.'

31 In section 151 (deductions from pay for maintenance of wife or child), in subsection (1)—

(a) after 'wife' (in the first place) insert 'or civil partner', and
(b) for 'wife' (in the second place) substitute 'wife, civil partner'.

Naval Discipline Act 1957 (c 53)

32(1) Section 101 (service of proceedings for maintenance etc) is amended as follows.

(2) In subsection (5)(a) and (b), after 'wife' insert 'or civil partner'.

(3) In subsection (5A), after paragraph (a) insert—

'(aa) references to the civil partner of a person include, in relation to an order made in proceedings in connection with the dissolution or annulment of a civil partnership, references to a person who would have been his civil partner if the civil partnership had subsisted; and'.

Courts-Martial (Appeals) Act 1968 (c 20)

33 In section 48A (appeals on behalf of deceased persons), in subsection (3)(a), for 'widow or widower' substitute 'widow, widower or surviving civil partner'.

SCHEDULE 27

SECTION 261(1)

MINOR AND CONSEQUENTIAL AMENDMENTS: GENERAL

Explosive Substances Act 1883 (c 3)

1 In section 6 (inquiry by Attorney-General, and apprehension of absconding witnesses), in subsection (2), for 'husband or wife' (in both places) substitute 'spouse or civil partner'.

Partnership Act 1890 (c 39)

2 In section 2 (rules for determining existence of partnership), in rule (3)(c), after 'widow' insert ', widower, surviving civil partner'.

Law of Distress Amendment Act 1908 (c 53)

3 In section 4(1) (exclusion of certain goods), after 'husband or wife', insert 'or civil partner'.

Census Act 1920 (c 41)

4 In the Schedule (matters in respect of which particulars may be required), in paragraph 5 after 'as to marriage' insert 'or civil partnership'.

Trustee Act 1925 (c 19)

5(1) Amend section 31(2)(i) (trust on reaching 18 or marrying under that age of accumulations during infancy) as follows.

(2) In sub-paragraph (a)—

(a) after 'marries under that age' insert 'or forms a civil partnership under that age', and

(b) for 'or until his marriage' substitute ', or until his marriage or his formation of a civil partnership,'.

(3) In sub-paragraph (b), after 'marriage' insert ', or formation of a civil partnership,'.

(4) In the words after that sub-paragraph, after 'marriage' insert 'or formation of a civil partnership'.

6 In section 33(1)(ii)(a) and (b) (trust to maintain principal beneficiary and his spouse and issue on failure of protective trust under paragraph (i)), for 'wife or husband' substitute 'spouse or civil partner'.

Law of Property Act 1925 (c 20)

7 In section 205(1)(xxi) (which defines 'valuable consideration' as including marriage), after 'includes marriage' insert ', and formation of a civil partnership,'.

Judicial Proceedings (Regulation of Reports) Act 1926 (c 61)

8(1) Amend section 1 (restriction on publication of reports of judicial proceedings) as follows.

(2) In subsection (1)(b), for 'or for restitution of conjugal rights' substitute 'or for the dissolution or annulment of a civil partnership or for the separation of civil partners'.

(3) Omit subsection (5).

Population (Statistics) Act 1938 (c 12)

9 In the Schedule (particulars which may be required), in paragraph 2—

  (a) in paragraph (a), for 'or divorced;' substitute ', divorced, a civil partner or former civil partner, and, if a former civil partner, whether the civil partnership ended on death or dissolution;', and
  (b) in paragraph (b), after 'surviving spouse' insert 'or civil partner'.

Landlord and Tenant (Requisitioned Land) Act 1942 (c 13)

10 In section 13(1) (definition of 'member of the family'), after 'the wife or husband of the tenant,' insert 'the civil partner of the tenant,'.

Limitation (Enemies and War Prisoners) Act 1945 (c 16)

11 In section 2 (interpretation), in the definition of 'statute of limitation', after the entry relating to the Matrimonial Causes Act 1973 insert—

  'section 51(2) of the Civil Partnership Act 2004,'.

Statistics of Trade Act 1947 (c 39)

12 In section 10 (information from persons entering or leaving the United Kingdom by air), in subsection (1), after 'marriage' insert 'or civil partnership'.

Marriage Act 1949 (c 76)

13(1) Amend section 1 (marriages within prohibited degrees) as follows.

(2) In subsection (1), for the words from 'between a man' to 'the said Part I,' substitute 'between a person and any person mentioned in the list in Part 1 of Schedule 1'.

(3) In subsection (2), for the words from 'between a man' to 'the said Part II,' substitute 'between a person and any person mentioned in the list in Part 2 of Schedule 1'.

(4) In subsection (4), for the words from 'between a man' to 'the said Part III' substitute 'between a person and any person mentioned in the list in Part 3 of Schedule 1'.

(5) In subsection (5) for paragraphs (a) to (d) substitute—

    '(a) in the case of a marriage between a person and the parent of a former spouse of that person, after the death of both the former spouse and the former spouse's other parent;
    (b) in the case of a marriage between a person and the parent of a former civil partner of that person, after the death of both the former civil partner and the former civil partner's other parent;
    (c) in the case of a marriage between a person and the former spouse of a child of that person, after the death of both the child and the child's other parent;
    (d) in the case of a marriage between a person and the former civil partner of a child of that person, after the death of both the child and the child's other parent.'

(6) Omit subsections (6) to (8).

14 In section 27 (notice of marriage), in subsection (3), for 'the name and surname, marital status, occupation, place of residence and nationality of each of the persons to be married' substitute 'the

name and surname, occupation, place of residence and nationality of each of the persons to be married, whether either of them has previously been married or formed a civil partnership and, if so, how the marriage or civil partnership ended'.

15 In section 28A (power to require evidence), for subsection (3) substitute—

'(3) "Specified evidence", in relation to a person, means such evidence as may be specified in guidance issued by the Registrar General—

(a) of the person's name and surname,
(b) of the person's age,
(c) as to whether the person has previously been married or formed a civil partnership and, if so, as to the ending of the marriage or civil partnership, and
(d) of the person's nationality.'

16 In section 78(1) (interpretation), in the definition of 'child', after ''child'' insert ', except where used to express a relationship,'.

17 For Schedule 1 (kindred and affinity) substitute—

'SCHEDULE 1
KINDRED AND AFFINITY

PART 1
PROHIBITED DEGREES: KINDRED

1(1) The list referred to in section 1(1) is—

Adoptive child

Adoptive parent

Child

Former adoptive child

Former adoptive parent

Grandparent

Grandchild

Parent

Parent's sibling

Sibling

Sibling's child

(2) In the list 'sibling' means a brother, sister, half-brother or half-sister.

PART 2
DEGREES OF AFFINITY REFERRED TO IN SECTION 1(2) AND (3)

2 The list referred to in section 1(2) is as follows—

Child of former civil partner

Child of former spouse

Former civil partner of grandparent

Former civil partner of parent

Former spouse of grandparent

Former spouse of parent

Grandchild of former civil partner

Grandchild of former spouse

PART 3
DEGREES OF AFFINITY REFERRED TO IN SECTION 1(4) AND (5)

3 The list referred to in section 1(4) is as follows—

Parent of former spouse

Parent of former civil partner

Former spouse of child

Former civil partner of child.'

Maintenance Orders Act 1950 (c 37)

18(1) Amend section 16 (application of Part 2) as follows.

(2) After subsection (2)(a)(viii) insert—

'(ix) Part 1, 8 or 9 of Schedule 5 to the Civil Partnership Act 2004, Schedule 6 to that Act or paragraph 5 or 9 of Schedule 7 to that Act;'.

(3) After subsection (2)(b)(ix) insert—

'(x) an order made on an application under Schedule 11 to the Civil Partnership Act 2004;'.

(4) After subsection (2)(c)(ix) insert—

'(x) Part 1, 7 or 8 of Schedule 15 to the Civil Partnership Act 2004, Schedule 16 to that Act or paragraph 5 or 9 of Schedule 17 to that Act;'.

Births and Deaths Registration Act 1953 (c 20)

19 In section 41 (interpretation), in the definition of 'relative', after 'by marriage' insert 'or civil partnership'.

Pharmacy Act 1954 (c 61)

20 In section 17(c) (benevolent fund: distressed relatives eligible for relief), for 'widows,' substitute 'surviving spouses, surviving civil partners,'.

Registration of Births, Deaths and Marriages (Special Provisions) Act 1957 (c 58)

21 In section 1 (records of deaths, births and marriages among armed forces and service civilians and their families overseas), in subsection (1), for 'and marriages solemnised,' substitute 'marriages solemnised and civil partnerships formed,'.

Maintenance Orders Act 1958 (c 39)

22(1) Amend section 4 (variation of orders registered in magistrates' courts) as follows.

(2) In each of subsections (5A) and (5B) (application of section 60(4) to (11) of the Magistrates' Courts Act 1980), for 'and section 15(2) of the Children Act 1989' substitute ', section 15(2) of the Children Act 1989 and paragraph 42 of Schedule 6 to the Civil Partnership Act 2004'.

(3) In subsection (6B) (no application may be made for variation under the Act of certain registered orders), after '1984' insert 'or under Schedule 7 to the Civil Partnership Act 2004'.

Offices, Shops and Railway Premises Act 1963 (c 41)

23 In section 2 (exception for premises in which only employer's relatives or outworkers work), in subsection (1), after 'wife' insert ', civil partner'.

Industrial and Provident Societies Act 1965 (c 12)

24(1) Amend section 23 (nomination to property in society) as follows.

(2) In subsection (2), for 'husband, wife,' substitute 'spouse, civil partner,'.

(3) After subsection (6) insert—

'(7) The formation of a civil partnership by a member of a society revokes any nomination made by him before the formation of the civil partnership; but if any property of that member has been transferred by an officer of the society in pursuance of the nomination in ignorance of a civil partnership formed by the nominator after the date of the nomination—

(a) the receipt of the nominee shall be a valid discharge to the society, and
(b) the society shall be under no liability to any other person claiming the property.'

25 In section 25 (provision for intestacy), in subsection (2), after 'widower' insert ', surviving civil partner'.

Criminal Appeal Act 1968 (c 19)

26 In section 44A (appeals in cases of death), in subsection (3)(a), after 'widower' insert 'or surviving civil partner'.

Theft Act 1968 (c 60)

27(1) Amend section 30 (husband and wife) as follows.

(2) In subsections (4) and (5), after 'wife or husband' in each place except paragraph (a)(ii) to the proviso to subsection (4) insert 'or civil partner'.

(3) At the end of paragraph (a)(ii) to the proviso insert

'or

(iii) an order (wherever made) is in force providing for the separation of that person and his or her civil partner.',

and omit 'or' at the end of paragraph (a)(i) to the proviso.

(4) For the heading to section 30 substitute 'Spouses and civil partners'.

28 In section 31 (effect on civil proceedings and rights), in subsection (1)—

(a) for 'wife or husband' substitute 'spouse or civil partner', and

(b) for 'married after the making of the statement or admission) against the wife or husband' substitute 'married or became civil partners after the making of the statement or admission) against the spouse or civil partner'.

Domestic and Appellate Proceedings (Restriction of Publicity) Act 1968 (c 63)

29(1) Amend section 2 (restriction of publicity for certain matrimonial etc proceedings) as follows.

(2) In subsection (1), after paragraph (d) insert—

'(da) proceedings under Part 9 of Schedule 5 to the Civil Partnership Act 2004 (provision corresponding to the provision referred to in paragraph (c) above);

(db) proceedings under section 58 of the 2004 Act (declarations as to subsistence etc of civil partnership);'.

(3) In subsection (3), after '(1)(d)' insert 'or (db)'.

Civil Evidence Act 1968 (c 64)

30 In section 14 (privilege against incrimination of self or spouse)—

(a) in subsection (1)(b), for 'husband or wife' substitute 'spouse or civil partner', and

(b) in the heading, after 'spouse' insert 'or civil partner'.

Gaming Act 1968 (c 65)

31 In Schedule 2 (grant, renewal, cancellation and transfer of licences), in paragraph 35A(8)(a) for 'wife or husband' substitute 'spouse or civil partner'.

Medicines Act 1968 (c 67)

32 In section 114 (supplementary provisions as to rights of entry and related rights), in subsection (4), for 'married) the husband or wife' substitute 'married or a civil partner) the spouse or civil partner'.

Employers' Liability (Compulsory Insurance) Act 1969 (c 57)

33 In section 2(2)(a) (persons whom employer is not required to insure) after 'husband, wife,' insert 'civil partner,'.

Administration of Justice Act 1970 (c 31)

34 In Schedule 8 (meaning of 'maintenance order' in Part 2 of the Act and in the Maintenance Orders Act 1958), after paragraph 14 insert—

'15. An order for periodical or other payments made under Schedule 5, 6 or 7 to the Civil Partnership Act 2004.'

Attachment of Earnings Act 1971 (c 32)

35 In Schedule 1 (maintenance orders to which the 1971 Act applies), after paragraph 14 insert—

'15 An order made under Schedule 5 to the Civil Partnership Act 2004 (financial relief in the High Court or a county court etc), for periodical or other payments.

16 An order made under Schedule 6 to the 2004 Act (financial relief in magistrates' courts etc), for maintenance or other payments to or in respect of a civil partner or child.'

Criminal Damage Act 1971 (c 48)

36 In section 9 (evidence in connection with offences under the 1971 Act)—

(a) for 'wife or husband' substitute 'spouse or civil partner', and
(b) for 'married after the making of the statement or admission) against the wife or husband' substitute 'married or became civil partners after the making of the statement or admission) against the spouse or civil partner'.

Immigration Act 1971 (c 77)

37 In section 5(4) (members of another's family for purposes of deportation)—

(a) in paragraph (a), after 'his wife' insert 'or civil partner,' and
(b) in paragraph (b), after 'her husband' insert 'or civil partner,'.

Local Government Act 1972 (c 70)

38 In section 95 (pecuniary interests for purposes of section 94), after subsection (3) insert—

'(4) In the case of civil partners living together the interest of one civil partner, shall, if known to the other, be deemed for the purpose of section 94 above to be also an interest of the other.'

39 In section 96 (general notices and recording of disclosures for purposes of section 94), in subsection (1), after 'spouse' (in each place) insert 'or civil partner'.

Matrimonial Causes Act 1973 (c 18)

40 In section 11 (grounds on which marriage is void), at the end of paragraph (b) insert 'or a civil partner'.

41(1) Amend section 14 (marriages governed by foreign law or celebrated abroad under English law) as follows.

(2) In subsection (1), at the beginning insert 'Subject to subsection (3)'.

(3) After subsection (2) insert—

'(3) No marriage is to be treated as valid by virtue of subsection (1) if, at the time when it purports to have been celebrated, either party was already a civil partner.'

42 In section 24A (orders for sale of property), in subsection (5), after 're-marriage of' insert ', or formation of a civil partnership by,'.

43(1) Amend section 28 (duration of continuing financial provision orders in favour of party to marriage, and effect of remarriage) as follows.

(2) In subsection (1)(a) and (b) after 'remarriage of' insert ', or formation of a civil partnership by,'.

(3) In subsection (2)—

(a) after 'remarriage of' insert ', or formation of a civil partnership by,', and
(b) after 'the remarriage' insert 'or formation of the civil partnership'.

(4) In subsection (3), after 'remarries whether at any time before or after the commencement of this Act', insert 'or forms a civil partnership'.

(5) In the heading to section 28, after 'remarriage' insert 'or formation of civil partnership'.

44 In section 35 (alteration of agreements by court during lives of parties), in subsection (4)(a) and (b), after 'remarriage of' insert ', or formation of a civil partnership by,'.

45(1) Amend section 38 (orders for repayment in certain cases of sums paid after cessation of order by reason of remarriage) as follows.

(2) In subsection (1)—

    (a) in paragraph (a), after 'remarriage of', insert ', or formation of a civil partnership by,', and
    (b) in paragraph (b), after 'remarriage' insert 'or formation of the civil partnership'.

(3) In subsection (6)—

    (a) in paragraph (a), after 'remarriage of' insert ', or formation of a civil partnership by,' and
    (b) in the words following paragraph (b), after 'had remarried' insert 'or formed a civil partnership'.

(4) In the heading to section 38, after 'remarriage' insert 'or formation of civil partnership'.

46 In section 52 (interpretation), after subsection (3), insert —

    '(3A) References in this Act to the formation of a civil partnership by a person include references to a civil partnership which is by law void or voidable.'

Fair Trading Act 1973 (c 41)

47 In section 30 (offences in connection with exercise of powers under section 29), in subsection (6) for 'married) the husband or wife' substitute 'married or a civil partner) the spouse or civil partner'.

Slaughterhouses Act 1974 (c 3)

48 In section 10 (temporary continuance of licence on death), for 'his personal representative, or of his widow or any other member of his family, until the expiration of two months from his death,' substitute 'the deceased's personal representative, or widow or widower or surviving civil partner or any other member of the deceased's family, until the end of two months from the deceased's death,'.

Health and Safety at Work etc Act 1974 (c 37)

49 In section 20 (powers of inspectors), in subsection (7), for 'husband or wife' substitute 'spouse or civil partner'.

Consumer Credit Act 1974 (c 39)

50 In section 165 (obstruction of authorised officers), in subsection (3), for 'married) the husband or wife' substitute 'married or a civil partner) the spouse or civil partner'.

51(1) Amend section 184 (associates) as follows.

(2) For subsection (1) substitute—

    '(1) A person is an associate of an individual if that person is—

        (a) the individual's husband or wife or civil partner,
        (b) a relative of—

    (i)   the individual, or

    (ii) the individual's husband or wife or civil partner, or

  (c) the husband or wife or civil partner of a relative of—

    (i)   the individual, or

    (ii) the individual's husband or wife or civil partner.'

(3) In subsection (2), after 'husband or wife' insert 'or civil partner'.

(4) In subsection (5)—

  (a) omit the word 'and' immediately before 'references',

  (b) for 'or wife;' substitute 'or wife, and references to a civil partner include a former civil partner;', and

  (c) for 'had been a child born to him in wedlock' substitute 'were the legitimate child of the relationship in question'.

Friendly Societies Act 1974 (c 46)

52(1) Amend section 66 (power of member to nominate person to receive sums payable on his death) as follows.

(2) In subsection (5)(a), for 'husband, wife,' substitute 'spouse, civil partner,'.

(3) After subsection (7) insert—

  '(7A) The formation of a civil partnership by a member of the society or branch revokes any nomination previously made by that member under this section.'

Rehabilitation of Offenders Act 1974 (c 53)

53 In section 7 (limitations on rehabilitation under the 1974 Act, etc), in subsection (2)(c), after 'the marriage of any minor,' insert 'or the formation of a civil partnership by any minor,'.

Sex Discrimination Act 1975 (c 65)

54 In section 82(5) (general interpretation: meaning of 'near relative')

  (a) after 'wife or husband' (in both places) insert 'or civil partner', and

  (b) for 'by affinity)' substitute 'by marriage or civil partnership)'.

Race Relations Act 1976 (c 74)

55 In section 78(5) (general interpretation: meaning of 'near relative')—

  (a) after 'wife or husband' (in both places) insert 'or civil partner', and

  (b) for 'by affinity)' substitute 'by marriage or civil partnership)'.

Criminal Law Act 1977 (c 45)

56 In section 2 (exemptions from liability for conspiracy), in subsection (2)(a), after 'spouse' insert 'or civil partner'.

Domestic Proceedings and Magistrates' Courts Act 1978 (c 22)

57 In section 4 (duration of orders for financial provision for a party to a marriage), in subsection (2)—

(a) after 'remarriage of' insert ', or formation of a civil partnership by,', and

(b) after 'the remarriage' insert 'or formation of the civil partnership'.

58(1) Amend section 35 (orders for repayment in certain cases of sums paid after cessation of order by reason of remarriage) as follows.

(2) In subsection (1)—

(a) in paragraph (a), after 'remarriage of' insert ', or formation of a civil partnership by,', and

(b) in paragraph (b), after 'that remarriage' insert 'or the formation of that civil partnership'.

(3) In subsection (7)—

(a) in paragraph (a), after 'remarriage of' insert ', or formation of a civil partnership by,', and

(b) in the words following paragraph (b)—
  (i) after 'the remarriage' insert 'or the formation of that civil partnership', and
  (ii) after 'had remarried' insert 'or formed a civil partnership'.

(4) In the heading to section 35, after 'remarriage' insert 'or formation of civil partnership'.

Interpretation Act 1978 (c 30)

59 At the appropriate place in Schedule 1 (words and expressions defined) insert—

> '"Civil partnership" means a civil partnership which exists under or by virtue of the Civil Partnership Act 2004 (and any reference to a civil partner is to be read accordingly).'

Protection of Children Act 1978 (c 37)

60 In section 1A (marriage and other relationships), in subsections (1)(a) and (2)(a) after 'were married' insert 'or civil partners of each other'.

Credit Unions Act 1979 (c 34)

61(1) Amend section 31(1) (interpretation) as follows.

(2) After the definition of 'charitable' insert—

> '"civil partner" includes former civil partner;'.

(3) In the definition of 'relative'—

(a) in paragraphs (a), (b) and (c), after 'spouse' insert 'or civil partner', and

(b) in the words following paragraph (c), for 'a child born in wedlock' substitute 'the legitimate child of the relationship in question'.

Estate Agents Act 1979 (c 38)

62 In section 27 (obstruction and personation of authorised officers), in subsection (4), for 'husband or wife' substitute 'spouse or civil partner'.

63(1) Amend section 32 (associates) as follows.

(2) In subsection (2), after 'spouse' insert 'or civil partner'.

(3) In subsection (3)—

(a) omit the word 'and' immediately before 'references',

(b) for 'reputed spouse;' substitute 'reputed spouse, and references to a civil partner include a former civil partner;', and

(c) for 'had been a child born to him in wedlock' substitute 'were the legitimate child of the relationship in question'.

Magistrates' Courts Act 1980 (c 43)

64 In section 59 (orders for periodical payments: means of payment), in subsection (7)(b), after 'Domestic Proceedings and Magistrates' Courts Act 1978' insert 'or Schedule 6 to the Civil Partnership Act 2004'.

65(1) Amend section 65 (meaning of family proceedings) as follows.

(2) After subsection (1)(c) insert—

'(ca) Schedule 2 to the Civil Partnership Act 2004;'.

(3) After subsection (1)(ee) insert—

'(ef) paragraphs 69 to 72 of Schedule 5 to the Civil Partnership Act 2004;'.

(4) After subsection (1)(j) insert—

'(ja) Schedule 6 to the Civil Partnership Act 2004;'.

Disused Burial Grounds (Amendment) Act 1981 (c 18)

66 In section 9 (interpretation), in the definition of 'relative', for 'husband or wife' substitute 'spouse or civil partner'.

Forgery and Counterfeiting Act 1981 (c 45)

67 In section 5 (offences relating to money orders, share certificates, passports, etc), in subsection (5)(l)—

(a) after 'adoptions, marriages' insert ', civil partnerships', and

(b) for 'register marriages' substitute 'issue certified copies relating to such entries'.

Supreme Court Act 1981 (c 54)

68 In section 18(1) (restrictions on appeals to Court of Appeal), before paragraph (g) insert—

'(fa) from a dissolution order, nullity order or presumption of death order under Chapter 2 of Part 2 of the Civil Partnership Act 2004 that has been made final, by a party who, having had time and opportunity to appeal from the conditional order on which that final order was founded, has not appealed from the conditional order;'.

69(1) Amend section 72 (withdrawal of privilege against incrimination of self or spouse in certain proceedings) as follows.

(2) In subsection (1), after 'spouse' insert 'or civil partner'.

(3) In subsection (3), for 'married after the making of the statement or admission) against the spouse' substitute 'married or became civil partners after the making of the statement or admission) against the spouse or civil partner'.

70 In paragraph 3 of Schedule 1 (business assigned to Family Division of High Court), after sub-paragraph (h) insert—

'(i) all civil partnership causes and matters (whether at first instance or on appeal);

(j)   applications for consent to the formation of a civil partnership by a minor or for a declaration under paragraph 7 of Schedule 1 to the Civil Partnership Act 2004;

(k)   applications under section 58 of that Act (declarations relating to civil partnerships).'

British Nationality Act 1981 (c 61)

71 In section 3(6)(a) (registration as British citizen of minor whose parents' marriage has terminated etc), after 'marriage' insert 'or civil partnership'.

72 In section 6(2) (naturalisation of person married to British citizen), after 'is married to a British citizen' insert 'or is the civil partner of a British citizen'.

73 In section 10(2)(b) (registration as British citizen after pre-1983 renunciation of citizenship), after 'has been married to' insert ', or has been the civil partner of,'.

74 In section 12(5) (renunciation: persons who have married deemed of full age), after 'has been married' insert ', or has formed a civil partnership,'.

75 In section 17(6)(a) (registration as British overseas territories citizen of minor whose parents' marriage has terminated etc), after 'marriage' insert 'or civil partnership'.

76 In section 18(2) (naturalisation of person married to a British overseas territories citizen), after 'is married to such a citizen' insert 'or is the civil partner of such a citizen'.

77 In section 22(2)(b) (naturalisation as British overseas territories citizen after pre-1983 renunciation of citizenship), after 'has been married to' insert ', or has been the civil partner of,'.

78(1) Amend paragraphs 4(d) and 8(d) of Schedule 1 (requirements for naturalisation under sections 6(2) and 18(2)) as follows.

(2) In the paragraph (f) set out in each of those provisions, after 'to whom the applicant is married' insert ', or of whom the applicant is the civil partner,'.

Forfeiture Act 1982 (c 34)

79 In section 3 (application for financial provision not affected by forfeiture rule), in subsection (2), for paragraph (b) and the word 'and' immediately preceding it substitute—

'(b) sections 31(6) and 36(1) of the Matrimonial Causes Act 1973 (variation by court in England and Wales of periodical payments orders and maintenance agreements in respect of marriages);

(c) paragraphs 60(2) and 73(2) of Schedule 5 to the Civil Partnership Act 2004 (variation by court in England and Wales of periodical payments orders and maintenance agreements in respect of civil partnerships); and

(d) section 13(4) of the Family Law (Scotland) Act 1985 (variation etc of periodical allowances in respect of marriages and civil partnerships).'

Representation of the People Act 1983 (c 2)

80(1) Amend section 14 (service qualification) as follows.

(2) In subsection (1)(d), for 'wife or husband' substitute 'spouse or civil partner'.

(3) For subsection (1)(e) substitute—

'(e) is the spouse or civil partner of a person mentioned in paragraph (b) or paragraph (c) above and is residing outside the United Kingdom to be with his or her spouse or civil partner,'.

81 In section 16 (contents of service declaration), for 'wife or husband' substitute 'spouse or civil partner'.

82 In section 59 (supplemental provisions as to members of forces and service voters), in subsection (3)(b), for 'by him and any wife of his or, as the case may be, by her and any husband of hers,' substitute 'by that person and any spouse or civil partner of that person'.

83 In section 61 (other voting offences), in subsection (4), for 'husband, wife,' substitute 'spouse, civil partner,'.

84 In section 141 (duty to answer relevant questions), in subsections (1)(a)(i) and (2)(a), for 'husband or wife,' substitute 'spouse or civil partner,'.

85(1) Amend Schedule 1 (parliamentary elections rules) as follows.

(2) In rule 11(4), for 'wife or husband' substitute 'spouse or civil partner'.

(3) In rule 35(2), for 'husband (wife),' (in both places) substitute 'spouse, civil partner,'.

(4) In rule 39(3)(b), for 'husband, wife,' substitute 'spouse, civil partner,'.

(5) In rule 44(2)(b), for 'wives or husbands' substitute 'spouses or civil partners'.

Mental Health Act 1983 (c 20)

86 In—

(a) section 12 (general provisions as to medical recommendations), in subsection (5), in the words following paragraph (e), and
(b) section 25C (supervision applications: supplementary), in subsection (10),

after 'husband, wife' insert ', civil partner'.

Mobile Homes Act 1983 (c 34)

87 In section 3(3) (succession to agreements to which Act applies), for 'or widower' (in each place) substitute ', widower or surviving civil partner'.

88 In section 5(3) (meaning of 'member of another's family')—

(a) after 'spouse,' insert 'civil partner,'
(b) in paragraph (a), after 'marriage' insert 'or civil partnership', and
(c) in the words after paragraph (b), after 'as husband and wife' insert 'or as if they were civil partners'.

Dentists Act 1984 (c 24)

89 In section 41(4) (family or representatives may carry on deceased dentist's business for three years), for 'his widow' (in each place) substitute 'his surviving spouse or his surviving civil partner'.

Matrimonial and Family Proceedings Act 1984 (c 42)

90(1) Amend section 12 (applications for financial relief after overseas divorce etc) as follows.

(2) In subsection (2) (no application may be made after remarriage), for 'remarries' substitute 'forms a subsequent marriage or civil partnership,'.

(3) For subsection (3) substitute—

'(3) The reference in subsection (2) above to the forming of a subsequent marriage or civil partnership includes a reference to the forming of a marriage or civil partnership which is by law void or voidable.'

91 In section 32 (meaning of 'family business' etc), after the definition of 'family proceedings' insert—

> '"civil partnership cause" means an action for the dissolution or annulment of a civil partnership or for the legal separation of civil partners;'.

92 After section 36 insert—

'36A Jurisdiction of county courts in civil partnership causes and matters

(1) The Lord Chancellor may by order—

> (a) designate any county court as a civil partnership proceedings county court, and
> (b) designate, as a court of trial, any county court designated as a civil partnership proceedings county court.

(2) In this Part of this Act 'civil partnership proceedings county court' means a county court designated under subsection (1)(a) above.

(3) A civil partnership proceedings county court shall have jurisdiction to hear and determine any civil partnership cause, subject to subsection (4) below.

(4) A civil partnership proceedings county court shall have jurisdiction to try a civil partnership cause only if it is designated under subsection (1)(b) above as a court of trial.

(5) The jurisdiction conferred by this section on a civil partnership proceedings county court shall be exercisable throughout England and Wales, but rules of court may provide for a civil partnership cause pending in one such court to be heard and determined—

> (a) partly in that court and partly in another such court, or
> (b) in another such court.

(6) Every civil partnership cause shall be commenced in a civil partnership proceedings county court.

(7) Every civil partnership cause shall be heard and determined in a civil partnership proceedings county court unless, or except to the extent, it is transferred to the High Court under—

> (a) section 39 below, or
> (b) section 41 of the County Court Act 1984 (transfer to High Court by order of High Court).

(8) The Lord Chancellor may by order designate a civil partnership proceedings county court as a court for the exercise of jurisdiction in civil partnership matters under Schedule 7 to the Civil Partnership Act 2004.

(9) The power to make an order under subsection (1) or (8) above shall be exercisable by statutory instrument.

36B Jurisdiction of civil partnership proceedings county courts as respects financial relief and protection of children

(1) Subject to subsection (2) below, a civil partnership proceedings county court shall have the following jurisdiction—

    (a) a jurisdiction to exercise any power exercisable under—

        (i) section 63 of the Civil Partnership Act 2004 (restrictions on making of orders affecting children), or

        (ii) Schedule 5 to that Act (financial relief in the courts), other than Part 12 (arrears and repayments) and paragraph 73 (alteration of maintenance agreements by court after death of one party),

in connection with any application or order pending in, or made by, a civil partnership proceedings county court;

    (b) a jurisdiction to exercise any power exercisable under—

        (i) Part 9 of that Schedule (failure to maintain: financial provision (and interim orders)), or

        (ii) paragraphs 69 to 71 of that Schedule (alteration of maintenance agreements by court during lives of parties);

    (c) if designated under section 36A(8) above, jurisdiction to exercise any power under Schedule 7 to that Act.

(2) Any proceedings for the exercise of a power which a civil partnership proceedings county court has jurisdiction to exercise by virtue of subsection (1) above shall be commenced in such civil partnership proceedings county court as may be prescribed by rules of court.

(3) Nothing in this section shall affect the jurisdiction of a magistrates' court under paragraphs 69 to 71 of Schedule 5 to the Civil Partnership Act 2004.

36C Consideration of agreements or arrangements

Where rules of court make provision for the purposes of section 43 of the Civil Partnership Act 2004 with respect to any power exercisable by the court on an application made under that section before an application is made for a dissolution or separation order, the rules shall confer jurisdiction to exercise the power on civil partnership proceedings county courts.

36D Assignment of circuit judges to civil partnership proceedings

The jurisdiction conferred by the preceding provisions of this Part of this Act on civil partnership proceedings county courts, so far as it exercisable by judges of such courts, shall be exercised by such Circuit judges as the Lord Chancellor may direct.'

93 For section 38(3) (transfer of family proceedings from High Court to county court) substitute—

'(3) Proceedings transferred under this section shall be transferred to such county court as the High Court directs, subject to subsections (3A) and (3B) below.

(3A) Where a matrimonial cause or matter within the jurisdiction of a divorce county court only is transferred under this section, it shall be transferred to such divorce county court as the High Court directs.

(3B) Where a civil partnership cause or matter within the jurisdiction of a civil partnership proceedings county court only is transferred under this section, it shall be transferred to such civil partnership proceedings county court as the High Court directs.'

94 In section 39(2) (family proceedings transferable to the High Court), for 'or divorce county court' (in each place) substitute ', divorce county court or civil partnership proceedings county court'.

95 In section 40(4)(b) (enforcement in High Court of orders of divorce county court), after 'a divorce county court' insert 'or a civil partnership proceedings county court'.

96(1) Amend section 42 (county court proceedings in principal registry of Family Division) as follows.

(2) In subsection (1)—

    (a) after 'Sections 33 to 35' insert 'and 36A to 36C',
    (b) after 'section 34(2)' insert 'or 36B(2)', and
    (c) after 'divorce county court' insert 'or civil partnership proceedings county court'.

(3) After that subsection insert—

    '(1A) Subsection (2) below applies to—

        (a) the jurisdiction in matrimonial causes or matters conferred by sections 33, 34 and 35 above on divorce county courts, and
        (b) the jurisdiction in civil partnership causes or matters conferred by sections 36A, 36B and 36C above on civil partnership proceedings county courts.'

(4) In subsection (2), for the words from the beginning to 'on divorce county courts' substitute 'A jurisdiction to which this subsection applies'.

(5) For the words in subsection (2) after paragraph (b) substitute the following new subsection—

    '(2A) Rules of court may make provision—

        (a) for treating, for any purposes specified in the rules, matrimonial causes and matters pending in the registry with respect to which the jurisdiction mentioned in subsection (1A)(a) above is exercisable as pending in a divorce county court,
        (b) for treating, for any purposes specified in the rules, civil partnership causes and matters pending in the registry with respect to which the jurisdiction mentioned in subsection (1A)(b) above is exercisable as pending in a civil partnership proceedings county court, and
        (c) for the application of section 74(3) of the Solicitors Act 1974 (costs) with respect to proceedings treated as mentioned in paragraph (a) or (b) above.'

(6) In subsection (3), for 'subsection (2)' substitute 'subsection (2A)'.

(7) After subsection (3) insert—

    '(3A) Where, by virtue of rules under subsection (2A) above, a civil partnership cause or matter is pending in the registry as in a civil partnership proceedings county court, any ancillary or related proceedings which could be taken in a civil partnership proceedings county court and which are not of a description excluded by the rules from the operation of this subsection may be taken and dealt with in the registry as in a civil partnership proceedings county court.'

(8) After subsection (4) insert—

    '(4ZA) The principal registry shall be treated as a civil partnership proceedings county court—

        (a) for the purposes of any provision to be made by rules of court under section 36A(5) above;

(b) for the purpose of any provision to be made under section 36B(2) above prescribing the county court in which any proceedings are to be commenced; and

(c) for the purpose of any transfer of family proceedings under section 38 or 39 above between the High Court and a civil partnership proceedings county court.'

(9) In subsection (4A), after 'in any matrimonial cause or matter' insert ', or in any civil partnership cause or matter,'.

(10) In subsection (5), for paragraphs (a) and (b) substitute—

'(a) as regards service of process—
  (i) as if proceedings commenced in the principal registry in a matrimonial cause or matter had been commenced in a divorce county court, and
  (ii) as if proceedings commenced in that registry in a civil partnership cause or matter had been commenced in a civil partnership proceedings county court; and
(b) as regards enforcement of orders—
  (i) as if orders made in that registry in the exercise of the family jurisdiction conferred by sections 33, 34 and 35 above on divorce county courts were orders made by such a court, and
  (ii) as if orders made in that registry in the exercise of the family jurisdiction conferred by sections 36A, 36B and 36C above on civil partnership proceedings county courts were orders made by such a court.'

(11) After that subsection insert—

'(5A) For the purposes of subsection (3A) above, proceedings—

(a) are "ancillary" to a civil partnership cause if they are connected with the cause, and
(b) are "related" to a civil partnership cause if they are for protecting or otherwise relate to any rights, or the exercise of any rights, of—
  (i) the civil partners as civil partners, or
  (ii) any children of the family.'

Police and Criminal Evidence Act 1984 (c 60)

97(1) Amend section 80 (compellability of accused's spouse) as follows.

(2) In subsections (2), (2A) and (3), for 'wife or husband' (in each place) substitute 'spouse or civil partner'.

(3) After subsection (5) insert—

'(5A) In any proceedings a person who has been but is no longer the civil partner of the accused shall be compellable to give evidence as if that person and the accused had never been civil partners.'

(4) In the heading to section 80, after 'accused's spouse' insert 'or civil partner'.

98 In section 80A (rule where accused's spouse not compellable)—

(a) for 'wife or husband' substitute 'spouse or civil partner', and
(b) in the heading, after 'spouse' insert 'or civil partner'.

Companies Act 1985 (c 6)

99 In section 203 (notification of family and corporate interests), in subsection (1), after 'spouse' insert 'or civil partner'.

100(1) Amend section 327 (extension of section 323 to spouses and children) as follows.

(2) In subsection (1)—

    (a) in paragraph (a), after 'wife or husband' insert 'or civil partner', and

    (b) in the words following paragraph (b), after 'as the case may be,' insert 'civil partner or'.

(3) In the heading to section 327, after 'spouses' insert ', civil partners'.

101(1) Amend section 328 (extension of section 324 to spouses and children) as follows.

(2) In subsections (1)(a) and (2)(a), after 'wife or husband' insert 'or civil partner'.

(3) In subsection (3)—

    (a) in paragraph (a), after 'spouse' insert 'or civil partner', and

    (b) in paragraph (b), after 'spouse' insert 'or civil partner' and after 'wife, husband,' insert 'civil partner,'.

(4) In the heading to section 328, after 'spouses' insert ', civil partners'.

102 In section 346 (connected persons) in subsection (2)—

    (a) in paragraph (a), after 'spouse,' insert 'civil partner,',

    (b) in paragraph (c) after 'spouse' (in both places) insert 'or civil partner'.

103 In section 430E (associates), in subsection (8) after 'spouse' insert 'or civil partner'.

104(1) Amend section 742A (meaning of 'offer to the public') as follows.

(2) In subsection (3)(a)(iii), after 'widower' insert 'or surviving civil partner'.

(3) In subsection (6)(a), after 'spouse' insert 'or civil partner'.

105 In Schedule 7 (matters to be dealt with in directors' report), in paragraph 2B(3), after 'spouse' insert 'or civil partner'.

Enduring Powers of Attorney Act 1985 (c 29)

106 In section 3 (scope of authority etc of attorney under enduring power), in subsection (5)(a), for 'or marriage' substitute ', marriage or the formation of a civil partnership'.

107 In Schedule 1 (notification prior to registration of instrument creating power of attorney), in paragraph 2(1)—

    (a) in paragraph (a), after 'wife' insert 'or civil partner', and

    (b) in paragraph (e), after 'widower' insert 'or surviving civil partner'.

108 Paragraphs 106 and 107 apply in relation to the exercise of powers under enduring powers of attorney created before the passing of this Act as well as in relation to those created on or after its passing.

Food and Environment Protection Act 1985 (c 48)

109 In Schedule 2 (officers and their powers), in paragraph 2A(4), after 'spouse' insert 'or civil partner'.

Child Abduction and Custody Act 1985 (c 60)

110 In section 24A (power to order disclosure of child's whereabouts), in subsection (2), after 'spouse' insert 'or civil partner'.

Airports Act 1986 (c 31)

111 In section 20 (powers of investment and disposal in relation to public airport companies), in subsection (6)(b), after 'widowers' insert ', civil partners, surviving civil partners'.

Insolvency Act 1986 (c 45)

112 In section 215 (proceedings under sections 213, 214), in subsection (3)(b), after 'marriage' insert 'or the formation of a civil partnership'.

113 In section 283A (bankrupt's home ceasing to form part of estate), in subsection (1)—

(a) in paragraph (b), after 'spouse' insert 'or civil partner', and

(b) in paragraph (c), after 'spouse' insert 'or former civil partner'.

114 In section 313 (charge on bankrupt's home), in subsection (1), after 'former spouse' insert 'or by his civil partner or former civil partner'.

115 In section 313A (low value home: application for sale, possession or charge), in subsection (1)—

(a) in paragraph (a)(ii), after 'spouse' insert 'or civil partner', and
(b) in paragraph (a)(iii), after 'spouse' insert 'or former civil partner'.

116 In section 329 (debts to spouse), in subsection (1), after 'spouse' (in each place) insert 'or civil partner'.

117 In section 332 (saving for bankrupt's home), in subsection (1), after 'former spouse' insert 'or by his civil partner or former civil partner'.

118 In section 335A (rights under trusts of land), in subsection (2)(b)—

(a) for 'bankrupt's spouse or former spouse' substitute 'bankrupt's spouse or civil partner or former spouse or former civil partner', and
(b) in sub-paragraphs (i) and (ii), for 'spouse or former spouse' substitute 'spouse, civil partner, former spouse or former civil partner'.

119 In section 339 (transactions at an undervalue), in subsection (3)(b), after 'marriage' insert 'or the formation of a civil partnership'.

120 In section 366 (inquiry into bankrupt's dealings and property), in subsection (1)(a), after 'former spouse' insert 'or civil partner or former civil partner'.

121 In section 423 (transactions defrauding creditors), in subsection (1)(b), after 'marriage' insert 'or the formation of a civil partnership'.

122(1) Amend section 435 (meaning of 'associate') as follows.

(2) For subsection (2) substitute—

'(2) A person is an associate of an individual if that person is—

(a) the individual's husband or wife or civil partner,
(b) a relative of—
    (i) the individual, or
    (ii) the individual's husband or wife or civil partner, or
(c) the husband or wife or civil partner of a relative of—
    (i) the individual, or

(ii)   the individual's husband or wife or civil partner.'

(3) In subsection (3), after 'husband or wife' insert 'or civil partner'.

(4) In subsection (8), at the end insert 'and references to a civil partner include a former civil partner'.

Building Societies Act 1986 (c 53)

123 In section 70 (interpretation), in—

(a) subsection (2)(a) and (c), and
(b) subsection (4),

after 'spouse' (in each place) insert 'or civil partner'.

Family Law Act 1986 (c 55)

124 In section 33 (power to order disclosure of child's whereabouts), in subsection (2), after 'spouse' insert 'or civil partner'.

125 In section 50 (non-recognition of divorce or annulment in another jurisdiction no bar to remarriage), for the words from 're-marrying' to the end substitute 'forming a subsequent marriage or civil partnership in that part of the United Kingdom or cause the subsequent marriage or civil partnership of either party (wherever it takes place) to be treated as invalid in that part.'

Consumer Protection Act 1987 (c 43)

126 In section 47 (savings for certain privileges), in subsection (2), after 'spouse' insert 'or civil partner'.

Criminal Justice Act 1988 (c 33)

127 In section 160A (marriage and other relationships), in subsections (1)(a) and (2)(a), after 'were married' insert 'or civil partners of each other'.

Companies Act 1989 (c 40)

128 In section 52 (meaning of 'associate'), in subsection (2)(a) after 'spouse' insert 'or civil partner'.

Children Act 1989 (c 41)

129(1) Amend section 8 (residence, contact and other orders with respect to children) as follows.

(2) After subsection (4)(b) insert—

'(ba) Schedule 5 to the Civil Partnership Act 2004;'.

(3) After subsection (4)(e) insert—

'(ea) Schedule 6 to the Civil Partnership Act 2004;'.

130 In section 48 (powers to assist in discovery of children who may be in need of emergency protection), in subsection (2), after 'spouse' insert 'or civil partner'.

131 In section 50 (recovery of abducted children etc), in subsection (11), after 'spouse' insert 'or civil partner'.

132 In section 98 (self-incrimination), in subsections (1) and (2), after 'spouse' insert 'or civil partner'.

Local Government and Housing Act 1989 (c 42)

133 In section 19 (members' interests) in subsection (7), after 'spouse' insert 'or civil partner'.

134 In section 69 (companies subject to local authority influence), in subsection (6)(c), after 'spouse' insert 'or civil partner'.

Opticians Act 1989 (c 44)

135 In section 29(1) (family or representatives may use deceased optician's title for three years), in paragraphs (b) and (d), for 'his widow' substitute 'his surviving spouse or his surviving civil partner'.

Food Safety Act 1990 (c 16)

136 In section 43 (continuance of registration or licence on death) in subsection (2), for the words from 'the deceased's personal representative' to 'his death' substitute

'the deceased's personal representative, or widow or widower or surviving civil partner or any other member of the deceased's family, until the end of—

(a) the period of three months beginning with the deceased's death'.

Courts and Legal Services Act 1990 (c 41)

137 In section 10 (family proceedings in magistrates' courts and related matters), in subsection (1), after 'Domestic Proceedings and Magistrates' Courts Act 1978' insert 'or Schedule 6 to the Civil Partnership Act 2004'.

138 In section 58A (conditional fee agreements: supplementary), omit 'and' at the end of subsection (2)(f) and insert—

'(fa) Chapter 2 of Part 2 of the Civil Partnership Act 2004 (proceedings for dissolution etc of civil partnership);

(fb) Schedule 5 to the 2004 Act (financial relief in the High Court or a county court etc);

(fc) Schedule 6 to the 2004 Act (financial relief in magistrates' courts etc);

(fd) Schedule 7 to the 2004 Act (financial relief in England and Wales after overseas dissolution etc of a civil partnership); and'.

Broadcasting Act 1990 (c 42)

139 In paragraph 1(2) of Part 1 of Schedule 2 (restrictions on the holding of licences)—

(a) in paragraphs (a) and (d), after 'husband or wife' (in each place) insert 'or civil partner', and
(b) at the end insert 'and references to a civil partner shall include a former civil partner'.

Local Government Finance Act 1992 (c 14)

140(1) In section 9(1)(a) (joint and several liability for council tax of married couple resident in same dwelling), after 'is married to' insert ', or is the civil partner of,'.

(2) After section 9(3) insert—

'(4) For the purposes of this section two persons are civil partners of each other if they are of the same sex and either—

(a) they are civil partners of each other; or
(b) they are not civil partners of each other but are living together as if they were civil partners.'

(3) In section 18(1)(b) (power to make regulations to deal with death of a person liable for council tax as a spouse under section 9), after 'spouse' insert 'or civil partner'.

Friendly Societies Act 1992 (c 40)

141 In section 77 (information on appointed actuary to be annexed to balance sheet), in subsection (3)(a), after 'spouse' insert 'or civil partner'.

142 In section 119A (meaning of 'associate'), in subsection (1)(a), after 'wife or husband' insert 'or civil partner'.

143 In Schedule 2 (the activities of a friendly society), in Head A, in class II—

(a) in the second column (description), after 'Marriage' insert ', civil partnership', and
(b) in the third column (nature of business), after 'sum on marriage' insert 'or on the formation of a civil partnership'.

Trade Union and Labour Relations Act 1992 (c 52)

144 In section 23 (restriction on enforcement of awards against certain property), in subsection (3)(b) for 'the wife' substitute 'the spouse or civil partner'.

145 In section 241 (intimidation or annoyance by violence or otherwise), in subsection (1)(a), for 'wife' substitute 'spouse or civil partner'.

146 In section 292 (death of employee or employer), in subsection (3)(b), after 'widow,' insert 'surviving civil partner,'.

Charities Act 1993 (c 10)

147 In Schedule 5 (meaning of 'connected person' for purposes of section 36(2)) in paragraph 1(e) after 'spouse' insert 'or civil partner'.

Pension Schemes Act 1993 (c 48)

148 In section 101E(1)(b) after 'or widower' insert 'or surviving civil partner'.

Pension Schemes (Northern Ireland) Act 1993 (c 49)

149 In section 97E(1)(b) after 'or widower' insert 'or surviving civil partner'.

Disability Discrimination Act 1995 (c 50)

150(1) In section 23 (exemption for small dwellings), amend subsection (7) as follows.

(2) In the definition of 'near relative'—

(a) after 'spouse' insert 'or civil partner', and
(b) for 'by affinity)' substitute 'by marriage or civil partnership)'.

(3) For the definition of 'partner' substitute—

'"partner" means the other member of a couple consisting of—

> (a) a man and a woman who are not married to each other but are living together as husband and wife, or

> (b) two people of the same sex who are not civil partners of each other but are living together as if they were civil partners.'

Employment Rights Act 1996 (c 18)

151 In section 57A (time off for dependants), in subsection (3)(a), after 'spouse' insert 'or civil partner'.

Family Law Act 1996 (c 27)

152(1) Amend section 64 (provision for separate representation for children) as follows.

(2) Omit 'or' at the end of subsection (1)(c).

(3) At the end of subsection (1)(d) insert

'or
> (e) Schedule 5 or 6 to the Civil Partnership Act 2004.'

Trusts of Land and Appointment of Trustees Act 1996 (c 47)

153 In paragraph 3 of Schedule 1 (family charges), after 'in consideration of marriage' insert 'or the formation of a civil partnership'.

Civil Procedure Act 1997 (c 12)

154 In section 7 (power of courts to make orders for preserving evidence etc), in subsection (7), after 'spouse' insert 'or civil partner'.

National Minimum Wage Act 1998 (c 39)

155 In section 14 (powers of officers), in subsection (2), for 'married, the person's spouse' substitute 'married or a civil partner, the person's spouse or civil partner'.

Access to Justice Act 1999 (c 22)

156 In Schedule 2 (community legal service: excluded services), in paragraph 2(3)(d), after 'Domestic Proceedings and Magistrates' Courts Act 1978' insert 'or Schedule 6 to the Civil Partnership Act 2004'.

Welfare Reform and Pensions Act 1999 (c 30)

157(1) Amend section 23 (supply of pension information in connection with divorce etc) as follows.

(2) After subsection (1)(a)(i) insert—

> '(ia) financial relief under Schedule 5 or 7 to the Civil Partnership Act 2004 (England and Wales powers in relation to domestic and overseas dissolution of civil partnerships etc),'.

(3) In subsection (1)(a)(ii)—

   (a) after '1984' insert 'or Schedule 11 to the 2004 Act', and

   (b) at the end, omit 'or'.

(4) In subsection (1)(a)(iii) for '(corresponding Northern Ireland powers);' substitute

   '(Northern Ireland powers corresponding to those mentioned in sub-paragraph (i)), or

      (iv) financial relief under Schedule 15 or 17 to the 2004 Act (Northern Ireland powers corresponding to those mentioned in sub-paragraph (ia));'.

(5) In subsection (1)(b), for 'or (iii)' substitute '(ia), (iii) or (iv)'.

158(1) Amend section 24 (charges by pension arrangements in relation to earmarking orders) as follows.

(2) After paragraph (a) insert—

   '(aa) an order under Part 1 of Schedule 5 to the Civil Partnership Act 2004 (financial provision orders in connection with dissolution of civil partnerships etc) so far as it includes provision made by virtue of Part 6 of that Schedule (powers to include provision about pensions),'.

(3) At the end of paragraph (b) omit 'or' and after paragraph (c) insert

  ', or

    (d) an order under Part 1 of Schedule 15 to the 2004 Act so far as it includes provision made by virtue of Part 5 of that Schedule (Northern Ireland powers corresponding to those mentioned in paragraph (aa)).'

159(1) Amend section 28 (activation of pension sharing) as follows.

(2) After subsection (1)(a) insert—

   '(aa) a pension sharing order under Schedule 5 to the Civil Partnership Act 2004,'.

(3) After subsection (1)(d) insert—

   '(da) an order under Schedule 7 to the 2004 Act (financial relief in England and Wales after overseas dissolution etc of a civil partnership) corresponding to such an order as is mentioned in paragraph (aa),'.

(4) In subsection (1)(f)—

   (a) at the end of sub-paragraph (i) insert 'or between persons who are civil partners of each other', and

   (b) at the end of sub-paragraph (iii) insert 'or (as the case may be) on the grant, in relation to the civil partnership, of decree of dissolution or of declarator of nullity'.

(5) In subsection (1)(g), after 'divorce etc)' insert 'or under Schedule 11 to the 2004 Act (financial provision in Scotland after overseas proceedings)'.

(6) In subsection (1)(h) for 'Northern Ireland legislation, and' substitute 'the Matrimonial Causes (Northern Ireland) Order 1978 (SI 1978/1045 (NI 15)),'.

(7) After subsection (1)(i) insert—

     '(j) a pension sharing order under Schedule 15 to the 2004 Act, and

     (k) an order under Schedule 17 to the 2004 Act (financial relief in Northern Ireland after overseas dissolution etc of a civil partnership) corresponding to such an order as is mentioned in paragraph (j).'

(8) In subsection (7)(a), omit 'matrimonial'.

(9) In subsection (8)—

(a) in paragraph (a), after 'divorce' insert ', dissolution', and
(b) at the end of paragraph (b) insert 'or, where the order is under Schedule 11 to the 2004 Act, the date of disposal of the application under paragraph 2 of that Schedule'.

(10) In subsection (9)—

(a) omit 'matrimonial', and
(b) in paragraphs (a) and (b)(i), after 'divorce' insert ', dissolution'.

160(1) Amend section 34 ('implementation period') as follows.

(2) In subsection (1)(b)(i), omit 'matrimonial'.

(3) In subsection (2)—

(a) omit 'matrimonial', and
(b) in paragraph (b), after 'divorce' insert ', dissolution'.

161(1) Amend section 48 (activation of benefit sharing) as follows.

(2) After subsection (1)(a) insert—

'(aa) a pension sharing order under Schedule 5 to the Civil Partnership Act 2004,'.

(3) After subsection (1)(d) insert—

'(da) an order under Schedule 7 to the 2004 Act (financial relief in England and Wales after overseas dissolution etc of a civil partnership) corresponding to such an order as is mentioned in paragraph (aa),'.

(4) In subsection (1)(f)—

(a) at the end of sub-paragraph (i) insert 'or between persons who are civil partners of each other', and
(b) at the end of sub-paragraph (iii) insert 'or (as the case may be) on the grant, in relation to the civil partnership, of decree of dissolution or of declarator of nullity'.

(5) In subsection (1)(g), after 'divorce etc)' insert 'or under Schedule 11 to the 2004 Act (financial provision in Scotland after overseas proceedings)'.

(6) In subsection (1)(h) for 'Northern Ireland legislation, and' substitute 'the Matrimonial Causes (Northern Ireland) Order 1978 (SI 1978/1045 (NI 15)),'.

(7) After subsection (1)(i) insert—

'(j) a pension sharing order under Schedule 15 to the 2004 Act, and
(k) an order under Schedule 17 to the 2004 Act (financial relief in Northern Ireland after overseas dissolution etc of a civil partnership) corresponding to such an order as is mentioned in paragraph (j).'

(8) In subsection (6)(a), omit 'matrimonial'.

(9) In subsection (7)—

(a) in paragraph (a), after 'divorce' insert ', dissolution', and
(b) at the end of paragraph (b) insert 'or, where the order is under Schedule 11 to the 2004 Act, the date of disposal of the application under paragraph 2 of that Schedule'.

(10) In subsection (8)—

    (a) omit 'matrimonial', and
    (b) in paragraphs (a) and (b)(i), after 'divorce' insert ', dissolution'.

Immigration and Asylum Act 1999 (c 33)

162 After section 24 insert—

'24A Duty to report suspicious civil partnerships

(1) Subsection (3) applies if—

    (a) a registration authority to whom a notice of proposed civil partnership has been given under section 8 of the Civil Partnership Act 2004,
    (b) any person who, under section 8 of the 2004 Act, has attested a declaration accompanying such a notice,
    (c) a district registrar to whom a notice of proposed civil partnership has been given under section 88 of the 2004 Act, or
    (d) a registrar to whom a civil partnership notice has been given under section 139 of the 2004 Act,

has reasonable grounds for suspecting that the civil partnership will be a sham civil partnership.

(2) Subsection (3) also applies if—

    (a) two people register as civil partners of each other under Part 2, 3 or 4 of the 2004 Act in the presence of the registrar, and
    (b) before, during or immediately after they do so, the registrar has reasonable grounds for suspecting that the civil partnership will be, or is, a sham civil partnership.

(3) The person concerned must report his suspicion to the Secretary of State without delay and in such form and manner as may be prescribed by regulations.

(4) The regulations are to be made—

    (a) in relation to England and Wales, by the Registrar General for England and Wales with the approval of the Chancellor of the Exchequer;
    (b) in relation to Scotland, by the Secretary of State after consulting the Registrar General of Births, Deaths and Marriages for Scotland;
    (c) in relation to Northern Ireland, by the Secretary of State after consulting the Registrar General in Northern Ireland.

(5) "Sham civil partnership" means a civil partnership (whether or not void)—

    (a) formed between a person ("A") who is neither a British citizen nor a national of an EEA State other than the United Kingdom and another person (whether or not such a citizen or such a national), and
    (b) formed by A for the purpose of avoiding the effect of one or more provisions of United Kingdom immigration law or the immigration rules.

(6) "The registrar" means—

    (a) in relation to England and Wales, the civil partnership registrar acting under Part 2 of the 2004 Act;
    (b) in relation to Scotland, the authorised registrar acting under Part 3 of the 2004 Act;

(c) in relation to Northern Ireland, the registrar acting under Part 4 of the 2004 Act.'

163 In section 166 (regulations and orders), in subsection (6)(b) after '24(3)' insert ', 24A(3)'.

Representation of the People Act 2000 (c 2)

164(1) Amend Schedule 4 (absent voting in Great Britain) as follows.

(2) In paragraph 3(3)(c), for 'his spouse,' (in both places) substitute 'his spouse or civil partner,'.

(3) In paragraph 6(6), for 'husband, wife,' substitute 'spouse, civil partner,'.

Financial Services and Markets Act 2000 (c 8)

165 In section 422 (controller), in subsection (4)(a), after 'spouse' insert 'or civil partner'.

166 In Schedule 11 (offers of securities), in paragraph 16(2), after 'wife, husband, widow, widower' insert ', civil partner, surviving civil partner,'.

Land Registration Act 2002 (c 9)

167 In section 125 (privilege against self-incrimination), in subsection (2), after 'spouse' insert 'or civil partner'.

Enterprise Act 2002 (c 40)

168 In section 127 (associated persons), in subsections (4)(a) and (c) and (6), after 'spouse' (in each place) insert ', civil partner'.

169 In section 222 (bodies corporate: accessories), in subsection (10), after 'spouse' in paragraphs (a), (c), (d) and (e) (in each place) insert 'or civil partner'.

Licensing Act 2003 (c 17)

170 In section 101 (minimum of 24 hours between event periods), in subsection (3)(a) and (d), after 'spouse' insert 'or civil partner'.

Local Government Act 2003 (c 26)

171 In paragraph 2(1)(a) of Schedule 4 (spouse of employee of the Valuation Tribunal Service disqualified for appointment as member of the Service), after 'is married to' insert 'or is the civil partner of'.

Courts Act 2003 (c 39)

172 In section 76 (further provision about scope of Family Procedure Rules), in subsection (2)(b), after 'divorce county court' insert 'or civil partnership proceedings county court (within the meaning of Part 5 of the Matrimonial and Family Proceedings Act 1984)'.

Sexual Offences Act 2003 (c 42)

173(1) Amend section 23 (sections 16 to 19: marriage exception) as follows.

(2) At the end of subsection (1)(b) insert 'or civil partners of each other'.

(3) In subsection (2), for 'were lawfully married at the time' substitute 'were at the time lawfully married or civil partners of each other'.

(4) In the heading to section 23 for 'marriage exception' substitute 'exception for spouses and civil partners'.

174(1) Amend section 28 (sections 25 and 26: marriage exception) as follows.

(2) At the end of subsection (1)(b) insert 'or civil partners of each other'.

(3) In subsection (2), for 'were lawfully married at the time' substitute 'were at the time lawfully married or civil partners of each other'.

(4) In the heading to section 28 for 'marriage exception' substitute 'exception for spouses and civil partners'.

175(1) Amend section 43 (sections 38 and 41: marriage exception) as follows.

(2) At the end of subsection (1)(b) insert 'or civil partners of each other'.

(3) In subsection (2), for 'were lawfully married at the time' substitute 'were at the time lawfully married or civil partners of each other'.

(4) In the heading to section 43 for 'marriage exception' substitute 'exception for spouses and civil partners'.

SCHEDULE 28

SECTION 261(2)

CONSEQUENTIAL AMENDMENTS: SCOTLAND

PART 1
AMENDMENTS OF THE SUCCESSION (SCOTLAND) ACT 1964 (C 41)

1 In section 1(2) (intestacy: saving for legal rights or prior rights), after 'spouse' insert 'or civil partner'.

2 In section 2(1)(e) (intestacy: succession rights of surviving spouse)—

    (a) for 'or a wife' substitute ', wife or civil partner', and
    (b) after 'spouse' insert 'or civil partner'.

3 In section 5(1) (representation on intestacy), for 'or spouse' substitute ', spouse or civil partner'.

4 In section 8 (prior rights on intestacy in dwelling house and furniture), in subsections (1), (3) and (4), after 'spouse' (in each place, including the provisos to subsections (1) and (3)) insert 'or civil partner'.

5 In section 9 (prior right to financial provision on intestacy)—

    (a) in subsection (1), for 'or wife, the surviving spouse' substitute ', wife or civil partner the survivor', and
    (b) in the proviso to that subsection and in subsections (2), (3), (4) and (6), after 'spouse', (in each place) insert 'or civil partner'.

6 In section 10(2) (calculation of legal rights), for 'jus relicti, jus relictae or legitim' substitute 'legal rights'.

7 In section 15(2)(a) (transfer of heritage in satisfaction of claim to legal rights or prior rights), after 'spouse' insert 'or civil partner'.

8 In section 16(2) (transfer of interest of tenant notwithstanding condition prohibiting assignation), after 'spouse' insert 'or civil partner'.

9 In section 31(1) (presumption of survivorship in respect of claims to property)—

(a) after 'spouse' insert 'or civil partner', and
(b) in paragraph (a), after 'wife' insert 'or civil partners to each other'.

10 In section 36(1) (interpretation), in the definition of 'prior rights', after 'spouse' insert 'or civil partner'.

PART 2
AMENDMENTS OF THE FAMILY LAW (SCOTLAND) ACT 1985 (C 37)

11 In section 1(1) (obligation of aliment), after paragraph (b) insert—

'(bb) a partner in a civil partnership to the other partner,'.

12(1) Amend section 2 (actions for aliment) as follows.

(2) in subsection (2), after paragraph (a) insert—

'(aa) for dissolution of a civil partnership, separation of civil partners or declarator of nullity of a civil partnership,'.

(3) In subsection (9), after 'wife' insert 'or the partners in a civil partnership'.

13 In section 6(1) (interim aliment)—

(a) in paragraph (a), for 'party' (in both places) substitute 'person',
(b) after paragraph (b) insert—

'(c) in an action for dissolution of a civil partnership, separation of civil partners or declarator of nullity of a civil partnership, by either partner against the other partner,'.

14(1) Amend section 8 (orders for financial provision) as follows.

(2) In subsection (1)—

(a) after 'either party to the marriage' insert 'and in an action for dissolution of a civil partnership, either partner', and
(b) in each of paragraphs (a) to (c), for 'marriage' substitute 'action'.

(3) In subsection (5), after 'marriage' insert 'or the partners in a civil partnership'.

15(1) Amend section 9 (principles to be applied in deciding what order if any to make for financial provision) as follows.

(2) In subsection (1)—

(a) in paragraph (a), at the end insert 'or as the case may be the net value of the partnership property should be so shared between the partners in the civil partnership',
(b) in paragraph (b), for 'party' (in each place) substitute 'person',
(c) in paragraph (c), the existing words 'after divorce, for a child of the marriage under the age of 16 years' become sub-paragraph (i), after that sub-paragraph insert—

'(ii) after dissolution of the civil partnership, for a child under that age who has been accepted by both partners as a child of the family,',

and for 'parties' substitute 'persons',
(d) in paragraph (d), for 'party' (in both places) substitute 'person', the existing words 'the date of the decree of divorce, to the loss of that support on divorce' become sub-paragraph (i) and after that sub-paragraph insert—

'(ii) the date of the decree of dissolution of the civil partnership, to the loss of that support on dissolution,' and

(e) in paragraph (e), for 'party' substitute 'person', after first 'divorce' insert 'or of the dissolution of the civil partnership,' and after second 'divorce' insert 'or dissolution'.

(3) In subsection (2), in the definitions of 'economic advantage' and 'contributions', after 'marriage' insert 'or civil partnership'.

16(1) Amend section 10 (sharing of value of matrimonial property) as follows.

(2) In subsection (1)—

(a) after 'property' insert 'or partnership property', and
(b) for 'the parties to the marriage' substitute 'persons'.

(3) In subsection (2)—

(a) omit first 'matrimonial',
(b) for 'the parties or either of them' substitute 'one or both of the parties to the marriage or as the case may be of the partners',
(c) in paragraph (a), after 'property' insert 'or before the registration of the partnership so far as they relate to the partnership property', and
(d) in paragraph (b), at the end insert 'or partnership'.

(4) In subsection (3)—

(a) in paragraph (a), for 'parties' substitute 'persons', and
(b) in paragraph (b), at the end insert 'or for dissolution of the civil partnership'.

(5) After subsection (4) insert—

'(4A) Subject to subsection (5) below, in this section and in section 11 of this Act "the partnership property" means all the property belonging to the partners or either of them at the relevant date which was acquired by them or by one of them (otherwise than by way of gift or succession from a third party)—

(a) before the registration of the partnership for use by them as a family home or as furniture or plenishings for such a home, or
(b) during the partnership but before the relevant date.'

(6) In subsection (5)—

(a) for 'party' (in each place) substitute 'person', and
(b) at the end insert 'or partnership property'.

(7) In subsection (6)—

(a) in paragraph (a), for 'parties' substitute 'persons' and at the end insert 'or partnership property',
(b) in paragraph (b), after 'property' insert 'or partnership property', for 'parties' substitute 'persons' and at the end insert 'or partnership',
(c) in paragraph (c), for 'party' substitute 'person',
(d) in paragraph (d), after 'property' insert 'or partnership property' and for 'matrimonial' substitute 'family', and
(e) in paragraph (e), at the end insert 'or the dissolution of the civil partnership'.

(8) In subsection (7), for 'parties' (in both places) substitute 'persons'.

17(1) Amend section 11 (factors to be taken into account) as follows.

(2) In subsection (2)—

    (a) in paragraph (a), for 'party' (in both places) substitute 'person', and

    (b) in paragraph (b), after 'property' insert 'or the partnership property'.

(3) In subsection (3)(g), for 'parties' substitute 'persons'.

(4) In subsection (4)—

    (a) in each of paragraphs (a) and (c), for 'party' substitute 'person',

    (b) in paragraph (b), for 'party prior to divorce' substitute 'person prior to divorce or to the dissolution of the civil partnership', and

    (c) in paragraph (d), for 'parties' substitute 'persons'.

(5) In subsection (5)—

    (a) in paragraph (a), for 'party' substitute 'person',

    (b) in paragraph (b), at the end insert 'or of the civil partnership',

    (c) in paragraph (c), for 'parties during the marriage' substitute 'persons during the marriage or civil partnership', and

    (d) in paragraph (d), for 'parties' substitute 'persons'.

(6) In subsection (6), for 'party' substitute 'person'.

(7) In subsection (7), after 'party' insert 'to the marriage or as the case may be of either partner'.

18(1) Amend section 12 (orders for payment of capital sum or transfer of property) as follows.

(2) In subsection (1)—

    (a) in paragraph (a), at the end insert 'or of dissolution of a civil partnership', and

    (b) in paragraph (b), for 'decree of divorce' substitute 'the decree'.

(3) In subsection (4), the existing words 'either party to the marriage' become paragraph (a) and after that paragraph insert the following paragraph—

      '(b) either partner,'.

19(1) Amend section 12A (orders for payment of capital sum: pensions lump sums) as follows.

(2) In subsection (1)—

    (a) for '("the liable party")' substitute 'or a partner in a civil partnership ("the liable person")', and

    (b) in paragraph (a), after 'property' insert 'or the partnership property' and for 'party' substitute 'person'.

(3) In subsection (2), for '("the other party")' substitute 'or as the case may be to the other partner ("the other person")'.

(4) In each of subsections (3) to (8), for 'party', wherever it occurs, substitute 'person'.

20(1) Amend section 13 (orders for periodical allowance) as follows.

(2) In subsection (1)—

    (a) in paragraph (a), at the end insert 'or of dissolution of a civil partnership',

    (b) in paragraph (b), for 'decree of divorce' substitute 'the decree', and

    (c) in paragraph (c), for 'decree of divorce' substitute 'such decree'.

(3) In subsection (4), after 'executor' insert ', or as the case may be either partner or his executor,'.

(4) in subsection (7)—

    (a) in paragraph (a), for 'party' substitute 'person' and for 'party's' substitute 'person's', and

    (b) for paragraph (b) substitute—

> '(b) shall cease to have effect on the person receiving payment—
> > (i)   marrying,
> > (ii) entering into a civil partnership, or
> > (iii) dying,
>
> except in relation to any arrears due under it.'.

21(1) Amend section 14 (incidental orders) as follows.

(2) In subsection (1), at the end insert 'or of dissolution of a civil partnership'.

(3) In subsection (2)—

    (a) in paragraph (c), after 'marriage' insert ', or as the case may be the partners,',

    (b) in paragraph (d), the existing words 'the matrimonial home' become sub-paragraph (i), after that sub-paragraph insert 'or' and the following sub-paragraph—

> '(ii) the family home of the partnership,',

    and for 'party to the marriage' substitute 'person',

    (c) in paragraph (e), for 'parties' substitute 'persons', the existing words 'the matrimonial home' become sub-paragraph (i) and after that sub-paragraph insert 'or' and the following sub-paragraph—

> '(ii) the family home of the partnership,',

    (d) in paragraph (g), for 'party to the marriage' substitute 'person', and

    (e) in paragraph (h), at the end insert 'or in any corresponding settlement in respect of the civil partnership'.

(4) In subsection (3), for 'decree of divorce' substitute 'the decree'.

(5) After subsection (5) insert—

> '(5A) So long as an incidental order granting a partner in a civil partnership the right to occupy a family home or the right to use furnishings and plenishings therein remains in force then—
>
> > (a) section 102(1), (2), (5)(a) and (9) of the Civil Partnership Act 2004, and
> > (b) subject to section 15(3) of this Act, section 111 of that Act,
>
> shall, except to the extent that the order otherwise provides, apply in relation to the order in accordance with subsection (5B).
>
> (5B) Those provisions apply—
>
> > (a) as if that partner were a non-entitled partner and the other partner were an entitled partner within the meaning of section 101 or 106(2) of that Act as the case may require,
> > (b) as if the right to occupy a family home under that order were a right specified in paragraph (a) or (b) of section 101(1) of that Act, and
> > (c) with any other necessary modification.'

(6) In subsection (7), at the end insert 'or of dissolution of a civil partnership'.

22(1) Amend section 16 (agreements on financial provision) as follows.

(2) In subsection (1)—

(a) after 'marriage' insert 'or the partners in a civil partnership', and

(b) after 'divorce' insert 'or on dissolution of the civil partnership'.

(3) In subsection (3)—

(a) after 'marriage' insert 'or the partners in a civil partnership',

(b) after first 'divorce' insert 'or on dissolution of the civil partnership',

(c) in paragraphs (a) to (c), for 'party' and 'party's' (in each place) substitute, respectively, 'person' and 'person's', and

(d) after second 'divorce' insert 'or of dissolution of the civil partnership'.

23(1) Amend section 17 (financial provision on declarator of nullity of marriage) as follows.

(2) In subsection (1)—

(a) after first 'marriage' insert 'or of a civil partnership',

(b) after first 'divorce' insert 'or for dissolution of a civil partnership',

(c) after second 'marriage' insert 'and "action for dissolution of a civil partnership" includes an action for declarator of nullity of a civil partnership', and

(d) for 'and "divorce"' substitute ', "divorce" and "dissolution of a civil partnership"'.

(3) In subsection (2)—

(a) after first 'marriage' insert 'or of nullity of a civil partnership', and

(b) at the end insert 'or civil partnership'.

24 In section 18(1) (orders relating to avoidance transactions), for 'party' (in both places) substitute 'person'.

25 In section 21 (award of aliment or custody where divorce or separation refused)—

(a) for 'or separation' substitute ', separation or dissolution of a civil partnership', and

(b) for 'parties' substitute 'persons'.

26(1) In section 22 (expenses of action)—

(a) for 'party to a marriage' substitute 'person',

(b) for paragraph (a) substitute—

'(a) an action for aliment brought—
   (i)   by either party to a marriage, or
   (ii) by either party in a civil partnership,

   on his own behalf against the other party or partner,',

(c) in paragraph (b), after 'separation' insert '(whether of the parties to a marriage or the civil partners in a civil partnership)',

(d) after paragraph (b) insert—

'(bb) an action for dissolution of a civil partnership, declarator that a civil partnership exists or declarator of nullity of a civil partnership,', and

(e) after fifth 'marriage' insert 'or the other partner in the civil partnership'.

27 In section 24(1) (marriage not to affect property rights or legal capacity)—

(a) after fifth 'marriage' insert 'or civil partnership',

(b) in paragraph (a), after 'marriage' insert ', or as the case may be the partners in the civil partnership,', and

(c) in paragraph (b), for 'the parties to the marriage' substitute 'those parties or partners'.

28(1) Amend section 25 (presumption of equal shares in household goods) as follows.

(2) In subsection (1)—

(a) after first and third 'marriage' insert 'or civil partnership', and
(b) after second 'marriage' insert 'or the partners in a civil partnership',

(3) In subsection (2), the existing words 'the parties were married' become paragraph (a) and after that paragraph insert—

'(b) the partners were in civil partnership,', and

(4) In subsection (3)—

(a) for 'in any matrimonial' substitute 'or civil partnership in any family', and
(b) after second 'marriage' insert 'or the partners'.

29 In section 26 (presumption of equal shares in money and property derived from housekeeping allowance)—

(a) after first 'marriage' insert 'or civil partnership',
(b) after second 'marriage' insert 'or as the case may be of a partner in a civil partnership', and
(c) after second and third 'party' insert 'or partner'.

30 In section 27(1) (interpretation)—

(a) at the appropriate places insert—

'"civil partnership", in relation to an action for declarator of nullity of a civil partnership, means purported civil partnership,',

'"partner", in relation to a civil partnership, includes a person who has a partner in a civil partnership which has been terminated and an ostensible partner in a civil partnership which has been annulled,', and
(b) in the definition of 'family', at the end insert 'and in relation to a civil partnership means the members of the civil partnership together with any child accepted by them both as a child of the family.'

PART 3
AMENDMENTS OF THE BANKRUPTCY (SCOTLAND) ACT 1985 (C 66)

31 In section 16(4) (presentation of petition for recall of sequestration), for 'section 41(1)(b)' substitute 'sections 41(1)(b) and 41A(1)(b)'.

32 In section 17(8)(b) (duties of clerk of court in relation to recall of sequestration), after '41(1)(b)(ii)' insert 'or 41A(1)(b)(ii)'.

33 In section 20(4) (powers of interim trustee in relation to obtaining information as to debtor's assets)—

(a) in paragraph (b), after 'spouse' insert 'or civil partner', and
(b) after 'debtor, spouse' insert ', civil partner'.

34 In section 32(3)(b) (the expression 'relevant obligations'), at the end insert 'or former civil partner'.

35 In section 34(7) (gratuitous alienations: saving for operation of Married Women's Policies of Assurance (Scotland) Act 1880), at the end insert 'including the operation of that section as applied by section 132 of the Civil Partnership Act 2004'.

36(1) Amend section 40 (power of permanent trustee in relation to debtor's family home) as follows.

(2) In subsection (2), after paragraph (a) insert—

'(aa) the needs and financial resources of the debtor's civil partner or former civil partner;'.

(3) In paragraph (d) of that subsection, for 'paragraph (a) or (b)' substitute 'paragraphs (a) to (b)'.

(4) In subsection (4)—

(a) in paragraph (a), after 'spouse' (in each place) insert 'or civil partner',
(b) in paragraph (b), after 'spouse' (in each place) insert 'or civil partner', and
(c) in paragraph (c)(i), after 'spouse' (in each place) insert 'or civil partner'.

37 After section 41 insert—

'41A Protection of rights of civil partner against arrangements intended to defeat them

(1) If a debtor's sequestrated estate includes a family home of which the debtor, immediately before the date of issue of the act and warrant of the permanent trustee (or, if more than one such act and warrant is issued in the sequestration, of the first such issue) was an entitled partner and the other partner in the civil partnership is a non-entitled partner—

(a) the permanent trustee shall, where he—
   (i) is aware that the entitled partner is in civil partnership with the non-entitled partner; and
   (ii) knows where the non-entitled partner is residing,

   inform the non-entitled partner, within the period of 14 days beginning with that date, of the fact that sequestration of the entitled partner's estate has been awarded, of the right of petition which exists under section 16 of this Act and of the effect of paragraph (b) below; and
(b) the Court of Session, on the petition under section 16 of this Act of the non-entitled partner presented either within the period of 40 days beginning with that date or within the period of 10 weeks beginning with the date of sequestration may—
   (i) under section 17 of this Act recall the sequestration; or
   (ii) make such order as it thinks appropriate to protect the occupancy rights of the non-entitled partner,

   if it is satisfied that the purpose of the petition for sequestration was wholly or mainly to defeat the occupancy rights of the non-entitled partner.

(2) In subsection (1) above—

"entitled partner" and "non-entitled partner" have the same meanings as in section 101 of the Civil Partnership Act 2004;

"family home" has the meaning assigned by section 135 of the 2004 Act; and

"occupancy rights" means the rights conferred by subsection (1) of that section 101.'

38 In section 44(1)(b) (request for order requiring private examination of certain persons before sheriff)—

(a) after 'debtor's spouse' insert 'or civil partner', and
(b) after 'such spouse' insert ', civil partner'.

39 In section 51(3)(b) (meaning of 'postponed debt'), at the end insert 'or civil partner'.

40 In section 74 (interpretation), in each of subsections (2) and (4), for 'husband or wife' (in each place) substitute 'husband, wife or civil partner'.

41(1) Amend Schedule 1 (determination of amount of creditor's claim) as follows.

(2) In paragraph 2(1)(a), the words 'in the case of spouses (or, where the aliment is payable to a divorced person in respect of a child, former spouses)' become paragraph 2(1)(a)(i).

(3) At the end of paragraph 2(1)(a)(i) insert

> ', or
>
> > (ii) in the case of civil partners (or, where the aliment is payable to a former civil partner in respect of a child after dissolution of a civil partnership, former civil partners),'.

(4) In paragraph 2(2), after 'divorce' insert 'or on dissolution of a civil partnership'.

PART 4
MISCELLANEOUS AMENDMENTS

Damages (Scotland) Act 1976 (c 13)

42(1) In Schedule 1 (definition of 'relative'), amend paragraph 1 as follows.

(2) In sub-paragraph (a)—

    (a) after 'spouse' (in both places) insert 'or civil partner', and
    (b) at the end insert 'or in a relationship which had the characteristics of the relationship between civil partners'.

(3) After sub-paragraph (e), omit 'and'.

(4) After sub-paragraph (f), insert

> 'and
> > (g) any person who, having been a civil partner of the deceased, had ceased to be so by virtue of the dissolution of the civil partnership'.

Marriage (Scotland) Act 1977 (c 15)

43 Amend section 3 (notice of intention to marry) as follows—

    (a) in subsection (1), after paragraph (a) insert—

> '(aa) if he has previously been in civil partnership and the civil partnership has been dissolved, a copy of the decree of dissolution or annulment;', and

    (b) in subsection (2), after 'paragraph (a)' insert ', (aa)'.

44 In section 5(4)(b) (ground on which there is a legal impediment to a marriage), at the end insert 'or in civil partnership'.

Presumption of Death (Scotland) Act 1977 (c 27)

45(1) Amend section 1(3) (jurisdiction of Court of Session to entertain action of declarator) as follows.

(2) In paragraph (b)(i), after 'spouse' insert 'or civil partner'.

(3) After paragraph (b) insert

'; or

    (c) in a case where the pursuer in the action is the civil partner of the missing person, the following conditions are met—

        (i) the two people concerned registered as civil partners of each other in Scotland; and

        (ii) it appears to the court to be in the interests of justice to assume jurisdiction in the case.'

46(1) Amend section 3 (effect of decree) as follows.

(2) In subsection (1), after 'marriage' insert 'or of a civil partnership'.

(3) In subsection (3)—

    (a) after first 'marriage' insert 'or civil partnership', and
    (b) for 'the dissolution of the marriage' substitute 'its dissolution'.

Administration of Justice Act 1982 (c 53)

47 In section 13(1) (interpretation), in the definition of 'relative', after paragraph (a) insert—

'(aa) the civil partner or former civil partner;'.

Rent (Scotland) Act 1984 (c 58)

48 In Schedule 1 (statutory tenants by succession)—

    (a) in paragraph 2, after 'spouse' (in both places) insert 'or civil partner' and after 'spouse's' insert 'or civil partner's', and
    (b) in paragraph 6, after 'spouse' (in both places) insert 'or civil partner'.

49 In Schedule 1A (statutory or statutory assured tenants by succession: certain cases), in paragraph 2—

    (a) in sub-paragraph (1), after 'spouse' (in both places) insert 'or civil partner' and after 'spouse's' insert 'or civil partner's',
    (b) in sub-paragraph (2), at the end insert 'and a person who was living with the original tenant in a relationship which had the characteristics of the relationship between civil partners shall be treated as the civil partner of the original tenant', and
    (c) in sub-paragraph (3), after 'couples)' insert 'or under section 101 of the Civil Partnership Act 2004' and after 'spouse' insert ', or as the case may be as the surviving civil partner,'.

Mental Health (Scotland) Act 1984 (c 36)

50(1) Amend section 53 (definition of 'relative' and 'nearest relative') as follows.

(2) In subsection (1)(a), at the end insert 'or civil partner'.

(3) In subsection (4)—

    (a) in paragraph (b), for 'or wife' substitute ', wife or civil partner' and after 'spouse' insert 'or civil partner', and
    (b) in paragraph (c), after 'wife,' insert 'civil partner,'.

(4) After subsection (5) insert—

'(5A) In this section "civil partner" includes a person who is living with the patient in a relationship which has the characteristics of the relationship between civil partners (or, if the patient is for the time being an in-patient in a hospital, was so living until the patient was admitted), and has been or had been so living for a period of not less than 6 months; but a person shall not be treated by virtue of this subsection as the nearest relative of a partner in a civil partnership unless the civil partner of the patient is disregarded by virtue of paragraph (b) of subsection (4) of this section.'

(5) In subsection (6)(b)—

(a) after 'married patient' insert 'or of a partner in a civil partnership', and
(b) after 'wife' insert ', or as the case may be the civil partner,'.

51 In section 54 (children and young persons in care of local authority), for 'or wife' substitute ', wife or civil partner'.

Housing Associations Act 1985 (c 69)

52(1) Amend section 105 (meaning of 'member of a person's family') as follows.

(2) In subsection (1)(a)—

(a) after 'spouse' insert 'or civil partner', and
(b) at the end insert 'or in a relationship which has the characteristics of the relationship between civil partners'.

(3) In subsection (2)(a), after 'a relationship by marriage' insert 'or civil partnership'.

Debtors (Scotland) Act 1987 (c 18)

53 In section 106 (interpretation), in paragraph (a) of the definition of 'maintenance order'—

(a) after 'divorce' insert 'or on dissolution of a civil partnership', and
(b) after 'marriage' insert 'or of nullity of a civil partnership'.

Housing (Scotland) Act 1987 (c 26)

54 In section 83 ('members of a person's family')—

(a) in subsection (1)(a), after 'spouse' insert 'or civil partner',
(b) in subsection (2)(a), after 'marriage' insert 'or by virtue of civil partnership', and
(c) in subsection (3), after 'references to' insert 'that person's civil partner or to'.

Civil Evidence (Scotland) Act 1988 (c 32)

55(1) Amend section 8 (evidence in actions concerning family relationships, etc) as follows.

(2) In subsection (2), for 'separation or declarator of marriage, nullity of marriage' substitute 'for dissolution of civil partnership, for separation of spouses or of civil partners, for declarator of marriage or of nullity of marriage or of civil partnership or for'.

(3) After subsection (3) insert—

'(3A) Subject to subsection (4) below, in any action for dissolution of civil partnership, separation of civil partners or declarator of nullity of civil partnership, the evidence referred to in subsection (1) above shall consist of or include evidence other than that of a partner in the civil partnership (or purported civil partnership).'

(4) In subsection (4), after '(3)' insert 'or (3A)'.

Housing (Scotland) Act 1988 (c 43)

56(1) Amend section 31 (right of succession of spouse) as follows.

(2) In subsection (1), after 'spouse' (in both places) insert 'or civil partner'.

(3) In subsection (3)(b), after 'spouse' insert 'or civil partner'.

(4) In subsection (4)—

   (a) the existing words from 'as his' to the end become paragraph (a), and
   (b) after that paragraph insert the following paragraph—

      '(b) in a relationship which had the characteristics of the relationship between civil partners shall be treated as the tenant's civil partner'.

57 In Part 1 of Schedule 5 (grounds on which sheriff must order possession), in paragraph (b) of ground 1, after 'spouse's' insert 'or civil partner's'.

Crofters (Scotland) Act 1993 (c 44)

58 In section 61(2) (interpretation), for 'or husband' substitute ', husband or civil partner'.

Civil Evidence (Family Mediation) (Scotland) Act 1995 (c 6)

59 In section 1(2) (inadmissibility in civil proceedings of information as to what occurred during family mediation), after paragraph (c) insert the following paragraph—

      '(cc) between partners in a civil partnership or persons in a purported civil partnership concerning matters arising out of the breakdown or termination of their relationship,'.

Children (Scotland) Act 1995 (c 36)

60(1) Amend section 12 (restrictions on decrees for divorce, separation or annulment affecting children) as follows.

(2) In subsection (1), the existing words 'divorce, judicial separation, or declarator of nullity of marriage' become paragraph (a) and after that paragraph insert 'or' and the following paragraph—

      '(b) dissolution or declarator of nullity of a civil partnership or separation of civil partners,'.

(3) In subsection (4)—

   (a) the existing words from 'the parties' to the end become paragraph (a) (with the existing paragraphs (a) and (b) becoming sub-paragraphs (i) and (ii)), and
   (b) after the new paragraph (a) insert 'or' and the following paragraph—

      '(b) the partners in a civil partnership, means a child who has been accepted by both partners as a child of the family which their partnership constitutes.'.

61 In section 54(2) (reference to the Principal Reporter by court), after paragraph (a) insert—

      '(aa) an action for dissolution or declarator of nullity of a civil partnership or separation of civil partners;'.

Sexual Offences (Amendment) Act 2000 (c 44)

62 In section 3(2)(c) (abuse of position of trust: defence), after 'to' insert ', or in civil partnership with,'.

Housing (Scotland) Act 2001 (asp 10)

63 In section 31(c) (effect of work on rent)—

(a) after 'spouse' insert 'or civil partner', and
(b) for 'husband and wife except that the persons are of the same sex' substitute 'civil partners'.

64(1) Amend section 108 (meaning of 'family' etc) as follows.

(2) In subsection (1)(a), after 'spouse' insert 'or civil partner'.

(3) In subsection (2)(a), after 'marriage' insert 'or by virtue of civil partnership'.

65(1) Amend Schedule 2 (grounds for recovery of possession of house) as follows.

(2) In paragraph 5—

(a) in sub-paragraph (a), after 'spouse' insert 'or civil partner', and
(b) in sub-paragraph (b), for 'husband and wife except that the persons are of the same sex' substitute 'civil partners'.

(3) In paragraph 15—

(a) in sub-paragraph (a), for '(or former spouse)' substitute 'or civil partner (or former spouse or former civil partner)', and
(b) in sub-paragraph (b), for 'husband and wife except that the persons are of the same sex' substitute 'civil partners'.

66 In Schedule 3 (succession: qualified persons), in paragraph 2(1)(a)—

(a) in sub-head (i), after 'spouse' insert 'or civil partner', and
(b) in sub-head (ii), for 'husband and wife except that the persons are of the same sex' substitute 'civil partners'.

Criminal Justice (Scotland) Act 2003 (asp 7)

67(1) Amend section 14 (victim statements) as follows.

(2) In subsection (10)(a), at the end insert 'or civil partner'.

(3) For subsection (11) substitute—

'(11) In subsection (10)(b), "cohabitee" means a person who has lived with the victim—

(a) as if in a married relationship; or
(b) in a relationship which had the characteristics of the relationship between civil partners,

for at least six months and was so living immediately before the offence (or apparent offence) was perpetrated.'

Agricultural Holdings (Scotland) Act 2003 (asp 11)

68(1) Amend section 71 (meaning of 'family') as follows.

(2) In subsection (2)(a), after 'spouse' insert 'or civil partner', and

(3) In subsection (3)(a), after 'marriage' insert 'or by virtue of civil partnership'.

Mental Health (Care and Treatment) (Scotland) Act 2003 (asp 13)

69(1) Amend section 254 (meaning of 'nearest relative') as follows.

(2) In subsection (2)(a), at the end insert 'or civil partner'.

(3) In subsection (3), after 'spouse' insert 'or civil partner'.

(4) In subsection (7)(a)(ii), for 'husband and wife except that the person and the relevant person are of the same sex' substitute 'civil partners'.

70 In section 313(5)(a)(ii) (defence in respect of sexual offence), after 'spouse' insert 'or civil partner'.

SCHEDULE 29

SECTION 261(3)

MINOR AND CONSEQUENTIAL AMENDMENTS: NORTHERN IRELAND

Interpretation Act (Northern Ireland) 1954 (c 33 (NI))

1 In section 46 (miscellaneous definitions), in subsection (2), after the definition of 'barrister-at-law' insert—

> '"civil partnership" means a civil partnership which exists under the Civil Partnership Act 2004 (and any reference to a civil partner shall be construed accordingly);'.

Trustee Act (Northern Ireland) 1958 (c 23 (NI))

2(1) Amend section 32(3)(a) (trust on reaching 18 or marrying under that age of accumulations during infancy) as follows.

(2) In sub-paragraph (i)—

(a) after 'marries under that age' insert 'or forms a civil partnership under that age', and
(b) for 'or until his marriage' substitute ', or until his marriage or his formation of a civil partnership,'.

(3) In sub-paragraph (ii), after 'marriage' insert ', or on formation of a civil partnership,'.

(4) In the words after that sub-paragraph, after 'marriage' insert 'or formation of a civil partnership'.

3(1) Amend section 34(1)(b) (trust to maintain principal beneficiary and his spouse and issue on failure of protective trust under paragraph (a)(ii)) as follows.

(2) In sub-paragraphs (i) and (ii), for 'wife or husband' substitute 'spouse or civil partner'.

(3) In sub-paragraph (ii), after 'married' insert 'or formed a civil partnership'.

Perpetuities Act (Northern Ireland) 1966 (c 2 (NI))

4(1) Amend section 3 (uncertainty as to remoteness) as follows.

(2) In subsection (4)(a), after 'spouse' insert 'or civil partner'.

(3) In subsection (5)(f), after 'spouse' insert 'or civil partner'.

5(1) Amend section 5 (condition relating to death of surviving spouse) as follows.

(2) After 'spouse' insert 'or civil partner'.

(3) In the heading to section 5, after 'spouse' insert 'or civil partner'.

Office and Shop Premises Act (Northern Ireland) 1966 (c26 (NI))

6 In section 2 (exception for premises in which only employer's relatives or outworkers work), in subsection (1), after 'wife' insert ', civil partner'.

Maintenance and Affiliation Orders Act (Northern Ireland) 1966 (c 35 (NI))

7 In section 10 (orders to which Part 2 of the Act applies), in subsection (2), after paragraph (h) insert—

> '(i)   paragraph 2(1)(a) or (d), 33, 34(3) or 36(1)(a) or (d) of Schedule 15, Schedule 16, or paragraph 9 of Schedule 17 so far as that paragraph applies Part 1 of Schedule 15, to the Civil Partnership Act 2004;'.

8(1) Amend section 13 (variation of orders registered in courts of summary jurisdiction) as follows.

(2) In subsection (5A), after '1980' insert 'or paragraph 42 of Schedule 16 to the Civil Partnership Act 2004'.

(3) In subsection (7B), after '1989' insert 'or paragraph 9 of Schedule 17 so far as that paragraph applies Part 1 of Schedule 15'.

Census Act (Northern Ireland) 1969 (c8 (NI))

9 In the Schedule (matters of which particulars may be required), in paragraph 5, after 'marriage' insert 'or civil partnership'.

Theft Act (Northern Ireland) 1969 (c 16 (NI))

10(1) Amend section 29(1) (effect on civil proceedings and rights) as follows.

(2) For 'wife or husband' substitute 'spouse or civil partner'.

(3) For 'married after the making of the statement or admission) against the wife or husband' substitute 'married or became civil partners after the making of the statement or admission) against the spouse or civil partner'.

Industrial and Provident Societies Act (Northern Ireland) 1969 (c 24 (NI))

11(1) Amend section 22 (nomination to property in society) as follows.

(2) In subsection (2), for 'husband, wife,' substitute 'spouse, civil partner,'.

(3) In subsection (6)—

(a) for 'marriage' substitute 'formation of a marriage or civil partnership by';
(b) after 'before the marriage' insert 'or civil partnership was formed';
(c) for 'a marriage contracted' substitute 'the formation of a marriage or civil partnership'.

12 In the definition of 'member of the family' in section 101(1) (interpretation), for 'husband, wife,' substitute 'spouse, civil partner,'.

Land Registration Act (Northern Ireland) 1970 (c18 (NI))

13 In Schedule 11 (matters required to be registered in the Statutory Charges Register), after paragraph 45 insert—

'46 An order under paragraph 67(2) of Schedule 15 to the Civil Partnership Act 2004 to the extent that by virtue of paragraph 69(1)(b) of that Schedule it renders liable to be set aside at the instance of an applicant for financial relief a disposition of any land in Northern Ireland which is specified in the order.'

Leasehold (Enlargement and Extension) Act (Northern Ireland) 1971 (c 7 (NI))

14 In section 1 (general right to acquire fee simple or to obtain extension of lease), in subsection (3)(f)(i) to (iv), after 'spouse' insert 'or civil partner'.

15 In section 19 (restrictions on right to extension of lease or to acquire fee simple), in subsection (1)(a)(i), after 'spouse' insert 'or civil partner'.

Civil Evidence Act (Northern Ireland) 1971 (c 36 (NI))

16(1) Amend section 10 (privilege against incrimination of self or spouse).

(2) In subsection (1), for 'husband or wife' substitute 'spouse or civil partner'.

(3) In the heading to section 10, after 'spouse' insert 'or civil partner'.

Local Government Act (Northern Ireland) 1972 (c 9 (NI))

17 In section 30 (relatives of councillors), in subsection (6) (relevant family relationship)—

(a) after 'husband and wife' insert 'or civil partners';
(b) after 'husband or wife' insert (in both places) 'or civil partner'.

18 In section 146 (interpretation: pecuniary interests), in subsection (2) (interests of spouses living together)—

(a) after 'spouses' insert (in both places) 'or civil partners';
(b) after 'spouse' insert (in both places) 'or civil partner'.

Employer's Liability (Defective Equipment and Compulsory Insurance) (Northern Ireland) Order 1972 (SI 1972/963 (NI 6))

19 In Article 6(a) (persons whom employer is not required to insure) after 'husband, wife,' insert 'civil partner,'.

Births and Deaths Registration (Northern Ireland) Order 1976 (SI 1976/1041 (NI 14))

20 In Article 2(2) (interpretation), in the definition of 'relative', after 'by marriage' insert 'or civil partnership'.

Sex Discrimination (Northern Ireland) Order 1976 (SI 1976/1042 (NI 15))

21 In Article 2(6) (meaning of 'near relative')—

(a) after 'wife or husband' (in both places) insert 'or civil partner', and
(b) for 'by affinity)' substitute 'by marriage or civil partnership)'.

Pharmacy (Northern Ireland) Order 1976 (SI 1976/1213 (NI 22))

22 In Article 3(3)(e)(iii) (objects of Pharmaceutical Society include providing relief for distressed relatives), for 'widows,' substitute 'surviving spouses, surviving civil partners,'.

Criminal Damage (Northern Ireland) Order 1977 (SI 1977/426 (NI 4))

23(1) Amend Article 11 (evidence in connection with offences under the Order) as follows.

(2) For 'wife or husband' substitute 'spouse or civil partner'.

(3) For 'married after the making of the statement or admission) against the wife or husband' substitute 'married or became civil partners after the making of the statement or admission) against the spouse or civil partner'.

Judicature (Northern Ireland) Act 1978 (c 23)

24 In section 31 (remittal and removal of proceedings), in subsection (7)(b), after '1882' insert 'or section 191 of the Civil Partnership Act 2004'.

25(1) Amend section 35(2) (restrictions on appeals to Court of Appeal from High Court) as follows.

(2) After paragraph (e) insert—

'(ea) from a dissolution order, nullity order or presumption of death order under Chapter 2 of Part 4 of the Civil Partnership Act 2004 that has been made final, by a party who, having had time and the opportunity to appeal from the conditional order on which the final order was founded, has not appealed from that conditional order;'.

(3) In paragraph (g)(iv), after 'matrimonial cause' insert ', a conditional order in a civil partnership cause'.

26(1) Amend section 94A (withdrawal of privilege against incrimination of self or spouse in certain proceedings) as follows.

(2) In subsection (1), after 'spouse' insert 'or civil partner'.

(3) In subsection (3), for 'married after the making of the statement or admission) against the spouse' substitute 'married or became civil partners after the making of the statement or admission) against the spouse or civil partner'.

Health and Safety at Work (Northern Ireland) Order 1978 (SI 1978/1039 (NI 9))

27 In Article 22 (powers of inspectors), in paragraph (7), for 'husband or wife' substitute 'spouse or civil partner'.

Matrimonial Causes (Northern Ireland) Order 1978 (SI 1978/1045 (NI 15))

28(1) Insert after Article 2(4)—

'(4A) References in this Order to the formation of a civil partnership by a person include references to a civil partnership which is by law void or voidable.'

29 In Article 13 (grounds on which marriage is void), at the end of paragraph (1)(d) insert 'or a civil partner'.

30(1) Amend Article 17 (marriages governed by foreign law or celebrated abroad under certain enactments or common law) as follows.

(2) In paragraph (1), at the beginning insert 'Subject to paragraph (3)'.

(3) After paragraph (2) insert—

> '(3) No marriage is to be treated as valid by virtue of paragraph (1) if, at the time when it purports to have been celebrated, either party was already a civil partner.'

31(1) Amend Article 30 (duration of continuing financial provision orders in favour of party to marriage, and effect of remarriage) as follows.

(2) In paragraph (1)(a) and (b) after 'remarriage of' insert ', or formation of a civil partnership by,'.

(3) In paragraph (2)—

(a) after 'remarriage of' insert ', or formation of a civil partnership by,', and
(b) after 'the remarriage' insert 'or formation of the civil partnership'.

(4) In paragraph (3), after 'remarries whether at any time before or after the commencement of this Article', insert 'or forms a civil partnership'.

(5) In the heading to Article 30, after 'remarriage' insert 'or formation of civil partnership'.

32 In Article 37 (alteration of agreements by court during lives of parties), in paragraph (4)(a) and (b), after 'remarriage of' insert ', or formation of a civil partnership by,'.

33(1) Amend Article 40 (orders for repayment in certain cases of sums paid after cessation of order by reason of remarriage) as follows.

(2) In paragraph (1)—

(a) in sub-paragraph (a), after 'remarriage of' insert ', or formation of a civil partnership by,', and
(b) in sub-paragraph (b), after 'remarriage' insert 'or formation of the civil partnership'.

(3) In paragraph (6)—

(a) in sub-paragraph (a), after 'remarriage of' insert ', or formation of a civil partnership by,', and
(b) in the words following sub-paragraph (b), after 'had remarried' insert 'or formed a civil partnership'.

(4) In the heading to Article 40, after 'remarriage' insert 'or formation of civil partnership'.

Rehabilitation of Offenders (Northern Ireland) Order 1978 (SI 1978/1908 (NI 27))

34 In Article 8 (limitations on rehabilitation), in paragraph (2)(c), after 'marriage,' insert 'civil partnership,'.

Criminal Appeal (Northern Ireland) Act 1980 (c 47)

35 In section 47A (appeals in cases of death), in subsection (3)(a), after 'widower' insert 'or surviving civil partner'.

County Courts (Northern Ireland) Order 1980 (SI 1980/397 (NI 3))

36 In Article 10 (general civil jurisdiction), after paragraph (3) insert—

> '(3A) Except as provided by the Civil Partnership Act 2004, a county court which is not a civil partnership proceedings county court shall not have jurisdiction to hear any cause or matter to which that Act applies.'

37 In Article 14 (jurisdiction in equity matters), in paragraph (j), after '1882' insert 'or section 191 of the Civil Partnership Act 2004'.

38 In Article 39 (capacity of parties), in paragraph (2)(d), after 'marriage, death or bankruptcy of' insert ', or the formation of a civil partnership by,'.

Domestic Proceedings (Northern Ireland) Order 1980 (SI 1980/563 (NI 5))

39 In Article 6 (duration of orders for financial provision for a party to a marriage), in paragraph (2)—

  (a) after 'remarriage of' insert ', or formation of a civil partnership by,', and
  (b) after 'the remarriage' insert 'or formation of the civil partnership'.

40(1) Amend Article 40 (orders for repayment in certain cases of sums paid after cessation of order by reason of remarriage) as follows.

(2) In paragraph (1)—

  (a) in sub-paragraph (a), after 'remarriage of' insert ', or formation of a civil partnership by,', and
  (b) in sub-paragraph (b), after 'that remarriage' insert 'or the formation of that civil partnership'.

(3) In paragraph (8)—

  (a) in sub-paragraph (a), after 'remarriage of' insert ', or formation of a civil partnership by,', and
  (b) in the words following sub-paragraph (b)—
    (i)   after 'the remarriage' insert 'or the formation of that civil partnership', and
    (ii) after 'had remarried' insert 'or formed a civil partnership'.

(4) In the heading to Article 40, after 'remarriage' add 'or formation of civil partnership'.

Judgments Enforcement (Northern Ireland) Order 1981 (SI 1981/226 (NI 6)

41 In Article 4 (judgments to which Order applies), in paragraph (e), after '1980' insert 'or Part 1, 2 or 6 of Schedule 16 to the Civil Partnership Act 2004'.

42 In Article 6 (judgments to which Order does not apply), in paragraph (c), after 'matrimonial jurisdiction' insert 'or by the High Court or a civil partnership proceedings county court in the exercise of its civil partnership jurisdiction'.

43 In Article 7 (The Enforcement of Judgments Office), in paragraph (3), after 'domestic' insert 'or civil partnership'.

44 In Article 25 (taking custody of goods under a money judgment), in paragraph (2)(b), after 'spouse' insert 'or civil partner'.

45 In Article 32 (property which may be seized), in paragraph (d), after 'spouse' (in each place) insert 'or civil partner'.

46 In Article 33 (property exempt from seizure), in paragraph (a), after 'spouse' (in each place) insert 'or civil partner'.

47 In Article 36 (where seizure may be effected), in paragraph (a)(i), after 'spouse' insert 'or civil partner'.

48 In Article 38 (power of entry under order of seizure), after 'spouse' insert 'or civil partner'.

49 In Article 44 (interpleader), in paragraph (1), after 'spouse' insert 'or civil partner'.

50(1) Amend Article 96A (maintenance orders in the High Court and divorce county courts) as follows.

(2) In paragraphs (1), (3)(a), (7) and (9) after 'divorce county court' insert (in each place) 'or civil partnership proceedings county court'.

(3) In the heading to Article 96A, for 'divorce' substitute 'certain'.

51(1) Amend Article 98 (power of courts to make attachment of earnings orders) as follows.

(2) In paragraph (a)(i), after 'matrimonial' insert 'or civil partnership'.

(3) In paragraph (a)(ii), after 'matrimonial jurisdiction' insert 'or a civil partnership proceedings county court in the exercise of its civil partnership jurisdiction'.

52(1) Amend Article 107 (committal for default) as follows.

(2) In paragraph (1)(c), after 'matrimonial jurisdiction' insert 'or by the High Court or a civil partnership proceedings county court in the exercise of its civil partnership jurisdiction'.

(3) In paragraph (2)(a)(ii), after 'matrimonial' insert 'or civil partnership'.

Legal Aid, Advice and Assistance (Northern Ireland) Order 1981 (SI 1981/228 (NI 8))

53 In Article 14(4) (resources of person's wife or husband treated as resources of that person), for 'wife or husband' substitute 'spouse or civil partner'.

54 In Part 1 of Schedule 1 (proceedings for which legal aid may be given), in paragraph 3(b), after '1998' insert 'or Schedule 16 to the Civil Partnership Act 2004'.

Magistrates' Courts (Northern Ireland) Order 1981 (SI 1981/1675 (NI 26))

55 In Article 85 (orders for periodical payment: means of payment), in paragraph (8)(a)(ii), after '1980' insert ', the Civil Partnership Act 2004'.

56 In Article 86 (revocation, variation, etc, of orders for periodical payment), in paragraph (1), after '1980' insert 'and paragraph 42 of Schedule 16 to the Civil Partnership Act 2004'.

57 In Article 88 (nature of domestic proceedings), after paragraph (dh), insert—

> '(di) under paragraph 54 of Schedule 15 to the Civil Partnership Act 2004 or under Schedule 16 to that Act;'.

58 In Article 98 (enforcement of orders for periodical payment of money), in paragraph (11)(i), after '1980' insert 'or Schedule 16 to the Civil Partnership Act 2004'.

59 In Article 99 (enforcement of orders for payment of money other than periodical payments), in paragraph (11), after '1980' insert 'or Part 1, 2 or 6 of Schedule 16 to the Civil Partnership Act 2004'.

60 In Article 143 (appeals in other cases), after paragraph (3) insert—

> '(4) Paragraph (1) is also subject to paragraph 8(2) of Schedule 16 to the Civil Partnership Act 2004 and Article 31(1) of the Domestic Proceedings (Northern Ireland) Order 1980 as applied by paragraph 46 of that Schedule.'

61 In Article 164 (appearance by counsel or solicitor), in paragraph (3), for 'husband, wife' substitute 'spouse, civil partner'.

Criminal Attempts and Conspiracy (Northern Ireland) Order 1983 (SI 1983/1120 (NI 13))

62 In Article 10 (exemptions from liability for conspiracy), in paragraph (2)(a), after 'spouse' insert 'or civil partner'.

Forfeiture (Northern Ireland) Order 1982 (SI 1982/1082 (NI 14))

63 In Article 5 (application for financial provision not affected by the forfeiture rule), at the end of paragraph (2)(b) insert

'and
   (c) paragraphs 53 (variation of secured periodical payments order) and 66 (alteration of maintenance agreements by court) of Schedule 15 to the Civil Partnership Act 2004'.

FAMILY LAW (MISCELLANEOUS PROVISIONS) (NORTHERN IRELAND) ORDER 1984 (SI 1984/1984 (NI 14))

64(1) Amend Article 18 (prohibited degrees of relationship) as follows.

(2) In paragraph (1), for the words from 'between a man' to 'that Table' substitute 'between a person and any person mentioned in the list in Part 1 of the following Table'.

(3) For the Table in paragraph (1) substitute—

'PART 1
PROHIBITED DEGREES OF RELATIONSHIP

Adoptive child

Adoptive parent

Child

Former adoptive child

Former adoptive parent

Grandparent

Grandchild

Parent

Parent's sibling

Sibling

Sibling's child

PART 2
DEGREES OF AFFINITY REFERRED TO IN PARAGRAPHS (2A) AND (2B)

Child of former civil partner

Child of former spouse

Former civil partner of grandparent

Former civil partner of parent

Former spouse of grandparent

Former spouse of parent

Grandchild of former civil partner

Grandchild of former spouse

PART 3
DEGREES OF AFFINITY REFERRED TO IN PARAGRAPHS (2C) AND (2D)

Parent of former spouse

Parent of former civil partner

Former spouse of child

Former civil partner of child'.

(4) In paragraph (2)—

    (a) in sub-paragraph (b), for the words 'brother or sister' substitute 'sibling';
    (b) in sub-paragraph (c), after the word 'marriage' insert 'or civil partnership'.

(5) In paragraph (2A), for the words from 'between a man' to 'that Part II' substitute 'between a person and any person mentioned in the list in Part 2 of that Table'.

(6) In paragraph (2C), for the words from 'between a man' to 'that Part III' substitute 'between a person and any person mentioned in the list in Part 3 of that Table'.

(7) In paragraph (2D), for sub-paragraphs (a) to (d) substitute—

    '(a) in the case of a marriage between a person and the parent of a former spouse of that person, after the death of both the former spouse and the former spouse's other parent;
    (b) in the case of a marriage between a person and the parent of a former civil partner of that person, after the death of both the former civil partner and the former civil partner's other parent;
    (c) in the case of a marriage between a person and the spouse of a child of that person, after the death of both the child and the child's other parent;
    (d) in the case of a marriage between a person and the former civil partner of a child of that person, after the death of both the child and the child's other parent.'

Credit Unions (Northern Ireland) Order 1985 (SI 1985/1205 (NI 12))

65(1) Amend Article 2(2) (interpretation) as follows.

(2) After the definition of 'board of directors' insert—

    '"civil partner" includes former civil partner;'.

(3) In the definition of 'member of the family'—

    (a) in paragraphs (a), (b) and (c), after 'spouse' insert 'or civil partner', and
    (b) in paragraph (ii), for 'a child born in wedlock' substitute 'the legitimate child of the relationship in question'.

66(1) Amend Article 17 (nomination to property in credit union) as follows.

(2) In paragraph (2), after 'wife,' insert 'civil partner,'.

(3) In paragraph (6)—

    (a) for 'marriage of' substitute 'formation of a marriage or civil partnership by';

(b) after 'before the marriage' insert 'or civil partnership was formed';

(c) for 'a marriage contracted' substitute 'the formation of a marriage or civil partnership'.

Mental Health (Northern Ireland) Order 1986 (SI 1986/595 (NI 4))

67(1) Amend Schedule 1 (persons by whom a medical recommendation or medical report under Article 12 may not be given) as follows.

(2) In paragraph 3, after 'spouse,' insert 'civil partner,'.

(3) In paragraph 4, after 'spouse' insert 'or civil partner'.

Companies (Northern Ireland) Order 1986 (SI 1986/1032 (NI 6))

68(1) Amend Article 10A (meaning of 'offer to the public') as follows.

(2) In paragraph (3)(a)(iii), for 'widow or widower' substitute 'surviving spouse or surviving civil partner'.

(3) In paragraph (6)(a), after 'spouse' insert 'or civil partner'.

69 In Article 11 (employees' share scheme), in paragraph (b), for 'wives, husbands, widows, widowers' substitute 'spouses, civil partners, surviving spouses, surviving civil partners'.

70 In Article 211 (notification of family and corporate interests), in paragraph (1), after 'spouse' insert 'or civil partner'.

71(1) Amend Article 335 (extension of Article 331 to spouses and children) as follows.

(2) In paragraph (1)—

(a) in sub-paragraph (a), after 'wife or husband' insert 'or civil partner', and

(b) in the words following sub-paragraph (b), after 'as the case may be,' insert 'civil partner or'.

(3) In the heading to Article 335, after 'spouses' insert ', civil partners'.

72(1) Amend Article 336 (extension of Article 332 to spouses and children) as follows.

(2) In paragraphs (1)(a) and (2)(a), after 'wife or husband' insert 'or civil partner'.

(3) In paragraph (3)—

(a) in sub-paragraph (a), after 'spouse' insert 'or civil partner', and

(b) in sub-paragraph (b), after 'spouse' insert 'or civil partner' and after 'wife, husband,' insert 'civil partner,'.

(4) In the heading to Article 336, after 'spouses' insert ', civil partners'.

73 In Article 354 (connected persons) in paragraph (2)—

(a) in sub-paragraph (a), after 'spouse,' insert 'civil partner,',

(b) in sub-paragraph (c), after 'spouse' (in both places) insert 'or civil partner'.

74 In Article 423E (associates), in paragraph (8) after 'spouse' insert 'or civil partner'.

75 In Schedule 7 (matters to be dealt with in directors' report), in paragraph 2B(3) (immediate family), after 'spouse' insert ', civil partner'.

Enduring Powers of Attorney (Northern Ireland) Order 1987 (SI 1987/1627 (NI 16))

76 In Article 5 (scope of authority etc of attorney under enduring power), in paragraph (5)(a), for 'or marriage' substitute 'marriage or the formation of a civil partnership'.

77(1) Amend paragraph 2(1) of Schedule 1 (persons entitled to receive notice) as follows.

(2) In head (a), after 'wife' insert 'or civil partner'.

(3) In head (e), after 'widower' insert 'or surviving civil partner'.

78 Paragraphs 76 and 77 apply in relation to the exercise of powers under enduring powers of attorney created before the passing of this Act as well as to those created on or after its passing.

Matrimonial and Family Proceedings (Northern Ireland) Order 1989 (SI 1989/677 (NI 4))

79(1) Amend Article 16 (applications for financial relief after overseas divorce etc) as follows.

(2) In paragraph (2) (no application may be made after remarriage), for 'remarries' substitute 'forms a subsequent marriage or civil partnership,'.

(3) For paragraph (3) substitute—

'(3) The reference in paragraph (2) to the forming of a subsequent marriage or civil partnership includes a reference to the forming of a marriage or civil partnership which is by law void or voidable.'

Insolvency (Northern Ireland) Order 1989 (SI 1989/2405 (NI 19))

80(1) Amend Article 4 (meaning of 'associate') as follows.

(2) For paragraph (2) substitute—

'(2) A person is an associate of an individual if that person is—

    (a) the individual's husband or wife or civil partner,

    (b) a relative of—
        (i) the individual, or
        (ii) the individual's husband or wife or civil partner, or

    (c) the husband or wife or civil partner of a relative of—
        (i) the individual, or
        (ii) the individual's husband or wife or civil partner.'

(3) In paragraph (3), after 'husband or wife' insert 'or civil partner'.

(4) In paragraph (8), at the end insert 'and references to a civil partner include a former civil partner'.

81 In Article 179 (proceedings under Article 177 and 178), in paragraph (3)(b), after 'marriage' insert 'or the formation of a civil partnership'.

82 In Article 286 (charge on bankrupt's home), in paragraph (1), after 'former spouse' insert 'or by his civil partner or former civil partner'.

83(1) Amend Article 302 (debts to spouse) as follows.

(2) In paragraph (1), after 'spouse' (in each place) insert 'or civil partner'.

(3) In the heading to Article 302, after 'spouse' insert 'or civil partner'.

84 In Article 305 (saving for bankrupt's home), in paragraph (1), after 'former spouse' insert 'or by his civil partner or former civil partner'.

85 In Article 312 (transactions at an undervalue), in paragraph (3)(b), after 'marriage' insert 'or the formation of a civil partnership'.

86 In Article 337 (inquiry into bankrupt's dealings and property), in paragraph (1)(a), after 'former spouse' insert 'or civil partner or former civil partner'.

87 In Article 367 (transactions defrauding creditors), in paragraph (1)(b), after 'marriage' insert 'or the formation of a civil partnership'.

Police and Criminal Evidence (Northern Ireland) Order 1989 (SI 1989/1341 (NI 12))

88(1) Amend Article 79 (compellability of accused's spouse) as follows.

(2) In paragraphs (2), (2A) and (3), for 'wife or husband' (in each place) substitute 'spouse or civil partner'.

(3) After paragraph (5) insert—

'(5A) In any criminal proceedings a person who has been but is no longer the civil partner of the accused shall be compellable to give evidence as if that person and the accused had never been civil partners.'

(4) In the heading to Article 79, after 'accused's spouse' insert 'or civil partner'.

89 In Article 79A (rule where accused's spouse not compellable)—

(a) for 'wife or husband' substitute 'spouse or civil partner', and
(b) in the heading, after 'spouse' insert 'or civil partner'.

Companies (Northern Ireland) Order 1990 (SI 1990/593 (NI 5))

90 In Article 54 (meaning of 'associate'), in paragraph (2)(a) after 'spouse' insert 'or civil partner'.

Food Safety (Northern Ireland) Order 1991 (SI 1991/762 (NI 7))

91 In Article 42 (continuance of registration or licence on death), in paragraph (2), for the words from 'the deceased's personal representative' to 'his death' substitute

'the deceased's personal representative, or widow or widower or surviving civil partner or any other member of the deceased's family, until the expiration of—

(a) the period of 3 months from the date of the deceased's death'.

Industrial Relations (Northern Ireland) Order 1992 (SI1992/807 (NI5))

92 In Article 23 (recovery of sums awarded in proceedings involving trade unions and employers' associations), in the definition of 'provident benefits' in paragraph (3), for 'wife' substitute 'spouse or civil partner'.

Pension Schemes (Northern Ireland) Act 1993 (c 49)

93 In section 97E (discharge of liability where pension credit or alternative benefits secured by insurance policies or annuity contracts), in subsection (1)(b), after 'or widower' insert 'or civil partner'.

Family Law (Northern Ireland) Order 1993 (SI 1993/1576 (NI 6))

94(1) In Article 12 (family proceedings rules), amend paragraph (3)(g) as follows.

(2) After '1978' insert 'or a civil partnership cause within the meaning of section 190(3) of the Civil Partnership Act 2004'.

(3) After 'that Article 48' insert (in both places) 'that section 190(3)'.

(4) After 'divorce county court' insert 'or civil partnership proceedings county court'.

Children (Northern Ireland) Order 1995 (SI 1995/755 (NI 2))

95 In Article 8 (residence, contact and other orders with respect to children), after paragraph (4)(h) insert—

> '(i) Chapter 2 of Part 4 of, or Schedule 15, 16 or 17 to, the Civil Partnership Act 2004'.

96 In Article 50 (care orders and supervision orders), in paragraph (4), for 'married)' substitute 'married or a civil partner)'.

97 In Article 67 (powers to assist in discovery of children who may be in need of emergency protection), in paragraph (2), after 'spouse' insert 'or civil partner'.

98 In Article 69 (recovery of abducted children, etc), in paragraph (11), after 'spouse' insert 'or civil partner'.

99 In Article 166 (appeals), at the end of paragraph (2)(b) insert

'or
> (c) where the county court is a civil partnership proceedings county court exercising jurisdiction under the Civil Partnership Act 2004 in the same proceedings'.

100 In Article 171 (self-incrimination), in paragraph (2), after 'spouse' insert 'or civil partner'.

Trade Union and Labour Relations (Northern Ireland) Order 1995(SI1995/1980 (NI12))

101 In Article 125 (intimidation or annoyance by violence or otherwise), in paragraph (1)(a), for 'wife' substitute 'spouse or civil partner'.

Employment Rights (Northern Ireland) Order 1996 (SI 1996/1919 (NI 16))

102 In Article 85A (time off for dependants), in paragraph (3)(a), after 'spouse' insert 'or civil partner'.

103 In Article 248 (institution or continuance of tribunal proceedings), in paragraph (5)(b), for 'widow or widower' substitute 'surviving spouse, surviving civil partner'.

Registration of Clubs (Northern Ireland) Order 1996 (SI 1996/3159 (NI 23))

104 In Schedule 1 (provisions to be included in rules of club), in paragraph 11, for 'husband, wife' substitute 'spouse, civil partner'.

Race Relations (Northern Ireland) Order 1997 (SI 1997/869 (NI 6))

105 In Article 23(7) (exceptions: meaning of 'near relative')—

(a) after 'spouse' (in both places) insert 'or civil partner', and
(b) for 'by affinity)' substitute 'by marriage or civil partnership)'.

Fair Employment and Treatment (Northern Ireland) Order 1998 (SI 1998/3162 (NI 21))

106 In Article 30(7) (exceptions: meaning of 'near relative')—

(a) after 'spouse' insert 'or civil partner', and
(b) for 'by affinity)' substitute 'by marriage or civil partnership)'.

107 In Article 69(3)(c) (interpretation: connected person), after 'wife or husband' (in each place) substitute 'or civil partner'.

Welfare Reform and Pensions (Northern Ireland) Order 1999 (SI 1999/3147 (NI 11))

108(1) Amend Article 21 (supply of pension information in connection with divorce etc) as follows.

(2) After paragraph (1)(a)(i) insert—

'(ia) financial relief under Schedule 15 or 17 to the Civil Partnership Act 2004 (powers in relation to domestic and overseas dissolution of civil partnerships etc);'.

(3) In paragraph (1)(a)(ii), after '1984' insert 'or Schedule 5 or 7 to the 2004 Act'.

(4) In paragraph (1)(a)(iii), after '1984' insert 'or Schedule 11 to the 2004 Act'.

(5) In paragraph (1)(b), after '(a)(i)' insert ', (ia)'.

109(1) Amend Article 22 (charges by pension arrangements in relation to earmarking orders) as follows.

(2) After paragraph (a) insert—

'(aa) an order under Part 1 of Schedule 15 to the Civil Partnership Act 2004 (financial provision orders in connection with dissolution of civil partnerships etc) so far as it includes provision made by virtue of Part 5 of that Schedule (powers to include provision about pensions),'.

(3) At the end of paragraph (b) omit 'or' and after that paragraph insert—

'(bb) an order under Part 1 of Schedule 5 to the 2004 Act so far as it includes provision made by virtue of Part 6 of that Schedule (England and Wales powers corresponding to those mentioned in paragraph (aa)), or'.

110(1) Amend Article 25 (activation of pension sharing) as follows.

(2) After paragraph (1)(a) insert—

'(aa) a pension sharing order under Schedule 15 to the Civil Partnership Act 2004,'.

(3) After paragraph (1)(b) insert—

'(ba) an order under Schedule 17 to the 2004 Act (financial relief in Northern Ireland after overseas dissolution etc of a civil partnership) corresponding to such an order as is mentioned in paragraph (aa),'.

111(1) Amend Article 31 ('implementation period') as follows.

(2) In paragraph (1)(b)(i), omit 'matrimonial'.

(3) In paragraph (2)—

(a) omit 'matrimonial', and

(b) in sub-paragraph (b), after 'divorce' insert ', dissolution'.

112(1) Amend Article 45 (activation of benefit sharing) as follows.

(2) After paragraph (1)(a) insert—

'(aa) a pension sharing order under Schedule 15 to the Civil Partnership Act 2004,'.

(3) After paragraph (1)(b) insert—

'(ba) an order under Schedule 17 to the 2004 Act (financial relief in Northern Ireland after overseas dissolution etc of a civil partnership) corresponding to such an order as is mentioned in paragraph (aa),'.

Housing (Northern Ireland) Order 2003 (SI 2003/412 (NI 2))

113 In Article 85 (meaning of exempt disposal), after paragraph (3)(d) insert—

'(e) Part 2 of Schedule 15 or 17 to the Civil Partnership Act 2004;.'

Marriage (Northern Ireland) Order 2003 (SI 2003/413 (NI 3))

114(1) Amend Article 5 (power to require evidence) as follows.

(2) In paragraph (3)(c), after 'marital' insert 'and civil partnership'.

(3) After paragraph (3) insert—

'(4) In paragraph (3)(c), "marital and civil partnership status", in relation to a person, means whether that person has previously formed a marriage or a civil partnership, and if so, whether that marriage or civil partnership has ended.'

115 In Article 6 (objections), in paragraph (6)(b), after 'married' insert 'or a civil partner'.

Access to Justice (Northern Ireland) Order 2003 (SI 2003/435 (NI 10))

116 In Article 39 (conditional fee agreements: supplementary), in paragraph (2) (definition of 'family proceedings'), after sub-paragraph (f) insert—

'(g) Chapter 2 of Part 4 of, or Schedules 15, 16 or 17 to the Civil Partnership Act 2004,'.

In Schedule 2 (civil legal services: excluded services), in paragraph 2(d)(i), after '1998' insert 'or Schedule 16 to the Civil Partnership Act 2004'.

Firearms (Northern Ireland) Order 2004 (SI 2004/702 (NI 3))

117 In Article 2(2) (interpretation), in the definition of 'relative'—

(a) in paragraphs (a) and (b), for 'spouse or former spouse' substitute 'spouse, former spouse, civil partner or former civil partner';
(b) after 'as husband and wife' insert 'or as if they were civil partners';
(c) after 'married to each other' insert 'or were civil partners of each other'.

SCHEDULE 30

SECTION 261(4)

REPEALS AND REVOCATIONS

Family provision	
Short title and chapter	*Extent of repeal*
Inheritance (Provision for Family and Dependants) Act 1975 (c 63)	In section 3(2), 'and,' immediately following paragraph (b).

Housing and tenancies	
Short title and chapter	*Extent of repeal*
Housing Act 1980 (c 51)	In section 54(2)(b), 'or' at the end.
Housing Act 1985 (c 68)	In each of sections 39(3)(c), 89(3)(a)(ii), 90(3)(a)(ii), 91(3)(b)(ii), 99B(2)(e)(ii), 101(3)(c)(ii) and 160(3)(c), and paragraph 1(2)(c)(iii) of Schedule 6A, 'or' at the end.
Landlord and Tenant Act 1987 (c 31)	In section 4(2)(c)(v), 'or' at the end.
Housing Act 1988 (c 50)	In paragraph 4(4)(c) of Schedule 11, 'or' at the end.
Housing Act 1996 (c 52)	In sections 15(6)(c), 133(3)(a)(ii), 134(2)(a)(ii) and 160(2)(e)(ii) and (3)(d)(ii), 'or' at the end.

Family Homes and Domestic Violence	
Short title and chapter	*Extent of repeal*
Family Law Act 1996 (c 27)	In section 63(1), the definition of 'matrimonial home rights'.
	In Schedule 7, 'or' at the end of paragraph 4(a) and paragraph 7(6).
	In Schedule 8, paragraphs 48(3), 53(2)(b) and 59(2)(b), and 'and' immediately preceding paragraphs 53(2)(b) and 59(2)(b).

Family provision: Northern Ireland	
Title and number	*Extent of revocation*
Inheritance (Provision for Family and Dependants) (Northern Ireland) Order 1979 (SI 1979/924 (NI 8))	In Article 5(2), 'and' immediately following sub-paragraph (b).

Family homes and domestic violence: Northern Ireland	
Title and number	*Extent of revocation*
Family Homes and Domestic Violence (Northern Ireland) Order 1998 (SI 1998/1071 (NI 6))	In Article 2(2), the definition of 'matrimonial home rights'.
	In Schedule 2, 'or' at the end of paragraph 4(1)(a).

Discrimination	
Short title and chapter	*Extent of repeal*
Sex Discrimination Act 1975 (c 27)	Section 1(4).

Discrimination	
Short title and chapter	*Extent of repeal*
Sex Discrimination (Northern Ireland) Order 1976 (SI 1976/1042 (NI 15))	Article 3(4).

Social security, child support and tax credits	
Short title and chapter	*Extent of repeal or revocation*
Child Support Act 1991 (c 48)	In section 8(11), 'or' at the end of paragraph (e).
Child Support (Northern Ireland) Order 1991 (SI 1991/2628 (NI 23))	In Article 10(11), 'or' at the end of sub-paragraph (dd).
Social Security Contributions and Benefits Act 1992 (c 4)	In section 37(4) 'or' at the end of paragraph (a).
	In section 38(3), 'or' at the end of paragraph (b).
	In section 39A(2) and (5), 'or' at the end of paragraph (a).
	In section 39B(5), 'or' at the end of paragraph (a).
	Section 85(1).
	In section 137(1), the definitions of 'married couple' and 'unmarried couple'.
Social Security Administration Act 1992 (c 5)	In section 74A(5), the definitions of 'married couple' and 'unmarried couple'.
Social Security Contributions and Benefits (Northern Ireland) Act 1992 (c 7)	In section 37(4), 'or' at the end of paragraph (a).
	In section 38(3), 'or' at the end of paragraph (b).
	In section 39A(2) and (5), 'or' at the end of paragraph (a).
	In section 39B(5), 'or' at the end of paragraph (a).
	Section 85(1).
	In section 133(1), the definitions of 'married couple' and 'unmarried couple'.
Social Security Administration (Northern Ireland) Act 1992 (c 8)	In section 72A(5), the definitions of 'married couple' and 'unmarried couple'.
Jobseekers Act 1995 (c 18)	In section 35(1), the definitions of 'married couple' and 'unmarried couple'.
Child Support Act 1995 (c 34)	In section 10(7), the definitions of 'married couple' and 'unmarried couple'.
Child Support (Northern Ireland) Order 1995 (SI 1995/2702 (NI 13))	In Article 4(7), the definitions of 'married couple' and 'unmarried couple'.
Jobseekers (Northern Ireland) Order 1995 (SI 1995/2705 (NI 15))	In Article 2(2), the definitions of 'married couple' and 'unmarried couple'.
State Pension Credit Act 2002 (c 16)	In section 17(1), the definitions of 'married couple' and 'unmarried couple'.
Tax Credits Act 2002 (c 21)	In section 48(1), the definitions of 'married couple' and 'unmarried couple', and 'and' at the end of the definition of 'tax year'.
State Pension Credit Act (Northern Ireland) 2002 (c 14 (NI))	In section 17(1), the definitions of 'married couple' and 'unmarried couple'.

Minor and consequential amendments: general	
Short title and chapter	*Extent of repeal*
Judicial Proceedings (Regulation of Reports) Act 1926 (c 61)	Section 1(5).
Marriage Act 1949 (c 76)	Section 1(6) to (8).
Theft Act 1968 (c 60)	In section 30(4), 'or' at the end of paragraph (a)(i) to the proviso.
Consumer Credit Act 1974 (c 39)	In section 184(5), 'and' immediately before 'references'.
Estate Agents Act 1979 (c 38)	In section 32(3), 'and' immediately before 'references'.
Courts and Legal Services Act 1990 (c 41)	In section 58A, 'and' at the end of subsection (2)(f).
Family Law Act 1996 (c 27)	In section 64, 'or' at the end of subsection (1)(c).
Welfare Reform and Pensions Act 1999 (c 30)	At the end of section 23(1)(a)(ii), 'or'.
	At the end of section 24(b), 'or'.
	In sections 28(7)(a) and (9), 34(1)(b)(i) and (2) and 48(6)(a) and (8) 'matrimonial'.
Gender Recognition Act 2004 (c 7)	In Schedule 4, paragraph 2.

Consequential amendments: Scotland	
Short title and chapter	*Extent of repeal*
Damages (Scotland) Act 1976 (c 13)	In Schedule 1, 'and' at the end of paragraph 1(e).
Family Law (Scotland) Act 1985 (c 37)	In section 10(2), first 'matrimonial'.
Adults with Incapacity (Scotland) Act 2000 (asp 4)	In section 87, in subsection (1), in the definition of 'nearest relative', ', subject to subsection (2),' and subsections (2) and (3).

Minor and consequential amendments: Northern Ireland	
Title and number	*Extent of revocation*
Welfare Reform and Pensions (Northern Ireland) Order 1999 (SI 1999/3147 (NI 11))	At the end of Article 22(b), 'or'.
	In Article 31(1)(b)(i) and (2), 'matrimonial'.

INDEX

References are to paragraph numbers.